CONTEMPORARY
Heroes
and
Heroines
Book IV

CONTEMPORARY
Heroes and Heroines

Book IV

DANA R. BARNES, EDITOR
LEIGH ANN DeREMER, ASSOCIATE EDITOR

GALE GROUP

Detroit
New York
San Francisco
London
Boston
Woodbridge, CT

Tualatin H. S. Media Center

STAFF

Dana R. Barnes, *Senior Editor*

Laura B. Avery, Leigh Ann DeRemer, *Associate Editors*

Bridget Travers, *Managing Editor*

Maria L. Franklin, *Permissions Manager*
Margaret Chamberlain, *Permissions Specialist*

Mary Beth Trimper, *Manager, Composition and Electronic Prepress*
Evi Seoud, *Assistant Manager, Composition Purchasing and Electronic Prepress*
Dorothy Maki, *Manufacturing Manager*
Rhonda Williams, *Buyer*

Robert Duncan, Dan Newell, *Imaging Specialists*
Randy Bassett, *Image Database Supervisor*
Pamela A. Reed, *Imaging Coordinator*
Dean Dauphinais, *Senior Editor, Imaging & Multimedia Content*
Michael Logusz, *Graphic Artist*

Cover Photos: Nat "King" Cole (AP/Wide World Photos), Mia Hamm (Reuters/Rick Wilking/Archive Photos), King Hussein I (Library of Congress), Camryn Manheim (AP/Wide World Photos), and Diego Rivera (The Estate of Carl Van Vechten).

ISBN 0-7876-3262-7

10 9 8 7 6 5 4 3 2 1

Contemporary Heroes and Heroines, Book IV

Advisory Board

Contents

Edward Abbey
Writer and environmentalist 1

Muhammad Ali
Championship boxer diagnosed with Parkinson's disease 6

Salvador Allende
Former president of Chile; first democratically elected
Marxist leader 12

Cleveland Amory
Writer and animal-rights activist 18

Lance Armstrong
Bicyclist; won the 1999 Tour de France after recovering from
advanced testicular cancer 24

Hanan Ashrawi
Spokesperson for Palestinian people and advocate for peace
in the Middle East 31

Isaac Asimov
Science fiction writer 38

Leo Hendrik Baekeland
Inventor of plastic 44

Carlos Filipe Ximenes Belo
Roman Catholic priest; winner of 1996 Nobel Peace Prize for
his role in East Timor's struggle for independence 50

Tim Berners-Lee
Inventor of the World Wide Web 56

Elizabeth Blackwell
First female physician in the United States 61

Niels Bohr
Physicist who made significant contributions to
understanding the structure of the atom 68

Antonia Brico
Pianist and orchestra conductor 74

x

Heroes and Heroines
Listed by Area of Endeavor

ARTISTS AND PHOTOGRAPHERS
Dorothea Lange
Diego Rivera
Charles M. Schulz

AVIATION AND SPACE
Jacqueline Cochran
James Doolittle
Ellen Ochoa
Scott O'Grady

BUSINESS
Bill Gates
Lillian M. Gilbreth
John Maynard Keynes
Giorgio Perlasca
Steve Wozniak

CIVIL RIGHTS ACTIVISTS
William Sloane Coffin, Jr.
James Farmer
Theodore Hesburgh
Vilma Martinez
Constance Baker Motley
Randall S. Robinson
Walter F. White

EDUCATION
Joe Clark
Theodore Hesburgh

ENTERTAINMENT AND PERFORMING ARTS
Antonia Brico
Nat "King" Cole
Ella Fitzgerald
Danny Kaye

Camryn Manheim
Rosie O'Donnell

ENVIRONMENT
Edward Abbey
Carol M. Browner
Denis Hayes

EXPLORERS AND ADVENTURERS
Richard E. Byrd
Ranulph Fiennes
Betrand Piccard and Brian Jones

INVENTORS
Leo Hendrik Baekeland
Tim Berners-Lee
R. Buckminster Fuller
Robert K. Jarvik
Charles "Swede" Momsen
Steve Wozniak

JOURNALISTS
Katherine Meyer Graham
Charlayne Hunter-Gault
Bill Moyers
Barbara Walters

MEDICINE
Elizabeth Blackwell
Michael DeBakey
Robert Peter Gale
Robert K. Jarvik

MILITARY
Max Cleland
James Doolittle
Dwight D. Eisenhower
Scott O'Grady

NOBEL PEACE PRIZE RECIPIENTS

Carlos Filipe Ximenes Belo
John Hume and David Trimble
Jose Ramos-Horta

POLITICS

Salvador Allende
Max Cleland
Elizabeth Dole
Dwight D. Eisenhower
Hiram L. Fong
Henry B. Gonzalez
King Hussein I
Carolyn McCarthy
Patsy T. Mink
Constance Baker Motley
Luis Muñoz Marín
Pablo Neruda
Bill Richardson
Mary Robinson
Margaret Chase Smith
L. Douglas Wilder

RELIGION

William Sloane Coffin, Jr.
Maximilian Kolbe

SCIENCE

Niels Bohr
Thomas R. Cech
Fang Lizhi
R. Buckminster Fuller
Robert Goddard
Edwin Hubble
Clyde W. Tombaugh

SOCIAL ISSUES

Cleveland Amory
Hanan Ashrawi
Karel and Jozef Capek
David Dellinger
Dith Pran
Henry Chee Dodge

Fang Lizhi
Reg and Maggie Green
Frances E.W. Harper
LaDonna Harris
Danny Kaye
Juliette Gordon Low
Betty Mahmoody
Carolyn McCarthy
Thich Nhat Hanh
Rosie O'Donnell
Emmeline Pankhurst
Leonard Peltier
Giorgio Perlasca
Jose Ramos-Horta
Bill Richardson
Walter J. Turnbull
Dan West

SPORTS

Muhammad Ali
Lance Armstrong
Alice Coachman
Mia Hamm
Carl Lewis
Rebecca Lobo
Pele
Harold "Pee Wee" Reese
Cal Ripken, Jr.
Gene Stallings

TECHNOLOGY

Tim Berners-Lee
Bill Gates
Steve Wozniak

WRITERS

Edward Abbey
Cleveland Amory
Isaac Asimov
Will and Ariel Durant
William Faulkner
Frances E.W. Harper
Zora Neale Hurston
Ursula K. Le Guin
Pablo Neruda

Individuals Profiled in
Contemporary Heroes and Heroines

These profiles appear in the original *Contemporary Heroes and Heroines,* Contemporary Heroes and Heroines, Book II **and** *Contemporary Heroes and Heroines, Book III.*

Hank Aaron
Jim Abbott
Ralph Abernathy
James G. Abourezk
Ansel Adams
Gerry Adams
Joy Adamson
Jane Addams
Madeleine Albright
Roald Amundsen
Marian Anderson
Maya Angelou
Susan B. Anthony
Corazon Aquino
Oscar Arias Sanchez
Louis Armstrong
Neil Armstrong
Arthur Ashe
Joan Baez
Robert D. Ballard
Christiaan Barnard
Clara Barton
Ben & Jerry
Irving Berlin
Joseph Bernardin
Leonard Bernstein
Daniel and Philip Berrigan
Mary McLeod Bethune
Stephen Biko
Dietrich Bonhoeffer
Margaret Bourke-White
Bill Bradley
Jim Brady
Sarah Brady
Gwendolyn Brooks
Christy Brown
Les Brown

Pearl Buck
Ralph Bunche
Chris Burke
Susan Butcher
Frances Xavier Cabrini
Helen Caldicott
Ernesto Cardenal
Dale Carnegie
Ben Carson
Rachel Carson
Jimmy Carter
Rosalynn Carter
George Washington Carver
Mary Cassatt
Chai Ling
Challenger Crew
Wilt Chamberlain
Cesar Chavez
Dennis Chavez
Shirley Chisholm
Winston Churchill
Roberto Clemente
Bessie Coleman
Eileen Collins
Francis S. Collins
Marva Collins
Kenneth H. Cooper
Aaron Copland
Mairead Corrigan and Betty Williams
Bill Cosby
Norman Cousins
Jacques Cousteau
Francis Crick
Walter Cronkite
Marie Curie
Dalai Lama
Jacques d'Ambroise

Clarence Darrow
Benjamin O. Davis, Jr.
Morris Dees
F.W. de Klerk
Vine Deloria, Jr.
Diana, Princess of Wales
Walt Disney
Tom Dooley
Dave Dravecky
Charles R. Drew
W.E.B. Du Bois
Katherine Dunham
Amelia Earhart
Marian Wright Edelman
Albert Einstein
Duke Ellington
Jaime Escalante
Medgar Wiley Evers
Anthony S. Fauci
Jose Feliciano
Zlata Filipovic
Alexander Fleming
Betty Ford
Dian Fossey
Terry Fox
Anne Frank
Betty Friedan
Millard Fuller
Indira Gandhi
Mohandas K. Gandhi
Gabriel Garcia Marquez
Lou Gehrig
Bob Geldof
Althea Gibson
Elizabeth Glaser
John Glenn
Evelyn Glennie
Jane Goodall
Mikhail Gorbachev
Billy Graham
Dick Gregory
Florence Griffith Joyner
Veronica Guerin
Clara Hale
Alex Haley
Alice Hamilton
Dag Hammarskjold
Armand Hammer
Lorraine Hansberry
Barbara Harris
Vaclav Havel
Stephen W. Hawking
Jim Henson
Matthew Henson
Katharine Hepburn
Thor Heyerdahl

Grant Hill
Edmund Hillary and Tenzing Norgay
Bob Hope
John Hope
Dolores Huerta
Langston Hughes
Lee Iacocca
Daniel Inouye
Bo Jackson
Jesse Jackson
Mae Jemison
Ann Jillian
Steven Jobs
Pope John XXIII
Pope John Paul II
Mother Jones
Barbara Jordan
Michael Jordan
Chief Joseph
Jackie Joyner-Kersee
Frida Kahlo
Helen Keller
John F. Kennedy
Robert F. Kennedy
David Kessler
Craig Kielburger
Billie Jean King
Martin Luther King, Jr.
Henry Kissinger
Helmut Kohl
C. Everett Koop
Ron Kovic
Maggie Kuhn
Louis Leakey
Mary Leakey
Richard Leakey
Greg LeMond
John Lennon
Candy Lightner
Liliuokalani
Maya Lin
Charles A. Lindbergh
Greg Louganis
George Lucas
Shannon Lucid
Sean MacBride
Anne Sullivan Macy
Malcolm X
Nelson and Winnie Mandela
Wilma Mankiller
Mickey Mantle
Thurgood Marshall
Marlee Matlin
Spark M. Matsunaga
Osceola McCarty
Margaret Mead

Golda Meir
Rigoberta Menchu
Chico Mendes
Karl Menninger
James Howard Meredith
Kweisi Mfume
Dorie Miller
Billy Mills
Toni Morrison
Grandma Moses
Mother Teresa
Farley Mowat
Kary Mullis
Audie Murphy
Joseph Murray
Ralph Nader
Patricia Neal
Paul Newman
Harrison Ngau
Julius K. Nyerere
Sandra Day O'Connor
Georgia O'Keeffe
Edward James Olmos
J. Robert Oppenheimer
Jesse Owens
Gordon Parks
Rosa Parks
Linus Pauling
Robert E. Peary
I.M. Pei
Claude Pepper
Itzhak Perlman
Pete Peterson
Colin Powell
Leontyne Price
Yitzhak Rabin
A. Philip Randolph
Jeannette Rankin
Christopher Reeve
Sally Ride
Pat Robertson
Paul Robeson
Jackie Robinson
Fred Rogers
Oscar Romero
Eleanor Roosevelt
Franklin Delano Roosevelt
Theodore Roosevelt
Wilma Rudolph
Salman Rushdie
Bill Russell
Albert Sabin
Anwar Sadat
Carl Sagan
Andrei Sakharov
Jonas Salk

Margaret Sanger
Oskar Schindler
Pat Schroeder
H. Norman Schwarzkopf
Albert Schweitzer
Jan C. Scruggs
Pete Seeger
Betty Shabazz
Alan Shepard
Karen Silkwood
Beverly Sills
Mitch Snyder
Aleksandr Solzhenitsyn
Steven Spielberg
Benjamin Spock
Standing Bear
Gloria Steinem
Aung San Suu Kyi
Maria Tallchief
Corrie ten Boom
Margaret Thatcher
Dave Thomas
Helen Thomas
Jim Thorpe
Harry S. Truman
Harriet Tubman
C. DeLores Tucker
Ted Turner
Desmond Tutu
Terry Waite
Lech Walesa
Alice Walker
Mary Edwards Walker
Raoul Wallenberg
Wang Dan
Booker T. Washington
Annie Dodge Wauneka
Ida B. Wells-Barnett
Ryan White
Elie Wiesel
Simon Wiesenthal
Roy Wilkins
William Griffith ("Bill W.") Wilson
Oprah Winfrey
Stevie Wonder
Tiger Woods
Carter G. Woodson
Frank Lloyd Wright
Wilbur and Orville Wright
Harry Wu
Chuck Yeager
Jeanna Yeager and Dick Rutan
Muhammad Yunus
Babe Didrikson Zaharias

Preface

Aguide to twentieth century figures and their achievements, *Contemporary Heroes and Heroines, Book IV* carries on in the tradition established by its predecessors, *Contemporary Heroes and Heroines, Contemporary Heroes and Heroines, Book II,* and *Contemporary Heroes and Heroines, Book III,* by furnishing biographical portraits of people whose activities reflect a variety of heroic traits. Included are inspiring profiles of prominent figures in many fields of endeavor, from art to technology, from conservation to social activism, all in one volume. It's the only reference source that brings together in one place lively sketches of contemporary figures collected around the theme of heroism.

Variety of Figures Profiled Helps Define
Contemporary Heroism

The heroes and heroines profiled in this volume were chosen after public and school librarians were surveyed for their help in identifying heroic figures of the twentieth—and expanding into the twenty-first—century. The survey yielded a wide range of individuals for inclusion. From boxing champion **Muhammad Ali**, to civil rights activist and judge **Constance Baker Motley**, to astronomer **Edwin Hubble**, this collection represents many fields of endeavor. International in scope, *Contemporary Heroes and Heroines, Book IV* includes essays on Puerto Rican governor **Luis Muñoz Marín**, Palestinian peace advocate **Hanan Ashrawi**, and Mexican artist **Diego Rivera**. The survey's results also demonstrate the spectrum of qualities that are considered heroic. Of course, no individual embodies every heroic ideal, but each listee was selected on the basis of a heroic aspect evident in her or his accomplishments.

Like hot air balloonists **Betrand Piccard and Brian Jones**, some listees face an element of risk in contributing to modern life, while others, such as talk-show host **Rosie O'Donnell**, combine talent and charitable work to garner both prominence and wide admiration. Some listees, like physician **Robert Peter Gale**, illustrate an altruistic type of heroism, joining those—like environmentalist and Earth

Day founder **Denis Hayes**, for example—who make a significant contribution to contemporary society. **Charlayne Hunter-Gault**, the first African American to attend the University of Georgia, and economist **John Maynard Keynes** are among the heroines and heroes profiled in this volume who were selected for the lasting nature of their accomplishments, and, like Nobel Peace Prize winner **Carlos Filipe Ximenes Belo**, others were chosen for the example they provide of achieving goals without violating another's rights to freedom, life, and dignity.

Graceful determination in the face of overwhelming obstacles characterizes the activities of listees such as pianist and orchestra conductor **Antonia Brico**, human-rights activist **Dith Pran**, television journalist **Barbara Walters**, Vietnam veteran **Max Cleland**, organ donation promoters **Reg and Maggie Green**, and bicyclist **Lance Armstrong**, who won the Tour de France less than three years after being diagnosed with advanced testicular cancer. While some figures profiled—like **William Faulkner, Emmeline Pankhurst**, and **King Hussein I**—enjoy enduring status, other listees—like **Camryn Manheim, Cal Ripken Jr.**, and **Elizabeth Dole**—are active entering the twenty-first century.

The changing nature of heroism is reflected in the demand for entries on people who might not have been included in a book like *Contemporary Heroes and Heroines* twenty or thirty years ago. In 1960, for example, it would have been difficult to predict how enormously popular and influential cartoonist **Charles M. Schulz** and his *Peanuts* comic strip would become. **Mia Hamm, Rebecca Lobo,** and **Alice Coachman** have each contributed to the expansion and increased popularity of women's sports, serving as role models for the next generation of young female athletes. Activists such as former Navajo tribal leader **Henry Chee Dodge**, gun-control advocate **Carolyn McCarthy**, political dissident **Fang Lizhi**, and **Betty Mahmoody**, who works to prevent international child abductions, all show heroic qualities through their actions based on their beliefs. The increased role of technology in daily life is attributable to individuals such as **Bill Gates, Tim Berners-Lee,** and **Steve Wozniak**. And the inclusion of soldiers such as former President **Dwight D. Eisenhower**, pilot **James Doolittle**, and **Scott O'Grady**, who survived six days in Bosnian territory without detection, is testimony to the nation's continuing respect for the military.

Entry Format Sets the Stage for World-Class Research

- A vivid photograph, a telling quote, and a "vital statistics" box open each entry in *Contemporary Heroes and Heroines, Book IV*, giving you an immediate sense of the person whose profile you're about to read. Addresses are included so that you can contact a favorite heroine or hero directly.

- You'll look forward to reading the appealing essays, which provide an overview of the lives of the heroines and heroes and highlight their remarkable achievements.

- Source citations at the end of each entry lead you to more information about the heroine or hero.

Features Put the Information You Need in the Limelight

- With its unique focus, *Contemporary Heroes and Heroines, Book IV* furnishes essays compiled with heroic criteria in mind. To capture the essence of each listee as well as to ensure accuracy, the editor has consulted autobiographies and biographies as well as newspaper and magazine articles of current and historical interest, thus eliminating the need to search for information scattered in a variety of sources.

- The primary table of contents in *Contemporary Heroes and Heroines, Book IV* includes a brief descriptor that matches a listee with his or her claim to fame.

- A second table of contents grouping biographees by category is headed "Heroes and Heroines Listed by Area of Endeavor." It allows you to scan names in a desired field and learn more about who has made a lasting contribution in a given arena.

- Following this alternative table of contents is a list of people who appeared in previous volumes of *Contemporary Heroes and Heroines,* demonstrating the breadth of coverage in these unique works.

- The volume's general Index lists key words, places, events, awards, institutions, and people cited in the essays, making it easy to trace a common thread through several profiles. It also contains references to biographees in previous volumes of *Contemporary Heroes and Heroines*—just look for the abbreviation "CHH", "CHH-2", or "CHH-3" after a name to know that you'll need to consult an earlier volume for an essay on that particular person.

Put *Contemporary Heroes and Heroines, Book IV* on Your Team

- If you're a student researching contemporary heroic figures, no other source will present you with short, readable essays collected according to a heroism theme.

- Working as a researcher in current events, history, or popular culture, you'll turn to *Contemporary Heroes and Heroines, Book IV* for the biographical material that personalizes the topic you're investigating.

- As an educator, member of the media, or interested general reader, when a "local hero" makes the news, you'll appreciate the backdrop provided by *Contemporary Heroes and Heroines, Book IV* that puts it all in perspective.

Available in Electronic Formats

Diskette/Magnetic Tape. *Contemporary Heroes and Heroines* is available for licensing on magnetic tape or diskette in a fielded format. The database is available for internal data processing and nonpublishing purposes only. For more information, call 800-877-GALE.

On-line. *Contemporary Heroes and Heroines* is available on-line as part of the Gale Biographies (GALBIO) database accessible through LEXIS-NEXIS, and is also included in the *Biography Resource Center*.

Make Your Contribution—Send Suggestions

The editors welcome your comments and suggestions for future editions so that we can best meet the needs of the greatest number of users. Readers are cordially invited to write us at the following address:

The Editors
Contemporary Heroes and Heroines
Gale Group, Inc.
27500 Drake Road
Farmington Hills, MI 48331

Or, call toll-free at 800-877-GALE

Edward Abbey

"If a label is required, say that I am one who loves the unfenced country."

Born January 29, 1927, in Home, Pennsylvania, Edward Abbey was a combative writer and naturalist whose works of fiction and nonfiction exposed the enemies of the American wild and fueled the sentiments of radical environmentalist groups. He died March 14, 1989, in Oracle, Arizona.

Edward Abbey was best known for his hard-hitting, frequently bitter, usually irreverent defense of the world's wilderness areas. Anarchistic and outspoken, he was called everything from America's crankiest citizen to the godfather of modern environmental activism. Abbey himself strenuously resisted any attempt to classify him as a naturalist, environmentalist, or anything else. "If a label is required," Burt A. Folkart quoted him as saying in the *Los Angeles Times,* "say that I am one who loves the unfenced country." His favorite places were the deserts and mountains of the American West, and the few people who won his respect were those who knew how to live on that land without spoiling it. The many targets of his venom ranged from government agencies and gigantic corporations responsible for the rape of the wild country, to cattlemen grazing their herds on public lands, to simple-minded tourists who, according to Abbey, defile the solitude with their very presence.

Abbey was born January 29, 1927, on a small farm in Home, Pennsylvania, the son of Paul Revere, a farmer, and Mildred (Postlewaite) Abbey, a teacher. He hitchhiked west in 1946, following one year in the U.S. Army. Captivated by the wide-open spaces of Arizona, New Mexico, and Utah, he stayed there, studying philosophy and English at the University of New Mexico. In the early years of his writing career Abbey worked a variety of odd jobs, including that of road inspector for the Forest Service and ranger for the National Park Service. The experiences he gained in those positions were the foundation of his first notably successful book, *Desert Solitaire,* which was published in 1968.

Desert Solitaire opens with a truculent preface, in which the author expresses his hope that serious critics, librarians, and professors will intensely dislike his book. In the body of the book, which compresses many of Abbey's experiences with the Park Service and Forest Service into the framework of one cycle of the seasons, readers find both harsh criticism and poetic description, all related to the landscape of the West and what mankind is doing to it. Freeman Tilden, reviewing *Desert Solitaire* in *National Parks,* recommended the book, "vehemence, egotism, bad taste and all. Partly because we need angry young men to remind us that there is plenty we should be angry about. . . . Partly because Abbey is an artist with words. There are pages and pages of delicious prose, sometimes almost magical in their evocation of the desert scene. . . . How this man can write! But he can do more than write. His prehension of the natural environment—of raw nature—is so ingenuous, so implicit, that we wonder if the pre-Columbian aborigines didn't see their environment just that way."

While it never made the bestseller lists, *Desert Solitaire* is credited as being a key source of inspiration for the environmental movement that was growing in the late 1960s. Abbey's no-holds-barred book awakened many readers to just how much damage was being done by government and business interests to so-called "public" lands, as did the many other essay collections he published throughout his career. But an even greater influence may have come from his 1975 novel, *The Monkey Wrench Gang.* Receiving virtually no promotion, it nonetheless became an underground classic, selling half a million copies. Within the comic story, which follows the misadventures of four environmentalist terrorists, is a serious message: peaceful protest is inadequate; the ecology movement must become radicalized. The ultimate goal of the Monkey Wrench Gang—blowing up the immense Glen Canyon Dam on the Colorado River—is one Abbey seemed to endorse, and his book provides fairly explicit instructions to anyone daring enough to carry it out. The novel is said to have inspired the formation of the real-life environmental group Earth First!, which impedes the progress of developers and loggers by sabotaging bulldozers and booby-trapping trees with chainsaw-destroying spikes. Their term for such tactics: "monkey-wrenching."

A sequel to *The Monkey Wrench Gang,* completed shortly before Abbey's death, was published posthumously in 1990; *Hayduke Lives!* finds most of the cast of the earlier novel settled comfortably into middle-class lives, only to be galvanized into action again by the reappearance of their leader, thought to be long dead.

Abbey's personal favorite of his more than twenty books was the bulky, largely autobiographical novel *The Fool's Progress.* "From the outset of this cross-country story it seems almost impossible to separate Edward Abbey from his narrator," observed Howard Coale in the *New York Times Book Review.* "The harsh, humorous, damn-it-all voice of Henry Lightcap is identical to the voice in the author's many essays." In Coale's opinion, the book was too "self-involved" to be a really successful work of fiction, although it contained some excellent descriptive passages.

Two of Abbey's novels were made into films during his lifetime. *The Brave Cowboy,* written in 1958, was adapted for film and released in 1962 as *Lonely Are the Brave,* starring Kirk Douglas. *Fire on the Mountain,* for which Abbey was awarded a Western Heritage Award for Best Novel in 1963, was put on film in 1981.

Abbey died of internal bleeding due to a circulatory disorder on March 14, 1989, in Oracle, Arizona, and was buried in a desert in the southwestern United States. Reviewing Abbey's body of work after his death, many environmentalists and critics concluded that his nonfiction works were his most powerful. *"Desert Solitaire* stands among the towering works of American nature writing," stated Grace Lichtenstein of the *Washington Post Book World.* "Abbey's polemic essays on such subjects as cattle subsidies and Mexican immigrants, scattered through a half-dozen volumes, remain so angry, so infuriating yet so relevant that they still provoke arguments among his followers. As for his outdoors explorations, no one wrote more melodic hymns to the red rocks and rivers of the Southwest; no one ever defended them with more elan. It is in those nonfiction odes to the wilderness, by turns cantankerous and lyrical . . . that Abbey lives, forever."

Sources

➤ Books

Bishop, James, Jr., with Charles Bowden, *Epitaph for a Desert Anarchist: The Life and Legacy of Edward Abbey,* Atheneum, 1994.
Contemporary Literary Criticism, Gale Research, Volume 36, 1986; Volume 59, 1990.
Hepworth, James, and Gregory McNamee, editors, *Resist Much, Obey Little: Some Notes on Edward Abbey,* Dream Garden Press, 1985.
McCann, Garth, *Edward Abbey,* Boise State University, 1977.
Peterson, David, editor and author of introduction, *Confessions of a Barbarian: Selections from the Journals of Edward Abbey, 1951-1989,* original drawings by Abbey, Little, Brown, 1994.
Ronald, Ann, *The New West of Edward Abbey,* University of New Mexico Press, 1982.

➤ Periodicals

Chicago Tribune, February 14, 1988, Section 14, p. 3; November 29, 1988; March 15, 1989; February 12, 1990.
Christian Science Monitor, July 27, 1977.
Harper's, August, 1971; February, 1988, pp. 42-44.
Los Angeles Times, October 22, 1980; January 3, 1988 (opening quote).
Los Angeles Times Book Review, June 17, 1979; May 16, 1982, p. 1; November 29, 1987, p. 10; January 24, 1988, p. 12; May 15, 1988, p. 14; November 20, 1988, p. 3; September 2, 1989, p. 8; January 7, 1990, p. 1; March 26, 1995, p. 6.
Nation, May 1, 1982, pp. 533-35.

National Observer, September 6, 1975, p. 17.

National Parks, February, 1968, pp. 22-23.

National Review, August 10, 1984, pp. 48-49.

New Yorker, July 17, 1971.

New York Times, June 19, 1979; March 15, 1989.

New York Times Book Review, January 28, 1968, p. 7; July 31, 1977, pp. 10-11; August 5, 1979, pp. 8, 21; December 14, 1980, p. 10; May 30, 1982, p. 6; April 15, 1984, p. 34; December 16, 1984, p. 27; February 28, 1988, p. 27; May 1, 1988; December 18, 1988, p. 22; May 7, 1989, pp. 44-45; February 4, 1990, p. 18; July 8, 1990, p. 28; January 27, 1991, p. 32; December 11, 1994, p. 11; June 11, 1995, p. 18; March 17, 1996, p. 32.

Time, November 28, 1988, p. 98.

Washington Post, December 31, 1979; January 5, 1988.

Washington Post Book World, March 24, 1968; June 25, 1979; May 30, 1982, p. 3; April 1, 1984, p. 9; April 3, 1988, p. 12; December 31, 1989, p. 12; January 28, 1990, p. 5; April 1, 1990, p. 8; April 22, 1990, p. 12; June 10, 1990, p. 15.

Muhammad Ali

"I'*ve got Parkinson's syndrome. I'm in no pain. . . . If I was in perfect health—if I had won my last two fights—if I had no problem, people would be afraid of me. Now they feel sorry for me. They thought I was Superman. Now they can say 'He's human, like us. He has problems.'"*

Born January 17, 1942, as Cassius Marcellus Clay, Jr., Muhammad Ali earned a reputation as a man dedicated to his goals and beliefs. After an illustrious boxing career—including three world heavyweight boxing championships—Ali was diagnosed with Parkinson's disease. Address: Ali Farm, Berrien Springs, MI 49103.

Muhammad Ali and his "float like a butterfly, sting like a bee" style of fighting dominated the world of heavyweight boxing for a decade and a half. As a teenager named Cassius Clay, he won the gold medal in the light heavyweight division at the 1960 Olympic Games. He later earned the title of world heavyweight champion, and became internationally famous for his confidence both in and out of the boxing ring. But when Ali lit the flame to open the 1996 Olympic Games in Atlanta, Georgia, his arm visibly shook as he raised the torch. The former fighter suffers from Parkinson's disease, a condition probably caused by the blows he received from opponents. Throughout his busy and sometimes controversial public life, Ali remains one of the most famous and popular athletes of the twentieth century. A consummate showman, he used to call himself "the Greatest," and many of his fans believe that the nickname fits.

Born Cassius Clay in Louisville, Kentucky, Ali was raised in a middle-class neighborhood, the eldest of two sons born to Cassius Marcellus Clay Sr. and Odessa (Grady) Clay. Ali's father supported his family as a sign and mural painter, while his mother worked as a domestic. Ali worshiped with his family on Sundays at Mount Zion Baptists Church and attended school with brother Rudolph Valentino Clay (now Rahaman Ali) at DuValle Junior High School and Central High School in Louisville. Ali was a rather poor student, which he blames on his preoccupation with boxing as a boy. Regrettably, Ali has confessed that he wished he had put forth more effort academically, because he has struggled as a slow reader his entire life.

Ali began boxing when he was 12 after his bicycle was stolen. He reported the theft to policeman Joe Elsby Martin, who invited Ali to train in boxing. Martin supervised the training of young boxers and had a television show called *Tomorrow's Champions*. He arranged for Ali to train with Fred Stoner, who taught him to move with the speed and grace of a dancer. Ali would be indebted to this man for teaching him the fine skills to become a powerful and great boxer.

In high school, Ali became a very successful amateur boxer, winning 100 out of 108 matches and earning six Kentucky and two national Golden Glove championships, as well as two Amateur Athletic Union Championships. He went on to compete at the 1960 Olympics in Rome, where, Ali would admit later, he mastered his renowned skill at ring chatter geared to distract and frustrate his opponent. At age 18, Ali won the Olympic gold medal in boxing in the light heavyweight category. Upon returning to Louisville, he signed a lucrative fifty-fifty split contract turning him into a professional boxer.

Early on as a professional, Ali attracted media attention by boasting about his abilities to secure the heavyweight title for himself, although he was only ranked nine on the list of heavyweight contenders. He immediately captured public and professional interest with his strength of character and wit, exemplified through the catchy and arrogant rhymes he would spout off to sports journalists and potential competitors. Not only was Ali a young master at the sport, he was a master of the public relations that was integral to attracting audiences and media recognition. In 1964, Ali told *Sports Illustrated*, "If you wonder what the difference between [other heavyweight boxers] and me is, I'll break the news: you never heard of them. I'm not saying they're not good boxers. Most of them. . . can fight almost as good as I can. I'm just saying you never hear of them. And the reason for that is because they cannot throw the jive. Cassius Clay is a boxer who can throw the jive better than anybody."

Still going by his birth name, Cassius Clay, Ali fought Sonny Liston for the world heavyweight championship title. The match in Miami attracted a lot of hype, largely due to Ali's boastful rhymes and insults towards Liston. It worked to place boxing once again at the forefront of American sporting attractions. It was weeks prior to this competition that Ali began his famous rhyming chant, "float like a butterfly, sting like a bee." Ali exhibited great grace and beauty of strength and control on the mat as he threw forceful punches at Liston and skillfully danced away from his opponent's jabs. At the age of 22, Ali beat Liston to become boxing's heavyweight champion of the world. The fight was a solid beginning to Ali's long career as the noble and "pretty" prince of boxing.

It was not long into Ali's professional career that he became active politically and socially. Disgusted with racism in America, he tossed his Olympic gold medal into a river after he was refused service at a soda fountain counter because he was black. Ali's fist wife reported him saying in the *Philadelphia Inquirer*, "That gold medal didn't mean a thing to me if my black brothers and sisters were treated wrong in a country I was supposed to represent." Having been inspired by Malcolm X while in Miami, Ali decided about this time to join the Nation of Islam. Cassius Clay, Jr. was given the name Muhammad Ali by Elijah Muhammad, his new title meaning "beloved of Allah."

Ali defended his heavyweight title by defeating Liston again at a rematch in June of 1965 with a knockout punch to the side of the head. The blow not only stunned Liston but onlookers as well. Sports writers wrote of how the perfection of speed and force in that punch demonstrated to the world that Ali was a rare caliber of boxer. Its power lifted Liston's left foot clear off the mat.

Despite his talent as a boxer, Ali was loathed by many in America when it became public knowledge that he had become a Muslim. Adding to America's aversion to this was the stance he took as a conscientious objector to America's involvement in the war in Vietnam. He refused to cooperate with the draft, and as a result, in May of 1967, he was stripped of his title and boxing license by the World Boxing Association and charged for violating the Selective Service Act by the government. He told the press, "I ain't got no quarrel with them Viet-Cong. No Viet-Cong ever called me nigger." "Patriotic" boxing fans and sports journalists participated in a tremendous outcry against him. Reflecting upon this period, Jack Olsen explained in *Sports Illustrated*, "The noise became a din, the drumbeats of a holy war. TV and radio commentators, little old ladies. . . bookmakers, and parish priests, armchair strategists at the Pentagon and politicians all over the place joined in a crescendo of get-Cassius clamor." Ali commented to *Sports Illustrated's* Edwin Shrake, "I'm giving up my title, my wealth, maybe my future. Many great men have been tested for their religious beliefs. If I pass this test, I'll come out stronger than ever." Sentenced to five years in prison and released on appeal, Ali's conviction was overturned three years later.

Ali returned to the ring. His first fight after the Supreme Court decision was against Jerry Quarry in November of 1970 in Atlanta. Ali won by knocking out Quarry in the third round. After the reinstatement of his New York license, Ali fought Joe Frazier, the reigning heavyweight champion, in New York in March of 1971. Ali lost this fight—his first defeat as a professional—and Frazier retained the title. By the end of his career, Ali had fought Joe Frazier twice more. These three bouts have been one of the most widely discussed series in the sport because of their intensity and duration.

In 1974 Ali avenged his loss to Frazier with a unanimous decision victory. This retaliation did not earn Ali the title, however, since newcomer George Foreman had dethroned Frazier as the champion. Ali arranged to fight for the title against Foreman in Kinshasa, Zaire, a bout billed as the Rumble in the Jungle. Because Foreman was younger, stronger, and larger as well as being considered the hardest hitter in boxing, he was favored to win. Ali employed a tactic called the rope-a-dope, in which he rested against the ropes while Foreman pummeled him with little success for almost eight rounds. Foreman expended energy while Ali bided his time. When Ali finally came off the ropes, he landed a quick succession of combinations, including a stiff right that sent the champ to the canvas where he was counted out seconds before the end of the round. Ali had regained the title.

In September of 1975, for the third time, Ali fought the unrelenting Joe Frazier. The fight was billed as the Thrilla in Manila and Ali won when Frazier was unable to answer the bell for the final round. Although Ali lost a title defense early in 1978 to Leon Spinks, he later defeated Spinks in a rematch to win his title for the third time. On June 26, 1979, at the age of 37, Ali retired as champion with a professional record of 59 victories and three defeats.

Because of his lavish lifestyle, Ali found himself in need of money. In 1980 he returned to the ring to fight Larry Holmes for the World Boxing Council (WBC) title and a guaranteed purse of $8 million. When Ali was unable to answer the bell for the eleventh round, Holmes won with a technical knockout. One year later Ali boxed professionally for the last time, when he fought Trevor Berbick. One month before his fortieth birthday, Ali was defeated for the fifth time in his professional career.

After losing the fight to Holmes, Ali's health appeared to be on a rapid decline: he seemed sluggish and weak in motor skills. Initially he was misdiagnosed as having a thyroid condition. Upon another medical evaluation in 1982, Ali began treatment for Parkinson's disease at the University of California. Doctors later expressed speculation that Ali had been indeed battling a form of Parkinson's brought on by repetitive trauma to the head, but only an autopsy would confirm their analysis.

Near the end of Ali's boxing career, he steered toward political activism and philanthropic work. In 1980, he supported Jimmy Carter and the Democratic Party, even working at the Democratic National Convention in New York. In February of 1985, he functioned as a lay diplomat, attempting to secure the release of four kidnaped Americans in Lebanon. Ali also met with leaders in the Soviet Union and Africa and founded the World Organization for Right, Liberty, and Dignity (WORLD).

At the 1996 Olympic Games in Atlanta, the world and his country honored Ali by choosing him to light the Olympic torch during the opening ceremonies. In 1999, Ali became the first boxer to ever appear on the cover of a Wheaties box.

Ali is the father of nine children and has been married four times. He lives with his fourth wife, Yolanda, who also acts as his manager, in Berrien Springs, Michigan. During the late 1990s, the quest of Ali's daughter, Khaliah Ali, towards a career in boxing was greatly publicized in the media. Although he has publicly expressed disapproval over women participating in the sport, Khaliah continued to follow in the footsteps of her champion father.

Sources

> **Books**

Ali, Muhammad with Richard Durham, *The Greatest*, 1975.
Lipsyte, Robert, *Free to Be Muhammad Ali*, 1978.
Roberts, James B. and Alexander G. Skutt, *The Boxing Register: International Boxing Hall of Fame Official Record Book*, McBooks Press, 1997.
Suster, Gerald, *Champions of the Ring: The Lives and Times of Boxing's Heavyweight Heroes*, Robson Books, 1992.

> **Periodicals**

Business Week, April 12, 1999, p. 47.
Esquire, September 1996, p. 138.
Jet, January 27, 1997, pp. 32-33; September 29, 1997, p. 46.
New York Times, October 20, 1996, p. 2; September 14, 1997, p. 34.
New York Times Magazine, July 17, 1988 (opening quote).
Philadelphia Inquirer, August 12, 1990.
Sports Illustrated, February 1964; December 20, 1976; April 25, 1988; September 29, 1997, p. 16.

Salvador Allende

*"*H*istory is on our side, and it is made by the people."*

Born July 26, 1908, in Valparaiso, Chile, Salvador Allende Gossens was the first democratically elected Marxist leader in history. He died under suspicious circumstances during a coup led by Chile's military on September 11, 1973.

When Salvador Allende became the first Communist politician to come to power after open, freely contested national elections, he planned to set Chile on the course of his "Chilean Way" to socialism. He was hailed as the successor to Marx, Lenin, and Mao, but respected all the more for the peaceful political triumph he engineered that gave him the country's presidency. Three years later, the 65-year-old was slain in one of the bloodiest coups in the history of contemporary South America.

Allende was born on July 26, 1908 in Valparaiso, Chile, the narrow, mountainous country's largest port. His father, Salvador Allende Castro, was a lawyer, and the families of both parents had long been active on Chile's national scene. One grandfather, an official in the Masons, had founded Chile's first secular school; another was a famed doctor and war hero. Allende—who took his mother's name, as customary in the Spanish-settled country—was educated at several different schools, both in Valparaiso and other locales. Finishing at the age of 16, he enlisted in the military, and entered the Coraceros Cavalry Regiment in another coastal city, Viña del Mar.

Allende moved to Santiago, the capital city, to enroll in the medical school of the University of Chile. He quickly proved himself an active and academically achieving student, but he also credited this phase of his life for awakening in him a political awareness. Indeed, the medical students as a whole were known for their leftist activities, "because we lived in the poor neighborhoods near the school, and we learned very quickly that good health is something you buy, and many people cannot pay the price," he told *New York Times Magazine* writer Norman Gall. He read the works of Marx and Lenin, became an active participant in the student occupation of the university, and was even jailed on two occasions. He was ousted for a time from the medical school, but permitted to resume his studies.

After earning his degree in 1932, Allende could not find a job as a physician. He was the only applicant for one post, but was repeatedly turned down; instead he took jobs at a mental hospital, a dental school, and even worked in the coroner's office. Performing autopsies, he said, "gave me a lesson for the rest of my life," he told Gall, for he witnessed firsthand just how poverty ravaged a body, in comparison to those who had lived and died well.

Allende remained active politically during his first years as a doctor, founding the Chilean Socialist Party in 1933. Four years later, he was elected to the lower house of Chile's legislature, the

Chamber of Deputies, where he quickly established himself as a champion of the poor with the introduction of bills to improve public-health funding and ease some of the other institutionalized problems of Chile's desperately poor. Because of his background, he was named Minister of Health in 1939 in the cabinet of a leftist president. After a massive earthquake in 1939, he was appointed to head the national relief effort.

Allende blamed capitalism for the miserable conditions under which many people lived in Chile, though the country could boast one of the oldest and most stable democracies in Latin America. In its Andes mountains were rich mineral deposits, and American mining companies had played an influential role in Chilean politics for decades. The mines produced one-quarter of the world's copper supply, but little of that wealth found its way to the majority of Chileans. Despite its seeming affluence and even a national health care system, Chile was still plagued by alarmingly high rates of malnutrition and reducible diseases. The nation could also boast a sizable amount of arable land, but there was little large-scale agriculture, and instead it imported wheat, meat, and other staples at high prices. It had 3,000 miles of Pacific Ocean coastline, but there was no commercial fishing industry at all. Many Chileans lived in dire poverty, and housing shortages in the cities created huge slums of squatters, which were known as *callampas,* or mushrooms.

Throughout his long political career, Allende asserted that the capitalist system was willing, but unable to solve such suffering, simply by nature of the system itself. Only Marxism, which he asserted was less a political doctrine than a way of interpreting data about poverty, social conditions, and their relation to a nation's resources, could relieve such poverty and inequality. Capitalism could not create a better life for Chileans, Allende told the *New York Times Magazine,* "because the system is exhausted and does not allow for more . . . because we are a colonial nation. Dependent on . . . imperialist capital. For this reason, to be a revolutionary means to break this economic, cultural and political dependence."

Allende won election to the upper chamber of the Chilean national legislature, the Senate, in 1945. In 1952, he made his first bid for the nation's presidency, allying with the then-outlawed Communist Party in the country; he came in last. In 1958, he ran once again on the Communist (again an official party) ticket, and lost a close race this time. Six years later, he was trounced by a friend from his boyhood, Christian Democrat leader Eduardo Frei. By the time the 1970 elections neared, Cold War politics were being played out in countries like Chile on a dangerous scale. Both the United States and its allies in Western Europe, and the Communist powers of the Soviet Union and China, were actively interfering in the internal politics of several nations around the globe in an attempt to create spheres of influence.

By 1970, even Chile's middle class were living in poverty. Government office workers earned just $30 or $40 a month, and had to buy clothes and even shoes on credit. Allende campaigned this fourth time on a platform that planned widespread reforms to alleviate unemployment and rampant inflation. Allende and his Unidad Popular Party—a coalition of liberals, Socialists, Communists, and some Christian Democrats—also gained support for their promise to nationalize certain industries, undertake serious agrarian reform, and replace Congress with a more democratically chosen People's Assembly.

The United States was worried about the upcoming elections in Chile, especially with registered Communist Party members in the country reaching a high of 60,000. Anti-Communist doctrine often asserted that in a free election, few would vote in a Communist government, which made the seizure of power by violence or civil war a necessity (as with the U.S.S.R., China, and Cuba). Nevertheless, Chile still maintained cordial relations with the United States, and the large number of diplomats and employees of the mining industry helped provide cover for the CIA's plans to influence the September, 1970 elections. They took place under the arms of Chile's military forces to ensure fairness, however, and Allende's Unidad Popular won a plurality, but not a majority; it was customary for a joint session of Congress to select the frontrunner, and again, covert U.S. actions tried to influence the outcome.

The CIA also helped rouse trouble by other means in the days following the election and before the confirmation by Congress. A financial panic occurred, and many upper-class Chileans fled the country with all their money. Yet Congress would only confirm Allende as president for the next six years if he agreed to a series of amendments to the constitution that would safeguard personal and political freedoms. He did, and was inaugurated on November 3, 1970. He became the first freely elected Marxist in the Western hemisphere, coming to power without a revolution, coup, or outside intervention.

Allende immediately set about implementing what he termed a "republic of the working class." In July of 1971, he signed a historic amendment to the constitution that gave Chile control over its mineral wealth, which took much of the power away from the American mining companies. He reestablished diplomatic ties with Cuba, led Chile as the first South American nation to establish relations with China, and nationalized several industries, among them the vital coal and steel concerns. He even authorized a Ford Motor Company automobile manufacturing plant to be taken over by the state. The government also began buying stock in banks with government funds, and bought out two major foreign lenders; from Chile's large landholders, the government seized 2.5 million acres for agrarian reform. But extremist leftists opposed some of his policies, and Chile was changing too quickly for others; strikes and economic turmoil prevailed.

Yet Allende's most troubling source of opposition came from the armed forces, which were controlled by a conservative cadre of officers. In September of 1973, the group of generals and anti-Communist politicians called for his resignation, and he refused; on the morning of September 11, Chileans who lived in the numerous coastal cities along the Pacific woke up to see the Chilean navy in full strength in their harbors. The fleet had been amassing for a planned annual joint exercise with the U.S. Marines, but once at sea, soldiers were informed that a coup was about to take place.

Fighting broke out everywhere across the country, and it would end as the bloodiest coup in twentieth-century South American history. Allende's presidential bodyguard contingent fought to defend his life, and a battle for the center of Santiago raged. All important government offices and ministries were located within a few short blocks. Late in the morning, Allende spoke from La Moneda, the presidential palace. He condemned the leaders of the coup, and declared his refusal to surrender. "I will pay with my life for the loyalty of the people," he said. "And I will tell you I am certain the seed which has been planted in the conscience of thousands and thousands of Chileans shall not be totally uprooted. They are strong, they are able to subdue us, but social processes cannot be detained by either crime or force. History is on our side, and it is made by the people."

Later that day, Chilean Air Force jets began bombing the palace; tear gas assaults followed, and Allende himself fired a submachine gun from the windows to defend the seat of government. Realizing their cause was hopeless, Allende surrendered, and was found dead in the formal Independence Hall of La Moneda, the victim of a self-inflicted gunshot wound. His family was allowed to hurriedly bury a sealed coffin; when his widow, Hortensia Bussi Allende, asked that the coffin be opened, a pane of glass revealed a face swathed in bandages underneath. In the end, 5,000 Chileans died in the coup, and Army chief of staff Augusto Pinochet Ugarte assumed control of the country. Over a quarter-century of repression and human-rights abuses followed.

Sources

➤ Books

Sandford, Robinson Rojas, *The Murder of Allende and the End of the Chilean Way to Socialism,* translated from the Spanish by Andrée Conrad, Harper & Row, 1976.
Varas, Florencia and José Manuel Vergara, *Coup! Allende's Last Day,* Stein and Day, 1975.

➤ Periodicals

New York Times, September 12, 1973, p. A1.
New York Times Magazine, November 1, 1970, p. 26.

Cleveland Amory

"The mark of a civilized person is how he treats what's underneath him."*

Born September 2, 1917, in Nahant, Massachusetts, Cleveland Amory was a writer, humorist, social historian, and outspoken animal-rights activist who was perhaps best known for his affectionate tales of a stray cat he rescued and named Polar Bear. He died of an abdominal aneurysm at his home in New York City, New York on October 14, 1998.

A self-described "curmudgeon" whose crusty demeanor belied his deep love of animals, Cleveland Amory was one of the world's most famous animal-welfare activists. He championed the notion that "animals have rights, too," and repeatedly called on his fellow human beings to recognize and halt the suffering of both domestic and wild animals. It was Amory's firm belief that if people demonstrated a little more compassion for other living creatures, the world might be a better place for everyone.

Born in the resort town of Nahant, Massachusetts, but raised in Boston, Cleveland Amory was the son of Leonore Cobb Amory and Robert Amory, a textile manufacturer descended from a long line of prosperous merchants. He thus enjoyed a privileged upbringing as a member of one of Boston's most socially prominent and well-to-do families. Amory attended Milton Academy before heading off to Harvard University, where he edited the *Harvard Crimson* newspaper during his senior year. After graduating in 1939, he worked very briefly as a reporter for the *Nashua Telegraph* in Nashua, New Hampshire, and the *Arizona Star* in Tucson, then served as managing editor of the *Prescott Evening Courier* in Prescott, Arizona. Amory moved back east later that same year and settled in Philadelphia, where he became associate editor of the *Saturday Evening Post*, the youngest person ever to work for the magazine in that capacity. When the United States entered World War II in 1941, he left his job to serve in Army Intelligence.

Amory launched his free-lance career as a writer in 1943. Over the next decade-and-a-half, he turned out several classic works of social history that earned him a reputation as a sardonic observer of life among the upper class. His first book, *The Proper Bostonians* (1947), poked good-natured fun at his hometown's wealthiest and most notable residents, from colonial days onward. Amory followed that with a novel, *Home Town* (1950), that satirized the business of book publishing, then returned to social commentary in 1952 with *The Last Resorts*, a bitingly witty look at the favorite seasonal getaways of American high society. In 1960, he published a book entitled *Who Killed Society?* that charted the rise and fall of the upper class.

Amory was involved in a variety of other journalistic endeavors during his long career. He was a social commentator on the NBC-TV "Today" show from 1952 to 1963 and chief critic for *TV Guide* from 1963 to 1976. He also contributed a column to the *Saturday Review* from 1952 to 1972, wrote and delivered a daily radio essay entitled "Curmudgeon at Large," and served as senior contributing editor to *Parade* magazine from 1980 until his death.

But it was Amory's animal-rights work that eventually took center stage in his life and brought him a different kind of fame. His interest in the field dated back to his days as a newspaper reporter when he covered a bullfight on the Mexican border that left him so sickened and angry that he picked up a cushion and threw it at the matador. He subsequently "joined just about every animal society I could find," he told interviewer Jean W. Ross of *Contemporary Authors*. Finally, in 1967 he established his own New York City-based animal welfare group, the Fund for Animals. "We speak for those who can't" was (and still is) its motto, and to that end, the Fund conducted a four-pronged assault on the abuse and exploitation of both domestic and wild animals involving "litigation, legislation, education, and confrontation," according to its founder.

Amory served without pay as the president of the Fund for Animals and was its chief spokesperson. In his writings and during his appearances on television and radio programs, he sharply criticized his fellow human beings for causing animals to suffer and for remaining indifferent to their suffering. In short, observed *Detroit News* reporter Chris Rizk, "For those of us who were too shy or too worried to stand up and defend our vegetarianism or pick a fight with those who wouldn't stop hunting, he picked up the gauntlet."

Indeed, the Fund for Animals has been in the forefront of many a battle over the years. During the early 1970s, for example, Amory and his supporters worked to gain passage for a number of significant pieces of federal legislation, including the Endangered Species Act, the country's strongest wildlife protection law. The Fund also took its message directly to consumers in 1974 with its "Real People Wear Fake Fur" advertising campaign featuring a number of celebrities.

The Fund's tactics grew bolder in 1979 when members traveled to the eastern coast of Canada to stop the clubbing of baby seals prized by hunters for their fur. As Amory explained in his interview with Ross, "We painted them with a red organic dye which is harmless to the seals but makes their coats worthless for what the sealers wanted to beat them to death for." The incident garnered worldwide attention and remains one of the Fund's most famous attempts to stop a practice it deemed unnecessarily cruel.

It was during this period that Amory published a hard-hitting condemnation of society's treatment of animals entitled *Man Kind?: Our Incredible War on Wildlife* (1974). He directed most of his rage at those who trap and kill for sport as well as those who exploit animals for their meat, fur, and other products. Often credited with igniting the anti-hunting movement in the United States, *Man Kind?* provoked much heated discussion and was even the subject of an editorial in the *New York Times.* In addition, it served as the inspiration for the CBS-TV documentary "The Guns of Autumn."

The Fund for Animals adhered to its activist agenda during the 1980s, launching what is perhaps its best known rescue effort at the beginning of the decade—saving nearly 600 burros scheduled to be shot by the National Park Service in Arizona's Grand Canyon. This massive four-year project involved capturing the threatened animals and then airlifting them out of the canyon. Similar burro rescues later took place at the China Lake Naval Weapons Center and the Death Valley National Monument region, both in California. In 1983, the Fund turned its attention to saving the lives of some 3,000 goats at a U.S. Navy weapons facility on an island off the California coast near San Diego. In each instance, the animals had been targeted for death as "nuisances."

During the late 1980s and throughout the 1990s, Amory and the Fund took on hunting and hunters. Through lawsuits and public-pressure campaigns, they were able to block a special hunting season on wolves in Minnesota, for instance, and also managed to halt black bear hunting for one season in California. They even persuaded state officials in Montana to ban the hunting of bison that wandered outside the boundaries of Yellowstone National Park. They subsequently focused on ending grizzly bear hunting in Montana, elk hunting in Arizona, black bear hunting in Colorado, Wyoming, Florida, and Maryland, "canned" hunts of exotic species on Texas game ranches, and pigeon shoots in Florida, North Carolina, and Pennsylvania. During this same period, the Fund also took action against commercial trapping, bear wrestling, cockfighting, and the killing of coyotes, foxes, bobcats, and other forms of wildlife in hunting contests.

Domestic pets also benefited from the Fund's attention through the years. Amory was especially sensitive to the challenges faced by shelters overflowing with kittens and puppies as well as adult cats and dogs. He actively promoted adopting pets from shelters and encouraged people to have their dogs and cats spayed or neutered. To that end, in 1996 the Fund opened its own high-volume, low-cost spay and neuter clinic in New York City.

Amory's most enduring legacy, however, may well turn out to be the trio of books he wrote about Polar Bear, a starving, bedraggled cat he rescued from a New York City alley on Christmas Eve 1977. All three titles—*The Cat Who Came for Christmas* (1987), *The Cat and the Curmudgeon* (1990), and *The Best Cat Ever* (1993)—sold millions of copies and enjoyed lengthy stays on the bestseller list. Each painted a humorous and heartwarming portrait of the special relationship that developed between the two over time. Amory was heartened by the public's response to the story of Polar Bear, remarking in his interview with Ross that "if I were responsible for a lot of cats coming out of shelters . . . I would feel that was the best thing I had done."

Some people, however, might single out another Amory project as perhaps the "best thing" he ever did. In 1980, he and the Fund for Animals purchased a large tract of land in eastern Texas to serve as a refuge for hundreds of abused and abandoned animals of every conceivable type. Named the Black Beauty Ranch in honor of one of Amory's favorite books, it was the fulfillment of a lifelong dream. "The animals are not here to be looked at," he declared to a reporter for *People*. "They're here to be looked after." At Black Beauty Ranch, the animals—many of them from the Fund's own rescue campaigns as well as from private owners, zoos, circuses, and research laboratories—are allowed to live out their lives with dignity. Amory wrote about this ambitious undertaking and profiled many of the animals cared for at the sanctuary in his final book, *Ranch of Dreams* (1997).

On many occasions during his life, Amory was asked if he thought animals had souls that went to heaven after death. He even debated the question once with a Catholic priest early in his animal-rights career. "I told the good father that if he and I were going in the future to some wonderful Elysian Field and the animals were not going to go anywhere, that was all the more reason to give them a little better shake in the one life they did have," he recalled in his interview with Ross. And if there was any doubt about what Amory believed, it was put to rest following Polar Bear's death in 1992. Etched on his beloved cat's stone monument at the Black Beauty Ranch are the words, "'Til we meet again."

Amory died of an aneurysm at the age of 81 on October 14, 1998. He remained active right up until the end, spending the day in his office at the Fund for Animals and then passing away in his sleep later that evening. His ashes were scattered around Black Beauty Ranch, where his headstone stands next to that of Polar Bear. Staffers at both the Fund for Animals and the Black Beauty Ranch have vowed that Amory's work will continue, "just the way Cleveland would have wanted it."

Sources

➤ On-line

"Animal Timeline," *Fund for Animals,* http://www.fund.org/timeline.html (January 23, 2000).
"Author Cleveland Amory: Lifetime Leader for Animals," *Fund for Animals,* http://www.fund.org/amory.html (January 23, 2000).
"Fund for Animals President Cleveland Amory Dies at 81," *Fund for Animals,* http://www.fund.org/news/amory.html (January 23, 2000).

➤ Books

Amory, Cleveland, *Ranch of Dreams: The Heartwarming Story of America's Most Unusual Animal Sanctuary,* Viking, 1997.
Contemporary Authors New Revision Series, Volume 29, Gale, 1990 (opening quote).

➤ Periodicals

Detroit News, October 21, 1998.
Economist, October 24, 1998.
New York Times, October 16, 1998, p. B11.
People, August 22, 1983; December 8, 1997; November 2, 1998, p. 62.
Texas Monthly, January 1999, p. 52.
U.S. News and World Report, February 5, 1990, p. 35.

Lance Armstrong

"❞**I**❝*f I never had cancer, I never would have won the Tour de France. I'm convinced of that. I wouldn't want to do it all over again, but I wouldn't change a thing."*

Born September 18, 1971, in Plano, Texas, Lance Armstrong made a remarkable recovery from advanced testicular cancer to win the 1999 Tour de France. Address: Lance Armstrong Foundation, PO Box 27483, Austin, TX 78755-2483.

A s winner of the 1999 Tour de France, Lance Armstrong is not only an American success story for his cycling talents, but also because of the seemingly insurmountable obstacles he overcame on his way to achieving this goal. After chalking up several notable victories at events like the World Road Race Championship, Thrift Drug Triple Crown, and Tour DuPont, Armstrong was dubbed the "Golden Boy" of American cycling and credited with restoring national pride in the sport, long dominated by Europeans. However, in 1996, at age 25, he was stricken with cancer in the prime of his career. Remarkably, Armstrong used the same determination in fighting the disease as he had in his competitions in order to beat back the tumors in his testicles, lungs, abdomen, lymph nodes, and brain. He managed to overcome the odds not only to survive, but also to return to his career and ride to victory at several more contests, including the world's most respected cycling event.

Armstrong was born on September 18, 1971, in Plano, Texas, a suburb of Dallas. His parents split up when he was very young, and his mother Linda—who had her only child when she was just 17 years old—then married Terry Armstrong. They later divorced as well, and Armstrong's mother married technical recruiter John Walling in 1992. His mother, whom Alexander Wolff in *Sports Illustrated* described as a "5 ft. 3 in., 100-pound steel magnolia," worked as a secretary to provide for her son when her marriages did not work out, displaying a tenacity that rubbed off on her son. As Armstrong told Wolff, "She instilled all her drive, motivation and toughness in me."

Athletic from a tender age, when Armstrong was in fifth grade, he began running six miles a day after school and entering weekend races with a mix of youth and adults. Throughout the years he would amass several ribbons and trophies for his age groups. He later took up swimming. He tried sports like baseball, football, and basketball, but he was better at endurance events than those requiring coordination. At age 13, Armstrong began competitive cycling and combined his three favorite activities to begin entering triathlons, contests which include a 1,000-meter swim, 15-mile bike ride, and three-mile run. Also at 13, he won the Iron Kids Triathlon and became a professional triathlete at age 16. In high school, he twice became the national sprint-course triathlon champion back-to-back in 1989 and 1990, and in 1988 *Triathlete* magazine named him rookie of the year.

Soon, Armstrong realized that his favorite part of triathlons was being on the bike—it was his strongest activity, and others noticed this as well. When he was a senior at Plano East High School, the U.S. Olympic development team invited Armstrong to train with them in Colorado Springs, Colorado. This required taking six weeks off of school to train, and he was told he could not graduate if he did so. Risking his diploma for the time being, Armstrong joined the Subaru-Montgomery team coached by Eddie Borysewicz, who had led the 1984 Olympic team. Armstrong eventually took private classes and graduated from high school in 1989.

The summer following his graduation, Armstrong qualified for the 1990 junior world team and subsequently placed eleventh in the World Championship Road Race, posting the best time of any American since 1976. He also earned second place at the national team time trials that year. In 1990, before turning 19, he moved to Austin, Texas, mainly because he enjoyed the lively music scene there. Also that year, he became the U.S. national amateur champion, in addition to winning the First Union Grand Prix and the Thrift Drug Classic, both of which are usually won by professionals. In 1991, Armstrong competed in the Tour DuPont, then the longest and most difficult stage race, covering 1,085 miles over 11 days. He finished in the middle of the pack, but many held high hopes for the newcomer. That same year, Armstrong won Italy's 11-day Settimana Bergamasca race. Although Italian fans threw tacks on the road to slow him down, he won by more than a minute, defeating an Italian competitor.

In 1992, Armstrong finished second in the U.S. Olympic time trials and raced in the Summer Olympics in Barcelona, Spain. Though he was favored to win, in a rare slump, he came in a disappointing fourteenth in that 115-mile road race. Undeterred, he turned professional immediately after the Olympics, joining the Motorola team on a paid basis. In his first pro event, the San Sebastian Classic, in Spain, he came in dead last out of 111 competitors in the daylong event, but insisted on finishing. Though he was crushed, he signed up for a World Cup race in Zurich, Switzerland, two weeks later, in which he placed second and stunned the European racing world.

Armstrong continued to put in a strong showing in 1993, winning several titles, including cycling's coveted "Triple Crown" with victories at the Thrift Drug Classic, the Kmart West Virginia Classic, and the CoreStates Race (the U.S. Professional Championship). For this accomplishment, he received a $1 million bonus, which he shared with his Motorola teammates, who were ranked among the top five in the world. This was the first time ever that an American team had reached this high of a position in cycling.

In July of 1993, Armstrong started off powerfully in his first Tour de France, considered by many to be the world's most prestigious race. He won the eighth stage of the 21-stage race, only the fifth American and the third-youngest to win a stage, but then sunk to 62nd place and eventually pulled out. Earlier that year, he came in second in May at the Tour DuPont, a 12-stage race, which was a respectable showing, especially for a 21-year-old racer. Most cyclists are thought to be in their prime in their mid-twenties, because they have had more time to hone their mental skills by this point, in addition to developing their physical strength.

The following month, August of 1993, in the most important success of his career up to that point, Armstrong prevailed at the World Road Race Championship in Oslo, Norway. This one-day event covered 161 miles and was rendered more difficult and dangerous that year by pouring rain. The slick roads caused Armstrong—now the leader of the Motorola team—to crash twice, but his teammates drafted him for a while and allowed him to restore his composure and strength. (Drafting is when a rider takes the rear position in a team, thus obtaining the benefit of wind blockage.) By the end of the race he broke away from the lead pack and finished in 6 hours, 17 minutes, and 10 seconds.

Armstrong's performance at the World Road Race Championship made him the youngest person ever, and the second American, to win this contest. "The day changed my life," Armstrong told Leigh Montville in *Sports Illustrated.* "The expectation levels grew." In an unorthodox move, the new world champion brought his mother onto the victory stand with him. The achievement also prompted Norway's King Harland to invite Armstrong to pay him a visit. However, the king did not extend the courtesy to the cyclist's mother, so he turned down the offer. King Harland later changed his mind, and both Armstrong and his mother attended the reception.

At his next Tour DuPont in 1994, Armstrong again placed second and came in seventh in the world championship road race. He also took second place at the San Sebastian Classic in Spain as well as a race in France. Before the 1995 Tour DuPont, according to Montville, Armstrong stated, "I don't want to finish second again." In the past, his weakness in this contest was in the time trials, when riders race against the clock alone, rather than competing against others. This time, Armstrong noted to Montville, "I think I'm stronger. I've never felt better. I just hope I can keep this form for as long as it takes." Sure enough, Armstrong pulled through this time, winning three of 12 individual stages and coming in two minutes ahead of his closest rival in the race, Viatcheslav Ekimov of Russia, who had defeated him the previous year.

After this victory, Motorola teammate Fabio Casartelli hit a wall in the 1995 Tour de France and died from head injuries, prompting Armstrong to ride even harder. He again won a stage of the race this time, although he later came in 36th, but it marked the first time he had finished. He also won the San Sebastian Classic that year, making him the first American to win a World Cup road race. He took this contest again in 1996, in addition to the Fleche Wallone in Belgium.

Also in 1996, Armstrong won his second Tour DuPont with the Motorola team and set records for 10 career stage victories, 5 stage wins, 14 top-three finishes, 11 consecutive days as race leader, largest margin of victory (at 3 minutes, 15 seconds), and fastest average speed in a time trial (at 32.9 miles per hour). In addition, he rode again for the 1996 U.S. Olympic team in Atlanta, Georgia, placing sixth in the time trials and 12th in the road race. The races seemed to fatigue him more than usual, and earlier that summer he was unable to finish the Tour de France, as he came down with bronchitis.

Despite these disappointments, Armstrong remained seventh-ranked in the world and in 1996 signed a contract with France's Team Cofidis. That October, though, in a shock to cyclists and athletes everywhere, he was diagnosed with testicular cancer that had spread to his abdomen, lungs, and lymph nodes. After experiencing severe pain in a testicle and coughing up blood, he saw the doctor and had the testicle removed the next day. Armstrong then gave up red meat, dairy products, and coffee, and began aggressive chemotherapy. Even with as far as the cancer had spread, he was given a 65 to 85 percent chance of survival. "I might have a bald head and not be as fast," he commented, "but I'll be out there. I'm going to race again."

In yet another blow, however, doctors soon discovered tumors on Armstrong's brain. His odds of survival dipped to 50-50, then to 40 percent. The surgery to remove them was a success, though, and, after more chemotherapy treatment, Armstrong was declared cancer-free in February of 1997. Though his lungs were scarred, he was determined to get back on his bike. When Cofidis canceled his contract and yanked his $600,000 annual salary, he became a free agent but did not attract any interest. Finally he managed to snag a position worth about $200,000 with the United States Postal Service team; he called the pay cut "an 80-percent cancer tax," reported Todd Balf in *Bicycling*.

By 1998, Armstrong was back in competition and looked to be in good condition. He took fourth place at the World Road Race Championships and won the Cascade Classic, the Rheinland Pfalz Rundfardt, the Spring 56K Criterium, and the Tour of Luxembourg. He also placed second at the First Union Invitational. By the summer of 1999, Armstrong was ready to compete again in the Tour de France, made up of 2,290 miles of exhausting terrain. Though it was a victory for Armstrong to even be competing in the event, he captured even more attention when it began to look like he was going to win. He was not demoralized by rumors, circulated in the French press, that his amazing comeback was assisted by performance-enhancing drugs, especially since frequent blood and urine tests showed no trace of such substances.

In an awe-inspiring finish, Armstrong ended up winning the Tour de France 7 minutes and 37 seconds ahead of his nearest rival, Alex Zulle of Switzerland. He dominated the race from the start, becoming only the second American to win the contest, and posted an average speed of 40.2 kilometers an hour, or 25 miles per hour, breaking the record of 39.9 kilometers per hour set in 1998. The victory was not only uplifting due to Armstrong's cancer fight, but also as a matter of national pride, since he was riding with an American-sponsored team—the U.S. Postal Service team, which had not even won a stage in its first two Tour de France outings in 1997 and 1998—and seven of the nine members were American. Greg LeMond, the other American Tour de France champion, had ridden with French teams when he won in 1986, 1989, and 1990.

At five feet, ten inches and 158 pounds, Armstrong is broad-shouldered and has short brown hair. He owns a million-dollar home in Austin named "Casa Linda" after his mother. He helped design the Mediterranean-style home, which took two years to plan and build, and splits his time between there and a house in Nice, France. Armstrong established the Lance Armstrong Junior Olympic Race Series in 1995 in order to promote cycling and racing among American youth, and in 1996 he founded the Lance Armstrong Foundation for Cancer, to benefit cancer research and promote early cancer detection and awareness. In 1998, Armstrong married Kristin Richard, a former public relations executive he met through his cancer foundation. They had their first child, Luke David, on October 12, 1999, using sperm that was frozen before

Armstrong began chemotherapy. His autobiography is due out from Putnam in 2000, and a film based on his life is in the works as well.

Sources

➤ On-line

Lance Armstrong Online! (official web site), http://lancearmstrong.com (October 25, 1999).
United States Postal Service Pro Cycling Team (official web site), http://uspsprocycling.com (October 25, 1999).

➤ Periodicals

Bicycling, July 1995, p. 50; August 1996, p. 28; February 1997, p. 44; July 1997, p. 86; January-February 1998, p. 52; May 1998, p. 21.
Men's Fitness, October 1998, p. 102.
New York Times, July 25, 1999, sec, 2, p. 23; July 26, 1999, p. D1.
People, October 28, 1996, p. 56; August 9, 1999, p. 62.
Publisher's Weekly, August 30, 1999, p. 12.
Sporting News, August 9, 1999, p. 63.
Sports Illustrated, May 24, 1993, p. 50; July 4, 1994, p. 52; May 15, 1995, p. 32; May 20, 1996, p. 48; October 21, 1996, p. 19; August 9, 1999, p. 68 (opening quote).
Texas Monthly, December 1996, p. 116.
Time, July 22, 1999, p. 66.
U.S. News & World Report, August 9, 1999, p. 60.

Hanan Ashrawi

"**O**ur parents were the dispossessed. We are the disinherited. What I want for our children is independence and freedom."

Born October 8, 1946, in Nablus, Palestine, Hanan Ashrawi first gained international prominence during the late 1980s as a spokesperson for the Palestinian point of view in the ongoing struggle between Arabs and Israelis in the Middle East. Address: c/o Miftah, P.O. Box 38588, Jerusalem 97800.

One of the most influential women in the Arab world—and certainly the most recognizable—is Hanan Ashrawi, who has championed the cause of the Palestinian people for more than three decades. Her emergence as an international spokesperson is all the more remarkable considering that she is a Christian woman in a society dominated by Muslim men. Yet as a reporter for *People* once observed, Ashrawi is "perhaps the most sophisticated weapon the Palestinians have ever fielded against Israel." Since first attracting widespread public attention in 1988, she has proven to be especially skilled at changing the image of her people from that of menacing terrorists to sympathetic victims of violence and repression.

Hanan Mikhail Ashrawi was born October 8, 1946, in the town of Nablus in what was then Palestine (now Israel). She is the youngest of five daughters of Dauod Mikhail, a physician, and his wife, Wadi'a Ass'ad, a nurse. The demands of Dauod Mikhail's profession, coupled with political instability in the region, forced the family to move frequently during the first few years of Ashrawi's life. Eventually, the Mikhails were able to settle in Dauod's hometown of Ramallah, a part of Palestine that came under Jordanian control in 1951. There young Hanan enjoyed a privileged upbringing surrounded by numerous relatives and friends.

Dauod Mikhail was a social and political liberal who took a leading role in Palestinian affairs and helped establish the Palestine Liberation Organization (PLO). His activities did not always find favor among Jordanian authorities, and as a result, he was jailed several times throughout Ashrawi's childhood. Years later, she acknowledged that his willingness to take such a courageous stand on behalf of his people was a major source of inspiration to her as she herself took up the struggle for Palestinian self-determination.

Dauod Mikhail held progressive views on other matters as well. He had a deep respect for women and their abilities and thus raised his daughters to become educated and independent members of society, a concept that was very much at odds with the customs of the time. Ashrawi received her elementary and secondary schooling at a Quaker school for girls in Ramallah before heading off to Lebanon and the American University of Beirut in the late 1960s to major in English.

Ashrawi's political awakening occurred during her college years. Despite her firsthand knowledge of the Palestinian situation, she had always been somewhat sheltered from its harsher aspects. All of that changed, however, in the wake of the 1967 Arab-Israeli war when Israeli troops occupied the West Bank, which had been

Jordanian territory, and the Gaza Strip, which had belonged to Egypt. Suddenly the so-called "Palestinian question" became very personal for Ashrawi, whose hometown of Ramallah was located on the West Bank. As she later recalled in her autobiography, *This Side of Peace*, "Overnight, I had become an 'exile,' and most of my family remained under occupation. . . . The era of resistance had taken on a new urgency and momentum. Thus began a momentous transition in my life in which activism was the key."

Ashrawi joined the General Union of Palestinian Students (GUPS), an organization of young men and women who, like her, were eager to bring about the liberation of Palestine. She acted as the group's spokesperson, wrote pamphlets and leaflets, helped organize clandestine women's revolutionary groups, conducted political consciousness-raising classes, and escorted reporters during their visits to Palestinian refugee camps.

Following her graduation from the American University in 1970 with a master's degree in literature, Ashrawi literally had nowhere to go. She could not remain in Lebanon without a visa or a work permit, and Israeli authorities had denied her request for a permit to return to Ramallah. She then learned that as the top student in her class she had been chosen to receive a doctoral scholarship to the university of her choice. Within a month Ashrawi was on her way to the University of Virginia at Charlottesville, where she studied medieval and comparative literature and earned her doctorate in English literature.

Under the terms of an Israeli amnesty that allowed Palestinian exiles to rejoin their families in the West Bank, Ashrawi was finally able to go home in 1973. She then accepted a teaching position in the English department at Birzeit University and settled into academic life. She also allied herself with student groups and took part in their demonstrations on behalf of the Palestinian cause and peaceful coexistence with Israel. Outside the university, she organized feminist study groups and held consciousness-raising sessions to address the special problems faced by women in the male-dominated Arab culture.

In 1975 Ashrawi married Emile Ashrawi, a photographer, artist, and filmmaker, and by 1981 they were the parents of two daughters. Ashrawi thus spent the late 1970s and early 1980s tending to her growing family while also fulfilling her responsibilities at the university and remaining politically active.

Ashrawi's devotion to the Palestinian cause took on added urgency during the 1980s as the Israelis moved to consolidate their power in the West Bank and the Gaza Strip. More and more Israeli citizens began settling in the occupied zones, sparking tensions between the Palestinians and the newcomers. Palestinian protests were often answered with violent crackdowns. The last straw for many Palestinians came during Israel's 1982 invasion of Lebanon when Lebanese Christian militiamen allied with Israel brutally massacred hundreds of Palestinian refugees at two camps in Beirut. The incident radicalized Ashrawi as nothing before had ever done.

It was not until the late 1980s, however, that people outside the Middle East started to take notice of the plight of the Palestinians. In December 1987, acts of civil disobedience and low-level violence that came to be known as the *intifada*, or uprising, broke out in the Gaza Strip among Palestinians fed up with the occupation. News footage of rock-throwing protesters was broadcast around the world, underscoring the impression in some people's minds that the Palestinians were little more than terrorists fueled by hate.

Into this volatile situation stepped Ashrawi, who quickly emerged on the international scene as one of the chief spokespersons for the Palestinians. (Although she was chosen to fill that role by PLO leader Yasser Arafat, she is a political independent who has never been an official member of the group.) Especially memorable was her appearance on the ABC-TV news program "Nightline" in April 1988. A strikingly self-confident and articulate woman garbed in modern, western-style attire, Ashrawi presented the Palestinians' case with dignity and passion, and in the process she helped forge a new and more positive image of her people that stood in stark contrast to what most television viewers were accustomed to seeing. She won many new admirers as a result of her appearances on various news programs that year, even among Israeli observers.

Beginning in the spring of 1991, Ashrawi participated in private discussions with U.S. Secretary of State James Baker on the subject of an Arab-Israeli peace agreement. By this time, however, sympathy for the Palestinians' position had weakened considerably due to their support for Iraq in the Persian Gulf War earlier that same year. The Israelis flatly rejected the idea of inviting PLO delegates to any formal peace talks, a condition Ashrawi found untenable. Eventually, an agreement was reached between the two parties that allowed an advisory team of Palestinians from the PLO (including Ashrawi) to accompany the official Palestinian delegation.

Thus was launched a fitful journey toward peace that has frequently stalled, occasionally lurched forward, and often slipped backward throughout the 1990s and into the new century. Little came of the 1991-92 talks (known as the Madrid conference), but in 1993, following a series of top-secret meetings held in Oslo, Norway, Israeli prime minister Yitzhak Rabin and PLO leader Yasser Arafat reached an historic accord that specified the terms of limited Palestinian self-rule and gradual Israeli withdrawal from the West Bank.

Throughout this tumultuous period, Ashrawi continued to take an active role in the peace process as an official member of the Palestinian delegation at various conferences, where she frequently upstaged her fellow negotiators with her straightforward, no-nonsense style. She also addressed numerous international gatherings and published many articles. Consequently, her words and her face became identified more and more with the Palestinian people. Often she was the only voice of calm and reason amid the harsh rhetoric of others around her, which garnered her even more respect.

This rankled the Israelis, who resented the favorable attention she received. It also annoyed some Palestinians who felt she gave in too easily to both the Israelis and the Americans. Some fundamentalist Muslims among the Palestinians also did not like the fact that a woman—a Christian woman, no less—held such a high-profile position on behalf of "their" cause. Still others felt that her upper-class background made it impossible for her to understand the plight of the refugees. But Ashrawi was immensely popular with ordinary Palestinian people and capitalized on her rapport with the West to create a new image of them as the victims of violence rather than the perpetrators. "I feel a very strong need to convey the human quality, the real image of our people, that never came through before," she remarked in a *Time* article. "I am never far away from Palestinian reality."

After the signing of the Oslo accord in 1993, Ashrawi resigned from her position on the Palestinian negotiating team and announced that she would no longer be the PLO's official spokesperson. She also declined to serve in the newly formed Palestinian National Authority (also known as the Palestine Authority), an interim government charged with supervising affairs in Palestinian territory. Some saw this as evidence of a falling out with Yasser Arafat over the terms of the agreement with Israel (which she did not wholeheartedly support), but Ashrawi insisted that she just felt it was time for her to move on. She then turned her attention to a human rights group she had founded, the Palestinian Independent

Commission for Citizens' Rights. In addition to investigating both Israeli and Palestinian human rights violations, the commission addressed issues such as women's rights and religious tolerance.

The late 1990s were marked by several major events that threatened to derail the fragile peace process, including the November 1995 assassination of Israeli Prime Minister Yitzhak Rabin and the May 1996 election of his replacement, Benjamin Netanyahu, a vociferous critic of both Yasser Arafat and the PLO. After Netanyahu took office, the peace process more or less came to a halt when he began reneging on promises Rabin had made to Arafat. Even after Netanyahu lost a re-election bid in May 1999 to Ehud Barak, who had pledged to restart the peace process, serious disagreements continued.

Meanwhile, in January 1996 the Palestinian National Authority held its first-ever elections. To no one's surprise, Yasser Arafat triumphed in the presidential contest. Voters also chose Hanan Ashrawi to serve on the Palestinian Legislative Council; Arafat subsequently named her to his cabinet as minister of higher education. But almost from the start the new government was riddled with corruption. So profound was the anger and disgust among the Palestinian people by mid-1998 that Arafat reorganized his cabinet in an attempt to appease reform-minded members of the Legislative Council. Ashrawi, who was inexplicably switched to the post of minister of tourism in the shuffle, became so fed up with Arafat's failure to address the inadequacies of his administration that she resigned from the cabinet in August 1998.

In January 1999, Ashrawi founded Miftah: The Palestinian Initiative for the Promotion of Global Dialogue and Democracy, an organization devoted to "reinforcing the Palestinian nation-building process and the evolution of statehood to ensure democratic practice, the rule of law and respect for human rights," according to information available at its website. She balances her responsibilities as secretary general of Miftah with those she still holds as a member of the Palestinian Legislative Council, thus maintaining "one foot in the government and one in civil society," noted Diana Digges in a *Cairo Times* article.

Now that the Palestinians' armed struggle appears to be winding down, Ashrawi is fully committed to the political struggle that lies ahead, even though the future outlook by all accounts is gloomy at best. The Palestinian Authority faces ongoing problems with corruption, a crippled economy, and an ever-widening gulf between the old PLO establishment and ordinary Palestinian people. The key to overcoming these difficulties, Ashrawi told Digges, is to foster a change in mentality and establish a civil society as soon as possible. "We need public debate, freedom of the press, transparency, meritocracy," she explained. "We have to get rid of political patronage, nepotism and tribalist loyalties." In short, concluded Ashrawi, "We cannot continue to justify or rationalize our own shortcomings. It is up to us to ensure a democratic system. The moment you give up on that, there's no hope."

Sources

➤ On-line

"About Miftah," *Miftah: The Palestinian Initiative for the Promotion of Global Dialogue and Democracy,* http://www.miftah.org/AboutM/Index.html (March 2, 2000).

➤ Books

Ashrawi, Hanan, *This Side of Peace: A Personal Account,* Simon & Schuster, 1995.
Encyclopedia of World Biography, 2nd edition, Gale, 1998.
Victor, Barbara, *A Voice of Reason: Hanan Ashrawi and Peace in the Middle East,* Harcourt, 1994.

➤ Periodicals

Cairo Times, September 2-15, 1999.
Christian Century, February 7, 1996.
Commonweal, October 8, 1993; June 16, 1995.
Grand Rapids Press, January 6, 1997.
Interview, July 1995.
Mother Jones, March-April 1993.
People, March 9, 1992 (opening quote).
Time, May 25, 1992; August 17, 1998, p. 20.
U.S. News and World Report, January 22, 1996.

Isaac Asimov

"I *have been fortunate to be born with a restless and efficient brain, with a capacity for clear thought and an ability to put that thought into words. None of this is to my credit. I am the beneficiary of a lucky break in the genetic sweepstakes."*

Born c. January 1, 1920, in Petrovichi, Russia, Isaac Asimov was one of the most prolific writers of the twentieth century. He made his most significant contributions to the science fiction genre. He died on April 6, 1992, in New York City, New York.

Regarded as one of the best science fiction writers ever, Isaac Asimov redefined the genre, in part because of his knowledge of science fact. A trained chemist, he also wrote numerous volumes of nonfiction, including many books explaining science to the average person. In addition, he worked in other fiction genres, including mysteries. During his lifetime, Asimov wrote and edited hundreds of books, making him one of the most prolific writers of the twentieth century.

Born around January 1, 1920 (the exact date is unknown), in Petrovichi, Russia, Asimov was the son of Judah and Anna Rachel Berman Asimov. The middle-class, Russian-Jewish couple emigrated to the Brooklyn borough of New York City when Asimov was three years old. The family also included Asimov's brother, Stanley, and sister, Marcia. In 1928, Asimov became an American citizen.

Judah Asimov worked different jobs until he bought a candy store in 1926. He and his wife worked long hours running the business, leaving them with little time to devote to family activities. Asimov himself worked in the candy store after school, which curbed his social life considerably. But the experience shaped his work habits for life.

Asimov showed exceptional intelligence at an early age. He learned to read English on his own by the age of five. A few years later, he mastered Yiddish with some help from his father. Asimov was very conscious of his abilities, however, which made him somewhat arrogant, as he later admitted. Furthermore, he did not have good social skills and was not especially popular with his classmates. Yet he did well enough in school to skip several grades.

Asimov began writing stories at the age of 11, influenced by the pulp magazines (primarily science fiction) that his parents sold in the candy store. His father did not approve of these publications, but Asimov managed to convince him that those with "science" in the title were educational. He was a voracious reader of other forms of literature as well and checked out many books from the local library.

While still in high school, Asimov published his first story, "Little Brothers," in the school's literary journal. A few years later, in 1934, he graduated from Boys High School in Brooklyn at the age of only 15. Asimov contemplated pursuing a career as a writer, but his parents discouraged such dreams. They expected him to become a doctor.

To that end, Asimov attended Columbia University's Seth Low

Junior College from 1934 to 1936 before transferring to the primary campus. He earned his B.S. in chemistry in 1939. By then, Asimov had also begun to write science fiction stories.

In 1938 Asimov submitted several of his early stories to John Campbell, the editor of *Astounding Science Fiction*. Campbell did not publish these stories right away, but he passed along editorial comments to the young writer that proved helpful. Asimov reworked these stories and also produced new ones. In 1939 he finally sold a short story to Campbell entitled "Marooned Off Vesta." Asimov continued to rely on Campbell as an editor and his magazine as a forum until the early 1950s, when the protégé surpassed his mentor.

Despite the sale of "Marooned" and other stories, Asimov felt the pressure of his parents' expectations. He applied to medical schools but was rejected. Deciding to resume his education, he entered the graduate chemistry program at Columbia University and earned his M.A. in 1941. His literary ambitions had not disappeared, however, and the same year he earned his degree he published the short story "Nightfall" in *Astounding Science Fiction*. Nearly 30 years later, the Science Fiction Writers of America voted it the best science fiction story ever written.

Also during this period, Asimov began working on what became one his crowning achievements as a science fiction writer—a series of short stories featuring robots. He had started writing robot stories as early as 1939 and devised his famous Three Laws of Robotics (also known as the Robot Rules) in 1940. These rules governed the behavior of robots in human interaction in all of his subsequent work. Asimov's best known robot short stories were collected in the 1950 cycle *I, Robot*.

After earning his master's degree, Asimov continued his education in Columbia's Ph.D. program. His studies were interrupted, however, when the United States entered World War II in December 1941. From 1942 to 1945 Asimov held a civilian job as a junior research chemist at the Naval Air Experimental Station in Philadelphia. It was the first time he had worked anywhere other than in his father's candy store.

While living in Philadelphia, Asimov met the woman who would become his first wife, Gertrude Blugerman. They married on July 26, 1942, and eventually had two children, David and Robyn.

Though Asimov was worried about being drafted, he continued to write. He began work on what became "The Foundation Trilogy," his best known series of novels. They were published in installments during the early 1950s.

Asimov was finally drafted at the very end of World War II, after Japan had been defeated. His time in the army was brief, however, and by 1946 he had returned to his studies. He finished his Ph.D. in chemistry at Columbia in 1948. While he still wanted to pursue a career as a writer, he was unsure if he could making a living at it, even though he published fairly regularly.

Asimov had often clashed with his superiors at Columbia and therefore could not get a satisfactory job at that institution. In 1949 he was hired by Boston University's medical school to teach biochemistry to first-year students. He was not at all familiar with the subject but regarded teaching as a job that would enable him to support his family.

Meanwhile, Asimov continued to grow and improve as a writer. In 1950 he published his first novel, *Pebble in the Sky*, finally impressing his father. Asimov then published the three "Foundation" novels: *Foundation* (1951), *Foundation and Empire* (1952), and *Second Foundation* (1953). Asimov often incorporated his educational and intellectual interests into his science fiction writing.

Asimov also branched out from science fiction with nonfiction works such as science textbooks and science books for the general public. It was while writing a biochemistry textbook in 1951 that Asimov came to the conclusion that he did not want to do anything but write. Yet he continued to teach to support his family. Though he did not like most of his colleagues and did only minimal research, Asimov did move up through the academic ranks. By 1955, he had achieved tenure as an assistant professor.

In 1957, Asimov's poor attitude and disdain for his colleagues led university officials to fire him. Because he had tenure, however, he retained his title and kept up his affiliation with the school. Asimov did not seek out another teaching position. Instead, he turned to writing full time because he was finally earning enough to afford to do so. He worked long hours at his craft for most of the rest of his life, beginning every day at 7:30 a.m. and ending around 10 p.m. He also developed the habit of rewriting every piece only once after producing the first draft on a typewriter.

Asimov's interests as a writer continued to change and expand. Though he had basically stopped writing science fiction by the mid-1950s, he began contributing a column to the *Magazine of Fantasy and Science Fiction* in 1958 that appeared until just a few years before his death. But for the most part, Asimov devoted his energy to writing nonfiction. He was especially proud of his ability to explain science to a general audience in books such as *Asimov's New Guide to Science.*

Asimov also wrote on topics other than science. He produced biographies and biographical reference books, histories that ranged from the ancient Greeks to the nineteenth century, mysteries, and even a book on British playwright William Shakespeare entitled *Asimov's Guide to Shakespeare.* He also wrote and edited a number of anthologies.

Asimov attributed his success as a writer to his ability to write with clarity. "I make no effort to write poetically or in a high literary style," Mervyn Rothstein of the *New York Times* once quoted him as saying. "I try only to write clearly and I have the very good fortune to think clearly so that the writing comes out as I think, in satisfactory shape."

Asimov's writing did not garner him much favor with mainstream literary critics, but the science fiction community (among others) embraced him. In 1967 he was awarded the American Association for the Advancement of Science-Westinghouse Science Writing Award. At the urging of an editor, Asimov once again starting writing the occasional science fiction story or novel during the late 1960s. When he published these works—such 1972's *The Gods Themselves*—they often won awards.

While Asimov's stature as a writer of merit was rising and his output was increasing (by 1969, he had written and edited 100 books), his personal life was in turmoil. In 1970 he left Boston and returned to New York City. Three years later, he ended his unhappy marriage to Blugerman and then married psychiatrist Janet Opal Jeppson.

Asimov's fame as a science fiction writer prompted the launching of *Isaac Asimov's Science Fiction Magazine* in 1976, to which he contributed editorials. Even Boston University wanted to capitalize on his success. Though he had taught only occasionally through the years, in 1979 he was promoted to full professor and encouraged to establish closer ties to the institution.

By the late 1970s, Asimov had begun looking back over his long career. Having kept a detailed diary since the age of 18, he started writing his autobiography, which was ultimately published in three volumes. He also revisited his earlier successes in science fiction, producing a fourth book in the "Foundation" series in 1982 entitled *Foundation's Edge* that became his first best-seller. Asimov also wrote more robot books, including *The Robots of the Dawn* (1983). His later titles combined the two sub-genres. By 1984, Asimov had written 300 books.

After suffering a heart attack in 1977 and undergoing triple bypass surgery in 1983, Asimov's health was questionable at best. Nevertheless, he continued to write books at a furious pace. He died of heart and kidney failure on April 6, 1992, at New York University Hospital. By the time of his death, he had written and edited over 500 books, a testimonial to the skill and determination of a man who lived only to write.

Sources

➤ Books

Bleiler, E.F., *Science Fiction Writers,* Scribner, 1982, pp. 267-75.

Boerst, William J., *Isaac Asimov: Writer of the Future,* Morgan Reynolds, Inc., 1999.

Encyclopedia of World Biography, 2nd edition, Volume 1, Gale, 1998, pp. 338-41.

Garraty, John A. and Mark C. Carnes, editors, *American National Biography,* Volume 1, Oxford University Press, 1999, pp. 687-89.

Hipp, James W., editor, *Dictionary of Literary Biography Yearbook: 1992,* Gale, 1993, pp. 286-99.

Mooney, Louise, editor, *Newsmakers: 1992 Cumulation,* Gale, 1992, pp. 558-59.

➤ Periodicals

Daily Telegraph, April 7, 1992, p. 19.

New York Times, April 7, 1992, p. B7 (opening quote).

Time, December 19, 1988, p. 80.

U.S. News & World Report, April 20, 1992, p. 25.

Leo Hendrik Baekeland

*"*I*f I had to live my life over again I would not devote it to develop new industrial processes; I would try to add my humble efforts to use Science to the betterment of the human race."*

Born November 14, 1863, in Ghent, Belgium, chemist Leo Hendrik Baekeland created the first durable synthetic compound, and with it launched the modern plastics industry. He died on February 23, 1944.

L eo Hendrik Baekeland was one of the most illustrious scientist/entrepreneurs of his day, in an era rife with such great inventors. A Belgian immigrant who grew immensely wealthy by developing the first-ever synthetic material in the world, Baekeland had little patience with the fame and fortune that came his way as a result. Had his General Bakelite Corporation not been sold in 1939, his heirs would have become one of the richest families in the United States.

Baekeland was born in 1863 in Ghent, Belgium, the capital of the country's Flemish-speaking half. His father, Charles, was a shoemaker who, like many of his humble social status, never learned to read. He may have likely drank as well, forcing his only son Leo to take on much of the business himself by the time he was 12 in order to support the impoverished family. Baekeland was expected to continue in this profession for the rest of his life. His mother, however, had worked as a maid for well-to-do families as a young woman, and witnessed firsthand how much more pleasant were the lives of the moneyed; she instilled in her son a clear distaste for poverty as well as an ambition to lead a better life.

Reportedly Baekeland was also influenced by a Flemish translation of Ben Franklin's autobiography, which provided inspirational advice for young readers, urging them to study diligently in school, for instance, and save their earnings, no matter how meager. While in school, Baekeland tutored other students for money, and his natural academic abilities earned him a scholarship to Ghent University. He became the youngest student in its history, and earned two degrees, concluding with a doctorate in chemistry in 1884.

By the following year, Baekeland became a member of Ghent University's chemistry faculty, and had also met his future wife, Celine Swarts, who was the daughter of one of his former professors. Nicknamed "Bonbon," she was an attractive, vivacious woman, and their engagement represented, with Baekeland's degree, entry into the European academic bourgeoisie. After a few years, however, he applied for and received a travel scholarship to the United States, but not long after their arrival Bonbon discovered that she was expecting; Baekeland sent her back to Belgium in the belief that both she and the infant would benefit from access to her family and its resources. She and the baby, born in 1890 and named Jenny, spent the next two years there; extant letters reveal that Baekeland worried greatly about his financial circumstances during this era, and felt he was unable to support a family. He worked on a number of inventions, none of which earned him a steady income.

Bonbon was adamant, however, and likely sailed back to her husband around 1892. They would have two more children, George and Nina, but Jenny died at the age of five. By then Baekeland had perfected a type of chemically treated paper that allowed photographers to use artificial light to develop their images. The new medium had opened up an entirely new world of images, and during these decades grew dramatically in popularity. In 1888, the box camera and roll film were introduced, and further galvanized the art form by making it accessible to the average citizen of means. Baekeland called his paper Velox, and photographers found it a far more reliable and convenient way to develop film, especially with the advent of electric light. Velox made its inventor a small fortune with the company he had founded in 1893 to manufacture and sell it, the Nepera Chemical Co. Six years later, the Kodak Company bought Nepera and Velox from Baekeland for nearly $1 million.

That same year, Baekeland won a coveted appointment at Columbia University. He spent the next 17 years there as a research professor, but the post allowed him the freedom to pursue other profitable experiments in his home laboratory. With his newfound wealth, he purchased an estate outside Yonkers, New York, on the banks of the Hudson River. Called Snug Rock, it boasted palatial living quarters with stained-glass windows, a giant sunken bathtub, sweeping views, and several outbuildings. One of them Baekeland renovated into a state-of-the art lab, and ensconced himself inside. He wrote in his journals that he wished for solitude, that his family's lifestyle was less extravagant. Coming from a poor background, he considered himself a simple man happy to have achieved his station in life as a respected scientist and academic. He had no further aspirations toward wealth or fame, and resented the trappings of success. A large house, for instance, was necessary if a woman of Bonbon's status wanted to entertain, and a staff of servants were then obligatory to keep it functioning. "What do we want such a large house for, and why all these servants?," Baekeland wrote in his journal, according to a 1985 book by Natalie Robins and Steven M. L. Aronson about the Baekeland family and a sensational 1972 murder titled *Savage Grace.* "Why all that complicated trash of unnecessary furniture? All this complication becomes more and more irksome to me."

Baekeland instead occupied himself with a new project: developing a cost-effective substitute for shellac. Made from the resin of the Asian lac beetle, shellac had been a useful compound for coating wood. The world, however, was becoming increasingly wired for electricity, and shellac had become vital to the new industry because it made an excellent insulator for wires and switches. The cottage industry in Southeast Asia could not keep up with the demand—it took 15,000 beetles six months to make one pound—and the cost of shellac was rising precipitously. Scientists knew that a resinous material could be concocted by mixing two compounds, phenol and aldehyde.

From 1904 to 1907, Baekeland and his research assistants logged three years of failed experiments with various combinations of phenol and aldehyde; in his lab he heated them, but when they cooled they were either too hard or too soft. But when he blended carbolic acid and formaldehyde in what he called a "bakelizer," an iron vessel he had designed that allowed him to regulate the temperature and pressure of his compounds, he found the substance, though not varnish-like, had possibilities. It was a hard, translucent, moldable material, and he christened it "Bakelite."

Bakelite was the first synthetic product in history, created entirely in a laboratory, and caused a sensation when Baekeland introduced at the New York meeting of the American Chemical Society in 1909. His peers gave him a standing ovation. In his demonstration, he showed Bakelite to be lightweight, durable and unbreakable, easily molded into almost any form. Baekeland obtained a patent and founded the Bakelite Corporation in 1910 to create applications for the revolutionary material, whose official name was polyoxybenzylmethylenglycolanhydride. Bakelite was soon being used in hundreds of products for the consumer and industrial sectors. Toothbrushes, billiard balls, lamps, phonograph records, pens, machine parts, costume jewelry, automobile components, and buttons were just some of the hundreds of products made with Bakelite during these years. Streamlined Art Deco radios and telephones made from Bakelite in the 1920s and '30s became valuable collectibles later in the century.

Other companies made inferior versions of Bakelite, and Baekeland instigated a series of drawn-out patent wars. He tenaciously held his ground, as well as the Patent No. 942,699 for "Method of Making Insoluable Products of Phenol and Formaldehyde," and in the end he merged with several rivals. The Baekeland family, of course, grew even more wealthy, but as he aged, Leo Baekeland became increasingly eccentric and miserly. His son George attended Cornell University and entered the family business by the 1920s, but father and son, drastically different in temperament, were never close. Once George threatened to leave the company if his salary was not raised, and notified his father in writing. Baekeland replied in kind.

"I desired to set an example to the others of our staff and not give them an opportunity of thinking that you might be favored as the son of a president," he wrote on May 5, 1928. Urging his son to stay with the family business, he instead offered him half of his own salary, which George accepted.

Celine Baekeland was felled by a series of strokes in her later years, which left her partially paralyzed and a virtual invalid. After selling General Bakelite to the Union Carbide Corporation in 1939— a decision urged by George, who wanted to get out of the business— Baekeland spent increasing amounts of the year at his Florida home in Coconut Grove. The sale of the company did not diminish the vast Baekeland fortune, but it was an unwise move, because the wartime applications for Bakelite multiplied. It was even used in the making of the first atomic bomb in the 1940s. His grandchildren recalled him as a delightful, charming man who wore white from head to toe, including inexpensive white sneakers. On hot days, he liked to walk into his swimming pool fully clothed, in front of houseguests, and then upon emerging explain the scientific principle of condensation, and how it was the best way to keep cool. He ate everything from a can—primarily soup and sardines, both at room temperature—and devoted himself to creating a profusion of tropical trees and plants on his grounds with the help of a neighbor who was a famed botanist.

Baekeland died in February of 1944 of a cerebral hemorrhage, but had suffered from senile dementia for a number of years. A year after his death, 400,000 tons of plastic were being manufactured in the United States; by the end of the twentieth century, 50 million tons of it were being produced annually around the world. In some ways the invention of plastic had created a throwaway, artificial culture that was drastically opposite of everything Baekeland believed. The fortune proved disastrous for later generations as well: Baekeland's great-grandson Antony spent several years in a psychiatric hospital after murdering his mother—the daughter-in-law of George—and later killed himself in prison in 1981. The irony of his death by suffocation using a plastic bag was not lost on the media. As Leo Baekeland wrote to a friend in 1934, according to *Savage Grace*, "If I had to live my life over again I would not devote it to develop new industrial processes; I would try to add my humble efforts to use Science to the betterment of the human race."

Sources

➤ Books

Robins, Natalie and Steven M. L. Aronson, *Savage Grace,* William Morrow & Co., 1985.

➤ Periodicals

New York Times, February 24, 1944.
Time, March 29, 1999, pp. 80-84.
U.S. News and World Report, August 17, 1998, pp. 38-43.

Carlos Filipe Ximenes Belo

"With or without Indonesia, East Timor can stand alone and can thrive."

Born February 3, 1948, in Baucau, East Timor, Bishop Carlos Filipe Ximenes Belo shared the 1996 Nobel Peace Prize for his efforts to end a long and violent clash with neighboring Indonesia. Address: IPJET for East Timor, Gruttohoek 13, 2317WK, Leiden, The Netherlands.

Carlos Filipe Ximenes Belo was awarded the 1996 Nobel Peace Prize with fellow activist Jose Ramos-Horta for their leadership roles in the East Timorese struggle for independence. Belo, a Roman Catholic priest, strongly advocated nonviolent resistance, lest any more lives be lost on this Indonesian island that had, since 1975, clashed with forces sent to annex it. Leading the large number of East Timorese Catholics who opposed the aggression dictated by Jakarta—seat of the world's largest Muslim nation— Belo called himself the "Voice of the Voiceless," and worked determinedly to make the international community aware of the horrific human-rights abuses taking place in his country.

Timor is one of the vast Indonesian archipelago's 3,000 islands. Stretching across the Indian Ocean between southeast Asia and Australia, Indonesia is one of the planet's most populous countries, but the east and west halves of Timor were colonies of Portugal and the Netherlands, respectively, until 1950. That year, the Dutch sector became part of the newly created nation of Indonesia. East Timor, however, remained a colony of Portugal, and here Belo was born on February 3, 1948, in the village of Wailakama. His father, Domingos Vaz Felipe, was a school teacher, but the family retained strong ties to its heritage as rice farmers. The second from last of six children, Belo learned to shepherd water buffalo as a child, a job that he likely had to take in order to contribute to the household after the death of his father.

Nevertheless, Belo's academic gifts were apparent at an early age, and he was educated at East Timor's Roman Catholic missionary schools. Deciding to enter the priesthood, he left in 1973 to study in Portugal, came back for a short time to teach at a school in Fatumaca belonging to the religious order of the Salesians, but had returned to Europe in 1975, the year that much of the major strife in East Timor began. Belo studied at a seminary in Lisbon, then its Catholic University, and journeyed to Rome to enter the Pontifical Salesian University. He was ordained a priest of the Salesian order in Lisbon in 1980. The following year, he returned to East Timor as director of the Fatumaca College.

Much had changed in his absence. In 1974, a democratic coup overthrew Portugal's long dictatorship, and nearly all of its overseas colonies attained sovereignty. East Timor declared its independence in 1975, and the majority of the country, largely a Roman Catholic populace, favored self-rule as opposed to joining Indonesia, where repressiveness was the rule under the military regime of General Suharto. A minority of Muslims in East Timor, however, wished to join the Indonesian federation, and this gave Indonesian military forces an excuse to cross the border. East Timor was officially annexed in 1976 and proclaimed the 27th province of Indonesia, but its "official" status was never recognized by the United Nations. An ongoing guerrilla war began.

As opposition to the Indonesian annexation increased among the estimated 650,000 residents of East Timor, more of them converted to Catholicism as a statement of political resistance. Belo encountered his first taste of the repressive policies of the Indonesian government, who became determined to stamp out the nationalist movement, as the director of the Fatumaca College. Human rights abuses increased, and the presence of largely Muslim troops fostered great discontent. Entire villages, as Belo discovered, were devoid of men, who had been forcibly conscripted into the Indonesian army. In other cases, the rural communities were slaughtered by the army, all crops and cattle seized, and the villages burned. Though Belo became aware of torture and other crimes committed by the government, he was initially reluctant to become politically involved, feeling that this was not his true calling as a Catholic priest.

In 1983, Belo was named apostolic administrator of Diocese of Dili, the main East Timor city, which made him, in effect, leader of all Catholics in East Timor. He offered his services as a conciliator to military authorities as concerns about human rights violations grew, but his effort was sharply rebuffed. In 1988, he was consecrated as the Bishop of Lorium, Italy, an important promotion in Roman Catholic hierarchy. The Vatican could not name a bishop for East Timor, a place that was in the midst of such tremendous political instability, but by elevating him to a bishopric, Pope John Paul II demonstrated his support for the East Timorese plea for self-rule.

Belo soon became a focal point for the nationalist cause, along with Jose Ramos-Horta, who fled after the 1976 annexation and led the East Timorese resistance movement, called Fretilin—short for Revolutionary Front for an Independent East Timor—from Australia. The bishop began condemning human rights violations in his sermons, aiding dissidents, and encouraging East Timorese culture. The violence continued, however, and by some estimates a third of East Timor's population perished over the years. Few people outside of international watchdog groups were aware of the calamity, since the Jakarta government made entry into or exit from East Timor extremely difficult.

Under such siege conditions Belo penned a 1989 letter to the

Secretary-General of the United Nations, Javier Perez de Cuellar, asking for help. There was no concrete action taken on the matter until 1994, but the letter did cause others to take notice of the situation in East Timor, and by the early 1990s, the demonstrations and violence in the area were coming under media scrutiny. A massacre in November of 1991 served as a turning point for Fretilin and Belo: a peaceful protest of mostly teenage East Timorese at the Santa Cruz cemetery near his residence was fired upon by the army, and 271 unarmed protesters died. Belo sheltered others fleeing the melee, then personally escorted them home; many were never seen again. "No one can speak. No one can demonstrate. People disappear. . . . For the ordinary people, there is no freedom, only a continuing nightmare," Belo said in 1995, according to the *National Catholic Reporter.*

Belo increased his involvement in the movement tremendously after this incident. He began to work—secretly, of course—with Ramos-Horta, and helped smuggle witnesses to Switzerland. There, they testified about the Santa Cruz massacre before the U.N. Human Rights Commission, which increased international pressure on the Indonesian government to grant the East Timorese some measure of political independence. Because of his efforts, Belo found himself the object of government surveillance, with his phone lines tapped and requests for travel visas increasingly difficult to obtain. He was named a finalist for the Nobel Peace Prize in 1994, and was nominated again the next year; among his many champions was South African Archbishop Desmond Tutu.

In 1996, Belo and Ramos-Horta shared the Nobel Peace Prize for their life-threatening work in support of East Timorese independence. The bishop, said Nobel Committee chair Francis Sejersted, "has become much more than a mediator: this man of peace has also become a rallying point for his sorely tried people, a representative of their hope for a better future." The honor accorded Belo and Ramos-Horta was condemned by the Indonesian government in Jakarta, but over the next few years, there were some modest concessions made. The Indonesian government established a human-rights commission for East Timor to investigate charges of abuse, and two military personnel were even court-martialed and tried for murder, though they received light sentences. Indonesia also agreed to negotiations with Portugal, to be overseen by the U.N.

After General Suharto was ousted from office at the end of 1998, a new president agreed to elections in East Timor. Nearly ten years after Belo had written to beg for an U.N.-sponsored referendum on the sovereignty issue, on August 30, 1999, East Timorese cast votes to determine their future. As expected, the autonomy package from Indonesia was rejected in favor of full independence. The election results sparked serious fighting, with renegade pro-Indonesia militia groups from West Timor carrying out a wave of violence. Thousands of East Timorese were forced across the border against their will by heavily armed gangs. Belo's house in Dili was fired upon while he was inside, and after he was forced to flee, it burned to the ground. After two weeks of rioting, the Jakarta government conceded it had lost control of the situation, and asked the U.N. to send a peacekeeping force.

Invited by his Salesian superiors, Belo spent a few weeks in Lisbon while order was restored in East Timor. The retreating Indonesians looted and set fire to much of the country, and a U.N. transitional administration for independence as well as several aid groups began to provide help to the homeless, injured, or those separated from their families. Though Belo was still absent, his years of leadership were an important source of strength for the East Timorese. In early October, supporters gathered at the courtyard of his wrecked Dili home, and wept at a statue of the Virgin Mary that remained amidst the rubble.

Belo returned before the end of the month, and on October 31, 1999, the first Sunday of freedom in East Timor, he led a religious procession down the main road at the waterfront. This occurred just hours after the last Indonesian tanks used the same thoroughfare to exit the country, and Belo called for a new era of peace with its neighbor. Cheers from the crowd, however, erupted when he remarked that after 24 years of Indonesian occupation of East Timor, the country was economically and physically decimated— but not spiritually. "With or without Indonesia, East Timor can stand alone and can thrive," the *New York Times'* Seth Mydans quoted Belo as saying, and the bishop also thanked his many international supporters. "Without you, we would never have survived."

Sources

➤ Periodicals

America, December 14, 1996, pp. 6-7; April 24, 1999, p. 4.
Christian Century, January 4, 1995, p. 10; October 30, 1996, p. 32-33.
Der Spiegel, October 14, 1996.

Maclean's, October 21, 1996, p. 37.
National Catholic Reporter, October 11, 1996, p. 24.
New York Times, September 13, 1999; October 4, 1999; November 1, 1999 (opening quote).
New York Times Book Review, December 19, 1999, p. 7.
Peace Review, March 1999, pp. 171-176.

Tim Berners-Lee

*"*W*e are forming cells within a global brain, a place where the whim of a human being and the reasoning of a machine coexist."*

Born June 8, 1955 in London, England, Tim Berners-Lee invented the World Wide Web and went on to champion the rights of computer users to universal information access. Address: World Wide Web Consortium, MIT/545 Technology Square, Cambridge, MA 02139.

During an era when technology and commerce became increasingly interconnected, Tim Berners-Lee won renown for his idealistic principles as well as his innovative vision. As the inventor of the computer codes that created the World Wide Web in 1990, he stood to make a fortune from this revolutionary breakthrough. Instead, he established the World Wide Web Consortium to help maintain a single standard of computer communication for all users. In a low-profile but still determined manner, he has continued to help guide the evolution of cyberspace.

Berners-Lee has been hailed as a visionary for his ideas about how the computer can bring people together. He has stressed cooperation between software manufacturers and promoted the role of the World Wide Web as a decentralized, egalitarian force. "The openness of the Web is a powerful attraction," he said in an interview with *Technology Review*. "Everyone can not only read what's on the Web but contribute to it, and everybody is in a sense equal. There's a sense of boundless opportunity."

Born in London, England, Timothy J. Berners-Lee is the son of Conway and Mary Berners-Lee. His mathematician parents met while working on the development of England's first commercial computer, the Ferranti Mark 1, in the 1950s. Tim was raised with a love of science and listened to family discussions of imaginary numbers at mealtime. (It may also be of significance that the mother of the future inventor of the World Wide Web used to rescue spiders from the family bathtub.)

As a child, Berners-Lee constructed a model of the Ferranti computer out of cardboard boxes. He later built an actual computer with a soldering iron and an old television while a student at the Queen's College at Oxford University, from which he graduated in 1976. He went on to work for several British firms designing communications systems and software before venturing forth as an independent consultant.

From June through December of 1980, Berners-Lee served as a consultant software engineer at CERN, the European Particle Physics Laboratory in Geneva, Switzerland. It was here that he created Enquire, an experimental computer program that would lead to the World Wide Web. At first, his goal was to devise a program to link all of his computer files together. This evolved into building links between the computers of other CERN scientists. Early on, he saw the possibilities of expanding the program still further. "The larger vision had taken firm root in my consciousness," he recalled in his 1999 memoir *Weaving The Web*. "Suppose I could program my computer to create a space in which anything could be linked to anything. All the bits of information in every computer at CERN, and on the planet, would be available to me and to anyone else. There would be a single, global information space. . . A web of information would form."

Berners-Lee left CERN in 1981 to take a position as a software designer with Image Computer Systems Ltd., then returned to CERN on a fellowship in 1984. He resumed work on Enquire and explored ideas that would develop it further. Building upon the work of designer Theodore Nelson in the 1960s, he refined the concept of hypertext, which allowed users to locate documents through text links. Berners-Lee took this several steps further and created HyperText Markup Language (HTML), a common coding system for words, pictures and sound. He also devised Universal Resource Locators (URLs), which gave documents easily-located addresses. The HyperText Transfer Protocol (HTTP) was yet another refinement, a program for moving information to and from any computer with greater accuracy and speed. The World Wide Web was a combination of these innovations.

"What was really new with the Web was the idea that you could code all the information needed to find any document on the network into a short string of characters," Berners-Lee told *Technology Review*. "The notion that all these tagged documents from computers all over the world could share a common naming and addressing 'space' was what made hypertext links so much more powerful." At first, he attempted to give the rights to the Web software to the French government, who refused unless funding from the European Community was provided as well. What happened from there was almost as dramatic a development as the invention of the Web itself: Berners-Lee and CERN colleague Robert Calliau posted the free Web software on the Internet in the summer of 1991. The software spread rapidly and, with the innovation of the Mosaic browser by future Netscape cofounder Marc Andreessen in 1993, it exponentially grew in use by the middle of the decade.

Rather than launch his own company to personally benefit from his ideas, Berners-Lee left CERN in 1994 to found the World Wide Web Consortium (or W3C) at the Massachusetts Institute of Technology (MIT) in Boston. A loosely-knit nonprofit organization of scientists in industry and academia, W3C seeks to keep the Web intact in the face of competing business interests. As the director of the consortium, Berners-Lee has refrained from business ventures of his own."People have sometimes asked me whether I am upset that I have not made a lot of money from the Web," he wrote in *Weaving The Web.* "What is maddening is the terrible notion that a person's value depends on how important and financially success-ful they are, and that that is measured in terms of money. . . . That suggests disrespect for the researchers across the globe developing ideas for the next leaps in science and technology."

During the 1990s, Berners-Lee received numerous honors, includ-ing the MCI Computerworld/Smithsonian Award for Leadership Innovation and the Mountbatten Medal of the National Electronics Council. In 1999, *Time* selected him as one of the 100 greatest minds of the twentieth century. Profiles of Berners-Lee in the press have noted that his unpretentious manner has not changed with his growing fame. A highly private man, he avoids discussing his wife and two children in interviews.

On topics relating to the Web, however, Berners-Lee is quite outspoken. Among his concerns is that standards for Web page design may be changed to make some pages only readable by certain browsers, breaking down the universality of the Web. He regrets that more people can browse the Web than can create their own pages. Still, he sees hope for the future. Among other develop-ments, he envisions advanced software that can be acquired by Internet users free of charge, simply by wandering the Web. The ultimate goal, he feels, is fostering as much two-way communica-tion as possible.

"I have (and still have) a dream that the web could be less of a television channel and more of an interactive sea of shared knowl-edge," he said during an October 1995 symposium at MIT. "I imagine it immersing us as a warm, friendly environment made of the things we and our friends have seen, heard, believe or have figured out. I would like it to bring our friends and collegues closer, in that by working on this knowledge together we can come to better understandings."

Sources

➤ On-line

"Hypertext and Our Collective Destiny"; "Longer Bio for Tim Berners-Lee," *W3C,* http://www.w3.org (March 8, 2000).

➤ **Books**

Berners-Lee, Tim, *Weaving The Web,* Harper, 1999.

➤ **Periodicals**

Chicago Sun-Times, December 5, 1999, p. LI56.
Daily Telegraph, November 11, 1999, p. 8; November 14, 1999, p. 4.
Forbes, November 15, 1999, p. 314 (opening quote).
Scientific American, December 1997, p. 34.
Technical Communication, November 1996, p. 376.
Technology Review, July 1996, p. 32.
USA Today, October 31, 1999, p. 4.

Elizabeth Blackwell

"If society will not admit of woman's free development, then society must be remodeled."

Born February 3, 1821, in Bristol, England, Elizabeth Blackwell defied the social conventions of her day to become the first female physician in the United States. She died of a stroke on May 31, 1910, in Hastings, England.

Elizabeth Blackwell came of age at a time when most women felt an excessive modesty and deep sense of shame about their bodies and how they functioned. When they fell ill—especially with a so-called "female complaint"—they chose to suffer in silence rather than subject themselves to an examination by a male doctor. Yet the notion of a *female* physician was laughable, if not downright scandalous, even to an enlightened thinker like Blackwell. Eventually, however, she began to wonder if her search for meaning and purpose in life might find fulfillment in the study of medicine. With that goal in mind, Blackwell challenged the prevailing wisdom that members of her gender were not suited for such work and proceeded to shatter a number of significant barriers on her way to becoming the first female physician in the United States.

Born in 1821 in the bustling seaport town of Bristol, England, Elizabeth Blackwell was the third of nine surviving children of Samuel, the owner of a successful sugar refinery, and Hannah Lane Blackwell. Both Samuel and Hannah were devout Methodists and strong advocates of social reform, especially regarding equal rights for women. Consequently, all five Blackwell daughters received the same education as the four Blackwell sons. Elizabeth thus grew up with an inquisitive mind and a fiercely independent streak that would serve her well during the years ahead.

In 1832, an economic depression nearly wiped out Samuel's business and left England in a state of turmoil. Deciding it was time to strike out in a new direction, he and Hannah and the Blackwell clan set sail for the United States. They settled first in New York City, where Samuel opened a sugar refinery and the entire family became involved in the growing antislavery movement. Later, they moved across the Hudson River to Jersey City, New Jersey.

Fire destroyed the sugar refinery in 1836, plunging the family into debt and leaving Samuel extremely depressed. (He subsequently became physically ill as well with what was probably malaria.) Two years later, he moved his wife and seven of their children to Cincinnati, Ohio, to set up a refinery that relied on sugar beets instead of sugar cane. But his health grew steadily worse, and he died in August 1838.

Samuel's death left the Blackwells in truly dire financial straits. Elizabeth and her two older sisters opened a boarding school in their home to help support their mother and their siblings. By 1845, the family had settled most of their debts, and Elizabeth was finally free to pursue her own dreams.

After a brief and not very pleasant stint as a schoolteacher in Kentucky, Blackwell returned to Cincinnati but soon found herself restless and bored. Then a visit to a sick friend named Mary Donaldson propelled her in a totally unexpected direction. Donaldson, who was dying of uterine cancer, remarked that she would have found it much easier to cope with both the physical and emotional pain of her illness if she had had a female physician. She suggested that Blackwell might want to consider going into medicine, an idea the young woman found preposterous given her gender and the fact that "the physical structure of the body and its various ailments filled me with disgust."

Yet Donaldson's words left an impression on Blackwell. Since she had already decided never to marry, she knew that she was going to have to make her own way in the world. And she had a deep yearning to do important work of some kind. While Blackwell was well aware that the path before her was full of obstacles, she felt it would be a moral victory for women everywhere if she succeeded in becoming a physician—and she was determined to succeed.

Blackwell spent the next couple of years teaching to earn money for medical school. In 1847, she sent out more than two dozen applications and met with rejection from administrators who regarded her with amusement, derision, or both. Therefore Blackwell could hardly believe it when she was accepted at New York's Geneva College. What she did not know was that the administration had been opposed to admitting her but hesitated turning her down for fear of offending a prominent Philadelphia doctor who had written her a letter of recommendation. They left the decision to the students instead, figuring the young men would certainly say no. But as a joke, the students unanimously voted in favor of allowing her to enroll. Thus, in November 1847, Blackwell became the first female medical student in U.S. history.

Blackwell graduated from medical school with top honors in 1849. Afterward, she worked at a charity hospital in Philadelphia to gain more practical experience treating patients. Faced with virtually no opportunities for further education in the United States, Blackwell decided to head for Paris, France, then a center of advanced work in the field of medicine. (Her ultimate goal was to become a surgeon.) First, however, she stopped off in her native England for a visit, where—to her surprise—the "daring little doctress from America" was greeted as somewhat of a celebrity.

Arriving in France in late May 1849, Blackwell encountered strong resistance from male physicians who refused to allow her to train with them. She was dealt yet another setback when she contracted a serious infection that left her blind in one eye, ending her dream of becoming a surgeon. Blackwell then headed back to England and a position at a London hospital, where she spent a year attending lectures, observing operations, treating patients, and reviewing cases with other doctors and students. She also became acquainted with a number of prominent English intellectuals, artists, and scientists during her stay, including Florence Nightingale, the founder of modern nursing and a pioneer in the field of hospital reform.

Blackwell finally returned to the United States in 1851 and settled in New York City, where she hoped to open a small private practice. But she had a difficult time convincing prospective landlords that her credentials as a physician were legitimate. When she finally found one who was willing to rent space to her, she encountered a new set of problems—namely the fears, prejudices, and hostility of her neighbors. Men hurled insults at her, and women avoided her on the street. Obscene letters flooded her mailbox. Worst of all, no patients came, and the local medical establishment flatly rejected her overtures.

Unfazed, Blackwell borrowed money from friends to establish a clinic in the slums of lower Manhattan. The New York Dispensary for Poor Women and Children opened its doors in 1853 and was soon overflowing with patients. Helping to shoulder the heavy workload during those first few months was Blackwell's younger sister, Emily, a medical student.

Faced with increasing financial pressures, Blackwell bought a house that was big enough to serve as both her home and her clinic. Meanwhile, she had become acquainted with a young woman named Marie Zakrzewska who also wanted to be a physician. The two worked together for a while and proved to be extremely compatible. Blackwell then secured Zakrzewska's admission to medical school at Western Reserve Medical College in Cleveland, Ohio. But her friend's departure reminded Blackwell of what a lonely life she led. So in late 1854, she adopted a seven-year-old orphan named Kitty.

By 1856, Blackwell was in practice with "Dr. Zak" and Emily, who had recently returned from studying in Europe. Together, the three physicians began working toward a goal they all shared— establishing the first hospital in the United States *for* women that was staffed entirely *by* women. In May 1857, after struggling to raise funds and convince others their plan was a viable one, they opened the doors to the New York Infirmary for Indigent Women and Children.

Elizabeth handled most of the administrative chores at the facility and supervised ongoing fund-raising activities. Emily devoted herself entirely to patient care, as did Dr. Zak. The infirmary was a success almost from the beginning as nearby residents sought medical treatment, many for the first time in their lives.

Around this same time, Blackwell's friends in England began pleading with her to come back and help them advance the cause of female physicians in Great Britain. Thus, in mid-1858 she turned over all of her responsibilities to Emily, and she and Kitty headed overseas. During the year she spent in England, Blackwell wrote, lectured, and visited hospitals across the country.

Blackwell returned to the United States in 1859 and resumed her work with enthusiasm. Together she and her sister moved the infirmary into bigger and better quarters in 1860. (By that time, Dr. Zak had left to teach at a college in Boston.) She then set out to fulfill a new dream—establishing a medical school for women. The outbreak of the Civil War during the spring of 1861 forced her to shelve those plans, however. Instead, she and Emily devoted their attention to recruiting and training women who had volunteered to serve as nurses for the Union Army.

After the war ended, Blackwell turned her attention to expanding the infirmary's outpatient efforts, especially in the area of public health and hygiene. To that end, she instituted an innovative inspection program in which a trained health worker visited the poor in their homes and offered basic health care and advice on maintaining proper sanitation.

Blackwell then revived her dream of opening a medical school for women. By 1868, she had raised the necessary funds, and in September of that year, the Women's Medical College of the New York Infirmary held its first classes. Elizabeth herself was on the faculty as professor of hygiene, and Emily taught obstetrics and women's diseases.

Having fulfilled her goals, Blackwell considered returning to Great Britain at the request of her friends there, who reported that efforts to train female physicians had been stymied by fierce opposition from male doctors. Thus, in 1869 she went to London, where she promptly opened a medical practice and lectured extensively on hygiene, nutrition, family planning, and sex education. She also campaigned for safer working conditions as part of her overall strategy to promote healthier living. In 1874 she co-founded the London School of Medicine for Women and served briefly on its faculty until illness forced her to resign.

While convalescing, Blackwell wrote a guide to sex education for young people that became a bestseller upon its release in 1876 and again when it appeared in the United States in 1879. That same year, she and Kitty moved into a cottage overlooking the English Channel, and there they remained for the rest of Blackwell's life. She continued to write, lecture, and direct reform efforts for a wide variety of medical, social, and moral causes ranging from sex education and birth control to prostitution and vivisection. She also maintained her private medical practice until 1894.

Blackwell visited the United States for the last time in 1906 at the age of 85. The following summer, while vacationing in Scotland, she fell down a flight of stairs and sustained severe injuries from which she never fully recovered. She spent the final few years of her life in declining physical and mental health and died of a stroke on May 31, 1910. Over a long and productive career spanning more than 50 years, Blackwell had fulfilled her dreams while inspiring those of countless other young women who, like her, were eager to make a difference in the world and not about to let convention stand in their way.

Sources

➤ On-line

"Elizabeth Blackwell, 1821-1910," *National Women's Hall of Fame,* http://209.105.130.97/blkwele.htm (January 27, 2000).
"Elizabeth Blackwell Award," *Hobart and William Smith Colleges,* http://www.hws.edu/NEW/bwaward/history.html (January 27, 2000).
"Women's Voices: Quotations from Women," *About.com: Women's History,* http: // womenshistory.miningco.com / education/ womenshistory/library/qu/blqublac.htm (January 28, 2000; opening quote).

➤ Books

Blackwell, Elizabeth, *Pioneer Work in Opening the Medical Profession to Women: Autobiographical Sketches,* Source Book Press, 1980.
Brown, Jordan, *Elizabeth Blackwell,* Chelsea House, 1989.

Hays, Elinor Rice, *Those Extraordinary Blackwells: The Story of a Journey to a Better World,* Harcourt, 1967.

Kline, Nancy, *Elizabeth Blackwell: A Doctor's Triumph,* Conari Press, 1997.

Ross, Ishbel, *Child of Destiny: The Life Story of the First Woman Doctor,* Harper, 1949.

Niels Bohr

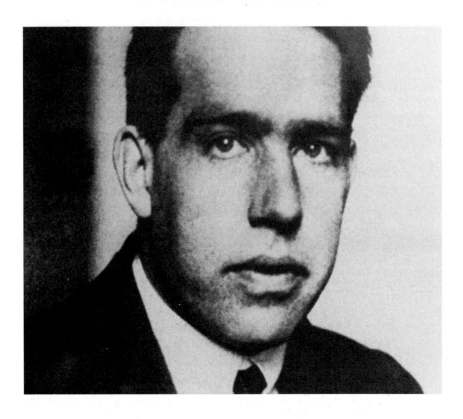

*"*I*t is wrong to think that the task of physics is to find out how nature is. Physics concerns what we can say about nature."*

Born October 7, 1885, in Copenhagen, Denmark, Niels Henrik David Bohr offered the "Copenhagen Interpretation," or principle of complementarity, in quantum physics theory. His school of thought, he argued, was relevant equally to physics and philosophy. He died November 18, 1962, in Copenhagen.

Niels Bohr received the Nobel Prize in physics in 1922 for the quantum mechanical model of the atom that he had developed a decade earlier, the most significant step forward in scientific understanding of atomic structure since English physicist John Dalton first proposed the modern atomic theory in 1803. Bohr founded the Institute for Theoretical Physics at the University of Copenhagen in 1920, an institute later renamed for him. For well over half a century, the Institute was a powerful force in the shaping of atomic theory. It was an essential stopover for all young physicists who made the tour of Europe's center of theoretical physics in the mid-twentieth century. Also during the 1920s, Bohr thought and wrote about some of the fundamental issues raised by modern quantum theory. He developed two basic concepts, the principles of complementarity and correspondence, that he said must direct all future work in physics. In the 1930s, Bohr became interested in problems of the atomic nucleus and contributed to the development of the liquid-drop model of the nucleus, a model used in the explanation of nuclear fission.

Niels Henrik David Bohr was born on October 7, 1885, to Christian and Ellen Adler Bohr, the second of three children. His father was a distinguished professor of physiology at the University of Copenhagen and the primary influence of young Bohr's interest in science. His mother came from a wealthy, distinguished Jewish family; her father, D. B. Adler, founded the Commercial Bank of Copenhagen and the Jutland Provincial Credit Association. As a child, Bohr also displayed an inherent interest and aptitude in figuring out how things work, and had a knack in repairing household appliances, such as clocks. When he was not studying at the Grammelholm School in Copenhagen, Bohr excelled as a youngster as a strong soccer player.

In 1903 Bohr entered the University of Copenhagen. A brilliant and eager student, he gained notice academically through his telling research regarding the surface tension of water, experimenting with a vibrating jet stream. His work earned him a gold medal by the Royal Danish Academy of Science in 1907. That same year he achieved his bachelor of science degree; in 1909 he completed a master of science degree. He earned his doctorate only three years later in 1911, defending his thesis on the electron theory of metals and showing that while classical physical principles were sufficiently accurate to describe the qualitative properties of metals, they failed when applied to quantitative properties. He then went to work with a scientist he deeply respected, J. J. Thompson, who discovered the electron, at Cavendish Laboratory of Cambridge

University. However, not long into his research there, Bohr discovered profound professional differences between himself and Thompson, and he left Cambridge to join Ernest Rutherford at the University of Manchester, where he remained until 1916. It was here that Bohr developed his theory of the electronic structure of the hydrogen bomb, an accomplishment that would earn him universal fame.

In 1911, Rutherford proposed a new model of the atom, in which all the atom's positive charge was concentrated in the nucleus. The electrons were located at relatively great distances outside the nucleus, traveling in orbits around it. The classical theory of physics, which is a mathematical description of nature, held that a moving charged particle should radiate energy. Therefore, electrons orbiting a nucleus should gradually give off all their energy and spiral into the nucleus. But this did not happen, and Rutherford could not explain what prevented it from happening in his model.

Bohr proposed quantum theory as a solution. Quantum theory was first put forth by Max Planck in 1900 and developed by Albert Einstein in 1905 and 1907. Bohr considered the question of atomic spectra. It was assumed among scientists that the heating of an element produces a pattern of lines, or line spectrum, but no one had studied in depth about what the lines' relationship might be with atoms. Bohr built on research regarding lines in the hydrogen spectrum conducted by German physicist Johann Balmer in the 1880s, using the mathematical formula Balmer applied to figure out line frequencies. Next, Bohr considered black-body radiation: a black-body object absorbs electromagnetic energy, then releases radiation in thermal energy. Planck had concluded that in some cases energy could be released, not in continual waves, but in bundles called quanta. The energy of a quantum depended on the frequency of the wave. Bohr adopted Planck's theory into Rutherford's model, suggesting that electrons could travel around the nucleus without radiating energy, provided they remained in certain restricted orbits. Applying Balmer's equation, he proposed that an electron could move from one orbit to another by gaining or losing one quantum or several quanta of energy. He could predict the frequency of radiation as to when electrons make various possible energy-level transfers within the atom. Although his model could only apply to the hydrogen atom, providing a theoretical explanation for Balmer's formula of the wavelengths of the lines in the hydrogen spectrum, Bohr's proposal was significant in that is solved a problem in classical physics by applying quantum theory. It was soon dubbed as "quantum mechanics" and was fundamental to the study of physics in the twentieth century.

In 1912 Bohr returned to the University of Copenhagen as an assistant professor of physics. In the same year he married Margrethe Norland, with whom he later had four sons (two others died in infancy): Hans, Erik, Aage, and Ernest. (Aage shared a 1975 Nobel Prize for his work on the structure of the atomic nucleus.) Bohr published his theory of the planetary atom in 1913, which contained an important addendum to his earlier hypothesis. The Balmer formula was insufficient in predicting line frequencies with helium atoms. Bohr found that an equation inherent in line frequency prediction known as the Pickering series could predict this type of frequency, and he rewrote the Balmer formula to reflect this. Soon after, scientists in England studied helium and found Bohr's hypothesis accurate. Further impressed with Bohr's genius, Rutherford offered him a post at Manchester, which he accepted and kept from 1914 to 1916. He then returned to the University of Copenhagen, where a position as chair of theoretical physics was created for him.

In 1920, Bohr founded the Institute for Theoretical Physics (renamed the Institute of Atomic Studies) at the University of Copenhagen, where he would serve as director for four decades and which would become the most important institute of its kind in Europe, attracting brilliant minds from around the world. As a leading intellectual in physics himself, Bohr continued his work in making new discoveries in physics and postulating new ideas. Bohr's approach, soon adopted by many in the field and relevant even into the twenty-first century, would be known as the Copenhagen Interpretation. Recognized as an international leader in the field, he was awarded the 1922 Nobel Prize in Physics for his achievement in developing the quantum mechanical model of the atom. In the prize's presentation speech, offered by Professor S. A. Arrhenius, Chairman of the Nobel Committee for Physics, Bohr was lauded as having "found the right roads to fundamental truths, and in so doing you have laid down principles which have led to the most splendid advances, and promise abundant fruit for the work of the future."

In 1927, Bohr introduced his idea of complementarity in explaining physical phenomena, another very significant theoretical contribution to the field. His theory contended that a light wave demonstrates characteristics of a wave and a particle; therefore, it cannot be understood exclusively as a wave or as a particle—it must be studied as both. Subsequent to and linked to complimentarity is Bohr's idea of correspondence: any conclusion drawn from quantum physics must not conflict with observations of the real world;

conclusions drawn from theoretical studies must correspond to the world described by classical physics.

In the 1930s Bohr became interested in nuclear physics and set out to contribute ideas in this subfield. He developed the "liquid drop" model of the nucleus, which assumes that the forces that operated between protons and neutrons making up the atomic nucleus could be compared to the forces that operate between the molecules making up a tiny drop of liquid. Bohr postulated that the atom's nucleus should be viewed as constantly changing shape in response to forces working inside it. His model was instrumental in explaining the process of nuclear fission—the spitting of the atomic nucleus, discovered in 1938.

Political turmoil in Europe due to Nazi expansionist aims affected Bohr's work and threatened his life, as he was of Jewish heritage on his mother's side. After his deep involvement in assisting in the transport of Jewish colleagues and acquaintances out of Denmark and away from the Nazi threat of extermination between 1939 and 1942, Bohr himself escaped with his family in September 1943, after learning that he was being hunted by the Nazis. They fled in a fishing boat to Sweden and then dangerously flew to England on a Mosquito bomber, which lacked an oxygen system. The Bohr family then ventured to the United States, where Bohr and his son became involved in the Manhattan Project, the top-secret mission to build the world's fist atomic bombs.

After World War II, Bohr became chairman of the Danish Atomic Energy Commission and a founding member of the European Center for Nuclear Research in Geneva. He sought to bring under control the dangers posed by nuclear weapons. In 1957, he received the first Atoms for Peace award by the Ford Foundation for his efforts in promoting peaceful uses of atomic energy. Bohr also helped found the Nordic Institute for Theoretical Atomic Physics (Nordita) in Copenhagen. Nordic was designed to provide a forum for cooperation among Scandinavian physicists.

Although Bohr was required in Denmark to retire in 1955 at age 70, he retained his post as director of the Institute for Theoretical Physics. He died on November 18, 1962. He worked until the end of his life, having just two days prior to his death conducted a meeting of the Danish Royal Academy of Sciences. Bohr was honored with many awards and distinctions during his life, including the Max Planck Medal of the German Physical Society in 1930, the Hughes (1921) and Copley (1938) medals of the Royal Society, the Franklin Medal of the Franklin Institute in 1926, and the Faraday Medal of the

Chemical Society of London in 1930. He was elected to over 20 prestigious scientific academies worldwide, such as Cambridge, Oxford, Manchester, Edinburgh, the Sorbonne, Harvard, and Princeton.

Bohr's lasting philosophical and theoretical contributions to physics were critical to the development of the field even at the beginning of the twenty-first century. In *Scientific American*, Bohr's contributions were praised by Philip and Phyllis Morrison, who wrote, "What did Bohr think of the embryonic cosmology of expanding space? His prescient answer is as fresh as today's news: we can hope to understand the cosmos only as we understand the elementary particles." By attempting to explain how the large and the small are joined, according to the Morrisons, "what Bohr foresaw [was] the wondrous loop where microcosm and macrocosm begin to explain each other step by step."

Sources

➤ On-line

"Biography of N.H.D. Bohr," www.nobel.se/laureates/physics-1922-1-bio.html (December 23, 1999).
"Bohr, Niels," www.phys.virginia.edu/classes/usem/origin/notes/05/bohr.html (December 22, 1999).
"Copenhagen Interpretation," www.treasure-troves.com/physics/CopenhagenInterpretation.html (December 23, 1999).
"Niels Henrik David Bohr," www-groups.dcs.st-and.ac.uk/~history/Mathematicians/Bohr_Niels.html (December 22, 1999).
"Prize Presentation," www.nobel.se/laureates/physics-1922-press.html (December 23, 1999).

➤ Books

Herbert, N., *Quantum Reality: Beyond the New Physics,* Anchor Press/Doubleday, 1985 (opening quote).

➤ Periodicals

Science News, January 11, 1986, p. 26.
Scientific American, December 1999.

Antonia Brico

*"**I** do not call myself a woman conductor. I call myself a conductor who happens to be a woman."*

Born June 26, 1902, in Rotterdam, Netherlands, Antonia Brico was a pianist, orchestra conductor, and teacher who waged a lifelong battle against sexism in the world of classical music. She died August 3, 1989, in Denver, Colorado.

D uring the 1930s, one of the most promising young performers on the classical music scene was Antonia Brico, a pianist
whose ultimate goal was to become an orchestra conductor.
But in her quest to become the first woman ever to serve as the
permanent director of a major symphony orchestra—one of the
most prestigious posts in the world of music—she encountered a
wall of resistance. Virtually no one in the conservative, male-
dominated profession was in favor of the idea of a female conductor. Thus, despite the sheer force of her personality, determination,
and talent, Brico was never able to break through the wall, a failure
she once described as a "perpetual heartbreak." Yet at the very least
she was a pioneer who helped clear a path for those who came
after her.

As she herself tells the story in the book *There Was Light,* Antonia
Brico was the daughter of a young Dutch woman (a member of a
"respectable" family from Amsterdam) who fell in love with an
Italian man who worked as a piano player in a nightclub. He
deserted her when she became pregnant, and she was forced to give
up their child to avoid disgracing her family. As an infant, Antonia
was taken in by a married couple named Wolthuis who renamed
her Wilhemina. Around 1907 they moved to the United States and
settled in Oakland, California.

The Wolthuises turned out to be abusive parents both physically
and emotionally, so Brico's childhood was not a happy one. Her one
escape was music, a passion she discovered when she was 10 and
fingered the keys of a piano for the first time. She later had the
chance to attend some concerts and was particularly fascinated by
the conductor's role. "I thought, how wonderful—with a little magic
wand you can make beautiful music," she later recalled in *Newsweek.* Hoping that their daughter might prove to be talented enough
to earn some money as a vaudeville performer, the Wolthuises
signed her up for piano lessons. But their interest in nurturing her
abilities quickly evaporated after they learned that vaudeville shows
did not feature classical music.

The teenager continued studying piano on her own, however,
amazing her high school teachers with her playing skills and grasp
of music theory. In 1919, determined to continue her education
despite her parents' objections, she enrolled at the Berkeley campus
of the University of California. The Wolthuises responded by
throwing her out of the house, leaving her to fend for herself at the
age of 17.

Having parted ways with her family, she began calling herself

Antonia Brico, which was probably the name she had been given at birth. She then set her sights on becoming a concert pianist and managed to stay in college with the help of scholarships, a full-time job at a variety store, and a part-time job as a waitress. She supplemented her earnings by giving recitals and also worked as an assistant to Paul Steindorff, who, in addition to serving as the director of the university's music program, was also the director of the San Francisco Opera. Brico developed a serious interest in conducting as a result of her association with Steindorff, and by the time she graduated (with honors) in 1923 with a bachelor of arts degree in music, she had made up her mind that she would one day lead a major symphony orchestra.

After completing her undergraduate education, Brico studied privately in New York City for two years with pianist Sigismund Stojowski. She then applied to the prestigious Master School of Conducting at the Berlin State Academy of Music and in 1927 became the first American (man *or* woman) to be admitted. Brico remained in Europe for the next five years and studied under several prominent teachers, including Karl Muck, who had been director of the Boston Symphony Orchestra prior to becoming head of the Hamburg Philharmonic. Muck mentored the promising young conductor and in 1928 helped her obtain a position as coach for the Bayreuth Wagner Festival.

Brico made her conducting debut in 1930 with the prestigious Berlin Philharmonic. Her appearance garnered good reviews, and later that same year she returned briefly to the United States to conduct performances of both the Los Angeles and the San Francisco symphonies. But her failure to win a permanent conducting post in Los Angeles prompted Brico to head back overseas. Over the next few years, she guest-conducted throughout Germany as well as in Poland and the Balkans, earning acclaim in the process for her energy and mastery of technique. None of these engagements offered the security of a permanent position, however, and as the economic downturn known as the Depression worsened and she received fewer invitations to conduct, Brico often teetered on the brink of poverty and despair. Furthermore, the rise of Adolf Hitler and Nazism was making it increasingly dangerous and difficult for her to travel and perform in Germany. So Brico left for the United States, arriving in New York City with no money and no job prospects.

Brico's fortunes soon took a turn for the better, however, when two prominent New York society matrons approached her about conducting a concert at the Metropolitan Opera House. On January 10, 1933, Brico made her New York debut conducting the Musicians' Symphony Orchestra. This in turn led to other engagements with groups throughout the United States, from Washington, D.C., to California. During this same period, she also directed the Works Progress Administration Symphony.

In late 1934, a group of about 15 female musicians who had been playing together for several months approached Brico and asked her to become their leader. She agreed, and from that ensemble she created the 85-member New York Women's Symphony Orchestra. (After several male musicians joined in 1939 it was renamed the Brico Symphony Orchestra.) Brico conducted the group's first major concert on February 18, 1935, at the Town Hall in New York City. The performance met with widespread acclaim and was quickly followed by two additional public concerts as well as an invitation to take part in a full second season at Carnegie Hall later that same year. Once again Brico and the New York Women's Symphony Orchestra earned rave reviews, this time for a presentation of Verdi's *Requiem.* The group continued to perform until disbanding shortly after the United States entered World War II in December 1941.

Brico spent the late 1930s and early 1940s serving as a guest conductor for a number of different orchestras and other musical events in the United States and directing several choral groups in the New York City area. In 1937, for example, she directed the New York Hippodrome Opera's production of *Hansel and Gretel,* making her the first woman ever to conduct a performance by a major New York opera company. The following year she achieved another milestone when she became the first woman to conduct the New York Philharmonic Symphony Orchestra. In 1945 Brico's work took her to Denver, Colorado, where she guest-conducted the Denver Civic Orchestra, directed the annual opera sponsored by the *Denver Post,* and taught a course on Wagnerian operas at Colorado College.

Throughout this entire period, Brico still harbored dreams of securing a permanent post as a conductor. She was sure that such an opportunity had finally come her way during her visit to Denver, where the Denver Civic Symphony Orchestra (later known as the Colorado Symphony Orchestra) was in the midst of transforming itself into a full professional orchestra. Part of that transformation involved securing the services of a director, and Brico presented herself as a candidate. Her conversations with members of the orchestra board left her with the impression that the job was hers, so she quickly wrapped up her affairs in New York City and relocated to Denver. But to her great disappointment and despite her stellar qualifications, she learned soon after her arrival that the orchestra board had no intention of giving the conductor's post to a woman, no matter how well suited she might be. In fact, board members denied ever offering her a job and insisted that they had never even invited her to audition for them.

This rejection left Brico heartbroken, but faced with the need to earn a living, she decided to remain in Denver and teach piano and voice to the city's most talented young people. Her exclusive Brico Studio quickly attracted about 70 students, all of whom were expected to adhere to their teacher's high standards of excellence. The most promising musicians also had to learn to play a second instrument in addition to mastering the piano.

Brico herself remained a lifelong student of music. She developed especially close associations with noted Finnish composer Jean Sibelius, who regarded her as the foremost interpreter of his work, and Dr. Albert Schweitzer, the famous humanitarian, theologian, philosopher, and physician who was an expert on organist and composer Johann Sebastian Bach. In fact, Brico visited Schweitzer on several occasions at his jungle hospital in Africa to study Bach.

In addition to her teaching career and her own studies, Brico continued to conduct orchestras and give performances as a pianist, primarily in various European countries. She also served as the permanent conductor and music director of the Denver Business-men's Orchestra (renamed the Brico Symphony Orchestra in 1969), an amateur group established in 1947. Her other responsibilities included leading the Denver Opera Association, the Women's String Orchestra, and the Boulder Philharmonic and serving as music director of Denver's Trinity Methodist Church.

In 1963, the Denver Symphony Orchestra once again found itself searching for a new conductor. Brico had been earning praise for years for her work with the Denver Businessmen's Orchestra and was the favorite choice of many in the community who felt she deserved the post. But the position eventually went to a man amid some speculation that at the age of 61, Brico was too old for the job.

More than a decade later, however, Brico emerged from near obscurity to bask in the spotlight following the release of an Academy Award-winning documentary about her life entitled *Antonia: A Portrait of the Woman* (1974). A project of one of her former piano students, folksinger Judy Collins, and film editor Jill Godmilow, the documentary was described by a writer for *Newsweek* as "a touching but unsentimental profile of an indomitable, humorous and forthright musician, who after a promising beginning is ignored by the music establishment." The attention Brico received led to several major conducting engagements at venues such as the Hollywood Bowl, the Lincoln Center in New York City, and the Kennedy Center in Washington, D.C. Unfortunately, by this time her gifts were not what they once had been. After an initial flurry of interest, the invitations soon stopped coming, and Brico resumed her quiet life in Denver.

Brico's final years were marked by increasingly eccentric behavior tinged by mounting bitterness and regret over the sexist attitudes that had stymied her career. In 1985 she was persuaded to retire from her post with the Brico Orchestra. Guest conducting engagements then ended for the most part, too, as did her work with students of piano and voice, many of whom had already drifted off to study elsewhere. On January 30, 1988, Brico was leaving a Judy Collins concert when she slipped on some ice and broke her hip and her shoulder. The injuries led to an overall decline in her health, and she died in a Denver nursing home on August 3, 1989.

Music had been Brico's only passion in life. It was a love she shared with her many students, some on whom went on to have outstanding careers of their own. One in particular—July Collins—was deeply moved and dismayed by the depth of Brico's pain during the making of *Antonia: A Portrait of the Woman*. The experience left Collins feeling especially indebted to her teacher because Brico had never allowed her sorrow and frustration to overwhelm her art. "There were only a couple of influences in my life that were female," observed Collins in a *New York Times* article, "and Brico was the major one."

Sources

➤ **Books**

Neuls-Bates, Carol, editor, *Women in Music: An Anthology of Source Readings from the Middle Ages to the Present*, Northeastern University Press, 1996.
Stone, Irving, editor, *There Was Light*, Doubleday, 1970.
Varnell, Jeanne, *Women of Consequence: The Colorado Women's Hall of Fame*, Johnson Books, 1999.

➤ Periodicals

Newsweek, August 18, 1975, pp. 52-53.
New York Times, September 15, 1974, pp. 15-16; August 5, 1989, p. 10
    (opening quote).
Time, October 21, 1974; November 10, 1975, p. 59.

➤ Other

Antonia: A Portrait of the Woman (documentary film), Rocky Moun-
    tain Productions, 1974, 20th anniversary re-release, Direct Cine-
    ma, 1994.

Carol M. Browner

"Our families—and particularly our children—have inspired many of us in our work to protect this nation's environment."*

Born December 16, 1955, in South Miami, Florida, Carol M. Browner was the head of the Environmental Protection Agency during the presidency of Bill Clinton. Address: 209 6th St. S.E., Washington, D.C. 20006.

When President Bill Clinton appointed Carol M. Browner head of the federal Environmental Protection Agency, she became only its second female leader. Browner had previously worked on environmental issues for the state of Florida. She is known for toughness as well as her ability to balance the needs of nature with the demands of business.

Born December 16, 1955, in South Miami, Florida, Browner is the daughter of Michael Browner and Isabella Harty-Hugues. Both of her parents were professors at Miami-Dade Community College. An immigrant from Ireland, her father was an English professor, while her mother taught social science. Browner's parents were divorced when she was still very young.

As a child, Browner and her two siblings, younger sisters Michelle and Stephanie, had limited access to television. Though Browner enjoyed reading, she also liked the outdoors, especially family hikes in different parts of Florida, including the Everglades. She also did a little painting outside.

After high school, Browner entered the University of Florida where she studied English. She graduated in 1977, and immediately entered the University of Florida's law school. She graduated in 1979, and was admitted to the Florida bar in 1980.

Right out of law school, in 1979, Browner was hired as the general counsel for the Government Operations Committee for the Florida House of Representatives. She spent the next four years working on legislation that eased Florida's ability to acquire land.

In 1984, Browner left Florida for Washington, D.C., and a position with Citizen Action. This was a left-leaning political group founded by consumer advocate Ralph Nader. As associate director, Browner helped lobby Congress and other politicians on environmental issues as well as those related to political campaign funding, children, and labor. Two important campaigns called for the federal government to mandate family leave and health care.

While working for Citizen Action Browner met her future husband, Michael Podhorzer. He also worked at the group as a health care issues specialist. They were married in 1987 and eventually had one son, Zachary.

By the time of her marriage, Browner had left Citizen Action to work for a United States Senator from Florida, Lawton Chiles. She was employed as his chief legislative aide from 1986 to 1988. Among her environmental accomplishments was her assistance in arranging an expansion of the Big Cypress National Preserve via a land swap. In this time period, Browner also worked for the Democratic staff of the Senate Energy and Natural Resources Committee as legal counsel.

In 1988, Browner joined the staff of another United States senator, Al Gore, Jr. The Tennessee senator employed Browner as legislative director for three years. Gore was particularly interested in environmental issues, and Browner helped develop the 1990 amendments to the Clean Air Act. She helped draft legislation in other areas as well.

When Browner's former employer Chiles was elected governor of Florida, she opted to return home. In 1991, Chiles offered her the position of Secretary of the Department of Environmental Regulations for the State of Florida. Chiles told Ronald Begley of *Chemical Week* that he saw Browner as "a coalition builder with a unique ability to pull together diverse interests." Expectations were high for Browner because the agency she took over was extremely troubled. Browner was up to the challenge and accomplished much in her two-year tenure.

The Department of Environmental Regulations was the third largest such agency in the United States with a budget of $650 million. One big problem on the bureaucratic level was the high rate of turnover among the 1,500 employees, a trend Browner changed for the better. The agency became one of Florida's most active.

Among Browner's accomplishments in Florida were several deals that showed her ability to work with big business while addressing the concerns of environmentalists. The most significant involved Walt Disney World, which owned acres of wetlands. In exchange for allowing Walt Disney to develop 400 acres of this wetland, the company paid out $40 million to reclaim another 8,500 acres of wetlands. This land was used to created a wildlife refuge. Browner also negotiated a compromise on Clean Air Act legislation with large Florida companies.

Not all of Browner's decisions sat well with both environmentalists and business interests. Her work with the Kissimmee River restoration project did not please environmentalists. Sugar cane farmers were not happy about the ecological restoration project involving the Everglades and the Everglades National Park. The $1 billion project was intended to purify and restore the natural water flow to the Everglades National Park, thereby restoring the Everglades. It was one of the largest ecological restoration projects in the United

States. Farmers were not happy because they would be responsible for much of the cost, though environmentalists were satisfied.

Browner was not always successful, however. She pushed for a minimum recycled content in certain products as well as a tax on products for hazardous waste site cleanup, but neither happened. Despite such setbacks, Browner's reputation as a fair negotiator and intelligent environmental administrator grew rapidly.

When Bill Clinton was elected president of the United States in 1992, Browner left Florida to work as a member of his transition team. In 1993, she was named the director of the Environmental Protection Agency (EPA), a federal agency created by President Richard M. Nixon in 1970 by executive order. The EPA was created to carry out Congress's environmental provisions. She was the second woman to head the EPA (the first was Anne Gorsuch Burford during the Reagan administration), and its youngest administrator in the short history of the agency.

Browner's appointment pleased environmentalists. Richard Miniter of *Insight on the News* quoted J. Michael McCloskey of the Sierra Club as saying "Carol Browner's appointment is like a breath of fresh air after 12 years of choking smog." Business interests were more cautious.

When Browner was appointed, she was quoted by Ronald Begley of *Chemical Week* as saying "at a time when environmental protection and restoration will finally receive the attention and commitment they deserve—when we will finally move beyond the false tradeoff between growth and environmental protection to a sustainable economic future." As in Florida, Browner had to reform the EPA, with its $7 billion budget and 17,000-20,000 person staff. The previous administrations had not been as environmentally friendly as Clinton's promised to be.

One big problem was that the EPA and businesses had an adversarial relationship, in part because the agency previously made decisions very slowly, negatively affecting companies. Browner wanted to make the EPA more business friendly by making the process of developing and policing regulations better, making decisions on a more timely basis, and making environmental positions unified with other federal regulatory agencies. Browner was well aware of the importance of consistent policies from her work in Florida.

Browner's work in Florida influenced EPA policy in another way. She realized that environmental protection plans would necessarily vary from state to state, and she wanted to give them the latitude to develop their own policies under the EPA's auspices. As she told *EPA Journal,* "There are many issues where states really are best suited to decide how to strike that final balance. As a national agency looking at the entire country, we must come up with rules that fit Florida, Maine, Hawaii, Alaska, and Iowa, to pick random states. There are similarities between those states, but there are also great dissimilarities."

In Browner's first years with the EPA, she had to deal with the renewal of two key acts. The Conservation and Recovery Act had expired in 1990. The act covered incinerators and solid toxic waste and their impact on the environment. Browner and the EPA increased what was covered by the Toxic Release Inventory and issued the Chemical Manufacturing Rules. These rules were to cut chemicals that produced smog by one million tons annually. In 1994, Browner handled the renewal of Superfund, which funded the clean up of toxic waste sites, and chemical accidents and emergencies.

Throughout her tenure, Browner was accused of expanding the power of the EPA beyond its original intent. This was a point of controversy. For example, she set up several offices within the EPA. In 1993, the Office of Environmental Justice was created. It supplied grants to scientists to study how industrial pollutants affected poor communities. A few years later, the Office of Children's Health Protection was created to develop a national plan that addressed how children could be guarded from environmental risks.

Browner was often attacked for being difficult, though her power was not denied. In 1997, she pushed tough new clean air rules and got them, though the pressure on her was difficult. Browner wanted to reduce ozone levels in cities, though the cost was high up front. Some questioned her scientific support and her numbers, but Browner prevailed for the moment. (Some of the rules were later overturned by the courts, and were still being fought out at the turn of the century.) Steve J. Milloy, executive director for The Advancement of Sound Science Coalition, told Pranay B. Gupte and Bonner R. Cohen of *Forbes* that "Carol Browner is the best hardball player in the Clinton Administration. She has the 105th Congress completely intimidated by her debating skills and her sheer grasp of facts, however questionable. She eats their lunch."

Browner's skills in negotiation and organization led to speculation in 1999 that she might run for the United States Senate from Florida. Whether or not she ever decides to run for office, she keeps her environmental priorities in perspective. When appointed to head the EPA, she told Richard Miniter of *Insight on the News,* "I want my son to be able to grow up and enjoy the natural wonders of the United States in the same way that I have."

Sources

➤ **Books**

Collins, Louise Mooney, editor, *Newsmakers: 1994 Cumulation,* Gale Research, 1994, pp. 86-89.
Encyclopedia of World Biography, volume 3, second edition, Gale Group, 1998, pp. 50-52.
Parry, Melanie, editor, *Larousse Dictionary of Women,* Larousse, 1996, p. 106.
Who's Who of American Women: 1999-2000, Marquis Who'sWho, 1998, p. 126.

➤ **Periodicals**

The Brownsfields Report, September 23, 1999, p. 4.
Chemical Week, December 23, 1992, p. 6; June 9, 1999, p. 11.
E, December 1993, p. 14; April 1994, p. 36.
EPA Journal, January-March 1993, pp. 6, 9 (opening quote).
Forbes, October 20, 1997, p. 170.
Insight on the News, February 8, 1993, p. 6.
The Oil Daily, December 14, 1992, p. 1; May 16, 1997, p. 1; May 28, 1999.
Science, January 21, 1994, p. 312; July 29, 1994, p. 599.
Time, July 7, 1997, p. 32.
Washington Monthly, November 1999, p. 36.

Richard E. Byrd

"No one who has ever seen new lands rising above the prow of a ship, or above a running dog team, or through the shine of a propeller, can easily deny the pull."*

Born on October 25, 1888, in Winchester, Virginia, Richard E. Byrd was known for his groundbreaking explorations of the Arctic and Antarctica. He died on March 11, 1957, in Boston, Massachusetts.

A pioneer in aviation, Richard E. Byrd was the first to fly over both the North and South Poles. While his journey to the Arctic was controversial, his well-organized expeditions to Antarctica provided much new knowledge about the continent. Byrd also made significant contributions in naval aviation and was regarded as one of the greatest heroes of the twentieth century during his lifetime.

Born on October 25, 1888, in Winchester, Virginia, Richard Evelyn Byrd was the son of Richard Evelyn Byrd and Eleanor Bolling Flood Byrd. His father was a lawyer, and his family was prominent in Virginia politics. Byrd was the middle of three brothers, one of whom, Harry, became a United States senator.

Even as a child, Byrd enjoyed adventures and exploration. An athletic youngster, he played war games with his brothers in the woods near their home. He had a real-life adventure at the age of about 12 or 13 when a family friend who was working as a United States circuit judge in the Philippines invited Byrd for a visit. Traveling alone, Byrd stayed in Manila for a year, then went around the world. It was around this time that Byrd first dreamed of one day conquering the North Pole.

When Byrd returned to the United States, he entered Shenandoah Valley Military Academy. His college education took him to several different institutions. He attended the Virginia Military Institute from 1904 until 1907, then decided to transfer to the University of Virginia, where he remained for only a year before entering the U.S. Naval Academy in 1908.

At the Naval Academy, Byrd was active in several sports, including football, gymnastics, tennis, and wrestling. He severely injured himself several times, breaking bones in the right ankle at least twice. He graduated in 1912, placing sixty-second in a class of 155.

After graduation, Byrd received a commission in the Navy and served on the USS *Wyoming* with distinction. After saving two men from drowning in the Caribbean, he was given a Congressional Life Saving Medal and a commendation letter from the Secretary of the Navy. But then an event from his past came back to haunt him. In a shipboard accident, Byrd again injured his right ankle, which left him with a permanent limp.

Despite this setback, Byrd went on with his life. He married his childhood sweetheart, Marie Donaldson Ames, in 1915, and eventually they had four children. Byrd also received another work assignment, this time as an aide to Navy Secretary Josephus Daniels on the USS *Dolphin.* However, his ankle injury interfered with his ability to do his job properly, forcing him to retire from the Navy with a medical disability in March 1916. He continued to serve as a retired officer on active duty, and thanks to his family's influence, he even received a promotion to lieutenant j.g. His first assignment was in Rhode Island, where he worked as the administrator of the state's naval militia.

When the United States entered World War I, Byrd began flight training in 1917 through the Navy and was a full-fledged naval aviator by 1918. During the war, he was stationed in Nova Scotia, Canada, where he set up air bases and was in command of two stations that were involved in anti-submarine patrols.

It was during this period that Byrd first became interested in navigation techniques for use over water. He wanted to be the first person to cross the Atlantic in an airplane. To that end, he invented a bubble sextant, which featured an artificial horizon to be used by those navigating over water. Byrd thought such technology could be useful in transporting certain types of aircraft to Europe as part of the war effort.

Navy rules did not allow Byrd to join the crew that ended up making the first transatlantic flight in 1919. By that time, he had become the Navy's liaison officer to Congress, a position he held until 1923. One of his assignments involved drafting the legislation that created the Bureau of Aeronautics. Byrd also continued to work in flight more directly, spending part of 1921 in England experimenting with dirigibles.

By the mid-1920s, Byrd had a new goal: he wanted to be the first person to fly over the North Pole. While serving with the Bureau of Navigation during the 1920s, Byrd went to Greenland as part of the 1925 MacMillan Polar Expedition, which piqued his interest in the Arctic. Because the Navy would not support his efforts, however, he left the military to pursue his quest on his own.

Byrd drummed up private funding for his adventure, later dubbed the Byrd Arctic Exploration. When he arrived in Greenland in 1926, he discovered there were several other groups preparing to beat him to the Pole. Accompanied by co-pilot Floyd Bennett in a plane called the *Josephine Ford,* Byrd made the flight in 15 hours and bested his rivals by three days. This he accomplished despite the fact that his plane experienced some engine trouble because of an oil leak and was nearly forced to go back. Byrd claimed to have circled the

North Pole several times but did not leave any physical markers to prove it.

While most people in the United States regarded Byrd and Bennett as heroes, some raised doubts about whether the two men had really made it to the Pole. Skeptics believed his flight was too short to have reached his goal. Nevertheless, Byrd was awarded the Congressional Medal of Honor for his accomplishments.

Many years later, in 1996, a newly discovered diary of Byrd's once again prompted questions about what he had actually achieved during his Arctic expedition. In one particular entry, a passage that had been erased but that was still readable suggested the flight was actually 100 to 150 miles short of reaching the pole.

Before he turned his attention to conquering the Antarctic, Byrd finally fulfilled one of his earlier ambitions. In 1927, he accompanied a crew on a flight across the Atlantic about a month after aviator Charles Lindbergh made his famous solo flight. This time, however, Byrd was not trying to beat Lindbergh or anyone else. Instead, he wanted to prove the practicality of scheduled, for-profit transatlantic flights. Circumstances almost sabotaged his efforts when events during the flight took a dangerous turn. In addition to compass problems, he and the crew encountered heavy fog, and the plane was forced to make a crash landing after 42 hours and 4200 miles. Byrd broke his arm in the process and went on to receive the Medal of Valor from the mayor of New York City.

Byrd's next goal was to be the first to reach the South Pole. Because of his previous successes, he was able to raise significantly more money than he had for his North Pole expedition. Byrd and his large crew began their journey to Antarctica in late 1928 and set up a base camp there dubbed "Little America" on January 1, 1929.

In November 1929, Byrd and several other crew members flew to the South Pole and then headed back to the camp. While on their historic flight, they mapped and photographed about 150,000 square miles of territory. They also observed certain zoological, meteorological, and geological features of Antarctica and even discovered some mineral deposits.

When Byrd returned to the United States after his expedition, he was again hailed as a hero. By order of Congress, he received a promotion to rear admiral. He was also was awarded the Navy Cross and the Patron's Medal of the Royal Geographical Society.

Byrd returned to Antarctica in 1934 with an even larger crew to do more scientific work. This expedition logged many scientific firsts. In addition to doing more mapping (of the continent's outline) and making more astronomical, meteorological, and geological observations, Byrd and his men measured the ice thickness in several places and collected physical data.

The biggest accomplishment of Byrd's second trip to Antarctica also proved to be the most dangerous. While there, he helped to build a permanent weather station named the Bolling Advance Station. After sending his crew away because of supply problems, Byrd spent several months alone at the station. During that time, he nearly died from carbon monoxide poisoning caused by a faulty stove. Alarmed by his incoherency during radio contacts with his base camp, his crew tried to rescue him three times before finally succeeding. An exhausted Byrd returned to the United States in 1935.

Byrd made his third trip to the Antarctic in 1939. This time, he was sponsored by the U.S. government, thus marking the first time in 100 years that officials had agreed to underwrite such an expedition. Byrd was in charge of a crew that was responsible for additional mapping of the continent and for establishing a permanent base. The expedition ended in 1941 when the United States entered World War II.

During the war, Byrd, who had been called up to serve again in the Navy, worked primarily in the Pacific theater. There he helped develop new air routes and air bases to prepare for an Allied campaign to retake islands captured by the Japanese. Byrd also contributed to efforts in the European theater by studying the use of aerial support for ground troops. After the war ended, Byrd resumed the peace activities he had been involved in prior to the outbreak of hostilities. For example, he helped found the Iron Curtain Refugee Campaign for the International Rescue Committee (IRC). From 1950 until his death, Byrd served as the honorary chair of the IRC's board of directors.

Byrd returned to Antarctica two more times during the postwar period. In 1946, he led 4,000 men in Operation Highjump and completed another mapping operation. Nearly a decade later, from 1955 to 1956, Byrd surveyed Antarctica for the U.S. Antarctic Programs to prepare for an International Geophysical Year expedition to the area in 1957. Two of his objectives were to determine whether aircraft could land at the pole and whether an observation station could be built there.

Byrd never saw the fruits of his labor, however. He died in his sleep on March 11, 1957, in Boston, Massachusetts, not long after receiving the Medal of Freedom from the U.S. Department of Defense. But the memory of him lives on in Antarctica. In 1965 a bust of Byrd was dedicated on the frozen continent in honor of his achievements.

Sources

➤ Books

Baker, Daniel B., editor, *Explorers and Discovers of the World*, Gale, 1993, pp. 98-100.

Byrd, Richard Evelyn, *Discovery: The Story of the Second Byrd Antarctic Expedition*, Putnam, 1935 (opening quote).

Deplar, Helen, editor, *The Discoverers: An Encyclopedia of Explorers and Exploration*, McGraw-Hill, 1980, pp. 87-89.

Encyclopedia of World Biography, 2nd edition, Volume 3, Gale, 1998, pp. 186-87.

Garraty, John A. and Mark C. Carnes, editors, *American National Biography*, Volume 4, Oxford University Press, 1999, pp. 133-35.

Garraty, John A. and Jerome L. Sterntein, editors, *Encyclopedia of American Biography*, 2nd edition, HarperCollins, 1998, pp. 163-64.

Hoyt, Edwin P., *The Last Explorer: The Adventures of Admiral Byrd*, John Day, 1968.

Magill, Frank N., editor, *Great Lives from American History: American Series*, Volume 1, Salem Press, 1987, pp. 373-77.

Waldman, Carl and Alan Wexler, *Who Was Who in World Exploration*, Facts on File, 1992, pp. 105-07.

➤ Periodicals

New York Times, May 9, 1996, p. A1.
St. Louis Post-Dispatch, May 9, 1996, p. A9.
Times (London), March 13, 1957.
Washington Post, May 9, 1996, p. A3; November 30, 1999, p. C13.

Karel and Jozef Capek

"Now I must help to educate the nation."*

Born on January 9, 1890, in Male Svatonovice, Bohemia (now Czech Republic), playwright and novelist Karel Capek died suddenly on December 25, 1938. His older brother, Jozef Capek—born in Male Svatonovice in 1887—was an early literary collaborator of Karel's before becoming a painter. Jozef died in a Nazi concentration camp just before the end of World War II.

Once published as The Brothers Capek, Karel and Jozef Capek were part of an emerging Czech avant-garde in the 1920s and '30s. Karel Capek is best remembered for his political satires and as the author of the play *R.U.R (Rossum's Universal Robots)*, while his older brother became a renowned painter and art critic. Karel died in 1938, just prior to the German invasion of his country; when the Nazi Gestapo found that the subversive writer had died, they took his brother into custody, who died just a few weeks before Bergen-Belsen, the concentration camp, was liberated.

Jozef was born in July of 1887, the first of three Capek children who grew up in Male Svatonovice, a village in the northwestern part of what later became the Czech Republic. In Male Svatonovice their father, Antonin, was a respected physician and Czech patriot. A sister, Helena, followed, and on January 9, 1890 Karel was born prematurely. Their mother, Bozena, suffered from hypochondria, and worried extensively about her youngest child, who was frail and sickly. Under the protective wing of his older brother, however, Karel led a relatively normal childhood with the usual adventures.

The pair, so close in age and interests, invented their own jargon as children, to which they sometimes reverted as adults. As a child, Karel began writing his homework answers in verse, while his brother showed an early talent for drawing. At the time, Czechoslovakia did not yet exist as a nation, and was part of the mighty Austro-Hungarian empire; in high school, Karel was expelled from one institution when his membership in a secret group of student anarchists was discovered.

In 1905, with Helena married and living in Brno, Karel moved in with her to attend school; after 1907, he joined his brother in Prague, who was by then studying art in that city. Their father had retired, and both parents moved to Prague as well, though Bozena Capek would later die tragically of a drug overdose with medication she used to calm her nerves. Karel enrolled at the venerable Charles University, while Jozef resisted his parents' coercive attempts to accept a job as manager of a textile factory. He later said that the literary collaboration with his brother began when Karel once threw a story away because he was dissatisfied with it, and Jozef rescued it from the trash and rewrote it. Their first short story to appear in print was "The Return of the Prophet Hermotinos," published in 1908 on the pages of the newspaper *Lidove noviny*.

In 1910, Jozef left Prague for further study in Paris. His brother followed him there, and came under the influence of the French modernist and surrealist poets. Karel was also becoming increasingly interested in political matters, having inherited a strong sense of Czech nationalism from his father. After receiving a doctorate in philosophy in 1915—and having been rejected for military service at the onset of the Empire's entry into World War I—Karel attempted to leave the country to "study" in Spain. There he hoped to drum up support for Czech independence, but the police refused, feeling that Karel's time spent in France already was a bit suspect.

In 1916, the first book to appear under the joint pseudonym "Brothers Capek" appeared in Prague. *The Luminous Depths* was a collection of short stories previously published in journals and newspapers. In 1918, Czechoslovakia emerged as an independent state, and the mood in Prague and elsewhere was an optimistic, heady one. After the end of the war, both brothers earned their living as journalists in Prague for several years, which offered them an excellent forum for their patriotic and somewhat left-wing views.

The Brothers Capek published another collection of short pieces, *The Garden of Krakonos,* in 1918, and around 1920 Karel met an actress and writer several years his junior, Olga Scheinpflugova, and the two fell in love almost immediately. By now, however, Karel's back problems had worsened, and a few vertebrae had even calcified. This made it difficult for him to turn his head, and he began walking with a cane; his doctors deemed marriage out of the question. The two continued their affair, however, while Karel's works for the stage gained him increasing renown. He directed several plays at the Prague Municipal Theater between 1921 and 1923 after the success of his first attempt at drama, *The Outlaw,* in 1920.

Capek's second play, *R.U.R.,* would earn him fame, though not quite fortune, for Czechoslovakia was not a signatory nation to international copyright treaty at the time, and he received no royalties when this popular, timely work appeared in translation on stages around the world. The satire is set at an island factory where automated drudge workers, called "robots," are manufactured; his brother Jozef had coined the term as Karel wrote *R.U.R.* to describe a machine modeled upon the human body, based on a Czech term used to characterize work that was boring or repetitive. In *R.U.R.,* Helena Glory, a humanitarian aide worker, arrives at the factory to agitate the robots to rebel. She claims they must have souls, and convinces a scientist to begin some modifications on new models. One of these new breeds suddenly issues the decree that the robots should exterminate the human race; chaos ensues, but in the end two of the robots do indeed link souls.

The work debuted in Prague in 1921 with a fantastical, Cubist-designed set, and went on to win acclaim in London and New York productions. In 1922 a play written by the two brothers, *From the Life of the Insects,* was also a success in Prague. It features almost no plot, but rather a series of interesting scenes in which certain species possess comical anthropomorphic characteristics. Over the next decade, however, the artistically inclined Jozef began to delve further into painting and art criticism, becoming particularly fascinated by ethnographic art. Karel continued writing for newspapers, feeling that journalism was a calling for him, a way to reach and educate Czechs and Slovaks. He had become a friend of Czechoslovakia's first president, T. G. Masaryk, and supported Masaryk's efforts at what he called *Statotvornost,* or "state-building." Karel, who once said, "Now I must help to educate the nation," recognized that the Czechs and Slovaks were not used to self-rule, and they possessed a sense of nationalism but not a national identity.

After 1925, Jozef and Karel lived in a multi-story flat they had built in the Prague neighborhood of Vinhorady. There they became famous for their annual "Friday Circle" gatherings, attended by many notable names from Czech politics and letters; even Masaryk was a frequent guest. In 1927, the final work under the pen name of the Brothers Capek was staged at Prague's National Theater. *Adam the Creator* was their reworking of the biblical tale of Adam and Eve. In this version, Adam is dissatisfied with God's work and argues that he could do a better job; God lets him, and predictably satirical results follow.

After 1927, Karel Capek wrote no more plays, and no further works with his brother. He concentrated on newspaper and journal essays, short sketches, travel writing, and fiction. He also began interviewing Masaryk for a biography, *Conversations with T. G. Masaryk,* which was published in three volumes between 1928 and 1935. Another work, critically acclaimed by later scholars, was the 1932 collection of articles *On Political Matters,* which included his infamous piece "Why I Am Not a Communist." Of his several novels, his best remembered remains the 1936 book *The War with the Newts.* The work was a satire on dictatorship, and contained several sly jibes at Adolf Hitler, the fascist leader of Germany since 1933.

Karel Capek finally married Scheinpflugova in 1935 after physicians pronounced his condition vastly improved. Jozef, meanwhile, continued his dual career as both writer and artist, penning *The Humblest Art,* a collection of essays on naive painting, and *The Art of Natural Peoples,* a groundbreaking look at the rich artistic traditions of non-Western cultures. With his six acclaimed novels, Karel

Capek was widely thought to be in line for the next Nobel Prize in literature in 1936. The Swedish Academy, however, was conservative and fearful of offending Nazi Germany; reportedly they asked him to write something not so clearly anti-fascist, "to which Capek replied he had already submitted his doctoral dissertation," noted Peter Kussi in the introduction to *Toward the Radical Center: A Karel Capek Reader.*

In the last years of his life, Karel Capek worked tirelessly to stem the rising threat of European fascism. He had the ear of many well-connected government officials, and he also had influential friends abroad. He even made broadcasts over the radio, urging for a peaceful solution to the Sudentenland crisis between Czechoslovakia and Germany. This mineral-rich part of Bohemia, where he had been raised, had been settled by many Germans in the Middle Ages, and for this reason Hitler now claimed it should lie inside the borders of Germany. Karel was invited to attend Moscow's May Day celebrations in 1938—the Soviets, too, were wary of fascism—but declined to go; Jozef, however, accepted. At a conference of European leaders in September of 1938—to which Czechoslovakia was not invited—it was decided to allow Germany to annex the Sudetenland. Capek, like many other Czechs with close ties to western Europe, was devastated by what many saw as those leaders' cowardice and prejudice toward Slavs. Soon he began receiving anonymous denunciations in the mail, and many urged him to leave the country.

Karel Capek contracted pneumonia late that fall, though he continued to work on what would become his last novel, *The Cheat.* The work skewers the vain, petty aspirations of a talentless composer who plagiarizes the work of others. Capek died, however, before he could complete it, on Christmas Day of 1938. As one of the country's leading writers, his reputation was accorded a grand state funeral with an official procession, but both the National Museum and the National Theater in Prague were too wary to accept the honors. A permit application for a public procession was submitted, and rejected; people lined the streets anyway.

The Nazis invaded Czechoslovakia in March of 1939, and were apparently unaware that Karel Capek had died. Scheinpflugova quickly burned all of his correspondence, and the Gestapo, frustrated that the opinionated writer was now out of their grasp, arrested Jozef Capek instead. He contracted typhus at the Nazi concentration camp at Bergen-Belsen, and died just a few weeks before the end of World War II. "Thus, in a sense, he continued to play his role of protector," noted William E. Harking in his literary biography *Karel Capek,* "enduring as proxy the agony which his younger brother had been spared."

Sources

➤ Books

Capek, Karel, *Toward the Radical Center: A Karel Capek Reader,* edited and with an introduction by Peter Kussi, Catbird Press, 1990.
Harkins, William E. *Karel Capek,* Columbia University Press, 1962.
Wellek, Rene, *Essays on Czech Literature,* Mouton & Co., 1963.

Thomas R. Cech

"Now that we know that RNA can both carry genetic information and serve as a catalyst, it seems possible that it was the key molecule at the origin of life."

American chemist Thomas R. Cech won the 1989 Nobel Prize in chemistry for his groundbreaking research on RNA (ribonucleic acid), a complex molecule associated with the control of chemical activities that occur in cells. He was born December 8, 1947, in Chicago, Illinois. Address: Department of Chemistry and Biochemistry, University of Colorado, P.O. Box 215, Boulder, CO 80309-0215.

American chemist Thomas Robert Cech challenged fundamental scientific beliefs with his research involving RNA (ribonucleic acid), which along with DNA (deoxyribonucleic acid) is one of the fundamental substances of all living things. Contrary to what was previously believed, Cech showed that RNA has catalytic properties and enzyme-like functions. For his revolutionary research, Cech shared the 1989 Nobel Prize in chemistry.

Cech was born on December 8, 1947, in Chicago, Illinois, the son of Robert Franklin Cech and Annette Marie Cerveny Cech. Robert Cech was a doctor, and Annette Cech was primarily a housewife. While their son was still an infant, they moved to Iowa City, Iowa, and it was there that Cech grew up. His father was very interested in science, especially physics, and he shared that fascination with his son. As a child, Cech was intrigued by minerals and rocks and wondered how they had come to be. By the time he was in junior high school, he had already been in contact with university-based geologists in search of answers to his questions.

After Cech graduated from high school, he entered Grinnell College, a small liberal arts institution in Iowa. He began his academic career studying physical chemistry, an outgrowth of his earlier interest in geology. As an undergraduate, Cech completed two prestigious research stints at Lawrence Berkeley Laboratory and Argonne National Laboratory. He later switched his major to biological chemistry, however, because the process of designing experiments and interpreting data moved more quickly than it did in physical chemistry. Cech graduated from Grinnell in 1970 with a B.A. in chemistry.

That same year, he married a fellow chemist, Carol Lynn Martinson, whom he had met at Grinnell. They eventually had two daughters, Allison E. and Jennifer N. Prior to starting a family, they both entered the chemistry Ph.D. program at the University of California at Berkeley. There Cech studied biophysical chemistry on a fellowship from the National Science Foundation. His studies focused on eukaryotic chromosomes (from an organism of one or more cells with clearly visible nuclei) and DNA, including chromosomic structure and characteristics of the DNA sequence organization.

Cech's doctoral thesis was also concerned with DNA, specifically in the mouse genome. He studied its organization and proprieties by purifying a DNA fragment, then visualizing it using an electron microscope. Cech subsequently published six papers on his research in scientific journals, an impressive number for a graduate student. Both he and his wife received their doctorates in 1975.

To enhance his understanding of biology, Cech then took a position at the Massachusetts Institute of Technology (MIT) as a National Cancer Institute fellow in molecular biology. Over the next two years, he continued to study DNA, using psoralen derivatives (light-sensitive compounds) to obtain his information. He focused his research on an organism known as Tetrahymena thermophila, a single-celled, ciliated protozoan. While this minute form of protoplasmic animal life is often found in ponds, it can easily be cultured in a laboratory environment for the purposes of scientific study. During his two-year stint at MIT, Cech produced four more papers for publication.

In January 1978, Cech was hired by the University of Colorado at Boulder as an assistant professor. He was soon promoted to associate professor, and by 1983 he had been named a full professor. He taught chemistry, biochemistry, and molecular cell and developmental biology. Soon after arriving in Colorado, Cech also began doing the research that would lead to his Nobel Prize.

Cech again used Tetrahymena thermophila to continue his study of genetic material, specifically gene expression and its regulation. He wanted to find out how DNA sends its instructions to the body of a cell so that its parts can be duplicated. The Tetrahymena thermophila was ideal for this type of study because it reproduced quickly and its structure was conducive to DNA extractions. But Cech's findings soon led him to turn away from focusing exclusively on DNA research to take up RNA biochemistry instead.

Just before Cech began this line of research, other scientists had made several relevant discoveries. It had been proven, for example, that DNA was different from end-product RNA. Scientist Philip Sharp also discovered what came to be called "introns," stretches of DNA that were non-coding. They were thought to be redundant.

It was generally believed that DNA was like a blueprint or template of the genetic code in the cell's nucleus. This coding was somehow imprinted on the three different types of RNA. The RNA, in turn, passively relayed the genetic coding to the enzymes or proteins of the cell. These then acted as the catalysts for chemical reactions that occurred in the cell. Scientists believed that RNA needed the presence of a protein or an enzyme for these reactions to take place. Cech refuted some of these assumptions with his research.

In the course of his work with Tetrahymena thermophila, he began looking for a protein or an enzyme that caused introns to be cut from RNA molecules after being copied from the DNA blueprints. The slicing of introns was a complex process, and in Cech's experiments, it happened rather quickly. He found that RNA did not need proteins or enzymes for the snipping to take place; it could act as its own catalyst. But it was not a catalyst in the true sense of the word. The RNA changed *after* the reaction, and, unlike a protein or enzyme, could only act upon itself and nothing else. Cech called the RNA catalyst a "ribozyme."

When Cech first began publishing his results during the early 1980s, he was not entirely sure his data was valid. His findings challenged every assumption about RNA, though some biologists had believed an RNA catalyst might someday be discovered. But after widespread debate in the scientific community and additional experiments, Cech's findings were proven correct.

In addition to overturning previous assumptions about chemistry and biology, Cech's discovery had several other implications. For example, there were potential applications in pharmaceutical and clinical areas. It could be used in gene technology to fight viruses, perhaps even the common cold. A new kind of genetic engineering could emerge based on RNA rather than DNA. It also launched the new research field of RNA enzymology.

Cech's discovery also changed the way scientists believe life on Earth began four billion years ago. Some have speculated that RNA could have been present in original cells before proteins or DNA. As Roger Lewin observed in *Science,* "For those interested in the origin of life, the existence of RNA catalysts offers an intriguing glimpse of a former, more primitive age when the full range of metabolic and genetic machinery had yet to evolve." As Cech's research came to be accepted and then built upon by other scientists such as Yale University professor Sidney Altman, it was frequently cited as being worthy of consideration for a Nobel Prize.

By the mid-1980s, Cech was beginning to receive numerous honors for his work, and he found himself in demand as a visiting lecturer at various institutions. In 1984 he garnered the Passano Foundation Young Scientific Award and the Harrison Howe Award. The following year, he was honored with a Guggenheim fellowship and the Pfizer Award in Enzyme Chemistry. His alma mater, Grinnell College, granted him an honorary Doctor of Science degree in 1987. That same year, Cech was elected to the United States Academy of Sciences; the following year, he was elected to the American Academy of Arts and Sciences. The greatest honor, however, came in 1989 when he was awarded the Nobel Prize in chemistry. He shared it with Sidney Altman, who had arrived at many of the same discoveries on his own while trying to answer a different set of questions. Cech's Nobel lecture was entitled "Self-Splicing and Enzymatic Activity of an Intervening Sequence RNA from Tetrahymena."

Cech had patented his biotechnology discovery in 1986. In 1989, however, two Australian scientists developed ribozymes that could shear specific genes, and they subsequently made a deal with a French pharmaceutical company that was interested in the technology. Cech then took them to court for violating his patent, and in 1991 he was granted a sweeping patent involving the use and synthesis of ribozymes. Some feared that this would stifle additional research, especially concerning viral diseases that might be able to be treated with the new technology. Cech later sold his licensing rights to United States Biochemical Corporation.

Since receiving the Nobel Prize, Cech has continued to study ribozymes and RNA's structure as well as the structure of chromosomes. He has also studied the enzyme telomerase, which helps protect the chromosomes of dividing cells, and has done some cancer cell research with other scientists. In 1987 Cech was named a research professor for the American Cancer Society. A year later, he was also named an investigator for the Howard Hughes Medical Institute, the largest private provider of funds for medical research and education in the United States. He held these positions concurrently with his faculty post at the University of Colorado, where in 1990 he was granted a distinguished professorship. Cech also served as a deputy editor of the well-known journal *Science* and worked with various biotechnical companies.

In the spring of 1999, Cech was named president of the Howard Hughes Medical Institute. His new position primarily involves managerial tasks such as determining how to allocate resources, but he negotiated an arrangement that will allow him to spend three weeks a month at the Institute in Chevy Chase, Maryland, and one week doing research at his laboratory in Colorado. As the chair of the Institute's board of trustees, Hanna H. Grey, was quoted as saying in U.S. Newswire upon Cech's appointment, "Professor Cech is a distinguished scientist of great accomplishment, with a profound understanding of the research world."

Sources

➤ **Books**

Daintith, John and others, editors, *Biographical Encyclopedia of Scientists,* 2nd edition, Institute of Physics Publishing, 1994, pp. 151-52.

James, Larylin K., editor, *Nobel Laureates in Chemistry, 1901-1992,* American Chemical Society/Chemical Heritage Foundation, 1993, pp. 745-49.

Magill, Frank N., editor, *The Nobel Prize Winners: Chemistry,* Salem Press, 1990, pp. 1236-46.

McMurray, Emily, editor, *Notable Twentieth-Century Scientists,* Gale, 1995, pp. 328-30.

➤ **Periodicals**

Chemical & Engineering News, December 4, 1989, p. 31.

Chemistry and Industry, November 6, 1989, p. 698.

Dallas Morning News, March 30, 1998, p. 4F.

Denver Post, October 19, 1995, p. A12.

Denver Rocky Mountain News, April 26, 1997, p. 22A.

Economist, October 21, 1989, p. 96.

Maclean's, October 23, 1989, p. 58.

New York Times, October 13, 1989, p. A10.

Science, January 20, 1984, p. 266; February 7, 1986, p. 545; October 20, 1989, p. 325; February 1, 1991, p. 521; April 2, 1999; October 8, 1999.

Science News, November 19, 1988, p. 326; October 21, 1989, p. 262.

ScienceNOW, March 24, 1999.

Scientific American, December 1989, p. 34.

Time, October 23, 1989, p. 73 (opening quote).

U.S. News & World Report, October 23, 1989, p. 20.

U.S. Newswire, March 24, 1999.

Joe Clark

"If you can conceive it, you can believe it, and you can achieve it."*

Born in Rochelle, Georgia in 1939, Joe Clark's radical and controversial discipline methods as an inner-city high school principal were portrayed in the 1989 movie *Lean on Me*. Address: Essex County Juvenile Detention Center, Director, Division of Youth Services, 208 Sussex Ave, Newark, NJ 07103.

S ince landing in the national spotlight as the inner-city high school principal patrolling the grounds of his school with a bullhorn and baseball bat, Joe Clark has been a controversial advocate of steering problem youth straight via the force of strict discipline. For many he is a hero; for others he is far too radical and abrasive. Educators, parents, students, and organizations who have lauded his methods and philosophy have honored him by bestowing him with awards, writing journalistic pieces, inviting him to speak at conferences and other events, and making a movie portraying his experience as principal at Eastside High, in Paterson, New Jersey— *Lean on Me.*

Joe Clark was born in Rochelle, Georgia, in 1939. He served in the U.S. Army Reserve from 1958-1966. During that time, in 1960, he earned his bachelor's degree from William Paterson College. He went on to serve on the Board of Education in Paterson, New Jersey, where he became school principal at PS 6, a troubled inner-city elementary school. He shortly earned a reputation as a principal who expected and got results from students. Admirers of Clark's style and effect on PS 6 referred to the school as the "Miracle on Carroll Street." In 1974 he received his master's degree from Seton Hall, and acted as language arts coordinator in Paterson from 1976-79. In 1982 Clark became principal of Paterson's Eastside High, a school with a predominantly black and Hispanic student body of 3,200. The school had a reputation for violence and poor academic scores. State officials had earlier tagged the school as on the verge of "educational bankruptcy."

Ruling with a delicate mix of firm, discipline-enforced control over and genuine affection for the students, Clark was honored by colleagues and associations with several awards, including: the NAACP Community Service Award, New Jerseyan of the Year by the Newark Star Ledger in 1983, Outstanding Educator of 1984 by the New Jersey Monthly, recognition in academic and disciplinary excellence at a presidential conference in 1985, the National School Safety Center Principal of Leadership Award in 1986, and the National Black Policemen's Association's Humanitarian Award in 1988.

During the late 1980s Clark became known around the country for his methods of raising students' enthusiasm for, participation in, and self-control at school. Rapidly his story was told in newspaper pieces and news television broadcasts across the United States. Though he developed and maintained an environment of strict adherence to authority at the school, expelling students whom he labeled "parasites" and "hoodlums, thugs and pathological deviants," he was able to appeal to students, who understood that he cared about their future and had confidence in their ability to be successful in school and in life. His tough love leadership earned him praise and admiration from students, teachers , and parents. And this charisma he mastered at Eastside was newsworthy around America, during a period of heightened concerns among politicians, academics, and parents over an American youth that was becoming increasingly more criminally and sexually active, as well as more likely to drop out of school. President Ronald Reagan praised Clark's brand of leadership and commitment as integral to managing inner-city schools in crisis. However, many voiced criticism of Clark's methods, declaring that his hard-line approach could not lead to real benefits in improving students' interest in learning.

In 1989 Clark wrote a book about his role as a high school principal entitled *Laying Down the Law: Joe Clark's Strategy for Saving Our Schools.* He described the atmosphere at the school upon his arrival as lawless. Fights frequently broke out in school hallways. Weapons were drawn against students and teachers alike. Drug dealers roamed freely throughout school grounds. Smoke from marijuana could be smelled in most corridors and restrooms. Graffiti was painted on walls inside and outside the school. The school building was in a shambles: broken windows, doors, and furniture. The process of learning was at a standstill as teachers, living in fear of retaliation by students, were unable to control their classrooms. Truancy and drop out rates had soared as academic scores plummeted. Clark was disgusted with the passivity of administrators and educators as they stood by and tolerated sub-standard academic performance and poor behavior, while the futures of students with potential were sacrificed. Residing in a crime infested area, Clark observed that kids who already encountered great obstacles outside of school were losing their one opportunity to acquire the skills they would need to improve their lives.

Clark knew that he had to work toward a broad objective of simply grabbing control of the school. First he went to work reorganizing the administrative structure of the school, firing administrators he felt were lazy or incompetent. He implemented a hierarchy for channeling various student problems, designating clearly defined responsibilities to specific members of the administration. He introduced strict student policies, including detention and suspension systems, student identification tags, a dress code, and foot traffic guidelines. He coordinated a major repair and renovation project of the building. He organized and increased security patrols to keep out the drug dealers. While he worked to transform Eastside, he kept his plans largely confidential, explaining in his book, "too often, an administrator kills or weakens a good plan by telegraphing in advance what he is going to do—instead of just doing it."

On the first day of his term as principal, Clark greeted the students with salutations made through a bullhorn, introducing himself and the new Eastside High School. He also told them, "What was, exists no more. Go to your classrooms. Please walk to the right." Adhering to the new, much stricter guidelines for discipline, Clark suspended 300 students during the first week of his tenure, for violations including assault, vandalism, talking back to teachers and administrators, wearing hats, and tardiness. Suspensions and expulsions were Clark's way of getting rid of the "hoodlums." Clark also fired teachers who did not support the new codes and guidelines.

When the Paterson School Board undertook insubordination proceedings against Clark for expelling over 60 "parasite" students in December of 1987, the controversy surrounding his model of leadership received widespread and deep attention among commentators and journalists nationally. The group Clark had expelled included many students over 18 who had not yet graduated, and Clark believed that these students were a bad influence on, even an obstacle for, other students at Eastside. Members on Paterson's School Board charged that Clark had violated these students' rights by expelling them on the basis that they did not graduate at the time students traditionally finish high school. They also sought to charge Clark with violating fire codes, as he had chained various exit doors throughout the school so that students were not as easily able to walk out of the building and skip their classes.

At the board meeting in January of 1988, many students and parents appeared and packed the room to support Clark. They chanted pro-Clark slogans, such as, "Without No Joe, Where Will We Go?" A representative from the Reagan Administration was present as well, who supported Clark and even offered him a position in the Office of Policy Development, in the event that the board was successful in ousting him out of his position as principal. Clark turned down the offer, maintaining his loyalty to Eastside and the Paterson District. He blamed the board for "making allowances for inner-city kids," and thereby, "making a bunch of parasites out of black and Hispanic kids." The proceedings were dropped against

Clark, who invited back some of the students who had been expelled.

However, a broader formal inquiry regarding the expulsions was instigated against Clark, which led to an even more intense debate nationally regarding control over problem students. Clark appeared on the cover of *Time* in February of 1988 and was interviewed on many television talk shows and news programs. The Reagan Administration continued to laud Clark; U.S. Secretary of Education, William J. Bennett, remarked, "Sometimes you need Mr. Chips, sometimes you need Dirty Harry." Educators, politicians, and parents who supported Clark's style described his methods and objectives as working to develop students into law-abiding citizens who would learn to respect authority and be successful in life. Those who condemned his tactics opined that he treated students as if they were the enemy. His approach would not truly rehabilitate problem students and lead them into success in the long run; he could only make troubled kids more angry, and they would eventually cease to tolerate his control over them. Criticism against him appeared increasingly in newspaper op-ed pieces, in which opponents regarded him as tyrannical and abusive towards students.

Clark remained at Eastside until June of 1989, two months after he underwent open-heart surgery. Many students and parents protested Clark's departure, initially treating it as the work of the school board. They carried sings and chanted, "If Mr. Clark leaves, we leave" and "We want Joe." Although he admitted that he indeed had difficulty performing his job the way he would like due to board-induced criticism and restraint, Clark made it clear that it was his will to resign. He soon began lecturing across the country on school management and discipline methods. In the same year, Clark's story was portrayed in the Warner Brothers film *Lean on Me,* starring Morgan Freeman.

In August of 1995, Clark began working as Director of the Essex County Youth House in Newark, New Jersey. He immediately implemented tough discipline and control measures against inmates. He refused to respond to a youth who did not address him as "Director Clark, Sir." A *New York Times* article quoted Clark's response to a boy who asked why inmates were not allowed to watch television: "Because you're here," he explained, "You are going to spend your time cleaning, mopping, studying, getting an education. We're going to transmogrify your souls, so when you go into your communities you will say, 'We are not going back again because Director Joe Clark is there and the man does not play.' That will be a message to the community." In October of 1996, Clark was once again charged with violating the rights of youths, when he was criticized by officials on the local, state, and federal levels for putting youths in handcuffs and leg irons as a disciplinary tactic. In *Jet*, Clark defended his actions, remarking, "I made them accountable for their diabolical behavior. They were not abused; they were not beaten; they were simply handled in a manner commensurate with their unacceptable behavior." Clark's tough love approach at the center continued to attract both criticisms and praises among parents and officials, just as it had at Eastside.

Sources

➤ Books

Clark, Joe, and Joe Picard, *Laying Down the Law: Joe Clark's Strategy for Saving Our Schools*, Regnery Gateway, 1989.

➤ Periodicals

Jet, September 4, 1995, p. 22; October 21, 1996, p. 8.
Nation, January 30, 1988, p. 109.
National Review, May 5, 1989, p. 18 (opening quote).
People, March 27, 1989, p. 51.
Time, February, 1998; March 13, 1989, p. 82.

Max Cleland

"There was a time I could have given up and let Uncle Sam take care of me, but I was raised to believe you can't expect help if you don't help yourself."

Born August 24, 1942, in Atlanta, Georgia, Max Cleland survived near-fatal injuries during the Vietnam War and has since pursued a career in public service in various government posts at the state and national level, including Georgia Secretary of State, head of the U.S. Veterans Administration, and U.S. Senator from Georgia. Address: 461 Dirksen Senate Office Building, Washington, D.C. 20510-1001.

On April 8, 1968, Captain Max Cleland of the U.S. Army was serving in Vietnam when his life took a sudden and almost fatal turn. As he picked up a grenade he thought he had dropped, it exploded in his right hand, ripping off his forearm and most of his right leg and mangling his left leg as well. For nearly two years Cleland struggled to recover physically as well as emotionally from his devastating injuries. Since then, he has steadfastly refused to let anything slow him down or deter him from his chosen career in public service.

A native of Atlanta, Georgia, who grew up in the nearby town of Lithonia, Joseph Maxwell Cleland (known simply as "Max" since childhood) was born on August 24, 1942, to Joseph Hugh Cleland and Juanita Kesler Cleland. Joseph, a salesman, and Juanita, a secretary, doted on their only child, who was a standout throughout his school years not only in academics and sports but also in extracurricular activities such as band and drama. "As far back as I could remember I wanted to live life to the fullest," Cleland later recalled in his autobiography, *Strong at the Broken Places*. "There was a deep, inner urge to challenge my limitations. . . . I wanted to be good at everything."

Following his graduation from high school in 1960, Cleland headed off to Stetson College, a liberal arts institution in Florida. There he struggled academically until finding his niche as a history major and as a member of the school's Army Reserve Officers Training Corps (ROTC) program. After receiving his bachelor of arts degree in 1964 and completing a year of graduate study in history and political science at Atlanta's Emory University, he joined the U.S. Army in October 1965 and was assigned to the Signal Corps as a second lieutenant. Eventually, he moved into a stateside desk job as a general's aide.

It was not long, however, before Cleland grew restless and bored. Not only did he crave excitement, he also felt guilty watching other young men his age being sent off to fight in Southeast Asia. Thus, despite the misgivings of his parents, friends, and even his commanding officer, Cleland volunteered for duty in Vietnam.

Cleland arrived in South Vietnam in June 1967 as a member of the First Air Cavalry Division. Stationed at a base camp in the country's central highlands, he was a platoon leader responsible for helping provide around-the-clock communications for the 15,000-man division. But his job quickly settled into a routine that seemed very distant from the war.

All of that changed, however, after February 1, 1968, which marked the beginning of a massive North Vietnamese invasion of South Vietnam known as the Tet Offensive. Cleland's division was hit hard as fierce fighting continued throughout the month of February. When the action suddenly shifted to an outpost in the northwestern part of the country called Khe Sanh, Cleland—who had recently been promoted to captain and had less than 90 days left on his tour of duty—volunteered to serve as a communications officer with an infantry battalion that had been assigned to help repel the enemy there.

The United States launched an air assault on Khe Sanh on April 1, 1968, and Cleland's signal team was sent in the following day. They came under attack almost immediately and fought back for most of the next five days and nights until the tide finally turned in their favor. On April 8, Cleland took a short helicopter flight with his men to a hill about 15 miles away from their camp to set up a radio relay station. After helping unload equipment, he spotted a grenade on the ground nearby. Figuring that he had probably dropped it, he bent over to pick it up.

Cleland recounted the next moments of his life in his autobiography. "A blinding explosion threw me backwards," he wrote. "The blast jammed my eyeballs back into my skull, temporarily blinding me. . . . My ears rang with a deafening reverberation. . . . When my eyes cleared I looked at my right hand. It was gone. . . . Then I tried to stand but couldn't. I looked down. My right leg and knee were gone. My left leg was a soggy mass of bloody flesh mixed with green fatigue cloth. . . . I tried to cry out to [my men] but could only hiss. My hand touched my throat and came back covered with blood. Shrapnel had sliced open my windpipe. I sank back on the ground knowing that I was dying fast. . . ."

Cleland managed to cling to life, but the severity of his injuries forced doctors to amputate both of his legs above the knee and his right forearm. He endured excruciating pain and serious infections as he slowly recovered, determined not just to survive but also to learn to walk again using artificial limbs. At the same time, he struggled with powerful emotions that veered from one extreme to the other—from gratitude that he was still alive to despair over his injuries. His turmoil was heightened by the fact that he had begun to question himself and his motives for serving in Vietnam as well as the purpose of the war itself.

Cleland spent 18 months in a series of hospitals healing from his wounds, undergoing rehabilitation, and battling depression. Doctors discouraged him from trying to learn to walk with artificial legs because the amputation of his arm meant that he would have difficulty using crutches; instead, they urged him to accept the idea of spending his life in a wheelchair. Cleland refused to give up, however, and after months of pleading, he finally received their consent to be fitted for artificial legs.

At that point, Cleland was transferred from Walter Reed Army Hospital in Washington, D.C., to a nearby Veterans Administration (VA) facility. But his experiences as a patient there left him angry and bitter. Reduced to a mere number without a name or rank, he encountered mostly indifference and bureaucratic red tape and very little concern for his physical or emotional well-being.

Cleland was nevertheless determined to live as normal a life as possible. He finally received his artificial legs in the spring of 1969 and by summer was walking again, albeit with much pain. He also taught himself how to drive a specially equipped car and even learned to swim and dance. But he was still unsure about what the future held for him and what kind of meaningful work he could do.

In December 1969, at the invitation of an acquaintance who was the executive director of the Paralyzed Veterans of America, Cleland testified before the U.S. Senate Committee on Veterans' Affairs about his own often bumpy road to rehabilitation and the special problems faced by veterans of the Vietnam war in general. As he explained to his audience, many soldiers like him had returned home with shattered bodies only to have to deal with the emotional pain of having sacrificed so much for such an unpopular cause.

By this time Cleland had regained much of his old confidence and independence. As a result of his appearance before the U.S. Senate, he received many letters that touched him deeply. Some asked him to share his story with others, and before long he was busy with speaking engagements, many of them back in his native Georgia. Gradually he came to believe that his calling was in public service.

In January of 1970, Cleland decided to run for the Georgia State Senate. As a Democrat in a Republican-led district, he was not expected to win. Yet that November he came out on top with more than 56 percent of the vote. At the age of 28, he thus became the youngest member of the Georgia State Senate and its only Vietnam veteran. Also victorious that year was Jimmy Carter, who had been elected governor of Georgia. He and Cleland became friends and allies as they worked on legislation aimed at helping the handicapped and veterans.

Cleland was re-elected to a second term in 1972 (the same year he decided to give up his artificial legs and opt for a wheelchair instead) but failed in a bid for the lieutenant governor's position in 1974. Several months later, in March 1975, he was offered a job on the staff of the U.S. Senate Committee on Veterans' Affairs. When Jimmy Carter was elected president in November 1976, he asked Cleland to head the Veterans Administration. The young man's first reaction was that he could never handle such an important position, but he eventually decided that perhaps he could provide the kind of leadership he felt the VA needed. Formally nominated by Carter in mid-February 1977, Cleland was confirmed by the Senate a week later and took office on March 2.

As head of the VA, Cleland focused on improving and expanding the medical treatment available at VA hospitals (especially for disabled veterans and those with alcohol and drug problems), streamlining the agency's bureaucracy (including computerizing the systems for keeping records and paying benefits), and providing more sensitive and compassionate care. He also advocated a bigger role for the VA in developing new treatments for veterans who had lost limbs or suffered spinal cord injuries. In addition, Cleland fought off pressures from both inside and outside the federal government to abolish or reorganize the VA in the name of efficiency and parcel out its functions to other agencies. Funding some of his more ambitious reforms proved troublesome, however, particularly given the budget constraints the VA was then facing.

Cleland remained head of the VA until Jimmy Carter left office in 1981. He then returned to Georgia, where in 1982 he was elected to the post of Secretary of State. Over the next 14 years, Cleland worked for campaign finance reform measures and took action against securities and telemarketing fraud. He also championed issues related to small business and established an information clearinghouse called the First Stop Business Information Center for would-be entrepreneurs and small business owners.

Cleland's next career move took him back to Washington and once again thrust him into the national political spotlight. When longtime Georgia politician Sam Nunn decided not to seek another term in the U.S. Senate in 1996, Cleland decided to run for his seat. He triumphed in the November election as an independent-minded moderate who appealed to both Democrats and Republicans.

Once in the nation's capital, the newly elected senator plunged headlong into his job. His belief that the goal of politics is to generate hope in people has prompted him to remain a strong advocate for veterans. As a member of the Senate Armed Services Committee and its Personnel subcommittee, he has spearheaded efforts to make improvements in health care, education, and retirement benefits for current and former members of the armed services and their families. In addition, Cleland has continued to look after the interests of small business owners through his work with the Senate Small Business Committee, focusing in particular on increasing funding for Women's Business Centers and lobbying for programs to help small businesses prepare for and recover from the impact of natural disasters. He has also served on the Senate Committee on Commerce, Science and Transportation as well as the Governmental Affairs Committee, which is involved in the struggle to enact significant campaign finance reform.

Despite the rigors of his job, which is made all the more exhausting on account of the daily challenges he faces as a triple amputee, Cleland thrives on the hard work and especially the personal contact with his constituents and his fellow politicians. "I feed off people—that gives me the energy," he explained to Charles Bowden of *Esquire*. "The worst thing you can do to me is put me in a corner and leave me alone. The air goes out of the balloon."

Sources

➤ On-line

"Max Cleland," http://cleland.senate.gov/index.html (February 22, 2000).

➤ Books

Cleland, Max, *Strong at the Broken Places: A Personal Story*, Chosen Books, 1980.

➤ Periodicals

Economist (US), October 26, 1996 (opening quote).
Esquire, August 1999.
Knight-Ridder/Tribune News Service, December 12, 1996.
Time, September 30, 1996, p. 31.

Alice Coachman

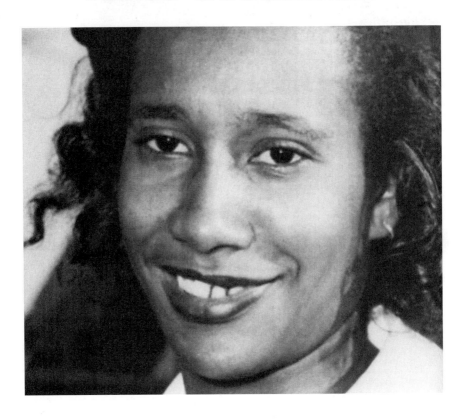

*"*__M__*y philosophy was if you beat me, you better set a record."*

Born on November 9, 1923, in Albany, Georgia, Alice Coach-man was the first African American woman to win a gold medal in the modern Olympics. Address: Tuskegee, Alabama.

In 1948, Alice Coachman because the first African American woman to win a gold medal in the modern Olympics. She won her only Olympic medal in the high jump event, and perhaps would have won more had the Olympics not been canceled in 1940 and 1944 because of World War II. Coachman competed in the United States from the late 1930s through the late 1940s, and continued to support others in track and field after her retirement. Coachman is considered a pioneer in track and field and a role model for African American women track stars.

Coachman was born on November 9, 1923, in Albany, Georgia, the fifth of ten children born to Fred and Evelyn (Jackson) Coachman. Fred Coachman was employed as a plasterer, while Evelyn worked in the home. As a child, Coachman set her sights on a career in entertainment, hoping to be like her heroes, child star Shirley Temple or jazz sax player Coleman Hawkins.

Athletic activities also caught Coachman's attention during her youth. She told Louise Jarvis of *Women's Sports and Fitness*, "It all started when my great-great-grandmother took me along on her walks. I'd skip and run ahead as fast as I could." Coachman soon became interested in a specific event—the high jump.

Coachman saw a men's track and field meet, and was especially intrigued by the high jump. When neighborhood boys were jumping over ropes for fun, Coachman was dared to compete. She did, and won.

People soon noticed Coachman's athletic abilities. Her fifth grade teacher urged her on. Coachman began practicing jumping over ropes on her own and at school. She easily beat all of the girls, and sought out competition among the boys, whom she beat, too. Coachman also enjoyed running and fighting.

Though Coachman was the highest jumper in her elementary school, her parents, especially her father, did not support her athletic interests. They did not believe a young lady should run or jump. Yet Coachman later credited her father for her toughness.

Despite the lack of support by her parents, Coachman persisted in following her dream. By the time she reached Madison High School in the late 1930s, Coachman competed in track and field with the encouragement of her teachers. While still in her mid-teens, Coachman competed in the famous Tuskegee Relays, in Tuskegee, Alabama.

Though only about 16 years old, a shoeless Coachman broke the high school and collegiate high jump record at the meet. This appearance led to a recruitment effort by Tuskegee Institute's track and field coach Cleve Abbott. At the time, the Tuskegee Institute was a center of education for African Americans.

After convincing her reluctant parents, Coachman enrolled at Tuskegee in 1939 or 1940. The Institute, which was both a preparatory high school and a college, had a strong women's college track program. Coachman was a scholarship student, but a working one. She had to perform tasks such as cleaning up the gymnasium and pool and rolling the clay tennis courts as part of her scholarship.

At Tuskegee, Coachman did not limit her athletic activities to track and field. She also played other sports, including basketball. Coachman was an All-American guard. But Coachman trained hardest in track and field, especially the high jump.

By the time Coachman came of age to participate in high-profile competitions in 1939, interest in women's track and field was waning. There was a lack of international competition because of the growing war in Europe. Yet Coachman managed to keep America's interest in the sport as well as increase Tuskegee's reputation for excellence.

Coachman only participated in racially integrated events, often barefoot. But she won numerous events and regularly set records. If World War II had not limited competition at the height of her abilities, many believe that Coachman would have accomplished even more.

Still, in 1939, Coachman won her first national women's outdoor high jump championship. She would win this event every year through 1948—a record that held up through the 1990s.

Two years later, in 1941, Coachman won the Amateur Athletic Union (AAU) indoor high jump event, with a jump of five feet one inch. Coachman won this even three times in the early 1940s, despite the fact that the AAU did not have competitions between 1938-40, and again from 1942-44.

Coachman won a total of 25 AAU events over the course of her career, some in events other than the high jump. In 1942, she won the national women's outdoor 100-meter dash. She won the dash again in 1945 and 1946, and finished second three times as well.

In 1943, Coachman graduated from Tuskegee's high school and won the AAU's women's outdoor 50-meter dash. She would win this event every year through 1947 as she attended Tuskegee

Institute as a college student in the dressmaking trade program. By the mid-1940s, Coachman was nationally recognized for her prowess in track and field events.

Coachman continued to work and train hard. In 1945, she won the AAU high jump at four feet eight inches and was the indoor 50-meter champion. She repeated both championships in 1946. Coachman was also a member for two national champion 4 x 100 meter relay teams and won the national individual high-point title several times. Her total number of national titles was more than almost any other American woman.

In 1947, Coachman transferred from Tuskegee to Albany State College. While studying for her bachelor's degree, Coachman tried out for the 1948 Olympic track and field team. These were the first Olympic games to be held since the Berlin Olympics of 1936.

The team trials were held on the campus of Brown University. Coachman made the team when, in spite of back pain, she shattered an American record by an inch and a half with her five feet four inches jump. Her record held up until 1960.

Coachman had never been outside the United States before her trip to London for the 1948 games. The 7-day trip by ship was hard on Coachman. She, like many of her teammates, suffered from seasickness the whole time, and she also had an injured hip. When the American Olympic team arrived in England, Coachman was surprised to learn that her reputation had preceded her. The sport was more popular there and Coachman's accomplishments were well known.

The high jump event was held on the last day of the London games. During her event, Coachman was locked in a duel with Great Britain's Dorothy Tyler. Both competitors set new Olympic records, but because Coachman had fewer misses, she won the event with her record five feet six and one-eighth inches jump. Coachman was the only American woman to win a medal at the 1948 games, and the first African American woman to win a gold medal in the Olympics.

Coachman's victory made her the toast of London, and she was praised by many Americans who lived there. Of her medal, Coachman told Yanick Rice of *Essence,* "I didn't realize how important it was. I had won so many national and international medals that I really didn't feel anything, to tell the truth. The exciting thing was that the King of England awarded my medal."

When Coachman returned to the United States, she continued to be lauded. She had an audience with President Harry S. Truman. The city of Albany held an Alice Coachman Day and named a street after her, and a parade was held in her honor.

However, because of the racial climate of the time in the South, the audience was segregated and she was not allowed to speak. Coachman was given presents by anonymous whites, who feared what other whites would think of them for giving presents to her. Still, her success led to an endorsement deal with Coca-Cola, making her the first African American woman to endorse an international product.

Soon after the Olympics, in 1949, Coachman retired from track and field competition. Only 26 years old, she quit while still in her prime because she had accomplished all of her sports-related goals. By the time of her retirement, Coachman had 31 national high jump and other track titles.

Coachman earned her bachelor's degree in home economics with a science minor from Albany State College in 1949. She also married N. F. Davis, and eventually had two children, Richmond and Evelyn, both of whom competed athletically. Coachman continued to be involved with athletics herself, but not as a competitor.

Coachman became a physical education teacher at high schools in several cities in Georgia, as well as two colleges. She coached both basketball and track while teaching. She also worked with the Job Corps, as a recreation supervisor, and as an art teacher at a Boy's Club. After retirement, Coachman lived in Tuskegee, Alabama.

The sports world did not forget Coachman's accomplishments. She was elected to numerous athletic halls of fame, including the National Track and Field Hall of Fame, Black Athletes Hall of Fame, and International Women's Sports Hall of Fame. Coachman did not forget what her athletic experience did for her, either. In 1994, she founded the Alice Coachman Track and Field Foundation. This organization supported Olympic athletes, both aspiring and retired, dealing with life problems.

When the 1996 Olympics were held in Coachman's native Georgia, she was one of those honored by the Olympic Women exhibit. It is, perhaps, because she lived by her own words of advice to young athletes that Coachman succeeded in her own Olympic games. She told Rice, "Don't let your dreams go away. Fight hard and have the guts to complete them."

Sources

➤ Books

Afro-American Encyclopedia, volume 3, Educational Book Publishers, 1974, p. 628.

Davis, Michael D., *Black American Women in Olympic Track and Field,* McFarland & Company, 1992, pp. 39-46.

Hanley, Reid M., *Who's Who in Track and Field,* Arlington House, 1973, p. 33.

Hickok, Ralph, *The Encyclopedia of North American Sports History,* Facts on File, Inc., 1992, p. 109.

Hine, Darlene Clark, editor, *Black Women in America: An Historical Encyclopedia,* volume 1, Carlson Publishing, 1993, pp. 255-56.

Hine, Darlene Clark, editor, *Facts on File Encyclopedia of Black Women in America: Dance, Sports and Visual Arts,* Facts on File, Inc., 1997, pp. 78-79.

Johnson, Anne Janette, *Great Women in Sports,* Visible Ink, 1996, pp. 87-90.

Oglesby, Carole A., editor, *Encyclopedia of Women and Sport in America,* Oryx Press, 1998, pp. 54-55.

Page, James A., *Black Olympian Medalists,* Libraries Unlimited, Inc., 1991, pp. 23-24.

Phelps, Shirelle, editor, *Contemporary Black Biography: Profiles from the International Black Community,* volume 18, Gale Group, 1998, pp. 28-31.

Sherrow, Victoria, *Encyclopedia of Women and Sports,* ABC-CLIO, 1996, pp. 60-62.

Smith, Jessie Carney, editor, *Notable Black American Women,* Gale Research, 1992, pp. 193-95.

The Women's Sports Encyclopedia, Henry Holt and Company, 1997, p. 99.

➤ Periodicals

Ebony, November 1991, p. 44.

Essence, January 1, 1996, p. 89.

Minneapolis Star Tribune, July 29, 1996, p. S4 (opening quote).

Newsday, August 14, 1994, p. 17.

Women's Sports and Fitness, June 1998, p. 80.

Jacqueline Cochran

"In every well-blended recipe for success will be
found, in addition to honesty and as main
ingredients, determination and tenacity and a sub-
stantial portion of skill and experience which come
with the trying."

Born May 11, 1910, in Pensacola, Florida (some sources say
Muscogee, Florida), Jacqueline Cochran was a pioneer in wom-
en's aviation. She died August 9, 1980, in Indio, California.

As an aviator, Jacqueline Cochran successfully challenged preconceived notions of what women could do in flight. She set numerous speed records and was the first woman to compete in several significant air races in the mid-1930s. Cochran was the first woman to fly faster than the speed of sound. She was also instrumental in getting the military to use women pilots during World War II. In addition to all of her aviation accomplishments, Cochran ran a successful cosmetics business.

Because Cochran's parents died when she was an infant and there are no records of her birth, the exact date she was born on is unknown. Cochran picked the day of May 11 at random and chose her last name from a telephone book. She could have been born as early as 1905 or as late as 1912. Her place of birth was either Pensacola or Muscogee, Florida.

Cochran was raised in poverty by foster parents. By the age of eight, she was already working in lumber mills in northern Florida. Her formal education was limited to a few years in school.

By the time Cochran was 15 years old, she had moved to Columbus, Georgia, where she worked in cotton mills. Wanting to move beyond the hand-to-mouth existence of her foster family, Cochran became an apprentice to a local hairdresser. Soon, she was working at a beauty shop to support herself.

One of Cochran's clients encouraged her to studying nursing. From 1925-28, Cochran completed the training in a Montgomery, Alabama-area hospital. Within a few years, Cochran moved first back to Pensacola, then on to beauty shops in Philadelphia and New York City.

While working at a Saks Fifth Avenue beauty shop, Antoine's, in 1932, Cochran met a multimillionaire businessman, Floyd Bostwick Odlum, who later became her husband. The banker and industrialist encouraged Cochran to learn to fly. She wanted to have her own business as a traveling cosmetics saleswoman.

Odlum bet Cochran that she could not get her certification during her six weeks off from Antoine's against the cost of the lessons. A natural at flying, Cochran won. Learning at Roosevelt Field, Long Island, she flew solo in two days and got her license within three weeks. By 1933, she had earned her commercial pilot's license and instructor's rating.

As planned, Cochran started her cosmetics company, the Jacqueline Cochran Cosmetics Company, in 1934 or 1935. She came up with much of her product line herself. Cochran used the profits from her company to finance her flying for many years.

Cochran began entering flying contests around 1934. She also appeared in some flying circuses. Cochran was tough from the beginning. One of her first planes had a problematic engine, forcing her to make numerous unscheduled landings. Yet she never parachuted from her plane. Once Cochran went up more than 30,000 meters in a plane with a non-pressurized cockpit. When she tried to inhale oxygen through a tube, it burst. Cochran came out of the flight unharmed.

Such experiences made Cochran resilient, a strength she would need as she began to enter air races. In 1934, she became the first woman to compete in the McRobertson London-to-Melbourne air race. She only made it to Bucharest, Romania, however, because of engine trouble.

The following year, Cochran became the first woman to compete in the annual Bendix Trophy transcontinental race. The Labor Day race, one of the most prestigious of its time, traversed the United States from Burbank, California, to Cleveland, Ohio. To even enter the race, Cochran had to convince many people that she could handle it, including all the other contestants.

However, Cochran almost had to drop out before the race began because she had problems with the power plant in her plane. Because no one would let her admit she had equipment problems, Cochran decided to fly anyway. Mechanical problems forced her to land in Arizona, and she might have had even more serious problems had she continued. Though Cochran did not win the Bendix Trophy, because of her efforts, women were allowed to compete from that point forward.

After Cochran married Odlum on May 11, 1936, and moved to Southern California, she continued to enter air races, but also began trying to set speed records. Though Cochran set many women-specific records, she was more concerned with setting general records. She was immediately successful and developed an international reputation.

In 1937, Cochran again entered the Bendix, winning the women's race and placing third overall. She also broke the international 1000 kilometers record, the women's national speed record, and the women's world speed record. For her efforts, she won her first Harmon Trophy from the International League of Aviators, as the outstanding woman pilot of the year. Cochran would go on to win this trophy every year through 1950 as well as 1953.

Cochran continued this trend in 1938 and 1939. She had her best showing at the 1938 Bendix Race, winning the race in a Seversky fighter though she had a gas intake malfunction. Cochran would continue to enter the race until the 1940s. In 1938, Cochran set two speed records, setting a record for women by crossing North America with a time of 10 hours, 12 minutes and 55 seconds. In addition to the Harmon Trophy, Cochran was also awarded the Mitchell Award for making the best contribution to aviation. She followed this up in 1939 by winning the Miami to New York air race, setting a new altitude record, and becoming the first woman to complete a "blind" landing.

After Cochran became president of the 99s, a female aviation group founded by Amelia Earhart, in 1940, she used her position to influence public policy in light of the growing threat of World War II. Before the United States entered the war, in June 1941, Cochran became the first woman to fly a warplane across the Atlantic Ocean. Her flying the Hudson V bomber from Canada to Great Britain was a stunt, however. Cochran wanted to show that women could fly war planes, while Great Britain needed to demonstrate how desperate it was for support. Cochran was not allowed to control the plane during take-off or landing however; a male co-pilot handled the controls during these maneuvers.

Cochran managed to prove something with this display. She and 25 other American women pilots soon went to Great Britain to serve in the British Air Transport Auxiliary (ATA). Captain Cochran and her counterparts flew military planes from the places they were manufactured in (usually North America) to their sites of deployment throughout Europe. Cochran spent 18 months serving in the ATA before returning home.

The United States had founded their own version of this program, called the Women's Auxiliary Ferrying Squadron (WAFS). Cochran was not selected to head it. Instead she was put in charge of a group that recruited and trained female pilots called the Women's Flying Training Detachment (WFTD). When WAFS and WFTD merged into one organization, Women Auxiliary Service Pilots (WASPS), Cochran was its director until the end of the war.

As in the ATA, these women delivered planes and also did much of the flying for the military within the United States. This freed more male pilots for combat duty. While in charge of these units,

Cochran wanted women to be treated equally to their male counterparts in the military, but this did not happen initially. Still, by the time the WASPS disbanded in 1944, more than 1,000 women flew for their country and 12,000 planes had been delivered.

After the war, Cochran wanted to work as a test pilot, but was only able to do so by working for one of her husband's companies, one which supplied the military with jets. She also continued to influence the military in other ways. Cochran was instrumental in making the Air Force a branch unto itself in the United States military. She joined the Air Force Reserves herself in 1948, and was a consultant for the Air Force, Federal Aviation Administration (FAA) and other aviation groups. Cochran managed to continue setting aviation records as well. For her efforts, she was named Pilot of the Decade.

Cochran's record breaking took a new turn when she became the first woman to break the sound barrier in May 1953. She was flying an F-86 Sabre Fighter with the first man to fly faster than sound—Chuck Yeager. While Cochran continued to break subsonic flying records, she also broke many supersonic records after this point as well.

Cochran's attentions also turned to space. In 1960, Cochran's friend, Dr. Randolph Lovelace, was running a private program to train women for National Aeronautic and Space Administration's (NASA) space program. Women pilots, including Cochran, were given the same test as men. Cochran also gave money from her cosmetics company so that 12 more women could take part. However, Cochran nor her colleagues made it to space. NASA did not even begin recruiting women until the late 1970s.

Not all of Cochran's attention was on aviation at this point. In 1956, she ran for a Congressional seat from California, but lost. She also still ran her cosmetics business until 1963, when it was sold.

Cochran set her last, and arguably most important, record on May 11, 1964. She set a new speed record for women, when she flew at 1,429 miles per hour—twice the speed of sound—in a Lockheed F-104 Starfighter. No woman flew faster at the time.

After retiring from the Air Force Reserves as a colonel in 1970, Cochran was inducted into the American Aviation Hall of Fame in 1971. She was the only living woman so honored. Around the same time, Cochran suffered a heart attack and had to have a pacemaker installed. This essentially ended her flying career.

Upon Cochran's death on August 9, 1980, in Indio, California, she had held more than 250 different aviation records. This was more than any man or woman. Yet as Robert A. Searles wrote in *Business & Commercial Aviation,* "Despite all the new ground she broke for women, she seemed more interested in breaking aviation records—taking chances and beating the odds."

Sources

➤ Books

Adamson, Lynda G., *Notable Women in American History,* Greenwood Press, 1999, p. 66.

Cochran, Jacqueline, *The Stars at Noon,* Little, Brown and Company, 1954 (opening quote).

Douglas, Deborah G., *United States Women in Aviation, 1940-1985,* Smithsonian Institution Press, 1990.

Garraty, John A. and Mark C. Carnes, eds., *American National Biography,* volume 5, Oxford University Press, 1999, pp. 117-18.

Hickcok, Ralph, *The Encyclopedia of North American Sports History,* Facts on File, 1992, p. 110.

Magill, Frank N., ed., *Great Lives from History: American Women Series,* volume 2, Salem Press, 1995, pp. 412-16.

McHenry, ed., *Her Heritage: A Biographical Encyclopedia of Famous American Women,* 1995.

Parry, Melanie, ed., *Larouse Dictionary of Women,* Larouse, 1996, p. 153.

Uglow, Jennifer, ed., *The Macmillan Dictionary of Women's Biography,* Macmillan, 1998, p. 132.

Welch, Rosanne, *Encyclopedia of Women in Aviation and Space,* ABC-CLIO, 1998, pp. 43-45.

Zophy, Angela Howard, ed., *Handbook of American Women's History,* Garland, 1990, p. 117-18.

➤ Periodicals

Business & Commercial Aviation, May 1988, p. 94.
Saturday Evening Post, May-June 1995, p. 58.
Smithsonian, August 1994, p. 72.

William Sloane Coffin, Jr.

"I *believe that God calls each of us to be a co-creator, to help make the crooked straight and the rough places plain, to exalt the valleys and not to be deterred by high mountains."*

Born June 1, 1924, in New York City, New York, William Sloane Coffin, Jr. is a Presbyterian clergyman and social activist who first garnered widespread attention during the civil rights and antiwar movements of the 1960s. Address: c/o Peace Action, 1819 H St., NW, #420, Washington, D.C. 20006.

Throughout his long and often stormy career, William Sloane Coffin, Jr. has espoused "a Christian philosophy that [makes] words and deeds inseparable," according to a *New York Times* reporter. In short, he has put his faith into action, prodding an entire nation to acknowledge and sometimes remedy what he believes are its moral failings regarding issues such as war, racism, and poverty. His brand of radical Christianity has angered some people who feel he should stick to the pulpit and stay out of politics; more than a few have criticized him as anti-American because he has dared to criticize the status quo and make overtures to so-called "enemies." But Coffin has persevered, secure in his conviction that "the best patriots are those who carry on not a grudge fight but a lover's quarrel with their country," as he once wrote in a *Nation* essay. It is a sentiment that has inspired a lifetime of social activism.

A native of New York City, William Sloane Coffin, Jr. was born June 1, 1924, to William Sloane Coffin, Sr. and Catherine Butterfield Coffin. By virtue of the elder Coffin's position as vice-president of a family-owned furniture store, young William, his older brother, and his younger sister grew up in an atmosphere of wealth and privilege. But the stock market crash of 1929 and subsequent economic downturn forced them to scale back their standard of living. The sudden death of William Sr. in 1933 dealt the family another blow and prompted Catherine Coffin to leave New York City with her children and start a new life in Carmel, California.

William Jr. attended public school in Carmel until he returned east in 1937 to spend the ninth grade at Deerfield Academy in Deerfield, Massachusetts. The following year he and his family went to Paris, where he studied with Nadia Boulanger in the hope of becoming a concert pianist. But the start of World War II in September of 1939 interrupted his plans, and the family soon headed back to the United States.

Coffin finished his high school education at Phillips Academy in Andover, Massachusetts. Following his graduation in 1942, he attended Yale University Music School for a year before joining the U.S. Army. He ended up in military intelligence with the rank of captain, serving as a liaison officer first with the French army and then with the Soviet army.

Coffin remained in the service until 1947, assisting with postwar duties that included helping repatriate 2,000 anti-Stalinist Russian soldiers who had been captured wearing German uniforms. At first, Coffin had little sympathy for the men, all of whom had chosen to fight for Adolf Hitler. But as he heard their horrific stories about the brutality of life under Stalin, he came to understand why they had deserted their own army and apparently betrayed their native land. The realization that they faced death or imprisonment upon their return to the Soviet Union sickened him, but he could not quite bring himself to defy his orders and sabotage the plan to send them back.

Guilt and shame over their fate and the part he played in it have plagued Coffin ever since, influencing not only his decision in 1950 to join the Central Intelligence Agency (CIA) so that he could oppose Stalin's regime but also his commitment to civil disobedience during the antiwar protests of the 1960s. As he explained in his memoir, *Once to Every Man,* "The forced repatriation of those two thousand Russians showed me that in matters of life and death the responsibility of those who take orders is as great as those who give them."

After his discharge from the Army, Coffin resumed his studies at Yale, this time as a political science major. (While he hoped to join the foreign service, he was also being actively recruited by the CIA.) But he soon found himself increasingly drawn to disciplines such as philosophy and theology that examined the human condition— especially the notion of good and evil—in more than just a political context. Although he recalled being "put off" by organized religion and "unimpressed" by the Christian students he knew, he had a change of heart after attending a conference at Union Theological Seminary at which Reinhold Niebuhr and several other theologians eloquently spoke of the vital role churches could play in remedying social injustice and other woes. Coffin left the conference committed to the idea of entering the ministry.

Upon his graduation from Yale in 1949, Coffin entered Union Theological Seminary. He remained there for a year until the outbreak of the Korean War in mid-1950 reignited his interest in fighting against communism. So he joined the CIA, spending three years in Germany contacting anti-Soviet Russian refugees and training them how to undermine the Soviet Union from the inside.

Returning to the United States at the end of his stint with the CIA, Coffin enrolled at Yale University Divinity School and earned his bachelor's degree in 1956, the same year he was ordained a Presbyterian minister. He then served for a year as chaplain at Phillips Andover Academy, followed by a year in the same position at Williams College. At Williams, he caused a stir on campus by actively opposing fraternities that discriminated against blacks and Jews.

In 1958, Coffin became chaplain at Yale University, where he remained for the next 18 years. His tenure coincided with a period of massive social upheaval in the United States, and his name became associated with some of the more famous activities and events of that era. During the early 1960s, for example, he became involved in the civil rights movement, which had begun challenging racial discrimination across the South on a number of different fronts. Coffin was one of the so-called "Freedom Riders," the name given to black and white activists who rode interstate buses to test enforcement of desegregation laws. Along with six other demonstrators, he was arrested in May of 1961 in Montgomery, Alabama, for disturbing the peace following one such bus ride. He was subsequently arrested on a number of other occasions for protesting against segregated facilities.

As the war in Vietnam escalated during the mid-1960s, Coffin teamed up with John Bennett, the president of Union Theological Seminary, and Abraham Heschel, professor of social ethics at Jewish Theological Seminary, to form Clergy and Laity Concerned about Vietnam (CALCAV), a nationwide organization of religious leaders from many faiths who were opposed to U.S. policy in Vietnam. (After the war ended, it became known simply as Clergy and Laity Concerned.) When their words failed to persuade government officials to negotiate an end to the conflict, they turned to civil disobedience, or rather, "a kind of radical obedience to conscience, to God, and . . . to the best traditions of [our] country," as Coffin declared in his memoir.

Coffin urged seminarians and young clergymen opposed to the war to give up their deferments and officially register as conscientious objectors and encouraged older members of the clergy to support the actions of their younger colleagues. He also called upon students against the war to organize and do likewise. In mid-1967 CALCAV issued a statement to its members pledging to assist draft resisters by offering them sanctuary in churches and synagogues. This action was followed in October by an antiwar protest in Boston at which nearly a thousand young men turned in their draft cards at a solemn church ceremony. About a week later Coffin and a handful of other prominent activists, including Dr. Benjamin Spock, took the cards gathered in Boston as well as hundreds more collected from other cities across the country and presented them to officials at the Department of Justice in Washington. Coffin, Spock, and three other protest leaders were subsequently arrested for advising young men how to avoid the draft and convicted in 1968. The charges were dropped after their convictions were overturned in 1970.

Coffin became a fixture at antiwar rallies, demonstrations, and teach-ins and even went to North Vietnam in 1972 to accompany three released American prisoners of war on their journey back to the United States. His activism disturbed some members of the administration at Yale and was especially infuriating to older alumni. His patriotism was frequently called into question, and on more than one occasion those who found his views unacceptable or embarrassing demanded that he be removed from his job. But Coffin remained at Yale until 1976, when he felt it was time to move on and tackle new challenges. As he recounted in his memoir, "I was struck by the fact that all major world problems seemed increasingly to be both international and interrelated. . . . Clearly the only viable future was a global one. Clearly the survival unit in our time was no longer an individual nation or an individual anything; it was the entire human race, plus its environment."

With that global view in mind, Coffin devoted himself during the remainder of the 1970s and throughout the 1980s and 1990s to a variety of human rights issues, including world hunger, poverty, overpopulation, and the arms race. From 1977 until 1987, he did so from the pulpit of New York City's Riverside Church, a multiracial and multiethnic congregation known for its commitment to social justice. At Riverside, Coffin continued his tradition of liberal activism by working on international arms control issues, pushing for more cooperation and unity among different religious faiths, aiding war refugees, and addressing urban problems such as juvenile crime, homelessness, poverty, and unemployment. He also made a point of welcoming members of the gay community into the church and condemned homophobia as the "last 'respectable' prejudice" within the religious community.

In December of 1979, Coffin once again made headlines for a controversial trip abroad. The destination this time was Iran, where militant Muslim students were holding a group of hostages at the American Embassy in Teheran following the revolution that toppled Shah Mohammad Reza and replaced him with a fundamentalist Islamic regime. Coffin and three other Christian clergymen went to Iran at the invitation of the country's ruling Revolutionary Council to hold Christmas services for the hostages and to see for themselves how they were being treated. Their visit and subsequent calls for a calm, faith-based approach to solving the crisis enraged those Americans who favored taking a stronger stand.

Coffin was not without his detractors at Riverside Church, some of whom complained that he was more political activist than theologian or minister. They were also critical of his administrative shortcomings. For the most part, however, Coffin was credited with boosting Riverside's membership and cementing its reputation for diversity and social action while making it a lively and energetic place to worship.

In mid-1987, remarking that at his age (he was then 63) "you've got, maybe, one biggie left," Coffin resigned from his post at Riverside Church to devote himself to the cause of world peace and nuclear disarmament. For the next several years, he served as president of SANE/FREEZE, a new Washington, D.C.-based organization formed by the merger of two existing groups, the Committee for a SANE Nuclear Policy and the Nuclear Weapons Freeze Campaign. (In 1993, SANE/FREEZE adopted the name Peace Action.) Coffin's tenure coincided with the breakup of the Soviet Union and the emergence of fledgling democracies in Russia and Eastern Europe. He therefore urged the United States, its allies, and the former eastern bloc nations to capitalize on these momentous events by dismantling the North Atlantic Treaty Organization (NATO) and the Warsaw Pact and halting the arms race.

Coffin retired as president emeritus of SANE/FREEZE in the early 1990s. Since then, he has taught and lectured across the United States and overseas, sharing his insights with a wide variety of audiences. His message reflects a relatively new strain of political thinking that acknowledges the existence of fundamental connections linking peace, social justice, and the environment. Cautioning that we are all living in "the shadow of Doomsday," Coffin urges his listeners to turn away from isolationism and become more globally aware or be prepared to face disastrous consequences. As he declared in a *Nation* essay, "No one is safe until all are safe."

Sources

➤ On-line

"Forty Years of Peace Action History" (chronology), *Peace Action*, http://www.webcom.com/peaceact/history.html (February 4, 2000).
"Peace Action: Forty Years of History" (narrative), *Peace Action*, http://www.webcom.com/peaceact/40th-history.html (February 4, 2000).

➤ **Books**

Coffin, William Sloane, *The Heart Is a Little to the Left: Essays on Public Morality*, Dartmouth College/University Press of New England, 1999.

Coffin, William Sloane, Jr., *Once to Every Man: A Memoir*, Atheneum, 1977.

➤ **Periodicals**

Grand Rapids Press, January 25, 1992, p. B1; January 25, 1997.

Nation, July 15, 1991.

New York Times, July 20, 1987, p. B3 (opening quote); December 21, 1987, p. B3.

Time, June 5, 1989.

Nat "King" Cole

*"*There won't be shows starring Negroes for a while. I think the time is not too far distant when things will be worked out, however."*

Born on March 17, 1919 (sources vary), Nat "King" Cole was a versatile jazz pianist and popular singer who became the first black to host his own television program. In addition to being revered for his unique and influential sound, marked by a low, husky quality, he is widely remembered for helping to break the race barrier in music. He died of lung cancer in Santa Monica, California, on February 15, 1965.

One of America's most beloved performers, Nat "King" Cole was the first African American to host his own radio and television programs, thus helping to remove obstacles for black entertainers. Even music in the 1950s was segregated, with works by and for blacks dubbed "race records," but Cole appealed to many whites as well. Though he is mainly remembered for his husky, breathy singing voice, he started out as a jazz pianist, but gained acclaim as a vocalist with his 1946 rendition of "The Christmas Song." His early trio has been recognized as a major force in leading music from the big-band, swing era into modern jazz. Cole's trademark tune was "Unforgettable." A 1965 *New York Times* obituary observed that his vocal quality had been described variously as "a syrupy slur" and "a soft evening breeze."

By many accounts, Nathaniel Adams Coles was born on St. Patrick's Day, March 17, 1919, in Montgomery, Alabama. However, as Leslie Gourse noted in the biography *Unforgettable: The Life and Mystique of Nat King Cole*, his birth year has also been placed at 1912, 1915, 1916 (the date on his official Selective Service form), and 1917 (the date on his first marriage certificate), but she reported that his sister, Evelyn Coles, "says definitely he was born in 1919." Gourse warned that many other dates in the musician's life have been questioned as well.

Cole was the son of Edward James Coles, Jr. and Perlina (Adams) Coles, and had five siblings: his older brother, Edward ("Eddie"); younger brothers Isaac ("Ike") and Lionel (also called Freddy); and sisters Eddie Mae and Evelyn. His mother had 13 children in all, but most died very young. Cole's father, a reverend at Beulah Baptist Church in Montgomery, moved the family (which did not yet include Isaac and Lionel) to Chicago in 1921. He had taken a job at the Second Progressive Baptist Church on the city's South Side, later called the True Light Baptist Church after its relocation to Forty-fifth Street and Dearborn.

At her husband's church, Perlina Coles served as choir director, and thus exposed her children to music early on. In fact, all four sons would grow up to play music, a fate that baffled their father, who came from a long line of preachers and deacons and could not fathom why none of them wanted to pursue religion. Cole's sister Evelyn would also perform, but not professionally; sister Eddie Mae died of pneumonia about six years after their move to Chicago. Cole taught himself to play piano by ear as a child, pumping out "Yes, We Have No Bananas" by about age four or five. At about age 12, Cole began taking formal piano lessons in order to learn how to read music, and became the organist at his father's church, as well as a member of the choir, a task he never relished.

By the time he was at Wendell Phillips High School, Cole had been inspired by the rich jazz and blues clubs in his neighborhood, much to the dismay of his father, who frowned upon secular music. "Pop was always preaching at us," Cole remarked to Richard G. Hubler in the *Saturday Evening Post*. "It was mother who finally convinced him that playing music for a living was an honest day's work." Cole especially admired Earl "Fatha" Hines, who played four blocks away at the old Grand Terrace. Cole and some friends formed a big band called the Rogues of Rhythm, and a quintet called Nate Coles and His Royal Dukes.

An avid sports fan and athlete, Cole also played football and baseball in high school and was talented enough to get letters of interest from a couple of minor-league teams. However, by this time, his brother Eddie, who had played bass with bandleader Noble Sissle and pianist Eubie Blake, had started a combo of his own, the Solid Swingers, and asked Cole to join him. His increasing musical responsibilities at night affected his studies, so Cole left school without a diploma, and began making records in 1936 with his brother.

The next year, the brothers joined a revival of *Shuffle Along* in Chicago, but when the show began touring, Eddie Coles turned down the offer to join it. Cole's girlfriend, Nadine Robinson, a chorus line dancer in the show, wanted to go on the road, though. During the tour, Cole, still a teenager by most reports, married Robinson, who was in her late twenties. Two months after beginning the tour, the show folded in Long Beach, California, but the couple decided to stay. Enjoying the warm weather and not wanting his father to see him at a low point, Cole stuck it out on the West Coast, telling Hubler, "It was a tough workout. I must have played every beer joint from San Diego to Bakersfield." His biggest paycheck during this time was five dollars a night.

Though Cole tried to form a new group, his efforts fell flat, and he ended up playing piano at the Los Angeles Century Club, where, as one story goes, a patron in jest placed a gold paper crown on his head and dubbed him "the King," thus providing his stage name. In the meantime, Robinson worked as a chorus girl and hostess in some of the clubs around Los Angeles. Eventually, Cole gained a following among other musicians who came to see him at the Century Club, and the owner of a club called the Sewanee Inn invited him to get a group together to play for a few weeks. One anecdote claimed that the manager here actually gave him the gold crown and nickname.

Though reports vary on how and when the band got together, it is certain that Cole assembled guitarist Oscar Moore and bassist Wesley Prince. Supposedly, drummer Lee Young was set to join as well, but was cut when he failed to show up on the first night. In any case, the trio, who began playing together in either 1937 or 1938, was originally billed as King Cole and His Swingsters, later changed to the King Cole Trio. They only earned $75 a week—$25 each—for their work there, so Cole played other gigs around Los Angeles at the time as well. Their intimate sound was unique in an era marked by big bands and blaring horn sections, but by 1940, they had gained enough of an audience to allow them to cut some records, both on their own and with vibraphonist Lionel Hampton. In 1941 they toured nationally and spent several months at some of New York City's best jazz nightspots.

Although Cole's group was mainly instrumental, he occasionally threw in a vocal for variation even though he did not care for his own voice, an opinion that he held even after becoming one of the most popular singers in the world. In 1943, the King Cole Trio had its first big hit with "Straighten Up and Fly Right," a song Cole based on one of his father's ever-present lectures. Their success continued with tunes like "Get Your Kicks on Route 66," "Sweet Lorraine," "It's Only a Paper Moon," "Frim Fram Sauce," and "For Sentimental Reasons." The trio also appeared in several Hollywood films, including *The Stork Club* (1945), *See My Lawyer* (1945), and *Breakfast in Hollywood* (1946).

However, Cole leaned away from jazz toward popular music with his version of Mel Torme's "The Christmas Song" (with its opening line, "Chestnuts roasting on an open fire . . . "), which was a huge hit in the winter of 1946-47. This recording, which was the trio's first to add a string section, was also the first to feature Cole as a singer, rather than a singing pianist leading a trio. Meanwhile, his marriage was in decline due to his attraction to a young singer. He and Robinson separated in 1946 and he married Maria Ellington on March 28, 1948, after his divorce. The couple had three daughters and adopted another son and daughter.

Around the time of his second marriage, Cole began to realize that his solo recordings were much more popular than those with his jazz trio, and the 1948 number-one hit "Nature Boy," which sold a million copies by the fall of that year and made him a household name, reinforced that. Ellington began to help him make the transformation into a major star. He went on to record "Mona Lisa" in 1950, and "Unforgettable," his trademark tune, in 1951. The King Cole Trio disbanded in 1955. Despite his fame and wealth, Cole and his new wife faced racial discrimination when they went to buy a home in 1948 in an upscale area of Los Angeles called Hancock Park. Neighbors banded together to keep them out, but the law was on their side. Several incidents of vandalism occurred there, but the furor eventually died down. The home was later seized by the Internal Revenue Service (IRS) when it was found that Cole owed back taxes, but he repaid his debt.

In the meantime, Cole was touring incessantly and also worked his way into radio and television, in addition to showing up in several films. In the summer of 1946, the King Cole Trio had substituted for Bing Crosby on *The Kraft Music Hall* radio program, and later that year they played on *The Wildroot Cream Oil Show.* Then, in 1956, Cole became the first African American to host his own television show. Although the program boasted good ratings, the network, NBC, could not find a sponsor and canceled it after a year. Discrimination due to race was seen as the main reason why no advertisers would sign on. The theory was that they all felt that marketing to blacks was a waste of money, and that it would alienate white customers. Cole was visibly upset, once noting, as Gourse reported, "Negroes, after all, constitute a very large buying market, and as an entertainer I know I'm salable to all kinds of people, not just one race." He concluded, "There won't be shows starring Negroes for a while. I think the time is not too far distant when things will be worked out, however."

In addition, when Cole appeared at a concert in Birmingham, Alabama, in 1956, a group of white men attacked him on stage. They were later prosecuted, and the incident drew more attention to the civil rights struggle. Though some criticized Cole for playing to segregated audiences, he responded by claiming that he would gladly join a boycott if all other black musicians agreed to it. The protest never materialized. According to Gourse, "[Cole] felt he could serve the cause of civil rights best by performing for white audiences." Though he continued to play in the South, he never returned to Birmingham; in another battle over race, he won some cases in which he sued some hotels for refusing to rent him a room due to his race.

Throughout his life, Cole was a heavy smoker. In 1964 he was diagnosed with advanced lung cancer and had his left lung removed in January of 1965. Treatments failed, and he died at age 45 on February 15, 1965, leaving his wife, Maria; adopted son Kelly; adopted daughter Carol; another daughter, Natalie; and twin daughters Timolin and Casey. Cole's daughter Natalie went on to a successful singing career of her own, claiming a number-one hit in 1991 with an unusual "duet" of "Unforgettable" with her father, a feat made possible by modern technology. The song was on the album *Unforgettable With Love,* which featured remakes of 22 Cole numbers in all; it sold eight million copies and garnered seven Grammy awards. Cole also won a Grammy in 1959 for "Midnight Flyer"; posthumously, he earned a Grammy lifetime achievement award in 1990, and was inducted into the *Down Beat* Hall of Fame in 1997.

Sources

➤ **Books**

Cole, Maria, with Louie Robinson, *Nat King Cole: An Intimate Biography,* William Morrow, 1971.
Contemporary Black Biography, volume 17, Gale Research, 1998.
Contemporary Musicians, volume 3, Gale Research, 1990.
Encyclopedia of World Biography, second edition, Gale Research, 1998.
Gourse, Leslie, *Unforgettable: The Life and Mystique of Nat King Cole,* St. Martins Press, 1991 (opening quote).
Notable Black American Men, Gale Research, 1998.

➤ **Periodicals**

Down Beat, December 1997, p. 30.
Entertainment Weekly, February 17, 1995, p. 72.
Life, February 26, 1965, p. 36.
Newsweek, July 15, 1957, p. 90; March 1, 1965, p. 81.
New York Times, February 16, 1965, p. 1; February 19, 1965, p. 35.
Saturday Evening Post, July 17, 1954, p. 30.
Time, July 15, 1957, p. 66.

Michael DeBakey

"I believe that in a society as rich as ours, each person has a basic, inherent right to good health."

Born September 7, 1908 in Lake Charles, Louisiana, Michael DeBakey has been a leader in cardiovascular medicine and a groundbreaking medical researcher since the 1930s. Address: Baylor College of Medicine, One Baylor Plaza, Houston, TX 77030.

As both an outstanding surgeon and a risk-taking research pioneer, Michael DeBakey ranks among the most respected living medical practitioners. Associated with Baylor College of Medicine in Houston, Texas for over a half-century, he has gained particular renown for achieving breakthroughs in artificial heart technology and bypass surgery. Known for maintaining a grueling professional schedule, his patients have included such world figures as the Duke of Windsor, Aristotle Onassis and Boris Yeltsin. Outside of the operating theater, DeBakey has been a champion of medical reform and a voice in favor of increased support for medical research.

DeBakey's years of prominence in medicine have brought both praise and controversy. His Baylor colleagues nicknamed him the "Texas Tornado" for his unstinting energy and dedication. "It would take other people five or six lifetimes to do what he's done," his partner Dr. George P. Noon told the *Lancet*. "He's very motivated, determined, focused, and tough." Over the years, DeBakey has earned a reputation as an exacting, sometimes temperamental co-worker. "I'm accused of being a perfectionist," he told *McCall's* writer Lyn Tornabene. "Well, I am. . . . If perfection is not needed when you are dealing with life and death, when is it?"

A native of Lake Charles, Louisiana, Michael Ellis DeBakey was one of six children born to Lebanese parents who left their homeland to escape religious persecution. His father, Shaker Morris DeBakey, taught him the disciplined work habits that served him well in later life. Among other properties, the elder DeBakey owned a drugstore, and it was there that Michael met local physicians and increased his desire to pursue medicine. His mother, Raheeja Zorba DeBakey, taught him expert sewing skills, which would aid him considerably as a surgeon.

DeBakey earned his medical degree at Tulane University, where he came under the mentorship of Dr. Alton Ochsner. While still a Tulane student in the early 1930s, he became an expert in blood transfusions and helped to develop a roller-pump that later became crucial in developing heart-lung machines. Together with Dr. Ochsner, he also became one of the first medical researchers to link lung cancer with cigarette smoking.

After completing his surgical training at the University of Strasbourg in France and the University of Heidelberg in Germany, DeBakey returned to the United States and joined the Tulane faculty in 1940. During World War II, he served in the U.S. Army, where he helped to set up mobile military army surgical hospitals (MASH units). His involvement with the military medical initiative continued after the war, when he played a leading role in creating the U.S. Veterans Administration Medical Center system. He was also instrumental in establishing the U.S. National Library of Medicine in 1949.

In 1948, he began teaching at the Baylor College of Medicine, advancing from chairman of the surgery department to president of the institution in 1969, then becoming chancellor ten years later. Even as he rose in the administrative ranks, DeBakey never put aside practicing surgery or conducting research. In 1953, he made medical history by using grafts of Dacron tubing in repairing aneurysms in the cardiovascular system. Later in the decade, he began pioneering work in arterial bypass procedures, which led to one of the first successful heart bypass operations in 1964.

DeBakey's early work with the roller-pump encouraged him to continue researching devices that could replace part or all of the human heart. In 1966, he developing a device to assist the left ventricle of a failing heart for a limited period. He continued to pursue his goal of creating a totally artificial heart during the following decades. In 1999, he prepared to begin clinical trials on a miniaturized heart pump, developed by DeBakey with assistance from NASA computer modeling technology.

As a surgeon, DeBakey's notoriety became world-wide by the 1960s. Celebrity patients increased his fame further, as did a 1965 international television broadcast of DeBakey performing open-heart surgery. Despite his access to wealth and power, he has directed fees for his services to a foundation that has contributed millions of dollars to Baylor's medical research program.

DeBakey remained at the forefront of medicine well past the age when most physicians retire. In 1987, he was honored by President Reagan with a prestigious National Medal of Science for "his pioneering medical innovations throughout his medical career." In 1996, at age 88, he flew to Moscow to serve as a consultant for Russian President Boris Yeltsin's quintuple bypass operation. He has continued to perform surgery into his 90s, as well as serve as Baylor's Chancellor Emeritus and director of the DeBakey Heart Center.

DeBakey's seemingly nonstop work schedule has amazed observers since his younger days. "He is a hard man to keep up with," wrote Tornabene in her 1969 *McCall's* profile. "From the time he appears on that third-floor hall [of Baylor's research center], it is twelve to sixteen hours before he will sit down again or eat. His pace has caused some of his staff to wonder whether he really is human." Just as his drive has not decreased, neither has his impatience with the failings of some of his colleagues."Maybe I should be more compassionate with people who do not think as fast as I can," he told Lawrence K. Altman of the *New York Times,* adding that "I have little tolerance for incompetence, sloppy thinking and laziness."

DeBakey has been active in working to bring medical care to more Americans. In the 1970s, he helped to establish a Houston high school for disadvantaged students seeking careers in health care. In the political arena, he has long maintained that government has a role in supporting health care for all Americans. During the 1960s, he advocated greater efforts to upgrade medical treatment in smaller U.S. cities, which brought him into opposition with the American Medical Association. DeBakey told *Time* in 1965 that "the Federal Government has already put a lot of money into medicine, and every physician in the United States is better off for it — better off than he ever was before." In 1999, he spoke out in support of unionizing physicians to help combat HMO abuses.

The year 2000 saw DeBakey continuing to perform surgery and engage in research. His commitment seemed undimmed after nearly 70 years in medicine. "What drives me?" he told *McCall's* in 1969. "Well, I know, as well as I know I am here this moment, that one day heart disease will be a matter of history. Like polio. Isn't that enough of a reason to keep moving? We are on the threshold of so many miracles."

Sources

➤ Periodicals

Lancet, April 24, 1999, p. 1420.
McCall's, May, 1969, p. 42 (opening quote).
New York Times, February 22, 1984, p. A11; June 26, 1987, p. A13; January 8, 1993, p. B4; November 4, 1996, p. A13; November 7, 1996, p. A13; September 1, 1998, p. F1.
Southern Medical Journal, September 1999, p. 934.
Time, May 28, 1965, p. 46.

➤ Other

Additional information was obtained from the public information office of Baylor College of Medicine.

David Dellinger

"There *are no comforts, no luxuries, no honors, nothing that can compare with having a sense of one's own integrity."*

Born August 22, 1915, in Wakefield, Massachusetts, David Dellinger is a nonviolent pacifist who has dedicated his life to the promotion of peace through his personal acts of courage. Address: c/o South End Press, 302 Columbus Ave., Boston, MA 02116.

An unwavering nonviolent pacifist, David Dellinger devoted his life to the promotion of peace through his writings, his organizational talents, and his personal acts of courage. He spoke up for what he believed and remained an active speaker throughout his lifetime.

David Dellinger was born in Wakefield, Massachusetts, on August 22, 1915. His father was a lawyer, a Yale law school graduate, and a Republican. In high school David was an outstanding athlete, long distance runner, and tournament-level golfer. He was also a superb student and already a confirmed pacifist. He graduated from Yale University as a Phi Beta Kappa economics major in 1936 and was awarded a scholarship for an additional year of study at Oxford University in England.

On his way to Europe he went to Spain, then in the middle of its civil war. Dellinger was so moved by the spirit of brotherhood among the Loyalist communist troops that he nearly joined them. Instead, he spent his year at Oxford, then returned to America for graduate work at Yale and religious training at the Union Theological Seminary.

In 1940 the U.S. government instituted the military draft in preparation for entering World War II, and David Dellinger became one of its first conscientious objectors. He refused to serve in the army. War, he said, was evil and useless. His alternative to war was brotherhood and the abolishment of capitalism. He served a one-year prison term, again refused to enlist, and was jailed for another two years. Upon leaving prison he married Elizabeth Peterson and embarked upon a career as a printer, a writer, a peace organizer, and, above all, a radical pacifist. Far from being the austere, serious prototype of a pacifist, Dellinger was a husky, happy man whom friends often described as a "cheery elf." He was a genial person of boundless energy and uncommon good sense.

Dellinger, A. J. Muste, and Sidney Lens became the editors of *Liberation* in 1956. It was a radical pacifist monthly magazine which stood for economic justice, democracy, and nonviolence, and it continued publication for 19 years. Its subscription lists grew as young Americans started to protest the nation's treatment of African Americans and the U.S. military incursion into Southeast Asia. Now, as one of the spokespersons for the American radical left, Dellinger made two journeys to Cuba in the early 1960s, reporting enthusiastically on what the Castro revolution had done for the Cuban people.

In April 1963, Dellinger participated in a "peace walk" in New York City during which those who favored peace clashed with other marchers over the Vietnam War, and Dellinger was cast into the forefront of anti-Vietnam politics. He worked in 1964 with Muste and two radical Catholic priests, Daniel and Philip Berrigan, to produce a "declaration of conscience" to encourage resistance to the military draft. A year later (August 1965), with Yale professor Staughton Lynd and Student Nonviolent Organizing Committee organizer Bob Parris, Dellinger was arrested in front of the U.S. Capitol leading a march for peace and was jailed for 45 days. Two months later Dellinger became one of the organizers of the National Coordinating Committee to End the War in Vietnam—the group which staged the huge anti-war marches in Washington D.C. in 1970.

Dellinger made two trips to China and North Vietnam in the fall of 1966 and the spring of 1967. In America he helped in the production of the famed March on the Pentagon of October 1967, which would later be memorialized by author Norman Mailer in his prize-winning *Armies of the Night*. Dellinger spent much of 1968 traveling to Cuba and preparing for demonstrations at the Democratic party national convention in August. When the Chicago police attacked the demonstrators, the federal government indicted all demonstration leaders (Dellinger, Rennie Davis, John Froines, Tom Hayden, Abbie Hoffman, Jerry Rubin, and Lee Weiner) for conspiracy to cross state lines to incite a riot.

In July 1969 North Vietnam decided, as it had twice before, to release a few U.S. prisoners of war, and Vietnamese leaders requested that Dellinger come to Hanoi to receive them. He and three others, including Rennie Davis, his co-defendant in the aftermath of the Chicago riots, flew to Hanoi in August and escorted the Americans back to freedom.

The 1969 trial of the Chicago Seven (known officially as *U.S. v. David Dellinger et al.*) was one of the most celebrated court cases of the 1960s. In order to disrupt the proceedings in Judge Julius Hoffman's courtroom and to attempt to place the Vietnam War itself on trial, the defendants wore outrageous clothing, carried anti-war signs, and replied bluntly to the court's capricious rulings. They were all found guilty by Judge Hoffman and, in addition, given innumerable contempt citations. But the entire trial was, on appeal, found to have been irrevocably tainted, and all "guilty" judgments were nullified.

By 1971 President Richard Nixon's planned withdrawal "with honor" of U.S. troops from Vietnam was lowering dissent on the home front. Dellinger was skeptical that there could be peace with honor because, as he saw it, the entire war had been without honor. He helped to plan the giant "Mayday" march on Washington, D.C. in spring 1971. But the next year American attention turned to the Watergate break-in, and Dellinger returned to his writing. *Liberation* ceased publication in 1975, and for the following five years he was the editor of *Seven Days* magazine. In the 1980s he moved to Peacham, Vermont, to teach at Vermont College and to write his memoirs, cheerfully referring to himself as a "failed poet, a flawed feminist, and a convinced pantheist."

Despite remaining an active protester and frequent public speaker, Dellinger found time to finish his memoirs and *From Yale to Jail: The Life Story of A Moral Dissenter* was published in 1993. In 1996, Dellinger and other activists who demonstrated at the 1968 Democratic National Convention had an opportunity of sorts to reprise the event. The 1996 Democratic National Convention was held in Chicago and attracted about 500 demonstrators protesting a host of causes. Dellinger was among them. He remarked to a reporter, "The numbers of people who came and the energy they had made it very successful. We made it clear there would be no violence."

Sources

➤ On-line

"David Dellinger," *Contemporary Authors Online,* http:// www.galenet.com (March 16, 2000; opening quote).

➤ Books

Dellinger, David, *From Yale to Jail: The Life Story of a Moral Dissenter*, 1993.
Dellinger, David, *More Power Than We Know: The People's Movement Toward Democracy*, 1975.
Dellinger, David, *Revolutionary Nonviolence*, 1970.

➤ Periodicals

Humanist, March 1997, p. 5.
Progressive, September 1993, p. 40.

Dith Pran

"I'm a one-person crusade. I must speak for those who did not survive and for those who still suffer."

Born September 27, 1942, in Siem Reap, Cambodia, Dith Pran is a human rights activist whose harrowing experiences during the communist Khmer Rouge regime in his native country were chronicled in the 1984 movie *The Killing Fields*. Address: c/o Dith Pran Holocaust Awareness Project, Inc., P.O. Box 1616, Woodbridge, NJ 07095.

For more than 20 years, Dith Pran has tirelessly sought justice for the estimated two to three million Cambodians who perished during the late 1970s under the brutal regime of the communist Khmer Rouge government. More than 50 of his relatives were among the dead, and he himself endured nearly five years of beatings and near-starvation before he finally managed to escape. Since then, he has made it his goal to inform as many people as possible about the ordeal of his fellow Cambodians and to do whatever it takes to bring the guilty to trial. "I am not a hero, and I am not a politician," Pran declared in a Knight-Ridder/Tribune News Service article. "I am a Cambodian Holocaust survivor, and I have to be a messenger."

One of six children of Dith Proeung and his wife, Meak Ep, Dith Pran was born in 1942 in Siem Reap, Cambodia, a provincial town located near the famous ruins of ancient temples at Angkor Wat. His father was a high-level public works official whose job as a road construction manager enabled the family to enjoy the comforts of a middle-class existence. Like many of his fellow Cambodians, Pran learned to speak French as a youngster (Cambodia was under French rule at the time) and later taught himself English as well.

After graduating from high school in 1960, Pran held a variety of jobs until he hired on as a translator for the United States Military Assistance Command soon after it was established in 1962. The presence of American military personnel in Cambodia coincided with the escalating U.S. involvement in the war in neighboring Vietnam. In that conflict, South Vietnamese troops and their American allies were pitted against communist forces from North Vietnam and their South Vietnamese sympathizers, a guerrilla army known as the Vietcong.

In 1965, however, Pran suddenly found himself out of work when South Vietnamese planes bombed villages along the Cambodian-Vietnamese border and Cambodia responded by severing its ties with the United States. He then served as an interpreter for a British film crew that was in the area making the movie *Lord Jim* and eventually went into the tourist business as a hotel receptionist near Angkor Wat.

Meanwhile, the war in Vietnam was steadily encroaching on Cambodian territory. Widespread government corruption and a shaky economy added to the country's instability. Finally, in March 1970, a right-wing coup led by a pro-U.S. military general named Lon Nol overthrew the existing regime of Prince Norodom Sihanouk. South Vietnamese troops invaded Cambodia in April with the help of secret bombing raids by the United States that destroyed numerous villages and killed a number of civilians. This in turn bolstered popular support for the communists in Cambodia, a group known as the Khmer Rouge. Before long a full-scale civil war had erupted.

The hostilities effectively shut down the tourist industry in Cambodia and left Pran without a job. Along with his wife, Ser Moeun, and their four children, he relocated to the nation's capital, Phnom Penh, and found work as an interpreter and guide for the many foreign journalists who were there covering the war. In addition to handling routine tasks such as booking hotel rooms, arranging for transportation, and obtaining press credentials, Pran displayed a knack for reporting. Bright, resourceful, and perceptive, he tracked down exactly the kind of information his clients needed.

In September 1972 Pran met someone whose life would become inextricably bound with his own—Sydney Schanberg, the Southeast Asia correspondent for the *New York Times.* The two men hit it off immediately. Both were deeply concerned about the impact of the war on the Cambodian people, and both had a burning desire to seek out the truth about the scope of the devastation, which U.S. officials were desperately trying to keep secret. Together they began to document the results of clandestine U.S. bombing raids and the suffering of refugees. Pran often resorted to bribes and subterfuge to obtain vital information and make sure that no one prevented Schanberg's stories from being wired out of the country.

By the spring of 1975 it was apparent that the Khmer Rouge were on the verge of toppling the Cambodian government. On April 12, as enemy soldiers closed in on Phnom Penh, the U.S. Embassy was evacuated. Schanberg decided to stay, however, so that he and Pran could continue to cover the fall of the city.

The Khmer Rouge captured Phnom Penh on April 17. Literally overnight, they plunged the country into an abyss of constant terror and unbelievable savagery. Their goal was to force Cambodia to revert to a primitive, agrarian society. Intellectual pursuits and professional careers were scorned. City dwellers were driven like livestock into rural areas to work on communes that were essentially slave labor camps. The Khmer Rouge deliberately separated families in many instances, taking children away from their parents and keeping husbands and wives apart. Those the Khmer Rouge regarded as their enemies were rounded up and taken away to be executed or, at the very least, beaten and tortured. Starvation and disease caused many more deaths, especially among the very young and the very old.

During the chaotic mass exodus from Phnom Penh, Pran and Schanberg remained on the move. As they were leaving a hospital accompanied by an American photographer and a British reporter, they were stopped by some heavily armed Khmer Rouge soldiers who confiscated their equipment and shoved everyone but Pran into a military vehicle. Fearing for his colleagues' lives, Pran explained again and again to the soldiers that Schanberg and the others were merely French journalists and that he was their driver. After pleading for several hours, he was finally able to persuade the soldiers to let them all go.

Pran and Schanberg spent the rest of the day watching helplessly as hordes of people were herded out of the city toward an uncertain fate. They then sought refuge in the French Embassy with other Westerners and Cambodians. Tensions escalated as Khmer Rouge soldiers periodically entered the compound and led away Cambodians targeted for execution. Meanwhile, Schanberg tried and failed to come up with a way to protect his friend and arrange for his evacuation. Thus, on April 20 Pran decided to leave on his own while he still could. (Schanberg was flown to Thailand 10 days later and in 1976 won a Pulitzer Prize—which he accepted in both his and Pran's name—for his articles on the fall of Phnom Penh.)

The next four-and-a-half years of Pran's life were a living hell. To avoid detection as an enemy of the Khmer Rouge, he passed himself off as a simple-minded taxi driver. By October 1975 he was part of a crew responsible for planting and tending rice fields. His typical day began at 4:00 a.m. and ended around 6:00 p.m., except during harvest season when everyone was required to work an additional two or three hours. Much of the time, food was so scarce that his daily ration of rice amounted to about a spoonful.

Under such conditions, Pran soon grew weak with hunger. One night, he stole some rice kernels but was caught in the act by other members of his commune. They beat him severely and then sentenced him to death until a member of the Khmer Rouge who had taken a liking to him intervened and persuaded his would-be executioners to show some mercy.

Pran subsequently held a series of different jobs. He carried dirt to build embankments for rice paddies, plowed using a team of horses, sawed down trees, and fished with hand nets. At one point, he also served as the cook for a group of 18 blacksmiths on the commune.

In late 1977 Pran was given permission to move to another nearby village. There his life improved somewhat when he became a houseboy to the head of the commune. In this role, he chopped firewood, carried water, washed clothes, cooked, and helped care for the children of the family.

Meanwhile, long-simmering ethnic tensions that for some time had touched off border clashes and other skirmishes between the Khmer Rouge and the Vietnamese erupted into a full-fledged war in 1978. Vietnamese troops captured Phnom Penh and its environs in January 1979 and drove out the Khmer Rouge. At last, Pran was able to return to Siem Reap, where he learned that most of the other members of his family were long dead; only his mother, one sister, a sister-in-law, and five nieces and nephews were still alive.

Pran soon went to work for the government the Vietnamese established in Siem Reap in a position similar to that of a mayor. He proved to be a very capable administrator whom the Vietnamese liked and trusted. In mid-1979, however, Pran was forced to resign his job when word got out that he had once worked for American journalists.

Increasingly uneasy about his future now that his past had come to light, Pran made up his mind to escape to Thailand. Over a period of several weeks, he edged his way toward freedom, and by mid-September 1979 he was within about 35 miles of the border. He then joined up with some other would-be escapees, and together they set out for Thailand through jungle and over rocky hills, dodging mines, booby traps, Khmer Rouge guerrillas, and Vietnamese patrols along the way.

To avoid arrest by Thai authorities, Pran donned the uniform of a Cambodian resistance fighter and entered Thailand on October 3, 1979. He headed immediately to a refugee camp, where he spoke to an American aid worker and asked her to relay his story to Schanberg in New York City. After years of hoping for the best while fearing the worst, the reporter was ecstatic to learn of his friend's escape. Schanberg left for Bangkok on the next available flight, and on October 9 the two men had an emotional reunion. "I am reborn," Pran declared through his tears, as Schanberg later recalled in *The Death and Life of Dith Pran*. "This is my second life."

Pran, however, was in very fragile health. Extremely thin, with rotting teeth, hands that shook from malnutrition, and badly infected legs and feet, he soon developed a fever. Diagnosed with malaria, he remained in Thailand for 10 more days undergoing treatment while *New York Times* staffers helped arrange for his departure. Finally, on October 19, he and Schanberg flew to the

United States and another reunion, this time with Pran's wife and children in San Francisco. (With Schanberg's help, they had fled Cambodia when Phnom Penh fell and settled in the United States.) The enforced separation they had endured took its toll on their marriage, however, and the couple eventually divorced.

Since regaining his health, Pran has been on a quest to publicize the atrocities of the Khmer Rouge and avenge the deaths of his fellow Cambodians. In addition to working as a photojournalist for the *New York Times*, he has given countless lectures and interviews, appearing before student groups, world affairs organizations, and on radio and television to share his story and discuss the plight of his people, most of whom are still struggling to recover from the Khmer Rouge years.

In 1984, moviegoers gained some sense of what Pran and his fellow Cambodians had experienced with the release of *The Killing Fields*, a film based on *The Death and Life of Dith Pran*, Sydney Schanberg's 1980 memoir. Pran was portrayed by Dr. Haing S. Ngor, a refugee Cambodian physician who was also a survivor of the labor camps. He and Pran became close friends after meeting at the film's premiere and worked together on Cambodian issues until Ngor was shot to death by a teenage Asian gang member outside his Los Angeles home in 1996.

Pran has visited Cambodia several times since his escape. His first trip was in 1989 with Ngor and other members of the Cambodian Documentation Commission, a human rights group that has tried to persuade the World Court to put the Khmer Rouge on trial for genocide. Due in part to the efforts of Pran and Ngor, the U.S. Congress passed the Cambodian Genocide Justice Act in 1994, and the U.S. Department of State gave a $500,000 grant to Yale University to catalog the atrocities, identify the perpetrators, and determine how to bring them to trial.

Pran is also the founder and president of the Dith Pran Holocaust Awareness Project, which seeks to alert the world to the horrors of the Cambodian genocide and warn against the reemergence of the Khmer Rouge, who have continued to stir up trouble in remote areas of the country and recruit new converts among the disgruntled and downtrodden. "The problems Cambodia faces are not only political but also economical and social. . . ," Pran declared on the website for his organization. "I try to awaken the world to the holocaust of Cambodia, for all tragedies have universal implications. . . . If Cambodia is to survive, she needs many voices."

Sources

➤ On-line

"Dith Pran: Cambodian Holocaust Survivor," *The Dith Pran Holocaust Awareness Project, Inc.: Spreading the Word of the Cambodian Genocide,* http://www.dithpran.org/dithbio.htm (March 8, 2000; opening quote).

➤ Books

Dith Pran, compiler, *Children of Cambodia's Killing Fields: Memoirs of Survivors,* Yale University, 1997.
Schanberg, Sydney H., *The Death and Life of Dith Pran,* Penguin, 1980.

➤ Periodicals

Knight-Ridder/Tribune News Service, February 15, 1994.
New York Times, August 15, 1989, p. A13.
New York Times Magazine, January 20, 1980; September 24, 1989.
People, December 10, 1984.
Reader's Digest, May 1997, pp. 60-66.
Time, February 24, 1986, p. 70.

Henry Chee Dodge

"I *would like to see them [all Navajos] make equal progress, but I am sure that it is only possible if we have one man at the head of the tribe, an active, strong, energetic and able man. . . . A uniform educational system, uniform treatment, uniform orders and regulations, and uniform progress would be the result."*

Born c. 1857 at Fort Defiance, Henry Chee Dodge was a famous Navajo tribal leader who dedicated himself to improving the quality of life for Navajos. He died on January 7, 1947, in Ganado, Arizona.

One of the most famous of the Navajo tribal leaders, Henry Chee Dodge made significant contributions to his community throughout his long life. He is known for his service as the first official Navajo interpreter, a role he played from the 1870s through the early 1900s; his many years as a head chief; and his position as the first chairman of the Navajo Tribal Council.

There is some dispute over what year Dodge was born, as well as about his parentage. Many historians show Dodge born in 1860 and the name of his father as Juan Anea (also known as Anaya, Cocinas or Cosonisas, and Gohsinahsu). Anea was a Mexican silversmith working for Captain Henry L. Dodge, the Navajo Indian Agent at Fort Defiance. However, in an 1888 sworn affidavit, Chee Dodge stated he was the son of a white army officer and a Navajo woman, was born at Fort Defiance, and was "about" 30 years old. In 1875, Augustus C. Dodge, brother of Henry L. Dodge, wrote that he "had a nephew then eighteen years old living at Fort Defiance, who was the son of a Navajo woman and of his brother," according to David M. Brugge in an essay, "Henry Chee Dodge: From the Long Walk to Self Determination." Since Henry L. Dodge was captured and killed by Apaches in late 1856, Brugge states the younger Dodge more likely was born about 1857 rather than 1860.

Dodge's mother, Bisnayanchi, was a Navajo-Jemez Pueblo woman from the Ma'iideshgizhnii [Coyote Pass] clan. She was married to Juan Anea during young Dodge's first few years of life. However, Anea died in 1862 during a Mexican raid. In 1863, Kit Carson forcibly moved the Fort Defiance Navajos to Fort Sumner at the Bosque Redondo to put an end to Navajo uprisings. During the Carson campaign, Bisnayanchi left her son in the care of a sister, then fled to Hopi territory, where she died sometime later.

Orphaned, Dodge was passed among his relatives for a time then was adopted by an eight-year-old girl and her grandfather, who found him alone and starving during the "Long Walk" to Fort Sumner. When Dodge returned to Fort Defiance with the rest of the Navajos in 1868, he lived with his mother's sister and her husband, a white man named Perry H. Williams, who taught Dodge English. He quickly learned English and Spanish, in addition to his native Navajo language. For a time, Dodge also lived with the new Indian Agent, W. F. M. Arny, who allowed Dodge to attend the Fort Defiance Indian School, where he learned to read and write.

Dodge first used his language skills as a translator while working at his uncle's trading post. He earned $5 a week, most of which he saved. He also worked for a time with a freight company moving goods from Santa Fe to the fort and assisted ethnologist Washington Matthews at Fort Wingate. Dodge became so proficient at translating and interpreting, and he understood the Navajo culture so well, that Agent Arny hired him in the late 1870s as the official Agency interpreter. In an effort to control crime among the reservation Indians, a police force was recruited in 1881. In 1883, Dodge was appointed chief of the Navajo patrol. He often acted as the agency interpreter during police investigations and helped to diffuse many potentially violent confrontations.

On April 19, 1884, Commissioner of Indian Affairs Dennis M. Riordan appointed Dodge to the job of head chief of the Navajos at Fort Defiance, a position held previously by the great war chief Manuelito. Later that year, Dodge and a delegation of other Navajo leaders traveled to Washington where they met with President Chester A. Arthur.

By 1890, Dodge had saved enough money from his various jobs to invest in a trading post and a sheep ranch. Near Crystal, New Mexico, he built a home at his ranch, which he called Tso Tsela ("Stars Lying Down"). Dodge and Stephen H. Aldrich became partners in the trading post at Round Rock in the Chinle Valley. Dodge managed the post and hired Charles Hubbell as a clerk. With his business established, Dodge finally decided to marry. His first wife, Asdzaa' Tsi'naajinii, he supposedly divorced after learning she was gambling heavily. However, records at the Saint Michaels Mission indicated that his first wife was the mother of Dodge's daughter, Josephine, who was the youngest of his children.

Most historians note Dodge then married Nanabah and her younger sister, K'eehabah, an accepted practice in traditional Navajo culture. They were the daughters of the woman who, as an eight-year-old child, adopted Dodge on the trip to Fort Sumner with her grandfather. Nanabah or her sister had a daughter named Mary in 1903, according to several written accounts about Dodge. However, the Mission records indicate that during his life, Dodge had a total of eight wives and six children, named Tom, Ben, Antoinette, Annie, Veronica and Josephine. Four of his wives were sisters and a fifth was a member of the sisters' clan, the Tse'njikini clan. Another wife was a cousin of the four sisters, but belonged to the Ta'neeszahnii clan. Until the Navajos converted to Christianity, polygamy was not only accepted, but expected.

Although his business and ranch took much of his time, Dodge continued to work at the Fort Defiance Agency as an interpreter. He helped the various Indian agents resolve disputes and encouraged

Navajo participation in mineral development and land rights issues and in a variety of federal programs. For example, in 1892, he helped Agent Dana L. Shipley obtain promises from a number of Navajo parents to send their children to the Fort Defiance government school. In 1907, he was a member of a committee that reviewed a request to lease land from the Shiprock Navajos. In September 1907, Dodge assisted the negotiations for surrender between federal troops and Little Singer, who had helped his wives escape jail and hid them and himself on Beautiful Mountain.

The Navajos did not have a centralized form of government until 1923. Dodge, however, envisioned such a government as early as 1918 when he corresponded with Cato Sells, Commissioner of Indian Affairs. Mary Shepardson, in "Development of Navajo Tribal Government," quoted Dodge as writing: "I would like to see them [all Navajos] make equal progress, but I am sure that it is only possible if we have one man at the head of the tribe, an active, strong, energetic and able man. . . . A uniform educational system, uniform treatment, uniform orders and regulations, and uniform progress would be the result."

In 1922, a three-man Navajo business council was formed to deal with requests for oil exploration leases in the Fort Defiance area of the reservation. Council members Dodge, Dugal Chee Bekiss, and Charley Mitchell, signed several oil leases for the jurisdiction. However, Indian Superintendent Evan Estap wanted more control over the leases and spread rumors that Standard Oil-owned companies had bribed Dodge to get leases signed. Estap, who was later fired over the issue, appointed former New Mexico Territorial Governor Herbert J. Hagerman to sign oil leases for all six of the Navajo jurisdictions.

Under somewhat restrictive orders, the first Navajo Tribal Council was formed and met on July 7, 1923, and Dodge was elected its first chairman on July 27. The council represented all nine of the Navajo districts with 12 delegates and 12 alternate members. They approved Hagerman's position, giving him the authorization to sign all oil and mineral leases in exchange for a federal promise to obtain more land for the Navajos.

Dodge served as chairman of the Tribal Council until 1928, when he stepped down to spend more time at his sheep ranch and trading post. During his years as chairman, he often found himself at odds with Jacob C. Morgan, a council member representing the San Juan Navajo jurisdiction. Morgan believed in assimilation, which often led him into confrontations with Dodge, who wanted a unified

Navajo nation. For example, in 1927, Dodge led a movement to use oil royalties to buy more land for the reservation. Morgan opposed the plan because he wanted to use the money for water development. Dodge was so upset after the council reached a compromise on the issue that he recommended the council be abolished.

While Dodge was chairman, the council steadily increased its power. It obtained the right to decide how oil lease royalties would be spent, approving a division of the royalties among the different jurisdictions, which, in turn, were allowed to determine how best to use that money within their jurisdictions. The council also opposed a federal move to use some of the funds to build a bridge off the reservation. In 1927, Dodge convinced Congress that the Navajos had a right to 100 percent of the oil royalties resulting from the oil reserves under the reservation. The Indian Oil Act of 1927, which Dodge supported, provided that states in which the oil was found would receive 37.5 percent of the royalties, but could spend those funds only on projects benefitting the Indians and only after first consulting with the Indians about those projects. Although Dodge was not a part of the Tribal Council during the next decade, he remained active in tribal politics.

Although the Indian Reorganization Act of 1934 provided the Navajos with more authority than in past years, it also allowed the Secretary of the Interior to limit the amount of livestock on Indian reservations. Overgrazing of reservation lands had been a problem for some years. In 1926, the Navajo Council had limited the number of horses allowed to graze on the reservation. In autumn of 1933, the Bureau of Indian Affairs (BIA) suggested that the Navajo reduce the number of sheep grazing on the reservation in an effort to reduce erosion. The government offered to buy ewes for about $1 per head, and many of the Navajo sheep ranchers agreed to cull their herds. Most of the ranchers, however, kept their most productive stock. A second stock reduction, funded by the tribe, was agreed to in the spring of 1934 but was apparently not implemented.

By 1936, stock reduction was resulting in hundreds of healthy sheep being slaughtered. In June, Dodge accused John Collier, head of the BIA, of causing hunger and sickness to spread among the Navajo as a result of the sheep reduction program. For a brief time, Morgan and Dodge formed an alliance to denounce Collier's continuing demands for more sheep reductions. During a Congressional hearing that year about expanding the boundaries of the reservation, Shepardson wrote that Dodge testified, "You take sheep away from a Navajo, that's all he knows. He isn't going to farm or anything like that; you might give a few acres to the poor ones, but stock raising is in their heart. That's their work. If you keep cutting down sheep after a while the Government will have to feed these people; give them rations; you know what that will cost." Collier later admitted that the reduction program was unfair to many Navajos.

Dodge's influence in the lives of the Navajos continued well into his eighties, when, in 1942, he was again elected as chairman of the Tribal Council. He was re-elected in 1946, but on January 7, 1947, Dodge died of pneumonia in Ganado, Arizona.

Sources

➤ Books

Biographical Dictionary of Indians of the Americas, Volume 1, American Indian Publishers, 1991.

Brugge, David M., "Henry Chee Dodge: From the Long Walk to Self-Determination," in *Indian Lives: Essays on Nineteenth and Twentieth Century Native American Leaders,* University of New Mexico Press, 1985.

Dictionary of American Biography, Supplement 4, 1946-1950, Scribner's, 1974.

Dockstader, Frederick J., *Great North American Indians,* Van Nostrand Reinhold, 1977.

Handbook of American Indians North of Mexico, Part 2, Rowman and Littlefield, 1975.

Native North American Almanac, Gale Research, 1994.

Shepardson, Mary, "Development of Navajo Tribal Government," in *Handbook of North American Indians,* Volume 10: Southwest, Smithsonian Institution, 1983 (opening quote).

Elizabeth Dole

"If you're not marching to your own tune, you're going to be marching to someone else's. You have to take control of your own life, set your own priorities, or someone will be happy to set them for you."

Born on July 20, 1936, in Salisbury, North Carolina, Elizabeth Dole has held many high-ranking positions in the United States government and has also served as president of the American Red Cross. Address: P.O. Box 58247, Washington, D.C. 20037.

One of the most accomplished women in American government, Elizabeth Dole's career has been marked by several successive accomplishments. She began her career as a consumer advocate and then public liaison, and went on to sit on the Federal Trade Commission. After Ronald Reagan became president in 1980, she became the first woman to hold a cabinet position during his administration, as he appointed her secretary of transportation. Once George Bush took office in 1988, she then became secretary of labor, and later ran the largest charitable organization in the country, the American Red Cross.

Throughout her career, Dole was also known as a tireless Republican crusader, most often on behalf of her husband, Senator Robert Dole, who threw his hat in the ring for the presidency several times. However, after her husband failed in all his bids, Dole took matters into her own hands and announced that she wanted to run in the 2000 elections. Though she withdrew her name by the end of 1999, citing financial reasons, Dole left a mark: Her effort made many think seriously about having a woman in one of the two major parties run for president. In the mainly male realm of politics, she has stood out for her motivation and rise through the ranks. "If you're not marching to your own tune, you're going to be marching to someone else's," Dole once remarked to Thomas Fields-Meyer in *People.* "You have to take control of your own life, set your own priorities, or someone will be happy to set them for you."

Dole was born Elizabeth Hanford on July 20, 1936, in Salisbury, North Carolina. Her parents, John Van Hanford and Mary Ella (Cathey) Hanford, ran a successful wholesale flower business in that small town near Winston-Salem, and also had a son, John, 13 years older than their daughter. Staunchly Methodist, they instilled in their children a strong work ethic while also providing luxuries such as private piano lessons, horseback riding instruction, and ballet classes. Dole, who began calling herself "Liddy" when she was a toddler, was always a precocious child who showed leadership qualities. Her first elected office was president of the Bird Club in third grade, and she formed a Junior Book Club in seventh grade. In high school she ran for class president even though that post was generally off-limits to girls. The school was not ready for times to change, however, and she never reached her goal.

After graduating from Boyden High School, Dole, wishing to follow in her brother's footsteps, applied only to Duke University, hoping to study political science. This concerned her mother, who had hoped she would pursue home economics. As Dole recalled in the book *The Doles: Unlimited Partners,* cowritten with her husband, Robert Dole, her mom "thought this would be a natural prelude to marriage and life next door." Contrary to her mother's wishes, Dole forged ahead as a political science major and graduated Phi Beta Kappa; she was also the president of her student body and voted May Queen.

In 1958, Dole began graduate studies at Harvard, earning a master's degree in education in 1960. She also briefly studied at Oxford University in 1959. She then worked as a secretary for North Carolina Senator B. Everett Jordan during the summer of 1960. Thanks to this connection, she ended up riding on a whistle-stop tour of the South with Democratic vice-presidential nominee Lyndon B. Johnson, despite grumbling from her father, a staunch Republican. In addition, Dole held a job at the Harvard Law School library while in graduate school.

During the summers of 1961 and 1962, Dole found work at the United Nations Public Information Section in New York, and began to think seriously about her future plans. She decided to try law school "as an experiment," as she put it in *The Doles,* adding, "I concluded that even a year at Harvard Law would be excellent training and background." Her mother, on the other hand, asked her, "Don't you want to be a wife, and a mother, and a hostess for your husband?" Dole remarked in her book, "I wanted to be all those things. In time. But just then I had other aspirations."

When she graduated from Harvard Law School in 1965, Dole was one of 24 women in a class of 550. The experience was a trial in itself: One of her professors steadfastly refused to call on women in class, and a male classmate told her she had no right to be there, insisting, "You're taking the place of a qualified man who will go out and do something with his education," as Maureen Orth reported in *Vogue.* After earning her degree, in 1967 she became the staff assistant to the assistant secretary for education at the Department of Health, Education, and Welfare. As she commented in *The Doles,* "While Bob Dole was voting against the Great Society, I was working for it." The Great Society was President Johnson's wide-ranging social initiative that established programs like Medicaid, Medicare, and Head Start. One of Dole's first assignments in the government was to organize a conference on education for the deaf.

After leaving that position, Dole practiced law for a short time as a public defender in Washington, D.C. Soon, though, she landed a spot in Johnson's Committee for Consumer Interests, and quickly became executive director. When Republican Richard M. Nixon became president in 1969, he renamed it the White House Office of Consumer Affairs, and kept Dole on board, even though she was a Democrat. She was appointed deputy assistant to the president for consumer affairs in 1971. During her time working under Nixon, Dole changed her affiliation to Independent, and later, after she married, registered as a Republican. She met her husband, then Senator Bob Dole of Kansas, in March of 1972. They began dating a couple years later and were married on December 6, 1975, when she was 39 and he was 53. He had one daughter, Robin, by a previous marriage, but they would not have any children together. Always on the go, they made their home in a two-bedroom apartment at the Watergate Hotel in Washington, D.C.

In 1973, Nixon appointed Dole as one of five members of the Federal Trade Commission, one of the oldest government watchdog groups. There, she became known for standing up for women, minorities, the poor, and the handicapped. When her husband threw his hat in the ring for the 1976 presidential race, she quit her job to help him campaign. Robert Dole eventually landed on a ticket as vice president with incumbent President Gerald Ford, who took office after Nixon's resignation due to the Watergate affair, but they were defeated in the election by Democrat Jimmy Carter. She resumed her position under President Carter, but stepped down again in 1979 to help her husband in the Republican primaries. He soon dropped out of the race, though, and Dole campaigned fervently for Ronald Reagan.

As a key member of President Reagan's transition team, Dole was rewarded with a post as head of the White House Office of Public Liaison, which required her to meet with all outside groups as a lobbyist for the president and to hear concerns and take them back to the White House. During this time, some criticized her for publicly supporting Reagan's opposition to the Equal Rights Amendment for women, but she replied by stating that her involvement in the top echelon of government was an important step for women on its own. After Drew Lewis resigned as secretary of transportation, Reagan—who had been criticized for not naming women to top positions—appointed Dole to fill the vacancy. Her nomination was approved 97-0 in the Senate and she was sworn into office in February of 1983.

Though Dole had no prior experience in transportation, she immersed herself in the issues and soon became known as the "Safety Secretary." She was credited with helping to push the legal drinking age up to 21 in order to cut down on drunk-driving incidents, lobbying for air bags and additional rear brake lights on vehicles, protesting deceptive airline scheduling, and adding more Federal Aviation Administration inspectors, among other efforts. She also headed the Coast Guard, thus becoming the first female head of an armed service. Still, some harped that she only won her job because Reagan needed to "showcase" women in his administration, according to Orth. Dole responded, "I've got 102,000 people working for me and a budget of $28 billion to run. I don't see how I could possibly be a 'showcase'!"

When Robert Dole took another stab at the running for president in 1988, Dole resigned once again to support him. She told Alessandra Stanley in *Time* that stepping down was "probably the most difficult decision of my life." By now, she and her husband were regarded as a "power couple" around Washington, not due to any kind of hobnobbing social life, but on the basis of their high rankings in the government. Both were so firmly entrenched in public service that, in 1984, a popular campaign button read, "Dole-Dole '88," indicating that some thought a husband-wife ticket would be a good idea (part of the allure of the ticket was that no one pointed out which Dole would be the top candidate).

After Robert Dole lost his bid for president in 1988, Dole campaigned for George H. Bush, who appointed her secretary of labor after his victory. This made her the only woman, and one of very few persons at all, to have held two different cabinet posts in separate administrations. Only 22 months into that job, she resigned to become president of the American Red Cross, the largest non-profit group in the United States and one responsible for half of the nation's blood supply. In that capacity, with a $1.8 billion annual budget, Dole oversaw 32,000 employees and 1.4 million volunteers. During her first year on the job, in 1991, she announced that she would not accept the $200,000 annual salary as a way to demonstrate her volunteer spirit and boost morale.

Again in 1996, Dole took a hiatus from her job to help her husband, who resigned from the Senate after winning the Republican presidential nomination. Throughout the run she insisted that she would return to her job if he won, which would have made her the nation's first working First Lady. Their witty, good-natured sparring on the campaign trail made her a popular partner; she was even more well-liked, according to polls, than her husband or his running mate, Jack Kemp. Though her husband's bid was unsuccessful, by this time some had begun to toss around her name as a good choice for a future presidential run, and she was not ruling it out.

Always regarded as warmer and more personable than her husband, not to mention having an impressive resume behind her, it was no surprise when Dole herself stepped down from her position at the Red Cross and began to campaign for the 2000 presidency. She entered the rigorous routine of the talk show circuit and other public appearances, but by October of 1999, she pulled out, citing that her lack of funds prohibited her from continuing. Early on, when Lynn Rosellini of *U.S. News & World Report* asked if she would consider a vice presidential slot, Dole replied, "Have you asked that question of the men? If I run, it'll be for president." However, after leaving the race, she refused to rule out the possibility, leaving open the potential for her name to be added to a ticket. After her withdrawal, candidate George W. Bush called her a "trailblazer" and noted in the *Dallas Morning News*, "She is an inspiration for a lot of women. She has made a mark on the political process."

Sources

➤ Books

Dole, Robert, and Elizabeth Dole, with Richard Norton Smith, *The Doles: Unlimited Partners*, Simon and Schuster, 1988.
Encyclopedia of World Biography, second edition, Gale Research, 1998.
Newsmakers 1990, issue 1, Gale Research, 1990.

➤ Periodicals

Dallas Morning News, October 21, 1999, p. 1A.
Insight on the News, July 24, 1995, p. 13.
Ladies Home Journal, August 1999, p. 44.
McCall's, April 1988, p. 131.
New Republic, February 1, 1999.
Newsweek, January 8, 1996, p. 36; August 19, 1996, p. 36.
New Yorker, January 22, 1996, p. 62.
New York Times, July 16, 1996, p. A1.
New York Times Magazine, October 13, 1996, p. 37.
People, June 24, 1991, p. 87; October 14, 1996, p. 50 (opening quote).
Time, September 21, 1987, p. 30; July 1, 1996, p. 30.

U.S. News & World Report, August 19, 1996, p. 26; March 15, 1999, p. 25; November 1, 1999, p. 34.
Vogue, October 1984, p. 110.

James Doolittle

"I *can honestly say that I've never felt fear."*

Born December 14, 1896 in Alameda, California, James Doolittle was a pilot who set two early transcontinental flying time records, pioneered advancements in aviation, led the Tokyo raid in 1942, and commanded the Eighth Air Force attack on Germany. He died on September 27, 1993, in Pebble Beach, California.

Geneviève James H. "Jimmy" Doolittle was one of the best-known American heroes of World War II. A daring aviator, planner, and commander, he led the 1942 U.S. Army Air Corps bombing raid on Tokyo, as well as other Japanese cities, that was credited with turning the tide of American wartime morale.

James Harold Doolittle was born in Alameda, California, on December 14, 1896, the only child of Frank, a carpenter, and Rosa Shephard Doolittle. Most of his youth was spent in Nome, Alaska, and Los Angeles, where he graduated from Manual Arts High School in 1914. Delicate as a child and small of stature, Doolittle nevertheless developed a love of adventure and a scrappy disposition, taking up motorbike riding and boxing as he grew older. His enthusiasm for homemade gliders developed into a lifelong commitment to aviation.

After two years at Los Angeles Junior College, Doolittle enrolled at the University of California at Berkeley to study mining engineering. He never completed his studies (several years later he was awarded a bachelor's degree, however), for in September 1917 he enrolled in the Signal Corps of the U.S. Army hoping to become a pilot. He was commissioned a second lieutenant on March 9, 1918. A few months earlier he had married Josephine "Joe" Daniels. They had two sons.

Doolittle saw no overseas duty during World War I, but remained in the service after the war ended and received a first lieutenant's commission in the Regular Army in 1920. A member of Billy Mitchell's team during the controversial bomber versus battleship tests of 1921, Doolittle himself emerged as a public figure in 1922 when he flew from Pablo Beach (near Jacksonville), Florida, to San Diego in less than 22 hours flying time, the first to span the continent in less than 24 hours. Nine years later, in the course of winning the Bendix Trophy race, he recorded the first transcontinental flying time of less than 12 hours. Doolittle, however, was much more than the daredevil aviator he was reputed to be, for at bottom he believed that one took chances in the air for a serious purpose: to further the usefulness of aviation. Selected to be one of the first participants in the army's new program in aeronautical engineering, he received a doctorate from Massachusetts Institute of Technology in 1925.

During the 1920s and early 1930s Doolittle, both as a student and as a pilot, made several important contributions to the advancement of aviation. Besides the two transcontinental speed records he established, he set additional speed records and in various ways added to the understanding of acceleration's effects. He became the first North American to fly across the Andes; and, perhaps most important, after further studies and research at the Full Flight Laboratory he made the first blind flight and landing on September 24, 1929. Doolittle's participation in the development and use of instruments such as the Sperry artificial horizon would do much to increase the safety of flying, enabling it to take place in varying weather conditions.

Given a major's rank in the reserves, Doolittle left active military service to join the Shell Oil Company in 1930. With his mother and mother-in-law in need of special medical attention he felt he needed the higher income he could earn in private industry. He did promotional and sales work for Shell and on occasion for Curtiss-Wright throughout the 1930s. Although he gave up racing in 1932, believing that after several close calls he had used up his luck, he remained active as a pilot.

With the start of World War II in Europe, Doolittle asked his long-time friend, General Henry "Hap" Arnold, who was now chief of the Army Air Corps, to return him to active duty. On July 1, 1940, Doolittle re-entered uniformed service as a major assigned to straighten out aircraft production bottlenecks. After America's entry into the war he sought combat duty but instead was attached to Arnold's staff with the rank of lieutenant colonel. This new position ultimately involved him in one of the war's most daring achievements—the April 1942 bombing of Tokyo.

The idea of avenging Pearl Harbor by bombing Japan itself had originated in the highest echelons of the navy, but accomplishing it posed a dilemma. The weakened American navy could not allow an aircraft carrier to approach within 400 miles of Japan, lest it be exposed to attack by shore-based Japanese planes. Nor did any standard American carrier plane of the time have the range to fly that distance with a bomb load and continue on to landing fields in China. Implementation of the plan therefore depended on using the Army Air Corps' new two-engine B-25 bomber.

Doolittle was put in charge of the intensive training required in flying such a large plane from the deck of a carrier—there was no possibility of landing on the carrier after completion of the mission—and managed to talk Arnold into letting him lead the attack itself. On April 18, 1942, the 16 planes he commanded flew from the carrier *Hornet* to bomb assorted targets in Tokyo and a few other Japanese cities and then on to landings in China. Although none of the planes landed intact in China, all but two of the crews reached safety. While some have considered the Doolittle raid, as it became known, strategically unsound in terms of the negligible damage it could inflict upon Japan, it was soon immortalized in the book and film *Thirty Seconds over Tokyo* and undeniably raised American morale while causing concern to the Japanese.

Doolittle was given a rare double promotion to brigadier general and then was awarded the Congressional Medal of Honor in a White House ceremony. He was sent to Europe to command Dwight Eisenhower's air units during the planned invasion of North Africa, after which Doolittle was promoted to major general. He had been coolly received by Eisenhower, but gradually won his commander's confidence and stayed with him throughout the remainder of World War II in Europe, in succession serving as commander of the Twelfth Air Force in North Africa (1942-1943), the Northwest African Strategic Air Forces, the Fifteenth Air Force during the Mediterranean campaigns of 1943, and, finally, from January 1944, of the Eighth Air Force based in England.

In his early commands Doolittle, who often flew missions himself, had been obliged to develop effective air forces, but the Eighth had already been built into a successful unit by its previous commander, Lieutenant General Ira Eaker. Nevertheless, Doolittle profited from the advent of more and better planes, particularly the P-51 fighter which allowed his forces to achieve air superiority over the heart of Germany itself. A firm believer in strategic bombing, Doolittle commanded the Eighth Air Force during its greatest successes: the first American bombing of Berlin, the sustained bombing campaigns against Germany's oil industry and various manufacturing and rail facilities, and finally the virtual destruction of the Luftwaffe, the German air force.

With the end of the war in Europe, Doolittle was ordered to Okinawa to establish with new planes and personnel what would in effect be a new Eighth Air Force, but Japan surrendered before it became operational. At 49 Doolittle was the youngest lieutenant general in U.S. service and the only reservist to reach that rank. Believing that he was not the right man to serve in a postwar air force due for retrenchment, Doolittle returned to reserve status in 1946 and resumed work for Shell. He remained a Shell vice president until 1958, taking occasional leave to do public service both for the Air Force and for various government bodies, among them a special board that President Truman named to report on airport safety and location.

After he left Shell, Doolittle settled in Santa Monica, California, served until 1961 as board chairman of the aerospace division of

TRW, then joined Mutual of Omaha. He had given up flying in 1961. Although much of Doolittle's career was spent in civilian pursuits, he will always be remembered for his pioneering achievements in aviation in the 1920s, for his successful command of the Eighth Air Force, and particularly for his leadership of the Tokyo raid in April 1942. Doolittle, recalled Arnold, "was fearless, technically brilliant, a leader who not only could be counted upon to do a task himself if it were humanly possible, but could impart his spirit to others."

Doolittle's contributions were recognized and honored by Presidents Ronald Reagan and George Bush. In Reagan's Farewell Address to the American People (1989) he said, "We've got to teach history based not on what's in fashion, but what's important: Why the pilgrims came here, who Jimmy Doolittle was, and what those 30 seconds over Tokyo meant." Later the same year, Doolittle was awarded the Presidential Medal of Freedom by President Bush. Doolittle died on September 27, 1993, at his son's home in Pebble Beach, California, following a stroke earlier that month.

Sources

➤ **On-line**

A&E Biography, http://www.biography.com (August 4, 1997).

➤ **Books**

Doolittle, James H. and Carroll V. Glines, *I Could Never Be So Lucky Again: The Memoirs of General James H. "Jimmy" Doolittle,* Bantam, 1991.
Glines, Carroll V., *Jimmy Doolittle, Daredevil Aviator and Scientist,* 1972.
Thomas, Lowell and Edward Jablonski, *Doolittle: A Biography,* Doubleday, 1976.

➤ **Periodicals**

National Review, November 1, 1993, p. 19.
People, October 11, 1993, p. 86 (opening quote).
Smithsonian, June 1992, p.112.
Tribune Books (Chicago), December 1, 1991, p. 4.

Will and Ariel Durant

"*We aim not so much to personalize history as to humanize it . . . .*"

Will Durant, born on November 5, 1885, in North Adams, Massachusetts, and his wife, Ariel Durant, who was born on May 10, 1898, in Proskurov, Russia, collaborated on one of the twentieth century's most ambitious projects, a multivolume history of the Western world. Married for 68 years, they died within two weeks of one another in late 1981.

Will and Ariel Durant devoted much of their married life to their epic series, *The Story of Civilization,* an 11-volume opus published between 1935 and 1975. A well-known philosopher and author before he began the project, Will Durant was a liberal-thinking intellectual like his wife, a Russian Jewish émigré. Ariel Durant assisted her husband in the research and organization process, but came to receive full author credit with the last five volumes. Together they shared the 1968 Pulitzer Prize for *Rousseau and Revolution,* the tenth installment in the series.

Born in North Adams, Massachusetts on November 5, 1885, William James Durant was the son of a chemical plant manager and raised in a devout Roman Catholic family of French-Canadian heritage. Given his intelligence, academic achievements, and piety, it was expected that he would enter the priesthood, but as he wrote in his 1927 autobiography, *Transition,* by the time he entered college, he was already an atheist as a result of his extensive reading from the shelves of philosophy, science, and other religions. "I continued to go to church, to confession and communion; I left no stone unturned, nor any lie untold, to conceal from my parents the loss of my theological innocence," Durant wrote.

Durant earned a degree from St. Peter's College in Jersey City, New Jersey, in 1907, and obtained a summer job as a newspaper reporter in New York City. Covering crime and the other by-products of urban poverty reinforced in him a growing belief in socialism, but he entered a seminary school for the priesthood that fall despite his misgivings. He spent a year and half at Seton Hall College, wracked with doubts still, and continued to read the "heretical" books that had led him to a new way of thinking—English philosopher Herbert Spencer, evolutionist Charles Darwin, and Dutch Jew Baruch Spinoza. Finally his superior, Monsignor Mooney, offered Durant a lay teaching position, which he accepted.

By 1911, Durant had begun teaching at the progressive Ferrer Modern School after becoming increasingly involved in radical currents then generating in and around New York's Lower East Side. The following year, his family read in the newspaper one day that the local bishop—the former Monsignor Mooney—had excommunicated Durant for a lecture in which he equated the origin of religion with sexual worship; his parents threw him out of the house, and he moved to a room over a saloon on West 19th Street in New York City. His name was also removed from the list of graduates from the college for more than two decades, and allegedly the Monsignor locked the library of the college, lest any other seminarian ever be tempted by unorthodox reading.

Around 1913, Durant met his future wife, a student of his, born Chaya Kaufman in Proskurov, Russia just 15 years earlier. Despite the 12-year age difference, the pair quickly fell in love and were married on Halloween of that year. Kaufman—who was soon nicknamed "Ariel" by her husband for her irrepressible energy after the Shakespearean sprite—had grown up in poverty in both the Ukraine and on the teeming tenement streets of New York. Economic hardships and pogroms (mass lynchings of Jewish people) had caused her father to emigrate first, leaving Ariel and her siblings behind with their mother, who grew tired of waiting for the promised money to join him. When she was just two, she and her family sailed to Liverpool first, but Ariel's contagious eye ailment, which had temporarily blinded her, caused her mother and siblings to be plucked off the ship for quarantine, while all their worldly possessions sailed on to New York without them. They eventually arrived in New York, and both parents eked out a meager living as newspaper vendors. Her mother grew increasingly dissatisfied with her lot in life, and became involved in the growing anarchist movement. She even moved out of her husband's home, and Ariel followed. It was during this time that she transferred from the chaos of the New York City public schools to the anarchist-inspired progressivism of the Ferrer School.

Though the Kaufman parents reminded their daughter that Durant was a Christian, and thus belonged to the same religion of those who murdered Jews back in the Ukraine, they gave their permission for the wedding. Will Durant entered the graduate program of Columbia University, while they lived an impoverished existence on Staten Island. After earning his Ph.D. in 1917, he became an instructor in philosophy at Columbia and published his first book, *Philosophy and the Social Problem*. From 1919 to 1926, the couple lived in Greenwich Village, where their daughter Ethel was born, and where Ariel Durant operated a tea room for several years. Increasing fame for her husband meant lecture tours that took him on long, cross-country train trips, and their marriage suffered during these separations. While in New York, however, Will Durant was jealous of his wife's thriving business, and the poets and artists whose work she sponsored; both suspected one another of extramarital dalliances.

After 1928, the Durants settled in a large, comfortable home in Great Neck, Long Island—financed in part by the success of his 1926 book, *The Story of Philosophy*—and came to a final disillusionment with their earlier socialist beliefs when they made a trip to Soviet Russia in 1932. By this point Will Durant had begun the exhaustive research for his proposed *Story of Civilization,* and his wife eventually gave up her Gypsy Tavern to assist him in his work. He hoped to write a work that would resonate with a general readership, not one aimed at the scholarly community.

Ariel Durant later noted that the organization of the source material for the project was more of a task than its gathering, which took two years: Durant had created an outline with hundreds of headings, splitting the first volume into geographic sections, then dividing into topics that included the government, arts, religion, and philosophy of each region. He handed out to his family, which now included a nephew they had adopted, Louis, his assembled research of 30,000 slips of paper. They were charged with the task of reading each slip and assigning it a Roman numeral notation corresponding with the outline. These were then arranged in shoeboxes by chapter. "We handed over them over to 'the Master,' and bade him turn them into a book," Ariel Durant wrote in *A Dual Autobiography.*

The first volume, titled *Our Oriental Heritage* and dedicated to Ariel, was published in July of 1935 to generally positive reviews. Some historians faulted the author, however, for factual errors, and warned of the inadvisability of tackling such an ambitious project—sixty centuries of Eurocentric history—for a popular audience. This and subsequent volumes issued every few years—*Caesar and Christ, The Age of Faith,* and *The Renaissance,* among several others, often became bestsellers and were a bookshelf staple in educated homes not just in America, as the volumes began appearing in foreign translation as well. Will Durant, wrote *Saturday Review* critic Garrett Mattingly, "parades the pageant of history before his readers with the gusto of a museum director exhibiting his treasures, and he comments on the sins and the scandals, the splendors and the terrors of his exhibits with a gentle wit and amused tolerance which is at once intimate and reassuring."

The Durants had relocated to Southern California during the 1940s, and continued to collaborate on the *Story of Civilization.* For volume 4, *The Age of Faith,* Ariel Durant had begun to conduct much of the research herself, for her husband was now in his seventies. With the 1961 publication of volume 7, *The Age of Reason Begins,* Ariel Durant began to receive joint author credit with her husband. That same year, the series began to be offered as a Book-of-the-Month club selection, which brought a financial windfall to the

Durants in royalty checks. They traveled extensively, and kept company with numerous other writers, philosophers, and contemporary luminaries.

Scholarly historians, however, continued to write scathing reviews of the volumes, faulting factual errors, use of biased sources, and lack of analysis. They were also criticized for injecting anecdotal passages in an attempt to portray events of the times. Will Durant defended one particularly sharp review in the *New York Times Book Review* with a rebuttal that read, in part: "History operates in events but through persons; these are the voice of events, the flesh and blood upon which events fall; and their human responses and feelings are also history. We aim not so much to personalize history as to humanize it . . . ."

Later volumes found more acceptance with the academic establishment, and even began appearing on required-reading lists for some college curricula. "We want to make history meaningful for ordinary readers," Will Durant explained later in a 1981 interview with John F. Baker in *Publishers Weekly.* "We need specialists who devote their time to research, and who work from first-hand materials, sure, but I reject the notion that only university professors can write history. There's room for an integral view, which looks at every aspect of an age—its art, its manners and morals, its philosophy, even its architecture—and shows how they all interrelate. That's how history works—it's not all in separate compartments."

The Durants' tenth volume, *Rousseau and Revolution,* received positive accolades from reviewers, and was awarded the 1968 Pulitzer Prize for general nonfiction. By this point the Durants had actually finished the manuscripts for the subsequent volumes in the series, which concluded with the 1975 title *The Age of Napoleon,* and began working on other literary projects. These included *The Lessons of History,* published in 1968, and *Interpretations of Life,* which followed two years later. The latter volume featured sketches on numerous luminaries from the world of literature, such as William Faulkner, Eugene O'Neill, and T. S. Eliot.

The Durants, who lived in Hollywood Hills for many years, were both awarded the Medal of Freedom from President Gerald R. Ford in 1977. After an earlier stroke, Ariel Durant died at home on October 25, 1981. Her husband, by then 95 years old and recovering from surgery in the hospital, was not told of her death. He died less than two weeks later.

Sources

➤ Books

American Women Writers: A Critical Reference Guide from Colonial Times to the Present, edited by Lina Maineiro, Ungar, 1979.

Durant, Will, *Transition: A Sentimental Story of One Mind and One Era,* Simon & Schuster, 1927.

Durant, Will and Ariel, *A Dual Autobiography,* Simon & Schuster, 1977.

➤ Periodicals

Publishers Weekly, November 20, 1981.

New York Times, October 28, 1981, p. B4; December 8, 1985.

New York Times Book Review, October 6, 1963 (opening quote).

Saturday Review, December 7, 1956.

Dwight D. Eisenhower

"All my life I have said what I meant, and meant what I said. No one will change that. All my life I had a deep and fundamental faith in my country, in its people, in its principles and in its spiritual value. No one will change that."

Born October 14, 1890, Dwight D. Eisenhower was an Allied military leader during World War II who went on to become the thirty-fourth president of the United States. He died on March 28, 1969, in Washington, D.C.

D wight D. Eisenhower served the United States in two important capacities around the middle of the twentieth century.
As a career military officer, he was a key leader in the Allies'
victory over the Axis powers in World War II. When he later became
the thirty-fourth president of the United States, he promoted world
peace from the perspective of a man who was very familiar with the
consequences of war. Eisenhower persevered in both careers despite setbacks that might have left others discouraged and dispirited.

Dwight David Eisenhower was born on October 14, 1890, in
Denison, Texas, the son of David Jacob and Ida Elizabeth Stover
Eisenhower. The third of seven sons, he was originally named
David Dwight, but his parents soon reversed the order to avoid
confusion with his father. David Eisenhower had moved his family
from Kansas to Texas to take a job on the railroad. But life still was a
struggle financially for the Eisenhowers in their new home, and
before long they headed back to Kansas. They settled in Abilene,
and it was there that Dwight Eisenhower spent the rest of his youth.
Even though his father found steady work at a local creamery, he
grew up in impoverished circumstances.

Abilene was a small, isolated, rural community that shaped
Eisenhower's outlook for the rest of his life. "Our pleasures were
simple—they included survival," Hugh Sidey of *Time* once recalled
him as saying. The Eisenhowers belonged to the River Brethren
Church, and religion was a prominent part of their daily lives.
David Eisenhower was very strict, and his wife was very devout.
Consequently, their son learned self-discipline and self-control at an
early age. He later said that he carried the lessons of his childhood
throughout his military and political careers.

As a youth, Eisenhower enjoyed many sports, including football
and baseball. He also liked camping and being outdoors. He enjoyed fighting, too, though it was forbidden by his religion. Additionally, Eisenhower was a good student whose favorite subject was
history. But sports were ultimately more important to the young
Eisenhower than academics, and they allowed him to indulge his
increasingly competitive nature.

After graduating from Abilene High School in 1909, Eisenhower
spent two years working at the creamery with his father. He wanted
to go to college but could not afford the tuition and fees. He then
made a deal with one of his brothers to help him earn his degree
with the understanding that his brother would return the favor. But
Eisenhower backed out of this arrangement when he learned he
could obtain a free college education through the military. Al-

though he wanted to attend the Naval Academy, he took an entrance exam that was designed for both the Naval Academy and the U.S. Military Academy at West Point. As it turned out, the Naval Academy did not want him, but West Point did. Eisenhower began his studies there in 1911.

At West Point, Eisenhower found it difficult to adjust to the orders and other demands of a cadet's life. In contrast to his experience in high school, he was a relatively mediocre student. He was still enthusiastic about sports, however, and managed to secure a spot on the football team. After he hurt his knee during the 1912 season and had to give up the game, he remained active by becoming a cheerleader.

When Eisenhower graduated in 1915, he ranked just sixty-first in a class of 164. He then received a commission as a second lieutenant in the infantry. While stationed at Fort Sam Houston in Texas, he met Mamie Doud, a socialite from Denver. They married on July 1, 1916, and eventually had two sons, one of whom—Doud—died of scarlet fever as a toddler. The other, John, survived to adulthood.

In 1917 America entered World War I, and Eisenhower hoped for a combat command in Europe. Instead he remained in the United States and was put in charge of instructing troops at a series of training camps. One of his stints was at Camp Colt, where he systematized the training of tank troops. A month before the war ended, Eisenhower was given his long-awaited European command, but by then he was no longer needed overseas.

Such disappointment was typical of Eisenhower's military career for many years. During the 1920s and 1930s, he developed a reputation as a solid staff officer through numerous successful assignments. Meanwhile, he also studied military science, graduating first in his class from the U.S. Army's Command and General Staff School and then completing additional course work at the Army War College in 1929 and the Army Industrial College in 1932. Eisenhower was eager to assume combat and troop command positions, but his demonstrated skills in office administration pigeon-holed him. So instead of heading out into the field, he became a senior aide to General Douglas MacArthur in 1932. Within three years, Eisenhower was working as MacArthur's assistant military advisor for the Philippine Commonwealth, a position he held until 1939.

By 1940, Eisenhower had only reached the rank of lieutenant colonel, and he feared the Army might force him to retire. While he was held in great esteem by his superiors, he was not sure if he would ever fulfill his own personal goals. However, he finally was given the opportunity to be a field commander that year for a brief period and proved himself able on the battlefield.

Eisenhower's chance to excel in a combat situation finally came during World War II. After the United States entered the conflict in December 1941, he was put in charge of the War Plans Division (later known as the Operations Division) of the War Department in Washington, D.C. At first he was consulted on policies and strategies for the Pacific theater based on his experience in the Philippines. He also had a hand in formulating larger strategies, including suggesting that it would be best for American forces to take the offensive in Europe and Africa while maintaining a defensive front in the Pacific. Soon he was promoted to one-star general.

One hallmark of Eisenhower's leadership abilities was already in evidence at this point in his career—he took responsibility for his decisions, no matter what the outcome. This quality garnered him tremendous respect among those who served with him and would become even more important as Eisenhower took on a larger role in the war effort. By 1942, he was in charge of all U.S. forces based in Great Britain.

Within a short time, Eisenhower was promoted to lieutenant general and put in charge of the joint operation between Great Britain and the United States to invade North Africa. Though Eisenhower's military decisions were somewhat controversial, most notably during the attempt to retake land in the area in November 1942, they helped the Allies conquer North Africa by the spring of 1943. Eisenhower then led Allied troops in a successful invasion of Sicily later that same year.

Eisenhower was soon rewarded with two promotions. First, he was made a four-star general, and in late 1943 he became the supreme commander of Operation Overlord, the code name given to a massive Allied operation aimed at liberating France from Nazi occupation. A skilled strategist, Eisenhower planned the invasion and supervised its launch on D-Day, June 6, 1944.

Just before Operation Overlord got under way, Eisenhower wrote a statement accepting full responsibility for the invasion in the event it failed. It was a success, however, and proved to be a key turning point in the war. It also cemented his popularity in the United States. As the Allies battled to reclaim Europe throughout the rest of 1944 and well into 1945, Eisenhower presided over events with uncommon cheerfulness, grace, and diplomacy. As Sidey of *Time* observed, "In war, Ike's magic was to inspire foot soldiers and generals alike, blending English lords with plain Americans . . . ."

Eisenhower was promoted to five-star general in 1944 as his troops headed for Germany. His strategy was used to defeat the Nazis at the Battle of the Bulge. Yet he was criticized for some of his decisions, such as declining to take Berlin at the very end of the war. The consequences of this decision became apparent later on during the Cold War, the decades-long standoff between the United States and the Soviet Union. But such mistakes did not diminish Eisenhower's contribution to changing the course of the war in Europe and bringing it to an end.

Eisenhower returned home in 1945 and was named the U.S. Army's chief of staff. He was not happy in the position, however, and retired from the military in 1948. He then wrote a book about his experiences during World War II entitled *Crusade in Europe* (1948). It was one of the most popular publications of its time, and its success provided him with a lifetime of financial security.

When Eisenhower left the service, many hoped he would run for president of the United States. He chose instead to serve as the president of Columbia University from 1948 until 1950. Eisenhower returned to his military roots in 1951 when President Harry S. Truman named him the supreme commander of Allied forces in Europe. This group was the forerunner of the North Atlantic Treaty Organization (NATO).

By 1952, Eisenhower's supporters had finally convinced him to run for president. Declaring himself a Republican, he won the election that year and again in 1956. He thus served two full terms, making him the first Republican to do so since Ulysses S. Grant in the late 1860s and early 1870s. A political moderate, he balanced the ticket with the more conservative and much younger Richard M. Nixon. Once in office, however, Eisenhower faced an uphill battle because the Democrats controlled Congress for six of his eight years as president.

Foreign policy was especially important to Eisenhower. In addition to ending the Korean War—albeit in a stalemate—he worked towards achieving peace with the Soviet Union. Though he met with Soviet leaders in 1955, he accomplished little in the Cold War atmosphere of the day. Nevertheless, he tried to keep the United States out of direct military conflicts while maintaining the nation's place in the world order. Though he was the first to involve the

United States in the civil war in Vietnam (an involvement that increased substantially under his successors), Eisenhower generally supported the right of other countries to self-rule.

On the domestic front, Eisenhower worked behind the scenes to derail Republican Senator Joseph McCarthy's efforts to expose alleged Communist sympathizers in the U.S. Department of State and the U.S. Army. Policy-wise, he continued President Franklin D. Roosevelt's New Deal in some areas, including expanding the social security program. He also approved the Federal Aid Highway Act of 1956, which created the interstate highway system. In 1960 Eisenhower established the National Aeronautics and Space Administration (NASA) as a response to the Soviet Union's 1957 launch of Sputnik, the first man-made space satellite.

When Eisenhower appointed Earl Warren to the U.S. Supreme Court, he did not know what a profound effect his choice would have on the racial climate in America. Warren was a key figure in the famous *Brown v. Board of Education* decision in 1954 that ended segregation in public schools. Though Eisenhower believed in segregation, he upheld and enforced the Court's decision. He also signed into law a somewhat weak civil rights act that dealt primarily with voting rights. Yet Eisenhower was the first president to hire African Americans to fill significant roles in his administration, including Ernest Wilkins as the assistant secretary of labor.

Eisenhower left office in 1961, and he and his wife then retired to homes in Gettysburg, Pennsylvania, and Palm Desert, California. He spent his time playing golf and writing three books of memoirs, *Mandate for Change* (1963), *Waging Peace: The White House Years* (1964), and *At Ease: Stories I Tell My Friends* (1967).

Eisenhower had a history of heart problems and even suffered a major heart attack while serving as president in 1955. He had several more heart attacks in 1968 before dying from congestive heart failure on March 28, 1969, in Washington, D.C., at Walter Reed Army Hospital. He was buried in Abilene, Kansas, near his library and memorial, the Eisenhower Center.

When Eisenhower left office in 1961, some observers judged him to be a weak president despite the strong economy, low inflation, and balanced budget. In the years since his death, however, historians have come to recognize him as one of the best presidents and world leaders the United States ever produced for his accomplishments on the battlefield and in the White House.

Sources

➤ Books

Commire, Anne, editor, *Historic World Leaders: North and South America,* Volume 4, Gale, 1994, pp. 250-55.

Encyclopedia of World Biography, 2nd edition, Volume 5, Gale, 1998, pp. 233-36.

Garraty, John A. and Mark C. Carnes, editors, *American National Biography,* Volume 7, Oxford University Press, 1999, pp. 374-79.

Garraty, John A. and Jerome L. Sternstein, editors, *Encyclopedia of American Biography,* 2nd edition, HarperCollins, 1998, pp. 339-41.

Gollagher, Elsie, editor, *The Quotable Dwight D. Eisenhower,* Droke House, 1967 (opening quote).

Magill, Frank N., editor, *Great Lives from History: American Series,* Volume 2, Salem Press, 1997, pp. 741-46.

Whitney, David C., *The American Presidents,* 7th edition, Prentice-Hall, 1990, pp. 291-301.

➤ Periodicals

American Heritage, December 1985, p. 49.

American Visions, February-March 1995, p. 36.

Forbes, June 2, 1997, p. S68.

Saturday Evening Post, November-December 1990, p. 86.

Time, October 29, 1990, p. 45; June 6, 1994, p. 36.

U.S. News & World Report, October 15, 1990, p. 65; March 16, 1998, p. 59.

Fang Lizhi

*"*P*eople got very excited when I told them there was total scientific freedom in the West. I got openly involved in the human rights movement. Even though I was a Party member, in one speech I dared to say that Marxism, at least in respect to science, was dated. No one had ever said that before, and it had a very strong impact on the intellectual community."*

Born on February 12, 1936, in Hangzhou, China, Fang Lizhi was an outspoken advocate for human rights and intellectual freedom in the midst of China's oppressive political climate. He was expelled from the Chinese Communist Party—twice— and exiled to the United States after the 1989 Tiananmen Square massacre. Address: Physics Dept., PAS Rm. 420D, The University of Arizona, Tucson, AZ 85721.

Fang Lizhi is an astrophysicist and political dissident who has spent most of his career in mainland China. Trained as a solid-state physicist, he later became involved in cosmology, a branch of astronomy concerned with space and time theory. In 1972 he published a paper on the big bang theory, previously a forbidden topic in China. An outspoken advocate for human rights and intellectual freedom since his days as a student, Lizhi sought political asylum at the United States Embassy after the 1989 Tiananmen Square massacre in Beijing, China. He relocated to the United States in 1990 and joined the Institute for Advanced Study in Princeton, New Jersey. In 1992, he became an associate professor of physics at the University of Arizona.

The son of a postal clerk, Fang Lizhi was born on February 12, 1936, in Hangzhou, China, to Fang Chengpu and Shi Peiji. Lizhi grew up in a politically unstable era in China, as power shifted from Japanese control first to the Nationalists and then to the Communists. At sixteen, Lizhi entered Beijing University to study theoretical and nuclear physics. He gained membership in the elite Chinese Communist Party (CCP) before graduating with highest distinction in 1956. He did graduate work in nuclear reactor theory at the Institute of Modern Physics Research.

But his academic success did not stop him from speaking out, and he called for democracy and freedom of expression while still a student. With Mao Zedong as China's leader, Marxist ideology pervaded politics, culture, and even science. Lizhi objected to the oppressive Marxist influence on physics, and in 1956 when Mao invited commentary from intellectuals, Lizhi promptly called for educational reform and academic freedom. After many academics had spoken their minds, thousands were imprisoned in labor camps; Lizhi was expelled from the CCP, but he was still allowed to help organize a new physics department at the University of Science and Technology (Keda) in Beijing. He taught electromagnetics and quantum mechanics and studied solid-state and laser physics. Lizhi married physicist Li Shuxian in 1961; the couple has two sons.

During China's Cultural Revolution (1966-1976), Mao sought to purge society of Western and traditional Chinese influences. Many intellectuals were punished for their beliefs, and in 1966 Lizhi endured a year of solitary confinement. He was then sent to Anhui Province to work in the mines and on the railroad until 1969. During this time he read Lev Landau's *Classical Theory of Fields* which led him to abandon solid-state physics for cosmology. In 1969, Lizhi was sent to teach astrophysics at a new branch of Keda in Hefei; he began writing again while he was there, but his articles were published under a pseudonym because of the political climate.

At the time Lizhi began studying astrophysics, publications about cosmology had been forbidden by the CCP. This prohibition, in place since 1949, was lifted in 1972, and Lizhi and others published an article on the big bang theory. The article was immediately condemned by the Communists because it contradicted the Marxist claim that the universe was infinite, but Lizhi and his colleagues were not punished. He continued his work throughout the 1970s in a gradually improving academic and political climate. In 1978, he was readmitted to the CCP and he won China's National Award for Science and Technology. At Keda he became the university's youngest full professor. He was allowed to travel and spent six months at Cambridge University in England. In 1985 he won the International Gravity Foundation Prize in the United States for a paper he had written with Humitako Sato on quasars and the history of the universe. Lizhi spent part of 1986 at Princeton's Institute for Advanced Study.

Lizhi has spent much of his career in astrophysics conducting theoretical research on the shape of the universe. He has been particularly concerned with topology, a mathematical discipline concerned with geometric point sets. Lizhi has likened cosmology to archaeology, because it reconstructs the history of the universe from physical evidence such as light that has been traveling for millions of years, cosmic background radiation, and the relationship between matter and antimatter. Lizhi has used topology to speculate on the shape the universe might have taken in the first fraction of a second after the big bang. His question is, as Hans Christian von Baeyer put it in *The Sciences*, whether the universe is "a ball or a doughnut," and his theoretical work in this area could help improve the scientific understanding of the future as well as the history of the universe in particular, whether the universe will continue to expand or whether gravity will eventually begin to pull it back together again.

Despite offers from many foreign universities and research institutions, Lizhi remained in China throughout the 1980s out of a strong sense of obligation. In 1984 Lizhi was appointed vice president of Keda. Lizhi and Guan Weiyan, Keda's president, drafted a plan to increase the power of the faculty and to foster freedom of speech on campus. They invited foreign visitors and encouraged students to study abroad, which was then consistent with national policy. Lizhi began to campaign throughout China for freedom of expression, but in 1986 a student campaign for democratic reforms turned into a series of large demonstrations in Beijing. Though they had actually discouraged the marches, Lizhi and Weiyan were blamed by the CCP for the activities. Lizhi was reassigned to a research position at the Beijing Observatory and in 1987 he was again expelled from the party.

Because of his long-standing role in encouraging democracy and promoting human rights, Lizhi was revered by the intellectual community in China. Although he played no role in the student demonstrations in Beijing's Tiananmen Square in 1989 and made no statements in support of them, the CCP considered Lizhi one of the perpetrators. On June 5, 1989, the day after troops massacred students in Tiananmen Square, Lizhi and his wife sought refuge in the United States Embassy in Beijing. They remained there for thirteen months, receiving permission to leave the country only after intense diplomatic pressure from the United States. In the summer of 1990 he was a visiting researcher at Cambridge University, where his family joined him, and he then accepted a position at the Institute for Advanced Study.

In 1991, Lizhi published in English an anthology of political and philosophical essays. The University of Arizona hired him as associate professor of physics in 1992. Maintaining his loyalty to China, Lizhi has expressed hope for progress in human rights there. Although he was a passionate spokesperson for greater political and personal freedom, he considered his role not that of a politician but that of a scientist and a person of conscience. In addition to his other honors, Lizhi received the Robert F. Kennedy Memorial Human Rights Award in 1989.

Sources

➤ Books

Newsmakers, Gale Research, 1988.

➤ Periodicals

China Quarterly, September, 1990, pp. 459-484.
New Scientist, July 21, 1990, p. 19.
Popular Science, August, 1996, p. 62 (opening quote).
The Sciences, March/April, 1991, pp. 10-12.
Time, August 20, 1990, pp. 12-15.

James Farmer

"R_eading scores don't respond to freedom march-_
es and income gaps don't respond to sit-ins.
That's why we must find new programs."

James Farmer, born on January 12, 1920, in Marshall, Texas, was one of the leaders of the civil rights movement during the 1960s. The original founder of the Congress of Racial Equality (CORE), he organized the historic 1961 Freedom Rides. He died on July 9, 1999, in Fredericksburg, Virginia.

One of the leading figures in the movement to end segregation in the United States, James Farmer founded the Congress of Racial Equality in 1942. As national director of this integral body during the 1960s, he was one of the "Big Four" in the civil rights struggle which included Martin Luther King, Jr. of the Southern Christian Leadership Conference, Whitney Young of the Urban League, and Roy Wilkins of the National Association for the Advancement of Colored People (NAACP). Dedicated to nonviolent protests, Farmer pioneered the tactic of the "sit-in" and also organized the famous Freedom Rides of 1961. His efforts earned him several awards during his lifetime, including the American Humanist Award in 1969 and the Presidential Medal of Freedom in 1998. He was also one of the first African Americans appointed to a high-ranking government post, and went on to write several books. His legacy rests on his participation in effecting major social changes in civil rights during his heyday, including desegregation and voting rights for blacks.

Born on January 12, 1920, Farmer was the son of James Leonard Farmer Sr. and Pearl Marion (Houston) Farmer. His father, a preacher, was thought to be the first African American in Texas to earn a doctorate. He received his degree at Boston University and could read, write, and speak French, German, Aramaic, Hebrew, Greek, and Latin. He taught theology and philosophy at various black colleges in the South, including Wiley College in Marshall, Texas, where Farmer was born. The family moved to Holly Springs, Mississippi, when he was six months old, where his father taught at Rust College, and lived in several other places before his father returned to Wiley College when Farmer was 13. His mother was formerly a teacher as well, before becoming a homemaker.

When Farmer was a toddler, he yearned to go to school like his sister, Helen, 17 months his senior. A quick learner, he could read, write, and count by the age of four, when he entered first grade. Before long, it was discovered that he was too advanced even for that level, so he was soon moved up to second grade with his sister, much to her chagrin. When Farmer was almost eight, his brother Nathaniel was born. Growing up in the confines of black academia, the family was rather sheltered from oppression, but it still cropped up at times and angered the young Farmer. When he was three, thirsty on a hot day, his mother explained that blacks were not allowed into certain stores to buy soft drinks. At other times, he saw his father, a distinguished and learned man, humiliated by racist whites.

At age 14, Farmer entered Wiley College, where his father was working as a professor and campus chaplain, on a full scholarship. A mostly "A" student, his instructors recognized his potential and challenged him even more. He was also inspired by his extracurricular activities on the debate team, drama league, and chemistry club, and was named class president his senior year. Despite his accomplishments, Farmer by this time was becoming more cognizant of the pervasive segregation that refused him service at restaurants and relegated him to the back entrance and balcony of the local cinema.

His activist spirit awakened, Farmer began to ponder his direction. Planning to become a doctor, he received a bachelor's degree in chemistry in 1938, but when he realized he became ill at the sight of blood, he searched for a new occupation. He went on to Howard University, where his father had accepted a job at the school of religion. Farmer decided to study for the ministry as well, planning to eventually become involved with the civil rights movement. Several of the best scholars of the time were on the faculty at Howard, including Ralph Bunche in political science, Carter G. Woodson in history, and Howard Thurman, professor of religion and Farmer's mentor. Through Thurman, he learned of the nonviolent protests of Mohandas Gandhi, who led the push for India's independence from Britain. Also during this time, Farmer was exposed to socialist thought by V. F. Calverton.

Farmer became conflicted about religion during his studies and wrote his graduate thesis on the relationship between racism and religion. Upon receiving his degree in divinity in 1941, he declined to be ordained as a minister. A conscientious objector during World War II because of his belief that war is immoral and also on the grounds that the military was segregated, he had gotten involved with the pacifist group Fellowship of Reconciliation (FOR) as a race relations secretary while in school. Afterward, he decided to continue working with them full-time in order to fight segregation, first in Chicago, then in New York City beginning in 1943. In 1945, he became an organizer for the Upholsterers International Union, and later worked as a representative for the American Federation of State, County, and Municipal Employees (AFSCME).

Meanwhile, in 1942, Farmer established an arm of FOR called the Committee of Racial Equality (CORE), later changed to Congress of Racial Equality. This group held the first "sit-in" at a restaurant in his neighborhood. When the eatery refused to serve Farmer, who went to have coffee with a white friend, they responded by amassing about 25 supporters, black and white, who returned and sat down at dinnertime. The whites were served without incident but the management told the African Americans that they would have to eat in the basement. The white people refused to eat, explaining that it would not be polite to start without their black friends. The manager called police, but the anti-discrimination laws were on the side of CORE, and the restaurant eventually served all of the patrons.

After this, CORE gained a national reputation for its nonviolent protests and by 1944 separated from FOR. Farmer acted as its unpaid national chairman, but his involvement was sporadic due to his obligations to his other paid union positions. Along with much of the civil rights movement, CORE's profile stayed low until the bus boycotts of 1956 in Montgomery, Alabama. Using his expertise in nonviolent tactics, in 1959 Farmer joined the NAACP to help with direct action programs. Soon, CORE was called to the front lines as sit-ins and other actions proliferated in the South, when students began to rally against segregation of lunch counters, schools, and other venues.

In 1961, CORE offered Farmer the paid post of national director. Soon after that, he launched one of his biggest initiatives, the Freedom Rides. Intrastate busing had been officially desegregated, but discrimination was still rampant on interstate lines in the South, so on May 4, 1961, Farmer and others set out from Washington, D.C. to challenge the practice of making blacks sit in rear seats and congregate in separate waiting rooms. They passed through Virginia, North and South Carolina, and Georgia, without incident, when Farmer got word that his father died. After he left the group, several riders were severely beaten in Alabama and the bus was firebombed. The resulting news coverage stirred much sympathy for the cause. As Farmer related in his autobiography, *Lay Bare the Heart*, "A common greeting among both whites and blacks had become, 'Hi. Got your bus ticket?'" Later, Farmer rejoined the riders, and most of them were arrested in Mississippi and jailed. Subsequently, U.S. Attorney General Robert Kennedy ordered the Interstate Commerce Commission to end bus segregation.

Tensions in race relations did not simmer down after this, however, and Farmer, as well as other black leaders, remained targets for violence. He and his family regularly received death threats. Meanwhile, a number of activist groups, including CORE, the NAACP, the Urban League, and others organized the historic 1963 March on Washington for Jobs and Freedom. Farmer was in jail at the time after being arrested while leading a march in Plaquemine, Louisiana. Once he was released, local youngsters organized another protest, but a backlash from law enforcement resulted in a violent melee. This, in turn, sparked more protests, during which blacks were beaten, poked with cattle prods, and tear-gassed. Farmer became a prime target for the police, and ended up sneaking out of town while hidden in a coffin in the back of a hearse. He observed in *Lay Bare the Heart*, "If any man says that he had no fear in the action of the sixties, he is a liar. Or without imagination."

By the mid-1960s, dissension within the ranks of the civil rights movement threatened its power. Some were growing impatient with nonviolent tactics, and the effort was plagued with infighting among different organizations and factions within the various groups. The assassinations of Malcolm X in 1965 and Martin Luther King Jr. in 1968 sent successive shock waves through the movement. Farmer resigned from CORE in 1966 and began to reap funds from his appearances on the lecture circuit (he had previously donated his fees to CORE), as well as holding a part-time position as professor of social welfare at Lincoln University, a black institution outside Philadelphia. He had also written his first book, *Freedom—When?*, in 1965.

In addition to teaching, Farmer formed and headed a literacy group for a time. In 1968 he ran for Congress on the Liberal party slate and received endorsement from the Republican party, but was defeated by a black woman, Shirley Chisholm. Subsequently, in 1969 he was appointed assistant secretary for administration in the Department of Health, Education and Welfare under President Richard Nixon, where he worked on affirmative action policies for the department. Weary of the bureaucracy, though, he resigned in December of 1970. Later, he joined a lobbying group with AFSCME. Throughout his life, he worked to improve conditions for blacks, realizing that although the heyday of the civil rights struggle had passed, problems continued. As he noted in a 1973 *Ebony* article, "Reading scores don't respond to freedom marches and income gaps don't respond to sit-ins. That's why we must find new programs."

In 1945, Farmer married Winnie Christie, but they divorced in 1946. He was then married in 1949 to Lula A. Peterson, and they had two daughters, Tami and Abbey. This mixed marriage drew criticism from both sides, but endured, even through this strain and Peterson's many health troubles—she was diagnosed with Hodgkin's disease even before the wedding. She died in 1977, and Farmer in

1979 began suffering from an eye ailment that eventually left him blind. He was also later in his life confined to a wheelchair. Despite his health problems, Farmer wrote several books on labor and race issues in addition to his enthusiastically received 1985 autobiography, and had lectured at Mary Washington College in Fredericksburg, Virginia, starting in 1984, as a living legend of the civil rights movement. He died on July 9, 1999, at age 79 at Mary Washington Hospital.

Sources

➤ Books

Contemporary Black Biography, volume 2, Gale Research, 1992.
Encyclopedia of World Biography, second edition, Gale Research, 1998.
Farmer, James, *Lay Bare the Heart: An Autobiography of the Civil Rights Movement,* Arbor House, 1985.
Notable Black American Men, Gale Research, 1998.

➤ Periodicals

Ebony, December 1973, p. 178 (opening quote).
Newsweek, January 10, 1966, p. 22.
New York Times, July 10, 1999, p. A1.
Washington Post, July 10, 1999, p. A1.

William Faulkner

*"*I*t is [the writer's] privilege to help man endure by lifting his heart, by reminding him of the courage and honor and hope and pride and compassion and pity and sacrifice which have been the glory of his past. The poet's voice need not merely be the record of man, it can be one of the props, the pillars, to help him endure and prevail.''*

Born September 25, 1897, in New Albany, Mississippi, William Cuthbert Faulkner (ne Falkner) came to be regarded as one of America's greatest and most prolific novelists. Inspired by and having written mostly about the South, he died in Byhalia, Mississippi on July 6, 1962.

Wiilliam Faulkner is considered one of the greatest American writers of the twentieth century. He spent most of his literary career in the South, which both inspired and informed his fiction. Faulkner chronicled the decline and decay of the aristocratic South with an imaginative power and psychological depth that transcends mere regionalism.

William Faulkner was born into a respected Southern family that played into Mississippi's history. Faulkner's great-grandfather and namesake, William Clark Falkner (Faulkner added the "u" to his last name later), had served with the Confederate Army, had been involved in the development of the American railroad, and had written a popular Southern novel, entitled *The White Rose of Memphis.*

A bright and precocious child, Faulkner was described by his family as a gifted storyteller, even as a very young child, so much so that it was difficult for even an adult to discern whether what young Faulkner was describing was an actual event that had taken place or a made-up plot he had hatched in his creative mind. He was a strong student as a younger child, but as he approached adolescence he scored increasingly poor marks. Bored with school, Faulkner was frequently truant and quit school in December of 1914. He returned to school the following fall so that he could play football, but when he was inflicted with a nose injury he quit school again, this time for good. During the winter of 1916, Faulkner worked briefly as a clerk at his grandfather's bank, First National Bank. During the same period, he frequented the campus of the University of Mississippi ("Ole Miss"), and befriended writers and intellectuals there. He wrote poetry and even contributed some of his drawings to the Ole Miss yearbook.

When the United States declared war against Germany, Faulkner tried to enlist, but was rejected due to his small stature (he stood only five feet five inches). He then traveled north to New Haven, Connecticut, to visit his friend, Phil Stone, a Yale-educated man Faulkner had come to know during his teens and who had served as a mentor for Faulkner's writing ambitions. Faulkner, under Stone's influence, came to appreciate the Balzac and French Symbolist poets. Eager to join the U.S. effort to defend France and its allies against the German threat, Faulkner, with Stone's assistance, launched a plan to sneak into military service by applying to the Royal Canadian Air Force with an affected British accent and forged letters of recommendation (at this time, he effectively changed his last name by applying to the force as Faulkner, rather than Falkner, his birth name). He succeeded in gaining acceptance into the RAF, but the war ended before he had opportunity to experience a tour of combat.

Faulkner returned to Oxford, Mississippi after his brief service in the RAF, and in 1919 he roamed the South, visiting Memphis and New Orleans. During his travels he spent a great deal of time writing poetry. He entertained new acquaintances with false yet glorious accounts of his days as a flying ace during the Great War. He attended Ole Miss and began publishing his poetry in the *Mississippian* and *Oxford Eagle*. In August, his poem "L'Apres-midi d'un faune" was published in *New Republic*. His somewhat eccentric manner and appearance on campus and lack of a steady occupation led to him being known around Ole Miss as "Count No Count." In November of 1920, Faulkner dropped out of Ole Miss. He worked at the university post office and continued telling fanciful tales orally and, more importantly, on paper, now in the genre of novel and short story.

Storytelling was Faulkner's way of connecting who he was and what the world around him was with who he wanted to be and what the world could be. He sported a number of different characters in the way he dressed and acted, according to his mood: he might have appeared as a genteel Southern aristocrat, a carefree rebel, or a seriously artistic Bohemian. As his writing developed, Faulkner became aware of his multifaceted personality and his skill in imagining and illustrating how a real event or character could have been or should have been. He became a novelist who never attempted to resolve human conflicts but to detail them in a good tale, which served its purpose not by providing answers, but by helping people to understand the complexities inherent in human conflict.

In 1924, Faulkner befriended novelist Sherwood Anderson, when he travelled to New Orleans to visit an old friend, Anderson's wife, Elizabeth Prall. Anderson encouraged Faulkner's writing in the form of the novel. Despite his energies in this alternate genre, Faulkner's collection of verse, *The Marble Faun*, his first book, was published shortly after he arrived in New Orleans. Sales were poor, and Faulkner pursued work on his novel, *Soldiers' Pay*, which, though not a commercial success, achieved praise in certain literary circles.

During the summer of 1925, Faulkner familiarized himself with many American literary expatriates in Europe, visiting Italy, Switzerland, France, and England. His experience in Europe must have inspired him, because when he returned to Oxford he embarked on a prolific writing career, publishing *Mosquitos* in 1927, *Sartoris* in 1928, *The Sound and the Fury* in 1928, *As I Lay Dying* in 1930, *Sanctuary* in 1931, and *Light in August* in 1932. At the time of publication, Faulkner's early novels were not very popular among the general reading public; during the beginning of an extreme national recession, American readers were seeking entertainment value in finding solutions to dilemmas such as unemployment and hunger. Faulkner's works did not offer practical fixes to these important and pressing problems in America. Rather, Faulkner examined the complexities of various human problems and faults, which tended further to disillusion readers who longed for literature that fit into a growing national mood of a "New Deal" hope for a brighter future. Others among the public faulted Faulkner's novels for having fascist leanings. These criticisms, coupled with a crippled economy, led to poor sales for Faulkner.

As he continued writing novels, Faulkner married Estelle Franklin and had two daughters, Alabama (born and died in 1931), and Jill (born in 1933). Struggling to pay the bills with his novel royalties alone, Faulkner worked as a Hollywood screenwriter, but never enjoyed the work very much. Some of the movies he wrote were *Today We Live* (1933), *The Road to Glory* (1936), *Banjo on My Knee* (1936), *Slave Ship* (1937), *Gunga Din* (1939), *To Have and To Have Not* (1945), and *The Big Sleep* (1946).

During the 1930s and 1940s, Faulkner continued to be productive in novel writing as well, creating some of his finest and most well-received works, including *Phylon* (1935), *Absalom, Absalom!* (1936), *The Unvanquished* (1938), *The Wild Palms* (1939), *The Hamlet* (1940), and *Go Down, Moses* (1942). Highly esteemed by writers and intellectuals in America and Europe, Faulkner's works became increasingly appreciated by a significant portion of the educated reading public. His work was particularly well received in France, where literary critics and philosophers—including Andre Malraux, Marice LeBreton, Jean Pouillon, and Jean-Paul Sartre—lauded him as a superior narrator of the human condition.

After a brief slump in the sales of his books due to the effects on the public mood and economy with the war effort during the early 1940s, Faulkner was able to resurrect an audience and interest in his writing in 1946 with the publication of *The Portable,* a collection of his previous works. In the foreword to the collection, editor Malcolm Cowley praised Faulkner as having an "imagination that has not been equaled in our time. . . "

Fifteen of Faulkner's novels take place in his mythical Southern setting of Yoknapatawpha County, contrived from an American Indian word meaning "water runs slow through flat land." Jefferson, its county seat, closely resembles Oxford, Mississippi. Nearby is Frenchman's Bend, the impoverished part of the county. Depicted in both the past and the present, Yoknapatawpha is populated with various kinds of people: the Indians who originally inhabited the land, the Southern aristocrats who worked their way into the landed gentry, poor farmers, carpetbaggers, and religious fundamentalists. Proud of his imaginary society, Faulkner penned in his map of Yoknapatawpha County in *Absalom, Absalom!:* "William Faulkner, Sole Owner & Proprietor."

Although Faulkner's works told tales of Southern American folk and life, he was hardly considered to be a provincial writer by critics at home and abroad. Arthur Edelstein considered the Yoknapatawpha collection "a hallucinated version of the Deep South which has escaped its local origins to become a region of the modern consciousness." What was particularly remarkable and effective about Faulkner's writing was his application of, even experimentation with, various narration styles and techniques, many of which he was the first to employ and would be imitated by future writers. He narrated from the point of view of the confused and weak, such as in *The Sound and the Fury;* he beamed the reader into different time periods of the story, usually out of chronological order of events; he omitted punctuation to communicate a specific flow speed and meter of the tale's information; he employed vague pronoun reference to model oral speech. Jean-Paul Sartre compared Faulkner's technique of the protagonist's frequent reflection of the past to that "of a passenger looking backward from a speeding car, who sees, flowing away from him, the landscape he is traversing. For him the future is not in view, the present is too blurred to make out, and he can see clearly only the past as it streams away before his obsessed and backward-looking gaze."

In 1949, Faulkner was awarded the Nobel Prize for Literature. Critics of his work fumed that he had been honored with such a prestigious literary award, citing his work as inaccurately and too negatively depicting American, especially Southern, life. However, Faulkner's stirring acceptance speech calmed the waves of controversy and literary debate among critics and readers, causing many to change their opinion of him seemingly overnight. He explained that it is the writer's duty and privilege "to help man endure by lifting his heart, by reminding him of the courage and honor and hope and pride and compassion and pity and sacrifice which have been the glory of his past. The poet's voice need not merely be the record of man, it can be one of the props, the pillars, to help him endure and prevail." Equally moving and meaningful to hearers were his words that man "is immortal, not because he alone among creatures has an inexhaustible voice, but because he has a soul, a spirit capable of compassion and sacrifice and endurance. The poet's, the writer's, duty is to write about these things. It is his privilege to help man endure by lifting his heart." After his acceptance speech, Faulkner went from being accused of promoting immorality to being lauded as a moral hero.

Faulkner's post-Nobel Prize novels appeared to be echoes of his acceptance speech and have been considered overly didactic by critics. Some of his works from this period are: *Requiem for a Nun* (1951); *A Fable* (1954), for which he was awarded the National Book Award for Fiction the same year; *Big Woods* (1955); and *The Reivers* (1962).

Faulkner wrote consistently throughout his lifetime. Recognizing his extraordinary talent to be so prolific, Faulkner wrote to a friend near the end of his life: "And now I realize for the first time what an amazing gift I had. . . . I don't know why God or gods or whoever it was, elected me to be the vessel. Believe me, this is not humility, false modesty: it is simply amazement." The trace that Faulkner left on American literature is extraordinary for its sheer volume and effect on the evolution of freedom in literary technique, as well as its quality in commentary on human nature at an abstract level. In an article in the *News & Observer*, J. Peder Zane praised Faulkner "as the most exalted American writer of the 20th century," and noted, "His 20 novels and scores of short stories constitute a body of work considered to have few peers for its depth and invention."

Sources

➤ On-line

"Faulkner Resources on the World Wide Web," http:// www.unf.edu/~alderman/faulkner.html (March 3, 2000).
"William Faulkner," http://www.olemiss.edu/depts/english/ ms-writers/dir/faulkner_william (March 3, 2000).
"William Faulkner Collections," http://www.lib.virginia.edu/special/colls/faulkner/html (March 3, 2000).
"William Faulkner Foundation," http://www.uhb.fr/Faulkner (March 3, 2000).

"William Faulkner on the Web," http://www.mcsr.olemiss.edu/~egjbp/faulkner (March 3, 2000).

"William Faulkner Society," http://www.utep.edu/mortimer/faulkner.mainfaulkner.htm (March 3, 2000).

"William Faulkner: Winner of the 1949 Nobel Prize in Literature," http://www.nobelprizes.com/nobel/literature/1949a.html (March 3, 2000; opening quote).

➤ Periodicals

News and Observer (Raleigh, N.C.), September 21, 1997.

Ranulph Fiennes

*"***W***hen your body begins to complain, you only have to think of the people who are depending on you to overcome the wet and wimpish side of your nature."*

Born March 7, 1944, in Windsor, England, Sir Ranulph Fiennes has embarked upon several arduous trips to some of the harshest corners of the globe, earning the designation "the world's greatest living explorer" from the *Guinness Book of World Records.* Address: Greenlands, Somerset, England TA24 7NU.

Ranulph Fiennes has been described as the last in a line of intrepid adventurers who place themselves in great danger in order to become the first to achieve a particular physical feat. For Fiennes, his best-known exploits have been an historic pole-to-pole circle of the earth's surface, and an epic trek across Antarctica in which he and another man carried everything they needed on sleds that weighed almost 500 pounds each. They did this for nearly a hundred days in subzero temperatures. England's Prince Charles, who was involved in the 1979-82 pole-to-pole journey as an official sponsor, once called Fiennes "mad but marvellous."

Fiennes, cousin to actor Ralph, was born Ranulph Twisleton-Wykeham-Fiennes in 1944 into a family that traced its ancestry and its wealth back to the Norman Conquest of Britain in 1066. A Fiennes ancestor was second in command to William the Conqueror, and famously beheaded England's King Harold in an act commemorated in the priceless Bayeaux Tapestry. A grandfather had served as governor of the Seychelles after living as a trapper in Canada, and Fiennes's own father died a heroic death as commander of a tank regiment in Italy during World War II. The death occurred just four months before Fiennes was born, and the legacy of a father he never knew would shadow his life. As a child, he resolved to follow in his father's footsteps as commander of the Royal Scots Greys regiment.

Fiennes grew up in South Africa with his mother, grandmother, and three older sisters, but was sent to Eton College as an adolescent. Eton is the best known of the rigorous private schools for boys in Britain, but like its ilk, is also somewhat infamous for the customary hazing amongst students. Fiennes, having grown up in a female-dominated household where he was adored, was termed a "tart" and bullied mercilessly by the other boys. He endured this for three years, until he learned how to box to save himself. The energies expended in defense meant that his grades suffered, and he did poorly in math, physics, and chemistry. Failing the university-qualifying exams barred him from entrance to the Officer Training College at Sandhurst, a great disappointment.

Fiennes eventually enrolled in a concentrated officer training course, and was able to enter the Greys. He commanded a tank troop in West Germany, but also worked as an adventure guide who conducted intense recreation trips, such as canoeing through Europe's rivers, for other military personnel. In 1965, he was recruited by Britain's Special Air Service (SAS), which carries out anti-terrorist activities, and offered a place in its rigorous selection course. One of his training assignments was to defend a nearby town in the event of a purported bank robbery, and Fiennes accidentally left some documents behind in a café one Sunday. Their discovery caused an uproar in the town, and he was nearly ejected from the course. After this incident, Fiennes then allowed himself to be drawn into a plan by one of his friends to blow up an artificial pond constructed by a film crew making the movie *Doctor Doolittle.* The police were alerted, however, and Fiennes escaped capture but his car did not. He attempted to speak with the constables to plead for it back—he was set to travel to Borneo the next morning for jungle training with the SAS—but they instead arrested him, and he was indeed booted from the SAS.

Fiennes returned to the Greys and his tank regiment, and spent two years in the Arabian peninsula as part of a special team of officers hired by the Sultan of Oman. A Marxist uprising in the Dhofar province was successfully quelled by the 300-man Oman army and its eleven British officers, which entailed deadly night ambushes. With his final year of service looming, Fiennes was in a quandary concerning his career opportunities. His only success, it seemed, had been as an adventure guide, and so he hired himself out as an expeditioneer and surveyor. He mapped a Norwegian glacier, led a 1969 expedition on the White Nile, and then canoed through British Columbia. In August of 1970, he married Virginia Pepper, whom he had known since childhood.

In 1972, his wife suggested that they make a trip around the world, and Fiennes scoffed at the idea, since the couple's financial situation was dire. No one had tried it vertically, she argued, and theorized that they could make contracts with a newspaper, a publisher, and a television company to sell the rights, which would finance the journey. It would be the first circumpolar expedition in history. Fiennes wrote of the seven years' work it took to make this happen in his 1983 book *To the Ends of the Earth: The Transglobal Expedition: The First Pole to Pole Circumnavigation of the Globe.* The planning alone was a herculean task, involving not just financial sponsorship but obtaining government permits, recruiting a crew, commandeering a ship, and then undergoing arduous physical training. The three-year trip began in September of 1979 in Greenwich, England, and went through Spain, the Sahara Desert, and along the southwestern coast of Africa before sailing to Antarctica. There Fiennes and his team used snowmobiles to cross the polar region, and then enjoyed the comforts of a large ship to sail across a long stretch of the Pacific Ocean. They disembarked at the Aleutian

Islands, and traveled overland through the Yukon Territory and the dangerous Northwest Passage region. They reached the North Pole on Easter Day of 1982.

Fiennes won great fame for his trek, and was hailed as the world's greatest living explorer. On some legs of the expedition, he and his team had conducted surveys of uncharted Antarctic territory, collecting measurement data which cartographers then used; just a few years later such old-fashioned scientific forays would be made obsolete by improved satellite imaging. Fiennes next vowed to conquer the North Pole "unsupported"—that is, without snowmobiles, airplane drops of food, or other aid. Crossing the Arctic Circle was far more difficult than the continent of Antarctica, however. The northern region is a mass of ice and ocean, not land, and the constant shifting of ice floes makes it exceedingly dangerous. Cracks can appear beneath without warning, and the presence of polar bears meant that a weapon had to be near at all time. Sometimes the wind would blow their camp backwards, halving the distance gained on a typical 13-hour trek. Even sleep was difficult, since the ice shrieked constantly.

During his four unsuccessful attempts to cross the North Pole between 1986 and 1990, Fiennes severely tested his physical limits. Once, after falling through to water, he suffered severe frostbite; later part of his toe came off when he removed his sock. Retinal damage was diagnosed, a vision impairment due to the high-intensity blue light of polar regions. On one occasion, sweat had caused his balaclava to freeze to his beard, and at camp he had yanked it down and off came the skin with it. On the last try, he nearly drowned.

Back in England, Fiennes spent several years as an aide to industrialist Armand Hammer, and led a trek in the early 1990s back to Oman to uncover the lost city of Ubar, described by second-century geographer Ptolemy. Fiennes chronicled this adventure in his 1992 book *Atlantis of the Sands: The Search for the Lost City of Ubar.*

In 1993, Fiennes and physician Mike Stroud completed what would become the explorer's most enduring achievement: they made an entirely unassisted trek across the Antarctic Continent. It was the longest ever such trip in the annals of exploration, and was planned as a fund-raising effort for a multiple sclerosis charity. For 97 days, Fiennes and Stroud lugged sleds bearing their food, fuel, and other supplies; each vessel weighed in at 485 pounds. The two also used cross-country skis and parachute sails to make the trek, and both men battled frostbite and the danger of hypothermia. Fiennes's physical problems were more acute, however, due to his age and previous exploits. His foot was so badly infected that his toes became a swollen mass of blackened flesh.

Starvation was another issue. They had planned enough rations to give them 5,000 calories a day, but actually required twice that for the strength of the task. Their 12-hour hauls, sometimes in temperatures that plummeted to 185 degrees below zero, were probably burning 8,000 calories a day in their systems. In the end, they were so emaciated and in so much physical pain that they barely slept. After trekking nearly 1,400 miles, they decided against crossing the Ross Ice Shelf—not technically part of the continent, but an adjacent area the size of France—since they had only nine days' rations left.

Fiennes was knighted by Queen Elizabeth II in 1993 for his endeavors, and has long been an active member of the Royal Geographic Society. He spent the next few years at home in England with his wife; the couple have a farm in Exmoor where their retinue of black animals includes Aberdeen-Angus cattle, Welsh Black Mountain sheep, several dogs and a cat. He wrote several books, including an 1994 autobiography, *Living Dangerously*, two quasi-novels, and *Fit for Life*, published in 1998.

In 1996, at the age of 52, Fiennes embarked upon an attempt to traverse Antarctica once more—but on a solo journey. The trip was tied to a heavily publicized fund-raising drive for Breakthrough, the British breast-cancer research charity, and once again, Fiennes planned to drag nearly 500 pounds on a sled. This time, however, he would be committed to traveling 18 miles a day for 110 days straight; more risky was the fact he would be utterly alone. There would be no one there to save him in the event he fell into a crevasse, or began to suffer the warning sings of impending hypothermia, which quickly disables its victims mentally, and in essence, leaves them for dead. Fiennes claimed that charity sponsorship for such feats was an ideal arrangement. "When your body begins to complain, you only have to think of the people who are depending on you to overcome the wet and wimpish side of your nature," he told Andro Linklater in an interview with the *Telegraph*. Fiennes was forced to abandon the cause, however, when a recurrence of kidney stones made him radio for rescue after 450 miles.

Sources

➤ Books

Fiennes, Sir Ranulph, *To the Ends of the Earth: The Transglobal Expedition: The First Pole to Pole Circumnavigation of the Globe,* foreword by H.R.H. Prince Charles, Arbor House, 1983.
Stroud, Mike, *Shadows on the Wasteland: Crossing Antarctica with Ranulph Fiennes,* Overlook Press, 1993.

➤ Periodicals

Geographical, November 1996, pp. 20-21; October 1999, p. S3, p. S7.

Ella Fitzgerald

"C*oming through the years, and finding that I not only have just the fans of my day, but the young ones of today—that's what it means. It means it was worth all of it."*

Born April 25, 1918, in Newport News, Virginia, Ella Fitzgerald became well known for her smooth, "scat" singing. She made over 200 recordings and won 13 Grammy awards before ill health forced her into retirement. She died June 15, 1996, at her home in Beverly Hills, California.

To her millions of fans around the world she was known simply as Ella, the first lady of song. In a six-decade career, Fitzgerald set the standard for jazz vocalists, and titillated non-jazz listeners with her "Songbook" albums and other forays into popular music. To many aficionados, certain songs simply cannot be sung by anyone else; Ella's were the quintessential version.

Ella Fitzgerald was born on April 25, 1918, in Newport News, Virginia. When she was an infant, she moved with her mother and stepfather to Yonkers, New York. A great music lover, her mother was a fan of radio musical shows and a collector of records by popular artists of the day, especially the Boswell Sisters. Throughout her childhood Fitzgerald dreamed of performing. Tragically, her mother died when she was only 15, and, according to a *New York Times* article, she was abused by her stepfather after her mother's death. She was given solace by an aunt in Harlem, where she earned money by running numbers and alerting prostitutes to approaching police officers. She landed in a reformatory school, the New York State Training School for Girls, where she was probably, like the other girls there in those days, subjected to frequent beatings by guards.

When Fitzgerald was 16, she appeared at an amateur night at the Apollo, dressed in scrubby clothes and men's boots, intending to perform a dance number. When she climbed on stage, however, she froze and lost her nerve to dance. She later described the incident this way: "The man said, 'do something while you're out there.' So I tried to sing 'Object of My Affection' and 'Judy,' and I won first prize." She was awarded $25 and was noticed by many in the business, including jazz musician and arranger Benny Carter.

Carter introduced the teen to the bandleader Fletcher Henderson, but Henderson failed to recognize Fitzgerald's potential for jazz greatness. Carter also notified talent scout John Hammond, who opted not to pursue representing her in the industry. Fitzgerald did manage to get an audition at CBS Radio, after which CBS executives hired her to appear on Arthur Tracy's radio show. However, CBS pulled the offer, because she was a minor and had no parent to sign the contract for her. Shortly after that, she performed in another contest at the Harlem Opera House, winning first prize of a week-long professional engagement, her first professional paying gig. This earned her attention by various other talent agents and producers.

In 1935 Bardou Ali, who worked for Chick Webb's band, introduced the 17-year-old Fitzgerald to Webb hoping that he would invite her to tour with the band. She recalled later, "Chick had a boy singer and didn't want a girl, and he grudgingly said, 'well, we're playing Yale tomorrow. Get on the band bus and, if they like you there, you've got a job.'" Audiences did like her, and she stayed on with the band, beginning with regular appearances at the Savoy Ballroom in Harlem. Fitzgerald's talent was appreciated by a greater audience through live broadcasts from the Savoy Ballroom.

In 1936, Webb's band, featuring Fitzgerald's vocals, recorded on the Decca label. Among these earlier recordings are: "Sing Me a Swing Song," "A Little Bit Later On," and "If You Can't Sing It, You'll Have to Swing It." Taking advantage of her youthfulness and equally youthful voice, Fitzgerald performed the nursery rhyme "A-Tisket A-Tasket" in 1938, which became a big hit and appeared on the Hit Parade for nearly a year.

When Webb died from tuberculosis in 1939, Fitzgerald took over as leader of the band, and soon Decca marketed her as a solo act, supported by the band. By this time jazz was rapidly becoming more mainstream, and soon Fitzgerald was regarded as a pop singer. John McDonough noted in *Down Beat*, ". . . she came of age in a time when jazz had moved to the center of popular music and brought with it the jazz musician's respect for and pursuit of technique and virtuosity."

In 1942, Fitzgerald performed with the band Four Keys, with whom she made one record, "All I Need Is You." However, most of the members were drafted into service to fight in World War II. Fitzgerald found herself touring road shows and appearing as a soloist at clubs around the United States. About this time she began experimenting with wordless vocal improvisation. Once when jamming with Dizzy Gillespie, Fitzgerald was asked to improvise. "I just tried to do what I heard the horns in the band doing," she explained. The improvisation technique she employed would be later popularized as "scat," her signature. Mikal Gilmore of *Rolling Stone* described Fitzgerald's mode of scat this way: "She developed a wild, gliding style of melodic extemporization and phonetic phrasing that was known as scat singing, and it established her as the most influential and admired vocalist in jazz next to Billie Holiday." Though jazz singers scatted before Fitzgerald, she developed and popularized the style. McDonough observed, "The origins of Fitzgerald's vocal improvising were rooted primarily in instrumental models, not vocal ones." Fitzgerald told *Ebony* in the mid-1940s (quoted by *Billboard*'s Jim Macnie): "These bop musicians have stimulated me more than I can say. I have been inspired by them, and I want the world to know it. Bop musicians have more to say than any other musicians playing today."

In 1946, Fitzgerald joined Jazz at the Philharmonic, a touring performance led by Norman Granz. From 1948 to 1952 she also sang in a jazz group led by double-bass player Ray Brown, whom she married in 1949. The couple divorced in 1953.

Granz had a great and positive influence on Fitzgerald, who was disappointed with Decca at the time. In 1955 Granz purchased Fitzgerald's recording contract from Decca so that she could record on his Verve label. He then produced Fitzgerald's series of "Songbook" albums. Each "Songbook" identified with a single composer, and the project earned her a great following among mainstream audiences. She also continued to record albums for Decca, the most popular being *Ella—Songs in a Mellow Mood, Lullabies of Birdland,* and *Sweet and Hot.* Jay Cocks of *Time* quoted Fitzgerald's earlier reflection of her "Songbook" recording: "Norman [Granz] felt that I should do other things, so he produced the Cole Porter Songbook with me. It was a turning point in my life." Cocks declared in the same article, "Those songbooks became the foundation of a legacy, the single source for a musical standard that Fitzgerald, as much as anyone, helped make timeless."

In 1955, Fitzgerald appeared on the cover of *Life* magazine. She was awarded numerous other honors during her lifetime, including ASAP's Pied Piper Award, the Urban League's Whitney Young Award, and honorary doctorates from Dartmouth, Washington, Princeton, Harvard, and Yale. She won the Esquire Gold and Silver awards in 1946 and 1947. She took first place in the *Down Beat's* Critics' Poll 18 years in a row, and she was voted first place in *Playboy's* poll for 13 years. She received 13 Grammy awards, including a Grammy Lifetime Achievement Award in 1967. Considered an icon in jazz, in 1979 she was lauded with a Kennedy Center Award. She was awarded the U.S. National Medal of Art in 1987 and the French Commandeur des Arts et Lettres in 1990. In 1989 the Society of Singers presented her with its first annual lifetime-achievement award, to be known from then on as "Ella." In 1974 the University of Maryland opened the Ella Fitzgerald School of Performing Arts.

Fitzgerald continued to tour in the United States and abroad throughout the 1970s and 1980s, performing in large arenas with orchestras, as well as small jazz clubs with a small ensemble of pianist, bassist, and drummer. However, beginning in the 1970s, Fitzgerald's eyesight began to fail considerably due to her battle with cataracts. In 1987 she underwent quintuple coronary bypass surgery after suffering congestive heart failure. Despite these health struggles, she continued to perform, earning high acclaim for keeping her artistic strength intact. After having both legs amputated below the knees as a result of complications due to diabetes, Fitzgerald completely retired from music in 1993.

Fitzgerald died early on Saturday, June 15, 1996, in her home, surrounded by family and friends. On the evening of Fitzgerald's death, music lovers were gathered at the Hollywood Bowl for the Playboy Jazz Festival. After the news of her death spread among the guests, the emcee, Bill Cosby, confirmed the news of her death and requested a moment of silence. In tribute to Fitzgerald, the Bowl's marquee was changed to read: "Ella, we will miss you." Musicians revised their sets in tribute as well.

Fitzgerald willed all of her properties and earnings to a trust fund she established, leaving nothing to family members or friends. Her Beverly Hills home sold for an estimated $2.5 million, and items from her estate were auctioned off, with the proceeds benefitting various children's, medical, and arts charities.

Numerous profiles and tributes were expressed by fans and music professionals, who lauded her as a giant in the music industry and in American pop culture. Gilmore summarized Fitzgerald's style and musical contributions in *Rolling Stone:* "It is true that Ella Fitzgerald sang in tones filled with joy, but her joy was not a simple thing—it was a joy born from her self-willed refusal to succumb to the limitation and degradation that her childhood had known." Jim Macnie of *Billboard* wrote, "Fitzgerald's sense of swing was deep. She could ride a groove or weave her wholly original patterns around and through the rhythms at hand. Her intonation was superb, her use of nuance expert, and her ability to quote other famous jazz solos entertaining."

Ira Gershwin once remarked: "I never knew how good our songs were until I heard Ella Fitzgerald sing them."

Sources

➤ **On-line**

"Ella Fitzgerald Pages," http://jump.to/ella (March 13, 2000).
"Ella Fitzgerald Tribute," http://www.public.iastate.edu/ ~vwindsor/Ella.html (March 13, 2000).

"'First Lady of Song' Passes Peacefully, Surrounded by Family," *CNN Showbiz*, http://www.cnn.com/SHOWBIZ/9606/15/fitz-gerald.obit/index.html (March 28, 2000; opening quote).

"The Last Jazz Great: Ella Fitzgerald, 1917-1996," *Salon*, http://www.salon.com/dec96/ella961216.html (March 13, 2000).

"Redsugar's Ella Fitzgerald Page," http://www.redsugar.com/ella/htm (March 13, 2000).

➤ **Periodicals**

Billboard, June 29, 1996, p. 9.

Down Beat, September 1996, p. 16; January 1999, pp. 76-77; July 1999, p. 96-97.

Jet, November 25, 1996, p. 54; March 17, 1997, p. 17.

People, July 1, 1996, p. 42; May 26, 1997, p. 33; December 6, 1999, p. 32.

Rolling Stone, August 8, 1996, p. 26; December 1996, p. 94.

Time, June 24, 1996, p. 83; June 8, 1998, p. 169.

Hiram L. Fong

*"*O*ur nation is the great pilot demonstration of the most lofty principles and ideals in history. . . . Our opportunity is to live up to these ideals."*

Born October 1, 1907, in Honolulu, Hawaii, Hiram L. Fong is an attorney and businessman who was the first Chinese American member of the U.S. Congress. He was chosen as the Republican senator from Hawaii just after it achieved statehood in 1959. Address: Finance Enterprises, Ltd., 1164 Bishop St., Honolulu, HI 96813.

One of the most distinguished and respected public figures in Hawaii, Hiram L. Fong is a self-made man who rose from very humble beginnings to became an attorney, businessman, and politician with more than a few groundbreaking achievements to his credit. Admirers laud him as a true American success story—ambitious, goal oriented, and successful despite the many obstacles he faced along the way. Fong also holds a special place in Hawaii's history as one of the first three legislators to represent the state after it entered the union in 1959. And to Asian Americans he is a source of pride as the first Chinese American to serve in the U.S. Congress, where he ardently championed the cause of brotherhood and the benefits of living in an ethnically diverse society.

Born Yau Leong Fong to illiterate Chinese immigrants Lum Fong and his wife, Chai Ha Lum, Hiram Leong Fong is a native of Honolulu, Hawaii. Both of his parents had left their homeland (his father at the age of 15, his mother at the age of ten) to work as indentured servants on one of Hawaii's sugar plantations. The seventh of 11 Fong children, Hiram grew up in a rough-and-tumble slum neighborhood of Honolulu and went to work picking beans at the age of four to help supplement his parents' meager income. He continued to do odd jobs during the rest of his childhood and teenage years, including shining shoes, selling newspapers, and caddying at a golf course.

Having to shoulder so much of the burden of helping to support his family meant that Fong sometimes had to miss school as a youngster. But he attended as often as he could and distinguished himself as a student with tremendous potential. Since attending college immediately after high school was out of the question due to financial reasons, Fong instead took a job as a clerk in the supply department at the Pearl Harbor Naval Shipyard. He remained in that post for three years and finally saved up enough money to enroll at the University of Hawaii. There he excelled in his studies (he graduated with top honors in only three years) and also found the time to hold a number of part-time jobs as well as pursue extracurricular activities such as editing the school newspaper and yearbook, competing on the debate team, and playing on several sports teams.

It was during this same period of his life that Fong changed his given name of Yau to Hiram in honor of the Reverend Hiram Bingham, the leader of the first group of Congregationalist missionaries who arrived in Hawaii from New England in 1820. Besides providing instruction in the Christian religion, they established the islands' first public schools and exerted considerable influence on the stability and development of the region. Fong greatly admired their accomplishments and embraced the Congregationalist faith himself.

Fong graduated from college in 1930 with a bachelor of arts degree and went to work as chief clerk of the suburban water department of the city and county of Honolulu. Within two years, he had set aside enough money from his earnings to pursue his next big dream—going to Harvard Law School. Armed with $2,000 in savings plus a $3,000 loan, he left for the U.S. mainland in 1932 and returned home three years later virtually penniless but with his educational goals fulfilled.

Fong then set his sights on establishing himself in his chosen profession. He worked briefly as a municipal clerk in Honolulu before teaming up with several other local attorneys of Japanese, Korean, and Caucasian descent to establish the city's first multiethnic law firm, a venture that proved to be very successful. Fong soon found himself in a much more comfortable financial position, enabling him to make a series of lucrative investments in real estate, insurance and financial firms, and a banana plantation. Before long, the young lawyer and entrepreneur was a millionaire. Freed from the burden of having to devote all of his time and energy to earning a living, Fong was able to pursue his growing interest in public service.

Fong launched his career in the public sector by working as a deputy attorney for both the city and county of Honolulu from 1935 until 1938. He then decided to run for the territorial House of Representatives and won election as a Republican. He served in that body for 14 years, spending three terms as speaker and two as vice-speaker. As a member of the territorial legislature, Fong made achieving statehood for Hawaii one of his top priorities.

Hawaii's strong religious, political, and economic ties to the west (especially Great Britain and the United States) dated back to 1778, the year England's Captain James Cook "discovered" the islands and opened them up for trade with the rest of the world. The U.S. influence began to dominate after the arrival of Christian missionaries from New England in 1820 and was strengthened during the 1830s when sugar emerged as an important export crop for Hawaii. (Americans developed and ran the plantation system for growing and harvesting sugar cane.) In 1893, a committee made up mostly of plantation owners and other businessmen overthrew Hawaii's Queen Liliuokalani and set up a temporary government headed by

Sanford B. Dole, a lawyer and the son of an American missionary. The Republic of Hawaii was created out of that temporary government the following year, and in 1898, the United States annexed Hawaii. It officially became a U.S. territory in 1900 and still held that status when Hiram Fong first took office.

Fong's political career was interrupted by World War II, which the United States entered in 1941 after the Japanese bombed Hawaii's Pearl Harbor naval base. During the conflict, he served with the U.S. Army Air Corps as judge advocate of the 7th Fighter Command of the 7th Air Force, rising to the rank of major. He subsequently spent nearly two decades as an officer in the U.S. Army Reserve and is also a retired colonel in the U.S. Air Force Reserve.

The postwar years saw renewed interest in making Hawaii a state. But a variety of internal factors worked against the statehood movement. There were, for example, widespread concerns about the amount of influence proponents of communism wielded within the islands' labor unions. (This was at a time when the United States was in the throes of anti-communist hysteria.) In addition, the many Hawaiians of Japanese descent aroused suspicion and fear among those who still regarded Japan as the enemy and the Japanese people as untrustworthy.

As an advocate of the principles of brotherhood and cultural understanding, Fong tried to defuse such tensions by emphasizing the positive aspects of Hawaii's ethnic diversity and racial harmony whenever possible. It was, in fact, a recurring theme throughout his political career. "We in Hawaii would like to believe that we are giving life to a community approaching the ideal of a world at peace and in concord," is how he put it in a 1960 speech to the National Conference of Christians and Jews that was reprinted in the *Congressional Record*.

His perseverance finally paid off on June 27, 1959, when islanders voted in favor of statehood. A month later, they elected Fong to one of the new state's two seats in the U.S. Senate; the other went to a Democrat named Oren E. Long. On August 21, Hawaii was officially proclaimed the fiftieth state. Three days later, a coin toss and drawing determined which new legislator—Fong or Long—would be considered Hawaii's "senior" senator and serve a longer term. Fong won and headed for the nation's capital for a five-and-a-half-year term.

A self-described liberal on social issues and a conservative on military matters and the national budget, Fong went against many of his Republican colleagues by strongly supporting major civil rights and antidiscrimination legislation, including the landmark Civil Rights Act of 1964, several bills that protected voters from discriminatory practices, and a measure that repealed provisions in the Internal Security Act that had been used during World War II to round up and imprison Japanese Americans in so-called "relocation" camps. As the highest-ranking Republican member of the Senate subcommittee on immigration and naturalization, he also advocated immigration reform and worked hard to gain passage of a 1965 bill that eliminated the old quota system, which had limited the number of new arrivals based on their race and national origin.

As a member of the powerful Senate appropriations committee, Fong played a key role in deciding how much of the federal budget should be allocated to education. He himself voted in favor of every education bill that ended up passing in the Senate during his tenure. In addition, he advanced Hawaii's interests in the areas of the environment, the economy, and international affairs and made sure that the country's newest state received fair and equal treatment from the federal government. Last but not least, Fong worked to establish better relations between the United States and the entire Asia-Pacific region by forging numerous cultural and economic exchanges. He was, in fact, instrumental in helping to establish and obtain financial backing for the East-West Center, an internationally known think tank based at the University of Hawaii.

Fong won election to the Senate two more times, once in 1964 and again in 1970, the same year he received the Horatio Alger Award in recognition of the success he had achieved despite adversity. He retired from politics in January 1977 but has remained very much involved in a variety of business and charitable activities. Fong typically spends his mornings working at Finance Enterprises, Ltd. (the financial services firm he founded and of which he is chairman), and his afternoons and weekends gardening at the 725-acre plantation he regards as his gift to the people of Hawaii. (In 1999, the Hawaii Visitors and Convention Bureau voted it the islands' best attraction.) At his direction, his foundations give away tens of thousands of dollars annually to assist local causes.

A beloved and popular figure in his home state, Fong—in defiance of his advancing years—is still looking forward to the challenges of the future. His mind is brimming with plans to expand and refine his gardens, for example. On the business front, he has turned his gaze to China, where he predicts continuing economic expansion will ultimately contribute to Hawaii's prosperity and ensure that it remains a popular tourist destination.

Sources

➤ On-line

"About Senator Fong," *Senator Fong's Plantation & Gardens,* http:// www.fonggarden.com/Senator%20Fong.htm (December 31, 1999).
"Fong Looks to China for Next Tourism Boost," *Honolulu Star-Bulletin,* http://www.starbulletin.com/1999/11/08/special/ story2.html (January 1, 2000).
"Hiram L. Fong," *Horatio Alger Association of Distinguished Americans,* http://www.horatioalger.com/member/fon70.htm (January 1, 2000).
"Hiram L. Fong: Former U.S. Senator 'Man of the Pacific,'" *Honolulu Star-Bulletin,* http://www.starbulletin.com/1999/10/01/news/ story8.html (January 1, 2000).

➤ Books

Zia, Helen, and Susan Gall, editors, *Notable Asian Americans,* Gale, 1995.

➤ Other

Congressional Record, 86th Congress, 2nd Session, Volume 106, Part 8, U.S. Government Printing Office, 1960, pp. 9971-9974; 94th Congress, 2nd Session, Volume 122, Part 25, U.S. Government Printing Office, 1976, pp. 32819-32829 (opening quote).

R. Buckminster Fuller

*"**I**f it is not so far to the moon, then it is not so far to the limits of the universe—whatever, whenever, or wherever they may be."*

Born July 12, 1895, in Milton, Massachusetts, R. Buckminster Fuller was a scientist, inventor, and futurist best known for his revolutionary geodesic dome. He died on July 1, 1983.

R. Buckminster Fuller belongs to a long list of innovative minds who failed to graduate from Harvard University. This futurist, engineer, inventor, architect, and poet was one of the most important visionaries of the twentieth century, though his genius came from a simple conviction about the power inherent in the structures and shapes in nature itself. Later in life, Fuller placed much of his energies and intellect into devising ways that life on the planet, which he called "Spaceship Earth," could be improved, despite what he felt was an entrenched opposition to progress by modern political entities.

Fuller was born Richard Buckminster Fuller, Jr. in Milton, Massachusetts, on July 12, 1895. He came from a long line of accomplished Fullers whose origins in New England dated back to Puritan times. Appropriately enough, Fuller was born with a minor vision impairment: extreme far-sightedness. This was not diagnosed, however, until he was four years old, and after being fitted with thick eyeglasses, Fuller was surprised to discover a world that appeared completely different from the one he had known up until then. Without the corrective lenses, he could see only large patterns and their colors; nearly everything else had been blurred. "I did not see a human eye or a teardrop or a human hair until I was four years old!," Fuller later wrote, according to Sidney Rosen's biography, *Wizard of the Dome.*

At the age of nine, "Bucky," as he was called, enrolled as a day student at a local private school, Milton Academy. He was perplexed by math and the theories his teachers set forth, but excelled in football, despite the fact that he had to play without his glasses. His pleasant adolescence, however, abruptly ended at age 13 with the death of his father. The family's fortunes were reduced considerably by the loss, and his mother worried about her son's nonconformist attitudes and penchant for spending money. Believing he lacked the determination to truly succeed in life, Caroline Wolcott Fuller often asked his uncles to lecture Bucky on the merits of hard work and playing by the rules.

Fuller, after earning top grades at Milton Academy, entered Harvard University in the fall of 1913 with some financial help from his uncles. Yet because of his precarious financial status, his classmates treated him shabbily. They also teased him about his appearance—he was only five feet, two inches in height, walked with a slight limp because one leg was shorter than the other, had a rather large head, and was lost without his thick-lensed spectacles. Virtually ostracized—even friends from his popular Milton Academy days now shunned him—he was turned down for membership in all the Harvard dining clubs. Overwhelmed, one day near midterm examinations Fuller impetuously went to the bank and withdrew the funds his family had deposited there for his semester's expenses. He took a train to New York City and checked into a luxury hotel, and lived lavishly in the company of Broadway chorus girls for a few days. His whereabouts were soon discovered, however, and he was expelled from Harvard.

Naturally the Fuller family was also tremendously disgruntled about this, and so it was decided to let Fuller have a taste of what life without a college degree might portend. He was sent to Sherbrooke, Quebec, to a cotton mill owned by a cousin, with the thought that some hard labor would improve his attitude. Fuller, however, loved the mill and its machinery, and his mechanical bent soon made him an able machine fitter. After another failed stint at Harvard, he tried to enlist in the armed forces at the onset of World War I, but was rejected because of his eyesight. He was eventually accepted into a special crash course at the U.S. Naval Academy at Annapolis, Maryland, and during that same year, in 1917, married Anne Hewlett, the daughter of a well-known painter, in a Long Island ceremony.

Fuller served as an ensign in the Navy until 1919, and was posted to a warship, which amazed him with its efficient use of resources. The Fullers became parents in 1918 with the birth of a daughter, Alexandra, but as an infant she was weakened by the devastating Spanish influenza epidemic that year, and never regained full health. She died four years later, and both parents were heartbroken. Living in Chicago while Fuller headed a building company founded by his father-in-law, another daughter, Allegra, was born. But the firm was bought out by another company in 1927, and Fuller was left with little savings and few employment prospects.

Drinking heavily, Fuller began to think of suicide, feeling an incompetent husband and poor provider, just as his family had predicted. Recognizing the rapid progress and scientific leaps being made during the era, however, Fuller told his wife that he was going to take some time off to "think," in the tradition of such philosophers as Henry Thoreau and Rene Descartes, to which she rather graciously agreed. For some two years, they lived in a poor section of Chicago and lived from funds drawn from their families' largesse.

Fuller had decided that it was possible for one individual to make a difference in the world, and resolved to let this goal determine how he would live his life. He already had some far-ranging ideas, and began sketching them out. One of the first was a "4D House," based on the idea that a dwelling could be as easily assembled and shipped by the same mass-production methods used by the burgeoning automobile industry. Hexagonal in shape, with 12 decks and anchored by tension cables to ground, Fuller's 4D house was revolutionary, but the architectural establishment was markedly disinterested. Fuller was dismissed as an amateur, since he had no formal training in the field, and the company he founded to manufacture eventually ran aground. Only Chicago's Marshall Field department store showed some interest, and it was one of its marketing experts who renamed it the "Dymaxion House."

Around 1930, the Fullers moved to Greenwich Village in New York City, and during this era Fuller came to know many progressive and modern minds of the day. He founded and edited a magazine he called *Shelter*, filled with many of his revolutionary ideas to alleviate the homelessness of the Great Depression, but it eventually folded, as did his company. A revolutionary streamlined car, also called the Dymaxion, was yet another failure for Fuller. From 1932 to 1936, he headed a company that would produce this three-wheeled vehicle, but an accident, at which the Dymaxion was not at fault, brought a slew of bad press and killed interest in it.

During the late 1930s, Fuller worked for the Phelps Dodge Company as a research and development specialist, and wrote his first book, *Nine Chains to the Moon*, in which he set forth many of his progressive ideas. If all humans stood on one another's shoulders, Fuller posited, the chain could stretch all the way to the moon and back nine times. "If it is not so far to the moon, then it is not so far to the limits of the universe—whatever, whenever, or wherever they may be," he theorized. He also worked on the staff of *Fortune* magazine as an emerging technologies writer.

With the onset of World War II, the military began to show interest in Fuller's ideas for lightweight, mobile shelter, and a Dymaxion design was used to shelter radar equipment in remote northern areas. In 1946, Fuller established the Fuller Research Foundation, and began thinking about shapes, distances, and how nature seemed to be based upon the principles of geometry. He founded another company, which he called Geodesics, that used the structural principal of adjacent tetrahedrons—triangles of equal size in a solid form—to create a vast, strong roof. He won a commission to use this concept with a showplace dome for the Ford Motor Company in Dearborn, Michigan, which did much to further his career.

Fuller also began designing entire structures based on geodesic principals. The units were stable, strong, yet light in weight and cost-effective to manufacture and ship. Construction could be done by nearly anyone, since the directions for assembly simply instructed workers to bolt blue ends to blue ends, and red ones to red ones. Geodesic domes began cropping up around the globe, and Fuller, having obtained a patent in 1954, was able to enjoy financial security for the first time in his life. He was nearly 60 years old.

Fuller became famous from this point in his career. After 1959 he was affiliated with Southern Illinois University, and was made an honorary life member of the American Institute of Architects in 1960. He even spent time as a professor of poetry at Harvard University—for years he had written many of his ideas in verse—and served as a special consultant to the National Aeronautics and Space Administration. He created a futurist model of a massive floating city, based on the tetrahedron, for the Department of Housing and Urban Development, and designed airports, theaters and auditoriums. Along the way he was feted with numerous academic and professional honors, fellowships, and degrees.

In his later years Fuller devoted himself to studying how the earth's resources could be best utilized to raise the standard of living for all citizens. He also devised what he called the World Game, conducted in conference settings with participants culled from the academic world and the social sciences. Utilizing banks of computers loaded with databases of global resources and human trends and needs that he had created, the World Game also used his "Dymaxion Airocean" map of the world—the first flat map of the planet with no distortion, which he had devised in the early 1940s. With these seminars, Fuller hoped that solutions to starvation, pollution, and hostilities among nations could be found.

During the 1960s and '70s, when a new generation of young adults were busy challenging entrenched conservatism and environmental degradation, the optimistic, always defiant Fuller was a particularly popular character of the times. He was adamant in the belief that science should be devoted not to weaponry, but to what he termed *livingry,* or improving the quality of life for the planet. "The politician is someone who deals in man's problems of adjustment," Fuller wrote in *Ideas and Integrities.* "To ask a politician to lead us is to ask the tail of a dog to lead the dog."

Fuller died on July 1, 1983, and his wife died less than two days later. Perhaps the best-known and most visited geodesic dome in the world is Epcot Center, a Walt Disney theme park in Orlando, Florida.

Sources

➤ **Books**

Fuller, Buckminster, *Ideas and Integrities: A Spontaneous Autobiographical Disclosure,* edited by Robert W. Marks, Prentice-Hall, 1963.
Kenner, Hugh, *Bucky: A Guided Tour of Buckminster Fuller,* William Morrow, 1973.
Rosen, Sidney, *Wizard of the Dome: R. Buckminster Fuller, Designer for the Future,* Little, Brown, 1969.

Robert Peter Gale

*"***W***e didn't learn all we could from Hiroshima and Nagasaki; we've not controlled the proliferation of nuclear weapons. Yet we have to learn. I hope Chernobyl will be the final lesson."*

Born October 11, 1945, in New York City, New York, Robert Peter Gale is a physician, medical researcher, and consultant who became internationally famous for his efforts to aid the victims of the Chernobyl nuclear disaster in 1986. Address: 11693 San Vicente Blvd., Suite 335, Los Angeles, CA 90049.

If Robert Peter Gale had not gone to the Soviet Union in 1986, he would be known today as a renowned physician and medical researcher with particular expertise in immunology, transplantation, and the treatment of leukemia. But the events surrounding the accident at the Chernobyl nuclear power plant in the Ukraine that year transformed Gale's life and added a new facet to his career, that of international medical consultant and humanitarian.

At the time of the Chernobyl accident, the United States and the Soviet Union were still Cold War adversaries, with nuclear weapons arsenals that threatened each other's survival. By working side by side with Soviet doctors in Moscow to save lives, Gale's efforts had considerable political as well as medical significance. "We as Americans don't know the Soviet people," he wrote in his 1988 book, *Final Warning: The Legacy of Chernobyl.* "We know the Soviet Union as a Communist country, but very few of us have considered who lives there apart from the context of their political system. For that reason, when people ask what was most important about my mission to Moscow, I'm inclined to answer: breaking down barriers."

Born in New York City, Robert Peter Gale is the younger of two sons of Harvey and Evelyn Gale. During his junior year at Hobart College in Geneva, New York, he decided to become a physician, and he went on to earn a medical degree from the State University of New York at Buffalo. While still in medical school, he traveled to Ethiopia and Thailand during the summers of 1968 and 1969 to assist at local health clinics. After earning his degree in 1970, Gale began his internship at the UCLA medical center in Los Angeles. A year later, he directed his energies towards earning his Ph.D. in microbiology and immunology with the idea of finding a cure for leukemia. To that end, he became a specialist in bone marrow transplants, at the time a brand-new procedure.

In 1973 Gale joined the faculty of the UCLA School of Medicine in the Department of Medicine, Division of Hematology and Oncology. Until 1986, he devoted most of his time to teaching, patient care, and laboratory research. He gained stature as the head of the UCLA Medical Center's transplant team, although controversy arose over several transplants he performed in 1978 and 1979. Gale contended that the transplants were medically necessary, but the National Institutes of Health Review Board formally admonished him for utilizing a treatment that was still considered experimental. By the mid-1980s, such transplants were accepted medical procedure.

The chain of events that would ultimately send Gale to the Soviet Union began on April 25, 1986, when an error in maintenance led to an explosion in one of the reactors at the Chernobyl nuclear power station in the Ukraine. The accident released more deadly nuclear material than the atomic bombs dropped on Hiroshima and Nagasaki combined. Plant workers and members of firefighting crews were among those most severely exposed to the radiation; all told, some 500 people were eventually hospitalized for treatment. The Soviet government waited 67 hours after the disaster took place to make an announcement. Gale was among those who heard the news via a local radio station on the morning of April 29.

Gale was highly qualified to offer assistance to the disaster victims. He knew that radiation destroys bone marrow, which in turn breaks down the immune system and produces leukemia-like symptoms. As chairman of the advisory committee for the International Bone Marrow Transplant Registry, he quickly sought and received authorization to offer aid to the Soviet Union. When the Soviets declined, Gale then contacted Dr. Armand Hammer, who had worked with him as the chairman of President Ronald Reagan's cancer advisory panel a few years earlier. Hammer had been doing business with the Soviets since 1921 and, as chairman of Occidental Petroleum Corporation, had signed a long-term, $20 billion fertilizer trade agreement in 1978. Gale phoned Hammer and asked him to convey his offer of free assistance to the Soviet government. Hammer did so, and on May 1 Gale received a call from the acting Soviet ambassador asking him to fly to Moscow as soon as possible. Gale thus became the first physician from the West to be invited by the Soviets to help cope with a crisis since World War II.

Events moved quickly once Gale arrived. After a briefing, he was taken to Moscow's Municipal Hospital Six to meet with the head of the Soviet medical team, Dr. Angelina Guskova. After determining which victims had the best chance of being saved, he requested that assistance and special equipment be brought in to help him perform the necessary bone marrow transplants. Two of the doctors for whom he requested visas, Dr. Richard Champlin and Dr. Paul Terasaki, were colleagues from UCLA. The third, Dr. Yair Reisner, was an Israeli biophysicist, which caused some political complications due to the tensions that existed between the Soviet Union and Israel at the time. In a few days, though, all three were allowed to come to Moscow. In addition, $80,000 worth of advanced medical equipment soon arrived from various Western countries.

Gale and his team put in long hours trying to save as many patients as they could. Racing against the clock, the medical team performed 19 transplants. Bureaucratic obstacles had to be smashed through literally as well as figuratively; at one point, Gale ordered a wall broken down at the hospital in order to move in a large piece of equipment. Chemotherapy, blood platelet transfusions, and antibiotics were also administered to patients. Of the 203 people who were treated for severe radiation sickness, 172 survived.

As Gale struggled against the terrible effects of radiation on his patients, he found himself the object of intense interest in the Soviet Union and elsewhere. On May 15, he appeared at a press conference at the Soviet Foreign Ministry and later had a meeting with General Secretary Mikhail Gorbachev. He was also contacted by Soviet Jews who asked him to help them emigrate to Israel and the United States. Though his wife, Tamar, was an Israeli, and he sympathized with those who wished to leave the Soviet Union, Gale knew that questioning Soviet policies carried risks. "I'm not Teddy Kennedy," he told Eric Lax in a 1986 *New York Times Magazine* interview. "If I become a nuisance to them, it makes for diminishing returns. It's impossible to know the right thing to do." On subsequent visits to Moscow, Gale managed to help several men and women leave the Soviet Union.

By the end of 1986, Gale had made four trips to the Soviet Union to perform additional operations and check on patients. His most dramatic visit was to the site of the Chernobyl disaster and to nearby Pripyat, a city of 45,000 that had been completely evacuated. A helicopter flight over its abandoned streets made a profound impression on Gale. "I thought, 'this is it—this is what we've been afraid of all these years: a city devoid of all human life because of radiation,'" he recalled in the *New York Times Magazine*. "I had a strong feeling that we were seeing history that I hoped we'd never see again."

Back in the United States, Gale kept in touch with Soviet authorities and worked to implement an agreement to monitor the 100,000 people who had lived within the risk zone around Chernobyl. He met with U.S. Secretary of State George Schultz and began to speak out on nuclear energy issues. Gale was urged to become an antinuclear activist, but that position was not entirely in line with his thinking. In *Final Warning*, for example, he advocated ending nuclear weapons testing and called for a careful, responsible use of nuclear power.

Gale's involvement with providing international medical aid did not end with Chernobyl. In 1987 he took part in medical relief efforts at a nuclear accident site in Goiania, Brazil. The following year, he went to Armenia to help earthquake victims, and in 1992 he visited Croatia and spoke out against the bombardment of hospitals there.

Gale's work as a medical researcher continued as well. In 1993, he left the UCLA Medical Center faculty to become senior physician and corporate director of bone marrow and stem cell transplantation at Salick Health Care Inc., a British-owned biosciences and pharmaceuticals company. Finding a cure for leukemia has remained his ultimate goal.

Sources

➤ On-line

Robert Peter Gale website, http://www.robertgalemd.com (January 25, 2000).

➤ Books

Gale, Robert Peter and Thomas Hauser, *Final Warning: The Legacy of Chernobyl,*Warner Books, 1988.

➤ Periodicals

Lancet, January 7, 1989, p. 38; February 17, 1990, pp. 401-402; January 4, 1992, p. 48.
Los Angeles Times, May 5, 1989, p.II7; May 2, 1996, p. 8.
Newsweek, May 26, 1986, p. 26.
New York Times, May 2, 1986, p. A9; April 26, 1987; November 2, 1987, p. A1; November 20, 1987, p. A13.
New York Times Magazine, July 13, 1986 (opening quote).

Bill Gates

"Software is changing the world, and through-out my lifetime that will continue. That's my life work."

As co-founder of the Microsoft Corporation, Bill Gates has been instrumental in the personal computer revolution as the leading software developer in the world. He devotes some of his vast wealth to philanthropic causes. He was born on October 27, 1955 (some sources say October 28), in Seattle, Washington. Address: Microsoft Corporation, 1 Microsoft Way, Redmond, WA 98052-8300.

At the beginning of the twenty-first century, Bill Gates was the wealthiest entrepreneur in the world. As co-founder of Microsoft Corporation, he developed software and operating systems for personal computers, a key factor in the explosive growth they have experienced since the 1980s. Though he has been criticized for not being more generous with his money, Gates has created and funded several philanthropic foundations that support projects in the fields of information science, education, and medicine.

Born on October 27, 1955 (some sources say October 28), in Seattle, Washington, William Henry Gates III is the son of William Henry Gates, Jr., and Mary M. Maxwell Gates. His father was a prominent lawyer in Seattle and a partner in the firm Shidler McBroom Gates & Lucas. His mother was involved in charity work and also served on the board of regents of a university and the boards of several corporations. The family also included Gates' older sister, Kristi, and younger sister, Libby.

Gates was an uncommonly bright youngster who demonstrated his intelligence at an early age. While attending Lakeside School in 1967, he became interested in computers and programming. With his friend and future business partner Paul Allen, he obtained some hands-on experience working for the school one summer creating a program that would generate student schedules.

During high school, Gates began to use his computer expertise to earn money. He had an after-school job at Computer Center Corporation looking for programming errors in the company's computer. He and Allen were also hired to study the electrical power requirements for their area, and to do so they created a computerized electricity grid. In addition, the pair founded a company called Traf-O-Data that studied the traffic patterns for nearby localities.

Besides these legitimate activities, Gates also did a little computer hacking in his youth. He came up with one of the first computer viruses and used it to crash the operating system of Control Data Corporation's CYBERNET computer system. Afterwards, Gates gave up computers for a year to devote time to his other interests. He was an Eagle Scout and spent one summer working as a Congressional page.

But Gates could not stay away from computers for long. He and Allen took leaves of absence during their senior year of high school to work in software development for TRW, a firm based in Vancouver, Washington. Nevertheless, after Gates graduated he decided that he was not going to work with computers any more.

Gates entered Harvard University in 1973 with the idea of becoming a lawyer, as his parents expected. For the next two years, he focused on his studies, though Allen kept trying to lure him back to computers. When the first microcomputer chip came out in 1975, Allen finally convinced his friend that they should stay ahead of the game and start their own company. Gates then left Harvard and never returned.

The first microcomputer, known as the Altair, was produced by MITS, a company based in Albuquerque, New Mexico. Gates and Allen were only 19 years old when they wrote a new version of the BASIC program for use in the new device, the so-called "personal computer" or PC. Their efforts impressed company officials, and before long the two young men had moved to New Mexico to work for MITS.

The following year, Gates and Allen founded Microsoft Corporation in Albuquerque with the goal of becoming the programmers for the microcomputer revolution. Success eluded them at first; five of Microsoft's original customers went bankrupt. But they began making money when they wrote programs for Commodore and Apple Computers. Gates and Allen sold their own version of 4K BASIC to suit different microcomputers. Microsoft thus became the first firm to devote itself entirely to creating software for personal computers, and a new industry was born.

By 1978, Gates and Allen had relocated their company to the Seattle area, setting up corporate offices in Bellevue, Washington. In 1980, Microsoft posted only $4-$8 million in sales, but it was about to become much bigger and broader in scope. IBM contracted with Gates that year to write an operating system for a personal computer then under development. He and his colleagues came up with MS-DOS (Microsoft Disk Operating System) by buying an operating system from a small local firm and then deconstructing and rewriting it to suit IBM. (Gates had never before coded an operating system.) Within a few years, IBM was using MS-DOS in almost all of its computers and continued to do so for many years until another Microsoft product called Windows took its place.

During the early 1980s, Gates and Microsoft began to design software for other companies. They also developed the first versions of software programs that would become industry standards, including Word, a word processing program. By this time, Gates no longer worked just on creating software. He was also involved in formulating business strategy, dealing with other manufacturers, and motivating his growing number of employees. He was determined to remain active in the technical aspects of the operation, however, so in 1982 he hired a president to run Microsoft on a daily basis. (He retained the titles of chief executive officer and chairman of the board.) Allen left the company the following year to receive treatment for Hodgkin's Disease.

By the mid-1980s Gates' success had begun to attract attention. In 1984, he received the Howard Vollum Award from Reed College in Portland, Oregon. Microsoft's profits that year were $15 million based on $100 million in revenues, and the software Gates had developed was installed on about two million computers. Only one year later, Microsoft posted nearly $163 million in sales, 20 percent of which were from MS-DOS alone.

Microsoft went public (that is, began to be traded on the New York Stock Exchange) in 1986. Gates personally held around 45 percent of the company's shares. With a net worth of approximately $390 million, he was ranked as one of the 100 richest people in America.

Gates had come to be known as a good business leader whose employees were unusually productive and loyal. He was regarded as a fair but rather intense boss. As his friend Nathan Myhrvold told Walter Isaacson of *Time,* "Every decision he makes is based on his knowledge of its merits. He doesn't need to rely on personal politics. It sets the tone."

Sometimes Gates was so far ahead of his time that his ideas did not meet with immediate success. In 1987, for example, Gates and Microsoft began promoting compact discs (CDs) for computers. These CD-ROMs could store more data than floppy disks and initially were going to be used for reference materials. At the time, however, many thought such technology was a waste. Only in the mid-1990s did Gates' vision finally catch on in a big way.

Also in 1987, Gates introduced Windows, a new operating system that would eventually replace MS-DOS as the primary operating system on the next generation of IBM PCs and their clones. Windows was easier to use than MS-DOS, which had been criticized for its complexity. But the program remained controversial for many years because of the bugs it contained. Nevertheless, sales continued to increase for Windows and other software innovations introduced by Microsoft. By this time, Microsoft was posting profits of $93 million, and Gates himself was worth over $1 billion.

By the early 1990s, some observers had begun to regard Gates and Microsoft with a very critical eye. They accused the company of stifling innovation in the software market in several different ways. For instance, there were charges that Microsoft swallowed up smaller firms to eliminate possible sources of competition. The company was also denounced for its habit of announcing new products well before they had been fully developed. This tended to cut into sales for companies that already manufactured similar products because some consumers opted to wait for the Microsoft version to appear. Finally, when the market for easy Internet access exploded in the mid-1990s, Gates responded rather belatedly to the trend by bundling Microsoft's version of Internet access software with his Windows operating system. Other companies with their own Internet access software strongly objected to this tactic, which they viewed as a not-so-subtle attempt by Microsoft to dominate the market and thus drive them out of business.

The controversy over Gates' business practices eventually led to charges that Microsoft was a monopoly. First the Federal Trade Commission launched an investigation, then the case was transferred to the Justice Department. Officials there spent two years assembling evidence to prove that Microsoft was indeed a monopoly. The federal government then sued Microsoft for violations of the Antitrust Act. The trial began in October 1998 and concluded during the summer of 1999, at which time Judge Thomas Penfield Jackson ruled that the company was a monopoly and therefore harmful to consumers and competition. As a result, there was speculation that Microsoft might have to be broken up into separate companies early in the twenty-first century.

Not all of Gates' life during the 1990s revolved around running Microsoft. On January 1, 1994, he married Melinda French, a former Microsoft marketing executive. With the births of his children, daughter Jennifer and son Rory, Gates began to address criticism that despite his status as one of the richest people in the world, he was not particularly generous with his money. Before 1997, much of what he donated went to places that already had large endowments. For example, he gave $15 million for a new computer center at Harvard University, one of the wealthiest educational institutions in the United States. And Microsoft's donation of computers to inner-city libraries was seen as a self-serving gesture since the libraries would probably end up purchasing the company's software to load on those computers.

Gates then founded the William H. Gates Foundation, which focused on health issues and nonprofit organizations in the Northwest. By 1999, however, all of Gates' charities had been folded into the Bill and Melinda Gates Foundation. Melinda Gates took a strong interest in the organization and its work on global health issues and education for underprivileged children. The Foundation gave $200 million to put computers in libraries located in impoverished areas and earmarked an additional $1 billion to set up the Gates Millennium Scholars Program, which provided funds for deserving students to attend the college of their choice. Another $750 million went to the development and distribution of vaccines to the world's children over a five-year period. As of 1999, the Foundation was worth $17 billion, making it the largest organization of its kind in the United States. Gates himself had a personal worth of $77 billion, primarily in Microsoft stock.

In early 2000, Gates stepped down as chief executive officer of Microsoft. While he remained involved in developing the overall strategy of the company, he wanted to focus more on product design. Previously, he had stated that he might want to leave Microsoft entirely around 2007 to devote himself exclusively to philanthropy. As Philip Elmer-DeWitt wrote in *Time*, "His is the ultimate revenge of the nerd. Outplotting, outprogramming and above all outthinking his competitors, he rose to the top of an industry that is driven by shifting alliances [and] rapid technological changes . . . . Nobody navigates these turbulent complexities better than Gates . . . ."

Sources

➤ Books

Encyclopedia of World Biography, second edition, volume 6, Gale, 1998, pp. 232-34.
Gareffa, Peter M., editor, *Contemporary Newsmakers: 1987 Cumulation,* Gale, 1988, pp. 126-28.
Ingham, John N. and Lynne B. Feldman, *Contemporary American Business Leaders: A Biographical Dictionary*, Greenwood Press, 1990, pp. 162-66.
Mooney, Louise, editor, *Newsmakers: 1993 Cumulation,* Gale, 1993, pp. 159-62.
Slater, Robert, *Portraits in Silicon,* MIT Press, 1987, pp. 263-71.

➤ Periodicals

Business Week, October 25, 1999, p. 80.

Newsweek, August 30, 1999, p. 38 (opening quote); August 30, 1999, p. 50; November 15, 1999, p. 52; November 22, 1999, p. 62; January 31, 2000, p. 61.

People, January 2, 1984, p. 36; January 17, 1994, p. 42; December 31, 1999, p. 75.

Time, December 25, 1995, p. 100; January 13, 1997, p. 44.

Vaccine Weekly, December 13, 1999.

Lillian M. Gilbreth

*"*W*hen my husband first told me he wanted to have six sons and six daughters, I asked how on earth anybody could have 12 children and continue a career. But my husband said, 'We teach management, so we shall have to practice it.'"*

Born May 24, 1878, in Oakland, California, Lillian M. Gilbreth was a pioneer in the field of industrial engineering, first in partnership with her husband, Frank Gilbreth, and then on her own after his death. The best-selling book *Cheaper by the Dozen* (1949) is an affectionate and humorous account of their family life. She died January 2, 1972, in Arizona.

A t a time when women were expected to be good wives, mothers, and homemakers and little more, Lillian M. Gilbreth was all that and *much* more. A lifelong career woman who, along with her husband, conducted groundbreaking research in time-and-motion study, she complemented his thorough knowledge of the mechanics of work with her own expertise in the human factors that contribute to an efficient and comfortable workplace. After his sudden death left her a widow at the age of 46 with a large family to support, she continued to carry out his dream by teaching the principles of engineering and scientific management to educators and business leaders throughout the world. Gilbreth was among the first to demonstrate that the behavior and performance of individual workers is inextricably linked to the quality of their work environment, a concept of modern industry that is now taken for granted. She also helped establish management as a science that could be codified and studied like any other discipline.

A native of Oakland, California, Lillian Evelyn Moller Gilbreth was born May 24, 1878, the oldest of nine surviving children of William Moller and Annie Delger Moller. The Mollers were quite well-to-do thanks to William's success as a businessman, first as the co-owner of a sugar refinery in New York City and then as a partner in a wholesale plumbing-supply firm in California after he and his wife moved west in the mid-1870s.

By her own account, Gilbreth was a painfully shy and introverted child who sought escape from her many fears in the pages of her favorite books. Because of her sensitive nature, she did not begin school at the customary age and was instead taught at home by her mother. Finally, at the age of nine she went off to public school for the first time. There she struggled socially but excelled academically. She was particularly fond of music and poetry and while still in high school penned the verses for the song "Sunrise," a popular tune of the 1890s.

After completing high school, Gilbreth attended the University of California and graduated with honors in 1900. (She was the first woman in the university's history to deliver the commencement speech.) She continued her education in New York City at Columbia University but became ill and eventually left school and returned home to California. Once she regained her health, Gilbreth enrolled again at the University of California and received her master's degree in 1902.

Later that same summer, her parents arranged for her to go on a trip to Europe with several other young women under the supervision of a local high school teacher named Minnie Bunker. Prior to the group's departure from Boston, Bunker introduced her traveling companions to her cousin, Frank Bunker Gilbreth, who offered to take the women sightseeing in his new car. A friendly, jovial man some ten years Lillian's senior, he was immediately smitten with her, as she was with him. They married in October 1904, thus beginning a personal and professional partnership that would endure for two decades.

The newlyweds settled in Boston, where Frank was already a well-known and highly respected construction engineer. In fact, he headed his own firm, which specialized in building bridges, factories, canals, and other major projects. He had begun his career right after high school as a bricklayer's helper, making so many suggestions during his very first week on the job about how to lay the brick faster and better that the foreman threatened to fire him. But Frank had found his calling in the science of time-and-motion study. By carefully examining the many different movements required to complete a specific task, an expert in time-and-motion study can apply scientific principles to improve speed and efficiency while reducing fatigue and injury. Frank proceeded to do just that on his bricklaying job, quickly rising to the position of foreman of his own crew and achieving such astonishing speed records that he was made superintendent. He also invented some helpful tools, including Gilbreth's Gravity Mixer (for cement) and a special moving scaffold system that kept bricklayers, their materials, and the wall they were working on within easy reach of each other. Before long, Frank went into business for himself.

After marrying Lillian, Frank wanted the two of them to work side-by-side. He therefore encouraged her to continue her education. She did so eagerly, learning from him about the construction trade and the systems he had developed to manage tasks more effectively. In addition, she began studying for her doctorate in psychology.

But Frank also wanted a large family (he thought six boys and six girls sounded about right), and, after some hesitation about how she could possibly handle a career and so many children, Lillian agreed. Recalling their decision many years later in her autobiography, *As I Remember,* she noted that Frank was able to persuade her that "the same principles of efficiency which worked out on the jobs should make the running of the household and the bringing up of a family easy."

Lillian ended up having a dozen children over the next 17 years.

As he had promised, Frank instituted a system designed to make the large, bustling household run as smoothly as possible. He often took moving pictures of his sons and daughters at work to analyze their motions and thus find ways to help them perform a task (washing dishes, for example) more quickly and efficiently. He set up process and work charts in the bathroom so that even the youngest children could record each morning when they had brushed their teeth, taken a bath, combed their hair, and made their beds. In the evening, each child noted his weight and plotted it on a graph before filling out the process charts to indicate whether he had brushed his teeth, washed his face, and done his homework. A family council met once a week to create a budget (a separate purchasing committee handled shopping duties) and assign regular chores; to earn extra money, the children submitted sealed bids for special jobs such as painting a fence or removing a tree stump. (The lowest bidder won the contract.) A utility committee monitored water and electricity usage and fined those who left a light on or a faucet running. A designated gift-buyer kept track of birthdays and other special occasions and bought presents.

"It was regimentation, all right," recalled one of the Gilbreth children years later in the memoir *Cheaper by the Dozen*. "But bear in mind the trouble most parents have in getting just one child off to school, and multiply it by 12. Some regimentation was necessary to prevent bedlam."

Meanwhile, Lillian continued to work with Frank whenever she could. Besides helping him develop and perfect his methods, she organized the material that went into the many technical papers and books he wrote (several of which are regarded as classics in the field of management), the speeches he delivered at countless professional meetings and conferences, and the seminars he held at factories, in offices, and at educational institutions throughout the world. She also handled advertising chores for his construction and consulting business and maintained his voluminous files of newspaper clippings, magazine articles, and research data. In addition, she managed to find time to complete the necessary course work and thesis for her doctorate, which she received from Brown University in 1915.

By that time, Frank had closed his construction business to concentrate exclusively on the work he and Lillian had been doing in the field of industrial management and time-and-motion study. (They had left Boston behind as well, settling in Providence, Rhode Island, in a house big enough to allow them to run their consulting firm largely from home; they later relocated to Montclair, New

Jersey.) With her expertise in psychology, Lillian focused less on the mechanical aspects of their findings and more on the human factors she felt were key to achieving contentment in the workplace—that is, on such things as the impact of worker fatigue on efficiency and how best to alleviate it, the ways machinery or a work area could be configured to accommodate someone with a physical handicap, or the benefits of brighter lighting, better air circulation, and well-designed equipment. Together she and Frank began conducting a summer course in scientific management attended by professors of psychology, engineering, economics, and other business-related subject areas.

In 1924, Frank Gilbreth died suddenly of a heart attack at the age of 56, leaving behind his wife and children, the youngest of whom was only two. Within days of his death, Lillian set sail for Europe to honor commitments he had made to speak at several conferences. She was determined to see that research on motion study continued and that it became a part of the curriculum at more and more colleges and universities.

To make it a little easier to tend to her family's needs, Gilbreth directed industrial engineering seminars at her home office from 1924 until 1930. She then joined the faculty of Purdue University, where she set up a time-and-motion study laboratory and was professor of management from 1935 until 1948. (She was the first woman to hold such a high position at an engineering school.) She served in the same capacity at Rutgers University and also lectured at Bryn Mawr. In addition, Gilbreth taught at the Newark College of Engineering from 1941 until 1943 and at the University of Wisconsin.

Gilbreth also contributed numerous articles to professional publications and wrote several books. Besides the four titles she collaborated on with her husband, she produced seven works of her own, including *The Psychology of Management, The Home Maker and Her Job, Normal Lives for the Disabled,* and *The Foreman and Manpower Management.* She published articles in popular magazines, too, especially on the topic of home management and raising children.

Gilbreth also served as a consultant to various government agencies and committees from the 1930s through the 1960s. During the Depression, for example, she offered advice on unemployment issues. With the start of World War II, she turned her attention to industrial production as the country's factories geared up to meet the demands of the armed forces. In the postwar era, her specialties included the rehabilitation of the physically handicapped (particularly those who had been disabled as a result of war injuries), civil defense, and aging.

Figuring out ways to make housework easier also fascinated Gilbreth. To that end, in one study she observed thousands of women cooking, opening cabinets, and washing dishes to help manufacturers determine the best heights for sinks and appliances. Of particular interest to her was the challenge of coming up with devices to help the handicapped function more comfortably and efficiently at home. Gilbreth carried out some of this research during the 1950s while serving as a consultant to the Institute of Rehabilitation Medicine at the New York University Medical Center. Her recommendations were also based in part on work Frank had done during and after World War I to help disabled veterans.

Gilbreth remained active in her profession almost up until her death in 1972 at the age of 93. "Age needn't determine what one is able to do," she once remarked. "It's really a matter of marshaling your resources, using time sensibly and well. I have taught that, and I have lived by that principle." Acknowledging that her life may have been "hectic" by most standards, she admitted enjoying it that way. "I've been lucky enough to inherit a good constitution and to have the motivation of knowing what I want to do," said Gilbreth as she looked back from the perspective of a great-grandmother. "Best of all, I grew up in a happy home, and now I have many happy homes." And to her credit, she also saw to it that her husband's quest for what he called the "One Best Way" to perform tasks and manage people survived him to inspire and instruct future generations.

Sources

➤ On-line

"Engineering Hero: Dr. Lillian M. Gilbreth," *New Jersey Society of Professional Engineers,* http://www.njspe.org/75a_Gilbreth.htm (December 2, 1999).
"Lillian Moller Gilbreth, 1878-1972," *National Women's Hall of Fame,* http://www.greatwomen.org/glbrth.htm (December 2, 1999).

➤ Books

Gilbreth, Frank B., Jr., and Ernestine Gilbreth Carey, *Cheaper by the Dozen,* Crowell, 1949.

Gilbreth, Lillian M., *As I Remember,* Engineering and Management Press, 1998.

Graham, Laurel, *Managing on Her Own: Dr. Lillian Gilbreth and Women's Work in the Interwar Era,* Engineering and Management Press, 1998.

Robert Goddard

"Work is in progress; there is nothing to report."

Born October 5, 1882 in Worcester, Massachusetts, Robert Goddard was a pioneering rocket scientist. He died on August 10, 1945, in Baltimore, Maryland.

Along with Russian Konstantine Tsiolkovsky and German Hermann Oberth, Robert Goddard was instrumental in the development of the science of rocketry in the twentieth century. Through innovative theories and much testing, Goddard laid the groundwork for modern rocketry, space flight, and many aspects of engineering. His many firsts in the field led to 214 patents in his name. Goddard accomplished these feats despite his constant illness and working in a self-imposed isolation from peer scientists.

Born Robert Hutchings Goddard on October 5, 1882, in Worcester, Massachusetts, he was the son of Nahum Danford Goddard and his wife, Fannie Louise Hoyt Goddard. Goddard's father was a bookkeeper for a machine knives manufacturer and machine shop owner, as well as an amateur inventor who encouraged his son's scientific pursuits. Goddard's mother was sick much of her life with tuberculosis.

Like his mother, Goddard also suffered from ill health. His respiratory diseases began in childhood. Because of the demands of his mother's disease, the family moved between Boston, its suburbs, and Worcester throughout Goddard's youth.

Despite Goddard's health problems, he liked to study, and was interested in rockets from an early age. His formal education was often interrupted by his illness so Goddard read about science and science fiction on his own when he could not be at school. Goddard's path in life was illuminated during an epiphanic moment in a cherry tree at home on October 19, 1899. Having read books like H.G. Wells's *War of the Worlds,* Goddard decided that he would devote his life to the serious study of rocketry.

Goddard managed to graduate from South High School in Worcester in 1904. His long absences due to illness prevented him from graduating before he was 21 years old. Goddard then entered the Worcester Polytechnic Institute, and as early as 1906, began investigating the mathematical practicality of rocketry.

While an undergraduate, Goddard tried to submit a paper for publication in prestigious and popular science publications like *Popular Science Monthly* and *Scientific American.* His article said that rockets could be propelled through outer space with heat and radioactive materials. The article was rejected. It would not be the first time Goddard's ideas would be so treated.

Goddard graduated from Worcester Polytechnic Institute with a B.S. in general science in 1908. He went on to do graduate work in physics at Clark University, which was near his home. He earned an

M.A. in 1910, then a Ph.D. in 1911. Goddard's studies were not limited to rocketry-related topics. He also studied electronics, including radio devices and the thermionic valve.

Goddard continued to work on his ideas for rocketry as well. In 1909, he began thinking about using liquid fuels as rocket propellants, instead of solids. His ideas at the time were focused on liquid hydrogen and liquid oxygen. The same year, Goddard devised the idea of a multi-stage rocket. Though he did not use these concepts immediately in his work, he thought about them for years and used them at key stages of development.

After finishing his Ph.D., Goddard went to Princeton University for a year, 1912-13, to do research at the Palmer Physical Laboratory. His year at Princeton was fruitful for his rocketry theories. He began examining how workable reaction engines were in vacuum tests, studies that would continue for many years. Goddard also began working out the mathematical side to the escape velocity of rockets and their reaching high altitudes.

Princeton would have made him an offer to stay at their institution, but for Goddard's lingering health concerns. He secured a position on the physics faculty at Clark University, however. Goddard was forced to take much of 1913 off as he contracted tuberculosis. At one point, doctors believed he only had two weeks to live. Goddard was told to slow down and take care of his health, but he did not then, nor at any point in his life.

When Goddard returned to his research, he began constructing rockets, primarily ship rockets and large rockets with solid fuels. By 1914, Goddard began receiving patents for his work. His first two patents were for a liquid-fuel gun rocket and a multistage step rocket, the latter the first of its kind. These patented ideas led to financial support for his experiments by the Smithsonian Institution.

During World War I, Goddard was hired by the United States Signal Corps to be the head of rocket research at the Mount Wilson Observatory in California. Though Goddard produced an anti-aircraft rocket and a solid-propellant bombardment, his most significant invention was not used until World War II. He worked on the basic ideas behind tube-launched rockets, which were called bazookas when they were made for combat in World War II.

After the war, Goddard returned to Clark and by 1919, was given a full professorship. He would remain affiliated with the institution through 1942. While teaching, Goddard continued to work on his rocketry, in both theory and fact.

In 1919, Goddard published one of his only papers, but it was extremely important. It was called "A Method of Reaching Extreme Altitudes," and appeared in *Smithsonian Miscellaneous Collections*. In the article, Goddard explained his mathematical theories behind the possibilities of rocket, propulsion and travel, and tried to prove its viability. Goddard essentially argued that a flash-powder missile could travel to the moon, an idea considered more science fiction that science feasibility at the time.

While the paper was scientifically momentous, it was misinterpreted by the media. Goddard was ridiculed in the media for his ideas, most notably in a *New York Times* editorial on January 13, 1920. Some thought he was crazy, others, a dreamer. Goddard was dubbed "the moon rocket man."

Such attitudes increased Goddard's tendency towards secrecy, though he already preferred to work on his own, and not in teams like most other scientists. He only worked with a few technicians (some of which he had sign non-disclosure agreements) as he worked out his theories of rocket propulsion.

By the early 1920s, Goddard began making progress in this direction. In 1921 or 1923, he started experimenting with liquid fuels, specifically, gasoline with a motivating force of oxygen. Within a few years, he developed a rocket motor that had used these liquid propellants. Goddard began setting off rockets, though most did not go very far.

On March 16, 1926, on the farm of an aunt near Auburn, Massachusetts, Goddard set off the first successful liquid-fuel rocket, which he dubbed Nell. He designed and built the four foot high, six inch wide rocket, which traveled at 60 miles per hour to a height of 41 feet. Goddard continued to build and test more sophisticated rockets throughout the late 1920s as he continued to receive funding for his work.

Goddard set off his last rocket in Massachusetts on July 17, 1929. This rocket was the first ever to have an instrument payload: an aneroid barometer, a thermometer, and a camera to take pictures of the other two instruments. The rocket's flight lasted about 18.5 seconds, rising about 90 feet, but the ensuing sound frightened neighbors. He was forbidden from shooting off rockets in Massachusetts again.

Goddard's rocket and the subsequent reaction from authorities in Massachusetts were covered by the media. He was again derided, with some pointing out that he missed the moon by a long shot. The cause of the retiring Goddard might have been hurt by such negative press, but it actually brought him to the attention of sympathetic supporters.

The most famous aviator of the era, Charles Lindbergh, was impressed by Goddard's theories and experiments. He helped the scientist obtain grants from the Guggenheim Foundation and family. In 1930, Goddard moved to a remote area of New Mexico, near Roswell, with his wife Esther Christine Kisk Goddard (whom he had married in 1924), and set up an experimental station.

While on several leaves of absence from Clark (from 1930-32, then 1934-42), Goddard spent his time in the desert trying to prove his theories. While he failed more often than not in his experiments, the ideas and successes that came from this time period were important accomplishments. Yet because Goddard worked under a cloak of secrecy, his work did not influence many of his contemporaries, especially in the United States.

In the New Mexico desert, Goddard's rockets became more sophisticated in their boosters and payloads. He reached speeds of 700 miles per hour and altitudes of up to 9000 feet. Many of his developments, while not always successes in his hands, were essential in the subsequent development of rockets and guided missiles. Even the ideas Goddard did not test, but merely theorized and speculated on, came to be used in advanced rocketry and space flight.

Among the many innovations Goddard devised were: gyro-stabilization apparatuses; clustered engines; using gimbal-mounted tail sections as a means of steering the rocket; devices that allowed for automatic firing and releasing; fuel-injection systems; and a new design for combustion chambers, among many others. Goddard published some of his findings in another paper for the *Smithsonian Miscellaneous Collections* in 1936. He never achieved his ultimate goal however: Goddard never got a rocket outside the Earth's atmosphere, perhaps, as some have speculated, because his testing methodology was flawed.

When the United States entered World War II, Goddard left New Mexico to work for the military in Annapolis, Maryland. He became the director of research at the Bureau of Aeronautics. Goddard left his primary rocket research behind for the moment, though he tried to show the potential in his work to them, but was turned down. Instead, he developed small rockets to help jets take off from aircraft carriers.

Ironically, after the war it was revealed that the engines of German V-2 rockets were based on Goddard's designs. Goddard had been professionally friendly with some of the German scientists and shared information with them before 1939. When these scientists came to the United States after the war, they told incredulous officials that they had learned everything from Goddard. Goddard himself was amazed when he inspected the engine in the V-2 rocket because it was exactly like his own.

After the war, Goddard returned to his rocket research and worked for Curtiss-Wright. However, he developed throat cancer, and died of the disease on August 10, 1945, in Baltimore, Maryland. Goddard's accomplishments were not really appreciated in his lifetime, perhaps in part because of his secrecy and because he did not reach the moon on his own. Yet his designs and patents were eventually used to send humans into outer space.

The impact of Goddard's work can be seen in several incidents a decade or so after his death. In 1960, the United States government paid more than $1 million to his estate to get the rights to his patents because so many were key to basic space technology. In 1962, the National Aeronautic and Space Administration (NASA) acknowledged his importance by naming a facility after him in Greenbelt, Maryland, the Goddard Space Flight Center. Most telling of all perhaps was that after a man walked on the moon in 1969, the *New York Times* apologized for its editorial from 1920.

Sources

➤ Books

Asimov, Issac, *Asimov's Biographical Encyclopedia of Science and Technology,* second revised edition, Doubleday & Company, Inc., 1982, pp. 688-89.

Emme, Eugene M., ed., *The History of Rocket Technology,* Wayne State University Press, 1964, pp. 19-23.

Encyclopedia of World Biography, volume 6, second edition, Gale Group, 1998, pp. 376-77.

Garraty, John A. and Mark C. Carnes, eds., *American National Biography,* volume 9, Oxford University Press, 1999, pp. 140-42.

Garraty, John A. and Jerome L. Sternstein, eds., *Encyclopedia of American Biography,* second edition, HarperCollins, 1998, pp. 448-50.

Gillispie, Charles Coulston, ed., *Dictionary of Scientific Biography,* volume 5, Charles Scribner's Sons, 1972, pp. 433-34.

Magill, Frank N., ed., *Great Lives From History: American Series,* volume 2, Salem Press, 1987, pp. 927-31.

➤ Periodicals

Technology and Culture, April 1995, p. 327.
Time, March 29, 1999, p. 99 (opening quote).

Henry B. Gonzalez

*"*If*a bill violates the constitutional rights of even one person, then it has to be struck down."*

Born May 3, 1916, in San Antonio, Texas, Henry B. Gonzalez is the first Texan of Mexican descent to be elected to the U.S. Congress. Over the course of his long political career, he earned a reputation as a feisty populist who championed the rights of those he perceived as underdogs. Address: 238 Kings Highway, San Antonio, TX 78212-2964.

During the nearly 40 years he represented his San Antonio constituents in the U.S. Congress, Henry B. Gonzalez— known affectionately to his admirers as simply "Henry B."—was one of the most colorful and unpredictable politicians in Washington, D.C. His "life's pursuit," as he once described it, was passionately standing up for the rights of minorities and others he felt were at the mercy of bigger and more powerful entities. That he did so at a time when discrimination against Hispanics (especially in Texas) was commonplace is a testament to his courage and his willingness to stay the course.

One of six children of Leonides and Genoveva Barbosa Gonzalez, Henry Barbosa Gonzalez was born May 3, 1916, in San Antonio, Texas. Only five years earlier, his parents had been forced to flee Mexico to escape a violent revolution. Prior to that, Leonides Gonzalez had been a successful businessman and mayor of the town of Mapimi in his native state of Durango. But relocating to San Antonio meant changing careers; in his new home, he became a journalist and eventually rose to the post of managing editor of *La Prensa*, at that time the only Spanish-language newspaper in the United States.

Gonzalez grew up in a lively household in which politics and philosophy were regularly debated and discussed. But times were difficult financially, so young Henry had to take on some part-time jobs while he was still in elementary school to help support his sister and his four brothers. Between going to class and working, he did not have much spare time. But what little he had he spent reading at the local public library.

Poverty was not the only obstacle Gonzalez faced as a youngster. He also encountered anti-Mexican prejudice that left him frightened and confused. Slurs and insults were plentiful, and, like many African Americans at that time (especially in southern states), he found himself excluded from "whites only" swimming pools, restaurants, and other public facilities.

After finishing high school, Gonzalez attended San Antonio Junior College, from which he graduated in 1937. He then headed to Austin and the University of Texas, where he studied engineering until he could no longer afford to stay. Returning home to San Antonio, he enrolled at St. Mary's University instead and earned his bachelor of arts degree and then, in 1943, a law degree. While he was still in school, Gonzalez married Bertha Cuellar; they eventually became the parents of eight children.

During the rest of the 1940s, Gonzalez worked at a variety of jobs that nudged him ever closer to a career in public service. After running his father's Spanish-English translation service for a while and serving as a public relations advisor for an insurance firm, he went to work for the local juvenile court system as assistant chief probation officer. In 1946, he was promoted to chief probation officer but promptly quit when his superiors refused to allow him to add a black person to his staff. Four years later he was appointed deputy family relocation director for the city of San Antonio's housing authority, a post in which he was responsible for helping find new homes for families whose slum neighborhoods were going to be demolished.

Gonzalez launched his political career around this same time when he entered the 1950 race for a seat in the Texas House of Representatives. Although he lost the election, he was not quite ready to give up on politics; in 1953, he tried out for the San Antonio City Council and emerged victorious. His most noteworthy accomplishment as a member of the council was winning passage of a law that ordered the city's recreational facilities to be desegregated.

In 1956, Gonzalez moved up another rung on the ladder when he won a seat in the Texas Senate, making him the first Mexican American in more than 100 years to serve in that body. Once in the state capital of Austin, he quickly made a name for himself among his fellow legislators as an outspoken liberal. He advocated doing more to clear slums, denounced a proposed state sales tax, and voiced strong opposition to a series of 10 bills designed to uphold the principles of racial segregation. In the latter case, he and another senator filibustered for a record 36 hours to stymie passage of the legislation; 9 of the 10 bills ultimately went down to defeat or were declared unconstitutional.

Setting his sights even higher, Gonzalez waged an unsuccessful campaign for governor of Texas in 1958. Three years later, he ran in a special election to fill the U.S. Senate seat left vacant when Lyndon B. Johnson was elected vice president. Gonzalez lost, but later that same year, he ran in yet another special election held to fill an unexpected vacancy in the U.S. House of Representatives. This time, Gonzalez won and headed to Washington, D.C., as the first Mexican American from Texas ever to serve in the House.

Gonzalez represented San Antonio and the surrounding area for the next 37 years, easily winning reelection each time. (He never faced an opponent in the Democratic primary and squared off against a Republican opponent in the general election on only six occasions.) This he accomplished while downplaying his ethnic origins. Pointing out that he had attracted support across a wide spectrum of voters, not just Hispanics, he argued that his responsibility as a member of Congress was to represent the needs and desires of *everyone* in his district. This stance angered more militant Mexican Americans who felt he should have been more active on their behalf; he was even dropped from membership in the Congressional Hispanic Caucus. Yet Gonzalez remained stubbornly independent throughout his long tenure.

One group he always stood up for was the underprivileged, regardless of race or ethnicity. A fierce supporter of minority interests, he sponsored legislation during the early years of his career that encompassed a wide variety of concerns, including civil rights, adult education and job training, the minimum wage, and the poll tax. In 1963, his impassioned speeches on the House floor helped defeat legislation that would have made it easier for large vegetable and fruit growers to exploit cheap farm labor from Mexico. He was also one of just a handful of Southern Democrats who supported the landmark Civil Rights Act of 1964. Later in his career, during the 1980s, he took up the cause of low-cost housing and vociferously defended it against attempts by the administration of President Ronald Reagan to scale back the modest programs then in existence.

On occasion throughout the 1970s and 1980s, Gonzalez's cantankerous and unpredictable nature prompted some observers to dismiss him as an eccentric has-been. During the late 1970s, for instance, he was preoccupied with investigating various conspiracy theories stemming from the assassinations of President John F. Kennedy and Martin Luther King, Jr. He even served as chairman of a special House panel that was looking into the matter. But he nearly derailed his own efforts when he abruptly fired the panel's chief counsel (with whom he had been feuding) and then resigned from the chairmanship in the ensuing turmoil. Later, on numerous occasions during the 1980s, he publicly railed against what he saw as corruption and abuse of power in the administrations of presidents Ronald Reagan and George Bush and even demanded that they be impeached.

Gonzalez came into his own again from 1988 until 1995 when he served as chairman of the powerful House Banking, Finance, and Urban Affairs Committee. In this position, his reputation for integrity, honesty, and independence served him well as head of the much-publicized investigation into the collapse of hundreds of savings and loan institutions, a crisis that reached its peak during the late 1980s. His committee conducted extensive hearings on the matter, and his persistent and effective questioning of the people called to testify clearly revealed the extent of the incompetence and deception that had led to the loss of billions of dollars. Afterwards, Gonzalez played a key role in drafting a special "bailout bill" that tightened government regulations pertaining to savings and loan institutions and provided funds to prosecute those suspected of wrongdoing. He then turned his attention to the banking industry and proposed reforms aimed at preventing a similar crisis there.

Gonzalez also used his banking committee chairmanship to improve enforcement of laws against the practice of redlining, or denying mortgages to buyers seeking housing in neighborhoods that are considered poor economic risks. In addition, he called upon banks to honor both the spirit and the letter of the law regarding their obligation to serve the communities in which they operate by fostering investment and development opportunities.

In 1994, Gonzalez had to give up the banking committee chairmanship when the Republicans gained control of the House in the mid-term elections. The transition from majority to minority status was a difficult one for him to make, however; he missed many meetings and seemed to have lost his enthusiasm. (He later attributed this uncharacteristic behavior to his wife's poor health, which required him to make frequent trips back to San Antonio.) Two years later, faced with criticism from some members of his own party that he was too old and too out of touch to continue serving on such an important committee, Gonzalez had to fight to retain his job as the top Democrat. He won that particular battle after delivering an emotional plea to his colleagues and promising to step down after the 1998 elections.

In late 1997, however, Gonzalez announced that he was retiring from Congress for health reasons after suffering from an infection that attacked his heart. But he did not immediately follow through with his plans; instead, he convalesced at home in San Antonio for some 14 months and then returned to Washington in September 1998 after declaring himself fit enough to serve out the remaining few weeks of his term in Congress. That he did, going out in typically feisty style by complaining about the Republican-led effort to impeach President Bill Clinton and dismantle programs he and other Democrats had helped create.

In a post-retirement interview with *Dallas Morning News* reporter Catalina Camia, Gonzalez reminisced fondly about his career. "The great privilege," he noted, "was to be able to serve . . . for consecutive sessions to carry out the aims and promises of the people." As Carlos Conde pointed out in an article published in another edition of the same Dallas newspaper, however, Gonzalez's legacy may not necessarily be shaped only by his many accomplishments as a legislator. Of greater importance, declared Conde, are intangibles such as "what he later came to symbolize and what he had the courage to do at a time when Latinos still were decades away from social and economic opportunities in Texas and elsewhere in the United States. . . . Most of today's Hispanic politicians never had to endure the indignities and struggles of trailblazers like Henry B. Gonzalez. . . . They reached Washington and their political prominence on a road made easier by men from an era when being an ambitious Latino was a risky task."

Sources

➤ On-line

Camia, Catalina, "Gonzalez Defeats 2 to Stay Top Democrat on Banking Panel," *Dallas Morning News,* http://www.archive.dallasnews.com (December 29, 1999).

Camia, Catalina, "Gonzalez Reflects on Long Career, Bemoans Impeachment," *Dallas Morning News,* http://www.archive.dallasnews.com (December 29, 1999).

Conde, Carlos, "Only Health Could Slow Henry B.," *Dallas Morning News,* http://www.archive.dallasnews.com (December 29, 1999).

Mittelstadt, Michelle, "Gonzalez Goes Back to Congress," *Dallas Morning News,* http://www.archive.dallasnews.com (December 29, 1999).

➤ Periodicals

Harper's, October 1992, pp. 84-96 (opening quote).
Hispanic, October 1989.
Mother Jones, July/August 1991, pp. 12-13.
Nation, June 1, 1992, pp. 740-741.
New Republic, April 11, 1994, pp. 14-17.
Texas Monthly, October 1992.

Katharine Meyer Graham

*"**W**atergate no doubt was the most impor- tant occurrence in my working life, but my involvement was basically peripheral, rarely di- rect. . . .What I did primarily was stand behind the editors and reporters, in whom I believed."*

Born June 16, 1917 in New York City, New York, Katherine Meyer Graham was publisher of the *Washington Post* during its publication of the "Pentagon Papers" and the Watergate scandal. Address: Washington Post Company, 1150 15th St NW, Washington, D.C., 20071-0002.

The American newspaper publishing industry has had its share of forceful, eminent personalities, and Katharine Meyer Graham is no exception. As heir to the *Washington Post* empire, Graham has been on convivial terms with a succession of presidents, while her roster of friends and acquaintances includes some of the most powerful names in the country. Such connections among the high and mighty, however, did not keep Graham from making the *Post* into one of the top newspapers in the country—which it was decidedly not when she assumed the reins after the death of her husband in 1963. Moreover, Graham came into power at a time when women were expected to remain on the sidelines of life as wives and mothers—as she had been trained. Graham struggled for many years to overcome her own self-doubts and self-imposed limitations.

Katharine Meyer Graham was born in New York City, New York on June 16, 1917, the fourth of five children born to Eugene Meyer, a banker, and Agnes Elizabeth (Ernst) Meyer, an author and philanthropist. In 1933, when Katharine was still a student at the Madeira School in Greenway, Virginia, her father bought the moribund *Washington Post* for $875,000. Already retired, Meyer purchased the paper because he had grown restless and wanted a voice in the nation's affairs. His hobby became the capital's most influential paper.

From an early age Katharine Meyer showed an interest in publishing. At the Madeira School she worked on the student newspaper. In 1935 she entered Vassar College, but the following year transferred to the University of Chicago, which she regarded as a more stimulating campus. During her summer vacations she worked on the *Washington Post*. After her graduation with a B.A. degree in 1938 she went to California to take a job as a waterfront reporter for the *San Francisco News*. She returned to Washington a year later and joined the editorial staff of the *Post,* where she also worked in the circulation department.

On June 5, 1940, she married Philip L. Graham, a Harvard Law School graduate and clerk for Supreme Court Justice Felix Frankfurter. Her husband entered the Army in World War II, and she gave up reporting to move with him from base to base. When he was sent overseas to the Pacific Theater, Katharine returned to her job at the *Post*. After his discharge in 1945, Eugene Meyer persuaded Philip Graham to join the *Washington Post* as associate publisher. Meyer, who had a warm relationship with his son-in-law, eventually turned the business over to him, selling all the voting stock in the company to the Grahams for $1 in 1948. Philip Graham helped his father-in-law to build the business, acquiring the *Post*'s competitor, the *Washington Times Herald,* in 1954, and in 1961 purchasing *Newsweek* magazine for a sum estimated to be between eight and 15 million dollars. He also expanded the radio and television operations of the company and in 1962 helped to establish an international news service.

Though the Graham marriage seemed a happy one, Phil Graham suffered from manic depression, which was left untreated until late—too late—in life. Combined with the mental illness was a proclivity toward ill health, and a penchant for drinking. He was often verbally abusive to Graham, and carried on liaisons with other women. Events reached a crisis point in 1962, when he announced that he was leaving Graham and their four children for a young, attractive reporter at *Newsweek*. He left their home and hired one of Washington's most feared attorneys to represent him in the divorce, which was predicted to turn ugly. Though both Grahams had been given the paper outright through gifts of controlling stock by 1948, Phil Graham had the majority and expected to keep his job—and the paper. Katharine Graham, meanwhile, vowed to fight to retain her ownership of the *Post*. "I was not about to give up the paper without a fight," she wrote in her book, *Personal History*. However, Phil Graham finally began undergoing long overdue psychiatric help, and returned to his wife and family. On leave from a nearby private sanitarium in August of 1963, he shot himself to death at the Graham farm in Virginia. It was his wife who discovered his body.

After her husband's death, Katharine Graham took over the presidency of the company. A prominent Washington matron who had devoted her time to the raising of her daughter and three sons, she had never lost her interest in the affairs of the family business. She studied the operations, asked questions, consulted with such old friends as James Reston and Walter Lippmann, and made the key decisions which helped to bring in skilled journalists to improve the quality of the paper. She selected Benjamin C. Bradlee, the Washington bureau chief for *Newsweek,* as managing editor in 1965.

Graham gave Bradlee, who later became executive editor, a free hand and backed him during the 1970s when the *Post* began making news as well as reporting it. In June of 1971 the *Post*, along with the *New York Times,* became embroiled with the government over their right to publish excerpts from a classified Pentagon study of U.S. military involvement in Vietnam compiled during President Lyndon Johnson's administration. A court order to restrain the publication of the documents led to an appeal to the U.S. Supreme Court and, in a decision judged a major victory for freedom of the press, the Court upheld the papers' right to publish the "Pentagon Papers."

Further controversy erupted when the investigative reporting team of Bob Woodward and Carl Bernstein began to probe the break-in at the Democratic National Headquarters at the Watergate apartment complex in June of 1972. Woodward's and Bernstein's articles in the *Post* linked the break-in to the larger pattern of illegal activities that ultimately led to the indictment of over 40 members of the Nixon administration and to the resignation of President Richard Nixon in August of 1974.

Graham, generally conceded to be the most powerful woman in publishing, held the title of publisher at the *Washington Post* starting in 1969. As chairman and principal owner of the Washington Post Company, she controlled the fifth largest publishing empire in the nation. In the period 1975 to 1985 profits grew better than 20 percent annually.

In 1979 Graham turned the title of publisher over to her son Donald. But she remained active in all areas of the business, from advising on editorial policy to devising strategies for diversifying the company's holdings, which included, in addition to the *Post* and *Newsweek*, the Trenton *Times*, four television stations, and 49 percent interest in a paper company. In Washington she was a formidable presence. Heads of state, politicians, and leaders in journalism and the arts gathered at her Georgetown home and weekends at her farm in northern Virginia.

Under Graham's leadership, the *Washington Post* grew in influence and stature until by common consent it was judged one of the two best newspapers in the country. It was read and consulted by presidents and prime ministers in the U.S. and abroad and exerted a powerful influence on political life. At the same time, the *Post*, which boasts a circulation of 725,000, served as a hometown paper for a general audience who enjoyed the features, cartoons, and advice columns.

Katharine Graham was described as a "working publisher." Determined to preserve the family character of the business, she took up the reins after the death of her husband and worked hard not only to build but to improve her publishing empire. A forceful and courageous publisher, she knew when to rely on the expertise of professionals and allowed her editors maximum responsibility, at the same time strengthening her publications by her willingness to spend to attract top talent in journalism and management. In

1997, Graham published her memoirs *Personal History,* which earned her a Pulitzer Prize for Biography in 1998.

Sources

➤ Books

Davis, Deborah, *Katharine the Great: Katharine Graham and the Washington Post,* 1979.
Felsenthal, Carol, *Power, Privilege, and the Post: The Katherine Graham Story,* 1993.
Graham, Katherine Meyer, *Personal History,* 1997.

➤ Periodicals

Commentary, August 1997, p. 46 (opening quote).
Editor & Publisher, June 1, 1991, p. 18; November 15, 1997, p. 17; October 30, 1999, p. 26.
Forbes, April 19, 1984; June 15, 1987, p. 145.
New Republic, February 28, 1983, p. 13.
New Statesman, July 4, 1997, p. 47.
Time, February 7, 1977; February 17, 1997, p. 24.

Reg and Maggie Green

"I've always taken hope from the idea that there's a lot you can do here in the world, and that what you do here can be about love rather than hate— kindness rather than cruelty.**"**

Reg (born January 31, 1929 in Accrington, England) and Maggie Green (born March 24, 1961 in San Francisco, California) turned the tragedy of their son Nicholas's murder into the gift of life by donating his organs after his death, and went on to become leaders in the international movement to promote organ donor awareness. Address: The Nicholas Green Foundation, P.O. Box 937, Bodega Bay, CA 94923.

R eg and Maggie Green became internationally famous because of a choice they made, one they never dreamed they would need to make. Following their seven year-old son Nicholas's murder during a botched robbery in Italy in 1994, they decided to donate his organs to seven Italians in desperate need of transplants. This act of kindness first inspired the Italian people, then became an ongoing crusade. The Greens called the wave of positive results that came out of their son's death the "Nicholas Effect." It became the turning point in their lives, and they continued to campaign for increased organ donation in honor of Nicholas's memory.

Up until tragedy struck his family's life, Reg Green was best known as a journalist in Britain and the United States. Born in the northern English town of Accrington, he grew up during the Great Depression and World War II years in modest circumstances. He attended college in Manchester and received a degree in economics at age 19. Several years later, he began an active career as a newspaper reporter and critic, serving on the staff of the *Birmingham Post* and *The (London) Times*. He also served as an economics commentator for the BBC. In 1970, he and his first wife Jane came to the United States, where he took a series of positions in public relations for corporate associations. He later became the founder and publisher of the Mutual Fund News Service, and became a United States citizen in 1995.

The Greens separated in 1984, and Reg moved from Washington D.C. to Northern California. After he and Jane divorced, Reg married Maggie Young, and the couple settled down to life in Bodega Bay, north of San Francisco. Their first child was a son, Nicholas, followed by a daughter, Eleanor. The family was a close and happy one, taking a particular delight in traveling together.

In the summer of 1994, the Green family took a vacation in southern Italy. On the night of September 29, while driving through Calabria in the southern tip of the country, the Greens's rented car was fired upon by robbers. Nicholas, sleeping in the back seat, was hit in the back of the head, although the family didn't realized it at that moment. The family outraced their attackers and discovered what had happened a few miles down the road. Nicholas was taken to a small local hospital, then to a larger one in Messina, Sicily. Doctors discovered that the bullet had lodged in the stem of his brain, and held out little hope for recovery.

Two days later, Nicholas was declared brain dead, and his parents agreed to donate his organs for transplant. The decision was made quickly and without difficulty. "When we saw Nicholas that day, it seemed perfectly obvious to us that this was the right thing to do," Reg Green recalled in an online interview with *CNN.com*. "His future had been taken away from him. It seemed even more important than ever that that future should be given to someone else." Seven Italian recipients received Nicholas's heart, kidneys, corneas, liver and pancreas.

Because of the low organ donor rate in Italy, Nicholas's story attracted a great deal of attention in the local news media. Phone calls and telegrams of sympathy and appreciation began to pour in. "It took the whole country by storm," Reg Green told writer Doug Hill in an interview included on the Nicholas Green Foundation's website. "I think that regardless of what we did or didn't do, there would have been that explosion of sympathy. They were horrified that a child had been hurt, many were ashamed." The Greens were interviewed on Italian television and received an award for their act of generosity from the mayor of Rome. Writing in the *New York Times*, Alan Cowell noted, "If there was a single idea that seized Italian commentators it was that, in a land with Europe's lowest record of organ-donation—and in a country not often known for selflessness—a lesson had been given."

The family returned to the United States, then flew back to Italy several months later to be further honored and to lend their support to local organ donation advocates. Both the Italian and the United States media covered the visit extensively. Among the honors they received was from the Bonino-Pulejo Foundation, an international charitable organization based in Messina. During this trip, the Greens met with six of the transplant recipients, amidst a flurry of press coverage. All of this served to extend the chain of positive actions that the Greens termed the "Nicholas Effect." An example of this was the quadrupling of organ donor cards signed in Italy immediately following the boy's death. In 1998, the Italian donation rate was more than double what it had been the year before his murder.

Back home in Bodega Bay, the Greens decided to keep working to promote organ donation awareness. Media attention continued in the United States, as Reg and Maggie wrote stories for or were interviewed by *Reader's Digest*, *Parents*, the *Economist* and other publications. The couple established the non-profit Nicholas Green Foundation to help spread information about organ donation and to support a range of children's causes. In addition, the Nicholas Green Distinguished Student Awards program was launched to recognize excellence in young children. Nicholas's memory was further honored with the dedication of a Children's Bell Tower north of Bodega Bay, featuring 100 bells of all shapes and sizes, including one cast in Italy and blessed by Pope John Paul II.

In 1999, Reg Green published *The Nicholas Effect*, an account of the events before and after the murder of his son. The book provided a loving portrait of Nicholas's life and described the family's tragedy with candor and humor. The book drew favorable reviews and praise for its eloquence and honesty. "I had tears in my eyes many times while I was writing it and some of it was wrenching, going back over Nicholas's death," Reg Green told interviewer Doug Hill. "But, for the most part, the loss of Nicholas has been so great that talking about it really doesn't make it worse. It was also nice to be able to put down on paper the happier times I remember too."

The Greens have continued to give lectures and meet with donor awareness groups in the United States and abroad. They helped to launch several new projects in the late '90s, including a Fulbright Scholarship to bring Italian physicians to the United States to study transplant techniques. Among the positive developments that the Greens point towards as examples of the "Nicholas Effect" is the establishment of a new transplant hospital in Sicily, with training and technical support from the University of Pittsburgh.

The cause of organ donation found a team of powerful advocates in Reg and Maggie Green. Beyond this, the life and death of Nicholas Green has touched people in even more universal ways. "There is one more thing that has struck me about this story," Reg Green said in his *CNN.com* interview. "It seemed to remind people all over the world how fragile young life is, therefore how precious. I said at the time I imagined parents giving their children an extra hug before they went off to school in the morning or reading an extra chapter to them at bedtime. I thought if that happened, Nicholas would say that this is the very best thing that could have come out of that story."

Sources

➤ **On-line**

"A Child's Death Gives Life to Seven Others,"*CNN interviews,* http://cnn.com (March 7, 2000).

"An Interview with Reg Green," *Nicholas Green Foundation*, http://www.nicholaseffect.com (March 7, 2000; opening quote).

➤ **Books**

Green, Reg, *The Nicholas Effect: A Boy's Gift to the World,* O'Reilly, 1999.

➤ **Periodicals**

Library Journal, May 1, 1999, p. 102.
Los Angeles Times, September 20, 1999, p. S2.
Omaha World-Herald, June 12, 1999, p. 11.
New York Times, October 9, 1994, p. 2.
San Francisco Chronicle, October 5, 1994, p. A20; February 8, 1996, p. A20.

➤ **Other**

Additional information for this profile was obtained from a telephone interview with Reg and Maggie Green in February of 2000.

Mia Hamm

"It's very important for young girls to have female athletes they can identify with."*

Born Muriel Margret Hamm, March 17, 1972, in Selma, Alabama, Mia Hamm played a pivotal role in promoting women's sports as a member of the U.S. women's national soccer team. Address: c/o Nike, Inc., Soccer Division, 1 Bowerman Dr., Beaverton, OR 97005-6453.

S occer player Mia Hamm has scored more goals during her career than any other player, male or female, in the history of the sport. This five-foot-five, 125-pound speed demon has run her opponents ragged as she has helped lead her college team, the U.S. national team, and the U.S. Olympic team to victories. Hamm became the first player to receive the U.S. Soccer athlete of the year award three times, in 1994, 1995, and 1996, and only the second player ever to receive the U.S. Soccer female athlete of the year award two years in a row, in 1994 and 1995. Even more astounding, she clinched the award again every year thereafter until 1998 as well. In the summer of 1999, Hamm once again proved to be an integral part of the national team, as she led the women to triumph over China for the World Cup.

In an age where soccer as well as women's sports are becoming popular for the first time, Hamm has ridden the wave to become a pioneer as well as an icon. Though soccer is one of the most closely followed sports worldwide, it only caught on in the United States beginning in the 1980s, when more young people began to play. In addition, the establishment of more professional female sports organizations, such as the Women's National Basketball Association, has started to wipe away the stigma of female athletes; they were previously perceived to be too "masculine." Salary-wise, they have a long way to go in order to catch up to their male counterparts, but the culture of female athletes is growing, which portends a brighter future. Female fans proudly wear Hamm's number 9 jersey and pull their hair back in ponytails, clamoring after her for autographs and high-fives, and the record-setting crowds are a good sign that people are more accepting of women's sports. Though the humble player is, by all accounts, uncomfortable with her status as a role model, Hamm noted to Jere Longman in the *New York Times Upfront,* "It's very important for young girls to have female athletes they can identify with."

Muriel Margret "Mia" Hamm was born on March 17, 1972, in Selma, Alabama, and moved frequently throughout her childhood because her father, Bill, was a colonel in the Air Force. The family, which includes her three sisters and two brothers, lived on bases in Texas, California, Virginia, and Florence, Italy. When Hamm was five, her parents adopted her brother Garrett, eight years old at the time, who was very athletic and a big influence on Hamm. "When he'd go play pickup football or baseball, I was always right behind him," she told Longman. "He always picked me for his teams." Her mother, Stephanie, a former ballerina, tried to steer her into dancing at a young age, but Hamm would have no part of it, preferring to play soccer instead. It was one of her father's passions: He would take the family to games in Italy, and back in the United States, he coached and refereed his children's teams.

Hamm got her start at age five on the soccer field in a co-ed pee-wee league in Wichita Falls, Texas. "Our team record wasn't very good, but I managed to score a lot of goals," she remarked in a *People* article. But she did not limit herself to one sport. On boys' teams, Hamm played baseball as a shortstop and pitcher, basketball as a point guard, and even football in seventh grade as a wide receiver and cornerback. "I was fast and could catch the ball," she explained to Kevin Sherrington of the *Dallas Morning News*. "My friends wanted me to play." She also put in time as a quarterback but did not enjoy it as much, although overall, she liked the sport. "I had a great time at it," she noted to Sherrington.

Hamm had her share of physical contact even in soccer, as the only girl in the boys' league. Her male opponents became angry when she scored and would then play rough and shove her down. Eventually she learned how to quickly get out of the way of a collision. Hamm was so talented at the sport due to her quick thinking as well as her dedication to practice—she would usually be on the empty field by 8 a.m. most mornings during the summer, trying to nail every shot possible. Coach Lou Pearce at Notre Dame High School in Wichita Falls was impressed and suggested she try out for something bigger.

By the time she was 14, Hamm was playing on an Olympic development team for John Cossaboon (even though women's soccer was not even declared an Olympic event at this time). He, in turn, called his friend Anson Dorrance, who was coaching the national team. He went to see her play and remarked in *People*, "I'd never seen speed like that in the women's game. She had unlimited potential." In 1987, at age 15 years, 140 days, Hamm joined the team as the youngest member ever, male or female, and made her first appearance on August 3, 1987. She scored her first goal with the team on July 25, 1990, versus Norway. After her sophomore year of high school, Hamm moved to Burke, Virginia, where she was a high school All-American. Then she enrolled at the University of North Carolina, where Dorrance was coaching. There, she earned a degree in political science in 1994, but in the meantime, she was ripping up the field as well.

Known as a soccer powerhouse, North Carolina cemented their reputation with Hamm on their side as she helped lead them to National Collegiate Athletic Association (NCAA) victories each of her four years there. She was a three-time All-American and set all-time conference records with 103 goals, 72 assists, and 278 points; her college number, 19, was retired in 1994. Hamm also became a star on the U.S. team that won the women's world championship in 1991, even though she was still the youngest player. During that game, she started five of six matches and scored two goals. In 1992 and 1993, she received the Missouri Athletic Club Award and Hermann Award and was named women's college player of the year, leading the NCAA with 32 goals and 33 assists.

In her senior year at North Carolina, Hamm found out that the Olympics had declared women's soccer a full-medal sport for the first time, to be included on the roster at the 1996 games in Atlanta, Georgia. She was ecstatic, now that she could follow in the footsteps of a couple of her heroes, gymnast Mary Lou Retton and track star Jackie Joyner-Kersee. "You hear all the cliches, that it's a dream come true," she remarked to Mike Spence of the Knight-Ridder/Tribune News Service. "Well, it is for myself and for every girl growing up who plays any sport." Not only did Hamm make it to the 1996 Olympics, she helped lead the team to the gold medal, pushing past China 2-1.

By this time, Hamm was considered the best player in women's soccer and became flooded with endorsement offers. Though shy by nature and reluctant to be made into such a public persona, she became convinced that her high profile would ultimately be a positive influence among young girls. She has made commercials for AT&T, Pert shampoo, Power Bars, and Nike, the latter of which even named a building in her honor at its headquarters in Oregon. In addition, Hamm helped market a special edition soccer Barbie doll for Mattel. But perhaps her most popular ad was the humorous spot for Gatorade in which she outperforms Michael Jordan in a number of sports—from soccer and basketball to fencing and ju-do—while the background music plays "Anything you can do, I can do better." In addition, after the Olympics, Hamm appeared on "Late Night with David Letterman" and in 1997, was the only female athlete to be named one of the 50 most beautiful people in the world by *People* magazine.

Women's soccer reached a new level during July of 1999 when much of the United States got wrapped up in following the Women's World Cup championships. After 120 minutes of scoreless play, including two nail-biting overtime periods, the game came down to a single penalty kick. Brandi Chastain finally kicked in a goal to squeak past China, 1-0. The event captured the attention of the nation and allowed everyone to rally around a winner. As Rick Reilly pointed out in *Sports Illustrated,* "Look at what our American men's international teams have done lately. Ryder Cup: humiliated. Presidents Cup: humiliated. USA Hockey: dead humiliated. World Cup: dead last." Not only was the team adored for their athletic prowess, they were admired for their well-roundedness as well. All team members had a college degree or were full-time students, and many were married with children.

Though the victory stirred much optimistic discussion about the future of women in sports, it also led to a flurry of debate about the sexuality of the female players. Many were critical that Chastain, immediately following her game-winning kick, tore her jersey over her head in a show of excitement. Though she was wearing a fully-covering sports bra top, she was the target of some who felt she was too immodest. Following that, she showed up in a men's magazine, *Gear,* covered by nothing but a soccer ball. Hamm managed to avoid much of the controversy, though the entire team did become a favorite of talk show host David Letterman, who repeatedly referred to them as "Babe City." Despite this side issue, the fact remained that the event had apparently gone far in promoting the idea of female sports: The final game between the U.S. and China was a sold-out event, drawing 90,185 fans, a record for a women's sporting event.

The year 1999 also marked an important personal milestone for Hamm. That year, she surpassed Elisabetta Vignotto of Italy, now retired, who had held the record of 106 for most goals scored in women's soccer. Also that year, the team went on to yet another championship. That October, they followed up their huge summer celebration by reigning at the U.S. Women's Cup tournament in Louisville, Kentucky, with a 4-2 win over Brazil. A 5-0 showdown against South Korea just a few days prior in Columbus, Ohio, had marked the team's twenty-third victory of the year, surpassing its year-old record for wins in a calendar year. In addition, another game in the series, in a 6-0 shutout against Finland, 36,405 people showed up to watch—the largest ever soccer crowd in Kansas City. This was a far cry from the old days before the Olympics, when the team would regularly play before just 5,000 or perhaps 10,000 spectators. Though Hamm had displayed a lackluster performance in some games earlier in the year, it appeared she was back on track by the year's end. By the time the 1999 U.S. Women's Cup contest was over, Hamm's goals had reached 114 and, undoubtedly, were bound to grow. At this point, she held the record for the most goals ever scored by a man or woman in all of soccer.

Hamm is married to Christian Corry, who is an officer in the U.S. Marine Corps, but they see each other infrequently due to her hectic travel schedule. In addition to her soccer games and product endorsements, Hamm keeps busy with the Mia Hamm Foundation, a nonprofit entity that she set up to raise funds to research bone marrow diseases and to assist young female athletes. Corporate partners Nike, Mattel, and Gatorade pitch in with special events as well. Much of Hamm's inspiration for the organization came from her brother, Garrett, who contracted a rare blood disease, aplastic anemia, in 1975 and died in 1997 at age 28. She has also written a book, *Go for the Goal,* 1999, which is ostensibly an autobiography but contains mainly self-help information and details on soccer.

Sources

➤ On-line

"U.S., Brazil win cup openers," *ESPN web site,* October 7, 1999, http://espn.go.com (October 12, 1999).
"Lilly, Hamm key U.S. rout of Finland," *ESPN web site,* October 8, 1999, http://espn.go.com (October 12, 1999).
"Hosts go 3-0 to capture U.S. Women's Cup," *ESPN web site,* October 10, 1999, http://espn.go.com (October 12, 1999).
"Mia Hamm," *Women's Soccer World web site,* http://www.womensoccer.com (October 11, 1999).

➤ Periodicals

Dallas Morning News, July 30, 1996, p. 20B.
Entertainment Weekly, July 16, 1999, p. 10.
Knight-Ridder/Tribune News Service, May 16, 1996; August 1, 1996; May 8, 1997.
Newsweek, July 19, 1999, p. 46.
New York Times, June 11, 1999, p. A1; June 20, 1999, sec. 1, p. 25; June 27, 1999, sec. 1, p. 21; July 11, 1999, sec. 1, p. 19.
New York Times Upfront, September 6, 1999, p. 32 (opening quote).
People, November 1, 1993, p. 63; May 12, 1997, p. 90.
Seventeen, June 1994, p. 42.
Sports Illustrated, July 5, 1999, p. 100.
U.S. News & World Report, June 21, 1999, p. 13.

Frances E.W. Harper

"The strongest nation on earth cannot afford to deal unjustly towards its weakest and feeblest members."

Born September 24, 1825, in Baltimore, Maryland, Frances E.W. Harper gained fame as a writer who worked in virtually every genre and as a lecturer on behalf of the antislavery movement, women's rights, and temperance. She died February 20, 1911, in Philadelphia, Pennsylvania.

One of the most remarkably versatile and talented African American women of the nineteenth century, Frances E.W. Harper was a popular and prolific poet, novelist, essayist, and author of short stories. She was also a superb public speaker, initially on behalf of the antislavery movement and later on her own as a crusader for racial uplift and moral reform. A pragmatic idealist who fused art and social action in both her written and spoken words, Harper devoted a lifetime to bringing about what she called "a brighter coming day" for all African Americans.

An only child, Frances Ellen Watkins Harper was born in 1825 to free parents in Baltimore, Maryland, which was then a slave state. Both her mother and her father were dead by the time she was three, so she was taken in by an aunt and uncle who tried to make her part of their large, close-knit family. But Harper was a quiet, pensive child by nature who years later still recalled the pain and loneliness of growing up without her mother.

Harper's uncle, William Watkins, was a deeply religious and politically active writer, minister, and educator who ran a highly respected school for free blacks in Baltimore. It was there that his niece received her formal education in subjects such as the Bible, classic literature, and public speaking. In addition, the curriculum stressed the virtues of leadership and service to others, which left a profound impression on Harper and contributed much toward shaping the character of the woman she would one day become.

Since higher education was a privilege only of the wealthy in those days, Harper left school at about 13 and went to work for a local family as a housekeeper, seamstress, and babysitter. Her employers owned a bookstore, however, and she was able to take advantage of that fact and continue to learn on her own by reading whatever caught her eye. Early on, she also showed a particular talent for writing; although scholars have not come across any copies, they believe she published her first collection of poems at about the age of 20.

Around 1850, as conditions worsened even for free blacks in Baltimore, William Watkins closed his school and moved his family to Canada. Harper left Maryland at about the same time and headed for Columbus, Ohio, where she had accepted a position in the vocational education program at the newly opened Union Seminary, an institution established by the African Methodist Episcopal Church that later evolved into Wilberforce University. A teacher of domestic science, she was the first female member of the faculty.

Harper remained in Columbus for about a year, then took another teaching job in Little York, Pennsylvania. Unhappy with her young, unruly pupils, she quickly resigned and moved on. Although she was homesick, she figured it was not wise to return to Baltimore due to her precarious status as a free black in a slave state. In addition, the stories she had heard from fugitive slaves of her acquaintance about the increasingly harsh and repressive treatment of blacks in the South left her depressed and unsure of what course her life should take.

By 1853, Harper had given up teaching to try another line of work. She definitely could not return to Maryland, because a new law there barred free blacks from entering the state and subjected those who did so to imprisonment or re-enslavement. Instead, she moved to Philadelphia, where she lived in a home that served as a station for the Underground Railroad. In this atmosphere of political and social activism, Harper joined the antislavery movement and began lecturing and producing poems and essays on abolitionist themes. Among her writings during this period was a response to the book *Uncle Tom's Cabin* by Harriet Beecher Stowe that brought her national attention from notables such as Frederick Douglass and William Lloyd Garrison, both of whom took an interest in her work and helped promote her as a writer and a lecturer.

On the strength of her formidable skills as a public speaker, Harper was hired by the Maine Anti-Slavery Society in 1854, thus becoming one of the first black women to serve as an abolitionist lecturer. Her territory encompassed New England and adjacent areas of Canada, although she also traveled as far west as New York, Ohio, and even Michigan. It was dangerous and extremely tiring work, but Harper excelled at it. Listeners described her as an articulate, dignified woman who could be quite passionate in her delivery but never to the point of losing her composure. She often incorporated some of her verse into her speeches, which helped develop her reputation as a poet.

Later that same year (1854), Harper published a book entitled *Poems on Miscellaneous Subjects*. Thanks in part to the recognition she already enjoyed as a lecturer, the collection was an immediate success. More than 10,000 copies were sold in three years, at which time a revised and enlarged version was released. (All in all, *Poems on Miscellaneous Subjects* was reprinted at least 20 times during Harper's life.) A pioneering work of African American protest poetry, the collection contains several of her most famous pieces ("The Slave Mother," for example) and addresses her favorite themes, including religious faith, personal integrity, abolitionism, temperance, civil rights, and racial pride.

From 1854 until 1860, Harper was an agent and lecturer for the Pennsylvania Society for Promoting the Abolition of Slavery. She observed a rigorous schedule, speaking two or three times every day throughout a large territory that included Ohio, Indiana, Illinois, and Michigan.

Meanwhile, the conditions under which blacks (especially those held in bondage) were forced to live grew more brutal and restrictive. Harper responded by becoming more militant, both in her writings and in her actions. Following John Brown's ill-fated raid on the arsenal at Harpers Ferry, West Virginia, in October 1859, she raised money and wrote letters in support of the imprisoned abolitionist and his followers. She also provided financial assistance to the Underground Railroad, and scholars believe she occasionally accompanied runaway slaves on their journey to freedom.

On November 22, 1860, in Cincinnati, Ohio, Frances Ellen Watkins married Fenton Harper, a young widower with three children. Using her savings, they were able to purchase a farm near Columbus, where Harper eventually gave birth to a daughter named Mary. The responsibilities of family life led her to curtail her writing and public speaking somewhat over the next few years, but all that changed in the wake of Fenton Harper's death around 1864. His widow subsequently lost their farm and most of their belongings to creditors, so to earn a living she returned to the lecture circuit. With the Civil War finally at an end, Harper discussed not abolitionism but the need to grant equal rights to newly freed slaves.

Audiences responded with a great deal of enthusiasm to Harper's ideas. Before long, she had teamed up with Frederick Douglass, Sojourner Truth, Susan B. Anthony, Elizabeth Cady Stanton, and other reformers to establish the American Equal Rights Association. But racism and sexism undermined the group's activities almost from the start. Harper discovered, for instance, that many white feminists tended to hold racist views about blacks (especially black men) and were largely indifferent to the concerns of black women. Furthermore, she learned that not all black men regarded black women as equals worthy of their respect and consideration.

As a result, Harper, an advocate of interracial cooperation, often found herself mediating between conflicting factions within the equal rights movement. Many of the disagreements erupted over which cause deserved top priority. Some reformers favored tackling the issue of securing voting rights for black men first, while others wanted to focus on obtaining the vote for women. Harper felt very strongly that black men had to be allowed to participate in the political system in order for the country to move forward, so she was willing to postpone efforts to bring about women's suffrage until black men's basic rights were guaranteed. An inability to settle this dispute ultimately contributed to the demise of the American Equal Rights Association.

From 1866 until 1871, Harper taught and lectured across the South, visiting 13 former slave states to share her message of moral reform, women's rights, and racial uplift with church groups, women's clubs, and other receptive audiences. She directed her remarks primarily to members of the emerging black middle class and urged them to make use of their new freedoms to improve themselves through education, self-discipline, and adherence to Christian principles. She also called for unity of the races to achieve common goals, pointing out that the future of the nation depended on everyone learning to live and work together in harmony.

During this same period, Harper also kept busy with her writing. In 1869, she published a serialized novel entitled *Minnie's Sacrifice,* and, later that same year, a collection of poetry on her favorite biblical character entitled *Moses: A Story of the Nile.* Two more poetry collections followed: *Poems* (1871), which is similar in theme to her 1854 book but more optimistic in outlook, and *Sketches of Southern Life* (1872), a major work of African American literature that combines the autobiography of a former slave with an oral history of slavery and Reconstruction.

Around 1871, Harper settled in Philadelphia, where she lived for the rest of her life. She continued to give speeches and write, meshing her political and social convictions with her literary creations as never before. In 1873, for example, she began writing a newspaper column in which a cast of fictitious characters discussed various moral dilemmas and issues of the day. From the late 1870s through the 1880s, Harper produced two novels and numerous essays and poems on temperance, a cause that had become increasingly important to her. Her best known novel, *Iola Leroy; or Shadows Uplifted,* appeared in 1892 to a fair amount of acclaim; in it she attempted to refute the negative stereotypes of blacks that populated most literature at that time. Harper published at least five collections of poetry after that, most of which were revised or enlarged versions of earlier works.

Harper kept busy with non-literary pursuits, too. She devoted some of her energies to the rehabilitation of juvenile delinquents and also worked on behalf of the elderly and the ill. The temperance movement claimed a great deal of her time as well. She served as superintendent of the so-called "colored branch" of both the Philadelphia and Pennsylvania chapters of the Women's Christian Temperance Union from 1875 until 1882 and directed the Northern United States Temperance Union from 1883 until 1890. Always a popular speaker, Harper continued to appear before women's groups in particular and was one of only four black women to address the Women's Congress at the Columbian Exposition of 1892.

Harper was also involved with a number of other groups, including the National Council of Women, the Universal Peace Union, the American Women's Suffrage Association, and the American Association of Education of Colored Youth. In 1896, she co-founded the National Association of Colored Women and served as vice-president and consultant for several years.

Health problems finally forced Harper to slow down during the last decade or so of her life. She died of a heart ailment in Philadelphia at the age of 85 on February 20, 1911. The "brighter coming day" she had envisioned so many years before still eluded African Americans, but that never diminished Harper's basic sense of optimism about the future. She placed her faith in those of strong moral character who were willing to continue the fight against ignorance, poverty, and other social evils. "More than the changing of institutions we need the development of a national conscience, and the upbuilding of national character," Harper declared to the women who gathered to hear her speak at the Columbian Exposition of 1892. "Men may boast of the aristocracy of blood, may glory in the aristocracy of talent, and be proud of the aristocracy of wealth, but there is one aristocracy which must ever outrank them all, and that is the aristocracy of character. . . ."

Sources

➤ Books

Anderson, Judith, *Outspoken Women: Speeches by American Women Reformers, 1635-1935*, Kendall/Hunt, 1984.
Foner, Philip S., editor, *The Voice of Black America: Major Speeches by Negroes in the United States, 1797-1971*, Simon & Schuster, 1972.
Gates, Henry Louis, Jr., and Nellie Y. McKay, editors, *The Norton Anthology of African American Literature*, Norton, 1997.

Hine, Darlene Clark, editor, *Black Women in America: An Historical Encyclopedia,* Carlson Publishing, 1993.

Lerner, Gerda, editor, *Black Women in White America: A Documentary History,* Pantheon Books, 1972.

Loewenberg, Bert James, and Ruth Bogin, editors, *Black Women in Nineteenth-Century American Life: Their Words, Their Thoughts, Their Feelings,* Pennsylvania State University Press, 1976 (opening quote).

Smith, Jessie Carney, editor, *Notable Black American Women,* Gale, 1992.

LaDonna Harris

"We Indians have dual citizenship. Not only are we citizens within our own tribes and are entitled to special resources under the treaties, but we are also entitled to everything any other citizen of the United States is entitled to."

Born February 15, 1931, in Temple, Oklahoma, activist LaDonna Harris has been an outspoken advocate since the 1960s on issues of concern to Native Americans, women, children, and the mentally ill. In 1970 she founded Americans for Indian Opportunity, and continued to lead that organization three decades later. Address: c/o Americans for Indian Opportunity, 681 Juniper Hill Road, Bernalillo, NM 87004.

As a member of the Comanche tribe whose father and husband of many years were non-Native Americans, LaDonna Harris has the benefit of experience in several different cultures. During the 1960s and 1970s, her work as an activist took her around the world, and she gained an even wider perspective. Her chief interest, however, has remained with her own people—not just the Comanche tribe, but all native peoples of the Americas.

In a 1997 profile of Harris, *New Mexico Business Journal* quoted her sardonic reference to the difficulties she repeatedly encountered in explaining the painful situation of Native Americans to white politicians in Washington. The article mentioned the "endless explanations of Indian history" which she has been required to give, explanations which Harris refers to as "Indian 101." Her own early experience was certainly an education, made doubly so by the fact that her father was a white Irish-American, and her mother a Comanche. Not long after Harris's birth in Temple, Oklahoma, on February 15, 1931, her father left her mother, in part because of the constant hostility they faced as a racially mixed couple.

Harris's grandparents raised her, and through their influence she grew up educated in both white and Indian culture. Her grandmother was a Christian, whereas her grandfather—a former Indian scout at Fort Sill, Oklahoma—was a tribal medicine man. But the two showed by their example of mutual respect for each other's beliefs that two cultures could exist side by side in harmony.

Harris's education, both in the larger American culture and in her own Native American one, continued when she entered elementary school. Until the age of six she spoke only the Comanche language, but when she entered public school she had to learn English. Meanwhile, in her home the primary influence remained the Comanche tradition.

Years later, in high school, she met the young man who would become her husband. Fred Harris was not a Native American, but like her, he had experienced poverty and hardship as the son of a sharecropper. He wanted to go to law school and run for public office, and after they were married, she helped put him through college and law school. The Harrises had three children: Kathryn, Byron, and Laura. Fred was elected first to the Oklahoma state senate, then to the U.S. Senate.

With Fred's election in 1965, the Harrises began to divide their time between Washington, D.C., and their home in Oklahoma. Perhaps this experience helped to expand Harris's vision to encompass national issues, because in 1965, she began an effort that mirrored the civil rights movement then making great strides on behalf of African Americans in the Southeast. But she was working in the Southwest, and she undertook her activities on behalf of Native Americans.

Operating from a base in the Oklahoma town of Lawton, Harris sought to bring together the state's tribes to combat segregation. This period saw the birth of an organization called Oklahomans for Indian Opportunity, which had members from 60 tribes. The group defined a set of goals which equated economic priorities with political ones, placing an emphasis on improvement of economic conditions for Native Americans while remaining committed to securing civil rights for them. Harris's work on this organization's behalf helped earn her recognition as "Outstanding Indian of the Year" for 1965.

Meanwhile, back in Washington, D.C., Harris's activities expanded. She became a nationally recognized advocate on behalf of Native Americans, and numerous groups sought her involvement in projects designed to assist the Indian population in achieving greater civil rights. Harris became involved with the National Rural Housing Conference, the National Association of Mental Health, the National Committee against Discrimination in Housing, and the National Steering Committee of the Urban Coalition, which she chaired.

In 1967 President Lyndon B. Johnson appointed Harris to lead the National Women's Advisory Council of the War on Poverty, an organization charged with assisting all Americans in enjoying the benefits of civil rights and economic prosperity. Johnson's administration created the National Council for Indian Opportunity, and in 1968 the president appointed Harris to a position with the new commission. Clearly Harris had come a long way from her humble beginnings in Oklahoma, and the coming years would see the expansion of her vision from a national to a global one.

Harris's appointment to the National Council for Indian Opportunity coincided with the end of Johnson's administration and the beginning of that of President Richard Nixon. In fact, the council did not actually meet for the first time until a year into Nixon's presidency—in January of 1970. Harris began to believe that Vice President Spiro Agnew, whose was responsible for the council, did not feel any great sense of urgency with regard to the issues it was intended to address. Finally she decided to leave the council.

During the early 1970s Harris became heavily involved in work both at home and abroad. A founding member of the National Women's Political Caucus, in 1970 she also founded Americans for Indian Opportunity (AIO), and assisted women's and Native American grassroots organizations in their efforts on behalf of their constituency groups. Another cause of interest to her was that of the mentally ill. Harris also became interested in the needs of native or indigenous peoples around the world, and traveled to Latin America, Africa, and the Soviet Union as a representative of the Inter-American Indigenous Institute. In this capacity, she participated in a number of conferences on world peace.

In 1975 President Gerald R. Ford named Harris to the U.S. Commission on the Observance of National Women's Year. But Harris's husband was retiring from the Senate, and the family decided that it was time to leave Washington, D.C. Instead of returning to Oklahoma, however, the Harrises moved to New Mexico, and the AIO relocated its offices with them. While concentrating her efforts more fully on the AIO, Harris also maintained her global vision. Thus when Cyrus Vance, secretary of state under President Jimmy Carter, offered her an appointment to the United Nations Education, Scientific, and Cultural Organization (UNESCO), she accepted.

In line with her interest in the cause of native peoples as a global and not merely national phenomenon, Harris had become interested in the U.S. Peace Corps as an effective instrument to assist in local development for indigenous peoples around the world. When President Carter appointed her to serve as special advisor to Sargent Shriver, who directed the Office of Economic Opportunity, she was able to realize this vision. The "Peace Pipe Project" trained Native Americans in skills necessary to assist in development of communities, then sent them to work in indigenous communities throughout the Western Hemisphere. The value of the Peace Pipe Project, which remained a limited effort, was that native peoples in other countries were more likely to trust the advice of another indigenous person than they were a white official.

While working with the Office of Economic Opportunity, Harris also introduced another initiative of interest specifically to Native Americans in the United States. Called the Council for Energy Resources Tribes, the program assisted tribes in acquiring the best possible monetary returns for the natural resources located on tribal lands. The council, which was not without its critics, also helped tribes protect those resources if the tribe chose not to exploit them.

In the 1980s and 1990s, Harris remained active with the AIO. She founded the National Indian Housing Council and the National Indian Business Association, but continued with the AIO as director, although daughter Laura Harris Goodhope also assisted with those responsibilities. According to a profile in the *New Mexico Business Journal*, Harris lived on the Santa Ana reservation near Bernalillo, outside of Albuquerque, New Mexico. Her home, owned by the reservation, also doubled as the main office of AIO. Divorced from her politician husband, Harris devoted most of her time to the organization.

Among the AIO's achievements in the 1990s was its work to strengthen tribal organizations for groups located as far apart as Alabama, Wisconsin, and Nebraska. Concern for the environment continued, and the AIO hosted regional meetings on that subject. With the greatly increased traffic on the "information superhighway" in the early 1990s, the AIO was quick to establish a significant Internet presence on behalf of Native Americans. It founded INDIANnet, which helps tribes and other groups set up Web pages and make the best possible use of the Internet's resources. The AIO, according to its own INDIANnet website, facilitated Harris's participation in the United States Advisory Council on the National Information Infrastructure, a group headed by Vice President Al Gore.

According to the *New Mexico Business Journal*, among the projects most important to Harris was the American Indian Ambassadors Program, funded by Kellogg's, the cereal manufacturer. Each year, advisors to the program choose some 30 young professional men and women from tribes throughout the United States. Each of the selectees serves as "ambassador" for a year, during which time he or she goes to Washington, D.C., and learns about the political process. The selectees also tour reservations around the country, and visit a selected tribal group in Central or South America.

Commenting on gaming, the federal policy that allows Indian reservations to operate casinos as a means of economic development, Harris has remained cautious. "I hate to see gaming of any kind used to support regular government," she told an interviewer for *New Mexico Business Journal*. "But the tribes have no other method that commands this degree of success." After 30 years as an activist, Harris remains positive about the future of Native Americans: "Exasperated—yes. Tired—maybe. But not angry," concluded the interviewer. "Despite years of dealing with Washington bureaucracy, despite funding cuts, run-arounds and red tape, Harris remains soft-spoken, optimistic, and certain that change for her people can occur."

Sources

➤ On-line

Americans for Indian Opportunity, Inc., http://indiannet.indian.com (March 28, 2000).

➤ Books

Harris, LaDonna, *LaDonna Harris: A Comanche Life,* University of Nebraska Press, 2000 (opening quote).
Harris, LaDonna, Margaret A. Fiore, and Jackie Wasilewski, editors, *Overcoming the Barriers to the Effective Participation of Tribal Governments in the Federal System,* American Institute for Interactive Management, 1989.
Notable Native Americans, Gale, 1995.
Schwartz, Michael, *LaDonna Harris,* Raintree Steck-Vaughn, 1997.

Denis Hayes

"*I have always felt that there is something to be offered by the environmental movement, by ecology as a science, that would transcend psychology and really transform in an almost religious way the ongoing principles of society.*"

Born August 29, 1944, in Wisconsin Rapid, Wisconsin, Denis Hayes organized the first Earth Day in 1970. Since that time, he has remained involved in environmental causes, including several subsequent Earth Day celebrations. Address: c/o Green Seal, PO Box 1694, Palo Alto, CA 94302-1694.

In 1970, Denis Hayes organized the first Earth Day, inaugurating an era of awareness about the environment that continues to this day. Hayes spent much of his life working to promote the use of solar energy, most importantly during his stint as the director of the Solar Research Institute. He was the first non-scientist to head a national laboratory in the United States. Hayes also was in charge of organizing other Earth Days, most notably the 1990 and 2000 anniversary celebrations.

Born Denis Allen Hayes on August 29, 1944 in Wisconsin Rapid, Wisconsin, Hayes was the son of Archibald John Hayes and his wife Antoinette Jacqueline. Hayes had two older siblings, a brother and sister, who were much older than him. When Hayes was six years old, the family moved to Washington state. He was reared in Camas, Washington, a town of 4,000 people. The town was plagued by sulfide aromas and runoff in the river from the local paper mill polluted the environment. As a child, Hayes reacted negatively to this pollution because it spoiled the beauty of the environment.

After graduating from high school, Hayes entered Clark College (located in Vancouver, Washington) in 1962. He had an identity crisis during his sophomore year, and chose to graduate with his AA (Associate Arts) degree in 1964. Instead of transferring to another school to complete his undergraduate degree, Hayes spent three years traveling around the world. He hitchhiked everywhere, working as needed in places like Japan and Hawaii. Hayes decided to come home after ending up in South West Africa, alone at both a literal and figurative crossroads.

When Hayes returned to the United States, he went back to school. He entered Stanford University in 1967, and became involved in the anti-war protest against American involvement in Vietnam. Hayes was also the student body president at some point, before graduating in 1969. Hayes then entered Harvard Law School, in a joint government-and-law program with the Kennedy School of Government.

While a law student at Harvard, he became involved with what eventually would be known as Earth Day. The idea for highlighting environmental issues on a national scale came from a United States Senator from Wisconsin, Democrat Gaylord Nelson. Nelson had been interested in the environment for years. During the presidency of John F. Kennedy, Nelson convinced the president to do a conservation tour of the country, but there was little interest generated.

This time, Nelson wanted to organize a nationwide series of

workshops on the environment. Nelson hired Hayes as one of three organizers (perhaps only for the Cambridge area) for his "Environmental Action" office. Hayes ended up taking over the whole operation beginning in January 1970. But the project took so much time to do it right that he quit law school and moved to Washington, D.C. Hayes' vision went well beyond what Nelson had first attempted.

The first Earth Day, April 22, 1970, was an unqualified success in the United States. More than 20 million Americans participated in some way, making Earth Day America's biggest public demonstration since the end of World War II. The participants were a diverse lot: everyone from disillusioned anti-war activists to militant environmentalists to corporations to average people. People sang songs, watched or marched in parades, and gave or listened to speeches. There were teach-ins about what pesticides and garbage were doing to the environment, and how air and water pollution was dangerous. There were also some publicity stunts.

The federal government also took notice of Earth Day. One member of the Cabinet, Secretary of the Interior Walter Hickel, had his staff take the day off to take part in the festivities. President Richard M. Nixon gave an anti-pollution speech, though he did not directly participate in Earth Day. Earth Day later had a legislative impact. The Clean Air Act eventually was passed by Congress. There were more clean water and toxic chemical reduction acts. Also as a result, the Environmental Protection Agency was created.

Earth Day began the environmental movement in the United States, but not quite in the way Hayes intended. Twenty years later, Hayes told Philip Shabecoff of the *New York Times*, "We hoped it would lead to a new kind of ideology, a new value system based on ecology and a reverence for life. Earth Day was translated into a series of local and regional issues, like dirty air in Los Angeles, concern in Chicago about the pollution of the Great Lakes and in New York about the Hudson River."

Hayes spent the next years trying to build on Earth Day and make it part of the environmental movement. Right after the initial Earth Day, he founded an environmental organization called Environmental Action. Later in 1970, they were successful in getting some anti-environment congressmen defeated in elections. But Environmental Action was not really successful in the long term. Many subsequent Earth Days were small affairs, until 1990, and Hayes was not directly involved with many of them.

Hayes continued to work in environmental issues. After marrying Gail Boyer in 1971, with whom he had a daughter, Lisa Antoinette, before their 1990 separation, Hayes primarily worked in alternative energy. He was a visiting scholar at the Smithsonian Institute from 1971-72. From 1974 to 1975, he was the director of the Illinois State Energy Office.

In 1975, Hayes was hired by Worldwatch Institute, an environmental organization that worked on research and policy. In the four years he spent there, Hayes became interested in solar power, among other alternate energy sources. He wrote a whole book about the subject, *Ray of Hope: The Transition to a Post-Petroleum World.* There was also a Sun Day celebrated on May 3, 1978. The following year, Hayes was awarded the Thomas Jefferson Medal for public service. It is the highest such honor in America for those under the age of 35.

Hayes left Worldwatch Institute in 1979 when then-President Jimmy Carter offered him a high-profile job. Hayes had already been working to get Carter to do more about solar energy, so he was tapped to head the Solar Energy Research Institute (SERI), located in Golden, Colorado. SERI was under the auspices of the United States Department of Energy, and had a budget of about $90 to 130 million. Hayes was given the job despite the fact that he was not a scientist, but a self-taught solar expert. He was the first non-scientist to head a national lab. Under Hayes leadership, SERI worked to design solar technology for use in homes, cars, and farming. Hayes himself believed that the United States would be using a significant amount of solar energy within 50 years.

Hayes' tenure at SERI was short. When Republican Ronald Reagan took office in 1981, Hayes was removed from his post. The 1980s proved to be low years for the environmental movement. After leaving SERI, Hayes spent a year as the Regents' Professor at the University of California at Santa Cruz. He then moved on to Stanford's civil engineering department in 1982 and another adjunct professorship.

While teaching at Stanford, Hayes also became a student. He completed his law degree there, earning his JD in 1985. After graduating, he went to work as a corporate attorney in the Bay Area for Cooley, Godward, Castro, Huddleston & Tatum. Hayes maintained his professorship through 1987.

In 1990, Hayes quit his job at the law firm to organize another Earth Day. It was not just the fact that it was the twentieth anniversary of the first that attracted him. He told Susan Reed of *People,*

"Our problems are more serious than they were in 1970. The ozone layer is being destroyed. Global warming is increasing. The rain forests are being cut down. We're poised at some crucial thresholds from which, if we cross them, we'll never return."

The 1990 Earth Day took place over four days, April 16-22. More than 3,600 cities in the United States participated as well as 130-160 countries around the world. Hayes wanted to be more inclusive than the 1970 version, involving minorities, labor, and businesses. There was much corporate sponsorship, though this was one of the areas which dismayed some critics. They believed that the 1990 Earth Day was really slick, with public relations firms, television specials, and product licensing. Others argued that Earth Day was really short term in its thinking: no solutions were provided. Earth Days continued throughout the 1990s.

Hayes' career returned directly to environmental causes after the 1990 Earth Day. On May 1, 1990, he began working as chair of Green Seal, Inc., a company he helped found earlier in the year. The company developed and identified products that were environmentally friendly as an educational tool for consumers. While maintaining his position with Green Seal, Hayes moved to Seattle in 1993 to direct the Bullitt Foundation. This foundation supports environmental causes. Hayes was also co-chair of the Coalition for Environmentally Responsive Economics (CERES), which tries to get corporations to become environmentally aware.

Hayes maintained his involvement with Earth Day as one of the key organizers of the 2000 Earth Day. He hoped that through the Internet, it would be the biggest one thus far.

As conservationist David Brower told Susan Reed of *People*, "In terms of the environment, Denis Hayes is undoubtedly the most important figure of his generation."

Sources

➤ Books

DeLeon, David, *Leaders from the 1960s: A Biographical Sourcebook of American Activism*, Greenwood Press, 1994 (opening quote).
Hayes, Denis, *Rays of Hope: The Transition to a Post-Petroleum World*, W.W. Norton & Company, 1977.
Who's Who in America: 1992-1993, Marquis Who's Who, 1992.

➤ Periodicals

E, April 1995, p. 10.
E Magazine, April 1, 1995, p. 30.
Earth Explorer, February 1, 1995.
Los Angeles Times, April 17, 1990, p. A23.
New York Times, April 16, 1990, p. B8.
People, April 2, 1990, p. 96.
PR Newswire, March 22, 1999.
Time, April 26, 1999, p. 63.

Theodore Hesburgh

*"*I* still intend to spread faith, hope, and love as widely as I can during whatever time I am given to live here on earth. These three virtues are the keys to peace and justice and to a better and more equitable world."*

Born May 25, 1917, in Syracuse, New York, Theodore Hesburgh was the long-time president of the University of Notre Dame and is an activist on behalf of civil rights and other social issues. Address: University of Notre Dame, 1315 Hesburgh Library, Notre Dame, IN 46556.

K nown as Father Ted (which he prefers), Theodore Hesburgh was president of the University of Notre Dame for 35 years. During his tenure, he boosted the school's national stature while ensuring that athletics did not take precedence over academics. Hesburgh also exercised his social conscience outside Notre Dame and worked for many years in the civil rights movement. In recognition of his accomplishments, he has received many awards and even holds the world's record for the number of honorary degrees granted to a single person (138 as of 1998).

Born on May 25, 1917, in Syracuse, New York, Theodore Martin Hesburgh is the son of Theodore Bernard and Anne Marie Murphy Hesburgh. By the time he was six years old, he knew he wanted to be a priest. He attended only Catholic schools while growing up, and after graduating from high school in 1934, Hesburgh began the process of becoming a priest by joining the Congregation of the Holy Cross.

From 1934 until 1937, Hesburgh attended the Holy Cross minor seminary at the University of Notre Dame. He went on to earn his Ph.B. (an undergraduate degree) from Gregorian University in Rome, Italy, in 1939. From 1940 until 1943, he did postgraduate work in theology at Holy Cross College in Washington, D.C. Finally, on June 24, 1943, Hesburgh was ordained as a priest. He then continued his education, earning his S.T.D. in 1945 from the Catholic University of America.

Hesburgh's career began in 1943 when he was assigned to serve as chaplain for the National Training School for Boys in Washington, D.C. He had no desire to become a parish priest; instead, he wanted to do missionary work in a foreign country. In 1944, however, he was sent to the University of Notre Dame, where he became the chaplain for student veterans returning from World War II.

A year after his arrival, Hesburgh began teaching, first as an instructor and then as an assistant professor of religion until 1948. He chaired the religion department from 1948 to 1949, at which time he moved up into the administrative ranks at the university as executive vice president. Three years later, in 1952, he was named president of Notre Dame. Hesburgh was only 35 years old at the time, and he was not sure he was ready to take on such a major responsibility. In fact, he did not really want the job—in part because he did not enjoy fundraising—but took it anyway because he had been asked to do so. Despite his original aspirations to the contrary, Hesburgh would end up spending the rest of his life at

Notre Dame. By the time he retired in 1987, he was one of the longest-serving university presidents in the United States during the twentieth century.

Hesburgh's immediate challenge was to make Notre Dame a better institution. At the time he became president, it was known primarily for producing a good football team and devout Catholics. It was not an academic powerhouse, not even among other Catholic schools, let alone on a national level. Hesburgh promptly cleaned house, firing many people in both the athletic and instructional departments. Years later, upon his retirement, he told Ezra Bowen of *Time*, "The very essence of leadership is you have to have a vision. It's got to be a vision you articulate clearly and forcefully on every occasion. You can't blow an uncertain trumpet."

Hesburgh began by recasting the football team in a somewhat different perspective. Though he did not particularly like the sport, he understood its revered place in the tradition of Notre Dame. "Intercollegiate athletics are important in the life of an institution," John Underwood of *Sports Illustrated* quoted him as saying, "but not all-important."

He forced his first coach, Frank Leahy, to follow eligibility requirements to the letter and without exception. Subsequent coaches were given five years to prove themselves with little interference from Hesburgh. Recruits had to meet high standards; they could not transfer into the program from another school or sit out a year to extend their eligibility to play. Hesburgh also made student-athletes accountable for earning their degrees. He kept the athletic department running without a hint of scandal throughout his tenure and established a tradition that most other schools could not hope to attain.

To improve Notre Dame's national academic stature, Hesburgh launched an ambitious program to enhance student life at the university. He increased faculty salaries to attract a better caliber of professors. He also oversaw the construction of 40 new buildings, only one of which was for athletics. (A library built in 1963 was named for him.) Hesburgh was similarly concerned with the moral well-being of Notre Dame students. He was proud of the fact, for example, that 93 percent of those who graduated from the university stayed married. And despite his disdain for the task, Hesburgh also became very good at fundraising. By 1986, the University of Notre Dame was ranked as one of the 36 most competitive schools in the country.

Hesburgh's success at Notre Dame brought him national prominence and invitations to serve on various boards and commissions. His first experience was on the board of the National Science Foundation in 1955. During the late 1950s, he was the Vatican's delegate to meetings of the International Atomic Energy Agency.

In 1957, Hesburgh took on an especially high-profile assignment when he accepted an appointment to the new U.S. Commission on Civil Rights. It had just been formed by President Dwight D. Eisenhower to recommend legislative solutions to racial problems. Eisenhower and his successors generally did not accept most of the group's recommendations, however, so Hesburgh used the commission as a forum in which he spoke out in favor of fair housing laws and busing schoolchildren to achieve racial integration.

Hesburgh chaired the commission from 1969 until 1972, the last three years of his tenure. In 1972, following the re-election of President Richard M. Nixon to a second term, Hesburgh and another member of the commission resigned in protest against the administration's poor civil rights record over the previous four years. Nixon had also angered Hesburgh during the election campaign by opposing fair housing legislation and forced busing in the hope of appealing to white voters in the South. This led to a very public disagreement between the two men. It was not the first time they had clashed; in 1969 Nixon had asked Hesburgh to head a poverty program, but the priest declined, citing in part the lack of civil rights progress in the United States under Nixon's leadership.

In 1964, in recognition of Hesburgh's work on the commission and other related activities, he was awarded the Presidential Medal of Freedom, the highest civilian honor in the United States. That same year, President Lyndon Johnson asked him to become the head of the National Aeronautics and Space Administration (NASA) and direct the U.S. space program. Hesburgh turned down the offer, however, partly because he felt that it was more appropriate for a layperson to fill the position.

Though Hesburgh generally supported the Roman Catholic Church and its tenets, he was not above publicly voicing his disagreement when he felt strongly about something. In 1967, concerned about the ability of the Church to interfere in university affairs, he helped change the rules about who ran Notre Dame. The Catholic Church, in the form of the Congregation of the Holy Cross, agreed to give up control to a board of trustees consisting of laypeople of all faiths. Notre Dame was the first Catholic university to do this, but many others followed suit. And while Hesburgh supported the Church's stand against abortion and sex outside marriage, he did not share the belief that birth control should be banned.

Hesburgh expressed similarly strong views on a number of other topics. In 1969, he again came to national prominence when he told students who were protesting against American involvement in Vietnam that they would be dismissed if they resorted to force or violence instead of words to make their point. Hesburgh himself opposed the war as well as the draft. On another domestic issue of note—feminism—Hesburgh came out in favor of the Equal Rights Amendment, and in 1972 he opened the doors of Notre Dame to women for the first time.

During the late 1970s, Hesburgh held several important posts on various commissions. From 1977 to 1979, he held a chair with the rank of ambassador in the U.S. delegation to the United Nations' Conference on Science and Technology for Development. From 1978 to 1981, he chaired the Select Commission on Immigration and Refugee Policy. (Hesburgh had been concerned with the plight of illegal aliens and migrant farm workers since the mid-1960s.) In 1979, Hesburgh served as chair of the Overseas Development Council. All told, Hesburgh held a total of 14 different presidential appointments throughout his career.

In 1987, Hesburgh retired from Notre Dame after heading the institution for 35 years and was named president emeritus. When he began his career, there were only 4,979 students (all men) and 389 faculty members at Notre Dame. When he retired, there were 9,675 students (one-third of whom were women) and 951 faculty members. The operating budget back in 1952 was $9 million. In 1987 it was $350 million.

After retiring, Hesburgh traveled for a year with friend and former Notre Dame athletic director Father Edmund Joyce. Upon his return to the university, he continued working in an advisory capacity. Hesburgh also regularly gave lectures, published books, and served on committees and boards, mostly related to social issues.

In 1987, Hesburgh delivered the commencement address at Notre Dame. "We don't know where we're going from here," he told the graduates, as reported by Dirk Johnson in the *New York Times.* "But there are battles yet to be won for justice—mountains to be climbed to overcome prejudice, ignorance, even human stupidity."

Sources

➤ Books

Encyclopedia of World Biography, 2nd edition, Volume 7, Gale, 1998.
Hesburgh, Theodore M. with Jerry Reedy, *God, Country, Notre Dame*, Doubleday, 1990 (opening quote).
Lungren, John C., Jr., *Hesburgh of Notre Dame: Priest, Educator, Public Servant*, Sheed & Ward, 1987.
Melton, J. Gordon, *Religious Leaders of America*, 2nd edition, Gale, 1999.
Ohles, Frederik and others, *Biographical Dictionary of Modern American Educators*, Greenwood Press, 1997.

➤ Periodicals

Economist, November 24, 1990, p. 103.
Fund Raising Management, October 1991, p. 78.
Indianapolis Star, December 7, 1997, p. A1.
Nation, August 16, 1986, p. 105; July 16, 1988, p. 45; October 10, 1988, p. 300.
National Catholic Reporter, December 15, 1995, p. 22; August 14, 1998, p. 18.
New York Times, November 15, 1986, sec. 1, p. 1; November 16, 1986, sec. 4, p. 24; May 14, 1987, p. D28; May 18, 1987, p. B6; January 6, 1991, sec. 7, p. 24.
Sports Illustrated, January 10, 1983, p. 58; September 22, 1986, p. 27; May 25, 1987, p. 17.
Time, May 18, 1987, p. 68.

Edwin Hubble

"We do not know why we are born into the world, but we can try to find out what sort of a world it is—at least in its physical aspects."

Born November 20, 1889, in Marshfield, Missouri, Edwin P. Hubble added integral knowledge to the field of astronomy, including the discovery of other galaxies and proof that the universe is constantly expanding. He died on September 28, 1953, in San Marino, California.

In simplified terms, astronomer Edwin P. Hubble basically discovered the universe. At a time when scientists did not believe any other galaxies existed outside the Milky Way, he proved otherwise, and also showed that the universe is expanding. He developed a mathematical model—known as Hubble's law—for observing this expansion. Though he was not the first to suggest that the universe is expanding, he was the first to recognize the existence of other galaxies and form a coherent theory and the law that proves it. Generally speaking, Hubble's law states that the further away a galaxy exists from our own, the faster it is moving away from us. This concept later became part of the big-bang theory of the creation of the universe. In his honor, the National Aeronautics and Space Administration (NASA) in 1990 launched the Hubble Space Telescope, a device that orbits 360 miles above the Earth's surface and was designed to collect data that would build upon Hubble's earlier findings.

Edwin Powell Hubble was born on November 20, 1889, in Marshfield, Missouri. His father, John Powell Hubble, was an insurance agent, and his mother, Virginia Lee (James) Hubble, had eight children in all; Hubble was the third. He learned to read and write before entering first grade, and was thus bored during his early years of school and tended to get into trouble. By fourth grade, though, he discovered literature such as *Alice in Wonderland, Tom Sawyer,* and Rudyard Kipling's *Jungle Books,* and he began to earn excellent marks.

Fond of playing outdoors and exploring nature, a nine-year-old Hubble was thrilled to learn that there would be a total lunar eclipse shortly after midnight on June 23, 1899. He stayed up late with a boyhood friend to watch it, in one of the earliest recorded incidents of his interest in astronomy. By this time, his father began to spend a good deal of time at his firm's regional office in Chicago, so in November of 1899, the family moved to Evanston, then later to Wheaton, both suburbs of Chicago. At age 11, two to three years younger than his classmates, Hubble entered the eighth grade, and went on to attend Wheaton High School. By his junior year, he was six feet, two inches tall, and displayed a knack for both academics and sports. He was a basketball hero, a member of the football team, and captain of the track team, excelling at the pole vault, high jump, discus, and more. Upon graduating in 1906 at age 16, he was granted a scholarship to the University of Chicago.

Although he had never advanced beyond algebra and geometry in school, Hubble studied analytical geometry, trigonometry, and chemistry in college, and was known to be a whiz at mathematics. In addition, he was profoundly affected by his studies with astronomy teacher Forest Ray Moulton. However, he still found time to play basketball and join the track team, and although he was a member of two championship teams, he was not the standout he was in high school.

By his junior year, Hubble earned the much-desired job of laboratory assistant to Robert A. Millikan, who later won the 1923 Nobel Prize for physics. Setting his sights on a Rhodes scholarship, Hubble rounded out his science and math courses with classes in political economics, languages, and public opinion. He received a bachelor's degree in 1910 and also that year was chosen as the Illinois Rhodes Scholar, which fully covered three years at Queen's College of Oxford University.

Bowing to pressure from his father, who had once tried to establish a law firm but failed, Hubble changed his path and studied law at Oxford. Holding no love for the courses, he found solace again in athletics, becoming captain and manager of one of Britain's first baseball teams, and once again winning honors in various track and field events. He earned his Bachelor of Arts in jurisprudence in 1912, and his father died in January of 1913, shortly after the family's move to Louisville, Kentucky. Hubble returned that year to the United States, and later perpetuated the tale that during this stage, he began practicing law part-time and never lost a case. However, Gale E. Christianson's biography, *Edwin Hubble: Mariner of the Nebulae,* quotes Hubble's sister Helen as once having said, "Where did that information come from? He never practiced law."

In the biography, Christianson reported that Hubble had started studying Spanish during his final year at Oxford, and upon his return to America, became a high school teacher in Indiana, responsible for Spanish, math, and physics courses, as well as coaching boys' basketball. His first year on the job, the team was undefeated. His students adored him, finding his newly acquired English mannerisms and dress exotic and attractive. However, Hubble's mind was elsewhere, and he returned to the University of Chicago in 1914 to pursue a doctorate in astronomy. There, he began research at the Yerkes Observatory in Williams Bay, Wisconsin, working under the director, Edwin B. Frost. In 1916, his family relocated to nearby Madison.

At Yerkes, Hubble was probably influenced by Vesto M. Slipher of the Lowell Observatory. Slipher had presented an exciting paper at the annual meeting of the Astronomical Society of America in

1914 that showed evidence that spiral nebulae (the term now refers to a galaxy, but at the time, it was used to describe any body that could not be called a star) were moving at the startling velocity of up to 1,100 kilometers per second, which indicated that the nebulae may not be part of the Milky Way galaxy. This came in an era when scientists held that the Milky Way constituted the entire universe.

Also during his time in graduate school, Hubble met astronomer George Ellery Hale, founder of the Yerkes Observatory and later the director of the Mount Wilson Observatory in Pasadena, California. Hale offered him a job on his staff after completing his doctorate, but Hubble was derailed by the onset of World War I in 1917. He graduated magna cum laude in mathematics and astronomy in May of 1917, then immediately joined the infantry and reported for active duty on August 15. He eventually achieved the rank of major and went overseas in 1918; he was discharged in 1919.

In the meantime, Hale kept a position open for Hubble at Mount Wilson Observatory, and he took his place there in September of 1919. He would remain at Mount Wilson for the rest of his life, except for a hiatus from 1942 to 1946, when he worked with the Ordnance Department in Aberdeen, Maryland, during World War II. There, he served as chief of exterior ballistics and director of the supersonic wind tunnel at the Ballistics Research Laboratory at the Aberdeen Proving Ground.

Early on, Hubble used the Wilson Observatory's 60-inch telescope to study objects in the Milky Way, but soon graduated to its brand-new 100-inch Hooker telescope in order to view and photograph a Cepheid variable star in the Andromeda nebula (now known as the Andromeda galaxy). Using data about the star's brightness, luminosity (how much light it gives off), and the distances of Cepheid stars within our own galaxy, Hubble calculated the distance from Earth to the Cepheid nebula, placing it at 900,000 light-years away, although later evidence would place that figure at 750,000 light-years. This was an enormous distance and clearly illustrated for the first time that there are other galaxies in the universe.

Continuing his research, Hubble discovered more Cepheids and eventually determined distances to nine other galaxies, and could view 75 million through the 100-inch Hooker telescope. He announced his findings at the Astronomical Society Meeting in December of 1924, provoking great debate, but immediately sealing his reputation as one of the top scientific minds. Incidentally, Hubble never used the term "galaxy," a word preferred by his rival, Harlow

Shapley; instead, he continued to call the bodies "nebulae." Today, scientists know that the universe contains tens of billions of galaxies beyond our own. By 1925, Hubble had come up with a system of categorizing these, based on whether they were "regular' or "irregular," spherical or elliptical, and other subdivisions. The classification system now being used is still based on Hubble's original ideas.

In the late 1920s, Hubble, building on the work of Slipher and Milton L. Humason, determined that the universe is in a constant state of expansion. By looking at various galaxies, he realized they were moving away from ours at a high rate of speed, and was able to correlate this velocity with distance to form what is called Hubble's law. This law, which states that the faster a galaxy is moving away, the further it is from Earth, would later be used to help formulate the Big Bang theory of the creation of the universe, an idea put forth by English astronomer Fred Hyle in 1950.

Hubble's law was incredibly revolutionary. Even legendary physicist Albert Einstein had altered his theory of general relativity to account for a static universe, although the theory itself seemed to suggest an expanding universe. In 1931, he visited Hubble at Mount Wilson, shook his hand, and acknowledged the earlier mistake in his theory. This caused Hubble's fame to soar even more. After World War II, Hubble devoted much of his effort to starting up the research program at California's Mount Palomar Observatory, which boasted the 200-inch Hale telescope, completed in 1948. Though Hubble never attended a church after his days at Oxford, he read numerous books on religion but never seemed to find a satisfactory answer about any kind of higher power. Christianson quoted him as saying, "The whole thing is so much bigger than I am, and I can't understand it, so I just trust myself to it; and forget about it." Hubble appeared to be solely devoted to the study of the physical realm, noting, according to Christianson, "We do not know why we are born into the world, but we can try to find out what sort of a world it is—at least in its physical aspects."

Hubble married Grace Burke Leib, a writer, in 1924. He amassed various honorary degrees and medals during his lifetime, and was known as a skilled speaker. Many of his lectures were compiled into book form. His hobbies included dry-fly fishing and collecting antique books about the history of science, and he was considered a civic leader. A member of his local library board for many years, he was also "enlisted to fight the smog menace," as a *New York Times* obituary put it, and served as president of the Pure Air Council of southern California. In his later years, Hubble developed heart trouble, but continued to work on *The Hubble Atlas of Galaxies*, a photographic guide to the classification of galaxies, which was finished after his death by colleague Allan R. Sandage. Hubble died of a coronary thrombosis, a type of stroke, at age 63 at his home in San Marino, California, on September 28, 1953.

Sources

> **Books**

Christianson, Gale E., *Edwin Hubble: Mariner of the Nebulae*, Farrar, Straus and Giroux, 1995 (opening quote).
Encyclopedia of World Biography, second edition, Gale Research, 1998.
Notable Twentieth-Century Scientists, Gale Research, 1995.

> **Periodicals**

National Geographic World, April 1998, p. 28.
New York Times, September 9, 1953, p. 29.
Physics Today, April 1990, p. 52.
Time, March 29, 1999, p. 124.
U.S. News & World Report, August 17, 1998, p. 48.

John Hume and David Trimble

"If we continue to blame people for the past, we're going nowhere. Everybody is a victim of our past . . . . We can only go forward."

In 1998, Irish politicians John Hume, a Catholic, and David Trimble, a Protestant, shared the Nobel Peace Prize for their efforts to find a solution to the conflict in Northern Ireland. Hume was born January 18, 1937, in Londonderry, Northern Ireland, and Trimble was born October 15, 1944, in Belfast, Northern Ireland. Addresses: 5 Bayview Terrace, Derry BT48 7EE, Northern Ireland (Hume); 2 Queen St., Lurgan, County Armagh BT66 8BQ, Northern Ireland (Trimble).

Throughout most of the twentieth century, the relationship between Catholics and Protestants in Northern Ireland has been marked by mutual hatred and distrust punctuated by frequent outbreaks of deadly violence. The seeds of the conflict go back some 400 years, but the most recent period of unrest, commonly referred to as "The Troubles," dates back to the late 1960s. At that time, Catholic civil rights activists began challenging discrimination by the Protestant majority against the Catholic minority in areas such as housing, employment, education, and social services. Riots broke out in several major cities, prompting the British government to send in army troops to restore order. Eventually, Great Britain suspended Northern Ireland's Parliament and imposed direct rule from London.

Irish nationalists, mostly Catholics committed to the notion of an unconditional reunion with the Republic of Ireland, looked upon the British soldiers as unwelcome invaders. The Catholic paramilitary group known as the Irish Republican Army (IRA) soon took up arms not only against the British forces but also against the Protestant unionists (also called loyalists) who were in favor of maintaining close ties to Great Britain and thus supported the crackdown. Bombings and other terrorist acts perpetrated by both sides followed and remain a problem into the new century. All in all, more than 3,500 people have died in the seemingly endless cycle of bloodshed and turmoil that has plagued Northern Ireland since "The Troubles" began.

Attempts to achieve a lasting peace proved largely ineffective until the mid-1990s, when a series of historic breakthroughs seemed to suggest that there might finally be a glimmer of light at the end of the tunnel. This optimism sprang in large part from the efforts of two Irish politicians on opposite sides of the fence, Catholic John Hume and Protestant David Trimble. Although markedly different in background, temperament, and philosophy, they had, over time, come to share a common goal—to bring an end to decades of misery and to lay the groundwork for a true and just sharing of power in their native land.

John Hume was born in 1937 in Londonderry (known simply as Derry to Catholics), Northern Ireland, the oldest of seven children. His father, Samuel Hume, toiled in a shipyard until after World War II, when he found it impossible to secure work because of rampant discrimination against Catholics. He remained jobless until his death in 1967, forcing Hume's mother, Anne Doherty Hume, to support her large family by laboring in a shirt factory.

The Humes were devoutly religious, so much so that young John considered becoming a priest and even attended the seminary for three years before deciding that he was not cut out for such a life. Instead, with the help of scholarships, he studied French and modern history at St. Patrick's College in Maynooth, receiving his bachelor's degree with honors. He then received his master's degree (also with honors) from National University of Ireland and went back to Londonderry to teach at St. Columb's College, a grammar school.

Despite his parents' lack of interest in political matters, Hume became active in community-based programs and self-help initiatives aimed at improving the lot of his fellow Catholics in Northern Ireland. In 1960, for example, he established a credit union to serve the local Catholic population, which was beholden to Protestant merchants who sold food and clothes on credit and charged exorbitant interest rates. It eventually grew into a national organization called the Credit Union League of Ireland. Hume was the league's president from 1964 until 1968, the year "The Troubles" began and sent the country into a social and economic tailspin.

Within just a few months the IRA had entered the fray, orchestrating bombings, ambushes, and other acts of terrorism against Protestant extremists who responded in kind. Alarmed by the veritable civil war that was tearing Northern Ireland apart, Hume resigned from his job to devote himself full-time to civil rights work in the tradition of nonviolent protest advocated by Martin Luther King Jr., a man he greatly admired.

Before long, Hume had made quite a name for himself as an activist. His supporters encouraged him to run for government office, and he reluctantly agreed. He won election to the Northern Ireland Parliament in 1969 and then the Northern Ireland Assembly in 1973. He left that post the following year and went on to become a member of the Northern Ireland Convention in 1976. In 1979 Hume moved into the leadership position of the Social Democratic and Labour Party (SDLP), which he had co-founded back in 1970 as an outgrowth of the credit union movement. That same year (1979) he was elected to the European Parliament, and in 1982 he became Londonderry's representative to the new Northern Ireland Assembly.

In 1983 Hume stepped into a much larger political arena when he was elected to the House of Commons in the British Parliament. Energetic but soft-spoken, he quickly assumed a prominent and influential role as the sole proponent of a moderate form of Irish nationalism that sought to create—through orderly, constitutional means—a Northern Ireland in which Catholics as well as Protestants participated equally in the governing process. Again and again, he stressed the virtues of reconciliation, accommodation, and living together in peace. "I have never believed in flag waving," he told Mary Pat Kelly of *Commonweal.* "I've always believed that the basic right of all is the right to existence, bread on your table and a roof over your head, and that it's an accident of birth what you're born and where you're born. And that accident of birth, whether it's race, nationality, or creed, should never be the source of hatred or conflict."

Hume's position was not popular with all his constituents, some of whom agreed with Sinn Fein, the IRA's political arm, that the only acceptable solution was for Great Britain to relinquish control of Northern Ireland and allow it to reunite with the overwhelmingly Catholic and independent Republic of Ireland. But Hume persevered in his efforts to tone down the rhetoric, stop the killing, and seek a balance between extremist points of view. In the process, he garnered a great deal of respect (even among his opponents) for his steadfast commitment to nonviolence. Peace proved to be elusive, however. As time went on, Hume became convinced that economic growth and social progress would be impossible to achieve and sustain without a sincere effort from those on both sides of the issue to lay down their arms and stay the course until their differences were resolved.

David Trimble came at the same problem from the perspective of an ardent Protestant unionist (or loyalist)—that is, a person who favors a semi-independent Northern Ireland with close ties to Great Britain. He was born William David Trimble in Belfast, Northern Ireland, in 1944 to William and Ivy Jack Trimble, both of whom had English Protestant backgrounds. Unlike Hume, whose family struggled against poverty, Trimble enjoyed a comfortable, middle-class existence. During the late 1960s, as the turmoil generated by "The Troubles" began sweeping across Northern Ireland, he was a law student at Queen's University of Belfast. Quiet and serious, he steered clear of the protests and devoted himself to his schoolwork. Trimble received his degree in 1968 but opted not to practice law. Instead, he became a lecturer at Queen's University, where he remained for the next two decades. He was promoted to senior lecturer in 1977 (a post he held until 1990) and also served as assistant dean of the law school.

Trimble first entered politics during the early 1970s as a member of the Vanguard Movement, a quasimilitary unionist party whose views were considerably to the right of Northern Ireland's largest and most significant Protestant party, the Ulster Unionist Party (UUP). Vanguard members vehemently opposed the Catholic civil rights movement and supported the use of deadly force against those who wanted an end to British control of Northern Ireland and unification with the Republic of Ireland. Trimble was elected to the Northern Ireland Convention in 1975 as a Vanguard candidate, but he gradually distanced himself from more inflammatory elements of the party and ended up joining the UUP in 1978. He subsequently served as its honorary secretary and during the late 1980s also headed two right-wing unionist groups, the Lagan Valley Unionist Association and the Ulster Society. During this period, Trimble was an advocate of civil disobedience and did not shy away from provoking violent confrontation, which he dismissed as an often "inescapable" part of such protests.

Trimble took on the responsibilities of higher office when he was elected to the British Parliament in 1990 as a UUP candidate. Like Hume, he was a hard-working politician who took an active role in the affairs of state. Yet unlike the even-tempered and conciliatory Hume, whose pacifist views lay at the heart of his quest for peace, Trimble quickly earned a reputation as an abrasive, unyielding hardliner prone to angry outbursts and decidedly undiplomatic behavior. A militant through and through, he made no attempt to hide his contempt for the IRA and Sinn Fein.

The paths of these two very different men did not really intersect until the mid-1990s, by which time both were well-established members of Parliament. But Hume had taken the first steps toward bringing about a peaceful resolution to the conflict in Northern Ireland as much as a decade earlier by establishing the New Ireland Forum, a commission made up of the SDLP and the country's three other major political parties whose leaders met to discuss ways of settling "the Irish question." He also worked diligently and persistently on behalf of the Anglo-Irish Agreement of 1985, which granted the Republic of Ireland a consultative role in the affairs of Northern Ireland. (It was soundly rejected by Trimble and other Protestant Unionists.)

Three years later, Hume sat down with Gerry Adams, the president of Sinn Fein (and, as a fellow Catholic, his chief political adversary), to begin discussing possible solutions to the stalemate. Throughout this extremely tense and dangerous period, Hume not only had to win over Unionists who distrusted him simply because he was willing to meet with suspected terrorists, he also had to answer to charges from Irish nationalists that he was a traitor to their cause for advocating a compromise on the issue of independence and for asking members of the IRA to lay down their weapons. In addition, he was criticized by fellow pacifists who wondered how he could possibly talk to Adams while the IRA continued its armed campaign. Explained Hume to interviewer Mary Pat Kelly of *Commonweal:* "I sat down and thought it through, and I decided if after twenty-five years and 20,000 troops that if I could save even one life by talking to one man I would do it."

The efforts of Hume and Adams to set aside their differences and develop a more friendly rapport finally paid off in 1993 when they teamed up with Ireland's prime minister, Albert Reynolds, to revive the Irish Peace Initiative, which outlined some basic principles and suggested ways of achieving peace. This in turn paved the way for the historic Downing Street Declaration later that same year in which Reynolds and British Prime Minister John Major affirmed that their governments would be willing to take part in multi-party peace talks if everyone involved agreed to adopt a policy of nonviolence.

While the declaration was embraced wholeheartedly by moderates in both Great Britain and Ireland, it received a much less enthusiastic reception in Northern Ireland, where both the Unionists and the Republicans rejected provisions calling for a cease-fire. Nevertheless, the Downing Street Declaration is regarded as the official beginning of the peace process, for in August 1994, the IRA announced an unconditional cease-fire and promised to join in on any talks. Protestant paramilitary forces followed suit six weeks later.

The cease-fire represented a tremendous victory for Hume, who received widespread praise for taking the huge personal and political risk of reaching out to the IRA and its supporters. But he was not quite ready to rest on his laurels. "Most people didn't believe me a year ago when I said this was going to happen," he remarked to a Knight-Ridder/Tribune News Service reporter. "But now that the violence has ended, the real challenge is ahead. What we need is a total re-examination of attitudes. Our past attitudes have brought us to where we are."

In May 1995 representatives of Sinn Fein and the British government held their first public talks on the subject of peace since 1973. But they deadlocked over the issue of IRA disarmament because the Republicans thought it was merely a ploy by the British that would make it possible for them to declare that the IRA had surrendered.

The situation grew even more tense in September 1995 when Trimble unexpectedly came out on top in an election to choose the leader of the UUP. Given his penchant for confrontation and his uncompromising nature, Irish nationalists and moderates and even liberal Unionists feared that he would completely derail the peace process and put an end to accommodation. In fact, Trimble had been drafted to head the UUP precisely because of his reputation for combativeness and his oft-stated refusal to sit down with Sinn Fein until it carried out more extensive decommissioning of weapons than even the British government had demanded.

It took more than Trimble's election, however, to deliver a near-fatal blow to the hope for peace. On February 9, 1996, the cease-fire—and the peace talks—ended when an IRA bomb exploded in London, killing two people. It was the first in a series of bombing attacks and other violent incidents committed by extremists on both sides of the Irish question throughout 1996 and well into 1997. As a result, both the British and Irish governments banned all high-level contacts with Sinn Fein until a new cease-fire agreement could be worked out. Meanwhile, negotiators from the United States, Great Britain, and Ireland toiled quietly behind the scenes to make that a reality.

The climate changed somewhat for the better in May 1997 when British voters turned their backs on the Conservative government of John Major and opted for Tony Blair and the Labour Party instead. Blair took immediate action on Northern Ireland, paying a personal visit and lifting the ban on British participation in talks with Sinn Fein. The IRA in turn called a cease-fire in July, and peace talks jointly sponsored by Ireland and Great Britain resumed in September 1997 under the chairmanship of former U.S. Senator George Mitchell.

For years, the Unionists had adamantly refused to sit down in the same room with anyone from Sinn Fein. This time, Trimble himself headed the UUP delegation after weeks of speculation about whether he would boycott the talks. Many observers saw this as evidence of a fundamental shift in Unionist policies. Indeed, Trimble himself had undergone some significant changes since being elected head of the UUP. Officials from both the United States and Great Britain had made a concerted effort to broaden his world view through travel and participation in international conferences on topics such as conflict resolution. (Previously, Trimble liked to brag that he had never set foot outside the United Kingdom.) While he remained a staunch Unionist who was still suspicious of Sinn Fein, he came to the talks with a decidedly different attitude that acknowledged the inescapable realities of the situation—namely, that the people of Northern Ireland were tired of violence and overwhelmingly in favor of all-inclusive peace talks. "We could have stayed back and waited for the talks to collapse without us," Trimble noted in a *Time* article. "But then we would have been accused of blocking peace."

Trimble stayed the course despite fierce opposition from belligerent far-right elements within his own party who denounced him as a traitor to the Protestant cause for "selling out" to the Catholic nationalists. He helped craft the historic power-sharing proposal that emerged from the discussions—dubbed the Good Friday Agreement (or Accord) because it was concluded on April 10, 1998, the Friday before Easter—and guided it through the approval process of his party, securing the backing of 72 percent of his membership in a vote held in late April. The following month, a referendum on the Good Friday Agreement went before all voters in Northern Ireland, 71 percent of whom endorsed it. An estimated 55 percent of them were Protestant, a definite triumph for Trimble.

Trimble's success cemented his position as leader of the UUP. It also paved the way for him to be named prime minister of the new power-sharing Northern Ireland Assembly after voters went to the polls in June 1998 and elected UUP members to more seats than any other party represented. But it was not as decisive a win as Trimble had wanted; the extreme right wing of the party won enough seats to cause considerable trouble, a scenario he found disturbing because of its implications for long-term peace.

Throughout the protracted peace talks, Hume remained mostly in the background, an unsung hero who helped draw the United States into the negotiations and persuade both President Bill Clinton and British Prime Minister Tony Blair to listen to what Gerry Adams and Sinn Fein had to say. Hume also played a key role in convincing the IRA to call the cease-fire in July 1997 that enabled the peace talks to get under way that fall and held private discussions with the various parties involved to help dispel the distrust among them. Around this same time, he declined a request to run for president of the Republic of Ireland (where he enjoyed considerable popularity), saying that he wanted to devote his full attention to the peace process in Northern Ireland.

The stress of all these activities took a toll on Hume's health, but it did not stop him from lobbying for passage of the May 1998 referendum on the Good Friday Agreement. As James Clarity of the *New York Times* noted, "He spoke to people in the street in a soft but firm voice, cajoling, arguing, not quite begging, shaking hundreds of hands, hugging scores of people, to sell to both Catholics and Protestants his well-known but often-rejected hope for a peaceful settlement of the sectarian violence." He also championed the new Northern Ireland Assembly in the June 1998 elections, declaring in *Time International,* "We have to create institutions that allow us to break down the barriers between our two deeply divided communities and begin the healing process." Hume and the SDLP did quite well at the polls, capturing 22 percent of the vote.

Two months later, the tenuous peace was put to the test when a bomb exploded in a crowded shopping district in the town of Omagh, Northern Ireland, killing 28 people, Catholics as well as Protestants. Believed to be the work of a terrorist splinter group calling itself the "Real IRA," the attack was the worst single atrocity since "The Troubles" began in 1968. But a crisis was averted when Gerry Adams and Sinn Fein quickly disavowed any advance knowledge of the event and strongly condemned it. Observers took that as a sign that the Good Friday Agreement could withstand some blows.

Both Hume and Trimble saw their hard work and sacrifices on behalf of the peace process in Northern Ireland rewarded later that same year when they shared the Nobel Peace Prize. Many observers saw Hume as an obvious choice; he had been in contention for the award for several years on account of his longstanding commitment to finding a nonviolent solution, and it was his vision that ultimately shaped the Good Friday Agreement. But there were some raised eyebrows over Trimble's selection because of his militant past. As the Nobel committee pointed out, however, his embrace of accommodation at a critical stage in the negotiations had demonstrated "great political courage," and his subsequent energetic campaigning for acceptance of the Good Friday Agreement was what persuaded Protestant voters in Northern Ireland to endorse it. Acknowledging that the peace process still faced a long and difficult road ahead, one member of the committee remarked, "We wanted to give it a push."

Since that momentous event, the road to peace in Northern Ireland has indeed proved treacherous. Major stumbling blocks remain, most notably the issue of decommissioning, or disarming paramilitary groups such as the IRA and its Protestant counterparts. (The stated goal in the Good Friday Agreement was to achieve decommissioning of all illegal weapons by May 2000.) The Unionists insist that disarmament is a must if reconciliation is to move forward, but the IRA has been dragging its feet in the belief that handing over its weapons would be tantamount to surrender. This stalemate in turn halted progress on other key parts of the Good Friday Agreement, such as the establishment of a Northern Ireland/ Republic of Ireland ministerial council and a British/Irish council.

Hume largely retreated from front-rank participation in politics after the Good Friday Agreement was reached. But Trimble has remained in the spotlight, initially as prime minister of the Northern Ireland Assembly. As a reporter for the *Economist* pointed out, however, the assembly was "an ungainly creature" from the start because it was essentially "an involuntary coalition of parties who do not like to talk to each other, boxed in by complex safeguards of sectarian interests." This made Trimble's job a veritable "high-wire act," in the words of the same reporter.

The battle over decommissioning raged throughout 1999 as Trimble refused to let Sinn Fein representatives take their place in the cabinet of the new assembly until the IRA began to disarm. Neither side budged, prompting exasperation among government officials of both Great Britain and the Republic of Ireland who were trying to keep the process moving forward. Great Britain then threatened to dissolve the assembly if the decommissioning issue were not settled by a certain date. Several deadlines came and went, however, and nothing changed. By mid-1999, talks had completely collapsed and plans to establish home rule in Northern Ireland were put on hold. To many observers, it appeared the ongoing crisis would indeed doom the peace deal.

In September 1999, however, Catholics and Protestants agreed to resume their discussions under the direction of U.S. Senator Mitchell, who had helped broker the Good Friday Agreement. The talks dragged on throughout the fall without notable progress until November, when the IRA issued a statement indicating for the first time that it was willing to discuss handing over its weapons as soon as a power-sharing government was formed that included Sinn Fein. Trimble responded to the IRA's historic concession with a statement of his own that the Unionists would drop their demand that IRA weapons had to be turned in before such a government could be established. To secure the support of his colleagues—many of whom were vehemently opposed to the idea of allowing a power-sharing government to be formed before the IRA gave up its weapons—he promised he would resign from the new cabinet if the IRA had not begun to disarm by February 2000.

With the impasse finally broken, representatives from the four main Protestant and Roman Catholic political parties immediately took steps to form Northern Ireland's first home-rule government since 1974. Trimble was named to the top post of first minister, and the SDLP's Seamus Mallon was made his deputy. (Although he was still a leading figure in the SDLP and could have had the job, Hume stepped aside in favor of Mallon because Mallon and Trimble had a better working relationship than he and Trimble did.) The official shift of power from Great Britain to the new Northern Ireland Assembly occurred on December 2, 1999, with the signing of the Good Friday Agreement into law. In it was a stipulation that any reunification of Northern Ireland with the Republic of Ireland can only come about if the proposal is put to a vote and wins the support of a majority of the people of Northern Ireland.

The euphoria over the return of home rule was short-lived, however. On February 1, 2000, a report issued by an independent commission overseeing the disarmament process revealed that the IRA had not given up any of its weapons and apparently had no intention of doing so. Trimble and his fellow Unionist Party representatives reacted angrily to the news by threatening to resign, thus forcing the new government to collapse. To head off that scenario, Great Britain shut down the fledgling body on February 11 and resumed direct rule from London, an action that left open the possibility that power could be restored to the still-intact cabinet at a later date once the deadlock over decommissioning had been resolved once and for all.

But as February gave way to March, prospects for the restoration of home rule in Northern Ireland remained gloomy. The IRA refused to begin disarming, insisting that it had never promised to do so and that it would not agree to a solution based on either British or Unionist terms. The leaders of all the main parties to the debate began meeting again in early March as they sought to establish common ground and iron out any obstacles to implementing in full the terms of the Good Friday Agreement. "We want to see that done . . . ," Trimble was quoted as saying in the *New York Times.* "We want to see clarity, an end to ambiguity, no more nods and winks, for people to know precisely and clearly where we stand." A dispirited and exasperated John Hume also lamented the lack of progress, declaring the time had come for "direct dialogue," according to a *New York Times* reporter.

All of the key players in the crisis (Trimble, Hume, Adams, and several others) gathered in Washington, D.C., on St. Patrick's Day 2000 for discussions they hoped would lead to a breakthrough. But there was no such breakthrough, and against this backdrop of continued uncertainty, violence returned to Northern Ireland in the form of shootings and other attacks by members of splinter guerrilla groups on both sides of the issue who oppose the peace process. Yet Trimble remained optimistic—and determined. "I don't think the peace process is ended," he told a Reuters correspondent (as reported in the *New York Times*) just before his departure for Washington. "It's difficult to see how the problems are going to be resolved when republicans haven't moved. But we're going to get out of it."

Sources

➤ Books

Newsmakers: 1987 Cumulation, Gale, 1988.
Newsmakers: 1999, Issue 4, Gale, 1999.

➤ Periodicals

America, June 20, 1998.
Christian Science Monitor, November 29, 1999; December 4, 1999, p. 15; February 7, 2000, p. 6.
Commonweal, October 21, 1994; November 20, 1998.
Detroit News, November 28, 1999, p. 9A; February 13, 2000, p. 15A.
Economist (US), March 26, 1988; October 24, 1998, p. 56; February 13, 1999; March 27, 1999, p. 59; May 22, 1999, p. 63; November 20, 1999, p. 65.
Forbes, August 14, 1995.
Grand Rapids Press, November 18, 1999. p. A18; November 30, 1999, p. A7; December 2, 1999, p. A3; February 2, 2000, p. A11; February 6, 2000, p. A15.
Knight-Ridder/Tribune News Service, December 10, 1994 (opening quote).
National Catholic Reporter, October 30, 1998, p. 28.
New Republic, May 4, 1998.
New Statesman, September 19, 1997; August 28, 1998.
New Statesman & Society, September 15, 1995.
Newsweek, October 26, 1998, p. 54.
New York Times, April 20, 1998; November 28, 1999; February 3, 2000; February 11, 2000; March 8, 2000; March 14, 2000; March 15, 2000; March 17, 2000.
Time, September 29, 1997.

Time International, July 6, 1998, p. 16; October 26, 1998, p. 34.
U.S. News & World Report, July 26, 1999, p. 36.

Charlayne Hunter-Gault

"We have to make room for all of the voices. . . I don't think you get at universal truth with one set of eyes. You need many."

Born February 27, 1942, in Due West, South Carolina, Charlayne Hunter-Gault is an award-winning journalist, broadcast correspondent and author who was the first African American woman to attend the University of Georgia. Address: CNN, One CNN Center, P.O. Box 195366, Atlanta, GA 30348-5366.

As a child, Charlayne Hunter-Gault was inspired by comic strip heroine Brenda Starr to become a reporter. By her early adulthood, she had made good on her dream, writing for such publications as the *New Yorker* and moving toward a career in broadcasting as well. By the end of the 1990s, she was world-renowned as a correspondent for PBS, NPR and CNN. Still, Hunter-Gault remains most famous as the first African American woman admitted to the University of Georgia, a landmark in the civil rights struggles of the 1960s. Her poise and quiet courage in the face of racism during this time foreshadowed her later determination to succeed as a print and broadcast journalist.

Born in Due West, South Carolina, Charlayne Hunter-Gault is the oldest of three children of Charles S.H. Hunter, Jr. and Althea Hunter. Her family moved to Covington, Georgia and, later, to Atlanta. Her father was a Methodist chaplain in the United States Army, and because of his long absences from his family, Hunter-Gault was largely raised by her mother and grandmother. The latter, who read three newspapers a day, was a special inspiration to her. Hunter-Gault wrote in her autobiography *In My Place* that, despite having only a third-grade education, her grandmother "developed a curiosity about the world and a love of learning. . . She was probably the first news junkie I ever knew."

Hunter-Gault's childhood was broadened by summertime visits with her relatives in New York City, and by a short residency in Alaska when her father was stationed there. But most of her teenage years were spent in Atlanta, where she attended Turner High School and became an honor student. Though she served as the editor of the school paper, she was advised against pursuing journalism as a career by her English teacher. Hunter-Gault recalled in *In My Place* that, "while she didn't say it in so many words, it was clear to me what she meant: Journalism is a white man's profession."

The only college in the state that offered a journalism degree at that time was the all-white University of Georgia in Athens. With the aid of lawyers from the NAACP Legal Defense and Education Fund and local civil rights activists, Hunter-Gault and fellow Turner graduate Hamilton Holmes challenged the university's admissions policies in federal court. While the case slowly progressed, she attended Wayne State University in Detroit for a year. Finally, in January 1961, she and Holmes won their lawsuit and were allowed to register. Hunter-Gault's first day on campus was greeted by jeers and racial slurs, and her first night in her dorm room was disrupted by rioting outside. She and Hamilton were initially suspended in the name of keeping the peace, then reinstated under court order. Hunter-Gault went on to graduate from the University of Georgia with a B.A. in journalism in 1963.

After her graduation, Hunter-Gault was hired by the *New Yorker*, working with renowned editor William Shawn as an editorial assistant and, later, as a contributor to its "Talk of the Town" section. As much as it pleased her to be part of the magazine's staff, she was hungry to prove herself in the rougher world of mainstream journalism. "It was very important to me to establish myself as a journalist," she told Mary Marshall Clark in an interview for the Washington Press Club Foundation. "I had been famous at nineteen for something that should ordinarily have required no effort other than, you know, getting good grades and getting into college. I was famous because I had walked onto the campus of the University of Georgia. I was famous for being black. . . . But I wanted to be famous for something that I could do, that rested really on my abilities."

Leaving the *New Yorker* in 1967, Hunter-Gault received a Russell Sage Fellowship to study social sciences at Washington University in St. Louis, Missouri. She kept her reporting skills active by covering the Poor People's Campaign in Washington, D.C. From there, she joined the staff of Washington's WRC-TV as an investigative reporter and anchorwoman in 1968. Before the year ended, she moved on to accept a position with the *New York Times*, covering stories primarily in Harlem. She soon earned recognition for her high journalistic standards and eye for detail. In 1970, she and Joseph Lelyveld received the *New York Times* Publishers Award for their account of a 12-year old heroin addict's tragic life and death. Hunter-Gault went on to win two more Publishers Awards, in 1974 and 1976.

For Hunter-Gault, one of the most significant moments during her nine years with the *Times* was her battle with its editorial board to substitute the term "black" for "Negro" in its pages. "It was the fight over perception," she recalled in her Washington Press Club Foundation interview. "This was a critical moment where many people in black America were saying that the term 'Negro' was derisive, derogatory and not appropriate." Eventually, she convinced the editors to adopt the change. To her, the issue touched upon the larger question of giving African Americans a greater voice in reporting the news. As she told the Washington Press Club Foundation, "I thought, it's a wonderful idea to have plurality in the newsroom, to have different kinds of people with different sets of experiences. But you have to use them."

Hunter-Gault continued to earn wide praise for her work, receiving the National Urban Coalition Award for Distinguished Urban Reporting and the Lincoln University Unity Award. She returned to broadcast journalism when PBS chose her as a correspondent and substitute anchor for its "MacNeil/Lehrer Report" news program in 1978. The show, later expanded into the "MacNeil/Lehrer NewsHour," allowed her to use her interviewing talents to a degree unusual for television. During her 19 years with the program (later renamed "The NewsHour with Jim Lehrer"), she particularly distinguished herself as a foreign correspondent covering Africa, the Middle East and the Caribbean. She was among one of the first correspondents to report from Grenada after its invasion by United States-led forces in 1983, and was one of only two journalists to conduct an extensive interview with Nelson Mandela after his release from prison in 1990. During her tenure with PBS she received two Emmys, as well as a George Foster Peabody Award for her work on "Apartheid's People," a NewsHour series examining South Africa.

In 1997, Hunter-Gault left PBS and became National Public Radio's chief correspondent for Africa. In this position, she covered such events as President Clinton's 1998 African visit and the ongoing conflicts in Angola and Rwanda. In 1999, she took on similar duties for CNN, working out of Johannesburg, where her husband, investment banker Ron Gault, served as managing director of J.P. Morgan, S.A.

Though her work became international in scope, Hunter-Gault continued to feel a deep connection with the American South. In 1988, she returned to the University of Georgia to become the first African American to deliver the school's commencement address. During the address, she touched upon her Southern heritage, noting that "only the South has ever been a true melting pot. Through our toil and our tumultuous history, we have become a definable people, sui generis in the way we talk, our preference for fried food and our humility as we fulfill our hopes and dreams." *In My Place,* published in 1992, was a poignant and insightful memoir of being black during the waning days of the South's segregation era.

Charlayne Hunter-Gault's personal story has mirrored the advances that blacks in America have made as a whole over the past four decades. In assessing those years, she has expressed both satisfaction and a desire to achieve still more. "We need to remember that it was only 30 years ago that so many of us got our first-class citizenship rights," she told Charisse Jones in a *Los Angeles Times* interview. "Thirty years is not a long time, on the one hand. But then, on the other hand, it's long enough for a lot more to have been done."

Sources

➤ On-line

Clark, Mary Marshall, "Charlayne Hunter-Gault: Interview #5," *Washington Press Club Foundation,* http://npc.press.org (January 27, 2000).

➤ Books

Hunter-Gault, Charlayne, *In My Place,* Farrar Straus Giroux, 1992.
Smith, Jessie Carney, editor, *Notable Black American Women,* Gale Research Inc., 1992.

➤ Periodicals

Los Angeles Times, November 30, 1992, p. E1 (opening quote).
New York Times, June 14, 1988, p. A27; December 16, 1992, p. C24; December 31, 1995, p. 6-24.

➤ Other

Additional information for this profile was obtained from MacNeil/Lehrer Productions and CNN biographical data, January 2000.

Zora Neale Hurston

"I *am not tragically colored. There is no great sorrow dammed up in my soul. . . . I do not belong to that sobbing school of Negrohood who hold that nature somehow has given them a lowdown dirty deal. . . . No, I do not weep at the world—I am too busy sharpening my oyster knife."*

Born January 7, 1903, in Eatonville, Florida, folklorist and novelist Zora Neale Hurston was best known for her collection of African American folklore, *Mules and Men* (1935), and her novel, *Their Eyes Were Watching God* (1937), in which she charted a young African American woman's journey for personal fulfillment. She died on January 28, 1960 at Fort Pierce, Florida.

Zora Neale Hurston managed to avoid many of the restraints placed upon women, blacks, and specifically black artists by American society during the first half of the twentieth century. And she did so with a vengeance by becoming the most published black female author in her time and arguably the most important collector of African American folklore ever. Hurston was a complex artist whose persona ranged from charming and outrageous to fragile and inconsistent, but she always remained a driven and brilliant talent.

One of eight children, Hurston was born in the idyllic setting of a town in central Florida named Eatonville. Eatonville was incorporated in 1886 as the first self-governed, all-black city in America. In her folklore classic *Mules and Men,* Hurston describes Eatonville as "a city of five lakes, three croquet courts, three hundred brown skins, three hundred good swimmers, plenty guavas, two schools, and no jail house," as well as the home of Joe Clarke's store porch. The porch became a stage as neighbors sat around on milk crates skillfully transforming simple gossip into folktales. Eatonville was a nurturing environment that provided a black child with rich traditions and a pride and joy in being black. The Hurstons built a comfortable home on five acres of lush land dotted with tropical fruit trees. The place was overrun with boisterous, barefoot children, and the young Zora was probably the loudest of them all. Lucy Ann Hurston, a former country school teacher, was delighted with her daughter's spiritedness. As Zora wrote in her autobiography, *Dust Tracks on a Road:* "Mama exhorted her children at every opportunity to 'jump at the sun.' We might not land on the sun, but at least we would get off the ground." Her father did not see it that way. "It did not do for Negroes to have too much spirit," he counseled, as related in Zora's autobiography. "The white folks were not going to stand for it."

A carpenter, three-term mayor, and moderator of the South Florida Baptist Association, Zora's father, Reverend John Hurston, was a well-respected man and—according to wisdom gathered on Joe Clarke's porch—the strongest and bravest man in the community. Reverend Hurston's words to his daughter were cautionary: the rest of the world was not like Eatonville. But it was the rest of the world that the child hungered for. As she recounted in her autobiography, one of her favorite pastimes was to sit atop a gatepost hailing down passing cars and impishly asking, "Don't you want me to go a piece of the way with you?"

Hurston was only nine when her mother died. It was a traumatic experience, one that strained the relationship between her and her father. Two weeks after her mother's death she was sent off to school in Jacksonville, Florida; her father quickly remarried. Hurston despised her stepmother and became even more estranged from her father, who reacted by requesting—unsuccessfully—that the school adopt his daughter.

By the age of 14, Hurston was on her own. She held a number of jobs as a domestic before being hired as the personal maid to a cast member of a traveling Gilbert and Sullivan troupe. The actors welcomed her into their family, and the 18 months she spent with them would be among her fondest memories.

With a new sense of worldliness, Hurston left the troupe in Baltimore, Maryland, and enrolled into the high school division of Morgan Academy (now Morgan State University). She graduated early and set her sights on the prestigious Howard University. Working as a waitress and as a manicurist in a black-owned, whites-only barbershop, Hurston managed to scrape together the tuition to enter Howard in 1918.

Hurston embraced college life. She excelled in classes she found interesting and failed in those she did not; she worshiped her teachers; and she fell in love. The target of her affection was Herbert Sheen, a fellow student who would go on to medical school. They eventually married in 1927, only to divorce two years later when their careers came between them.

In 1921 Hurston published her first story. "John Redding Goes to Sea" was accepted by Howard's distinguished literary-club magazine. Though the story is considered a naively written and overly dramatic saga, it was the necessary first step for the blossoming young writer. In *Zora Neale Hurston: A Literary Biography*, Robert E. Hemenway wrote, "Hurston was struggling to make literature out of the Eatonville experience. It was her unique subject, and she was encouraged to make it the source of her art."

By 1925 her struggle was beginning to pay off. At an awards dinner sponsored by *Opportunity: A Journal of Negro Life,* a National Urban League magazine, Hurston came away with second-place prizes for an Eatonville story and play, and she caught the interest of leading figures in what would be known as the Harlem Renaissance. The connections she made at that dinner opened doors. That year she moved to New York City, began a job as a personal assistant to famed novelist Fannie Hurst, and entered Barnard College on scholarship as its first and only black student.

The time was the Roaring Twenties. Sandwiched between the beginning of World War II and the Great Depression of 1930, the 1920s was America's carefree era. It was the Jazz Age, Charleston was the dance, and Prohibition was for many only an inconvenience whose remedy was speakeasy social clubs. For black Americans, the 1920s was also an era of extremes. While the Ku Klux Klan was reviving a campaign of terror in the North, South, and Midwest, New York City was in the midst of the Harlem Renaissance, a movement marking the emergence of numerous notable black writers. Hemenway wrote that for some, "Harlem became an aphrodisiac, a place where whites could discover their primitive selves." But the Harlem Renaissance was not merely a white fad. It is regarded as a spiritual revolution born in the cultural capital of black America, exploring and celebrating the African American heritage.

Joining the likes of Jean Toomer, Alain Locke, Countie Cullen, and her friend Langston Hughes, Hurston became one of the "New Negroes." They were the young black intellectuals who demanded equal billing for African American culture in American history. But many thought Hurston to hold a special status. As a product of a community with a thriving black folk life and as a talented young writer who would celebrate that culture through her art, she is said to have personified the movement and was dubbed the "Queen of the Renaissance."

Hurston's celebrity status grew easily. In a room full of people, she reportedly could draw an audience to her like a magnet. She used storytelling techniques that the masters on Joe Clarke's porch would have been proud of and brought to life the tragicomic Eatonville stories that became known as "Zora stories." But her popularity drew some criticism too. A writer for the *Washington Post* noted, "Among her faults, her peers felt, was a dependence on whites for approval." The *Washington Post* writer went on to quote Langston Hughes: "To many of her white friends, no doubt, she was the perfect 'darkie' in the nice meaning they give the term—that is, naive, childlike, sweet, humorous and highly colored Negro. . . . But, Miss Hurston was clever too."

In 1928 Hurston answered her critics in an essay entitled "How It Feels to be Colored Me." In it she wrote: "I am not tragically colored. There is no great sorrow dammed up in my soul. . . . I do not belong to that sobbing school of Negrohood who hold that nature somehow has given them a lowdown dirty deal. . . . No, I do not weep at the world—I am too busy sharpening my oyster knife."

After receiving a B.A. from Barnard, Hurston began graduate work at Columbia University under the tutelage of Franz Boas, the foremost anthropologist in America. She continued writing and seeing her short stories published in literary magazines, but her interest was shifting to anthropology. Boas was encouraging: he saw Hurston as a natural candidate to help fill the void in the study of African American culture.

Hurston's first folklore collecting trip to America's South was unfruitful, but it was only a false start to a decade of field work that would prove rewarding. The trip also directed the budding anthropologist to a largely unexplored and exciting subject: voodoo. Funded by Guggenheim fellowships and by her long-term relationship with a wealthy New York City patron, Hurston spent the next decade researching black folklore in the South and tracking conjure lore—a quest that took her from New Orleans, Louisiana, to Jamaica, and finally Haiti, where she photographed an apparent zombie.

The secret of Hurston's success as a collector was her genuine respect and growing belief in the voodoo religion. As an initiate in the field, Hurston was included in sophisticated rites that would have been off limits to most anthropologists. In 1938 she painstakingly documented her experiences in Jamaica and Haiti in *Tell My Horse.* In the book's foreword, novelist and poet Ishmael Reed noted, "Her greatest accomplishment is in revealing the profound beauty and appeal of a faith older than Christianity, Buddhism, and Islam, a faith that has survived in spite of its horrendously bad reputation and the persecution of its followers."

Two other books resulted from Hurston's days on the road. Her work of folklore, *Mules and Men,* focuses on her excursions to the South and is regarded as the best and most important book of its kind. Its pages are filled with what many consider the integral ingredients of America's black culture: stories, or "big old lies," songs, superstitions, and even "formulae of Hoodoo Doctors."

But Hurston's masterpiece and the book she is most identified with is her novel *Their Eyes Were Watching God,* the jewel that Hurston cut from her Eatonville experience. It is the story of a young black woman, Janie, following her through three very different relationships and her transformation into a self-sufficient, whole human being. In the novel Janie learns that there are "two things everybody's got tuh do fuh theyselves. They got tuh go tuh God, and they got tuh find about livin' fuh theyselves." It is a novel of affirmation. Writer Alice Walker is quoted on its cover: "There is no book more important to me than this one."

While the 1930s and 1940s brought Hurston her greatest professional successes, they didn't come without a price. In 1931 a bitter breakdown of Hurston's friendship with Langston Hughes occurred. Their relationship was the victim of a series of misunderstandings over the authorship of a play. The two had been collaborating on what they believed to be the first true Negro comedy. *Mule Bone: A Comedy of Negro Life* was finally dusted off and produced on Broadway in 1991—and immediately caused controversy. The play was another Eatonville story; the setting was Joe Clarke's store porch; and the dialect was authentic.

To many blacks who worried about their perception in today's society, the play's use of Southern black dialect was embarrassing and even offensive. In its defense, Dr. Henry Louis Gates, Jr. wrote in the *New York Times*, "By using the vernacular tradition as the basis of their play—indeed, as the basis of a new theory of black drama—Hurston and Hughes sought to create a work that would undo a century of racist representations of black people." Though *Mule Bone* was not a typical Broadway hit, it is said to have earned its place in American history.

In 1948, living in New York City and in her late fifties, Hurston was arrested on charges of molesting a young boy. The case was thrown out of court but not before the black press ran it as a front-page scandal. Hurston's spirit was scarred by the false accusation, but she persevered, continuing to work with her characteristic zeal. In 1950 she moved to Fort Pierce, Florida, and took on a series of jobs, among them a librarian, maid, and substitute teacher. She also wrote political essays for the *Saturday Evening Post* and *American Legion Magazine.* Impoverished—a now familiar circumstance—, overweight, and weak, she nevertheless was pursuing her publisher about a book in progress. In 1959 she suffered a stroke and was forced to move into a welfare home.

The author of seven books and more than fifty articles and short stories, a playwright and traveler, and an anthropologist and folklorist, the "Queen of the Renaissance" died quietly in the welfare home on January 28, 1960. In 1973 Alice Walker made a pilgrimage to Fort Pierce and placed a tombstone on the site she guessed to be Hurston's unmarked grave. The stone was inscribed: "Zora Neale Hurston, A Genius of the South."

Sources

➤ Books

Hemenway, Robert E., *Zora Neale Hurston: A Literary Biography*, University of Illinois Press, 1977.
Hurston, Zora Neale, *Dust Tracks on a Road*, Lippincott, 1942.

➤ Periodicals

Miami Herald, August 22, 1976.
Ms., March 1978.
New York Times, June 2, 1978; February 10, 1991.

King Hussein I

"**I** *want to hear the tracks of bulldozers, not tanks; the footsteps of travelers, not troops. Let war be banished from our lands forever, so that we may engage our minds and energies in the development of the area.*"

Born November 14, 1935, in Amman, Jordan, Hussein Ibn Talal, better known as King Hussein I of Jordan, was the Middle East's longest-ruling leader, serving as monarch for 46 years. His reign—which began in 1953 when Hussein was 18 years old—was noted for his friendly relations with the West and his ability to maintain stability in his own nation, which is entrenched in a region infamous for its strife. Hussein died of cancer on February 7, 1999.

Hussein ibn Talal became, at the age of 18, the king of the Hashemite Kingdom of Jordan, a strategic central state in the Middle East. He was regarded in the West as a moderate Arab leader. Perhaps his greatest achievement was a 1994 peace agreement with Israel.

King Hussein, born in Amman, was the scion of the illustrious Hashemite family from which the Prophet Mohammed sprang in the sixth century. His great-grandfather Hussein ibn Ali and his grandfather Abdullah were leaders of the Arab revolt against the Ottoman Empire during World War I. The latter was also founder of the modern state of Jordan, originally called Transjordan. Hussein's early life is described as happy but the family's lifestyle was not elaborate. They lived in a modest villa in what was still an unspoiled desert kingdom.

The young Prince Hussein attended primary and secondary schools in Amman, Egypt, and England, after which he was a student at Britain's Sandhurst. At Sandhurst he learned military principles and attitudes that helped in future years with his own Jordan Arab Army, which in turn became a key to his longevity on Jordan's throne. The most important formative influence on the prince, though, was his grandfather King Abdullah, who was his tutor and guide. From him Hussein learned both respect for tradition and openness to change. Crown Prince Talal, Hussein's father, suffered from schizophrenia and the King took a special interest in his grandson Hussein, the only member of the family King Abdullah believed could rule Jordan.

When Abdullah was assassinated in the Haram al-Sharif mosque in Jerusalem in 1951 Hussein was at his side, and the memory of that event would affect his personal attitude toward danger as well as his view of the significance of Jerusalem. Following the assassination, Talal, Hussein's father, was crowned king, but he was removed by the Jordanian parliament within a year due to his mental illness. After a brief regency in 1953 Hussein took the constitutional oath as king. In the 1980s he became the longest ruling head of state in the world.

The young Hussein inherited a country which was extremely poor, filled with refugees, and subject to the political turmoil that was characteristic of the Middle East. Considered a pawn of the West, the young king spent the early portion of his reign just trying to survive in a time when Arab nationalism was thriving. For Jordan, the results of the 1948 Arab-Israeli war were threefold. The West Bank of the Jordan River and its Palestinian population were included in the Hashemite Kingdom of Jordan; hundreds of thousands of refugees from other parts of Palestine found their way to Jordan; and the state of Israel was created on Jordan's western border. Within this context King Hussein faced challenges to his throne emanating from disgruntled citizens, from radical Arab nationalism and interference from neighboring Arab states, and from occasional conflicts with Israeli military forces in Jordan's West Bank. With the key support of the army, which was recruited from Jordan's tribes, and other loyal political leaders, King Hussein and his regime were able to consolidate control by the late 1950s, although they still faced periodic challenges. Despite political tumult and tensions, King Hussein's regime made strides in building up the country's social and economic infrastructure—most significantly in education, which paid off in the following decades.

The 1967-1970 period was undoubtedly the most threatening to King Hussein's rule. In 1967 King Hussein along with Egypt and Syria fought the Six Day War against Israel and was defeated. For King Hussein the defeat was a severe setback, because Jordan lost the West Bank which, despite its small size, contained half the country's people, a little less than half of the economic activity, and the important religious shrines of East Jerusalem and Bethlehem.

Equally important, this defeat gave rise to the Palestinian guerrilla movements. Initially they attacked the state of Israel, which would retaliate by hitting their camps in Jordan. In 1970 the guerrillas turned their attacks on the government of Jordan. At the same time a Syrian tank force threatened the country's northern border, creating a second front which Jordan's military had to defend. With diplomatic support from the United States, King Hussein won on both fronts, but not without considerable death and destruction, particularly in Amman in the struggle with the Palestinian guerrillas.

From 1967 through 1973 Jordan's economy suffered greatly as a result of the fighting and punitive actions on the part of some radical Arab regimes. In the post-1974 oil boom, however, Jordan's fortunes improved significantly. Jordan's trained population and loyal military performed valuable services for the Arab petroleum producing countries for which they were well paid. The king and his brother, Crown Prince Hassan, also sought and received grants and concessional loans from the same countries. The infrastructure built in the 1950s and 1960s allowed these funds to fuel economic expansion. Not only were there rapid advances in socioeconomic development in the 1970s and 1980s, but also King Hussein allowed his people personal and economic freedom in an environment of civil order. Neither of the Hashemite monarchs, however, has allowed extensive political freedom or participation. Apparently to fill this void, King Hussein recalled parliament in 1984 after a ten-year hiatus.

Another major theme during King Hussein's reign was his difficult search for peace with Israel in the context of a realization of the just rights of the Palestinians. In the aftermath of the 1967 war with Israel he was the chief Arab negotiator in the formulation of the United Nations Security Council Resolution 242 which stipulated the principle of exchange of territory for peaceful relations with Israel as well as the inadmissibility of acquisition of territory by war. In 1972 the king followed up on this resolution with a proposal for a United Arab Kingdom which would be composed of East Jordan and the West Bank, the latter of which would enjoy local autonomy under the Jordanian crown.

In 1974 Hussein surrendered leadership in negotiations over the West Bank and Jerusalem to the Palestinian Liberation Organization (PLO), which was recognized by the Rabat summit as the sole legitimate representative of the Palestinian people. Consistent with this position, he refused to participate in the autonomy talks envisaged by the Camp David agreements of 1978, which had in fact been rejected by the PLO. But when Egypt and Israel signed a subsequent peace treaty in 1979 Jordan became the first Arab nation to cut diplomatic ties with Egypt.

President Ronald Reagan's Middle East peace initiative of 1982 was similar to a combination of Resolution 242 and the Hussein 1972 proposal. In the following years, King Hussein worked at realizing the 1982 initiative through talks and negotiations with American, Arab, and Palestinian leaders. But peace remained elusive.

In the 1991 Persian Gulf War, which was prompted by Iraq's invasion of Kuwait, King Hussein remained neutral initially, but eventually supported Saddam Hussein. After Iraq's defeat, King Hussein's relations with surrounding nations and the West were strained.

In the mid-1990s Hussein relinquished his stranglehold over the government and permitted political parties to field candidates in the first multi-party elections since 1956. Another crucial change in Jordan's relations with its neighbors occurred in 1994, when Israel and Jordan ended their 46-year state of war with the signing of a peace treaty. After the signing of the historic treaty, Hussein admitted that the Six Day War of 1967 was a mistake. However, the road to peace was not smooth, especially after the assassination of Yitzhak Rabin, Israel's prime minister. Rabin's successors chose not to honor all of the peace accords and this caused Hussein much anger and loss of face within his own country.

In 1992, King Hussein suffered his first bout with cancer. When the cancer resurfaced in 1998, he spent six months at the Mayo Clinic in Minnesota being treated for non-Hodgkin's lymphoma. King Hussein died at the age of 63 on February 7, 1999. King Hussein was married to Queen Noor, the former Lisa Halaby, an American citizen and his fourth wife. They had two sons and two daughters. Previously the king had seven children (plus one adoption) from three earlier marriages. King Hussein's son Abdullah succeeded to the throne of Jordan following his father's death.

Sources

➤ Books

Current Leaders of Nations, Gale Research, 1998 (opening quote).
Hussein, King of Jordan, *Uneasy Lies the Head,* Heinemann, 1962.
Newsmakers 1997 Cumulation, Gale Research, 1997.
Newsmakers 1999, Issue 3, Gale Group, 1999.
Snow, Peter, *Hussein: A Biography,* Barrie and Jenkins, 1972.

➤ Periodicals

Chicago Tribune, February 7, 1999.
Foreign Affairs, November-December 1993, p. 45.
Houston Chronicle, March 12, 1997, sec. 1, p. 18.
Los Angeles Times, August 15, 1990, sec. 1, p. 1; March 31, 1991, sec. 1, p. 1; February 8, 1999.
New Leader, May 6, 1991, p. 5.
New Perspectives Quarterly, Fall 1996, p. 15.
New Republic, August 26, 1985, p. 16; August 14, 1994, p. 18.
New York Times, March 12, 1997, sec. 1, p. 1; February 6, 1999.
Time, July 26, 1982, p. 22; November 20, 1989, p. 50; November 5, 1990, p. 41.
Times (London), February 8, 1999.
USA Today, March 12, 1997, sec. 1, p. 1; February 7, 1999.
U.S. News and World Report, August 15, 1988, p. 34.
Wall Street Journal, March 17, 1997, sec. 1, p. 1.

Robert K. Jarvik

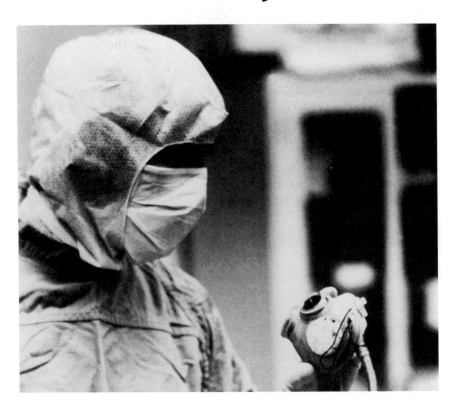

"If the artificial heart is ever to achieve its objective, it must be more than a pump. It must also be more than functional, reliable and dependable. It must be forgettable."

Robert Koffler Jarvik, born on May 11, 1946, in Midland, Michigan, designed and engineered the first artificial heart used as a permanent replacement in a human body. Though several patients' lives were prolonged with the device, it was more effective as a temporary measure for those awaiting a natural transplant. Address: Jarvik Heart Inc., 333 West 52nd St., New York, NY 10019-6238.

On December 2, 1982, doctors transplanted the first artificial heart intended to be a permanent replacement in a human body. This plastic and aluminum device, the Jarvik-7, was designed by biomedical engineer Robert Jarvik, a researcher who then worked with the University of Utah Medical Center. The heart was implanted into Barney Clark, a dentist with advanced heart disease who survived for 112 days after the operation. Several other direly ill patients subsequently received Jarvik-7 hearts as well, but none lived more than 620 days. The main benefits of using an artificial heart instead of transplanting a natural one were that there would be no wait for a human heart to become available, and there would be no chance of rejection of a foreign tissue. The obvious pitfall was that patients were forever connected to a compressed air machine via tubes.

Though the Jarvik-7 was eventually used as a stopgap measure for patients awaiting natural hearts, it marked a great leap forward in biomechanics, providing further hope that, eventually, those stricken with heart disease will no longer have to wait for organ transplants. Years after the first Jarvik-7 transplant, Jarvik continued to work on a new, tiny, self-contained device that would be implanted into a person's own diseased heart in order to make it function correctly. As he explained in a *Scientific American* article, "If the artificial heart is ever to achieve its objective, it must be more than a pump. It must also be more than functional, reliable and dependable. It must be forgettable."

Robert Koffler Jarvik was born on May 11, 1946, in Midland, Michigan. His parents, Norman Eugene and Edythe (Koffler) Jarvik, raised him in Stamford, Connecticut, where his father was a surgeon. As a child, Jarvik told Kristin McMurran in *People,* he was "a kid who was always mentally disassembling things and putting them back together." He built intricate model boats at age eight, and by his teens, joined his father in the operating room to watch surgeries. Before graduating from high school, Jarvik received his first patent, for an automatic stapler to be used during surgeries instead of having to manually clamp and tie blood vessels.

Entering New York's Syracuse University in 1964, Jarvik, who had always enjoyed the arts, especially sculpting, studied architecture and mechanical drawing. After his father developed heart disease and had to undergo surgery, Jarvik switched his major to pre-medicine. He graduated in 1968 with a bachelor of arts in zoology, but his grades were poor and he was rejected "probably 25" different times by medical schools in the United States, as Jarvik told Philip J. Hilts in the *Washington Post.* As he noted in a *Fortune* article, "I'm not a conventional thinker," and he conceded that he did not concentrate enough on his assigned work. Although he entered medical school at the University of Bologna in Italy, he left after two years and began attending New York University, earning a master of arts in occupational biomechanics in 1971.

Although Jarvik found work at a surgical supply house, he was still interested in becoming a doctor and applied for a job with the artificial organs program at a division of the University of Utah in Salt Lake City, hoping that working there would be his ticket to medical school. The director of the Institute for Biomedical Engineering and Division of Artificial Organs, Willem Kolff, was the reigning authority in the field and had invented the first kidney dialysis machine during World War II. He had been working on developing an artificial heart since the mid-1950s, and that was the main goal of his department at Utah. Jarvik began as his lab assistant, and Kolff did indeed help Jarvik win acceptance to the university's medical school. He earned his degree in 1976, and that year his father, who had been suffering from heart disease, died of an aneurysm.

At the time that Jarvik began working on the artificial heart, there had long been research on a permanent artificial heart, but only in recent years had accomplishments pointed to the possibility of success. An artificial lung had been developed by two researchers in Germany in 1855, and more than 30 types of heart-lung machines were devised by 1951, according to Jarvik in an article for *Scientific American.* He went on to note that a mechanical pump intended to replicate the function of both sides of the natural heart was employed in 1928 in England "to temporarily bypass the heart so that surgical procedures could be done on it."

Later, in 1952, a researcher at General Motors developed a mechanical heart that would allow a 50-minute surgery on the natural heart. However, Jarvik pointed out, this did not allow for the patient's lungs to oxygenate the heart, so the heart-lung machine was a better option for this use. Using a plastic model and compressed air, in 1957 Kolff was able to keep a dog alive for roughly an hour and a half, and gradually, with improvements, the time increased. By 1969, the first artificial heart was used in a human subject by Denton A. Cooley at the Texas Heart Institute, sustaining life for 64 hours until a natural heart was found and transplanted.

Though Jarvik heavily acknowledged the work of Kolff and others, he was the first to overcome some of the technical obstacles with the artificial heart. The item needed to be small and light-weight, gentle in pumping blood, but durable. Kolff had worked to create a device that would perform the pumping action and include a self-contained power supply, and he experimented with both electric and nuclear energy with little luck. Subsequently, he began to concentrate more on the pump and decided to rely on an outside power supply, although it meant that patients would have to be permanently hooked to a machine via tubes. One of the first mechanisms, designed by Clifford S. Kwann-Gett—also on Kolff's team—used a flexible rubber diaphragm and was activated by compressed air. Animals were able to live up to two weeks with that model. However, the diaphragm caused excessive clotting, which used up so much of the clotting factors in the blood that other wounds might suffer uncontrolled bleeding, which could possibly result in death.

By the 1970s, Jarvik had come up with a new design that was better tailored to the anatomy of the experimental animals. It featured layers of smooth polyurethane, called biomer, on aluminum bases. By the mid-1970s, he was working on a design for humans, and began testing it in calves and sheep. One of these devices kept alive a calf, named Alfred Lord Tennyson, for a record of 268 days. This heart simulated the two pumping chambers, called ventricles, and was attached to the atria, or upper chambers. It was powered by compressed air from a machine that was connected by tubes.

In 1981, Kolff asked for permission from the Food and Drug Administration (FDA) to implant the Jarvik-7 into a human. The initial request was denied but later approved, and in 1982 Barney Clark, a 61-year-old retired dentist, became the first person to receive the artificial heart. William C. DeVries headed the surgical team at the University of Utah Medical Center. Clark lived for 112 days before dying of multiple organ failure, but the Jarvik-7 was still working. In November of 1984, the second artificial heart recipient, William J. Schroeder, age 52, underwent the operation. His recovery was more hopeful, and he was able to move around for about three hours daily thanks to a portable battery pack the size of a camera bag that provided power for the air hoses. However, he soon suffered from strokes and was debilitated. Several subsequent patients received the heart, with one patient living a record 620 days. Others received the heart for short spans while they waited for natural hearts to become available for transplants.

Like many other contemporary medical issues, the procedure

was not without controversy. Some argued that at between $100,000 and $200,000 or more for the operation, the cost was too high, but proponents argued that other transplants and procedures were expensive as well. There were also ethical issues—opponents of the artificial heart noted that natural transplants were still superior, and thought that the operations were making human subjects into guinea pigs for experimentation with the Jarvik-7. They also argued about the patients' quality of life, but Jarvik responded in a *New York Times* article by Philip M. Boffey, "As a physician, I certainly don't think that I could submit a patient through this if I didn't believe that the quality of life would be better improved from what it was."

Back in 1976, fearing that public funding for their research may eventually run dry, Jarvik entered a private business venture with Kolff; later, in 1981, he was named president of another company of Kolff's called Symbion, Inc. However, in 1987, Jarvik left the University of Utah and Symbion to forge out on his own in the business world. After his departure, the FDA restricted the use of the artificial heart as a temporary measure, and in 1990, citing quality concerns and poor service from Symbion, withdrew approval entirely. Jarvik, meanwhile, moved to New York City and formed Jarvik Research, and later focused his energies into Manhattan-based Jarvik Heart, concentrating more on actual manufacturing than experiments.

By 1998, Jarvik was devoted to creating a new incarnation of the artificial heart called the Jarvik 2000. Unlike earlier models, which required removal of the natural heart, this device—the size of a C-cell battery—is inserted into the left ventricle and provides pumping action. "If you boost the output of the natural heart and keep it working," Jarvik explained to Scott Rathburn in *CNC Machining*, "you have the advantage that the heart still regulates the body's needs and the amount of blood flow the patient gets." Another benefit Jarvik saw was that by placing the Jarvik 2000 inside the heart, it lowered the risk of infection. As of 1999, the product was still being tested. Jarvik hoped that his new artificial heart would be able to function as a permanent replacement.

The Intellectual Property Owners, a trade association of inventors, in 1982 named Jarvik inventor of the year, which he remarked "was sort of funny," according to Hilts, since he really only helped develop it and did not even hold a patent on it. That same year, he received a Brotherhood Citation from the Utah chapter of the National Conference of Christians and Jews, the American Academy of Achievement's Golden Plate award, the John W. Hyatt award from the Society of Plastics Engineers, and the Utah Heart Association's Gold Heart award.

Jarvik was married in 1968 to journalist Elaine Levin, and they had two children—Tyler and Kate—but divorced in 1985. In August of 1987 he married Marilyn Vos Savant, who holds the world's highest intelligence quotient (I.Q.). At 228, she is 88 points smarter than the average genius. Vos Savant is an author best known for her weekly column in *Parade* magazine. Jarvik's hobbies include reading poetry, weightlifting, and snow skiing, both downhill and cross-country.

Sources

➤ **Books**

Contemporary Newsmakers, 1985 Cumulation, Gale Research, 1986.
Notable Twentieth-Century Scientists, Gale Research, 1995.

➤ **Periodicals**

CNC Machining, Fall 1998, p. 12.
Fortune, June 29, 1981, p. 78.
Maclean's, May 9, 1983, p. 41.
Newsweek, December 13, 1982, p. 73; December 10, 1984, p. 74; March 4, 1985, p. 72.
New York Times, December 3, 1982, pp. A1, A24; July 9, 1985, p. C8; November 12, 1985, p. C7; November 26, 1985, p. C3; December 3, 1985, p. C1.
People, December 16, 1985, p. 58; July 27, 1987, p. 46.
Science News, February 19, 1983, p. 119.
Scientific American, January 1981, p. 74 (opening quote).
Time, April 6, 1981, p. 67; December 10, 1984, p. 70; December 17, 1984, p. 79.
Washington Post, February 12, 1983, p. A2.

Danny Kaye

"I believe implicitly in the kind of work that UNICEF is doing for children throughout the world and . . . I had the greatest time I ever had in my whole life doing this."

Born on January 18, 1913, in Brooklyn, New York, Danny Kaye was an actor and entertainer who was also a long-time ambassador for UNICEF, the United Nations International Children's Emergency Fund. He died on March 3, 1987, in Los Angeles, California.

While Danny Kaye was known primarily for his contributions to the entertainment industry, he had a deep love for children that led to a long stint as an honorary ambassador for UNICEF, the United Nations International Children's Emergency Fund. Kaye spent more than four decades as an actor, singer and dancer on stage, screen, television and radio, often combining a childlike spirit with worldly charm. He then used his stardom to help raise funds for UNICEF and other charitable causes.

Kaye was born David Daniel Kaminski (some sources say Kominski) on January 18, 1913, in Brooklyn, New York. He was the son of Jacob Kaminski and his wife, Clara Newmerovsky Kaminski, both of whom were Jewish immigrants from the Ukraine. While Jacob Kaminski had been a horse dealer in his native country, he worked as a tailor in the United States. The Kaminskis struggled financially and were too poor to send their son to college to fulfill his dream of becoming a doctor.

Kaye was already dancing and singing for fun while a student at Thomas Jefferson High School. But during his sophomore year, he decided to drop out of school to pursue a professional career in entertainment. Accompanied by a friend who played guitar, Kaye hitchhiked to Miami Beach, Florida, to seek his fortune. The pair lasted only two weeks before returning to Brooklyn.

Upon his return, Kaye spent his evenings working private parties as an entertainer and held a variety of odd jobs during the daytime to support himself. He toiled as a soda jerk and even worked as an office boy for a dentist. He was fired from a job as an insurance appraiser when he made a mistake in addition that cost his employer thousands of dollars.

Kaye received his first professional break in 1929 when he was hired as a *tummler* at a resort in New York's Catskill Mountains called White Roe Lake. A *tummler* was an entertainer whose job was to provide constant amusement for guests at the resort, and Kaye did not disappoint—he was willing to do anything for a laugh. It was during this period that he took the stage name Danny Kaye. (He legally changed it in 1943.)

Kaye spent every summer at White Roe Lake through 1933 and earned $1000 per season. He went home to Brooklyn in the winter to audition for Broadway shows but never had any luck. Another break came his way in 1933, however, when he was asked to become part of the Three Terpsichoreans, a comedy and dance act. For the next few years, Kaye toured with them throughout Asia.

While on this extended tour, Kaye developed what would become part of his standard comic routine. Because many audience members did not understand English, he used wildly exaggerated facial expressions to underscore his point. He relied on a similar technique in his pantomimes and dance routines. The tour was very successful, but Kaye still could not find work in the United States upon his return in 1936. An eight-week tour of England turned out to be a disaster.

By 1939, Kaye was once again working at resorts. While employed at Pennsylvania's Camp Tamiment, he met Sylvia Fine, the resort's pianist and songwriter. Fine supplied him with material that suited his strengths. She became his lifelong collaborator, managing his career and helping him develop an act that would make him as popular at home as he had been in Asia.

Kaye finally made it to Broadway in late 1939 when he was featured in a show called *The Straw Hat Revue* that contained much of Fine's work. Kaye was very funny and garnered some favorable notices from both critics and audiences. He and Fine subsequently married on January 3, 1940, and later had one child, a daughter named Dena. Though the marriage lasted for the rest of Kaye's life, it was not an especially happy one.

At long last, Kaye's career started to take off. He appeared in a couple more Broadway musical shows that turned out to be quite popular, then achieved bona fide stardom in 1940 when he appeared in *Lady in the Dark* and performed the novelty song "Tschaikovsky." In this 38-second ditty, he recited the names of some 50 Russian composers at breakneck speed. His feat was the talk of the town, and audiences loved it.

When the United States entered World War II in 1941, Kaye wanted to join the military but was turned down due to back problems. Eager to contribute something to the war effort, he entertained troops in both the European and Pacific theaters as well as at bond rallies in the United States.

During this same period, Kaye branched out into film and radio for the first time. Though he had had film offers before, it was not until 1943 that he finally made his debut in a war comedy entitled *Up in Arms.* Two years later he hosted his own radio program on CBS called "The Danny Kaye Show." Though it received decent reviews, it did not remain on the air for very long.

In 1945, Kaye made his second film, *Wonder Man,* which defined his screen persona for years to come. In it he played twin brothers with totally opposite personalities, one serious and mild-mannered and the other brash and trouble-prone. In many of his most highly regarded movies, Kaye played more than one role, though his primary character was usually a meek victim of circumstance. He also did a significant amount of physical comedy.

Kaye made some of his best-known movies during the 1940s. They included *The Secret Life of Walter Mitty,* (1947) in which he played seven different roles, and *The Inspector General,* (1949) in which he played four roles. Yet Kaye was actually more famous for his stage work and one-man shows that enabled him to entertain audiences in person. As William A. Henry III wrote in *Time,* "Limber of face and graceful even in pratfalls, he was zany but gentle, making fun chiefly of himself." Kaye toured England every year from 1948 to 1952 and attracted sellout crowds.

Kaye continued to make movies during the 1950s. Arguably his best-known role was as Hans Christian Anderson in the 1952 film of the same title. While *White Christmas* (1954) did well at the box office and became a holiday classic, it was not a favorite among reviewers. The last of Kaye's 18 movies to receive critical acclaim was *The Court Jester* (1956), which some believe was the best film he ever made.

In 1954, Kaye became involved with UNICEF as their ambassador-at-large. His relationship with the organization came about almost by accident when he met the group's first executive director, Maurice Pate, on an airplane. At the time, many Americans were suspicious about the newly established United Nations (UN), the parent organization of UNICEF. Opponents tried to portray it as a tool of communism, a powerful accusation in an era dominated by Senator Joseph McCarthy and others determined to root out communist influence in every corner of American life. Kaye helped raise the public's awareness of UNICEF as a group devoted to the interests of children around the world and in the process improved the image of the United Nations as a whole.

In 1954 Kaye was featured in a short documentary about the work of UNICEF entitled *Assignment: Children.* It showed how much he traveled on the organization's behalf, sometimes flying his own plane to benefits and other events. In recognition of his work with UNICEF, Kaye was given a special Academy Award in 1955.

UNICEF was not Kaye's only charitable concern, however. In 1961, he began working as a guest conductor at concerts that raised funds for musicians' pensions. Over a 20-year period, Kaye's appearances raised an estimated $6-$10 million. Though he did not read music or regard himself as a true conductor, he took his job seriously. Yet physical comedy still played a part in his act. During performances of "The Flight of the Bumblebee," for example, Kaye often conducted with a fly swatter.

Kaye's career took a different turn in 1963 when he began to work on television as host and star of "The Danny Kaye Show," a variety program. It won four Emmys as well as a George Foster Peabody Broadcasting Award during its four-year run. Kaye also continued to appear in small film roles toward the end of the 1960s and did some stage work, including a stint as Noah in a 1970 Broadway production of *Two by Two.*

In 1975, Kaye undertook his most extensive campaign ever for UNICEF, flying in his own plane to 65 cities to drum up support for the organization. In fact, throughout the late 1970s and beyond he did very little else but work for UNICEF. He also indulged his love of baseball as co-founder and owner of a major league team, the Seattle Mariners.

Kaye had two significant television roles during the 1980s. He played a Holocaust survivor in *Skokie,* a 1981 made-for-television movie that earned praise for his powerful performance. Five years later, he was nominated for an Emmy for his appearance in a widely acclaimed episode of "The Cosby Show." He received a number of other awards as he neared the end of his life, including the 1982 Jean Hersholt Humanitarian Award from the Academy of Motion Picture Arts and Sciences. Kaye was also singled out for Kennedy Center Honors in 1984.

Kaye died of a heart attack brought on by internal bleeding and hepatitis on March 3, 1987, in Los Angeles, California. Upon his death, United Nations Secretary General Javier Pérez de Cuéllar was quoted by Eric Pace of the *New York Times* as saying, "He was truly a champion for children in every continent."

Sources

➤ Books

Burgess, Patricia, *The Annual Obituary 1987,* St. James Press, 1990, pp. 143-45.
Gareffa, Peter M., editor, *Contemporary Newsmakers: 1987 Cumulation,* Gale, 1988, p. 202.

Garraty, John A. and Mark C. Carnes, editors, *American National Biography,* Volume 12, Oxford University Press, 1999, pp. 411-12.
Gottfried, Martin, *Nobody's Fool: The Lives of Danny Kaye,* Simon & Schuster, 1994 (opening quote).
Shipman, David, *The Great Movie Stars,* Hill & Wang, 1980, pp. 287-90.

➤ **Periodicals**

Los Angeles Times, March 4, 1987, p. 1.
New York Times, August 16, 1981, section 2, p. 1; March 4, 1987; October 22, 1987, p. C28.
Time, March 16, 1987, p. 90.
United Nations Bulletin, May 15, 1954, p. 401.
United Nations Chronicle, June 1983, p. 76.

John Maynard Keynes

"This long run is a misleading guide to current affairs. In the long run we are all dead."*

Born June 5, 1883, in Cambridge, England, John Maynard Keynes was one of the most influential economists in the twentieth century, responsible for theories that were the basis for the modern economic system. He died April 21, 1946, at Tilton, his home near Firle, Sussex, England.

Through his writings on economics, John Maynard Keynes changed the course of capitalism with his so-called Keynesian Revolution. His ideas—which included deficit spending by governments to pump up lagging economies—were revolutionary at the time. Many believed that Keynes' economics were responsible for the end of the Great Depression. Keynes' writings are still studied today.

Keynes was born June 5, 1883, in Cambridge, England. He was the only son of John Neville and Florence Ada (nee Brown) Keynes. John Neville Keynes taught economics at Cambridge University. He was also involved in Cambridge's administration, including a stint as registrar. Florence Keynes served as the mayor of Cambridge at one time.

The education of Keynes began at Saint Faith's Preparatory School. He then attended Eton, one of Britain's most elite public schools. In his class, he was the second in mathematics, and first in the study of the classics. For his university education, Keynes chose to return to Cambridge, where he studied economics and some mathematics. Keynes chose to pursue economics so that he would be prepared for the civil service exam. When he took his exam, however, his lowest score was in economics.

After graduating from Cambridge, Keynes did get a job as a civil servant. He was employed in the India Office from 1906 until 1908, working on Indian currency problems as a junior clerk. At the time, India was a colony of Great Britain, part of the British empire. Keynes was rather bored by his job, though he did learn about the demands of government service.

In 1908, Keynes returned to Cambridge University. He spent the next seven years teaching economics at King's College. While at Cambridge, Keynes' career progressed in other areas. In 1911, he became an editor at the *Economic Journal,* a position he would hold until just before his death. Published by the Royal Economic Society, *Economic Journal* was one of the foremost publications of its kind. Keynes was given the post despite his young age and limited experience.

Keynes published his first book in 1913, based on his experiences in the India Office, called *Indian Currency and Finance.* It concerned the gold exchange standard. That same year, he was appointed to serve on the Royal Commission on Indian Currency and Finance.

Just after World War I began, in 1915, Keynes began working for the British Treasury on an unofficial basis. Later, it became official, and he was promoted to British Treasure representative. He consulted financial issues related to the war. To help France's struggling economy out, for example, Keynes suggested the National Gallery of Great Britain buy some of their works of art.

When the war ended in 1918, Keynes accompanied the prime minister of Great Britain, Lloyd George, to the peace negotiations in Versailles, France. Keynes was an official Delegate to the Paris Peace Conference. He ended up resigning in protest over the Versailles Treaty in June of 1919. Keynes believed that the reparations demanded of Germany were far too much for them ever to pay considering the restrictions the plan placed on their economy. Keynes believed this Treaty would eventually ruin Europe because it kept the Germans oppressed. (He would later be proven right, when World War II broke out 20 years later.)

Keynes also wrote a book on the subject entitled *Economic Consequences of Peace* (1919). In *Economic Consequences,* he was also critical of the fact that the treaty abandoned several economic factors existent before the war. They included an economy based on gold and low tariffs for trade. The book sold 84,000 copies, and was very controversial.

When the book was complete, Keynes went into private industry. He speculated on the foreign exchange and commodities market. Keynes began working at the National Mutual Life Insurance Company on the board in 1919, and by 1923, was the director of the board. (He resigned in 1938.) In 1923, Keynes also became the director of the Provincial Insurance Company, and the following year was named the director of the Independent Investment Company (remaining in both appointments until his death). Keynes also worked with two smaller investment companies, and made a lot of money for himself.

Keynes' money-making activities were not limited to businesses. He returned to Cambridge University in 1921, as King's College's second bursar. (A bursar is a college treasurer, who could invest funds.) Three years later, Keynes was promoted to first bursar, a position he would hold until death. His shrewd investments made King's College extremely wealthy. Keynes also continued to write books, including *Treaty on Monetary Reform* in 1923. Additionally, Keynes was married in this time period, to Lydia Lopokova, a ballerina who was a native of Russia.

In the middle of the 1920s, Keynes began formulating a new economic theory. At this point, governments of most countries in

Europe and the United States functioned on the principle of laissez-faire. This meant that businesses and industries were relatively unregulated by governments. Governments also wanted to keep their budgets balanced as much as possible. Debt was to be avoided. Keynes saw flaws in this thinking, and within ten years would publish a book that changed the way governments regarded their economies.

Before this book, Keynes published the two volumes of *Treatise on Money* in 1930. Though it was a difficult book, it had important moments of clear insight. Keynes argued that price stability and savings were more important than deflation (decreasing the amount of money in circulation so that it would be worth more). He also talked about what role interests rates played in the economy.

As the Great Depression started to put a stranglehold on the economies of the western world in the early 1930s, Keynes prepared to publish his most famous book, *The General Theory of Employment, Interest and Money* (1936). Many scholars believe it is one of the most important economic books ever written.

In *General Theory*, Keynes argued that laissez-faire economics would not solve the economic problems of the Great Depression and other depressions. Indeed the problem was not overproduction, as was commonly believed at the time. Instead, the lack of money meant that goods could not be distributed appropriately. Keynes offered several solutions to this problem, primarily related to employment.

To keep a capitalist economy going during such times, Keynes believed that governments should play a bigger role. Though he did not advocate their control of business and industry, Keynes believed governments should intervene so people would become employed again. He argued governments should not worry about staying out of debt, but spending money to stimulate the economy and create employment. The money would be spent on public works, increasing purchasing power.

This money would be above what a government took in from taxes, and create a deficit situation. But Keynes believed that this intervention would stabilize a capitalist marketplace because private investors would not invest in such a situation. Capital could not create demand when it did not exist. Keynes was sure the resulting rise in employment would make up for the deficit created.

When Keynes published *General Theory*, there were those who were doubtful about his combining capitalism with socialist principles. American president Franklin Delano Roosevelt tried everything to end the Great Depression. When he was elected in 1932, he promised to balance the budget by increasing taxes which should have ended the Depression. It only got worse. By the late 1930s and early 1940s, Roosevelt used some of the principles of Keynesian economics and the American economy seemed to improve.

Critics have pointed out that the United States was gearing up for World War II, and the resulting boost to the economy would have solved the problems of the Great Depression anyway. Despite such detractors, Keynes' ideas from *General Theory* were used by economists in the post-Depression and post-war years to formulate policies and further ideas. Keynes' work was influential for decades, not just for his ideas, but also for his balance of the practical and theoretical. Additionally, scholars admired his ability to formulate economic ideas that were in tune with economic realities, unlike many of his predecessors.

With World War II, Keynes returned to public service. He worked as a consultant to the chancellor of the exchequer (treasurer) in 1940, and was also a director of the Bank of England at the same time. Keynes had published his last book in 1940, *How to Pay for the War*, and used its principles in his work. For his accomplishments, in 1942, he was made a peer, the first Baron of Tilton.

After the war in Europe ended in 1944, Keynes participated in the international conference at Bretton Woods, New Hampshire, in 1944. The meeting focused on stabilizing the international economies and currencies in the post-war period. Keynes was one of the architects of what became the World Bank and International Monetary Fund (IMF). These organizations loaned money to poorer countries to help them develop economically.

At the end of the war, those who negotiated the peace settlement remembered what Keynes said at the end of World War I. Instead of making impossible demands on the economies of the losers, the Allies helped those who lost rebuild. With such public investing, those economies did much better. Great Britain's post-war Labour governments also based their economies on the principles set forth in *General Theory*, focusing on getting people employed.

After a history of heart problems, Keynes died of a heart attack April 21, 1946, at Tilton, his home near Firle, Sussex, England. He had just returned home from working on the IMF. He was survived by his wife, and the couple had no children. Robert B. Reich of *Time* quoted Arthur Burns, a one-time American economic advisor to

President Dwight D. Eisenhower, as saying "Keynes' thinking moved the world... as profoundly as Adam Smith's *Wealth of Nations* did in his time."

Sources

➤ **Books**

Carson, Thomas, editor, *Gale Encyclopedia of U.S. Economic History*, Gale Group, 1999.
Columbia Encyclopedia, Columbia University Press, 1993.
Davis, William, *The Innovators: The Essential Guide to Business Thinkers, Achievers and Entrepreneurs*, American Management Association, 1987.
Encyclopedia of World Biography, Gale Group, 1998.
Jeremy, David J., editor, *Dictionary of Business Biography*, volume three, Butterworths, 1985.
Moggridge, D.E., *John Maynard Keynes*, Penguin, 1976.

➤ **Periodicals**

Fortune, March 29, 1999, p. 136.
Newsday, March 13, 1994, p. 42.
Time, March 29, 1999, p. 136 (opening quote).

Maximilian Kolbe

"I'*d like to die in a knightly manner. . . I wish the same for you. For what nobler can I wish you?"*

Born on January 8, 1894, in Zdunska-Wola, Poland, Maximilian Kolbe was a Roman Catholic priest of the Franciscan order who died in a Nazi concentration camp on August 14, 1941.

A t the memorial site dedicated to those who died in the notorious German concentration camp at Auschwitz, Poland, is a special marker and shrine to one of the camp's earliest victims, Father Maximilian Kolbe. One of many Poles killed there before the Nazis expanded Auschwitz and it became, literally, a factory of death for European Jews, Kolbe gave his life so that a fellow internee, who was a husband and father, might be spared. He was canonized by the Roman Catholic Church in 1982.

Kolbe was born in the village of Zdunska-Wola, Poland, near Lodz, on January 8, 1894, and christened Rajmund. The middle of three sons, Kolbe was an obedient child who often prayed at the family's shrine to the Virgin Mary. Both of his parents were devout Catholics; his mother, Marianna, had wanted to become a nun as a teenager, but her family had no money to give as a dowry to a religious order, as was the custom at the time. His father, Juliusz, was a weaver and leader of the local chapter of a religious society for lay men, the Third Order of Franciscans.

The Kolbe family eventually moved to Pabianice, a larger town, where Marianna Kolbe opened a small store while her husband managed a small factory. As a young teen, Kolbe attended a business high school with his older brother Francis. During an Easter mass in 1907, the Pabianice priest announced in church that a new Franciscan seminary had opened in Lwow (then called Lemberg), and both Rajmund, then 13, and Francis decided to apply for admission. Their mother was in favor of this move to an all-boys' school; she was reportedly so eager to shield them from worldly temptations that they were not even allowed to speak to a member of the opposite sex without a reason.

When they reached the age of 16, it became necessary for the seminary students to decide whether they would pursue the priesthood. Kolbe doubted his calling, and thought he might like to join the army and become an officer, or study engineering. His mother convinced him otherwise, and he took the name of Maximilian and the Franciscan habit in September of 1910. He made his temporary vows a year later, and spent the next several years in training; he showed such promise that he was selected to travel to Rome, a great honor, for further study.

Kolbe arrived in Rome in the fall of 1912, and spent the next seven years there. He made his perpetual vows in 1914, and earned a doctorate in philosophy in 1915. In 1918 he was ordained a priest at Rome's S. Andrea della Valle Church. A year earlier, however, Kolbe had founded the Knights of the Immaculata Movement, on the day that Catholics in Rome were celebrating the 75th anniversary of a famous conversion of a French Jew to Roman Catholicism after the Virgin Mary had appeared before him. Kolbe, who often prayed to saints to whom the Madonna had appeared, was inspired that day to found a "Marian" movement for lay men and women. In Latin it was called the Militia Immaculatae, and its dual aims were to draw Catholics to an increased spirituality, and win converts from other faiths. The movement reflected the mood of the times: Europeans were shocked and demoralized by the carnage of World War I, and there was a decided anti-Catholic prejudice in the laws of many countries that the Knights hoped to eradicate.

After earning a second doctorate in 1919, Kolbe departed for Poland. For a time, he taught philosophy and church history at a Franciscan college in Krakow, but the Italian climate had worsened his already-frail health, and he was diagnosed with tuberculosis. He spent several months recuperating, and returned to Krakow in 1922. Here he won permission from his superiors to begin a small magazine for the organization, but they appropriated no money to publish. He was forced to solicit donations himself, a difficult task for this man who was by both nature and training a humble priest.

The Knight, however, became a success and circulation rose to 100,000 copies a month. In 1927, Kolbe convinced a local aristocrat to donate land near Teresin for a site that would be called Niepokalanow, or "City of the Immaculata." The seminary opened in 1929, and Kolbe then spent the next several years in Asia, where he built a similar site near Nagasaki, Japan. He returned to Poland in 1936, and entered once again into the thriving activities of the friars at Niepokalanow and the Knights elsewhere. Nearly 1,000 men lived or studied at the seminary, and the magazine was joined by a popular newspaper; there was also a radio station and plans for Catholic films.

Tensions in Europe were mounting, however, as German Chancellor Adolf Hitler annexed both part of Czechoslovakia and Austria. Not for the first time Kolbe predicted that war was imminent, and that the friars should prepare for the final of what he viewed as the three stages of life: preparation, activity, and suffering. "I think the third stage will be my lot shortly," he said to them at Niepokalanow a week before Germany invaded Poland, according to Diana Dewar's *Saint of Auschwitz: The Story of Maximilian Kolbe.* "I'd like to die in a knightly manner. . . I wish the same for you. For what nobler can I wish you? Christ himself said, 'Greater love hath no man than this, that he lay down his life for his friends.'"

The Nazi invasion set in motion World War II, and put an abrupt end to the publishing and educational work of the friars at Niepokalanow when Kolbe and several others were detained. Villagers who saw the priests sometimes offered them civilian clothing to help them escape, but they declined. When the friars returned to Niepokalanow, they found it ransacked, but began rebuilding. Kolbe now announced that their mission was to house, feed, and provide spiritual support for the thousands of Jewish and Polish refugees displaced by the German invasion. Soon Kolbe applied for permission to begin printing *The Knight* again, and the Gestapo, or German secret police, finally okayed a press run for a single edition that appeared in December of 1940. In the issue, Kolbe wrote of the need to believe in truth. "Find it, and be its servant . . . Not even the most powerful propaganda machine in the world can change truth." Within two months, Kolbe was arrested by the Nazis, who viewed many individual Roman Catholic priests—often the most influential, educated men in some Eastern European villages—as dissidents and a hindrance to the goals of the Third Reich.

Kolbe was sent first to a prison in Warsaw, then transported by cattle car to Auschwitz in May. On the way, he led the travelers in song and prayer. It was a labor camp, and the frail priest, who had been plagued by years of poor health, often was unable to perform the terrible workload assigned to him, such as carrying massive logs or even corpses. He was sometimes beaten, and often gave his meager rations—watery soup or bread made with sawdust—away to other internees who were in equally dire circumstances. He counseled fellow prisoners, heard confessions, and held mass, all under tremendous danger to his safety for continuing to practice his calling as a spiritual guide for others. At the end of July, a prisoner from his section escaped from a farm detail. Such escapes were relatively common, and to punish them, the camp commandants would select ten of their cellmates and condemn them to death.

Kolbe and the other men were not given their evening meal that day, and ordered to stand in formation until late into the night. They awoke early the next morning and were again forced to endure long hours under the hot sun, and it became apparent that the escapee was not going to return as a captive. Gestapo officers, who never even deemed to address a prisoner, then selected ten of them at random. One man chosen was a Polish army sergeant, who cried out, "My poor wife and children!" Kolbe stepped out of line and walked slowly toward one of the officers. He could have been shot on the spot for this transgression alone. The commandant barked, "What does this Polish pig want? Who are you?" Kolbe replied that he was a Catholic priest, and wished "to die for that man. I am old; he has a wife and children." The officer made a remark to the effect that the extermination of those unfit for labor was indeed official camp policy, and changed the list.

Kolbe then entered the terrible starvation bunker with the others, from which no one emerged alive. It was a dank cellar, and the men were stripped and given neither food nor water. When he and his cellmates entered, there were already 20 other condemned men inside. Kolbe had made this sacrifice not just to save one man, but to help many men in the most dire hours of their life, as they suffered a degrading, painful death and watched others around them succumb. The wretched conditions of the starvation bunker, noted one man assigned to empty their urine pails, were evident by the fact that many of the buckets were often empty. Kolbe prayed with the others incessantly, and survived nearly two weeks under such conditions. The Gestapo, wanting the bunker free for another round of condemned men, ordered that he and the other three be killed by lethal injection. Kolbe was the only one of these men still fully conscious. He was given an injection of carbolic acid on August 14, 1941, and his body cremated. He was 47 years old.

The man whose life he saved, Franciszek Gajowniczek, managed to survive both Auschwitz and another camp until the end of the war; he returned home to the news that his two sons had died. Gajowniczek devoted the rest of his life to spreading the religious tenets of Kolbe and the Knights of the Immaculata. The shrine to Kolbe at Cell 18, Block 11 of Auschwitz was dedicated in a ceremony by Pope John Paul II, the Church's first Polish leader, on a visit back to his homeland in 1979. The former Karol Wotylja was once the Archbishop of Krakow, the diocese in which Auschwitz is located. Kolbe's admission into the Roman Catholic canon of saints was one of the speedier ones of the modern era. Beatified in 1971, he was canonized by the same pope on October 10, 1982.

Sources

➤ **Books**

Dewar, Diana, *Saint of Auschwitz: The Story of Maximilian Kolbe,* Harper & Row, 1982.
St. Maximilian Kolbe: Apostle of Our Difficult Age, translated and adapted by the Daughters of St. Paul from the Italian biography

Beato Massimiliano Maria Kolbe by Rev. Antonio Ricciardi, St. Paul Editions, 1982.

Dorothea Lange

"*All my life I tried very hard . . . to make a place where . . . what I did would count.*"

Born on May 26, 1895, in Hoboken, New Jersey, Dorothea Lange was an influential American documentary photographer. She died on October 11, 1965, in Berkeley, California.

Through her photographs, Dorothea Lange created change in both photography and society at large. Her unsentimental pictures of those suffering from the economic effects of the Depression raised awareness about their situation and influenced the direction of social policy. Lange's photographic style was important in the development of photojournalism and social documentary photography.

Lange was born Dorothea Margaretta Nutzhorn in Hoboken, New Jersey on May 26, 1895. She was the eldest child and only daughter of lawyer Henry Martin Nutzhorn, and his wife Joanna Caroline Lange Nutzhorn. Both of Lange's parents were of German descent.

As a young child, Lange contracted polio. By the age of 7, the disease had left her with limping with her right leg. Called "Limpy" by other children, Lange was very ashamed of her disability throughout her childhood. It deeply affected her outlook on life. As an adult, Lange accepted her limp, and her handicap often made her accessible to those she wished to photograph who were themselves suffering.

Another trauma beset Lange's childhood several years later. When she was about 12 years old, her father abandoned the family. There is some speculation he might have embezzled funds from a client and wanted to avoid the scandal. Lange never saw or heard from her father again. Lange, her mother, and brother Martin all took on Joanna Nutzhorn's maiden name, Lange. (Some sources say that Lange took her mother's maiden name years later.)

After Lange's parents divorced in 1907, Lange, her mother and brother moved in with Lange's grandmother, Sophie Lange. Sophie Lange was a German immigrant and dressmaker, who ruled her home in Hoboken in a demanding, tyrannical manner. Lange did not spend much time at home to avoid the wrath of her grandmother.

Joanna Lange had worked as a clerk and a librarian prior to her marriage, and she took up the latter profession again after her divorce. She found a job in New York City's Lower East Side, where Lange was enrolled in school. Lange felt like an outsider, in part because of her limp, but also because she was one of the only Gentiles in her school.

Sometimes skipping school, Lange spent much time exploring New York City, observing the rich variety of life there: the museums, street life, etc. Lange saw a darker side when her mother became a social worker, doing investigations for a juvenile court judge. Lange would accompany her mother on visits to the Bowery and other harsh areas of the city.

By the time Lange graduated from Wadleigh High School for Girls in 1913, she knew she wanted to be a photographer, though she never took a picture nor owned a camera. To make her mother happy, though, Lange attended the New York Training School for Teachers from 1914 until 1917. At the same time, Lange did apprenticeships with professional photographers, including society lensman Arnold Genthe and theatrical photographer Charles H. Davis. She also took classes with photographer Clarence White, of the Photo-Secession group, at Columbia University. Soon Lange bought her own camera and two lenses. She converted a chicken coop into a darkroom for her use.

In 1918, Lange and a high school friend, Florence Bates, decided to go around the world. Lange sold photographs along the way, though the pair only made it to San Francisco, California. There, they were robbed of all their funds. Lange ended up spending the rest of her life in the Bay area.

To support herself, Lange soon found work as a photo finisher. She also became a member of a camera club. With funding from a friend, Lange established a photography studio at 540 Sutter Street in 1919 and slowly built up a clientele as a society photographer.

Lange's studio was often a gathering place for many artist friends. Among them was a painter, Maynard Dixon, who was 21 years older than her. They married on March 21, 1920, and eventually had two sons together, Daniel Rhodes and John Eaglefeather. Throughout the 1920s, Lange supported her family with her successful business, taking photographic portraits, primarily of society women.

The Stock Market Crash of 1929 marked the beginning of the Great Depression. For a while in this time period, the family lived in an artists' colony in Taos, New Mexico. On the family's return trip home, Lange noticed the troubling sight of migrants trying to escape their poverty. Lange soon became bored with taking pictures of the elite, and wanted to capture what was really happening in the world.

By 1931, Lange's marriage was in trouble, and she and Maynard Dixon separated. Their children were put in a boarding school. With no responsibilities, Lange began to wander the streets of San Francisco, recording the effects of the Depression on the average man and woman.

In 1934, Lange took one of her most important photographs, "White Angel Breadline." Her first social documentary photograph, it focused on a group of men gathered at a food line near her studio. When she exhibited "White Angel" and similar photographs, her work caught the attention of many people.

Among them was a social economist and professor, Paul Schuster Taylor. He was embarking on a project to document the lives of migrant workers for the California State Emergency Relief Administration. Lange's pictures were used to complement Taylor's written word. Their work helped change the lives of migrant workers, as the agency procured federal funds for the construction of sanitary facilities for them.

Lange and Taylor's partnership moved beyond work. After Lange divorced Dixon, Taylor and Lange were married on December 6, 1935. Taylor also taught Lange better techniques for dealing with her subjects, talking to them as she worked. Though her photographs were known as warm and sympathetic, Lange personally could be difficult.

In 1935, Lange was hired by the Historical Section of the Federal Resettlement Administration (later known as the Farm Security Administration) to document the conditions of those most affected by the Depression in the second half of the 1930s: migrant workers, tenant farmers, and share-croppers. For much of the next five years, Lange traveled through the south and west, including the Dust Bowl, taking photographs of these people and their poverty. Lange's photographs continued to affect public policy and change the public's opinion. The administration of President Franklin D. Roosevelt used them to garner support for their New Deal legislation.

One of the most poignant of Lange's photographs of this era was "Migrant Mother" (1936). For many, this photo, of this beat-down mother, a pea picker, and her starving children, summarized the Great Depression. "Migrant Mother" led to aid for the pea-pickers, and was also used on a world-wide basis to raise funds for medical supplies.

After a brief stint photographing collective cotton farms in the southwest for the Bureau of Agricultural Economics in 1940, Lange received a Guggenheim fellowship in 1941. She was one of the first photographers so honored, and began using the funds to take pictures of the American social scene in several rural communities. However, when the United States became directly involved in World War II, Lange's work was cut short.

Lange was hired by the War Relocation Authority to document Japanese-American internees in the early 1940s. Many American citizens of Japanese descent were put in internment camps during the war by the United States government. Lange took empathetic photographs of her subjects, which angered the American government. Her photos were essentially suppressed, and not widely seen until 1972.

Later during the war, from 1943-45, Lange also took photographs for the Office of War Information. Many were used in *Victory Magazine*. She was then hired by the State Department to take photographs of United Nations conferences' delegates. Her work was cut short when she became seriously ill with ulcers and had to be hospitalized. Lange did not take many pictures again until the early 1950s.

Lange's professional output after this point was focused on her family and everyday people. She took many pictures of the familiar, and did some photo essays for magazines such as *Life.* Lange also accompanied her husband on his work-related trips to Asia, Africa, the Middle East and South America in the late 1950s and early 1960s. She took pictures when she could, but was often still suffering from ill health.

While Lange worked on a one-woman show for New York City's Museum of Modern Art in 1964, she was diagnosed with cancer of the esophagus. Despite her poor health, she continued to work on the show, entitled "The American Country Woman" and put together a related book *Dorothea Lange Looks at the Country American Woman.* However, Lange died on October 11, 1965, in Berkeley, California, before the show's opening in 1966.

Though many admired and were inspired by Lange's photographs, she did not regard her work as art. Her gift was greater than that. As Louis C. Gawthrop wrote in *Society,* "The legacy of Lange, the visionary change agent, is a national portrait of unity through diversity."

Sources

➤ Books

Adamson, Lynda G., *Notable Women in American History*, Greenwood Press, 1999, p. 204.

Cullen-DuPont, Kathryn, *The Encyclopedia of Women's History in America,* Facts on File, Inc., 1996, pp. 114-15.

Encyclopedia of World Biography, second edition, volume 9, Gale Group, 1998, pp. 193-94.

Felder, Deborah G., *The 100 Most Influential Women of All Time: A Ranking Past and Present,* A Citadel Press Book, 1996, pp, 207-10.

Garraty, John A. and Mark C. Carnes, eds., *American National Biography,* volume 13, Oxford University Press, 1999, pp. 145-47.

Magill, Frank N., ed., *Great Lives from History: American Women Series,* volume 3, Salem Press, 1995, pp. 1066-70.

Meltzer, Milton, *Dorothea Lange: Life Through the Camera,* Viking Kestrel, 1985.

Parry, Melanie, *Larousse Dictionary of Women,* Larousse, 1996, p. 381-82.

Partridge, Elizabeth, *Restless Spirit: The Life and Work of Dorothea Lange,* Viking Press, 1998.

Sicherman, Barbara and Carol Hurd Green, eds., *Notable American Women: The Modern Period: A Biographical Dictionary,* Belknap Press, 1980, pp. 408-10.

Sufrin, Mark, *Focus on America: Profiles of Nine Photographers,* Charles Scribner's Sons, 1987, pp. 74-86.

Uglow, Jennifer, ed., *Dictionary of Women's Biography,* third edition, Macmillan, 1998, p. 311.

➤ **Periodicals**

PSA Journal, June 1995, p. 26.

Society, July-August 1993, p. 64 (opening quote).

The World and I, May 1, 1995, p. 142.

Ursula K. Le Guin

"The fantasist, whether he uses the ancient archetypes of myth and legend or the younger ones of science and technology, may be talking as seriously as any sociologist—and a good deal more directly—about human life as it is lived, and as it might be lived, and as it ought to be lived. For, after all, as great scientists have said and as all children know, it is above all by the imagination that we achieve perception, compassion, and hope."

Born October 21, 1929 in Berkeley, California, science-fiction writer Ursula K. Le Guin created fantastic worlds in which the author's strong-willed, feminist protagonists have increasingly taken center stage. Address: c/o Virginia Kidd Literary Agency, P.O. Box 278, Milford, PA 18337-0278.

An understanding of both anthropology and varied cultures informed the highly acclaimed science fiction writing of Ursula K. Le Guin. In such books as the *Earthsea Trilogy, The Lathe of Heaven,* and *The Left Hand of Darkness,* she created what Nancy Jesser in *Feminist Writers* called "an anthropology of the future, imagining whole cultural systems and conflicts." Eschewing the "pulp" aspects of most science fiction—brawny male heroes, compliant women, and over-the-top technology as both cause and solution to the world's problems—Le Guin was known for skillfully telling a story containing many layers of meaning beneath its calm exterior. Her *Earthsea* novels have been cited by several reviewers as characteristic of her work; an essayist in *Science Fiction Writers* commented that, as it was "constrained neither by realistic events nor by scientific speculation, but only by the author's moral imagination," the *Earthsea* books showed such characteristic themes from "questing and patterning motifs to [her] overall emphasis on 'wholeness and balance.'" Echoes of Taoism, Jungian psychology, ecological concerns, and mythos resonate throughout her written works.

Le Guin was born in Berkeley, California, on October 21, 1929. Her father, anthropologist Alfred L. Kroeber, was noted for his studies of the Native American cultures of California. Her mother, Theodora Kroeber Quinn, was a psychologist and, in her later years, a writer; she would be a particularly strong influence on her daughter, both as a writer and as a feminist.

Raised in an intellectually stimulating environment, Le Guin excelled at academics. After graduating from high school, she enrolled at Harvard University's Radcliffe College, where she received her bachelor's degree, in 1951, and was a member of Phi Beta Kappa national honorary. Course work in New York City, at Columbia University, followed. Le Guin was named a faculty fellow in 1952, and received a Fulbright fellowship to study in Paris in 1953, having earned her master's degree in romance literature of the Middle Ages and Renaissance from Columbia the previous year.

The year after she earned her master's degree at Columbia, Le Guin married the historian Charles A. Le Guin. The couple made their home in Portland, Oregon. They had two daughters and one son. Prior to raising her family, she got a job as a French instructor at Mercer University, in Macon, Georgia, before moving on to the University of Idaho for a brief period in 1956.

Le Guin's first written efforts consisted of poetry and short fiction. Her first published work was the story "April in Paris," which appeared in *Fantastic* magazine, in 1962, when she was 33 years old. Le Guin's first novel, *Rocannon's World,* would be published by Ace Books, in 1966. It was the first of many science fiction works she would write in the following decades, and the first of her five-volume "Hainish" series of novels. In the Hainish novels—*Rocannon's World, Planet of Exile, City of Illusions, The Left Hand of Darkness,* and *The Word for World Is Forest*—the author allowed readers to follow the physical and emotional journeys taken by her protagonists as they were confronted with cultures that had rules and systems radically different from their own. The Hainish were a race of beings from the planet Hain who have colonized all planets of the Universe that will sustain them. As each colony adapted to its new, unique environment, it developed differently, evolving distinctive physical and cultural traits in relation to other Hain colonies. Le Guin's protagonists must become, in a sense, amateur anthropologists in their attempts to understand and exist within new worlds as they journey between colonies, re-evaluating their own cultural assumptions in the process.

While most science fiction has traditionally been dismissed by critics, as well as serious students of literature, Le Guin's sophisticated, well-studied, yet immensely readable novels have been able to break the barrier and gain a mainstream audience and mainstream attention, perhaps because of her ability to weave fantasy elements into her gentle, often dispassionate prose. After the publication of the highly acclaimed *The Left Hand of Darkness* in 1969, 1971's *The Lathe of Heaven,* and 1974's *The Dispossessed: An Ambiguous Utopia,* Le Guin's work began to be taken seriously, even within academic circles.

With these novels, the author seriously explored the influence of gender roles and race on cultural attitudes, and focused on such backlashes as sexism and oppression in all of their forms. The juxtaposition of contrasting societies was a familiar motif: one society off balance, characterized by violence, injustice, and inequality; the other stable, just, and peaceful. This duality related to the universal duality reflected in such sources as the Christian belief in heaven and hell, or the Taoist philosophy of balanced opposites, the yin and yang. Le Guin's focus on this universal duality has allowed her fiction to speak to mainstream readers, particularly those not inducted into the heavy-duty technological concerns addressed in so-called "hard science fiction."

In her works after the Hainish novels, Le Guin began to broaden her talents, writing poetry, the short play *No Use to Talk to Me,* two volumes of literary criticism, and several children's books. In her imaginative Catwings series that includes *Catwings, Catwings Return, Wonderful Alexander and the Catwings,* and *Jane on Her Own,* she entertained younger readers with imaginary worlds containing flying cats and kittens. In Le Guin's adult novels written after the mid-1970s, she also began to stretch the boundaries of her so-called science fiction, creating the quasi-history of an anonymous nineteenth-century country in 1979's *Malafrena,* and again in the short stories collected in *Orsinian Tales,* and combining music (via an accompanying cassette), verse, anthropologist's notations, and stories in 1985's *Always Coming Home,* a book about the Kesh, future inhabitants of California who establish a new society after ecological Armageddon. In 1997, Le Guin published *Lao Tzu: Tao Te Ching: A Book About the Way and the Power of the Way,* a poetic version of the Taoist classic *Tao Te Ching,* and *The Twins, the Dream: Two Voices,* a collection of poems by Le Guin and Argentine poet Diana Bellessi where each has translated the other's work. She followed these endeavors with *Sixty Odd* in 1999, a book of poems primarily about nature. It contains a number of poems that examine aging and death, and the book concludes with 26 poem-portraits of people no longer in Le Guin's life.

Whether set in the past or future, each of Le Guin's novels actually addressed the present. Imbedded within the plot of her 1972 novel *The Word for World Is Forest,* thoughtful readers could easily discover solemn parallels to the Vietnam War era, as well as telling commentary about the destruction of the world's rain forests. The novel told of the reaction of the colonizing culture—the Terrans—to the peaceful, forest-dwelling tribes—the Athsheans (read "indigenous tribes of South America and Indonesia")—that they encountered in their new home. Because they fear the ways of the Athsheans, the Terrans react violently, destroying the homes of the forest dwellers in an effort to exterminate them and reap financial rewards.

Spanning Le Guin's career as a writer were her four award-winning *Earthsea* novels, which have been praised by critics as some of her most enjoyable works. Beginning with 1968's *A Wizard of Earthsea,* readers met the goat herder Ged, who lives on one of a kingdom of islands known as Earthsea, as he trains to become a practitioner of magic. In later novels in the series—*The Tombs of Atuan* (1970) and *The Farthest Shore* (1972)—Ged matured as both a man and a wizard, grappling with hubris, then flattery, before sacrificing his own powers to save his world. In the 1990s, *Tehanu: The Last Book of Earthsea,* which concluded the series and which Le Guin wrote as a response to criticism by feminists that her male protagonists were all powerful, and female characters merely helpers, an elderly woman and a young girl were featured. According to Charlotte Spivack in her appraisal, *Ursula Le Guin*, "Earthsea is a convincingly authenticated world, drawn with a sure hand for fine detail. [It is a] mature narrative of growing up, a moral tale without a moral, a realistic depiction of a fantasy world."

In addition to her prolific career as an author, Le Guin has taught writing workshops at numerous colleges around the United States, as well as in Australia and Great Britain. She has revised several of her early works, updating them in response to her growing feminist leanings. She has also been involved in the adaptation of several of her novels into motion pictures. The Public Television production of *The Lathe of Heaven* in 1980 benefitted from her adaptation of her own novel—the story about a man whose dreams alter reality—as well as her on-the-set production assistance. Le Guin's positive appraisal of the resulting film was a marked contrast to most authors' feelings about their work after a film crew gets through with it. The recipient of numerous awards, she continued to make her home in Oregon.

Sources

➤ Books

Bittner, James, *Approaches to the Fiction of Ursula K. Le Guin*, UMI Research Press, 1984.
Bleiler, E.F., editor, *Science Fiction Writers*, Scribner's, 1982.
Cogell, Elizabeth Cummings, *Understanding Ursula K. Le Guin*, University of South Carolina Press, 1990.
Concise Dictionary of American Literary Biography: Broadening Voices, 1968-1988, Gale Research, 1989 (opening quote).
Feminist Writers, St. James Press, 1997.
Greenburg, Martin H., and Joseph D. Olander, *Ursula Le Guin*, Taplinger, 1979.
Slusser, George Edgar, *The Farthest Shores of Ursula K. Le Guin*, Borgo Press, 1976.
Spivack, Charlotte, *Ursula Le Guin*, Twayne, 1984.

➤ Periodicals

Horn Book, April 1971, pp. 129-138.
Science-Fiction Studies, March 1976.

Carl Lewis

"When I run like Carl Lewis, relaxed, smooth, easy, I can run races that seem effortless to me and to those watching."

Born July 1, 1961, in Birmingham, Alabama, Carl Lewis was one of the twentieth century's greatest track and field athletes, winning nine Olympic gold medals over the course of his career. Address: Carl Lewis Internet Fan Club, PO Box 57-1990, Houston, TX 77257-1990.

By winning nine gold medals in four different Olympics, Carl Lewis ensured that he would be known as one of the best athletes of the twentieth century. The length of his career and breadth of his abilities (winning medals in the 100- and 200-meter dashes, long jump, and as a member of the 400-meter relay team) demonstrated the depth of his talent. Lewis has held several world's records in the long jump and 100-meter dash, and in 1984, became the first to win four gold medals in one Olympics since Jesse Owens in 1936.

Born Frederick Carlton Lewis, on July 1, 1961, in Birmingham, Alabama, he was the son of Bill and Evelyn (nee Lawler) Lewis. Both of his parents were high school teachers (his mother taught physical education, while his father taught social studies) and track coaches. While the couple attended the Tuskegee Institute, they both ran track. Evelyn Lewis was a world-class hurdler whose career was cut short by injury. Lewis had two older brothers, Mack and Cleve, and a younger sister, Carol.

When Lewis was two, the family moved to Willingsboro, New Jersey. There, his parents founded the Willingsboro Track Club to train young athletes—including their children—in 1969. Lewis was a late bloomer but from an early age, he was determined to become a track star. He did not fare well when he began entering track meets at the age of eight. Lewis was overshadowed early on by his siblings. His brothers (one in track, one in soccer) and his sister (track) were better athletes. Lewis's parents tried to turn his interests to music, but while he played cello, he continued to follow his track and field dreams.

Lewis's favorite event was the long jump. By the time he entered high school, he predicted that he would jump 25 feet. To practice, he marked the world record distance (29 feet 2 1/2 inches) for practice to meet his goal. As a junior at Willingsboro High School, Lewis jumped 25 feet and came into his own as an athlete. He competed in the national junior championships in 1978, winning the long jump event with a 25 feet, nine inch jump as well as the 100-meter dash with a time of 9.3 seconds. When Lewis graduated from high school in 1979, he was the top-rated high school athlete in track and field in the United States.

After graduation, Lewis entered the University of Houston on a track scholarship, quickly becoming a top-rated long jumper and 100-meter race runner. In 1980, he made the Olympic team but did not compete because the United States boycotted the event. When Lewis competed at the 1981 National Collegiate Athletic Association indoor championships, however, he proved he was a world-class athlete. Lewis became the first track and field athlete to win two events at such a championship. He was later awarded the Amateur Athletic Union's Sullivan Award. Lewis also set an indoor long jump world's record in 1981.

In 1982, Lewis left the University of Houston when he became academically ineligible. (He later completed his degree in broadcasting.) Lewis moved to California and began practicing and competing with the Santa Monica Track Club. He was coached by his University of Houston coach, Tom Tellez. Of Lewis, Tellez said to Barry Jacobs of *Saturday Evening Post,* "It doesn't make any difference if you're born with talent—you have to nurture it. At a very young age, Carl was a steady person. He's very coachable. He sees the things you're trying to teach him. He's thinking all the time."

Lewis was coachable in multiple events. In 1983, he won three events at the United States Outdoor Track and Field Championships: the long jump (at 28 feet 10 1/4 inches—second best jump ever), 100-meter dash (10.27 seconds) and 200-meter dash (19.75 seconds). Lewis was the first American since 1886 to win three events at a national outdoor championship. He went on to win three gold medals at the world championships in Helsinki, Finland, in the 100-meter, long jump and 400-meter relay.

Of his penchant for multiple events, Lewis told Jacobs of the *Saturday Evening Post,* "I like to do a lot of things. I always have. I don't like to go to a track meet, run one event and watch. I've always liked to be part of the show." Lewis's speed and seemingly adaptable abilities led to him being drafted for professional football (by the Dallas Cowboys) and professional basketball (by the Chicago Bulls), though he did not really play either sport.

By the time of the 1984 Summer Olympic Games in Los Angeles, California, there were high expectations for Lewis and his abilities. Just before the Olympics, Lewis set his first world record for the indoor long jump with 28 feet, 10 1/2 inches. He predicted his victories in multiple events at the games, and was ready to rake in endorsement money. (He already had endorsements in Japan with Nike and Fuji-Xerox). Though Lewis did win four gold medals—in the 100-meter dash (with a time of 9.99 seconds), 200-meter dash (19.8 seconds), long jump (distance of 28 feet 1/4 inch), and as part of the 4 x 100 relay team (37.83 seconds)—he drew much criticism. Some spectators and commentators were incensed that Lewis only did one jump to save strength and avoid injury, because he knew he would win with his distance. He did not go for the world's record so that he could run other events, an act some saw as selfish.

The general public, businesses and the press were not impressed by Lewis, despite his accomplishments. There were those who were offended by his self-created hype. Statements like the following, which was said to Tom Callahan of *Time*, did not help. Responding to his advisor Joe Douglas's statement to Callahan that "Carl Lewis will be as big as Michael Jackson," Lewis said "Physically, definitely. I can't sing as well as he does, and I don't think he can run as fast as I do, so I don't fear him, and there's no reason for him to fear me." Lewis appeared to be an athlete who was only in his sport for the money.

Lewis did not get the range of endorsements he expected. He had a contract with Nike in the United States, but it did not last long and the contract had to be settled out of court. Lewis had no other contracts in the United States, though he continued to endorse products in other countries. Lewis had other career plans in the works. By 1984, he had already studied acting seriously and had worked as an intern at a Houston television station for a few months. In 1985, he released an album in Japan, *The Feeling That I Feel*, which totally failed.

Lewis also continued to compete in national and world track and field events. He nearly always did well in the long jump and 100-meter dash, but lost the 200 at the 1986 national outdoor championships. But, by the time of the trials for the 1998 Summer Olympic Games in Seoul, Korea, Lewis faced stiff competition for the first time. He was seriously challenged in the long jump, jump for jump. Lewis also had a strong competitor in the 100-meter dash, with Canadian Ben Johnson.

At the Seoul games, Johnson beat Lewis in the 100-meter dash, though Lewis later won by default when it was revealed that Johnson had been using steroids. Lewis went on to win the gold in the long jump and the silver in the 200-meter dash. At the end of the 1988 Olympics, Lewis said that these would probably be his last, though they were not. He continued to win on the national and international level, especially in the long jump. But he was beat more often in other events. Lewis continued to diversify, however. In 1990, he wrote a book called *Inside Track*. He also began his broadcasting career by becoming the sports director for a Houston radio station.

Thus Lewis's accomplishments in the early 1990s seem all the more unreal. He won two key 100-meter races. He won the national outdoors event, then went on to set a world's record in the event at the 1991 world championships. He ran the event with a time of 9.86, though he was supposed to be past his prime at the age of 30. As Kenny Moore of *Sports Illustrated* wrote, "Lewis, the most theatrically expressive of performers, had contrived to summon his climatic performance just when it seemed he could astound us no more."

Redemption for Lewis came in the 1992 Summer Olympics in Barcelona, Spain. He only qualified for the long jump and 400-meter relay, and was regarded as an underdog in his favorite event. Lewis went on to win gold medals in both events, and the relay team set a new world's record. The American public finally embraced him, and Lewis finally got the American endorsement deals he wanted, including another deal with Nike.

Though Lewis continued to compete on a national and world level, he did not do as well. One particularly bad year was 1993 when he won only the bronze in the 200 in the world championships, in part because of lingering injuries from an automobile accident. Though 1994 was much better, by 1995, he was regularly losing to up-and-coming athletes. He only placed second in the long jump at nationals that year. Lewis was inconsistent at best, as his track career was in slow decline.

Lewis tried to make the Olympic team for the 1996 summer games in Atlanta, Georgia, for the long jump, 100-meter dash, 200-meter dash, and 400-meter relay team. But he only qualified in the long jump. Lewis did win the event with a jump of 27 feet 10 3/4 inches, making him only the second person to win the gold four times in the same event. With his nine gold medals, Lewis had tied the medal record for American track and field athletes.

Two ceremonies in 1997 marked Lewis's retirement from track and field. The official end was after a lap around the Olympic Stadium in Berlin, Germany, where Jesse Owens had won his four medals in 1936. Dorian Friedman of *U.S. News & World Report* quoted Lewis as saying "I feel so lucky. I've tasted ultimate success so I can leave without any regrets."

Lewis's life after retirement was rich with possibilities. He considered a run for political office or some other type of involvement with politics. He also wanted to do more acting and broadcasting work, as well as run his sportswear design company and help coach children. Lewis's track and field legacy will not be forgotten. As his coach, Tom Tellez, told Steve Wulf of *Sports Illustrated* in 1991, six years before his retirement, "Carl has been around for so long that maybe he's taken for granted, but to my mind, he is the greatest athlete we've ever had. Only Jesse Owens is in his class. To be among the very best long jumpers in the world for more than a decade is amazing enough, but to also be among the very best sprinters. . . it's incredible."

Sources

➤ **Books**

Encyclopedia of World Biography, volume nine, second edition, Gale Group, 1998, pp. 377-80.

➤ **Periodicals**

Ebony, May 1992, p. 60.
Jet, May 16, 1994, p. 47; November 11, 1996, p. 50.
Maclean's, July 27, 1992, p. 50.
Newsweek, June 17, 1996, p. 68.
People Weekly, August 6, 1984, p. 24; August 12, 1996, p. 92; September 19, 1998, p. 48.
Runner's World, August 1992, p. 62; July 1996, p. 42.
Saturday Evening Post, May-June 1984, p. 20.
Sports Illustrated, February 14, 1983, p. 87; June 27, 1983, p. 32; August 22, 1983, p. 16; June 4, 1984, p. 24; June 25, 1984, p. 22; August 13, 1984, p. 60; August 20, 1984, p. 22; May 27, 1985, p. 18; December 2, 1985, p. 18; June 30, 1986, p. 18; July 6, 1987, p. 20; August 1, 1988, p. 16; September 14, 1988, p. 22; October 10, 1988, p. 50; October 2, 1989, p. 25; June 25, 1990, p. 66; September 2, 1991, p. 22; December 23, 1991, p. 82; August 17, 1992, p. 40; August 9, 1993, p. 32; May 30, 1994, p. 62; September 19, 1994, p. 74; April 15, 1996, p. 84; August 5, 1996, p. 54; September 22, 1997, p. 26.
Time, July 4, 1983, p. 65; July 30, 1984, p. 52 (opening quote); August 13, 1984, p. 41.
U.S. News & World Report, September 8, 1997, p. 16.

Rebecca Lobo

"If kids call me a role model, that's fine—and I think it's good that there are females out there for kids to look up to."*

Basketball star Rebecca Lobo, born on October 6, 1973, became an icon for women's sports when she led the University of Connecticut to a perfect season and snagged the National Collegiate Athletic Association (NCAA) title in 1995, ticking off a long list of honors as the team's powerhouse. Riding heavily on the wave of her popularity, the Women's National Basketball Association—the first professional organization for women's basketball in the United States—opened for business in 1997. Address: c/o New York Liberty, Two Penn Plaza, New York, NY 10121.

At six feet, four inches tall, basketball star Rebecca Lobo should expect people to look up to her. However, she has become a standout not only for her height and her prowess on the court, but also for her wholesomeness, humility, and academic excellence. At the University of Connecticut (UConn), she led her team to a stunning National Collegiate Athletic Association (NCAA) championship. She became the first Big East basketball player to simultaneously earn Big East Player of the Year and Scholar-Athlete of the Year honors, and did this not once, but two consecutive times, in addition to numerous other accolades. Even more remarkably, throughout this rise she had to contend with watching her mother battle breast cancer, a frightening episode for her extremely close-knit family. In 1997, Lobo signed on to play with the New York Liberty in the inaugural season of the Women's National Basketball Association (WNBA), and was largely credited, along with a couple other core players, for boosting the interest in women's professional sports.

Born in northern Connecticut on October 6, 1973, Lobo and her family moved to Southwick, Massachusetts, just over the state line, when she was two. Her father, Dennis (who stands six feet, five inches tall), is a high school history teacher, and her mother, RuthAnn (at five feet, eleven inches), is a middle school counselor. They continued to work in Granby, Connecticut after the move, leading to a later conflict when both states wanted to claim Lobo as their local hero. Though she attended elementary school in Granby, Lobo went to high school in Massachusetts, but later entered the University of Connecticut. Her older siblings, Jason and Rachel, are tall as well, and both played college basketball.

As a child, Lobo and her siblings adored sports of all kinds, including stickball, soccer, Wiffle ball, and volleyball. She even donned mittens to box with her sister while her brother acted as referee. However, Lobo showed a particular affinity for basketball. In fact, in third grade, as she related in the book *Home Team,* she wrote a letter to Boston Celtics general manager Red Auerbach that read, "I really like watching the Boston Celtics play. You do a really good job. I want you to know that I am going to be the first girl to play for the Boston Celtics."

Although Lobo's parents instilled in her the idea that she could be anything she wanted to be, playing sports caused some difficulties. Early on, a teacher chastised her for being too much of a tomboy. And Lobo's mother knew that her daughter would never win a spot on the Celtics, but did not want to discourage her. So when the girls' community basketball team never got off the ground for lack of interest, Lobo's mother insisted she get a spot on the boys' team. Lobo did so well, she earned a starting position on the traveling team, too.

At Southwick-Tolland Regional High School, Lobo became a star in track, softball, and field hockey, not to mention basketball. In her first high school hoops game, starting on the varsity team as a freshman, she scored 32 points and eventually became the top scorer, male or female, in Massachusetts's history, with 2,710 points. Her single-game high was 62 points, which she regarded as an "embarrassment," as she told Rick Telander of *Sports Illustrated*, adding, "I mean, it's a team game." On top of this, she was an excellent student, graduating salutatorian of her class in 1991 and reaping offers from more than 100 colleges, including Notre Dame, Stanford, and the University of Virginia.

After high school, Lobo chose to attend UConn, partly because it was only about an hour from home. Also, she was impressed with Coach Geno Auriemma, who had taken the women's team to the NCAA Final Four tournament at the close of the 1990-91 season. However, Auriemma was not as thrilled with Lobo her first time out on the court. As the UConn Huskies met the University of California, she scored only ten points—not a bad start in general, but everyone had higher hopes for Lobo. By the end of the season, she was averaging 14.3 points and 7.9 rebounds per game, and was named rookie of the year in the Big East Conference. However, her team that year, holding a record of 23 wins to 11 losses, was eliminated from the NCAA tournament in the second round.

The next season, 1992-93, was a dark spot in Lobo's history with UConn because many of the team's key players graduated in 1992. They posted their worst record of her college career, at 18 wins, 11 losses, but since much of their success rested on her performance, her personal statistics rose to 16.7 points and 11.2 rebounds per game. During her junior year, the team improved to a 27-2 record for the regular season, but missed out on the Final Four contest when they lost to the University of North Carolina. However, Lobo this year averaged 19.2 points per game and posted some of the best statistics of her career, including shooting 54.6 percent of field goals and 73.8 percent of free throws.

Lobo managed to continuously improve her personal game and lead her team to victories despite a crushing blow: In December of 1993, after the Huskies won a game against the University of Virginia Cavaliers, her mother told her that she had breast cancer.

She immediately had a lumpectomy, but soon discovered she would need a mastectomy as well. She refrained from telling her daughter until Lobo had taken all of her final exams. Then, she arranged her chemotherapy treatments around the UConn basketball schedule so that she would not miss any games. Meanwhile, they kept the news from the public.

At the end of the 1993-94 season, Lobo was named Big East Player of the Year. At the awards banquet, as related in *Home Game,* she announced, "This is for my mother. She has been the real competitor this year, and this is for her." In addition, Lobo that year became the only Big East basketball player to earn that honor as well as the Scholar-Athlete of the Year award simultaneously. She was also named the Big East Tournament most valuable player, Kodak All-American, and Academic All-America.

During her senior year, Lobo's situation only got better. Her mother's cancer was in remission, and she continued to do well in her studies, making the dean's list every semester and eventually graduating with her bachelor of arts in political science. And of course, her game was going well, too. Gampel Pavilion at UConn sold 6,541 season tickets for the women's basketball season that year and averaged crowds of about 7,900—up 485 percent from 1991, before Lobo arrived—whereas numerous other schools were lucky to rouse any interest at all in the sport. Much of the attention was directed at Lobo, who was heavily credited with drumming up interest in women's sports, even though her coach, Auriemma, told Telander, "What is she great at? I can't say any one thing. But the sum of all the parts is unreal."

By the 1994-95 season's end, UConn was ranked number one, unseating the University of Tennessee for that position. They posted a 33-0 regular season record and continued through the NCAA playoffs undefeated, beating out Tennessee once again in the final game. Afterward, Lobo again won the Big East Player of the Year and Scholar-Athlete of the Year awards, as well as being named Big East Tournament most valuable player and Academic All-America. In addition, she was the Naismith National Player of the Year and Final Four most valuable player, won the Wade Trophy, and was tapped as Sportswoman of the Year by the Women's Sports Foundation. An undisputed national star, she was thrilled to be able to go jogging with President Bill Clinton. She was profiled in several publications and also appeared on David Letterman's talk show. In 1996, she cowrote with her mother the dual autobiography *Home Team: Of Mothers, Daughters, & American Champions.*

In addition, Lobo in 1996 toured with the USA Basketball Women's National Team, where she remained in the spotlight despite being a newcomer. Her solid home life, stellar academic performance, and all-around pleasant personality stood up to the glare. Another National Team member, Jennifer Azzi, remarked in *Women's Sports and Fitness,* "Rebecca's a good ambassador for the sport, and the attention she gets has been helping our team a lot." Lobo, in turn, noted in the same article, "If kids call me a role model, that's fine—and I think it's good that there are females out there for kids to look up to." During her time in 1996 with the team, they toured the world and won all 52 of their games in preparing for the Olympics. She was the youngest member of the Olympic team that captured the gold medal during the team's sixtieth consecutive victory, this one against Brazil at the games in Atlanta, Georgia.

After the Olympics, Lobo mulled over whether to pursue a sports broadcasting career, head to Europe to play there, or join the new professional league in the United States. Eventually she chose to join the WNBA, where she, Sheryl Swoopes, and Lisa Leslie were the key stars. Though she did not make it to the Boston Celtics, this was a big step in the evolution of women's sports, since there simply was no professional league in the nation before this. The interest in Lobo was one of the key reasons why the time was ripe to start one up, as she was a main focus of the marketing campaign for the new venture.

In 1997, Lobo's first season with the New York Liberty, her personal 102-game winning streak ended on her eighth game of the year as they fell to the Phoenix Mercury. Though she did not prove to be one of the top scorers over the next couple of years, she remained one of the best known. As Sally Jenkins put it in *Women's Sports and Fitness,* "If you want to talk across-the-board popularity and box office draw or a surefire familiar face for a commercial, Lobo remains the most in-demand star in the league."

A torn anterior crutiate ligament benched Lobo from June of 1999 through the rest of the season, but she kept busy regardless. In 1997, she began doing sports commentary for ESPN on the off season, and she has numerous endorsement deals with companies like Spalding, Mattel (promoting the WNBA Basketball Barbie), and General Motors. She even has her own shoe, the Reebok "Lobo." She also works with various breast cancer research and awareness groups. In addition to being popular among fans, the athlete is admired among teammates for her dry wit, her down-to-earth manner, and her generosity.

Sources

➤ **On-line**

WNBA web site, http://www.wnba.com (November 16, 1999).

➤ **Books**

Lobo, Rebecca, and RuthAnn Lobo, *The Home Team: Of Mothers, Daughters, & American Champions,* Kodansha, 1996.

➤ **Periodicals**

Good Housekeeping, May 1996, p. 22.
Newsday, January 23, 1997, p. A70.
New York Times, March 6, 1995, p. C1; January 23, 1997, p. B14.
People, March 20, 1995, p. 61.
Sport, July 1997, p. 46.
Sports Illustrated, March 20, 1995, p. 98.
Star Tribune (Minneapolis, MN), September 24, 1996, p. 1C.
Time, March 27, 1995, p. 68.
Washington Post, March 28, 1995, p. C1.
Women's Sports and Fitness, March 1996, p. 68 (opening quote); July 1999, p. 68.

Juliette Gordon Low

*"*I *like the organization and the rules and the pastimes, so if you find that I get very deeply interested you must not be surprised."*

Born on October 31, 1860, in Savannah, Georgia, Juliette Gordon Low was the founder of the organization that became known as the Girl Scouts of the United States of America. She remained vital to its growth up until her death on January 17, 1927.

To those who knew her, Juliette Gordon Low seemed an unlikely candidate to serve as founder and president of an organization for girls that taught them practical skills and leadership traits. Cheerful, eccentric, artistic, perennially late, and severely hard of hearing, she was many things, but a leader she was not. Yet Low persevered, and turned her failings into success, for she blithely dismissed others who criticized her or her seemingly grandiose plans, and planted prominent women in leadership positions by pretending that she just did not hear their protests to the contrary. Because of her, the Girl Scouts grew into the most important and respected association for young women in American history.

Born Juliette Magill Kinzie Gordon in Savannah, Georgia, in 1860, Low came from wealthy, illustrious families on both sides. Her paternal grandfather, a railroad tycoon, served as mayor of Savannah in the 1830s; her mother's family, the Kinzies, were one of the first Europeans to settle in what later became Chicago. Just a few months after her birth, the American Civil War erupted, and her father William Washington Gordon—a graduate of Yale College, slave-owner, and cotton broker—became an officer in the Confederate Army of the South. War brought severe hardship to Georgia, and Low's health suffered because of malnourishment during these early years. The family was later forced to flee to relatives in Chicago, where she and her sisters—Nelly and Alice—saw snow for the first time. But in the North, Low fell gravely ill. She recovered, but the near-loss induced her family to treat her with an indulgence that made her a rather willful child.

Nicknamed "Daisy," Low was a carefree teenager who loved animals and took care of as many strays as she could find. With her family's financial fortune revitalized after a few postwar setbacks, she led a comfortable life as one of Savannah's richest young women. Though she did poorly in math and spelling, she displayed a talent for art from an early age. At the age of 14, she was sent to a series of private schools for well-to-do young women, "finishing" at a New York City institution in 1879. She loved the school and the city, and convinced her mother to send her reluctant younger sister there as well. Tragically, Alice contracted scarlet fever while there and died, and Low forever blamed herself.

Over the next few years, Low divided her time between Savannah and traveling through Europe with her mother or another chaperon. This continued when she fell in love with Willie Low, a young Savannah-born man who had been raised in England. He was a spendthrift, a rake, and a drinker, and her parents were appalled. She was forced to keep her attachment to "Billow," as she called him, a secret for some time, and only after some financial negotiations between both fathers took place was a wedding date set.

Before the wedding, however, Low came down with an earache, and read about using a compound of silver nitrate that might cure it. She convinced her reluctant doctor to try it, but the nitrate only worsened her pain, and she lost her most of her hearing in that ear. The wedding took place on December 21, 1886 in Savannah, but again, tragedy struck: a grain of rice, from the hail tossed by guests as she and Billow departed for their honeymoon, became stuck in her other ear. It became infected, and an operation to remove it ruined that eardrum as well.

Low did not let her handicap diminish her interests or zest for life. The couple divided their time between a lovely home in Savannah, a charming country estate in England, and another abode in Scotland. An avid sportswoman, popular party-giver, and working artist, Low had also developed a charitable conscience, too. She frequently visited a local elderly woman—who had been shunned by the English villagers because she was thought to suffer from leprosy—with food, and read to her as well. Low's marriage, however, became an increasingly distressful part of her life. She learned she was unable to have children, and Billow began spending more time away from home; when they were together, he drank too much and teased her by speaking so low that she could not hear him.

At one point, her husband installed his mistress in their home in England, and announced his intention to divorce Low. Before the proceedings became final, however, Billow died; in a final humiliation, he had changed his will to omit Low. She contested this successfully in court, however, and then purchased a small home in England in addition to the one she had acquired as a newlywed in Savannah; she also maintained a place in Scotland.

By now, Low was 46, and had no real hobbies save for her art and travel. Her life changed in 1911, however, when she met the celebrated Robert Baden-Powell. Already knighted for his heroics during England's Boer War in South Africa, Baden-Powell was four years her senior, unmarried, and both were delighted by the number of interests they shared, including sculpture. B.P., as Low called him, had recently founded the Boy Scouts in England. The organization had been based on his experiences in South Africa during the war, when he recruited South African youths to carry messages and set up camp for the British soldiers. Baden-Powell brought this idea back to England with him, and founded a scouting organization that taught teenage boys outdoor skills, personal responsibility, and physical hardiness. Scouting spread rapidly across Britain, and a Girl Guide organization was set up by Baden-Powell's sister Agnes. Low wrote with enthusiasm to her family back home about scouting. "I like girls and I like the organization and the rules and the pastimes, so if you find that I get very deeply interested you must not be surprised," she declared.

Low founded her own Girl Guides patrol near her home in Glenlyon, Scotland with seven girls from the area. The first meeting took place in August of 1911, and one of them walked seven miles to get there. In London, Low began another patrol in a poor section of London, which was also a success. When she had to return to America, she told an accomplished woman she knew that she needed her to take over the London group. The woman protested vehemently, but Low pretended as if she had not understood a word she had said, and simply left her in charge. It was a tactic she used with much success in the United States as well after she formally founded her first American patrol, which met at her Savannah home on March 9, 1912. As the case in Britain, the group rapidly caught on with young women.

Those who had known Low for many years assumed that she would soon lose interest in her newest pet project. Her detractors were nearly proven right when she dropped out of contact for a time after the death of her father later in 1912; compounding her grief was the announcement from B.P. that he planned to marry Olave Soames, who had crossed the Atlantic with them that spring. But after comforting her grieving mother, Low went back to work with a sense of renewed purpose. The first American Girl Scout handbook, *How Girls Can Help Their Country*, was published, and did much to win new recruits; bereft until then of any productive yet fun organized activities save for church groups, the adolescents were enchanted by scouting's mix of practical skills and outdoor activities. There were tips on how to set up a tent, how to tie up a burglar with failsafe knots, and basic comportment conduct. Low also included skills tests to earn merit badges, which she herself designed and embroidered.

Low campaigned tirelessly on behalf of what became her national organization in June of 1913. After installing a friend there to run it—once more, cheerfully ignoring the woman's objections—she traveled around the United States to establish new troops, and the movement spread rapidly. To encourage middle-class young girls to learn how to milk a cow, cut firewood, and hike in the woods was all rather progressive for the time, but Low's own well-bred background and accomplishments added a certain luster to the organization.

Traveling back and forth across the Atlantic, and still working closely with the Baden-Powells, Low spent the next several years helping the organization grow. With America's entry into the war, the 10,000 Girl Scouts were recruited into the war effort. They made bandages, sold war bonds, staffed nurseries for women working in munitions factories, and even volunteered in hospitals. As a result, the number of girls wanting to sign up increased exponentially after the war, and with its expansion Low became a tireless fundraiser for the organization.

With the Baden-Powells, Low also worked to found an International Council of Girl Guides and Girl Scouts, which had its first meeting in London in 1919. She retired as president the next year, but remained active in the organization; she was particularly adept at obtaining donations of rural acreage to use as official Girl Scout camps. Diagnosed with cancer around 1923, she kept her illness a secret, but continued her involvement as best she could. One day in 1926, she informed her national director that the first World Encampment of Girl Scouts to be held in the United States would take place the following year on Girl Scout land in upstate New York. The director protested that there was no camp ready yet—no buildings, no water, and there were not even roads leading to it yet—and they could not possibly accomplish this feat in a year. At the suggestion that it be put off for two years, Low replied that she would not live to see it.

The first World Encampment to be held in North America indeed took place the following spring, and Low greeted the Baden-Powells and 56 foreign Girl Scout delegates at the New York City harbor and escorted them to the camp in Pleasantville, New York. In just more than a dozen years, her troop of 17 girls from Savannah had expanded to number 140,000 Scouts and troops in all 48 states. Over the next few months, however, Low grew quite ill. Before her death at her Savannah home on January 17, 1927, she was moved by a telegram sent from women at the Girl Scout headquarters in New York, which read, "You are not only the first Girl Scout, you are the best Girl Scout of them all!" Her birthday is celebrated by Girl Scouts of America as Scouts Founder's Day.

Sources

➤ Books

Brown, Fern G., *Daisy and the Girl Scouts: The Story of Juliette Gordon Low*, Albert Whitman & Co., 1996.

Kudlinski, Kathleen V., *Juliette Gordon Low: America's First Girl Scout*, Viking Kestrel, 1988.

Betty Mahmoody

"I *wanted to share my hard-learned lesson: that you can't pack your rights in a suitcase and take them wherever you go."*

Born c. 1949, Betty Mahmoody, author of *Not Without My Daughter*, is an activist who works to prevent international child abductions. She and her daughter were held captive by her husband in Iran for a year and a half before escaping. Address: One World: For Children, P.O. Box 1018, Owosso, MI 48867.

Activist Betty Mahmoody is the author of *Not Without My Daughter*, the true story of her experiences being held against her will by her husband in Iran. While she could have eventually found a way out of her situation, there was nothing legally she could do to help her daughter, Mahtob, who was a hostage as well. The book relates the details of their year and a half in Iran, including frightening tales of air strikes and oppression, not to mention the daily drudgery she faced and the filthy conditions they endured. Mahmoody also told of the ongoing tensions within her husband's extended family, who often treated her with contempt. Once she managed to free herself and her daughter by underground means, Mahmoody became a beacon for other parents and children trapped in their non-native countries. Thanks to her efforts, the United States passed legislation to help prevent international child abductions from happening to its citizens, and her ongoing lectures try to inform parents of this peril. Though Mahmoody appreciates the diversity of the world's cultures and does not urge anyone to forgo an international relationship out of fear, she noted in her second book, *For the Love of a Child,* "I wanted to share my hard-learned lesson: that you can't pack your rights in a suitcase and take them wherever you go."

Mahmoody was born Betty Lover on June 9, 1945, in Alma, Michigan, and grew up in rural mid-Michigan. Her father, Harold Lover, worked for one of the automobile companies, and her mother, Fern (Chase) Lover, owned a variety store for several years. Mahmoody was married young, just out of Chesaning High School, and had two sons, Joe and John, but the marriage ended in a bitter divorce. By age 28, she had found a job at ITT Hancock in Elsie, Michigan, as a night billing clerk. She worked her way up to running the entire office and was in line for a rewarding career in management. She also began attending Lansing Community College. However, by the time she was in her thirties, she began to suffer intense migraines and began to undergo physical therapy and manipulation treatments at Carson City Hospital.

While in the hospital, Mahmoody became attracted to her physician, an Iranian intern named Sayyed Borzog Mahmoody, nicknamed "Moody." They began to date after her treatments were over, and continued to do so while he was doing his residency at Detroit Osteopathic Hospital. When his residency was over, he was offered a job in anesthesiology with an attractive salary at Corpus Christi Osteopathic Hospital in Texas. They married on June 6, 1977 at a mosque in Houston. Mahmoody related in her book *Not Without My Daughter* that Moody was caring and loving throughout the courtship and after they married, and even applied for U.S. citizenship.

However, in Texas, Moody became involved with a group of Iranian students, and in early 1979, after the fall of the Shah of Iran and the rise of the Ayatollah Khomeini, he celebrated these events and began to change. He withdrew his application for U.S. citizenship and began to focus his energies on following the news, even listening intently to Iranian broadcasts over a short-wave radio. Though Mahmoody was becoming concerned about him, she loathed the idea of another divorce, and besides, discovered that she was pregnant. They had a daughter, Mahtob, in the fall of 1979. In 1980, they returned to Alpena, Michigan, but after Moody lost a three-year-old patient at Alpena General Hospital, his right to practice was revoked. After sinking into a depression, he found work at a clinic in Detroit, and the family moved to nearby Southfield and rented a home there.

In August of 1984, despite concerns, Mahmoody, now age 39, agreed to travel with her daughter, then age five, and her husband to his home in Iran for a two-week vacation. Once there, Moody basically held them hostage. When Mahmoody married an Iranian national, according to the laws of that country, she and her daughter became dual citizens, and they were not free to leave Iran without Moody's consent, since women have few rights there. Refusing to give in to her husband, who beat her and her daughter regularly, she tried to construct an escape plan. Eventually Moody agreed to let her return to America, but he would not allow her to take Mahtob.

Refusing to leave Iran by herself and most certainly relinquish custody of Mahtob, Mahmoody surreptitiously developed benevolent contacts, some of them Iranian, who tried to help her leave the country. Though most of the leads did not pan out, she finally found one man who paid $12,000 to professional smugglers to get her and her daughter out of Iran on the mere promise that Mahmoody would pay him back when she was home. They traveled a rough 900 miles in cars and trucks, on foot, and on horseback through the ice-cold mountains until they reached the U.S. embassy in Ankara, Turkey. They finally arrived back in Michigan in February of 1986.

In addition to yearning for safety for her and her daughter, there was yet another driving force that propelled Mahmoody not to give up hope of returning to America: Her father had been diagnosed with colon cancer in the early 1980s and given six months to three years to live. She desperately wanted to see him again before his death. As it turned out, her father fought the disease for five years, and finally died at age 66 on August 3, 1986, six months after his daughter and granddaughter had returned home.

Back in America, Mahmoody kept her end of the bargain to the man who helped them, borrowing the funds to repay him from a bank in Alpena, because her husband had wired all their savings out of Michigan shortly after their arrival in Tehran. She moved back in with her parents, and endured the looming threat of her husband returning to possibly abduct Mahtob, who lived under an assumed name from the age of seven until she entered ninth grade, or maybe harm Mahmoody or her family. Although she considered changing her identity and forming a new life, much like those in the federal witness protection program, she was told she would have to cut off ties with all of her friends and family, even her sons. She decided, as she stated in *For the Love of a Child*, "Moody had jailed us in Iran. I would not allow him to become our warden in America."

Shortly after her return from Iran, in March of 1986, Mahmoody joined with author William Hoffer, who had cowritten *Midnight Express*, the tale of an American drug smuggler's escape from a Turkish prison. They worked together for seven months on *Not Without My Daughter*. It received rave reviews and became a best-seller throughout North America, Europe, and Australia. In Germany, the work sold more than four million copies, and the nation named her their 1990 woman of the year. She and Mahtob also received the American Freedom Award in 1991, and she holds an honorary doctorate from Michigan's Alma College. The film version of *Not Without My Daughter* premiered on January 5, 1991, and starred Sally Field in the role of Mahmoody.

Though Mahmoody became a public figure due to the attention surrounding her book and movie, she continued to live in fear that her husband might return and kept her whereabouts private. At the time, there were no laws in place to protect a parent who suspected that the other parent might try to abduct a child; American laws generally only act in response to a crime already committed. One way to help parents regain custody was through the Hague Convention, which states that custody battles must be waged in the home country of the child. This only applied to nations that voluntarily ratified the convention, however. Thanks to the efforts of Mahmoody and others, American legislators responded to this threat, and in 1993, President Clinton signed a federal law to protect children from being abducted and taken overseas by a parent.

In addition, Mahmoody discovered that if she wanted a divorce, she was required to file in the county of her residence in case her husband wanted to go to court to contest it. She worked diligently to change this state law in Michigan, working closely with lawmakers on the issue, and once it passed in 1990, she filed for divorce in a different county. Michigan thus became the first state to have a law protecting residents in international divorce cases. Moody was notified of the action but did not reply, so the divorce became finalized in 1991 and Mahmoody has had no direct contact with him since leaving Iran.

Mahmoody's second book, *For the Love of a Child*, released five years after her first, provided information about her readjustment to life in America and her ongoing struggle in the legal system to protect herself and Mahtob. Much of the work, though, was devoted to telling stories of other parents who had similar experiences being held captive in foreign countries, or who had suffered the abduction of their children by the other parent. Seeing the large scope of the problem, Mahmoody devoted her energies to the cause of international child abduction, forming an organization called One World: For Children in 1990 with attorney Arnold Dunchock, the coauthor of her second book. This group, as she explained in *For the Love of a Child*, "promotes understanding of different cultures, provides counseling by left-behind parents for others whose children have been abducted, and refers these victims to agencies and professionals for further help."

Mahmoody funded One World: For Children for a while, but was unable to secure financial support from outside, so the organization began to function mainly as a referral agency, working in conjunction with the National Center for Missing and Exploited Children, among others. However, she noted in an interview for this profile, "I am still handling some individual cases, some high-profile cases that I feel can really make a difference." She also gets calls from the courts asking for her help, and she remains involved through her frequent lectures, speaking about abductions and at battered women seminars. In 1999 it was announced that she was joining the touring "Unique Lives" series in 2000, along with luminaries such as Gloria Steinem and Margaret Thatcher, and she was also scheduled to speak at a women's financial success conference in Germany. It marked the first time she would be a main speaker at an international conference in which she used an interpreter. In addition to her continued activism, Mahmoody enjoys the hobbies of gardening, quilting, and gourmet cooking.

Sources

➤ On-line

"Betty Mahmoody," *Contemporary Authors Online,* http://www.galenet.com (November 10, 1999).

➤ Books

Mahmoody, Betty, and William Hoffer, *Not Without My Daughter,* St. Martin's Press, 1987.
Mahmoody, Betty, and Arnold D. Dunchock, *For the Love of a Child,* St. Martin's Press, 1992 (opening quote).

➤ Periodicals

Ladies Home Journal, November 1998, p. 40.

➤ Other

Additional information for this essay was obtained from an interview with Betty Mahmoody on December 2, 1999.

Camryn Manheim

"I *just don't get it. If Art is supposed to imitate Life, why do they want all the actors to be thin? There are fat people in the world. Shouldn't there be a few of us actors to represent them?"*

Born March 8, 1961, Camryn Manheim is an actress best known for playing Ellenor Frutt on the television series *The Practice*, and has gained recognition for her activism regarding weight discrimination. Address: c/o William Morris Agency, 151 El Camino Dr., Beverly Hills, CA 90212.

Actress Camryn Manheim, who plays the strong-willed lawyer Ellenor Frutt on ABC's *The Practice,* has been widely praised for her refusal to perpetuate stereotypes of overweight people as sullen victims or jolly clowns. She also parlayed a successful one-woman stage show, *Wake Up, I'm Fat!,* into a bestselling autobiography of the same title, in which she chronicles her longstanding concern over her weight and her eventual acceptance of her size. As Manheim related in her book, she has realized that she is "an unofficial poster child for fat girls," and added, "I never intended to become the spokesperson for the fat-acceptance movement. But I did want to provide an alternative role model to young girls so they wouldn't feel such pressure to emulate the unrealistic beauty standard in our society."

On March 8, 1961, Debra Frances Manheim was born in Peoria, Illinois, a western suburb of Chicago. She later changed her first name to Camryn after graduating from college because she just never liked the name Debra, or Debi, as she was called. As a youngster spending her formative years in the 1960s, she identified with counter-culture leaders such as author/activist Angela Davis, musician Bob Dylan, and poet Allen Ginsberg. "I had always felt I was born ten years too late," Manheim lamented in her book, *Wake Up, I'm Fat!,* adding, "I would have been a good hippie."

Manheim's parents were forward-thinkers, too: Her father, Jerry Manheim, a math professor, had once been personally denounced by Senator Joseph McCarthy, who led the Communist "witch trials" in the 1950s. Manheim's dad and her mom, Sylvia, an elementary school teacher, relocated the family—which included two older siblings, brother Karl and sister Lisa—from the Midwest to southern California when Manheim was 11 years old. Her father had taken a job as dean of letters and science at California State University at Long Beach, and almost immediately, Manheim, who was thin up until this point, began gaining weight.

On the subject of her size, Manheim's parents were not as progressive. Her mother chastised her for hiding her figure in Levi's, telling her she looked like a truck driver. They persisted in helping her to slim down, as Manheim recalled to Gregory Cerio and Toby Kahn in *People:* "They tried everything from bribes to hypnotism." In another *People* article, she told Peter Ames Carlin and Monica Rizzo, "All they really wanted was for me to have everything. And they knew the world, as it was, would not offer a fat girl very much."

Though she was on the yearbook staff at Woodrow Wilson High

School, Manheim did not fit in with any particular clique at school and felt a desperate need to belong to something. After her parents took her to a Renaissance Faire, she immediately felt welcome. "I wanted to finally be in a world that devoured curvy women and honored them with due respect," she wrote in *Wake Up, I'm Fat!*. The next summer, at age 16, she ended up working at the festival for the first of four consecutive years. There, she wrote, "I learned to love my body, and I learned to love that others loved my body."

After graduating from high school, Manheim spent a semester at Cabrillo Junior College so that she could earn credits in language, which she needed in order to be accepted at a university. She studied sign language, then went on to the University of California at Santa Cruz, which she noted in her book "has the largest per-capita lesbian population in the country." (Although most of Manheim's friends were lesbians at this time and thought that she was as well, she noted in her book that she is heterosexual.) Having bought her first motorcycle at 16, she had long showed signs of nonconformity, and she felt at home in unconventional Santa Cruz. She joined a radical feminist group called the Praying Mantis Brigade (named for the insect that has a ritual in which the female eats the male after mating), and became an activist for a number of causes, landing in jail for civil disobedience more than once.

The Praying Mantis Brigade also staged an annual protest of the Miss California Pageant called the "Myth California Pageant." Manheim found it incredulous that "in a town dedicated to natural-ness, anti-materialism, feminism, liberalism and earthy values ar-rived a procession of capped teeth, long blond hair, and plastic surgery," as she remarked in *Wake Up, I'm Fat!*. After one particular-ly vehement demonstration, the event was moved from Santa Cruz to Pasadena.

After graduating in 1984, Manheim knew she was bound to pursue an acting career, despite the fact that appearance is an important consideration for performers. She had run a theater company in Santa Cruz and taught a class at the university, but yearned to expand her horizons. She was accepted at the Tisch School for the Arts at New York University (NYU) to work toward a master's degree in fine arts. However, once she arrived she learned that roughly one-third of the class would be "cut" after their first or second year and not allowed to complete their degree.

Comparing graduate school to "boot camp," as she described it in her book, Manheim had one professor who was especially vigilant in haranguing her about her weight. Another upbraided her for leaving class to use the restroom at one point. With the threat of being "cut" looming, Manheim tempered her normally defiant attitude, although not enough for the faculty, who chided her for her negativity and put her on academic probation. Finally, the chairperson of the program bluntly told her to consider losing weight. This was when, she admitted, she began using illegal amphetamines to help her become thin, while taking Valium at night to fall asleep.

Manheim later wrote in *Wake Up, I'm Fat!*, "I just don't get it. If Art is supposed to imitate Life, why do they want all the actors to be thin? There are fat people in the world. Shouldn't there be a few of us actors to represent them?" But at the time, she succumbed to pressure. Eventually, Manheim lost 80 pounds, becoming, as she revealed, "a wreck but a trimmed-down wreck, and that kept NYU happy." However, she still did not attract the kind of attention from agents and casting directors that many of her classmates had. After graduating in 1987, she almost died of an overdose of amphetamines, after which she turned her whole life around. Manheim quit smoking cigarettes and taking speed, but also gained back all of the weight she lost.

It was around this time, shopping for a dress for her ten-year class reunion, that Manheim uttered the words that would later become the title of her best-selling book. While in the dressing room at Bloomingdale's, she asked her mother to retrieve a size 22 dress from the rack. When she tried it on, it was way too small, and Manheim felt terrible about herself. When she took it off, she caught a glimpse of the size of the tag—16—and realized her mother had given her a smaller size on purpose so that she would feel even worse about herself. Manheim, as she revealed in her book, exited the dressing room and yelled, "Mom, WAKE UP ... I'M FAT!" Though Manheim distanced herself from her parents for a while due to their concern about her weight, she later reconciled with them.

Manheim started out in the theater as a reader, hired to play various parts in auditions opposite those who were actually trying out, and as a sign language interpreter. She eventually began landing small roles in films and on television episodes. She was cast in 1990's *Bonfire of the Vanities* and on the cop drama *Law & Order* in the early 1990s, then took a part as a sexually liberated woman in a health spa in *The Road to Wellville*, 1994, which she thought would be her breakthrough part. In it, she rides nude on horseback. Despite the lack of stereotyping in that film, the role led to a string of offers for characters she described in her book as "the put-upon, ugly, butt-of-the-joke fat girl." A couple of small roles in the movies *Jeffrey*, 1995, and *Eraser*, 1996, followed.

In the meantime, Manheim continued to act on stage; she had the opportunity to meet award-winning playwright Tony Kushner (*Angels in America*) while at NYU before he was famous, and his protégé, Michael Mayer, cast her in several productions. In 1993, Manheim's first lead role was in her one-woman show, *Wake Up, I'm Fat*, which was a hit off-Broadway, first at the Classic Stage Company, then at Second Stage, where it gained in popularity until moving to the Public Theater. Then in 1995, she won a *Village Voice* Obie award for playing Gemma in *Missing Persons*.

Riding the wave of these successes, Manheim then snagged an audition with television show creator David E. Kelley (*Ally McBeal, Picket Fences*), who was looking for someone to play a sassy, streetwise character for *The Practice*, a drama about a Boston law firm. She made such an impression on him—she boldly challenged him to a cribbage game, and later won—that he penned the character of Ellenor Frutt just for her, a role that suited her brash nature and did not relegate her to a stereotype. "I just didn't want to get stuck in the jolly fat-girl part for five years on some sitcom," she related to Stef McDonald in *TV Guide*.

The Practice premiered in 1997, and Manheim soon garnered attention for playing a character whose lines are not dictated by her size. Various articles applauded her for blazing new trails for larger actors, and Jefferson Graham in *USA Today* even pointed out that she "has romantic relationships with men—something large women aren't usually seen doing on TV." At the end of the first season, she received an Emmy Award for best supporting actress in a drama series. At the ceremony, she proudly lifted the statuette and proclaimed, "This is for all the fat girls!" Subsequently, *People* magazine named her one of the 25 most intriguing people of 1998. In 1999, Manheim picked up a Golden Globe Award as well. She has also appeared in several films, including *Romy and Michele's High School Reunion*, 1997; *Fool's Gold*, 1998; *Happiness*, 1998; and *Mercury Rising*, 1998.

Manheim earned a six-figure advance for her best-selling autobiography, published in 1999. She splits her time between Hollywood and New York City, but calls New York's East Village home—it is where she is registered to vote. As for the attention devoted to her size, she explained in *Wake Up, I'm Fat!*, "Look, I don't mind being described as fat. In fact, that's the whole point. But I hope there are more interesting aspects to my performances, and I would hope that in the future reviewers will focus on my acting and not my dimensions. The reason they don't mention that Tom Cruise is 5'8" in reviews is because it doesn't matter. And I hope that some day, my weight will be regarded as equally irrelevant."

Sources

➤ **Books**

Contemporary Theatre, Film and Television, volume 23, Gale Group, 1999.
Manheim, Camryn, *Wake Up, I'm Fat!,* Broadway Books, 1999 (opening quote).

➤ **Periodicals**

Dallas Morning News, May 15, 1998, p. 2C.
Entertainment Weekly, September 18, 1998, p. 67; May 7, 1999, p. 56.
In Style, June 1999, p. 282.
Maclean's, January 1, 1999, p. 62.
Ms., October/November 1999, p. 93.
Newsday, November 13, 1995, p. B7.
People, November 21, 1994, p; 145; December 28, 1998, p. 76; May 24, 1999, p. 73.
Publisher's Weekly, April 12, 1999, p. 67.
Star Tribune (Minneapolis, MN), September 27, 1998, p. 8E.
TV Guide, July 4, 1998, p. 24.
USA Today, August 26, 1998, p. 3D.

Vilma Martinez

"I'm successful because I have the confidence,
courage, and willingness to work hard for what
I want. This was taught to me by my family and by my
culture.''

Born October 17, 1943 (some sources say 1944) in San Antonio,
Texas, Vilma Martinez is a prominent lawyer and civil rights
activist. Address: Munger, Tolles & Olson, 3555 South Grand
Avenue, Los Angeles, CA 90071.

Throughout her entire career, Vilma Martinez has worked to promote civil rights, especially for Hispanic Americans. During the years she spent as president and lead counsel for the Mexican American Legal Defense and Educational Fund (MALDEF), she fought a number of significant court battles dealing with access to public education and the ballot box. Martinez's determination to seek fair treatment for those ignored or oppressed by governments and corporations dates back to her childhood and the prejudice she encountered as both a female and a Mexican American. Since then, she has made it her life's work to eliminate the legal obstacles preventing Hispanics and other minorities from fully participating in American society.

Born October 17, 1943 (some sources say 1944) in San Antonio, Texas, Vilma Socorro Martinez is the daughter of Salvador Martinez and Marina Piña. Her father, a carpenter, was originally from Mexico. Her Texas-born mother raised Martinez and her four younger siblings. When she was a very small child, Martinez also spent a great deal of time with her grandmother, who taught her to read and write Spanish.

Though she grew up in an ethnically integrated, working-class neighborhood, Martinez only spoke Spanish when she began her formal education. However, she quickly learned English and liked school, especially reading. She particularly enjoyed biographies, which she found inspirational. But as she grew older and sought greater academic challenges, she received virtually no encouragement from her teachers and counselors. In the Texas of her youth, her gender and ethnicity automatically relegated her to second-class status.

Martinez persisted despite such attitudes. In junior high school, she became an officer in the National Honor Society. When she expressed interest in attending an academically oriented high school, her counselor suggested that she try a vocational or trade high school instead. Martinez ignored the suggestion and went on to the school of her choice.

While attending Jefferson High School, Martinez found her career path. At the age of 15, she went to work for Alonso Perales, a famous Hispanic lawyer and activist who knew her father. Perales had served as an advisor to President Franklin D. Roosevelt and was an advocate for fair treatment for Hispanics. Martinez came to admire Perales and was inspired by his example to pursue a legal career.

When Martinez graduated from high school in 1961, she wanted to attend college. But her counselor refused to help her fill out the necessary forms. So Martinez took matters into her own hands and applied to the University of Texas. She not only was accepted, she was also granted a partial scholarship.

Despite objections from her father, who thought that she had no chance of reaching her goal and that she should just stay home and get married, Martinez entered the University of Texas in the fall of 1961. There she managed a full course load every semester (including summers) while also working 20 hours a week for the school. She earned her B.A. in political science in less than three years and graduated in 1964.

On the advice of a professor, Martinez decided to head east to continue her education to escape the kind of bias she was routinely subjected to in Texas. She then entered Columbia University Law School with the help of several scholarships. Though she still experienced some prejudice because of her gender (she was one of only 20 women in a class of 300), Martinez graduated in 1967 with her LL.B. and was admitted to the New York State Bar the following year.

Martinez's first job was with the National Association for the Advancement of Colored People (NAACP) as a staff attorney for the group's Legal Defense and Educational Fund. During the three years (1967 to 1970) she spent with the NAACP, she worked on many cases representing minorities and the impoverished. One especially important case Martinez handled was *Griggs v. Duke Power Company*, which went all the way to the U.S. Supreme Court and helped define affirmative action in the workplace. In *Griggs*, she argued that companies that demanded high school diplomas or intelligence tests from applicants were in violation of the Civil Rights Act of 1964 because such requirements had a disproportionate effect on minorities and were therefore discriminatory.

In 1968, Martinez was one of the founders and organizers of the Mexican American Legal Defense and Educational Fund (MALDEF). She continued her professional association with the NAACP while remaining active with MALDEF; for a time, she acted as the liaison between the two organizations. In 1969 Martinez also served as a consultant to the U.S. Commission on Civil Rights.

After leaving the NAACP in 1970, Martinez continued to work on behalf of civil rights issues and labor laws as an equal employment opportunity counselor for the New York State Division of Human Rights. In her job, she drafted and implemented regulations and procedures relevant to the rights of employees. Martinez then took her expertise into the private sector in 1971 when she hired on as a labor lawyer and litigation associate for the law firm Cahill, Gordon & Reindel.

As Martinez's professional career blossomed, her personal life experienced some transitions of its own. During the early 1970s, she married fellow lawyer Stuart Singer. They eventually had two sons, Carlos and Ricardo.

In 1973, Martinez moved to Los Angeles, California, to work full-time for MALDEF as the organization's president and general counsel. At the time, it was struggling financially because it had no regular funding. One of Martinez's primary goals, therefore, was to remedy this precarious situation. She gave MALDEF a structure that allowed it to expand and improve and created an endowment to ensure a steadier source of funding. She also turned to potential new sources of support, primarily corporate sponsorships and grants.

In addition, Martinez broadened the activities and goals of MALDEF. She established the Employment Litigation Project, the Education Litigation Project, and the Chicana Rights Project. She also launched an intern program that trained litigators in civil rights work. Martinez took steps to make MALDEF more diverse, too, in order to boost its power and impact as a civil rights organization of note.

During her tenure, Martinez argued several significant legal cases on behalf of MALDEF. In 1974, for example, she won a case of particular import to Hispanic children whose primary language was Spanish, not English. The judge's ruling guaranteed such students the right to a bilingual education in public schools. Several years later, in 1982, Martinez successfully argued another major education case, *Plyler v. Doe.* As a result of this decision, the state of Texas was ordered to allow the children of illegal aliens (many of whom worked as migrant workers) to attend public school free of charge. Previously, state law had required such children to pay $1,000 in tuition, a sum most of their families could not afford.

Martinez also devoted a great deal of attention to the issue of voting rights. In a landmark 1975 case, she contended that Mexican Americans should be covered by the anti-discrimination measures contained in the Voting Rights Act, which had originally been crafted to protect African Americans. Without such coverage, she insisted, election workers in areas with large Hispanic populations (such as certain parts of Texas and California) were free to use tactics aimed at discouraging or even preventing Mexican Americans from voting. Martinez also lobbied to make certain states print ballots in both Spanish and English.

In addition to her responsibilities at MALDEF, Martinez worked for a number of public entities in an advisory capacity during the 1970s. From 1975 until 1977, for instance, she served as a consultant to the Immigration and Naturalization Service. From 1975 to 1981, she was an unpaid consultant to the U.S. Bureau of the Census. Thanks to her efforts, a category for "Hispanic" was included on the 1980 census form for the first time. (The data collected ultimately had an impact on some electoral districts.) During this same period, Martinez was also a consultant for the U.S. Department of the Treasury. She has held many other such posts over the course of her career.

In 1976 California Governor Jerry Brown named Martinez a regent for the University of California system. Before leaving her post in 1990, she spent one term (1984 until 1986) as board chairperson. She was also the co-founder of the regents' Achievement Council, a group that worked to increase the number of minority students attending schools in the University of California system by helping them during their elementary and high school years.

Around 1982 Martinez decided to leave MALDEF to pursue a different course. In less than a decade at the helm of the organization, she had increased its budget from just under $1 million to $4.9 million. Meanwhile, the number of attorneys on the staff had grown to 23, allowing MALDEF to expand its efforts nationwide.

Eventually, Martinez became in partner in a Los Angeles-based law firm, Munger, Tolles & Olson, where she specialized in labor law. Though she was in private practice, she continued to honor her commitment to public service. She served on a number of boards and committees, including MALDEF's board of directors beginning in the 1990s. Martinez was also on several corporate boards, including Shell Oil and Anheuser-Busch, Inc. In addition, she spoke at law schools, academic institutions, and gatherings of business groups, and even considered running for political office. And in 1994 Martinez was on President Bill Clinton's short list for an appointment to the U.S. Supreme Court.

Over the years, Martinez has received numerous awards for her civil rights work, including an honorary degree from Amherst College, a Distinguished Alumnus Award from the University of Texas, and a Medal of Excellence from Columbia Law School. But

Martinez acknowledges there is much more work that needs to be done. As she told Sam Enriquez of the *Los Angeles Times*, "I'm still impatient . . . . There have been changes. . . . There ought to be more and they ought to be faster, and I've been saying that for a long time and will keep on saying it."

Sources

➤ **Books**

Codye, Corinn, *Vilma Martinez*, Raintree Publishers, 1990 (opening quote).
Encyclopedia of World Biography, Volume 18, Gale, 1999.
Meier, Matt S. and others, *Notable Latino Americans: A Biographical Dictionary*, Greenwood Press, 1995.
Meier, Matt S., *Mexican American Biographies: A Historical Dictionary, 1836-1987*, Greenwood Press, 1988.
Telgen, Diane and Jim Kamp, editors, *Notable Hispanic American Women*, Gale, 1993.

➤ **Periodicals**

Los Angeles Times, February 9, 1989, p. 8.

➤ **Other**

PR Newswire, September 13, 1993; December 9, 1996.

Carolyn McCarthy

"It's a simple safety lock. We have bills that make it impossible for children to get in an aspirin bottle. Do my colleagues not think we should do the same thing with a gun?"*

Born on January 5, 1944, in Brooklyn, New York, Carolyn McCarthy became an active gun-control advocate after the shooting death of her husband on a Long Island commuter train on December 7, 1993. Nearly three years after the tragedy, she was elected as representative of the Fourth Congressional District of New York. Address: 1725 Longworth Bldg., Washington, D.C. 20515.

When Carolyn McCarthy returned to her suburban Mineola, New York, home from a Christmas concert in early December of 1993, her brother Tom was waiting outside to tell her that her husband was dead and her son was seriously injured. The former nurse and homemaker would later learn that a gunman had shot 25 people on the Long Island commuter train they were riding, killing six, including her husband, Dennis. Prospects looked extremely bleak for her son Kevin as well, with doctors giving him only a ten percent chance of survival, and even then, they expected him to suffer severe brain damage. The normally mild-mannered McCarthy went into full gear to care for her son with a zeal, who eventually made almost a full recovery and was able to return to work. She then led a vehement campaign for gun control, and upon learning that her congressman was voting to repeal a ban on assault weapons for which she had helped lobby, she decided to take his place. McCarthy had been a registered Republican for a long time, but found that her party was not willing to support her. She switched tickets and ran as a Democrat, managing to unseat her district's representative, Dan Frisa, 57 percent to 41 percent. She was sworn in on January 1, 1997, just before she turned 53.

McCarthy was born Carolyn Cook in Brooklyn, New York, to Thomas and Irene Cook. Her father was a boilermaker and her mother was a homemaker who also held a job for a while as a salesperson. McCarthy and her family, which included three siblings, grew up in the suburban Long Island town of Mineola, New York, in a house where she would live her whole life and later raise her own son. As a youth, McCarthy enjoyed sports and considered becoming a physical education teacher. However, school was often difficult for her; years later she found out that she was dyslexic. The condition, which affects learning and reading skills, still plagues her.

When McCarthy was in high school, her career plans changed when her boyfriend was in a terrible car accident and his family hired a nurse to take care of him. The nurse asked McCarthy to assist her, and she was exposed to caring for a person. However, the boy died a few days later, and that very day, McCarthy applied to nursing school. She became a licensed practical nurse and devoted herself to caring for the people "nobody else would touch," as she noted to Jonathan Mandell in *Good Housekeeping*. Chronically ill patients, badly burned patients, all deserved the same high level of care, in her mind. "Even if a person was dying," she told Mandell, "you made that person comfortable, helped them cross over."

After starting her career, McCarthy met Dennis "Whitey" McCarthy at the beach. A tall blond man, McCarthy was from a large Irish-American family, just as his future wife was. She was a little reluctant to date him, since she was suburban and he lived in the city. But he pursued her, and they were married in 1967. Dennis McCarthy was an office manager at Prudential Securities in Manhattan who called his wife "Cookie," after her maiden name, Cook. Their only child, Kevin, was born in 1967, and he grew up to work as a computer analyst in the same firm as his father, riding the commuter train with him each day. Carolyn McCarthy, meanwhile, had left her job in the intensive care unit after a number of years to become an avid gardener and homemaker. Though the McCarthys divorced at one point, reportedly due to Dennis's problems with alcohol, they reunited and remarried. Active in the outdoors, McCarthy and her husband enjoyed fishing, skiing, and golfing, and spent much of their free time at a ski lodge in Killington, Vermont. They had agreed to buy some nearby property as a retirement getaway shortly before McCarthy's pleasant life was shattered.

On December 7, 1993, McCarthy came home at around 11 p.m. from an evening with a friend at a Christmas concert. She found her brother Tom on the front lawn, as well as a bare Christmas tree that she had asked her husband and son to set up in the house. After McCarthy asked why the tree was still in the driveway, McCarthy's brother told her the news. Dennis and Kevin McCarthy were riding the 5:33 Long Island Rail Road out of New York City's Pennsylvania Station to come home when a mentally ill gunman opened fire on 25 passengers in the car, killing six, including Dennis. Kevin was the worst of the injured, as well. About one-seventh of his brain was shot away, and much of the remaining was exposed and riddled with bullet and bone fragments. His hand was blown apart, too. As Kevin lay in a coma, doctors said he had a ten percent chance of pulling through, and even if he did live, he would probably be a vegetable.

McCarthy, however, was determined to help Kevin survive. She had lost her husband and best friend, and decided she was not going to lose her son as well. At the press conference after the shooting, she spoke up and told the doctor, "Excuse me, you're wrong. He will live. And he will move," she recalled in *Good Housekeeping.* McCarthy vigilantly attended to her son at the hospital, and a week later, he was able to speak. As the weeks progressed, he remained paralyzed on the left side and doctors assumed he would never be able to walk. McCarthy enlisted his friends in shifts to provide physical therapy, continuously moving his arms and legs so that they would not become stiff. He was eventually able to move his fingers on his right hand. Though his left hand and foot remained paralyzed, he learned to walk again with the aid of a brace, thanks in large part to his mother's constant push for him to become rehabilitated. Kevin even went back to work, taking the train daily, to the same job he held before the shooting, even working overtime. He told *Good Housekeeping* that his mother "is more outgoing now, more determined."

Once McCarthy learned more about the incident, she put her persistence to work. She found out that the gunman, Colin Ferguson, was carrying his 9-millimeter semiautomatic pistol illegally. He had purchased it in California and did not have a permit for it in New York. However, the 15-round magazine he was using was legal, and so were the destructive Black Talon bullets, designed to spread apart on impact in order to cause greater injury. McCarthy and other victims and victims' families filed lawsuits against the company that produced the gun, the bullets, and the clip, but it was thrown out. In addition, a governor's aide at one point asked her to lend support to a state bill to ban assault weapons. This experience fueled her spirit. As time progressed, McCarthy became a vehement activist.

Trying to garner support for her cause, McCarthy began speaking at rallies and lobbying Congress to ban assault weapons. "I couldn't change those events," McCarthy stated in the *Washington Post*, "but I could try to make sure it never happened again to anyone else." In 1994 the Crime Bill outlawed 19 such weapons, including the 15-round magazine that was used in her husband's shooting. Meanwhile, beginning in February of 1995, McCarthy and the other victims had to endure a horrific trial in which the defendant, Ferguson, acting as his own lawyer, sadistically questioned the very victims that he had wounded. He eventually received 200 years in prison.

After the trial, McCarthy found her battle was starting all over again when a new set of representatives in Congress planned to repeal the bill she worked so hard to get passed. She traveled to Washington, D.C. in order to bend some ears. Her own congressman, Republican Dan Frisa, voted to repeal the bill, despite what had happened on the train. Though he told McCarthy that he wanted to develop a more inclusive bill that would eliminate semiautomatic weapons altogether, McCarthy doubted his sincerity, because the bill seemed destined for failure. According to *Ms.*, McCarthy at the time commented to a friend, "I'm gonna run against this guy and I'm gonna beat this guy." The angry threat gradually became a serious idea. The longtime registered Republican found that her party was unwilling to encourage her, so McCarthy ran as a Democrat. "Carolyn is stronger politically than either the Democrats or Republicans because she's neither," former New York Mayor Mario Cuomo commented in the *Los Angeles Times.* "She is where most Americans are. They'll all call themselves something but they would prefer to tell you what they don't like about either party."

Throughout the race, Frisa and some media commentators criticized McCarthy as being a one-issue candidate. "At least I have an issue!" she retorted in *People.* Also, McCarthy pointed out that her lobbying efforts gave her insight into the workings of Washington, and she further responded by outlining her broader concerns in addition to gun legislation. "It's not about guns alone," she told Dan Barry in the *New York Times.* "It's about Head Start. It's about drug-free schools, it's about job opportunities." She learned the hard way about the flaws in the health care system when Kevin needed emergency treatment after the shooting, and has spoken out about reform in that industry. She has a strong pro-choice stance, and advocates spending for education, environmental protection, and welfare reform. All the other knowledge that she needs, she figured she could get on the job, just like the other freshman congressmen always have. "What did I know about guns three years ago?" McCarthy asked in *People.* "I learned. I had to." She also had an open mind on crime policy, stating that although she personally opposed the death penalty, she would vote for it if her constituents desired it.

On November 5, 1996, McCarthy unseated Frisa after his first term in office with 57 percent of the vote as opposed to Frisa's 41 percent. As the representative from the Fourth Congressional District of New York, she speaks for a generally suburban area on Long Island composed of a mix of working-class, upper-class, and upper-middle-class people. About a quarter of her constituents are African American and Latino and most commute into New York City for their jobs. About two out of three are registered Democrats. As a new representative, McCarthy did not land her preferred committee assignments to the House Commerce, Judiciary, Appropriations, or Ways and Means committees. She was instead placed on the House Education and Workforce Committee, which oversees the entire range of learning in the country from preschool to adult education, and the House Small Business Committee, designed to help and protect small businesses, especially in regards to financial assistance.

After starting her new career, McCarthy was not shy to ask for help. "In nursing, I learned never to be afraid to ask a question, because if you don't ask, someone could die," she told Jeffrey Zaslow in *USA Weekend.* In her first term, she worked with fellow New Yorkers Senator Alfonse D'Amato and Representative Peter T. King to draft a bill helping legal immigrants. Reflecting her pro-choice stand, she voted against a ban on partial birth abortions. She also supported funding for the National Endowment for the Arts and opposed military funding, school choice, and the requirement to notify parents when their children seek family planning. Though she fought for a law requiring child-proof safety locks on all handguns, the measure has not survived. The *New York Times Magazine* reported that she pointed out in an address on the House floor: "It's a simple safety lock. We have bills that make it impossible for children to get in an aspirin bottle. Do my colleagues not think we should do the same thing with a gun?"

In May of 1998, NBC aired a television movie, *The Long Island Incident,* based on McCarthy's life and the events surrounding the shooting and her subsequent political career. Initially, she was against the project, but then learned that since the information was in the public domain, it would be made without her consent if necessary. She cooperated closely with the writers and was allowed quite a bit of control with the script, and she and Kevin were on the set during much of the filming. McCarthy was also on track to write her autobiography, but it was later put on hold.

McCarthy was re-elected to a second term in 1998. In 1999, she received several honors, including being named one of *Newsday's* 100 Long Island Influentials, *Congressional Quarterly's* 50 Most Effective Legislators in Congress, *Ladies' Home Journal* list of America's 100 Most Important Women, and *Advertising Age's* list of "Most Impact by Women in 1999." The small-built, blond congresswoman has an apartment in Washington when she is not at home in Mineola. Though she misses her husband, Dennis, McCarthy told Tamara Jones in the *Washington Post,* "You have to keep moving forward."

Sources

➤ On-line

"Carolyn McCarthy Biography," U.S. House of Representatives

web site, http://www.house.gov/carolynmccarthy (March 30, 2000).

➤ Periodicals

Good Housekeeping, September 1996, p. 64.
Los Angeles Times, July 5, 1996, p. E1; May 3, 1998, p. 3.
Ms., September/October 1996, p. 19.
Nation, November 1, 1996, p. 15.
Newsday, February 26, 1998, p. B3; May 12, 1998, p. A34.
New York Times, April 12, 1996, p. B6; May 29, 1996, p. B1; October 12, 1996, p. B15; January 8, 1997, p. B6.
New York Times Magazine, June 22, 1997, p. 20 (opening quote).
People, September 9, 1996, p. 75.
USA Weekend, May 1-3, 1998, p. 26.
Washington Post, August 27, 1996, p. B1.

Patsy T. Mink

"If to believe in freedom and equality is to be a radical, then I am a radical. So long as there remain groups of our fellow Americans who are denied equal opportunity and equal protection under the law ... we must remain steadfast, till all shades of man may stand side by side in dignity and self-respect to truly enjoy the fruits of this great land."

Born December 6, 1927, in Paia, Maui, Hawaii, Patsy T. Mink was the first Asian American woman elected to Congress, serving numerous terms in the House of Representatives. Address: 2135 Rayburn Office Building, U.S. House of Representatives, Washington, D.C. 20515-1102.

A s an Asian American, Patsy T. Mink was the first woman of color elected to the United States Congress. Overcoming prejudice and sexism, Mink accomplished much in her political life. She was extremely active in issues related to education, working women, families, and children. Mink was a Democrat, though her penchant for voting with her conscience did not always endear her to her party.

Mink was born Patsy Takemoto on December 6, 1927, in Paia, Maui, Hawaii. Of Japanese descent, she was the daughter of Suematsu Takemoto and his wife, Mitama Tateyama. Her father worked for an irrigation company as a land surveyor. The family, which included Mink's elder brother Eugene, lived in a small town called Hamakuapoko during her formative years.

Mink started attending school at the age of four because of her brother. She followed him to school and would not leave, and was entered in the same grade as him though he was a year and a half older. Mink was very close to her brother, and they were constant companions as children. However, they grew up in a segregated environment in Hawaii where whites and Asians were separated on the islands.

The day after Mink's fourteenth birthday, the Japanese bombed Pearl Harbor, bringing the United States into World War II. On the mainland, many Japanese Americans were rounded up and put in prison camps, but this did not happen to the same degree in Hawaii because of their sheer numbers. Mink had studied at a Japanese language school after public school, but this was closed. (Public schools were also closed for a while, but only because of the bombing and safety concerns.) During the war, Mink's school was only open four days a week, and the students did war duty on the fifth.

Mink experienced and saw racial prejudice during the war. She was called names. Those who worked for Japanese language newspapers and were leaders in the Japanese-American community were questioned and sometimes arrested. Mink's father was among those interrogated. Mink aspired to be a medical doctor and was encouraged by her teachers at Maui High School. She received this support at school, despite her ancestry and her gender, both of which might have been problematic for some.

In 1943, she was elected president of the student body at Maui High School, the first girl to win it. Mink was an active student who participated in many extracurricular activities. When she graduated in 1944, she was named valedictorian. After graduation, Mink entered the University of Hawaii in Honolulu, where she spent the next two years working toward her goal. During this time period, the war ended.

In the fall of 1946, Mink transferred to Pennsylvania's Wilson College. Mink had a disappointing experience there because she was not used to the cold and because there was no pre-med program. After a semester, she transferred to the University of Nebraska at Lincoln. It was here that she experienced true segregation for the first time. She was assigned to the dormitory at the International House, where all non-whites were housed. She protested publicly in a letter to the editor, and instantly became the focal point of campus politics.

Mink was forced to leave Nebraska during the summer after a few months because she developed a serious illness, a thyroid condition that had to be operated on at home. Mink finished her education at the University of Hawaii, where she graduated with a BA in zoology and chemistry. Though she applied to many schools, Mink was not accepted to any of them in part because of her gender but also because of her race.

An alternate plan was formed. Mink decided instead to go to law school. She entered the University of Chicago in 1948, but only got in because of an error. Mink was admitted as part of the foreign student quota because someone there thought that Hawaii was a foreign country. Though Mink had a hard time adjusting to the demands of law school, she grew to like the intellectual challenge. She also met her future husband, John Mink, a geology graduate student there. They were married on January 27, 1951, and both graduated later that year.

When Mink searched for a position at a law firm, she had a hard time finding one, in part because she was married. In the meantime, she worked at the University of Chicago Law Library, and had their only child, daughter Gwendolyn Rachel Matsu Mink. With no law prospects in Chicago, Mink and her family returned to Hawaii in the summer of 1952. Even in Hawaii Mink still could not find work at a law firm, mostly because she was married with a child. This, despite the fact that she passed the Hawaii bar exam, making her the first Japanese-American woman lawyer in Hawaii.

As a result, she was forced to open her own practice. Mink's father got her a small office in a building, paying her rent while she built up a clientele. She attracted several clients, and taught business law at the University of Hawaii. In the fall of 1953, Mink became involved with Democratic party politics. At the time, Republicans had controlled Hawaii for many years, but the Democratic party was undergoing a reformation and revitalization.

Mink began her foray into politics in 1954 by organizing a branch of the Oahu Young Democrats, then a Hawaii version of the organization. While the Democratic party was doing well in the state, Mink ran for her first office in 1956, a seat in the Hawaii Territorial House and won without a problem. (Hawaii did not become a state until 1959.) One of her first accomplishments was the successful protest of the testing of nuclear weapons near Hawaii. In 1957, she was elected vice president of the Young Democrats of America.

In 1958, Mink decided to run for Hawaii Territorial Senate, and again won. She was named chairperson of the Educational Committee, beginning a long-time interest in education issues. These territorial legislative bodies were dissolved when Hawaii became a state in 1959, and Mink decided to run for the Hawaiian seat in the United States House of Representatives. Mink lost her first election when she was beat by Daniel Inouye. Though she vowed never to run again, she did.

Despite holding no office, Mink remained active in Democratic politics. She gave a well-received speech at the 1960 Democratic Convention in Los Angeles. Mink also continued her law practice until 1962 when she ran for the Hawaiian Senate. Again she became chair of the Educational Committee. Mink also sponsored an equal pay for equal work bill which would give women the same amount of money as men for the same jobs.

In 1964, Mink was ready for another shot at Congress. She ran for a seat in the House of Representatives, but was an extreme underdog with no press coverage and little support from her own party because she had already shown her independent streak. Mink easily won the primary then the general election, making her the first Asian American woman elected to Congress. Mink had to undergo another hard adjustment process. Of the 5,353 members of Congress, only 12 were women.

Mink persevered, and was elected every two years between 1964 and 1976. As a Congresswoman, Mink was heavily involved in civil rights, health care, issues related to women and children, and the war on poverty. She also worked on promoting federal aid for education, a concern of her's for many years. She was a member of the House Committee on Education and Labor. Mink always followed her conscience, even if her views were not popular.

Mink was against increased American involvement in Vietnam, despite the fact that Hawaii had many war-related jobs. Mink's view was shared by only a small minority in Congress, at least at first. Mink also joined the protest against gender barriers in Congress. In 1970, when G. Harrold Carswell was nominated by President Richard M. Nixon for the Supreme Court, Mink protested because he had made some anti-women rulings. Though she was the only one to testify against him, she started a snowball of sentiment against him. His appointment was denied in the Senate.

In 1972, Mink ran for president, but she did not expect to become elected. She wanted to use the forum to highlight issues—especially civil rights and social programs—and show that the idea of a female president was a serious possibility. Mink was on the ballot of the Oregon primary, though she only won two percent of the vote and withdrew her candidacy.

Mink was on the vanguard again in 1973. That year, she gave a speech in the House of Representatives asking that impeachment hearings begin for President Nixon on his Watergate scandal. Within several months the wheels were turned in motion, but Nixon resigned before the process could be completed. Two years later, Mink decided to run for the United States Senate. An underdog again, this time Mink lost. She left Congress after the 1976 election to serve in newly-elected-President Jimmy Carter's bureaucracy. Mink was named Oceans and Environmental Affairs' Assistant Secretary. She only stayed a year, then returned to Hawaii.

Mink stayed out of electoral politics for several years. She practiced law and taught at the University of Hawaii, speaking out on occasion if an issue was important to her. In the end, the lure of electoral politics proved too strong. In 1983, she was elected to the city council of Honolulu where she served two terms through 1987. Mink then lost two subsequent elections, when she ran for the governorship in 1986, then campaigned for the job of mayor of Honolulu in 1988.

Mink decided to make another run for a seat in Washington. In 1990 or 1991, Mink returned to the U.S. House of Representatives via special election when a seat was vacated. She picked up where she had left off more than a decade ago, continuing to fight for the rights of Hawaiians and women's rights. Mink again protested the appointment of a man with questionable conduct toward women to the Supreme Court. The nominee, Clarence Thomas, had been accused by his former co-worker, Anita Hill, of sexual harassment. Despite the objections of Mink and others, Thomas was appointed.

Mink was re-elected to her seat in the House several times through the 1990s, often with overwhelming majorities. In 1998, for example, she won with 69 percent of the vote. Mink was instrumental in the founding of the Congressional Asian Pacific Caucus, and served as chair beginning in 1995. At different times, she also served on the House Education Committee, Workforce Committee, House Budget Committee, and at one time was the ranking Democrat on Oversight & Investigations Committee. By 1996, she was the most senior Democratic woman in Congress.

The work Mink had done for people garnered her numerous accolades over the years, especially from women's groups. Mink accomplished much while remaining true to herself. As Sue Davidson wrote in *A Heart in Politics*, "She has reached her goals without leaving her ideals behind. She has never forsaken her passionate struggle for peace and for 'simple justice and equality'."

Sources

➤ Books

Davidson, Sue, *A Heart in Politics: Jeannette Rankin and Patsy T. Mink*, Seal Press, 1994 (opening quote).
Encyclopedia of World Biography: Supplement, volume 18, Gale Group, 1999, pp. 287-89.
Unterburger, Amy L., editor, *Who's Who Among Asian Americans: 1994-95*, Gale Research, 1994, p. 419.
Who's Who of American Women: 1999-2000, Marquis Who'sWho, 1998, p. 720.

➤ Periodicals

Denver Rocky Mountain News, May 12, 1997, p. 42A.
Gannett News Service, May 20, 1994; April 7, 1995.
Social Justice, Spring 1994, p. 159.

Charles "Swede" Momsen

"To *have your own ship, to take her to sea—and under it—what an experience that is! I wouldn't trade it for anything."*

Born June 21, 1895, Charles "Swede" Momsen was the inventor of several pieces of equipment related to diving and submarines that changed the nature of deep-sea lifesaving and exploration. In 1939 he directed a dramatic rescue using his inventions that saved a U.S. Navy submarine crew from certain death. He died May 25, 1967.

Though he toiled in relative obscurity without fanfare or publicity, Charles "Swede" Momsen was by some estimates the greatest inventor of deep-sea diving and submarine technology of the twentieth century. A career officer in the U.S. Navy, he had watched and waited in despair on more than one occasion as men he knew died aboard submarines trapped deep beneath the sea. Creating the kind of equipment that could save them became his goal. Yet it was a quest Momsen pursued largely on his own, with little financial or moral support from the military. His perseverance paid off in an especially dramatic way in 1939 when he and his inventions figured prominently in the rescue of 33 men trapped on a grounded submarine in the Atlantic Ocean off the coast of Maine.

Born June 21, 1895, Charles Bowers Momsen grew up in St. Paul, Minnesota, where his father was a businessman. As a youngster, he was intrigued by the book *Twenty Thousand Leagues Under the Sea,* an underwater adventure with science-fiction undertones written by French novelist Jules Verne in 1870. The exciting yarn sparked Momsen's interest in joining the Navy and attending the Naval Academy.

Momsen took the first step toward fulfilling his dream when he entered the Naval Academy in Annapolis, Maryland in 1914. During his freshman year, there was a cheating scandal that involved some of his fellow students. Academy officials responded by making exams much more difficult, and as a result, Momsen and many of his classmates flunked out of school. He managed to persuade his congressman to have him re-appointed to the academy in 1916, however, and three years later he graduated. It was during his time at Annapolis that Momsen acquired the nickname "Swede," though he was not of Swedish extraction. (His ancestors were Danish and German.)

When Momsen graduated, he was commissioned an ensign and assigned to the battleship *Oklahoma.* There he remained until 1921, when the Navy's submarine school began accepting new recruits for training. Even though he was advised against going into the submarine service because it was considered a less prestigious branch of the Navy, Momsen applied for the program and was accepted.

Life on board submarines of that era was far from pleasant. They were small, cramped, and had no amenities whatsoever. There was no fresh air, no heat, and no refrigeration. Furthermore, there were no toilets or showers and no laundry facilities. And if a submarine had the misfortune to sink to the ocean floor—something that happened with alarming regularity back then—there was no escape. Everyone on board faced a slow, agonizing death from asphyxiation.

By 1923, Momsen was a junior lieutenant, and he received his first submarine command with the O-15. While on a run during which he and his crew hoped to set a time record, the O-15 sank and became stuck on the ocean floor. Figuring he had nothing to lose, Momsen took a chance and fired water out of the torpedo tubes and successfully dislodged the sub. By 1925, he had been promoted again and given the command of the S-1 submarine out of the Navy's main base in New London, Connecticut.

After a series of submarine accidents in the mid-1920s claimed the lives of dozens of men (including many he had known since his days at the Naval Academy), Momsen felt compelled to take action. Experimenting on his own, he created a diving bell that could rescue crewmen from grounded submarines. It consisted of a steel rescue chamber that was lowered into the sea with cables and then attached to the submarine's hull over a special kind of escape hatch. Once the bell had been secured with bolts and suction to maintain the proper pressure, the hatch was opened and several people at a time could move from the submarine into the rescue chamber.

When Momsen first proposed the idea of his rescue chamber around 1925, he received some encouragement and support from his immediate superiors in the Navy. He then submitted it through official channels to higher-ups and waited in vain for months for some kind of response. Meanwhile, Momsen received a new assignment in the Navy's Bureau of Construction and Repair in Washington, D.C. Not long after starting his job, he was sorting through some papers on his predecessor's desk when he came across the documents he had passed along regarding his invention. Realizing that no one had ever even bothered to read through them, he began asking questions and campaigning for his own proposal. When Momsen finally received an answer, it was not the one he had wanted to hear; his design was declared impractical and unseaworthy. In the wake of yet another submarine disaster in which many lives were lost, Momsen almost quit the Navy but opted instead to try to build a diving bell on his own.

Before starting that project, however, Momsen came up with another idea around 1928 for a self-contained breathing apparatus that allowed people to move around underwater untethered. It consisted of two tubes, a bag, a mouthpiece, a nose clip, and some soda lime to filter out carbon dioxide. As with every one of his innovations, Momsen used himself as a test subject first. During this experimental phase, the Momsen Lung, as journalists dubbed it, enabled its creator to go down to the equivalent of about 300 feet below the water's surface.

To test the lung in actual undersea conditions, Momsen built his first crude diving bell. When newspaper reporters heard about what he was trying to do, they wrote of his determination to save trapped submarine crews. The Navy—which until then had been unaware of Momsen's activities—finally came through with some funding and officially sanctioned his work, albeit somewhat grudgingly.

Momsen's success with the lung earned him approval to develop and test his diving bell. Twice during the course of his experiments he nearly lost his own life. By around 1930, however, he had worked out the bugs and had a finished product. Yet the Navy declined to name the bell after him, deciding instead to call it the McCann Rescue Chamber. (Even the Momsen Lung was known in the Navy by a different name, the Submarine Escape Appliance.) Momsen was rewarded with the Distinguished Service Medal and the knowledge that the Navy was providing every submarine in the fleet with both Momsen Lungs and the type of escape hatches required for diving bell rescues.

Momsen spent the early 1930s training the Navy personnel in the use of the Momsen Lung and diving bell before joining the crew of the *Augusta,* a heavy cruiser assigned to patrol the waters off Asia. By late 1937, he was back in the United States, working at the Washington Navy Yard as head of an experimental deep-sea diving unit. It was here that he came up with another innovation aimed at helping prevent the bends, an extremely painful and sometimes fatal condition caused by the presence of too much nitrogen in the blood. If a diver has been in deep water for a long period of time and then tries to surface too quickly, gas bubbles are released into body tissues. This is turn causes severe joint pain and may affect the brain to the point where a diver cannot think clearly.

To combat the bends, Momsen developed a helium-oxygen mixture for divers to breathe. Early on in his experiments, he encountered some unexpected problems. But after conducting numerous tests over the span of many months, he finally hit upon the correct proportions in his helium-oxygen mixture that allowed divers to go down deeper and stay there for longer periods of time without ill effect.

Momsen and all of his innovations proved to be invaluable in a dramatic submarine rescue in 1939. On May 23 of that year, a new submarine called the *Squalus* was on a test run out of Portsmouth, New Hampshire, with 59 men aboard when it sank to the floor of the Atlantic Ocean, about 240 feet below the surface. Many hours passed before the Navy even knew the ship was missing.

Despite bad weather and some initial uncertainty over the exact location of the *Squalus,* Momsen was called upon to direct a rescue operation using his new equipment. It was the first time most of it had ever been put to the test in such a life-and-death situation. Thirty-nine hours later, 33 men who had been on board the *Squalus* were brought to safety via Momsen's diving bell. The remaining men could not be rescued; they had drowned when part of the submarine flooded at the time of the grounding. Meanwhile, the country had followed the story with great interest and trepidation as Navy personnel struggled against the odds to save their comrades beneath the sea.

As the first survivors reached the ship from which Momsen was directing their rescue, one of the inventor's colleagues made note of his strikingly calm demeanor. Yet as Peter Maas recounted in his book *The Terrible Hours: The Man Behind the Greatest Submarine Rescue in History,* he was anything but relaxed. "Perhaps I tried to appear calm, but to me this was the most exciting moment in my life," Momsen later wrote of the historic event in his personal notes. "Eleven years of preparation, combating skepticism and trying to anticipate all sorts of possible disasters—and then to have it telescoped into this one moment. Who could stay calm?" Momsen was subsequently involved in the salvaging of the *Squalus,* a difficult undertaking in and of itself.

Just a few months after the *Squalus* incident, World War II broke out in Europe. The tremendous significance of Momsen's achievement was therefore soon forgotten amid the other pressing news of the day. At the time the Japanese bombed Pearl Harbor and the United States entered the conflict in December 1941, he was already in Hawaii working as the operations officer of the Commandant Fourteenth Naval District. He remained in the Pacific theater, first organizing and then serving as the assistant chief of staff of the Hawaiian Sea Frontier.

Eventually, Momsen was promoted to captain and named head of Submarine Squadron Two. In this capacity, he came up with new submarine warfare tactics. He also put his life on the line one more time when the Navy began having problems with torpedoes that failed to explode on contact. Momsen himself dove into the water and retrieved one of the so-called "duds." Though he could have been blown up, he examined the torpedo and figured out how to fix it. He was later awarded the Legion of Merit for his efforts.

Not all of Momsen's accomplishments were quite so death-defying. In 1943 he was put in charge of reorganizing the Navy's notoriously inefficient mail system. Within three months, he had straightened out the difficulties. Later he was promoted to rear admiral and appointed assistant chief of naval operations for under-sea warfare.

During the early 1950s, before the end of the Korean War, Momsen came up with his last great invention, a new kind of submarine for the age of nuclear power. Because of his past experience in dealing with the Navy bureaucracy, Momsen decided to resort to a somewhat novel tactic when he pitched his idea to his superiors. He suggested they develop the vessel as a practice target for submarine hunter-groups. They found that acceptable and allowed development of the new submarine to proceed.

Older submarines had been able to stay underwater for long periods time, but they were behemoths that could neither move fast nor maneuver well. Momsen's radical new design was shaped like a fish. His prototype version, the *Albacore*, was completed in 1953, and it proved to be speedier and more nimble than any of its predecessors. Once it had demonstrated its prowess, it changed the direction of submarine technology and became the standard for most modern vessels.

Momsen retired from the Navy in 1955 with the rank of vice admiral. He then went to work as a consultant for companies interested in tapping into the ocean's mineral resources. Momsen died of cancer on May 25, 1967, in St. Petersburg, Florida. He was survived by his wife, Anne, and their two children. His son, Charles B. Momsen, Jr., followed in his father's footsteps and worked for the Navy in submarine research and development.

Momsen's legacy lives on in the diving innovations he developed that continue to be used every day. His helium-oxygen mixture, for example, is what deep-sea divers still use in their tanks to prevent the bends. Yet it was his invention of the diving bell and the subsequent rescue of the 33 men trapped aboard the *Squalus* that truly earned him a place in the pantheon of American heroes. "He was a Navy officer whom the Navy never really knew what to make of," observed Maas in a *Parade* magazine article on Momsen. "His deceptively composed demeanor disguised an extraordinary combination of visionary, scientist and man of action. He saw and dreamed things nobody else did—and made them a reality. Above all, however, [Momsen] was a human being who profoundly cared for his fellow man."

Sources

➤ **Books**

Maas, Peter, *The Terrible Hours: The Man Behind the Greatest Submarine Rescue in History*, HarperCollins, 1999 (opening quote).

➤ **Periodicals**

Minneapolis Star-Tribune, December 12, 1999, p. 14F.
New York Times, May 24, 1939; May 25, 1939.
Parade, September 26, 1999, pp. 4-5.
Saturday Evening Post, September 23, 1967.
Washington Post, October 26, 1999, p. C16.

Constance Baker Motley

"**W**e must not forget that **Brown** *brought down all segregation in the public domain and allowed the South to join twentieth-century America.*"

Born September 14, 1921, in New Haven, Connecticut, attorney Constance Baker Motley fought to abolish racial segregation as a key member of the National Association for the Advancement of Colored People (NAACP) Legal Defense and Educational Fund from the mid-1940s through the mid-1960s. In 1966, she became the first black woman named to a federal judgeship. Address: U.S. District Court, U.S. Courthouse, 500 Pearl St., New York, NY 10007-1316.

One of the unsung heroines of the American civil rights movement, Constance Baker Motley toiled for 20 years as an attorney for the Legal Defense and Educational Fund of the National Association for the Advancement of Colored People (NAACP). She played a role in most of the significant civil rights litigation of the 1940s, 1950s, and 1960s, battling racism and sexism. In courtrooms across the South, she met with both curiosity and hostility as a female lawyer from New York City who also happened to be black. Yet her thorough knowledge of the law, as well as her determined and direct nature, allowed Motley to rise above the emotional issues at hand and triumph in a series of cases that changed the course of U.S. history.

A native of New Haven, Connecticut, Constance Baker Motley was born in 1921, the ninth of 12 children. Her parents, Rachel Keziah Huggins Baker and Willoughby Alva Baker, had both immigrated to the United States from the Caribbean island of Nevis. Willoughby Baker worked as a chef at a private club affiliated with Yale University, and his modest earnings meant that the family usually had to struggle to make ends meet. Yet he and his wife aspired to a genteel, upper-middle-class existence in the British colonial style of their homeland.

Because her parents tended to socialize only with other blacks from the West Indies, Motley was largely unfamiliar with the African American experience until she reached high school and took classes that helped spark her interest in political affairs, race relations, black history, and, above all, the law. (She knew by the age of 15 that she wanted to be a lawyer.) During this same period, she also became involved in a variety of church and civic activities that brought her into contact with black people outside her family circle.

After graduating from high school with honors in 1939, Motley was able to attend college with the help of a local white businessman and philanthropist who had heard her speak at a community meeting and was impressed by her poise and intelligence. As a student at Fisk University in Nashville, Tennessee, she majored in economics and also gained a much deeper understanding of the problems blacks faced in a southern state with strict segregation laws. As a result, Motley developed a sense of solidarity with African Americans that she had never felt before.

Motley left Fisk in 1942 and completed her undergraduate studies at New York University the following year. She then enrolled in

Columbia University Law School in 1944 and graduated two years later.

Motley's legal career began in 1945 when the NAACP hired her to work for the group's Legal Defense and Educational Fund (LDF). Formed in 1939 to lead the NAACP's battle in the courts against segregation and discrimination, the LDF was headed by Thurgood Marshall, who would later become the first African American to serve as a U.S. Supreme Court justice.

The LDF was at that time challenging the "separate but equal" standard established in 1896 by the U.S. Supreme Court in the *Plessy v. Ferguson* case. In that ruling, the Court maintained that the state of Louisiana had the constitutional right to segregate railroad cars as long as the accommodations for blacks were "equal" to those for whites. The decision essentially legalized the concept of racial segregation and allowed it to flourish, especially across the southern United States.

Racial segregation in public schools was the LDF's chief target. Throughout the late 1940s and early 1950s, it filed one lawsuit after another charging that so-called "equal" facilities were inherently unequal by virtue of their separateness and therefore unconstitutional. As assistant counsel for the LDF beginning in 1949, Motley worked behind the scenes on virtually every one the cases. She conducted the necessary research, helped devise strategy, and prepared numerous briefs and other legal papers. The steady onslaught of litigation slowly but surely chipped away at racial segregation. The LDF's meticulous preparation and documentation soon became legendary in legal circles, as did their successes.

In 1950, Motley prepared the draft complaint for the case that evolved into one of the most famous antidiscrimination lawsuits in U.S. history—*Brown v. Board of Education of Topeka, Kansas.* Following several favorable Supreme Court rulings in cases involving discrimination at the college and university level, black parents had begun pressuring the NAACP to take action against segregation in the nation's public elementary and secondary schools. By 1951, five such cases had been filed across the country in different jurisdictions; when they reached the U.S. Supreme Court in 1952, they were consolidated under one name.

The LDF staff researched and prepared for *Brown* as they had never done before. Motley and her colleagues worked with a team of lawyers, psychologists, sociologists, historians, and others to formulate arguments for a case they knew even then would be a historic one. Their strategy was to demonstrate that segregation fostered feelings of inferiority in black children and thus had a harmful psychological effect on their ability to learn. "Defeat never entered my mind. . . ," Motley later declared in her autobiography, *Equal Justice Under Law.* "We all believed that our time had come and that we had to go forward. . . ."

Finally, on May 17, 1954, the U.S. Supreme Court ruled unanimously in favor of the LDF. While it did not expressly overturn *Plessy v. Ferguson,* the *Brown* ruling more or less signaled the end of public segregation in the United States. Yet in the aftermath of this stunning victory, Motley was often depressed as she contemplated how difficult it would be to implement the decision. In the South especially, there was ample evidence to indicate people were not about to accept integration willingly—or peacefully.

Throughout the rest of the decade and well into the 1960s, massive and often violent resistance to school desegregation did indeed occur in a number of southern states. Motley and the LDF became involved in scores of lawsuits filed by the NAACP, among them the infamous Little Rock, Arkansas, case in 1957 that ultimately prompted President Dwight Eisenhower to call in federal troops to protect nine black high school students who had to walk past an angry white mob to attend class. Motley played a key role in several other major cases during this same period, including one at the University of Georgia, where black students Charlayne Hunter (later a radio and television news reporter under the name Charlayne Hunter-Gault) and Hamilton Holmes sought admission. Beginning in 1961, Motley also took the lead in the case of James Meredith, who had been shut out of the University of Mississippi.

All of this activity coincided with the emergence of the civil rights movement, which forced a change in the LDF's mission and strategy. In the past, it had focused exclusively on attacking *public* racial discrimination because such cases were easier to support from a legal standpoint. But with the advent of student sit-ins at lunch counters across the South beginning in the early 1960s, the LDF found itself under pressure to spearhead attacks on *private* forms of racial discrimination as well. Before long, it had shifted its efforts from seeking legal redress in the courts to defending civil disobedience.

Motley often led the way in these battles as well. In 1963, for example, she successfully argued for the reinstatement of over 1,000 schoolchildren in Birmingham, Alabama, after the local school board expelled them for participating in massive student demonstrations. She also represented scores of "Freedom Riders" (the name given to people who rode interstate buses to test enforcement of desegregation laws) and served as counsel to Martin Luther King, Jr.

In 1961, Thurgood Marshall left the LDF to accept a federal judgeship. Motley was not chosen to replace him, however, because there was no support for the idea of giving the position to a woman. Instead, she was named to the new job of associate counsel, the second-highest post in the LDF. That same year, she argued her first case before the U.S. Supreme Court and won. All in all, Motley was victorious in nine of the ten cases she eventually tried before the highest court in the land.

Motley's life took a very different turn following the 1963 assassination of civil rights activist and NAACP field representative Medgar Evers. She had worked closely with Evers for several years, and his death left her shaken, angry, and convinced that blacks were paying too high a price to end segregation. She was also eager to spend more time with her husband, Joel Wilson Motley, and their 12-year-old son, Joel, Jr. Therefore, she resigned from the LDF to accept an invitation to run as a Democrat for the New York State Senate in a special election held in February 1964 to fill a vacancy. Motley came out on top, and in November of that same year easily won re-election in her own right. (She was the first black woman ever to serve as a New York State senator.) Once taking office, she concentrated on fighting racial discrimination in the areas of housing, employment, and education.

Motley switched gears politically in February 1965 when she was elected to fill a vacancy in the office of Manhattan borough president, making her the first woman ever elected to head any of the city's five boroughs. (At the time, it was also the highest political post ever held by a black in city government.) Motley stood for election in November 1965 for a full four-year term and won. She soon gained a reputation as one who was more than willing to "rock the boat" when she streamlined her office operations and introduced ambitious plans to redevelop and revitalize underprivileged neighborhoods, improve schools, and expand the local community's involvement in city planning.

An even greater honor came Motley's way in January 1966 when President Lyndon Johnson named her a judge in the U.S. District

Court for the Southern District of New York, the largest trial court in the country. Once again, she broke new ground as the first black woman appointed to the federal bench. However, her nomination encountered vehement opposition from conservative federal judges and politicians across the South. The confirmation process dragged on for seven months until she was finally approved and sworn into office in September 1966.

Since then, Motley has made a name for herself as a liberal jurist. Civil rights litigation accounts for a large percentage of her caseload. Many have been lawsuits filed by women, Hispanics, the poor, the elderly, the handicapped, and others who were empowered by the landmark Civil Rights Act of 1964 to seek redress for discrimination, especially in the area of employment. Motley became chief judge of the District Court in 1982 by virtue of her length of service; four years later, she stepped down upon reaching her sixty-fifth birthday and assumed senior status on the court.

From the perspective of one who has spent more than 50 years in the battle for civil rights, Motley sees the front shifting from the courtroom to the political arena. "Most of the problems blacks now face require political solutions," she told interviewer Floris Barnett Cash in *Notable Black American Women*. "The most pressing need among blacks is the need for greater political power." While she is optimistic that racism will one day cease to be an obstacle to success, she remains concerned about the growing economic underclass (black as well as white) and how its members can ever hope to escape poverty and isolation from mainstream society. As Motley noted in her autobiography, "What to do about those of all racial and ethnic groups left behind by our latest economic revolution will challenge us all."

Sources

➤ Books

Contemporary Black Biography, Volume 10, Gale, 1996.
Motley, Constance Baker, *Equal Justice Under Law: An Autobiography by Constance Baker Motley*, Farrar, Straus & Giroux, 1998 (opening quote).
Smith, Jessie Carney, editor, *Notable Black American Women*, Gale, 1992.
Williams, Jayme Coleman, and McDonald Williams, editors, *The*

Negro Speaks: The Rhetoric of Contemporary Black Leaders, Noble & Noble, 1970.

➤ Periodicals

New Yorker, May 16, 1994, pp. 65-71.
New York Times, January 26, 1966.

Bill Moyers

"What I have sought for 25 years to put on television is the conversation of democracy."

Born June 5, 1934, in Hugo, Oklahoma, Bill Moyers is a television documentarian, aide to Senator-then-President Lyndon B. Johnson, and Baptist minister whose work focuses on socially relevant issues. Address: 76 Fourth Street, Garden City, Long Island, NY 11530.

In his television documentaries produced for PBS and CBS, journalist Bill Moyers insightfully explores life in America and in the world. His intellectual approach to journalism and documentary has garnered Moyers a solid following and numerous awards. Moyers began his career working with President Lyndon B. Johnson, including a stint as his press secretary.

Born Billy Don Moyers on June 5, 1934, in Hugo, Oklahoma, he was the son of John Henry and Ruby (nee Johnson) Moyers. (Moyers later legally changed his name to Bill.) John Henry Moyers worked as a laborer. While Moyers was an infant, the family—which included Moyers' brother—moved to Marshall, Texas, a small town in the northeast corner of the state, near the border of Arkansas, Oklahoma, and Louisiana. Moyers liked listening to radio (later television) journalist Edward R. Murrow, who brought the world into his home in the small town.

In 1948, politician Lyndon B. Johnson spoke in Marshall's town square, and Moyers was present at the speech. He was impressed by the power of Johnson, though he did not hear much of what he said. Soon after, in 1949, Moyers began his career in journalism, working as a cub reporter at the local newspaper, the *News Messenger.* Moyers was still in high school, and moved up the ladder at the paper despite his tender age. After covering some local beats, Moyers became sports editor before graduating.

After graduating from high school in 1952, Moyers attended North Texas State University in Denton, Texas. While working on the university's newspaper during the school year, Moyers spent most of his summers writing for the *News Messenger.* Moyers had already decided that he wanted to be a political journalist. Moyers also spent his college years at North Texas State being active in the Baptist Student Union and student government.

Remembering the power of Johnson's speech, Moyers wrote him a letter while still a student. The letter reached the United States Senator, and in 1954, Moyers spent his summer working for him in Washington, D.C. This was the beginning of a long affiliation with the future president, however inauspicious. Moyers began the summer addressing envelopes before handling the senator's mail.

In 1954, Moyers transferred from North Texas State to the University of Texas at Austin, as recommended by Johnson. There, Moyers continued to focus on journalism. Though Moyers finally left the *News Messenger* behind, he continued to work full time. He became employed by KTBC, a radio and television network in Austin owned by Johnson's wife, Lady Bird, as an assistant news editor.

Moyers was also married that year, to Judith Suzanne Davidson on December 18, 1954. They eventually had three children together: William Cope, Alice Suzanne, and John Davidson. Though Moyers enjoyed his study of journalism, he was beginning to feel a religious call. He was not sure if he wanted to do journalism, politics, or, perhaps, the ministry.

After graduating with a bachelor's degree with honors in journalism in 1956, Moyers won a Rotary fellowship to study in Scotland for a year. He spent the time studying moral philosophy at the University of Edinburgh. When Moyers returned to the United States in 1957, he had a crisis of faith.

Moyers decided to abandon journalism and become a minister. While studying at the Southwestern Baptist Theological Seminary in San Antonio, Texas, Moyers worked in an Oklahoma church. He graduated with a B.D. (bachelors in divinity) in 1959. After spending a short time as lecturer in Christian ethics at Baylor University in Waco, Texas, Moyers had another crisis of faith, deciding that the ministry was not for him. He considered entering graduate school in American Studies, but instead returned to the employ of Johnson.

Moyers became the senator's special assistant from 1959 to 1960, then was his executive assistant during his campaign for the vice presidency in 1960 and after the election in 1961. The idea of public service still appealed to Moyers, however. In 1961, he became the associate director in charge of public affairs for the Peace Corps. The following year he was promoted to deputy director, a post he held for a year. Moyers garnered support for the Corps in Congress as well as from the public.

Moyers again returned to Johnson's side after President John F. Kennedy was assassinated in Dallas, Texas, in November 1963. Moyers had been in Texas at the time, and immediately offered Johnson his support. After Johnson took over the presidency, Moyers became his special assistant and number one aide from 1963-65. Johnson himself ran for president in 1964, and Moyers was instrumental in developing the president's Great Society slate of social programs as well as an aggressive campaign against Republican opponent Barry Goldwater.

In 1965, Moyers was promoted to press secretary, a position he held through December 1966. He left the Johnson administration when the war in Vietnam escalated because Moyers was against increased American involvement. Although Johnson did not want him to leave despite the disagreement, Moyers returned to print journalism.

Moyers was hired by *Newsday*, a Long Island-based publication, as its publisher in 1970. Before Moyers, the paper had a conservative bent and was somewhat unsuccessful. He changed the face and organization of the paper, bringing in new people and making it more liberal. The circulation of *Newsday* increased, and won two Pulitzer Prizes, the ultimate journalistic award. When the owner, Harry F. Guggenheim, was ready to sell *Newsday* in 1970, Moyers and others wanted to buy it. Guggenheim refused to sell it to them, and sold it to another group for less. Moyers left the paper soon after.

Moyers stayed in journalism and began doing what he would come to be known for. After leaving *Newsday*, he was approached to write a book on America. He embarked on a cross-country trip and wrote about his findings in 1971's *Listening to America: A Traveler Rediscovers His Country*. Moyers' next move was to television. He had become intrigued by the possibilities of television journalism while working in the Johnson White House, and when he was offered a position at New York City's WNET (National Education Television) in 1971, Moyers took the job without even asking about the salary.

Moyers became the host of *The Week*, a public affairs broadcast. The adjustment was hard for Moyers, but he soon thrived in the environment. By 1972, the program evolved into *Bill Moyers' Journal* and was aired on the Educational Broadcasting Corp. (later known as Public Broadcasting System, or PBS). As editor in chief of the show, Moyers shaped its content. *Bill Moyers' Journal* featured thoughtful interviews with intellectuals and episodes just about ideas, combining news with documentary. Moyers developed a reputation for respecting the humanity of his subjects while asking hard questions. The show did not just focus on national stories, but also on regional and local events.

In 1974, Moyers left the show for a while, and did a weekly column for *Newsweek* for a year. When he returned, the program was renamed *Bill Moyers' Journal: International Report*. It changed its focus to international issues, though still with intellectuals and ideas. CBS had been trying to recruit Moyers for its commercial broadcasts for several years, and finally succeeded in luring him away in 1976.

Moyers became the editor and chief reporter for *CBS Reports*, a forum for many of his documentaries. His 1977 documentary, *The Fire Next Door*, won several awards. Moyers' work for CBS was somewhat controversial. CBS wanted to tone down his report on baby food sold to third world countries for fear of offending advertisers. It was re-edited, though the report still ran. Another controversial piece was also very important. In *The Vanishing Family: Crisis in Black America*, Moyers had a lot of good material and wanted 90 minutes instead of the allotted 60. He threatened to quit to get the extra time he wanted. The documentary was very acclaimed; Michael Novak of *National Review* called it "one of the bravest TV documentaries ever made."

Because Moyers had so many problems working with CBS and because he wanted a weekly forum for his ideas, he returned to PBS in 1979, where he revived *Bill Moyers' Journal*. But all was not perfect at PBS: funding and time were big issues there. Moyers' documentaries were expensive and time consuming. Moyers explained the dilemma to an unnamed writer for *Broadcasting*, "I prefer the role of teacher and illuminator and there's not time available to do that on a regular basis. I understand the dynamic behind commercial broadcasting—the need to reach the largest possible audience, which means you have to go to a lower common denominator."

In 1981, Moyers returned to CBS for a five-year stint as a senior news analyst for *CBS Evening News*. He also did other jobs for CBS throughout the 1980s—including reports for *Our Times* and *Crossroads*, two CBS magazine series that featured the kind of documentaries Moyers did. Moyers' work was again controversial in the White House of Ronald Reagan. They perceived that he was trying to undermine them with stories like *People Like Us* which showed four families suffering because of welfare cuts.

While still at CBS, Moyers occasionally produced programs with PBS such as 1983's *Our Times with Bill Moyers*. In 1986, Moyers again began working for public television full-time after CBS became more entertainment than hard news oriented. He formed a production company with his wife, called Public Affairs TV, Inc. It produced the kind of documentaries and public affairs programming for public television that Moyers had been doing all along for PBS, and more. Moyers was now free to do long documentary series that explored big social, historical, and intellectual ideas.

Between 1986 and 1991, Public Affairs TV produced 136 hours of television. Early titles included *Bill Moyers: In Search of the Constitution* (1987); *Moyers: God and Politics* (1987); *A Walk Through the Twentieth Century with Bill Moyers*, a social history of America;

Marshall, Texas, Marshall, Texas, a documentary about whites and blacks and segregation in his hometown.

Later documentaries also included extremely successful companion books. In 1988, Moyers produced *The Secret Government* about the Iran-Contra scandal during the Reagan administration. He also simultaneously published a book under the same name. *Joseph Campbell and the Power of Myth* (1988) was a six-part documentary on one of the most influential but unknown professors of mythology and religion. The documentary attracted an audience of 30 million people, and the book was on the best seller lists for 74 weeks.

By early 1990s, there was some talk of Moyers running for political office himself, the presidency perhaps, but it did not happen. Instead, he continued to produce documentaries on a wide range of ideas. In 1993, he did a five-part series entitled *Healing and the Mind* on Eastern medicine, nontraditional therapies, and the connection between emotional and physical response. This was a huge ratings success. However, not all of Moyers' documentaries were successful. In 1995, he did *The Language of Life,* an eight-part documentary on poetry and the poetry subculture, readings and workshops. It was not as successful as most of Moyers' work.

In 1995, Moyers returned to commercial broadcasting with a brief stint on NBC and related networks. He worked as a news analyst for *NBC's Nightly News with Tom Brokaw* and hosted *Internight* on MSNBC beginning in 1996. Moyers continued to produce his documentaries for PBS, and several were rather personal. In 1996, he produced two on religious topics: *The Wisdom of Faith,* a five-part series about different religions, and *Genesis: A Living Conversation,* which in its 10 parts discusses the first book of the Bible. In 1998, he did an even more personal story, one involving his own family. *Moyers on Addition: Close to Home* talked about addiction to drugs and alcohol, something his eldest son had been struggling with for many years.

Over the course of his career, Moyers won almost every major and minor award for his kind of work, including four Peabody Awards. In 1995, he was inducted into the Television Hall of Fame. As Frank McConnell of *Commonweal* writes, "He's as much a public intellectual, serious and sensitive, as TV has so far produced. And 'public intellectual' is an honorable role."

Sources

➤ Books

Encyclopedia of World Biography, volume 11, second edition, Gale Group, 1998, pp. 214-16.
Mooney, Louise, editor, *Newsmakers: 1991 Cumulation,* Gale Research, 1991, pp. 290-93.

➤ Periodicals

Broadcasting, November 19, 1984, p. 95.
Broadcasting & Cable, February 6, 1995, p. 30.
Christianity Today, October 28, 1996, p. 28.
Commonweal, March 27, 1998, p. 20.
Fortune, January 18, 1988, p. 165; July 29, 1991, p. 177.
Insight on the News, July 22, 1996, p. 37.
The Nation, December 14, 1985, p. 639.
National Review, February 28, 1986, p. 47; March 10, 1989, p. 22.
New Republic, September 23, 1986, p. 9; August 19, 1991, p. 22.
Newsweek, October 21, 1996, p. 74.
Nieman Reports, Fall 1997, p. 49.
People Weekly, November 27, 1989, p. 64; March 15, 1993, p. 63.
Time, January 24, 1983, p. 68; April 7, 1986, p. 84; May 30, 1994, p. 21; October 28, 1996, p. 31, 66 (opening quote).
U.S. News & World Report, October 14, 1996, p. 69.

Luis Muñoz Marín

"I learned there is a wisdom among the people in the towns and countryside which education may lead, but cannot improve. I taught many of them something, but they taught me more."

Born February 18, 1898, in San Juan, Puerto Rico, Luis Muñoz Marín was the first freely elected governor of Puerto Rico and a significant figure in its becoming a commonwealth of the United States. He died April 30, 1980.

A significant figure in the politics of Puerto Rico, Luis Muñoz Marín's importance to the shaping of the modern state of Puerto Rico cannot be underestimated. In addition to his long stint as governor of Puerto Rico—1949 through 1965—it was Muñoz Marín who worked to get the island commonwealth status with the United States. Muñoz Marín believed the United States would be key to the future of Puerto Rico, and for better and worse, he has been proven correct.

Born José Luís Alberto Muñoz Marín on February 18, 1898, in San Juan, Puerto Rico, he was the only child of Luis Muñoz Rivera and Amalia Marín. Known as the George Washington of Puerto Rico, Luis Muñoz Rivera was an important political figure in the history of the island in his own right. Muñoz Rivera had been instrumental in getting Puerto Rico out from under Spain's control as a colonial possession. The year that Muñoz Marín was born, Puerto Rico was transferred to United States' rule as a result of the Spanish-American War. Muñoz Rivera also founded and owned a newspaper, *La Democracia*. Muñoz Marín's grandfather, Luís Ramon Muñoz Barios, had also been a politician.

Muñoz Marín spent the first three years of his life in Puerto Rico. When he was three years old, his family moved to New York City, where his father ran a newspaper about Puerto Rico, *Puerto Rico Herald*. The family returned to Puerto Rico when Muñoz Marín was eight years old. Muñoz Rivera was a minister in the first free government of the island. In 1910, Muñoz Rivera was sent to Washington, D.C., to represent Puerto Rico as resident commissioner. His wife and son accompanied him.

Muñoz Marín completed his education at a local boarding school, Georgetown University's prep school. His parents separated when he was a teenager, and Muñoz Marín spent a lot of time with his father, helping him learn English and write speeches. Like his father, Muñoz Marín enjoyed poetry and was given the nickname, "El Vate" or "The Bard." He also wrote essays. Muñoz Marín graduated from prep school in 1915, and he entered Georgetown University Law School the following fall.

When his father fell ill in 1916, Muñoz Marín returned to Puerto Rico with him. Muñoz Rivera died in 1916. After his father's death, Muñoz Marín returned to Washington, D.C., where he worked as the secretary for his father's successor, Félix Córdova Dávila. While holding down his day job, Muñoz Marín began working on his own writing. He submitted some of his father's writing for publication as well. He published two books in this time period: 1917's *Borrones*

(*Ink Blots*), which included a play as well as essays; and 1918's *Madre Haraposa* (*Mother in Rags*).

In 1918, Muñoz Marín moved to New York City to work as a poet and journalist. He took some playwrighting classes at Columbia University, and published poems in leading literary magazines. Muñoz Marín also founded a magazine of his own, *The Review of the Indies* (*La Revista de Indias*), which focused on the culture of Latin America. While living in New York City, Muñoz Marín married Muna Lee, an American poet and translator from Mississippi, on July 1, 1919. The couple eventually had two children, daughter Munita and son Luis Munóz Lee.

While maintaining his primary residence in New York City, Muñoz Marín returned to Puerto Rico for short stints throughout the 1920s. He became involved in the politics of the island, and his first political affiliation was with Puerto Rico's Socialist Party. When he returned to New York City from 1922 through 1926, Muñoz Marín wrote some articles about Puerto Rico and its struggles for important publications. In 1926, he came back to Puerto Rico to edit *La Democracia*, the paper his father had founded, for a year before going back to New York. Four years later, Muñoz Marín came back to Puerto Rico, again to work as an editor at his father's paper, but this time, he and his family stayed permanently.

In 1932, Muñoz Marín again became involved in politics. He was co-founder of the Liberal Party with others who had been part of the Union Party. At the time, he promoted independence for Puerto Rico, though his position on this subject would later change. Elections were held that year, and though the Liberal Party did not win the election as a whole, Muñoz Marín did win a seat in the Puerto Rican Senate. He had the opportunity to become Puerto Rico's next resident commissioner and return to the United States, but declined the offer. Puerto Rico was now his home.

With another official (Carlos Chardón, who was the chancellor of the University of Puerto Rico), Muñoz Marín came up with the Chardón Plan in the early 1930s. This was an economic plan for Puerto Rico. In 1935, the Chardón Plan was used by the Puerto Rican Reconstruction Administration. The U.S. government gave $70 million to make it work. This came about because Muñoz Marín had met with American President Franklin D. Roosevelt and his wife Eleanor in 1933, telling them about the problems on the island. Mrs. Roosevelt actually came to the island to see for herself in 1934. Later, President Roosevelt put Muñoz Marín on a commission to organize Puerto Rico's future.

In the mid-1930s, problems developed within the Liberal Party. There was tension between Muñoz Marín and the more conservative elements in the party. The United States was considering independence for Puerto Rico, but without solutions to the economic problems. Muñoz Marín did not want independence under these conditions, and for his opinions, was kicked out in 1937.

The following year, Muñoz Marín was a key organizer (and later head) of the Popular Democrat Party (Partido Popular Democrático, or PDP). The party's slogan was "Bread, land and liberty." Muñoz Marín and the PDP believed in the peasant, the common man and woman. They called for both economic and social reforms that would improve their lives. They focused on issues such as reforming land laws, and increasing the availability of medical services, electricity, and schools for the poor. PDP also wanted a closer relationship with the United States. It soon became one of Puerto Rico's major political parties.

In 1940 and 1944, Muñoz Marín was elected to the Puerto Rican Senate on the PDP ticket. One of his campaign promises was self-rule for Puerto Rico. He urged peasants who usually sold their votes for a significant amount of money to better their lives and vote for him instead, which they did. When he got into office, he and the PDP kept their promises. Muñoz Marín's popularity increased.

The United States decided in 1947 to allow Puerto Rico to elect their own governor. The following year, Muñoz Marín became Puerto Rico's first freely elected governor. As his political career was evolving, his personal life was also transforming. Muñoz Marín and his first wife divorced in 1947. Ines María Mendoza de Palacios had become his common law wife in 1940. After the divorce, the couple officially married and had two children, daughters Viviana and Victoria. The latter followed her father into politics and became a Puerto Rican senator.

Puerto Rico's status within the United States was also changing. By the late 1940s, Muñoz Marín did not want Puerto Rico to be another American state or an independent entity, but a commonwealth. This plan was accepted by the United States in 1950, and a constitution was drafted. But not all in Puerto Rico agreed with Muñoz Marín. There were assassination attempts on him as well as the president of the United States, Harry S. Truman. Despite their protests, Puerto Rico's commonwealth status became official in 1952. Commonwealth status meant that Puerto Rico had American military protection, some funding, and at least one representative in

Washington, but citizens did not pay federal taxes and could not vote for the president or Congress.

Muñoz Marín was re-elected governor twice in 1952 and 1956. He proposed another economic plan, one that expanded on the Chardón Plan. Called "Operation Bootstrap," Muñoz Marín proposed giving American businesses tax incentives and other perks to start or transfer their businesses to Puerto Rico. The plan became a model for other developing countries.

There were some vocal critics of Muñoz Marín's work, however. Some thought that the commonwealth status was a sham, and Puerto Rico should be free. Others said that between the commonwealth status and Operation Bootstrap, Puerto Rico was more dependent on the United States than ever. Critics also pointed out that while businesses were brought to the island, resources and revenues were also taken away. Puerto Rican companies' growth would be limited because they did not have the same breaks. These arguments were proven out to some degree because when the economy went sour, many companies did leave the country. By the 1960s, chronic unemployment in Puerto Rico was blamed on Operation Bootstrap.

Despite such problems, in 1963, Muñoz Marín was given the Presidential Medal of Freedom for all he did accomplish in Puerto Rico. But Muñoz Marín decided he had enough of the governership. He chose not to run again in 1964, though his many supporters wanted to nominate him again. Instead, he was elected to the Puerto Rican Senate, where he served through 1970.

After leaving politics, Muñoz Marín spent two years in Italy working on his autobiography and memoirs. When he returned in 1972, Muñoz Marín did not run again for office, but used his influence to renew the fortunes of the faltering PDP. He ensured their candidate was elected governor. Muñoz Marín retired from the political scene entirely in 1975, and he died on April 30, 1980. Two years after his death, his *Memorias, 1898-1940* was published.

Sources

➤ **Books**

Columbia Encyclopedia, Columbia University Press, 1993.
Encyclopedia of World Biography, volume 11, Gale Group, 1999.

Foner, Eric and John A. Garraty, editors, *The Reader's Companion to American History*, Houghton Mifflin Company, 1991.

Garraty, John A. and Mark C. Carnes, editors, *American National Biography*, volume 16, Oxford University Press, 1999.

Mann, Peggy, *Luis Muñoz Marín: The Man Who Remade Puerto Rico*, Coward, McCann & Geoghegan, Inc., 1976 (opening quote).

Meyer, Nicholas E., *The Biographical Dictionary of Hispanic Americans*, Facts on File, Inc., 1997.

➤ **Periodicals**

The Atlanta Journal and Constitution, December 13, 1998, p. A16.

Pablo Neruda

"Poetry is an act of peace."

> Born in 1904 in Parral, Chile, Pablo Neruda became his country's most celebrated literary and political figure. He died September 23, 1973, of heart failure in Santiago, Chile.

Winner of the 1971 Nobel Prize in literature, Pablo Neruda was not just Latin America's greatest living poet, but an ardent political activist who used his celebrity to call attention to social injustice. As a diplomat, senator, and leading citizen, Neruda denounced leaders of his and other South American countries whose policies helped maintain a sense of colonialism well into the twentieth century.

The poet took the pen name "Pablo Neruda" at the age of 14, and formally changed it in 1946. He was born Ricardo Eliezer Neftali Reyes y Basoalto on July 12, 1904, in Parral, Chile. Parral was situated in Chile's fertile wine-growing region, but his father, a railroad crew foreman, moved the family much further south to Temuco not long after the death of his wife from tuberculosis. A frontier settlement, Temuco was surrounded by dense woods and volcanoes, and the fantastical natural beauty made a deep impression on Neruda, even at an early age.

From his youth, Neruda was also interested in the plight of Chile's poorer classes. These included the Araucunian Indians in Temuco, who had been pushed south by the Spanish conquistadors in previous centuries, and still encountered discrimination from contemporary Chileans as well. An indifferent student, sometimes Neruda went to work with his father, and here he came to know the peasants and ex-convicts who quarried rocks for a living, men "made of iron," as he recalled in his *Memoirs.* He also developed a fascination with insects and the animal world in general. Once, he found a swan that had been beaten, and tried to nurse it back to health. For three weeks, he carried it daily to the river, and tried to teach it to fish for itself again. "But its sad eyes wandered off into the distance," he recalled, and the graceful bird eventually died in his arms.

Clearly Neruda was a dreamer, unlike other children, and sickly and frail as well for some years. His first attempts at poetry were encouraged by a local teacher in Temuco, Gabriela Mistral, who would later achieve some renown herself as a writer. By the time he was in his teens, his poetry was being published in local newspapers, though he had already adopted the Neruda pseudonym to avoid trouble with his family, who tried to discourage his literary ambitions. At the age of 16, Neruda entered a teachers' training school in Santiago, Chile's bustling capital. He loved the city and its rich array of diversions, lived in a rooming house and met other young poets, artists, and intellectuals, and again did rather poorly in his studies.

Neruda made a name for himself in 1921 when he won Santiago's Spring Festival poetry prize that year. His first volume was published as a result, *La cancion de la fiesta*, and he was heralded as a gifted young poet. Two years later, a second volume, *Crepusculario*, appeared, but he still had to sell his few pieces of furniture to pay for its printing. *Crepusculario*, which he later dismissed but scholars of his work value, was marked by a quiet tone and the use of conventional language. It had some surrealist tinges to it, but Neruda was also influenced by Walt Whitman during this period of his life. The volume was outside of the Latin American *Ultraismo* movement, but Neruda's verse soon moved toward it, and came fully to bloom with *Veinte poemas de amor y una cancion desesperada* ("Twenty Love Poems and a Song of Despair"), his acclaimed 1924 work. Concretely surrealist, the poems here are deeply passionate, and celebrate life in all its sensuous forms. A great success, it became a best seller, and was followed by several other volumes of poetry during the decade.

Many Latin American nations offered their poets honorary consulships abroad as an expression of official esteem, and in 1927 Neruda departed for Myanmar, then part of the British Empire. Posted in Rangoon, Neruda spoke little English, and was initially shocked by the squalor of urban life both there and then in Sri Lanka and Indonesia, his next postings. In 1930, he married Maruca Hagenaar Vogelzang, in Bali, with whom he would have a daughter who did not survive her childhood. On the two-month sea voyage back to Chile in 1932, he began writing verse for his most acclaimed work, *Residencia en la tierra*, published in two volumes beginning the next year; a third part, *Tercera residencia*, appeared in 1947. Translated as "Residence on Earth," the poems in this opus, heralded as the work of a contemporary Latin American master, reflect Neruda's impressions of a bleak, senseless world, one in which natural beauty and harmony have been ruined by civilization. The volume earned him international acclaim as well.

After 1933, Neruda was again posted as a diplomat, first in Buenos Aires, then to Thailand, Cambodia, and finally Spain in 1935. Here he was thrilled to find himself amidst Madrid's emerging Republican movement, and his work was already appreciated by these and other leftist-leaning European intellectuals. Neruda and a wildly popular Andalusian poet, Federico Garcia Lorca, founded a literary magazine with others, but they were forced to close it down when the Spanish Civil War erupted in 1936. The election of a leftist government that year launched an attack by a coalition of disenchanted conservative elements in Spain, led by

Fascist dictator Generalissimo Francisco Franco. The immediate violence and brutality of the civil strife forever politicized Neruda; even the famous Garcia Lorca was slain by members of Franco's army. Without receiving confirmation from the Santiago government, he declared Chile on the side of the Republicans, who had much support from Communist and Socialist groups around the world. He also wrote *Espana en el corazon: Himno a las glorias del pueblo en la guerra* ("Spain in the Heart: Hymn to the Glories of the People at War"), which enjoyed a legendary first press run at the hands of inspired Republican soldiers on the battlefield.

As a result, Neruda was recalled to Santiago, but was soon sent to Paris to help organize the Congress of Anti-Fascist Writers, and then began working to resettle Spanish refugees in Chile. The older Chilean diplomats in the Paris consulate thought this a terrible idea, and treated those who came to complete the necessary papers quite badly. They even shut off the elevator. Often, the visitors to Neruda's office at the consulate were ordinary workers maimed during the Spanish Civil War. "It broke my heart to see them come up to the fourth floor with such painful effort, while the cruel officials gloated over my difficulties," he wrote in his *Memoirs.*

During the early 1940s, Neruda served as the Chilean consul in Mexico City and, by the time he returned to his homeland in 1944, had officially joined Chile's growing Communist Party. Despite his many years abroad, little had changed in Chile in the interim: there were elegant avenues and residential sections in the cities, but crushing poverty in squalid suburban encampments and the arid mining regions of the countryside. In 1945, troubled mine workers from Antofagasta and Tarapacá asked him to run for a seat in the national senate, and he agreed.

The Antofagasta and Tarapacá areas were much like fiefdoms run by foreign corporations, who had been granted virtual free rein in the area through deals with the Chilean leadership. Copper, nitrate, and other minerals were extracted by Chilean peasants, who were forbidden any political representation. There were no political parties allowed, entry into these hardscrabble regions was difficult for an outsider to obtain, and the workers were paid in currency minted by the companies. The effort to unionize alone had cost many lives. Not surprisingly, Neruda became an outspoken champion for his constituency. A newly elected president launched reprisals against the Communist Party and, more brutally, against striking miners, and Neruda became his eloquent foe on the senate floor. He denounced the regime, was threatened with arrest, and went into hiding; from there he sent letters to the newspapers condemning the elected leadership, accusing it of selling the country outright to foreigners.

Facing indictment, Neruda fled the country for several years, and traveled extensively, including sojourns in the Soviet Union and China. He returned to Chile in 1953, and the events of the past decade had firmed his commitment to communism as a means of alleviating the suffering and hopelessness of the poor. This determination was reflected in his poetry, most notably with what many critics consider his masterpiece, *Canto general* ("General Song"), made available to the Spanish world in 1950. Its theme is justice in the New World, and its 340 poems recite a litany of Chilean and South American history, culture, and conquests. One celebrated section about the abandoned mountain city of Machu Picchu, the last Inca stronghold in Peru, even merited separate publication.

Throughout the next three decades, Neruda enjoyed a reputation as Chile's most respected literary figure. He lived on an oceanside retreat, Isla Negra, from which he wrote, but maintained a delightfully eccentric modern house in Valparaiso, where he entertained other renowned cultural and political figures. He married Matilde Urrutia in 1951, a well-known Chilean singer who became the subject of some of his verse. As his awareness of the lives and culture of the working class and rural poor grew, he entered a new literary phase, marked by a distinct stylistic shift. Beginning with the 1954 work *Odas elementales,* he wrote short paeans to ordinary objects and their beauty, such as air, the ocean, or even the pure wonder of a lemon or a taste of salt.

In addition to a growing number of volumes to his credit, Neruda also penned a five-volume memoir in verse, published on his sixtieth birthday in 1964, and served as president of the Union of Chilean Writers for several years. Still an ardent communist, he was nominated as a presidential candidate for the 1970 elections, but when the five leftist parties allied around leading Socialist candidate Salvador Allende, he withdrew and gave the coalition his support. After taking office, Allende named Neruda Chile's ambassador to France, and it was there that the poet learned he had been awarded the 1971 Nobel Prize for literature.

Neruda knew Fidel Castro and Ché Guevara, and continued to denounce American meddling in Chile, which reached its apogee in early September of 1973, when a military coup ousted Allende; Senate hearings in Washington later revealed that the Central Intelligence Agency had played a large part in the overthrow of the world's first freely elected Marxist government. Allende died under suspicious circumstances during the battle, and Neruda's residences were ransacked by soldiers. He was already ailing from prostate cancer, and died of heart failure after an operation at a Santiago hospital on September 23, 1973.

Sources

➤ **Books**

Neruda, Pablo, *Memoirs,* translated from the Spanish by Hardie St. Martin, Farrar Straus & Giroux, 1977.
Stainton, Leslie, *Lorca: A Dream of Life,* Farrar Straus & Giroux, 1999.

➤ **Periodicals**

Americas, January/February, 1998, pp. 22-27.

Thich Nhat Hanh

*"*We *have the tendency to run away from suffering and to look for happiness. But, in fact, if you have not suffered, you have no chance to experience real happiness."*

Born October 1926, in central Vietnam, Thich Nhat Hanh is a leading Zen Buddhist teacher, author and peace advocate, working internationally to promote nonviolent social activism since the 1950s. Address: Green Mountain Dharma Center, P.O. Box 182, Hartland Four Corners, VT 05049.

Through his advocacy of "engaged Buddhism," Thich Nhat Hanh has spread a humanitarian message to both world leaders and ordinary citizens across the globe. As a Vietnamese-born Buddhist monk, he watched as his country was torn apart by bitter warfare in the 1950s. Nhat Hanh sought to promote a "third way" between the North and South Vietnamese governments, bringing him into conflict with both sides. Exiled from his native land in 1967, he has gone on to promote change in social consciousness through an awakening of "mindfulness" in the individual. Though still barred from his homeland, he found increased interest in his teaching in the United States and elsewhere during the 1990s.

Nhat Hanh has made the unlikely transition from dealing with the sufferings of Vietnamese war victims to the spiritual afflictions of Western societies. To both, he has urged an engagement with, rather than a retreat from, the troubles of the world. "When you focus on yourself, you find many more problems," he told the *New Yorker*. "Not realizing the suffering around you in the world—I don't think that is a happiness. You feel loneliness and emptiness, and these are more unbearable than other kinds of suffering. The most effective medicine is an experience of the suffering around you. Then you heal."

Nhat Hanh was born in central Vietnam in October, 1926. One of six children, his father worked on village resettlement projects for the Vietnamese government. Growing up during his country's last days as a French colony, he was exposed to great poverty and starvation, which in part motivated him to become a monk at age sixteen. "It was a dream of a little boy to go out and learn Buddhism, to practice Buddhism in order to relieve the suffering of other people in society," he said of himself in a *San Francisco Chronicle* interview. "Later on, when I became a novice monk, I also learned and practiced by this kind of desire."

After completing his novitiate at age twenty, Nhat Hanh became a full monk and assumed the Buddhist title *thich*, an honorific similar to "reverend." His early adult years coincided with the outbreak of the Vietnam War, and as the conflict continued he was increasingly drawn to local Buddhist movements that sought to aid its victims. In 1950, he began working with the An Quang pagoda in Saigon, which advocated an early form of "engaged Buddhism." Ngo Dinh Diem, president of the Republic of Vietnam (South Vietnam), considered such Buddhist groups to be subversive to his government and sought to suppress them. Despite such opposition,

Nhat Hanh continued his activism and founded the School of Youth Social Service (SYSS) in 1964. This organization worked to rebuild bombed villages and establish schools and medical facilities. Gaining strength, the SYSS implemented its community-based program through a team of some 10,000 student volunteers. During this time, Nhat Hanh also furthered the cause by founding Van Hanh Buddhist University in Saigon and by publishing a weekly magazine.

As the Vietnam war continued, Nhat Hanh's advocacy of peace brought him worldwide attention. In 1966, he visited Pope Paul VI to gain the pontiff's support in ending the fighting. That same year he came to the United States, where he met with Defense Secretary Robert McNamara, Senator Edward Kennedy and other government officials. Nhat Hanh also made contact with Dr. Martin Luther King, Jr., who was impressed enough with his message to speak out in opposition of the Vietnam war at a May 1966 news conference in Chicago. The following year, King nominated Nhat Hanh for the Nobel Peace Prize.

While abroad, Nhat Hanh received word that the South Vietnamese government had barred his return. He received asylum in France and continued his efforts to promote peace and reconciliation in his native country. In 1969, when peace talks seeking an end to the Vietnam war began in Paris, Nhat Hanh attended as the leader of a Vietnamese Buddhist delegation. When the South Vietnamese government fell to communist forces in 1975, he led rescue efforts to aid the fleeing refugees and sponsored programs for support of orphans within the country.

Vietnam's communist government refused to allow Nhat Hanh to re-enter his homeland. Despite his exile, he has remained in contact with the Vietnamese through his writings. "In the beginning, I missed my country very much," he told the *San Francisco Chronicle*. "I used to dream of going back. But now I feel that I am home. Although I have been away for more than 30 years, my books, my tapes, have found a way back to Vietnam. . . . Many friends of ours visiting Vietnam from Australia, from Europe, report to me that my presence in Vietnam is very tangible, very real. So, I don't suffer because I cannot go home."

Among Nhat Hanh's most influential works has been *The Miracle of Mindfulness*, originally written as a long letter to Brother Quang, a SYSS member, in 1974. This book, later translated into English and other languages, was based upon the Buddhist Sutra of Mindfulness, which emphasizes full awareness of one's self and surroundings. Nhat Hanh emphasized in its pages the connection between a sense of living in the present moment and an increased compassion for others. "Mindfulness is the miracle by which we master and restore ourselves," he writes. "[It] is the miracle which can call back in a flash our dispersed mind and restore it to wholeness so that we can live each minute of life."

Nhat Hanh continued to write and publish into the 1990s. His nearly 85 titles have included works of poetry, novels, collections of short stories and a three-volume history of Vietnamese Buddhism. One book, *Being Peace,* has sold over 200,000 copies. He has also released tapes of his books and recordings of Buddhist chants as well.

In 1982, Nhat Hanh founded the Buddhist meditation community Plum Village in southern France. Besides offering a retreat setting for visitors, it has operated as a commercial plum orchard, donating its earnings to needy children in Vietnam. During the 1980s and 1990s, Nhat Hanh traveled from his home in Plum Village to lecture and lead retreats in over 30 countries, including the United States, Canada and Israel. "Everywhere I go, I urge people to stick to their roots," he told the *Jerusalem Post.* "You remain a Jew when you practice the teaching I offer and you become, maybe, a better Jew (or a Christian or a Hindu). You have to help make your tradition grow in the direction that will help the young people go back (to it), because I know that a person who gets uprooted from his tradition is an unhappy person." Among Nhat Hanh's more noteworthy appearances was at the 1995 State of the World Forum in San Francisco, where he led former U.S. President George Bush, ex-British Prime Minister Margaret Thatcher, former Soviet Union President Mikhail Gorbachev and other famous political figures in a half-day of mindful breathing and walking meditation.

1999 found Nhat Hanh involved in establishing the Green Mountain Dharma Center, a Buddhist retreat and future monestary located in rural Vermont. That year also saw efforts on his behalf by the U.S. State Department and other officials to persuade the Vietnamese government to allow him to return to his homeland to teach. One sticking point was Nhat Hanh's unwillingness to have his visit sponsored solely by Vietnam's government-sanctioned Buddhist organization. His outspoken views about his native country had not moderated with time. "People don't have anything to believe in," he said of Vietnam in a *Los Angeles Times* interview. "The economic situation is very bad and now social ills are increasing. How can the country have any chance of success if they don't allow the rebuilding of the spirit?"

Engagement in the world of human conflict has not dimmed Nhat

Hanh's spiritual focus. Touched by the suffering of his homeland, he has brought a depth of experience and compassion to his Buddhist message. At their core, his teachings are simple and universal. "People usually consider walking on water or in thin air a miracle," he wrote in *The Miracle of Mindfulness*. "But I think the real miracle is not to walk either on water or in thin air, but to walk on earth. Every day we are engaged in a miracle which we don't even recognize: a blue sky, white clouds, green leaves, the black, curious eyes of a child — our own two eyes. All is a miracle."

Sources

➤ Books

Nhat Hanh, Thich, *The Miracle of Mindfulness,*, Beacon Press, 1987.
Wuthnow, Robert, editor,*The Encyclopedia of Politics and Religion,* Volume II, Congressional Quarterly Inc., 1998.

➤ Periodicals

Jerusalem Post, May 22, 1997, p. 7.
Los Angeles Times, October 16, 1993, p. B4; September 11, 1999, p. B2.
Minneapolis Star Tribune, November 8, 1997, p. 7B.
Montreal Gazette, April 18, 1998, p. J7.
New Yorker, June 25, 1966, p. 21.
New York Times, October 16, 1999, p. A8.
San Francisco Chronicle, , October 1, 1995, p. 3 (Sunday Review section); October 12, 1997, p. 3/Z1 (opening quote).

➤ Other

Additional information for this profile was obtained from Parallax Press biographical materials, 2000.

Ellen Ochoa

"What everyone in the astronaut corps shares in common is not gender or ethnic background, but motivation, perseverance, and desire—the desire to participate in a voyage of discovery."

Born May 10, 1958, in Los Angeles, California, Ellen Ochoa became the first female Hispanic astronaut in 1990. Address: Lyndon B. Johnson Space Center, Mail Code CB, 2101 NASA Road 1, Houston, TX 77058-3696.

llen Ochoa first dreamed of taking part in a space flight during her graduate-school days, when several of her fellow students applied to the National Aeronautics and Space Administration (NASA) astronaut training program. While they did not make the final cut, she persevered throughout the lengthy and difficult selection process and finally achieved her goal in 1990, making her the first female Hispanic astronaut in NASA history. Since then, Ochoa has spent hundreds of hours in space as a member of three different shuttle crews performing vital research and taking part in historic firsts. Such high-profile success has made her a role model for students across the nation, an assignment Ochoa has accepted with pride and enthusiasm.

Although she was born in Los Angeles, California, Ellen Ochoa has always regarded the suburban San Diego community of La Mesa as her hometown. She, her sister, and three brothers grew up in a single-parent household headed by her mother, Rosanne; her father left the family when Ellen was in junior high school. Rosanne Ochoa was a firm believer in the value of education and the idea that a person can succeed at anything if he or she tries hard enough. (She herself took college classes over more than two decades while raising her family and eventually earned three degrees.) Ochoa was therefore encouraged to excel as far back as she can remember. She developed a love of math in particular and was an exceptionally good student, graduating from high school at the top of her class. In addition, Ochoa was (and still is) very fond of music and earned recognition during her teen years as a classical flutist.

Ochoa headed off to San Diego State University in 1975 and obtained her bachelor's degree in physics (with top academic honors) in 1980. She then went on to graduate school at Stanford University to study electrical engineering and was granted her master's degree in 1981 and her doctorate in 1985, all while performing as an award-winning soloist with the Stanford Symphony Orchestra.

Ochoa subsequently began working as a researcher for Sandia National Laboratories in Albuquerque, New Mexico, and, later, for NASA Ames Research Center at Moffett Field Naval Air Station in Mountain View, California. In both positions, she specialized in studying and developing optical systems for performing information processing, especially regarding space exploration. She is listed as co-inventor on three patents dating from this period of her career: one for an optical inspection system, a second for an optical object recognition method, and a third for a method to reduce noise in images. In her spare time, Ochoa also took flying lessons and became a certified private pilot.

Ochoa first applied to become an astronaut in 1985, and in 1987 she learned she had been chosen as one of the top 100 candidates under consideration for the training program. She was still employed at the NASA Ames Research Center when it was announced in January 1990 that she and 22 other candidates had made the final cut (out of a group that originally numbered about 2,000). Ochoa, whose father's parents were from Mexico, thus became the first Hispanic woman ever accepted into the elite astronaut corps.

Ochoa's training began in late 1990 at the Johnson Space Center in Houston, Texas. The program is physically and mentally demanding, encompassing academic subjects such as geology, oceanography, meteorology, astronomy, orbital mechanics, and medicine as well as land and water survival techniques and even parachuting. Each astronaut also devotes a significant percentage of his or her time to learning about the space shuttle itself, inside and out. Ochoa passed the rigorous course and officially became an astronaut in July 1991.

Ochoa participated in her first space shuttle mission aboard the *Discovery* in April 1993. During the nine-day flight, the five-person crew studied various atmospheric and solar phenomena to gain a better understanding of the earth's climate and environment, paying particular attention to the impact of certain factors on the ozone layer. As a mission specialist, Ochoa operated a remote robotic arm to deploy and then capture a satellite that had collected data on the velocity and acceleration of solar wind and the sun's corona. Observing the beauty of the universe from the shuttle's windows was an awe-inspiring experience, she later recalled. "I never got tired of watching the Earth, day or night, as we passed over it," she told a reporter for *Latina.* "Even though we brought back some pretty incredible pictures, they don't quite compare with being there."

In November 1994, Ochoa flew a second time in space, this time aboard the space shuttle *Atlantis* on a ten-day mission with a total crew of six, including a French representative of the European Space Agency. The sun was again the focus of attention as mission specialists gathered data on fluctuations in its energy output and the impact such variations have on the earth and ozone levels in the atmosphere. In her role as payload commander, Ochoa once again used the remote robotic arm to retrieve a satellite that had performed atmospheric research.

Her next space shuttle flight began on May 27, 1999, and culminated on June 6 of that same year. During her stay aboard the *Discovery,* whose seven-person crew included representatives from the Canadian Space Agency and the Russian Space Agency, Ochoa served as both a mission specialist and flight engineer. May 29 was a particularly momentous day during the journey in that it marked the first time the shuttle docked with the International Space Station. Ochoa's responsibilities included coordinating the transfer of nearly two tons of supplies such as clothing, sleeping bags, medical equipment, spare parts, and water from one craft to the other to prepare for the arrival in 2000 of the first crew to live on board the space station. She also operated the remote robotic arm during a lengthy space walk by two of her fellow astronauts.

By the end of 1999, Ochoa had logged nearly 720 hours in space. The veteran of three shuttle flights and countless hours of training compares the astronaut experience to the life of a student. "Being an astronaut allows you to learn continuously, like you do in school," she remarked in an article published in the *Stanford University School of Engineering Annual Report, 1997-98.* "One flight you're working on atmospheric research. The next, it's bone density studies or space station design." But she readily admitted that other components of space flight such as the launch, weightlessness, and seeing the earth from afar have a strong appeal as well: "What engineer wouldn't want those experiences?"

Between space shuttle flights, Ochoa has held a variety of other technical support positions with NASA at the Johnson Space Center in Houston. She has, for example, verified flight software, served as crew representative for robotics, and worked at Mission Control as spacecraft communicator. As assistant for space station to chief of the Astronaut Office for two years, Ochoa directed the crew involved in the international space station project, a high priority for NASA in 2000 and beyond.

Ochoa's contributions to the space program have garnered her several awards, including two Space Act Tech Brief Awards in 1992, Space Flight Medals in 1993, 1994, and 1999, an Outstanding Leadership Medal in 1995, and an Exceptional Service Medal in 1997. A number of other honors have come her way as well, among them the Women in Aerospace Outstanding Achievement Award, the Hispanic Engineer Albert Baez Award for Outstanding Technical Contribution to Humanity, and the Hispanic Heritage Leadership Award. In addition, Ochoa has served as a member of the Presidential Commission on the Celebration of Women in American History.

Ochoa is frequently asked to speak to students and teachers about her career and the success she has enjoyed as NASA's first Hispanic female astronaut. She regards this part of her job as an unexpected bonus and relishes the many chances she has had to inspire young people to study mathematics and science. "I never thought about this aspect of the job when I was applying, but it's extremely rewarding," she noted in the *Stanford University School of Engineering Annual Report, 1997-98.* "I'm not trying to make every kid an astronaut, but I want kids to think about a career and the preparation they'll need." As a parent herself (she and her husband, Coe Fulmer Miles, have a young son) and the daughter of a woman she has described as a "super-mentor," Ochoa is very much aware of her status as a role model, particularly among women and Hispanics. "I do as much speaking as I am allowed to do," she explained to Lydia Martin of Knight-Ridder Newspapers. "I tell students that the opportunities I had were a result of having a good educational background. Education is what allows you to stand out."

Sources

➤ On-line

"Biographical Data," *National Aeronautics and Space Administration, Lyndon B. Johnson Space Center,* http://www.jsc.nasa.gov/Bios/htmlbios/ochoa.html (December 18, 1999).
"Ellen Ochoa, PhD, '85, MS '81, Electrical Engineering: A Higher Education," *Stanford University School of Engineering Annual Report, 1997-98,* http://soe.stanford.edu/AR97-98/ochoa.html (December 18, 1999).
"La Primera Astronaut," *Latina Online,* http://www.latina.com/new/magazine/books/98/may/story (December 18, 1999).
"STS-56," *Space Shuttle Mission Chronology,* http://www-pao.ksc.nasa.gov/kscpao/chron/sts-56.htm (December 18, 1999).
"STS-66," *Space Shuttle Mission Chronology,* http://www-pao.ksc.nasa.gov/kscpao/chron/sts-66.htm (December 18, 1999).
"STS-96," *Space Shuttle Mission Chronology,* http://www-pao.ksc.nasa.gov/kscpao/chron/sts-96.htm (December 18, 1999).

➤ Books

Romero, Maritza, *Ellen Ochoa: First Hispanic Woman Astronaut,* Rosen Publishing Group, 1997.

➤ **Periodicals**

Hispanic, May 1990.
Knight-Ridder/Tribune News Service, December 1, 1993.
Latina, May 1998.
Sol de Texas, May 20, 1993.

➤ **Other**

The opening quote was provided by Ellen Ochoa from the text of a
speech she gave upon accepting an award from the Congressional
Hispanic Caucus.

Rosie O'Donnell

"I *think that to use my celebrity status to inspire or help or encourage children is really payback for all the celebrities who helped me so much through my childhood."*

Born March 21, 1962, in Commack, New York, Rosie O'Donnell is an actress, comedienne, and talk-show host who actively supports children's charities and Broadway theater. Address: The Rosie O'Donnell Show, NBC Studios, 30 Rockefeller Plaza, Suite 800E, New York, NY 10112-0002.

Dubbed "The Queen of Nice," Rosie O'Donnell is the host of a top-rated, syndicated television talk show, "The Rosie O'Donnell Show." After years of working as a stand-up comedienne and appearing in a few situation comedies, she was making inroads as a film actress when she decided to adopt a child and seek a more stable work schedule. Out of that desire to settle down came the deal for her talk show, which has ended up changing the face of daytime television. O'Donnell uses her celebrity status to call attention to the social causes she supports and sometimes turns her show into a forum for her opinions.

Born Roseann O'Donnell on March 21, 1962, in Commack, Long Island, New York, she is the daughter of Edward O'Donnell, Sr., and Roseann O'Donnell. Her father had immigrated to the United States from Belfast, Northern Ireland; he was an electrical engineer who designed spy satellite cameras. Her mother, after whom she was named, encouraged her eldest daughter's penchant for telling jokes and doing imitations. She also introduced young Rosie to Broadway musicals, which she soon embraced with a passion.

O'Donnell's world changed forever on March 17, 1973, when her mother died of pancreatic and liver cancer. She was buried on her daughter's eleventh birthday. O'Donnell's father became emotionally distant from his children after his wife's death, leaving Rosie and her four siblings (two older brothers, Edward, Jr., and Daniel, one younger sister, Maureen, and one younger brother, Timothy) to close ranks and take care of themselves. O'Donnell's preferred outlet for dealing with her grief was performing.

At school, O'Donnell was always a cut-up. Bubbly and popular, she was the prom queen, homecoming queen, and president of her class. She also did some acting as a member of the drama society and played sports, including baseball. When she graduated in 1980, her goal was to become a Broadway actress.

Comedy, however, proved to be O'Donnell's true calling. She made her stand-up debut in 1978 at the age of 16 when, on a dare, she performed on amateur night at a Round Table restaurant in Mineola, Long Island. She was immediately enthralled by the experience and continued to perform while still attending high school. Material was sometimes hard to come by, however, due to her youth and limited life experience.

Among the places O'Donnell appeared at was Huntington's East Side Comedy Club, which later relocated to Farmingdale, New York. Its manager, Richie Minervini, told Nancy Harrison of the

New York Times, "She came in and went on stage, and I'll tell you what. She had talent right off the bat. She wasn't really funny but she had a charisma. She had a presence. She had a desire."

Right after graduating from high school, O'Donnell began touring as a stand-up comedienne. Though she loved being on the road, she also wanted to pursue her education. She spent short periods at Dickinson College and Boston University, but by 1981 her college days had come to an end.

In 1984, O'Donnell received a break when she appeared on the television show "Star Search," which featured up-and-coming talent. She won five televised competitions and made it to the finalist level before losing to another contestant. But she won about $14,000, which enabled her to move to Los Angeles. O'Donnell then struggled to make it as an actress while continuing to do stand-up comedy.

O'Donnell made her television debut in 1986 when she appeared in the final season of the situation comedy "Gimme a Break" starring Nell Carter and Joey Lawrence. Her character was a neighbor who worked as a dental hygienist.

After "Gimme a Break" was cancelled in 1987, O'Donnell joined the adult music video channel VH-1 as a veejay around 1988. When veejays were phased out a year later, she stayed with the network as the host of "VH-1 Stand-Up Spotlight" beginning in 1990. For the next four years, O'Donnell produced the show and helped select the featured comedians, many of whom were looking for their first big break. She honored her own roots by often booking comics from Long Island.

While working for VH-1, O'Donnell continued to seek out acting roles. She returned to the television situation comedy format in 1992 as one of the stars of "Stand By Your Man," a show about two sisters who move in together when their husbands go to prison. Its run lasted only from April to August of that year.

O'Donnell also made her feature film debut in 1992 in *A League of Their Own.* This popular comedy about an all-women's baseball league that was formed during World War II also starred Geena Davis, Tom Hanks, and Madonna. O'Donnell's role was that of a wisecracking third base player named Doris Murphy. Her performance garnered good reviews—the best of her career, in fact.

As was the case in *A League of Their Own,* O'Donnell often played a lead character's best friend. In 1993's *Sleepless in Seattle,* for example, she was the confidante of star Meg Ryan's character. That same year, she also appeared in the buddy comedy *Another Stakeout* with Richard Dreyfuss and Emilio Estevez. She played a district attorney, and the other two were undercover policemen. All three of them were looking for a missing witness.

O'Donnell's film career really shifted into high gear in 1994. In addition to appearing in a movie version of the classic television series "Car 54, Where Are You?" and in the film *I'll Do Anything,* she took part in a live-action version of the television cartoon "The Flintstones" in the role of Betty Rubble, Wilma Flintstone's best friend. O'Donnell received praise as the best part of *Exit to Eden,* an offbeat comedy in which she played an undercover policewoman at a sexual fantasy resort. Also in 1994, her lifelong dream came true when she made her Broadway debut in a musical as Rizzo in *Grease.*

In 1995 O'Donnell, who had never married but very much wanted a family, decided to adopt a child. That spring she welcomed a son, Parker Jaren. She added a daughter, Chelsea Belle, in the fall of 1997, and another son, Blake Christopher, in the winter of 1999. "Being a mother is the most difficult and beautiful experience anyone can have," O'Donnell once remarked to a *People* reporter. "Through Parker, I have a greater capacity to love and feel life."

O'Donnell continued her film career for a while after Parker's arrival, playing a doctor in *Now and Then* in 1995 and the eccentric nanny in the movie version of the children's classic *Harriet the Spy* in 1996. Also in 1996, she appeared in *Beautiful Girls.* By this time, however, O'Donnell had decided that, as a new mother, she needed a more stable working environment, so she decided to return to television.

In late 1995, O'Donnell cut a deal for a new syndicated talk/variety show for which she would serve as both host and executive producer. Inspired by the talk shows she used to watch after school as a child such as "The Dinah Shore Show" and "The Mike Douglas Show," she wanted to do the type of program that would stand in stark contrast to the sex, sleaze, and occasional violence that characterized many of the other shows on the air at the time. As O'Donnell told Cynthia Littleton of *Broadcasting & Cable,* "I'm so thrilled to be given an opportunity to present my idea of talk variety. I promise there will be no fistfights."

Launched in June 1996, "The Rosie O'Donnell Show" was an immediate hit, and it went on to change the face of syndicated daytime talk television. Much of its success had to do with O'Donnell herself. Critics and audiences alike found her engagingly ordinary. She freely admitted her love of junk food, displayed an encyclopedic knowledge of television and popular culture, and worshipped celebrities (especially actor Tom Cruise) as a fan would. Writing of her appeal, Betsey Sharkey of *Mediaweek* observed, "O'Donnell's essential charm is her kick-off-your-shoes-and-stay-awhile sensibility. ... [She] is a master at making everyday life a laughing matter."

O'Donnell's achievement did not go unnoticed. Besides doing extremely well in the ratings, she won three consecutive Daytime Emmy Awards for Outstanding Talk Show Host from 1997 through 1999. Her impact was also measured in another way; before long, imitators of her mix of talk and variety had hit the airwaves, most notably "The Donny & Marie Show."

The show also helped O'Donnell become a household name across the United States. She then began to use her immense popularity and celebrity status on behalf of many causes, including breast cancer awareness, pro-choice initiatives, AIDS benefits, and homelessness. In 1997, she founded the For All the Kids Foundation to raise money for children's charities. She also promoted children's literacy through Rosie's Readers in 1999, a joint project with eToys. But her vehement anti-gun stance cost her at least one endorsement when she quit as a K-Mart spokesperson during the late 1990s after discovering that the discount chain sold guns.

O'Donnell also used her fame to promote interest in the theater. She often featured performers from Broadway musicals on her show, for example. She also hosted the Tony Awards on CBS-TV in 1997 and again in 1998 and gave a tremendous boost to, the program's typically anemic ratings. As TN Media's Stacey Lynn Koerner explained to Alan Frutkin of *Mediaweek*, "Rosie changed the whole way of thinking about the Tonys. She was the 'everyman' host, and that benefited the broadcast." O'Donnell also presided over the Grammy Awards (which honor those in the recording industry) in 1999 and 2000.

Despite her many personal and professional responsibilities, O'Donnell still managed to find a little time to devote to films. In 1998 she played a nun in *Wide Awake,* and in 1999 she provided a voice for the animated feature *Tarzan.* Though O'Donnell's primary project, "The Rosie O'Donnell Show," continues to evolve, she knows it will come to an end at some point. "I don't have any illusions that people aren't going to get sick of me," she told Paula Span of the *Washington Post.* "I know it's going to happen." Until then, O'Donnell reigns as the queen of the daytime talk and variety genre.

Sources

➤ Books

Collins, Louise Mooney, editor, *Newsmakers: 1994 Cumulation,* Gale, 1994.
Mair, George and Anna Green, *Rosie O'Donnell: Her True Story,* Birch Lane Press, 1997 (opening quote).
Parish, James Robert, *Rosie: Rosie O'Donnell's Biography,* Carroll & Graf Publishers, 1997.

➤ Periodicals

Brandweek, February 24, 1997, p. 1.
Broadcasting & Cable, November 27, 1995, p. 26; July 1, 1996, p. 38.
Mediaweek, January 15, 1996, p. 25; July 22, 1996, p. 18; January 13, 1997, p. 34; May 17, 1999, p. 16.
Newsweek, July 15, 1996, p. 44; January 17, 2000, p. 67.
New York Times, May 31, 1992, p. 13LI; June 20, 1999, section 2, p. 27.
People, July 20, 1992, p. 65; January 8, 1996, p. 15; December 30, 1996, p. 50; April 21, 1997, p. 68; June 2, 1997, p. 146; November 24, 1997, p. 51; December 1, 1997, p. 79; May 4, 1998, p. 7; January 11, 1999, p. 11; January 24, 2000, p. 58.
Publishers Weekly, June 2, 1997, p. 33; October 5, 1998, p. 46; October 18, 1999, p. 12.
Time, November 11, 1996, p. 102.
U.S. News & World Report, June 7, 1999, p. 9.
Variety, August 24, 1998, p. 5.
Washington Post, November 30, 1997, p. G1.

Scott O'Grady

"Most of the world's heroes are unsung. It's heroic to dare to make a difference in the world, whether you're defending your country or fighting fires or teaching children to read."

Born in 1965, Scott O'Grady was a captain in the U.S. Air Force when his F16 fighter jet was shot down over Bosnia in June of 1995. He spent six days evading capture before a dramatic rescue by helicopter, and returned home for a hero's welcome. Address: 1663 Prince Street, Alexandria, VA 22314.

When Captain Scott O'Grady's F16 aircraft was bisected by a Serbian surface-to-air missile during a routine NATO flight over northern Bosnia's United Nations-mandated no-fly zone, his military training and quick thinking helped eject him from the burning plane, land him safely, and ensure that he survived several days in enemy territory without detection or even serious physical deterioration. After his rescue, O'Grady made certain to point out that the true heroes of the story were the Marines who followed his radio distress signals, landed, and flew him to safety.

O'Grady was born in the New York City borough of Brooklyn in 1965. His father, William, was a radiologist who had served on-board a U.S. Navy ship during the Vietnam War. His family eventually settled in Washington state, where he played both soccer and, less ardently, football. He tried out for the latter team at Spokane's Lewis & Clark High School, though he weighed just 125 pounds. "I wasn't one of those golden boys," O'Grady wrote in *Return with Honor.* "Few things came easily to me. But . . . I hated to lose, or be passed over." He thought he might have a successful gridiron career as a place-kicker, and practiced for hours. When he was sent into a game for the first time, he missed the kick and landed on his back, "like Charlie Brown after Lucy swipes the ball away," he recalled in the autobiography.

Both O'Grady parents were recreational pilots, and he first flew with his father at the age of six; by the time he was a teenager, he was taking flying lessons himself. He dreamed of a career as a military pilot, but was rejected by the Air Force Academy on the basis of his Scholastic Aptitude Test scores. He spent a year at the University of Washington, but left to ski in the Idaho resort of Sun Valley, where he found work as a dishwasher to support himself.

O'Grady entered the ROTC program at Embry-Riddle Aeronautical University in Arizona, and worked toward a degree in aeronautical science. He won a coveted Air Force scholarship before his junior year, and with it came a contract for nine years' service. He still had to work hard to make up for some shortcomings, however: the night before his graduation, his visiting family wanted to take him to dinner, but he had to decline, since a professor had offered to raise his grade in a class if he re-wrote a paper. O'Grady worked late into the night to re-do it, "and when I walked up to get my diploma the next day, they added two words to my name: *cum laude,*" he remembered in *Return with Honor.*

When he entered the Air Force in 1989, O'Grady was selected for the Euro-NATO (North Atlantic Treaty Organization) Joint Jet Pilot

Training Program at a base in Texas. From there he was sent to Korea, where he first began flying the F-16C, a single-seater jet that could drop bombs as well as fire upon other planes. In 1994, he was transferred to the 555th Fighter Squadron, based in Aviano, Italy, in the Italian Alps.

O'Grady became part of a United Nations effort to enforce a no-fly zone over northern Bosnia by sending patrols of fighter jets to patrol the area. Called Operation Deny Flight, the attempt to create peace in the war-ravaged republics of the former Yugoslavia had logged 69,000 flights by June 2, 1995. On that day, O'Grady took off for his 47th Deny Flight mission, and he and the other F16 assigned to carry out that day's sortie were instructed to remain along a corridor in northwest Bosnia during their four- to six-hour mission. But tensions had increased in recent weeks, and NATO had struck a Bosnia Serb munitions depot; in return several U.N. peacekeepers were taken hostage, and they began threatening to shoot down NATO planes with one of their Soviet-built surface-to-air missiles.

After taking off at 1:15 p.m., O'Grady and the plane he was accompanying cruised above the narrow air corridor at nearly 400 m.p.h. in what appeared to be another routine mission. At three minutes after 3 p.m., however, his radar warning system notified him that his plane had been "spiked," or locked by enemy radar on the ground. Nine seconds later, he saw a red flash of light from his cockpit, and a second later he could feel his F16 take the hit of an SA-6 surface-to-air missile. It cleaved the entire plane in two. Still airborne, the cockpit and nose of O'Grady's bomber heaved upward from the shock, but it then began plummeting quickly. Flames were rapidly destroying what was left of the F16. "My console was disintegrating, breaking up before me, twisting and warping like plastic," O'Grady wrote in *Return with Honor*. He spied the ejection lanyard, a yellow rubber handle, between his knees, and pulled with the necessary force to eject his specially constructed seat from the airborne wreckage. "Had I delayed ejecting half a second, I might have been tossed helplessly around the cockpit," O'Grady wrote. "I might have spun into G-forces so high that my arms would have stalled of their own weight, too heavy to move."

O'Grady successfully ejected from the plane while nearly four miles above the ground. He dropped 26,000 feet, and pulled the parachute attached, fearing that the release had already been damaged, and if it did not work, he would not have time during his fall to fix it to save himself. The parachute, however, was a dead giveaway to the enemy, and he could see villagers watching his fall.

When he hit the ground, he ran toward a clump of trees, and quickly muddied his face and hands so that no skin would show. A few minutes later, Serbs with rifles came looking for him, and passed within just a few feet of where he lay motionless, face-down in the dirt.

O'Grady spent nearly a week hiding in a densely forested area that provided ideal cover. He remained inert during the day, since patrols were still looking for him on the first few days before heavy rains set in, and moved about at night looking for an ideal rescue spot. With him was an emergency kit with water, first aid supplies, and flares, which had been attached to his ejection seat, and he also had—strapped on him before takeoff in Aviano—a 9mm pistol and a tiny two-way radio with a Global Positioning System. He immediately began using it to make contact with the other NATO aircraft in the region, but was at first unsuccessful.

Meanwhile, Air Force chaplains and officers had notified both sets of his divorced parents, and with his younger brother and sister, the families held vigil. When the Serbian government announced on Saturday that they had captured O'Grady, the family was elated, for it meant he was still alive. O'Grady, meanwhile, was still hiding out, battling hunger, thirst and encroaching despair.

There were no food rations in O'Grady's kit, and he soon ran out of water. Thankfully it rained, which gave him rainwater to collect in some Ziploc plastic bags he had with him. But bad weather also kept other planes from flying over the area, including friendly NATO aircraft that could pick up the locating beep from O'Grady's radio. When he did use it, he worried that Serbian monitoring would be able to hear it and pinpoint his location. The first time he heard a response from an American voice, they could not hear his transmission. During the night, he searched for a high spot for better reception, and one near a clearing, too, where rescue helicopters might land.

To keep up his strength, O'Grady ate leaves, using a five-step test for poison content, brushing it first against his lips, and then keeping it in his mouth a full five minutes before swallowing. He also ate ants for protein. By June 6, Air Force personnel were certain they were receiving signals from the area, but were uncertain as to the source. To verify that it was indeed the downed pilot and not a Serb ruse, a stepped-up electronic intelligence plan was put into action, with CIA spy satellites aimed on the area, and infrared scanners searching for a heat source. Finally, at 2 a.m. on June 8, O'Grady made contact with a plane from his base that was on a Deny Flight mission. "I'm alive; help," O'Grady told the other pilot, Captain Thomas Hanford, who then asked him the name of his former squadron in Korea, to be sure it was actually O'Grady.

In the Adriatic, the 24th Marine Expeditionary Unit aboard the *U.S.S. Kearsarge* mobilized to rescue O'Grady. Sixty-one Marines boarded two giant helicopters, with two helicopter gunships accompanying them; also in the entourage of 40 aircraft were backup aircraft and electronic warfare planes. Flying into the no-fly zone over Bosnia around 6:30 a.m, pilots saw yellow smoke from a flare O'Grady had set off; the helicopters touched down, Marines jumped out to secure the perimeter, and the pilot of the second helicopter saw a bearded man, running through the fog toward them, carrying a pistol. O'Grady stopped, not knowing which one to approach, nor how to avoid the deadly rotors. He saw a sergeant waving him in to one, and once aboard, could only repeat the words "Thank you, thank you, thank you."

O'Grady's ordeal was not yet over—he was wrapped in a blanket to keep warm, and given a crash helmet, for the helicopters now began traveling an erratic path at 175 m.p.h. to avoid Serb fire. The crew of the *Kearsage* cheered when they landed. He had lost 25 pounds, and was suffering from trench foot. At a press conference at Aviano on Saturday, O'Grady broke down and wept when a recording was replayed of his and Hanford's first contact.

A few days later, O'Grady met with President Bill Clinton—who had waited for news of the pilot's rescue until late in the night, and then smoked a celebratory cigar on the White House balcony when it was confirmed—and began making the rounds of all the major network and cable news studios. He was pointed about not accepting the "hero" tag, crediting the Marine rescue squad from the *Kearsage* as the real heroes in the story. "By putting their bodies on the line and taking enemy fire, they gave me another shot at life," O'Grady wrote in *Return with Honor.* "Most of the world's heroes are unsung. It's heroic to dare to make a difference in the world, whether you're defending your country or fighting fires or teaching children to read."

Sources

➤ Books

O'Grady, Captain Scott, *Return with Honor*, with Jeff Coplon, Doubleday, 1995 (opening quote).

➤ Periodicals

Columbia Journalism Review, September 1995, p. 21.
Time, June 19, 1995, p. 20; June 26, 1995, p. 30.
Weekly Compilation of Presidential Documents, June 19, 1995, p. 1042.
World Press Review, September 1995, p. 23.

Emmeline Pankhurst

"I look upon myself as a prisoner of war."

Born on July 14, 1858, in Manchester, England, Emmeline Goulden Pankhurst led the suffragist movement in Britain during its most crucial period. She died on June 14, 1928.

For Emmeline Pankhurst, the battle to secure for women in Britain the right to vote became her life's work. Born into comfort, she rejected the constraints of her class and instead used her position to agitate for widespread reform. Founder of the Women's Social and Political Union in 1903, Pankhurst encouraged thousands of women to enter into a fight for enfranchisement that grew violent and deadly, and she and her daughters were repeatedly imprisoned for their roles as leaders.

Pankhurst was one of ten children of Robert Goulden, a partner in a Manchester textile firm, and Jane Quine, and was born at home on the outskirts of the famous industrial city in 1858. Both parents were supporters of various reform causes of the day, and Jane Goulden began taking her daughter to women's suffrage meetings when Pankhurst was in her early teens. Attempts to win voting rights for English women dated back to the 1840s, but faced strong opposition from politicians, the clergy, and several other powerful interests.

As a student, Pankhurst was gifted but rarely applied herself to her studies. She played the piano well, but shyness and a fear of public performance kept her from pursuing this. Back in Manchester in 1878 after a stint at a Paris finishing school, Pankhurst met prominent socialist lawyer Richard Pankhurst when she was 20. A London University graduate, atheist, and radical 24 years her senior, Dr. Pankhurst vociferously espoused abolition of the monarchy, separation of church and state, suffrage for women, and once termed the House of Lords a "public *abattoir* where the liberties and interest of the people have been butchered like the cattle of the field." Pankhurst, meanwhile, had emerged as an attractive young woman, with olive skin, dark hair, and violet eyes; she also had a love of fashionable clothes. Despite Dr. Pankhurst's personal misgivings about the institution of marriage itself—believing that it enslaved women—the two were wed in the winter of 1879.

They immediately began a family with daughter Christabel, born in 1880, followed by Sylvia two years later; a son they named Frank arrived in 1884, joined by a final daughter, Adela, the following year. The quick succession of pregnancies irreparably damaged Pankhurst's health, and she would suffer the rest of her life from neuralgia, migraines, and other disorders. Nevertheless, she worked alongside her husband in his political campaigns when he unsuccessfully stood for a seat in Parliament on several occasions. Hoping to free him from his law practice so that he might devote himself entirely to politics, Pankhurst opened a store in London with her sister Mary, where they sold artistic objects. When her four-year-old son died of diphtheria, she blamed herself and their reduced circumstances for the careless medical treatment he received. It made Pankhurst a defender of the poor for the rest of her life.

After conceiving another son, Pankhurst nearly died in childbirth in 1889 with Harry. That same year, she formed the Women's Franchise League at her home with a number of other prominent reformers. A severe recession hit the British economy in 1894, and widespread unemployment and subsequent misery greatly affected the working poor of Manchester, where the Pankhursts again lived. They founded a Relief Committee that operated several soup kitchens across the city, and Pankhurst used her position when elected a "Poor Law Guardian" in 1895 to agitate for workhouse reform. These institutions were the only official charitable measure to help the most unfortunate members of English society, but were abominable, unsanitary and cruel places to which the elderly and young, whose families could no longer afford to feed them, were sent, often to die.

By now the two elder Pankhurst daughters were reaching adulthood and becoming increasingly involved in political causes themselves. Richard Pankhurst died in 1898, leaving the family deeply in debt, and his widow was forced to sell much of their possessions. When friends tried to solicit donations to help her, Pankhurst refused, saying that such monies would be better used to construct a Socialist Hall in commemoration of her husband's achievements. To give her some income, Pankhurst was made a Manchester registrar of births and deaths, a job in which she met many young girls who had just become mothers. She was dismayed by the utter poverty an unmarried female as young as 13 might find herself in through rape or incest; in some cases the law stipulated that the purported father must pay a small maintenance sum, which rarely happened. A man could deny paternity by taking a friend before the court to swear that he, too, had enjoyed relations with her. If women were allowed a say in the political process, Pankhurst reasoned, such injustices would no longer be permitted.

Meanwhile, Christabel, studying law at Manchester University, became increasingly involved with a new generation of suffragists, which lured her mother back into the movement. In 1903, Pankhurst founded the Women's Social and Political Union (WSPU), which aimed to recruit large numbers of working-class women into the cause. Its slogan, which she coined, was blunt: "Votes for Women." The WSPU worked tirelessly to win the allegiance of Labour Party members of Parliament (MPs), but though it was a progressive party, it was uninterested in suffrage, since voting rights for men in Britain at the time were based upon property ownership; if women won the right to vote, it was thought, only landed, wealthier women would gain it, who would naturally support the opposing Tory (Conservative) Party.

Frustrated with the lack of progress made through conventional means, the WSPU soon became a militant organization. Pankhurst declaimed tirelessly at rallies, finally having conquered her fear of public speaking, and used her wealth of connections to personally lobby lawmakers. She and the other activists were often jeered at, manhandled by police, and even lewdly grabbed by crowds of hooligans. Still, their demands for voting rights gained tremendous support among British women of all classes, and the movement swelled. It grew increasingly volatile, however: Pankhurst called the first "Women's Parliament" in early 1907. Attempting to march toward the House of Commons, they battled with London mounted police all night, and after a third attempt the next year the government, fearful of its safety now, proposed to revive a law that banned gatherings of more than a dozen people who might present a petition to Parliament. It was called the Tumultuous Petitions Act and dated back to the late 1600s. With a severe limp, Pankhurst led a group of 12 on February 13, 1908, and was promptly arrested.

Prisons in England for both sexes were abysmal during this era. Pankhurst was strip-searched, bathed in filthy water, and locked in a dank cell with a plank for a bed. Nearing 50 years of age, she suffered a quick decline in health, and was sent to the prison hospital; one night, the woman in the next bed gave birth to a child, whose birth certificate would immutably read "born in prison" for the remainder of its life, a terrible stigma. Pankhurst later learned the woman was released soon afterward, and had been taken into custody on a baseless charge anyway. Again, such injustices fortified her resolve to gain for women a say in the legislative process. She told the governor of the jail that she and her forces would forever eradicate evils like prisons themselves. "Men have had control of these things long enough," she declared. "No woman with a spark of womanliness in her will consent to allow this state of things to go on any longer."

Pankhurst was soon released and returned to public speaking. After another arrest in the summer of 1908, she and the other WSPU detainees demanded that they be treated as political prisoners, and as such accorded some privileges. After her release, her son Harry, now grown, became ill from polio, and so Pankhurst accepted an invitation to lecture in the United States because the family needed the money for medical care. He died, however, not long after her return. "As we drove the sad way to his burial," wrote her daughter Sylvia in *The Life of Emmeline Pankhurst*, "she was bowed as I had never seen her."

During 1912, the WSPU began an organized campaign of window-breaking and rock-throwing. It kicked off on March 4, when Pankhurst took a taxi to the residence of the prime minister at 10 Downing Street, got out, and hurled a rock that shattered a window. At that same moment, as prearranged, hundreds of women on London's great commercial boulevards took hammers out of handbags and smashed plate-glass windows. Sheets of broken glass littered the streets, and the next day even the national museums were closed by decree.

For her part, Pankhurst was sentenced to nine months' imprisonment, and all detainees decided upon a hunger strike. Forcible feeding via a barbarous rubber tube was the official response, which caused a public outcry. She was released after refusing this torture, and the WSPU militant actions continued; railway stations were bombed, and "Votes for Women" greeted early-morning golfers, etched in acid in huge letters, across some of England's most famous greens. Her daughter Sylvia was also jailed and force-fed. Hoping to skirt the hunger-strikers and the uproar over tube-feeding, Parliament passed what became known as the "Cat and Mouse Act"— when hunger weakened them, they would be released, then reinterred when their strength regained with no credit for time already served.

Pankhurst took responsibility for the 1913 bombing of the house of government minister David Lloyd-George, and for it was sentenced to three years in prison. "I look upon myself as a prisoner of war," she told the court. She immediately joined the other suffragists in prison on their hunger strikes. She was re-arrested and re-jailed a number of times under the Act. The onset of World War I immediately halted all militant WSPU actions by Pankhurst's decree, and instead turned to assisting the war effort.

In early 1918, a Reform Bill, granting women over 30 the right to vote, passed both houses of Parliament. After forming the Women's Party with Christabel, Pankhurst spent time in Canada and ran an English tearoom on the French Riviera. Back in England in 1925, she joined the Tory Party and stood for election from London's poorest constituencies in its East End, which angered many of her former socialist associates as well as her daughter Sylvia. She even moved into the slum area, but her health declined and she died in a nursing home on June 14, 1918. A statue of Pankhurst stands in the Victoria Tower Gardens, outside the Houses of Parliament where she had led so many demonstrations.

Sources

➤ **Books**

Barker, Dudley, *Prominent Edwardians,* Allen & Unwin, 1969.
Pankhurst, E. Sylvia, *The Life of Emmeline Pankhurst: The Suffragette Struggle for Women's Citizenship,* T. Werner Laurie Ltd./Kraus, 1969.

Pele

"I would like to be remembered as a person who showed the world that the simplicity of a man is still the most important quality. Through simplicity and sincerity, you can put all humankind together."

Born Edson Arantes do Nascimento on October 23, 1940, this Brazilian athlete became indelibly associated with the game of soccer in the 1960s as its first superstar, Pele. Address: c/o FIFA, Case Postale 85, Zurich, CH-8030, Switzerland.

Often called the king of soccer, Pele is the game's most enduring and endearing star. With an astonishingly long career, a record number of goals, and some legendary scores to his name, this Brazilian is considered one of modern history's most celebrated athletes. "His nickname means nothing in any language but evokes images of genius and gentility in them all," noted a 1994 *Sports Illustrated* profile.

Edson Arantes do Nascimento was born on October 23, 1940, and named by his parents after American inventor Thomas Edison. The family lived in Tres Coracoes, an impoverished city in Brazil's interior, where his father, Dondinho—an avid soccer player—taught his son to play at a very early age. Because they were too poor to buy a real soccer ball, they played with a makeshift one, a large sock stuffed with rags. His family called him "Dico," but by the age of six, the other boys in his town with whom he played began calling him "Pele," a nonsense word in Brazilian Portuguese.

Pele soon developed a strong lure to the game. He often skipped school, preferring to be out of doors practicing, if not playing, with the other boys; he walked along railroad tracks to gather peanuts that had fallen off the freight cars, then re-sold them. With the profits from this enterprise he saved enough money to buy a genuine soccer ball. At the age of ten, his parents agreed to let him leave school, but with the condition that he find work. He began repairing shoes in town, earning about $2 a month. The job left him plenty of time to play soccer, which he did until late at night at times. Like his fellow athletes in town, he played barefoot.

Around 1952, Waldemar de Brito, a well-known Brazilian soccer player, saw Pele play with a group of factory workers, and was impressed with the 12-year-old's ability. Within a year, he had joined de Brito's junior team, and the day he was provided with the team uniform was one he remembered as "one of the thrills of my life," he said in *Pele! The Sports Career of Edson do Nascimento.* "I took the uniform home to show my parents. When I saw how proud my father was, I cried."

Over the next three years, Pele worked on perfecting his game with teammates and coaches. He became known as a tireless athlete, willing to practice longer than anyone else and keep at a certain maneuver until he perfected it. His dedication to the game was complete, and he led his team to the junior title in Brazil for three years in a row. This attracted the attention of Santos, a leading Brazilian professional team, but at first he was confined to the bench; his first foray onto the field with Santos came during a heated title match. The coach sent him to kick a penalty shot, which he missed. He was devastated.

Hours of practice followed, and Pele's skills progressed within a few short months. He scored his first career goal on September 7, 1956, and he was invited to join the Brazilian national team for its international games. Because of his age, he endured boos from the crowds, but when he scored a goal against Italy, he punched the air with his fist in excitement, which soon became his trademark. In the deadly seriousness of the World Cup championships in soccer, held every four years, Brazil's young star helped his country advance steadily to the finals in its 1958 bid. In the final match against Sweden, Pele scored one of most memorable goals in his entire career: his back was to the goalie and the net, and he caught a pass with his chest, let the ball roll down his left foot, then lifted it up over his shoulder, whirled around, and kicked it into net. The ball had never touched the ground. The crowd erupted in cheers at such a dazzling feat, and even Sweden's goalie applauded him. Brazil won that game as well as its first World Cup title.

By the early 1960s, Pele was a celebrity in Brazil. He continually set individual scoring records each season, and even studied geometry to help improve his game. Offered large sums of money to play outside the country, Pele was thwarted by any such move when Brazil's president officially declared him a national treasure in 1961. The proclamation effectively barred him from playing for another country's team. "This was a big honor for me, but I still paid income taxes," Pele told *Sports Illustrated* in 1994. He refused to accept lucrative endorsement offers from liquor or tobacco companies, as was common for athletes in the era, since he himself did not smoke or drink; shy by nature, he eschewed the wilder side of life for soccer athletes as well.

Pele was crushed when an injury forced him to sit out the 1962 World Cup games. But he also came to loathe the World Cup games for their intense, even violent play. He was often fouled by other players, which was usually the only way to halt his determined path to the net, and other players even kicked him. Such tactics reached a nadir during the 1966 World Cup games, when he was repeatedly kicked and even tripped; he suffered a serious knee injury when one player jumped on his leg after tripping him. It forced him out of the game, and Brazil lost. Still, he was the country's most famous celebrity by the mid-1960s, and a millionaire. He began investing his earnings in business ventures and real estate. He built low-income housing in Brazil, and supported his immediate family as well as the one he began with his wife, Rosemarie.

A national hero in Brazil, Pele also became an international star. In 1968, he traveled to Nigeria for a game, but there was a civil war raging with Biafra, an independently declared republic; a two-day truce was agreed upon, since both sides were in ardent agreement about their need to watch the game. In November of 1969, Pele scored the thousandth goal of his career, a historic feat that secured his place as the sport's all-time leading scorer; a top soccer star could only expect about 400 goals during his career, which usually only lasted about 5 years before injury and age forced him off the field. But Pele endured: he would enjoy a career that lasted more than 20 years, though he was not 40 when he retired.

After Brazil's third World Cup win in 1970, Pele quit the national team. He began to devote more time to youth soccer, and in a single year traveled across the globe speaking out on the benefits of the game for children. He played his last game with Santos on October 2, 1974, after announcing his retirement. He was earning nearly a million dollars a year, and during his last season, donated the entire sum to children's charities.

Brazilians, of course, were saddened by his retirement, but devastated when he arrived in the United States the next year to sign a three-year agreement with the North American Soccer League (NASL) franchise in New York, a team called the Cosmos. He was given $4.5 million to play a sport in a country that could not even attract a crowd of more than 10,000 for a game; with four other professional sports to watch, Americans paid little attention to soccer, which was viewed as utterly foreign. This was part of the lure for Pele—the underdog status of the game itself in the United States. "I looked and saw another mountain to climb," Pele reportedly said about his decision, according to *Sports Illustrated.*

Not surprisingly, attendance rose dramatically at New York Cosmos games, and they won the NASL title two years later. His last professional appearance, at an October 1, 1977 game at New Jersey's Meadowlands stadium, was actually a special match: Pele played the first half of the game for the Cosmos, and the second for his former team, Santos, who had been invited to America for the special occasion. A crowd of 76,000 was in attendance, and luminaries that day included Muhammad Ali, U.S. Secretary of State Henry Kissinger, and even Rolling Stones singer Mick Jagger; Pele's father Dondinho was also present. Before the game, Pele spoke to the crowd: "I want to take this opportunity to ask you to pay attention to the young of the world, the children, the kids," he said, according to the next day's *New York Times.* "We need them too much. . . . Love is more important than what we can take in life. Everything pass. Please say with me, three times—love, love, love!" The words "Love, love, love!" also flashed on the scoreboard, and with that, the game was underway. Pele scored his 1,281st career goal that day, and in a halftime ceremony gave his Cosmos jersey to his father.

Pele's two years in the United States accomplished what he hoped: the number of registered U.S. Soccer Federation players quadrupled. After his second retirement, he devoted himself to increasing interest in the game, and lobbied to bring World Cup soccer to the United States. In 1988, three sites emerged on the short list for the 1994 event: Brazil, Morocco, and United States. Pele urged that the U.S. be awarded the World Cup, and argued against Brazil's bid. "A country where millions of people are starving and which has the Third World's largest foreign debt cannot consider the sponsorship of a World Cup with government money," he declared, according to *Sports Illustrated.* He weathered a great deal of criticism across Latin America for this stance.

Pele has also been involved with UNICEF and other children's charities for a number of years. His first marriage ended in the late 1970s, and in 1994 he married Assiria Seixas Lemos. That same year, the World Cup finals were indeed played in the United States for the first time in history. Brazil won, though without Pele's legendary talents at the goal line. At times the target of criticism for the lucrative endorsements and deals his name and talents have brought him, Pele is resolved to using his fame to bring soccer to the youth of the world—perhaps remembering his own humble origins. "It is a mission," he said in *Sports Illustrated* in 1994. "I could make money without traveling so much. But to bring soccer to the countries where soccer is undeveloped, this is my passion. I want to see soccer all over the world. All people can be part of it. Poor people can play it. Other sports are so expensive for kids. But soccer is easy."

Sources

➤ Books

Hahn, James, and Lynn Hahn, *Pele! The Sports Career of Edson do Nascimento,* Crestwood House, 1981.

➤ Periodicals

New York Times, October 2, 1977 (opening quote).
Sports Illustrated, June 20, 1994, p. 86; September 19, 1994, p. 122.
Time, June 14, 1999, pp. 110-116.

Leonard Peltier

"I've got my dignity and self-respect, and I'm going to keep that, even if I die here."*

Born September 12, 1944, in Grand Forks, North Dakota, American Indian activist Leonard Peltier has been dubbed the "Nelson Mandela of North America" by political activists who are convinced that he was wrongly accused of and imprisoned for murdering two FBI agents on Pine Ridge Reservation in 1975. Around the world, supporters—including actor Robert Redford and activists from Amnesty International—have been working tirelessly toward gaining his release from prison, where he has served since 1977. Address: c/o The Leonard Peltier Defense Committee, P.O. Box 583, Lawrence, KS 66044.

With at least 50 FBI agents poised for combat on Pine Ridge Reservation, the fateful day of June 26, 1975, is described by Peltier's defenders as a battle between American Indian activists set on defending their treaty rights and U.S. government agents set on controlling territory in the interest of uranium mining. Between May 1973 and June 1975, 60 American Indians were murdered, 47 of whom were American Indian Movement (AIM) activists, and over 300 others are estimated to have been wounded during that period. On June 26, 1975, a shoot-out between FBI agents and AIM activists ensued, leaving two agents dead. Although federal prosecutors admitted to not being able to prove that Peltier fired the shots, they worked to build a case with evidence to support that he aided and abetted. Peltier was tried and convicted, and is now serving two life terms for premeditated murder.

Leonard Peltier's earliest childhood memories are of migrating through the Dakotas, working the potato fields with his large family. His father, Leo Peltier, who died in 1989, was three quarters Ojibwa and one quarter French. His mother, Alvina Showers, is half Lakota Sioux. Peltier's mother and father separated when he was four, and he and his younger sister went to live with his paternal grandparents, Alex and Mary Peltier. When he was older, he moved with his grandparents to Montana, but returned to North Dakota where he attended Wahpeton Indian School. He then moved in with his father on Turtle Mountain Reservation, where be became involved in traditional religious ceremonies. When he was 14 he participated in the sun dance, which is a significant Plains Indians religious renewal and purification ceremony. Involving self-torture to gain mystical vision and spiritual insight, the ceremony was outlawed in the United States, and Peltier and others were jailed for participating in it. The 1950s, a period that would be very influential on Peltier's activist spirit, brought many realities of the suffering and oppression of American Indians to the forefront for Peltier. He recalled in Bud and Ruth Schultz's article, "War Against the American Nation: Leonard Peltier," "When I was a teenager, I heard an old Ojibwa woman, a relative of mine, get up and speak at an Indian meeting. She was pleading for food for her children. 'Are there no more warriors among our men,' she asked, 'who will stand up and fight for their starving children?' That day, I vowed I would help my people the rest of my life."

When Peltier was 19, he moved to Oakland, California, to live with his mother, who had been sent there as part of the government's relocation program. Within a year, he became part-owner of an auto body shop in Seattle. During this period, he also became active in American Indian issues, participating in the Washington Indians' fishing rights campaigns. In 1970, Peltier participated in Indian rights demonstrations that would become increasingly popular throughout the decade. That year, he was involved with the take-over of surplus Indian land at Fort Lawton, outside Seattle.

Peltier joined the American Indian Movement in 1972, which was newly organized by Dennis Banks, Clyde Bellecourt, and other American Indian leaders who had been outspoken in the 1960s on American Indian and Alaska Native issues. Peltier was among the participants of the famed Trail of Broken Treaties March to Washington D.C. in November of 1972 and the subsequent takeover of the Bureau of Indian Affairs (BIA) headquarters. Early on AIM concerned itself with insisting that the U.S. government comply with terms of various treaties, most importantly the 1868 Fort Laramie Treaty, which recognized the sovereignty of Indian lands, specifically the Sioux. Infringements of the treaty on the part of non-Indians cost the Sioux most of their homeland, leaving them with a minuscule portion of what was rightly theirs, even according to U.S. treaty. After the incident at the BIA headquarters, the FBI tagged AIM as extremist, and AIM leaders, including Peltier, contend that they were harassed by the government thereafter.

In 1975 Peltier and other AIM members moved to Pine Ridge Reservation, which was the setting of the Wounded Knee siege of February 1973. AIM was responding to tensions on Pine Ridge between traditionalists and the followers of tribal chairman Dicky Wilson, who were known as the Guardians of the Oglala (Lakota) Nation—Dicky's GOONs. AIM members lived on the property of an elderly couple, Mr. and Mrs. Jumping Bull, and set up a camp where they planned activist strategies and enjoyed spiritual community and ceremony. Very importantly, their camp shielded traditionalist rivals of Wilson from harassment by his GOONs. Later in sworn testimony, FBI chief Clarence Kelly would describe the group as nonviolent and one that advocated sobriety and community improvement.

On the morning of June 26, 1975, FBI agents Ronald Williams and Jack Coler entered Jumping Bull's property to serve a warrant to a young Lakota man named Jimmy Eagle for an accusation that he stole a pair of cowboy boots. Events led to a car chase in the pursuit of Eagle. The agents radioed that Eagle was driving a red pickup truck and that they were in danger. "If you don't get here quick, we're gonna be dead," the agents transmitted to the FBI in Rapid City. A third agent, one of dozens on the reservation, reported to the site. Gunfire broke out. AIM members Bob Robideau and Norman Brown reported that the FBI fired first. The shootout ended with agents Williams and Coler dead—shot in the head—and a young Coeur d'Alene Indian named Joe Stuntz killed as well. FBI agents, BIA police, and other law enforcement agents moved in, and a stand-off ensued for the remainder of the day. Though authorities never investigated Stuntz's death, the deaths of the agents were followed immediately with a massive manhunt of about 350 federal agents.

In November of 1975, Robideau, Darrelle Butler, Eagle, and Peltier were indicted for the deaths of the agents. The men fled authorities with armed AIM members, hiding out for a period at the home of Leonard Crow Dog. Peltier entered Canada and requested political asylum there, arguing that the chance of him getting a fair trial in the United States was extremely unlikely. However, he was arrested in Alberta on February 2, 1976. With negotiations for Peltier's extradition delayed, Judge Edward McManus went ahead with the trial of Robideau and Butler, who had also been captured. Charges against Eagle were dropped. The trial, conducted in Cedar Rapids, Iowa, ended in a jury's verdict of "not guilty," after the defense successfully discredited the prosecution's weak and faulty arguments to prove that the two were guilty of aiding and abetting in the killings. AIM supporters celebrated the verdict, encouraged that Peltier could too be found "not guilty."

Peltier's extradition took place in December of 1976. The government built a case on a trio of conflicting affidavit statements from an American Indian woman named Myrtle Poor Bear, who, believed to be mentally unstable, claimed that she was Peltier's girlfriend. In her first statement, she professed not to have been at the camp. In the second, she declared that she was there and with Peltier. In the third, she offered more inconsistent details. In Robert Redford's documentary about the event and the government's case against Peltier, *Incident at Oglala*, Poor Bear recanted these sworn statements, explaining that she had been coerced by the FBI, who threatened to take away her daughter. She claimed that one agent threatened to make sure she ended up like Anna Mae Aquash, an activist who was found shot in the head on Pine Ridge in February of 1976, after she had pressured the government about its uranium mining on Pine Ridge and vowed that she would not cooperate with U.S. officials regarding Peltier's indictment.

Peltier's trial began on March 4, 1977, in Fargo, North Dakota. Judge McManus was replaced by Judge Paul Benson, who had been reversed by the Eighth Circuit Appeals Court for making anti-Indian statements during at least one of his previous trials. He repeatedly ruled against motions of the defense during the course of Peltier's trial. The largely circumstantial evidence of the prosecution centered around a single shell casing from a .223 caliber AR-15 rifle that was linked to Peltier. The prosecution also connected him to a red and white van in which Peltier was allegedly seen entering and leaving the Jumping Bull property. No one testified in court that they had seen Peltier commit the shootings. Evidence that the defense hoped to present to the jury regarding the war-like state on Pine Ridge, the persecution of AIM by the FBI, and FBI tampering of statements regarding the case were kept from the jury by Judge Benson's rulings. On April 18, 1977 the jury found Peltier guilty, and on June 1, Judge Benson sentenced him to two consecutive life terms in Marion Federal Penitentiary in Illinois.

A long series of unsuccessful appeals followed, the first in December of 1977, another in December of 1982, and the third and final on July 7, 1993. Attempts to appeal to the U.S. Supreme Court failed as well. However, there are several sources of doubt and inconsistency regarding the government's case against Peltier. Peltier's defense sought a retrial on the ground that documents obtained from FBI files under the Freedom of Information Act included suppressed evidence, including a statement on October 2, 1975 by an FBI ballistics experts that the gun alleged to have been Peltier's contained "a different firing pin" than that used in the killings. At a district court hearing in 1984, ballistics expert Evan Hodge testified that the teletype referred to other casings found at the scene. In addition, the description of the red pickup truck pursued by agents Williams and Coler was reneged by Agent Adams, who recalled seeing a red and white pick up. The defense claimed that Adams changed his statement so that the government could more easily pin the killings on Peltier, who owned a red and white van. The strongest source of inconsistency came from government prosecutor Lynn Crooks, who told the appeals court that, although the government tried Peltier for first-degree murder, it did not know this to be true. She explained that aiders and abettors are punishable to the same degree as principals. When the government could not prove that Peltier fired the shots, it seemed to be changing gears to make Peltier into an aider and abettor rather than a premeditated murderer. In 1990 journalist Peter Matthiessen, author of the book, *In the Spirit of Crazy Horse*, which was about the Peltier case, conducted an interview with a man who called himself Mr. X and claimed to have been the man who fired the shots that killed the agents.

Peltier's defense continues in its quest to gain Peltier's release. Supported by millions around the world, Peltier has been considered a political prisoner of the United States by many highly respected committees and individuals worldwide, including Amnesty International, Archbishop Desmond Tutu, the late Mother Theresa, Robert Redford, Jesse Jackson, Nelson Mandela, former U.S. Attorney General Ramsey Clark, and the late Fancois Mitterrand. Many supporters have signed petitions for his clemency and have rallied at peaceful demonstrations, including one of an estimated 3,000 people, on June 26, 1994, in Washington, D.C. In July of that year, a 3,800-mile Walk for Justice was overwhelmingly supported by people believing Peltier to be a victim of the government's quest to put any AIM member behind bars for the killings and to put an end to the Indian wars of the 1970s.

Leonard Peltier spends his time in prison responding to the many letters supporters send him and painting images, which are sold and made into prints to raise money for the Leonard Peltier Defense Committee. In 1999, his autobiography, *Prison Writing: My Life Is My Sun Dance,* was published. Fighting severe health problems, including the effects of a stroke and lockjaw, Peltier claimed in his book to gain his strength from his Indian heritage, and the spirituality therein, as well as his responsibility to make the best use of his situation and the publicity it attracts for the relief of conditions for his people.

Sources

➤ On-line

International Leonard Peltier Defense Committee, http// www.freepeltier.org (March 4, 2000).
Leonard Peltier, http://www.lpsg-co.org (March 4, 2000).

➤ Books

Encyclopedia of World Biography, second edition, Gale Research, 1998.
Matthiessen, Peter, *In the Spirit of Crazy Horse,* Penguin USA, 1983.
Newsmakers, volume 1995, issue 1, Gale Research, 1995 (opening quote).
Notable Native Americans, Gale Research, 1995.

Peltier, Leonard, edited by Harvey Arden, *Prison Writing: My Life Is My Sun Dance*, St. Martin's Press, 1999.

Schultz, Bud and Ruth Schultz, "War Against the American Nation: Leonard Peltier," in *It Did Happen Here: Recollections of Political Repression in America*, University of California Press, 1989; 213-229.

➤ **Periodicals**

Esquire, January 1992, p. 55.
Maclean's, July 27, 1992, p. 30.
Monthly Review, January 2000, pp. 57-60.
Nation, July 18, 1994, p. 76.
North American Review, May-August 1998, pp. 64-71.
People, May 4, 1992, p. 36.
Progressive, October 1999, p. 13.
Toronto Sun, May 30, 1999.

Giorgio Perlasca

"These people were in danger and I asked why must someone die because they are of another faith? I had a chance to do something. I couldn't refuse."*

Born in 1910 in Como, Italy, Giorgio Perlasca risked his life to save thousands of Hungarian Jews from deportation to Nazi concentration camps in World War II. He died August 15, 1992 in Padua, Italy.

One of the genuine heroes of the Holocaust, Italian business-man Giorgio Perlasca fought to save Jews in Hungary from Nazi forces during the last days of World War II. With little regard for his own safety, he impersonated a Spanish diplomat and issued thousands of travel documents that allowed Jewish victims of persecution to escape the country. After Hungary was liberated from Nazi control by Soviet forces, he made his way back to Italy and slipped into obscurity. It wasn't until the 1980s that he was honored by heads of state and private citizens alike for his courage and selflessness.

The son of a royal functionary, Perlasca was born the second of five children in the northern Italian town of Como. Moving to the coastal city of Trieste with his family, he was an indifferent student who showed few signs of having an outstanding future. Like many young Italians of his time, he was attracted to the strongly national-istic message of Fascism, and he volunteered to fight in Mussolini's Ethiopian campaign in 1935. A year later, he fought on the side of Fascist leader Francisco Franco during the Spanish Civil War. After his return to Italy, he was decorated for his service. Perlasca's military career was cut short, however, when he openly disagreed with Italy's anti-Jewish racial laws in 1938. "I couldn't understand the discrimination against the Jews," he told author Enrico Deaglio in his book *The Banality of Goodness.* "So many of my friends were Jews, in Padua, in Trieste, in Fiume. In Spain, the commander of a battery in my artillery regiment was a Jew, from Rome. . . " Though he never renounced his Fascist past entirely, Perlasca opposed an Italian alliance with Hitler and involvement in World War II.

By 1940, Perlasca had married Nerina Dal Pin and was working for a livestock importing firm. Exempt from military service, he was in Yugoslavia when war broke out and saw Nazi persecution of Jews and gypsies first-hand. In 1942, he relocated to Budapest, Hungary, a city relatively untouched by the fighting at that point. The following year, Italy signed a separate peace with the Allies, prompting German forces in Hungary to send Perlasca to an internment camp. Escaping, he made his way back to Budapest, which was under the control of Nazi SS troops. There, he sought out the Spanish embassy, which granted him citizenship in recognition of his earlier service to Franco.

Perlasca made friends with Spanish ambassador Angel Sanz-Briz and became involved in the consulate's efforts to keep Hungarian Jews from arrest by the Nazis. Together, they worked to extend Spanish legal protection to Jews and met with officials to thwart deportation efforts. The situation in Budapest grew more danger-ous as Soviet troops approached, and in November 1944 Sanz-Briz fled the country. Rather than abandon his rescue efforts, Perlasca decided to pose as the new Spanish ambassador. Working with remaining embassy employees, he began issuing documents of protection to Jews, brought them food and medicine and led them to safe houses. Thanks in part to his distinguished appearance and fluency in Spanish, he proved to be a convincing diplomat when negotiating with Hungarian and German officials. During one meeting, he convinced the Minister of Internal Affairs that the Spanish government would retaliate against Hungarian citizens living in Spain if the minister didn't allow Jews to remain under Spanish protection. Helping him in these efforts were representa-tives of other neutral nations, most notably Swedish envoy Raoul Wallenberg. During his two months of work, Perlasca protected more than 3,000 people from almost certain death at the hands of the Nazis.

The incident that stood out most for Perlasca involved the rescue of two twins one morning in December 1944. A long line of men, women and children were being herded into a railroad car for shipment to German camps. Perlasca arrived in a car flying a Spanish flag on its aerial and, scanning the scene, spotted a pair of curly-haired siblings in the middle of the line. "As they passed in front of me, I reached out and grabbed them, pulled them out of line, and threw them into the car," Perlasca recounted to Deaglio in *The Banality of Goodness*. "I yelled out, 'These two people are under the protection of the Spanish government!' A German major came over and wanted to take them back. I stepped in front of him and said, 'You have no right to take them! This car is Spanish national territory. This is an international zone!'" A shoving match between Perlasca and the soldier ensued. Finally, a German colonel interced-ed and allowed the children to leave, remarking coldly that "their time will come." After the colonel left, Raoul Wallenberg told Perlasca that the colonel was the infamous Adolf Eichmann, the officer in charge of the "final solution" for the Hungarian Jews.

Perlasca continued to masquerade as the Spanish consul until Russian forces took control of Budapest in mid-January 1945. In the midst of the chaos that followed, he was briefly detained by Russian troops, who forced him to dig up corpses from snow-covered streets. After he escaped, he was cited by the new Hungarian government for his "superhuman efforts on behalf of the oppressed and the persecuted." When he finally left Budapest in May 1945, he carried with him certificates recognizing his heroism. Among them was one presented by a delegation of Jews he had protected at a Spanish safe house, which read in part: "There are no words to praise the tenderness with which you fed us and with which you cared for the old and the sick. You gave us courage when we were on the verge of desperation and your name will never be missing from our prayers. May Almighty God reward you."

After his return to Italy, Perlasca faded from view for some 40 years. Like most European nations, his homeland was eager to put aside issues of guilt and responsibility raised during World War II, and the deeds of this Fascist veteran in Hungary were forgotten. "When I came back, I tried to tell the story, but it seemed like nobody believed it," he told Deaglio. ". . . And so it happened that, slowly but surely, I began to forget about it myself. I thought about it often, naturally, but I started to have my doubts. . . Were all the things I did in those few months really true?"

In 1987, Perlasca was living with his wife in a small apartment in Padua, Italy when he received a letter from Dr. Eveline Blitstein Willinger, who represented a group of Jewish Holocaust survivors. They sought to honor him for his work and, through their efforts, he began to receive belated recognition by governments around the world. Hungary was the first, awarding him the Gold Star at a special session of Parliament. In September 1990, he was presented with the Righteous Among the Nations of the World Award by the Yad V'Shem Holocaust Memorial in Jerusalem, an honor based upon extensive testimony by those Perlasca had rescued. He was also made an honorary citizen of Israel. That same year, he received the Medal of Remembrance of the United States Holocaust Memorial Council. And Spain — the nation he had "represented" — named him Knight Commander of the Order of Isabella by decree of King Juan Carlos.

Tributes to Perlasca in print and on television appeared in Italy, Hungary and elsewhere in the early 1990s. The publication of *The Banality of Goodness* in Italy in 1991 brought his story even greater attention. Gregory Conti, the book's English translator, wrote in a *Commonweal* article that Perlasca's heroism "reminds us . . . that the expression of human goodness in the struggle against human evil is an enterprise whose success requires not only courage and perseverance but also skill, craft, art, and imagination."

Perlasca died of a heart attack at his home in Padua on August 15, 1992. According to Deaglio, he had been changed little by the international attention he had received in his last years. To the end of his life, he made no special claims of heroism for his actions in

Budapest. "I did what I had to do," he told the *Jerusalem Post* in a 1987 interview (quoted in *The New York Times* in 1992). "I was lucky. I had friends among the Jews who were being killed by the Nazis. That gave me courage."

Sources

➤ Books

Deaglio, Enrico, *The Banality of Goodness: The Story of Giorgio Perlasca*, University of Notre Dame Press, 1998.

➤ Periodicals

Commonweal, December 3, 1999, p.10.
New York Times, September 6, 1990, p. B22; August 22, 1992, p. 10.
Publishers Weekly, June 1, 1998, p. 44.
U.S. News and World Report, March 21, 1994, p. 56 (opening quote).

Bertrand Piccard and Brian Jones

"*We didn't have to overcome nature. We had to harmonize with it. We put our capsule into a position where Mother Nature takes us into her arms.*"

Bertrand Piccard (born March 1, 1958, in Switzerland) and Brian Jones (born March 1947, in Bristol, England) completed a non-stop round the world trip in a balloon in 20 days, setting a world's record. Piccard is a psychiatrist from Switzerland, while Jones is a professional balloonist and balloon designer from Great Britain. Address: c/o John Wiley & Sons, Incorporated, 605 Third Ave., 4th Flr., New York, NY 10158-0012.

In 1873, French science fiction pioneer Jules Verne wrote a book entitled *Around the World in Eighty Days*, about a balloon voyage that circumnavigated the globe. In 1999, Bertrand Piccard and Brian Jones became the first to complete a non-stop round-the-world trip by a balloon. However, the trip only took 20 days and set several world's records. Both Piccard and Jones had spent many years ballooning, though they had other careers as well.

Piccard was born March 1, 1958, in Switzerland, into a family of pioneers of the sky and sea. His grandfather, Auguste Piccard, was the first man to enter the stratosphere in a balloon in 1931. He went nearly 10 miles high, or about 51,762 feet. Auguste Piccard, a physicist and professor at the University of Brussels, was also the inventor of the pressurized cabin.

Piccard's father, Jacques, was a pioneer under the sea. He built a bathyscaph, based on designs by his father, and set a record for diving depth. Jacques Piccard took the bathyscaph down 36,000 feet into the deepest part of the ocean, the Pacific's Mariana Trench, in 1960. Jacques Piccard also invented more undersea submersibles, including one specifically designed for tourists. Piccard's mother was more cerebral, interested in religion, psychology and philosophy.

Piccard was raised primarily in Europe, though because of his father's career, he spent two years in the United States during adolescence. Living in West Palm Beach, Florida, Piccard witnessed the launching of six Apollo space missions (Apollo 7 through Apollo 12), and met the astronauts. The experience made a deep impression on him, and he soon wanted to do something spectacular involving flight himself.

In 1974, Piccard became interested in hang-gliding, then a new sport in Europe. Hang-gliding involves gliding through the air harnessed to a very large kite-type object. Piccard specialized in aerobatics hang-gliding and was soon a champion in the sport. He also found the hang-gliding helped him do better in school. Piccard was training to become a psychiatrist at the University of Lausanne. He later used what he learned about self-awareness in hang-gliding in his private psychiatric practice, also based in Lausanne.

Piccard became interested in ballooning in the early 1990s. He was invited to be the co-pilot of a balloon in a race across the Atlantic Ocean because of his medical and hang-gliding skills. Piccard was soon hooked on the sport, and became a recognized champion.

Within a few years, he was interested in the challenge of going around the world non-stop in a balloon. With the support of his wife

Michéle (with whom he had three daughters, Estelle, Oriane, and Solange), Piccard pursued a sponsorship deal with Breitling, a Swiss watchmaking company. Through his relationship with the British balloon manufacturing firm, Cameron, Piccard met Brian Jones, who would co-pilot his only successful attempt at this feat.

Jones was born in Bristol, England, in March of 1947. His father worked as a lawyer's legal executive, while his mother was employed as a secretary. From an early age, Jones liked the outdoors and flying. When he was 16, he only earned one O-level, in English.

After working as a clerk at British Aerospace for a short time, Jones joined the Royal Air Force (RAF), hoping to become a pilot. However, his one O-level was not enough to qualify him for the program. Instead, he was trained as an administrative apprentice. Jones continued his education via the RAF Education section, and earned three additional O-levels. Jones tried to join pilot training again, but he was refused. He was retrained to become a loadmaster on transports then helicopters, and had numerous adventures.

In 1977, Jones retired from the Air Force. He found work as a salesman in the pharmaceutical industry, then as a trainer of salesmen. Later, Jones started a wholesale catering supply business, Crocks, with his sister Pauline. Eventually, the business expanded to include retail stores as well. Through Crocks, Jones met his wife Jo, with whom he had two children.

Jones became interested in ballooning in 1986, when he rode in one for the first time. After selling some of his retail business, he bought a balloon and taught himself to fly it. Jones looked to ballooning for his livelihood. He got a commercial license that allowed him to take people up in balloons. Later, he became a certified instructor to people who wanted to fly balloons. He also became an examiner and certifier for flight instructors via the National Training Officer. Jones had to approve relevant licenses given out by the Civil Aviation Authority of Great Britain.

In 1994, Jones and others founded High Profile Balloons, which ran balloons for businesses. He became involved with Piccard's sponsor, Breitling, in 1997 when they approached Cameron Balloons for support work for Piccard's flight. Jones played an organization role at Cameron, where he designed balloons. His wife Jo also became involved with the control team. In fact, the couple lived near Cameron's manufacturing headquarters. Before the record-setting flight, Jones had logged 1,200 hours in balloons.

Piccard had not been the first to want to try and fly around the world in a balloon in the late twentieth century, when technology developed to the point where such a feat was truly possible. There were a spate of attempts beginning in the early 1980s, about 20 between 1981 and 2000. Before Piccard and Jones, the only people to come close were two Americans, Don Ida and Maxie Anderson, in 1981. Ida and Anderson flew from Egypt to India, for a total of 2,676 miles.

Under the sponsorship of Breitling, Piccard made two attempts to go around the world with co-pilots other than Jones in the late 1990s. His attempt in Orbiter 1 lasted only six hours in 1997. In 1998, Piccard and his co-pilot flew Orbiter 2 for nine days before technical problems ended that flight. While Breitling was Piccard's sponsor, the company would not support many more failed attempts. Orbiter 3 was essentially Piccard's last chance.

There were problems with Orbiter 3 even before the balloon was in the air. Because of competition from other balloonists, Piccard was pushed into starting in March of 1999, after the traditional end of ballooning season. Piccard also had co-pilot problems. His scheduled co-pilot was Tony Brown, a citizen of Great Britain, who did not get along with Piccard. Jones, who had overseen production of the Orbiter 3 balloon at Cameron Balloons as a project manager, was a last-minute substitution and one that turned out for the best.

Positive aspects were also present when the Orbiter 3 took off on March 1, 1999, from Chateau d'Oex in the Alps of Switzerland. Piccard and Jones' weather team predicted favorable conditions in their pre-determined route. A year had been spent planning this best route to meet their goal. Piccard and Breitling learned from their mistakes, however, improving the design of the balloon based on previous experience.

The Orbiter 3 was 13 stories tall (about 180 feet high) and weighed about 18,000 pounds (about the same as a fighter plane). The balloon's envelope was filled with helium and air, while prone provided the heat that propelled it. Piccard and Jones lived inside a capsule that was 17.72 feet long, 9.35 feet high and went about 150 mph. The capsule contained a small water heater, a bunk, and a toilet. It was pressurized because of the altitudes at which they traveled.

The trip was not particularly problematic through eastern Europe and Asia. They crossed the Pacific in six days, though they encountered some slow winds and had some communication problems with mission control. Piccard and Jones' biggest challenge came over the Americas. They had some problems over Central America and the Caribbean. At one point, they were worried they might have to quit when they reached Puerto Rico.

The challenge of being in such a small space for a long period of time was daunting. Piccard and Jones' heater broke during the trip, and they suffered from extreme cold from that time forward. They also suffered from carbon dioxide build-up at one point. In order to cope with the stituation, Piccard used self-hypnosis, which he taught to Jones.

Even before they completed the circumnavigation of the globe, Piccard and Jones broke a record. It was flight duration without refueling, which they bested at 17 days, 18 hours and 25 minutes. Their trip around the world was only a few days longer, but fuel was low by the end.

Piccard and Jones completed the trip on March 20, 1999. The balloon flight had taken 19 days, one hour and 49 minutes. They had traveled 26,755 miles (42,647 km), which also set a record for longest trip without refueling. Though the pair technically only had to land in Mauritania to complete the journey, the pair chose to land near Mut, Egypt, which was much farther than they had to travel. Jones had wanted to land near the Great Pyramids at Giza, but the winds did not co-operate.

The trip also broke two other records. They broke the longest distance record for a balloon flight. The previous one was held by American Steve Fossett who traveled 14,000 miles in 1998. The pair also broke a duration record. Piccard and his Orbiter 2 co-pilot Andy Elsen set it with 233 hours and 55 minutes. Piccard and Jones attributed their success to good planning.

For their effort, Piccard and Jones won $1 million from Anheuser-Busch and the Budweiser Cup. After the flight, Piccard went back to his psychiatric practice, while Jones returned to Britain to continue working the balloons. In 2000, Piccard was named the United Nations Population Fund's Goodwill Ambassador. He's a spokesman in his native Switzerland and does goodwill tours. Upon his appointment, he said, according to an unnamed Reuters reporter, "Maybe one day . . . we can travel in a balloon around the world, look at the beauty of the world, and know that on the ground it is a little better also."

Sources

➤ Books

Piccard, Bertrand and Brian Jones, *Around the World in 20 Days: The Story of Our History-Making Balloon Flight,* John Wiley & Sons, 1999.

➤ Periodicals

Arizona Republic, March 22, 1999, p. A6.
Daily Telegraph, March 20, 1999, p. 12.
Library Journal, November 1, 1999, p. 92.
Life, May 1, 1999, p. 20.
Maclean's, March 29, 1999, p. 41.
Newsday, March 21, 1999, p. A3.
Popular Science, June 1999, p. 33.
Publishers Weekly, October 25, 1999, p. 66.
Reuters, November 11, 1999.
U.S. News & World Report, March 29, 1999, p. 72.
Washington Post, March 21, 1999, p. A1; March 23, 1999, p. A11; April 8, 1999, p. C1 (opening quote).

Jose Ramos-Horta

*"***I** *am Western government's biggest embarrass-*
ment. They are often patronizing to me, some-
times hostile; but they are never allowed to forget."

Born December 25, 1949, in Dili, East Timor, Jose Ramos-Horta
is a human rights activist who spent his life working to free his
native country from its Indonesian oppressors. After winning
the 1996 Nobel Peace Prize for his work, Ramos-Horta's goal
was reached in late 1999. Address: IPJET, Gruttohoek 13,
2317wk, Leiden, The Netherlands.

Living in exile most of his adult life, Jose Ramos-Horta worked tirelessly to free his native East Timor, a small nation located on half of an island between Indonesia and Australia. His exile began when Indonesia invaded and claimed East Timor for its own in 1975. Throughout the bloodshed that followed, Ramos-Horta worked to bring the attention of this problem to the world, an uphill battle which earned him the Nobel Peace Prize (shared with another East Timorese activist). After East Timor was finally free of Indonesia in 1999, Ramos-Horta was allowed to return to his country.

Ramos-Horta was born on December 26, 1949, in Dili, the capital of East Timor. He was one of ten children born to Francisco Horta and Natalina Ramos Filipe Horta. His father was a native of Portugal, the country that had originally colonized East Timor. Francisco Horta had been exiled to East Timor for political crimes (he had rebelled against the military dictatorship of Antonio Salazar), and married a native of East Timor, Natalina Ramos Filipe. Francisco Horta was not really part of Ramos-Horta's upbringing. He lived isolated from his family, obsessed with Portugal. Ramos-Horta and his siblings were primarily raised by their mother.

Though born in Dili, Ramos-Horta grew up on different parts of the island. He was educated at a Catholic mission school located in the remote village of Soibada beginning at the age of seven. Many children, including his siblings, were sent there for their elementary education. He spent seven years there, not seeing his family except during summers. Ramos-Horta did well though, unlike most, and was one of the few to continue his education. He went on to a school in Dili, and graduated from high school.

Ramos-Horta was a rabble-rouser from a young age. While beginning a career as a journalist, in about 1970, he was forced to leave East Timor for uttering anti-Portuguese sentiments in front of the wrong people. He completed part of his education while living in exile in Mozambique, and returned to East Timor in 1972. His education eventually included a stint at Oxford University on fellowship. There he studied international relations at St. Anthony's College. He also attended college in the United States in the 1980s. In addition to some time at Columbia University, he earned his M.A. in peace studies at Antioch College in 1984. The rest of his formal university education took place in Europe in Strasbourg's International Institute of Human Rights and the Hague Academy of International Law.

When Ramos-Horta returned to East Timor, he continued to work as a journalist. In the mid-1970s, events in Portugal seemed to indicate that East Timor would become independent soon. After a left-wing coup in 1974, Portugal gave up colonial claims to East Timor in August of 1975. When Portugal pulled out, Fretilin (Revolutionary Front for an Independent East Timor, or National Liberation Front for East Timor), an East Timorese group dedicated to independence, formed a government in September of 1975. Ramos-Horta was named foreign minister, though he was only 25 years old. At the time, he was the youngest government official of his caliber in the world.

Fretilin got support by appealing to the people. Ramos-Horta was quoted by John Pilger of *New Statesman & Society* as writing, "We criss-crossed the country. Our theme was simple. We spoke the language of the people: 'Are we human beings or sacks of potatoes to be sold to another country?'" Yet there were also accusations that Fretilin killed people from the other four independence groups vying for power in 1975.

The Fretilin government was short-lived. In addition to other independence groups, Indonesia, a much larger country which already controlled the western half of the island on which East Timor was located, wanted East Timor. On December 7, 1975, Indonesia invaded and took over East Timor. In the ensuing bloody battle, many died. Indonesia annexed East Timor the following year. Ramos-Horta barely escaped a few days before the invasion. He spent the next two-and-a-half decades in exile, representing Fretilin.

For Ramos-Horta, the Indonesian takeover had personal ramifications. Several of his siblings died by the end of the conflict as a direct result: three brothers (Guy, Guilherme, and Nuno) and one sister, Maria. Ramos-Horta worked to bring the problems in his native country to the world. From 1976 until 1989, he was Fretilin's official representative to the United Nations.

Though the United Nations and almost every country in the world (except Australia) did not recognize Indonesia's claim on East Timor, the conquerors carried out a systematic destruction of East Timorese culture that lasted from 1976 to about 1981. In addition to crushing those involved in underground resistance and independence, many were imprisoned and human rights were routinely violated. About a third of the native population died: 200,000 of a population of about 650,000. If the war did not kill them, starvation and disease did. Indonesia also brought in new settlers, giving them the best of what was available to further dilute the power of the native population.

Ramos-Horta's work to bring attention to the situation did result in some international outcry. The Roman Catholic Church supported East Timorese independence, because most of the populace was of that religion. (Indonesia was primarily Muslim.) Other supporters included Amnesty International. But Ramos-Horta could not get much media attention in the West, despite his best efforts. He called for countries like the United States, Great Britain and Australia to stop selling arms to Indonesia because they were used to kill his people. Ramos-Horta was unsuccessful on this front for many years.

Yet horrible events continued to occur in East Timor. In 1990, 150 independence demonstrators were arrested, jailed and tortured. On November 12, 1991, a crowd marched to the grave of a fallen East Timorese activist located in Santa Cruz cemetery. The Indonesian troops opened fire on them. While Indonesia claimed only 50 people died, others said the number was as high as 400. The event was later deemed a massacre.

By this time, Ramos-Horta's position at the United Nations had ended. His new homebase in exile was Sydney, Australia, where he held a faculty position at the University of New South Wales' law school beginning in 1990. That year, he founded the Diplomacy Training Programme, and served as its director and lecturer. (Some members of his family, including his mother and one sister, joined him in Sydney when they could escape.) His time at the university was limited, as freeing East Timor was his primary occupation. To that end, in 1991, he was special representative and co-chair of the National Council of Maubere Resistant, an umbrella organization for resistance groups.

Ramos-Horta affected some change by the mid-1990s. The United States started to limit their armaments sales to Indonesia. As early as 1992, Fretilin leaders (including Ramos-Horta) promoted a peace plan. Yet he and other East Timorese activists were not permitted to attend the Asia Pacific Conference on East Timor because of pressure placed on the host country, the Philippines, by Indonesia.

Despite such snubs, Ramos-Horta began to be recognized for his work. In 1993, he received the Professor Thorolf Raftol Human Rights Award. In 1995, he received the Gleitzman Foundation Award. In 1996, he received the UNPO Award. The biggest prize of all came in 1996 as well: the Nobel Prize. The Nobel committee wanted to bring attention to the problem in the hope of bringing about a solution.

Ramos-Horta shared the prize with another East Timorese activist, Bishop Carlos Felipe Ximenes Belo. Belo was a Catholic bishop who stayed in East Timor despite the harassment. Ramos-Horta did not feel worthy of the award. He told Keith Suter of *Bulletin of the Atomic Scientists,* "I feel humbled to be [honored] next to people like Nelson Mandela." Ramos-Horta thought it would have been better if the award had gone to another East Timorese activist, Jose Alexandre Gusmao, who had been imprisoned for many years.

Change was in the air. The United States stopped selling most arms to Indonesia right away. Indonesia had been ruled by an uncompromising dictator, President Suharto, through 1998, when he was removed from power. His successor, President B.J. Habibie, was open to changes in the situation. By 1999, it was finally agreed that the United Nations would sponsor elections in East Timor so the people could vote on their future. Habibie had offered the East Timorese broad autonomy within Indonesia as a province. The other option was independence.

Ramos-Horta wanted to go home badly over the years. He had considered just sneaking in, though he would be put in jail or killed immediately. In 1999, he initially was not allowed to go to East Timor to campaign for the referendum. He was allowed into Indonesia on June 26, after promising not to be too prominent. Ramos-Horta was willing to support anything as long as it was the end of violence.

Though there was some violence and intimidation even in the registration process, the vote occurred on August 30, 1999, and the East Timorese voted for freedom. Indonesian soldiers backed militias who responded with more violence and death. About 7,000 people died after the results were announced, but the independence of East Timor did not change.

Ramos-Horta was finally allowed to return to East Timor on December 1, 1999, after traveling around the world to promote the cause of rebuilding his native country. He also wanted the new government to be inclusive, balancing the interests of everyone, even the newcomers. The United Nations supervised the transitional period, which was expected to take three to five years.

Ramos-Horta planned to leave political concerns behind after December, and return to journalism. He immediately became involved in the formation of the East Timor News Agency. An unidentified long-time friend told Joe Leahy of *Maclean's* that "Horta's had a unique career. He's a supreme diplomat and he has taken on the diplomatic might of the Western world almost single-handedly." And he won.

Sources

> **Books**

Ramos-Horta, Jose, *Funu: The Unfinished Saga of East Timor*, Red Sea Press, 1987.
Thompson, Clifford, editor, *Nobel Prize Winners: 1992-1996 Supplement*, H.W. Wilson Company, 1997.
Who's Who 1999: An Annual Biographical Dictionary, St. Martin's Press, 1999.

> **Periodicals**

AP Online, December 18, 1999.
Bangkok Post, February 4, 2000.
Bulletin of the Atomic Scientists, January-February 1997, p. 47.
Businessworld, February 11, 2000.
Christian Century, October 30, 1996, p. 1031.
Contemporary Review, June 1997, p. 295.
Economist, December 14, 1996, p. 34.
Independent, December 2, 1999, p. 16.
Maclean's, October 21, 1996, p. 37.
Nation, November 4, 1996, p. 6.
New Statesman & Society, January 27, 1995, p. 17 (opening quote).
New York Times, October 12, 1996, section 1, p. 6.
Progressive, May 1, 1997, p. 29.
Reuters, June 26, 1999; August 30, 1999; February 13, 2000.
Seattle Times, November 11, 1999, p. A16.
Time, October 21, 1996, p. 47.
Time International, October 21, 1996, p. 30.
United Press International, June 14, 1999; August 6, 1999; September 16, 1999; September 17, 1999.
U.S. News and World Report, October 21, 1996, p. 32.
Washington Post, June 27, 1999, p. A23; September 9, 1999, p. A17.

Harold "Pee Wee" Reese

"I *don't care if this man is black, blue or striped. He can play and he can help us win. That's* *what counts."*

Born July 23, 1918, in Ekron, Kentucky, Harold "Pee Wee" Reese was a leader on the Brooklyn Dodgers team, playing a key role in the integration of baseball. Reese died on August 14, 1999, in Louisville, Kentucky.

Many have expressed the opinion that Harold "Pee Wee" Reese was the greatest player to ever wear a Brooklyn (later Los Angeles) Dodgers uniform. Though Reese was an exemplary player, both offensively and defensively, it was his role as team captain and leader that was often better remembered. Reese was the catalyst in the integration of major league baseball by showing his unwavering support for Jackie Robinson, the first African American to play in the league in the twentieth century.

Born Harold Henry Reese on July 23, 1918, on a farm in Ekron, Kentucky, he was the son of Carl Reese, a yard railroad detective with L&N Railroad. Reese grew up primarily in Louisville. He acquired the nickname "Pee Wee" in 1932 when he was national marbles champion. (A pee wee is a type of small marble.)

It was commonly believed that Reese was so nicknamed because of his small stature. While attending DuPont Manual High School, Reese did not play much baseball because of his size. He only played in five games during his senior year because he was only about five feet four inches tall and weighed about 120 pounds.

When he graduated from high school, Reese got a job working for the telephone company as a cable splicer. He continued to play baseball, however, primarily for the New Covenant Presbyterian Church in a church league. The Reese-led team was the best in 1937, and he caught the eye of a minor league club during the last game of that season.

The team was the Louisville Colonels, an independent AA squad in the America Association. Reese played for the team in 1938 and 1939, and acquired another nickname, the "Little Colonel." Though only five feet nine inches tall and 140 pounds, growing to 5 feet 10 inches tall and 160 pounds, Reese soon became the team's star shortstop. In 1939, he had a fielding percentage of .943, a batting average of .279, and led the association in triples with 18 and stolen bases with 35.

Impressed by his abilities, the Boston Red Sox bought the team to get the rights to Reese. Within a short time, he contract was sold to the Brooklyn Dodgers for $75,000 because the Sox already had a star shortstop in their player-manager Joe Cronin. Reese went to spring training with the Dodgers in 1940, and though still relatively small compared to many major league players, he made the team.

Reese's rookie season, however, was unspectacular. He played in only 84 games because of injuries, primarily a fractured heel. In those games, he managed a .272 batting average and a .960 fielding percentage.

By the 1941 season, Reese began to find his stride and soon became the team's spiritual leader. Though he still struggled with both his hitting and fielding—his batting average was a career-low .229, his fielding average was only .946 and he led the league in errors with 47—the Dodgers won the National League pennant and played in the World Series.

Reese rebounded from these struggles and soon became recognized for his abilities both defensively and offensively. He appeared in the All-Star Game in 1942, the same year he married Dorothy Walton. Together they had a daughter, Barbara, and a son, Mark.

World War II interrupted Reese's development as a player, however. Reese missed three whole seasons, 1943-45, when he served in the United States Navy as part of the war effort. When he left the service, he had reached the rank of Chief Petty Officer.

Reese returned to baseball after the war and continued to improve. The year 1947 was crucial both for Reese and major league baseball. That year the race barrier was broken when the Dodgers signed Jackie Robinson.

Reese played a role in the integration as early as spring training that year. He refused to sign a petition circulated by other Dodgers, led by Dixie Walker. The petition said that these players would not play if Robinson was on the team. Reese's refusal to sign stopped its circulation.

Yet Reese could have had several reasons to resent Robinson. Reese could have feared that Robinson would take his job since Robinson was also a shortstop. Steve Bailey in *The Columbian* quoted Reese as saying, "If he's man enough to take my job, I'm not gonna like it, but, dammit, black or white, he deserves it."

Reese was also a white Southerner, though he got along with everyone. Baseball historian Tot Holmes told Jon Thurber and Jason Reid of the *Los Angeles Times*, "The fact that Reese, a Southerner, befriended Robinson made a great deal of difference to his Dodger teammates." Yet Robinson was still berated by some of them as well as the players on other teams and the crowds where they played.

One of the best instances of how Reese led by example occurred during a Dodgers game in Cincinnati, a city near Reese's home. After Robinson was pelted with negative words and objects, Reese put his arm around Robinson's shoulder. This action silenced everyone, and is seen by many as a turning point in the public acceptance of Robinson.

Of this incident, Martin Weil of the *Washington Post* quoted Jackie Robinson as saying, "Pee Wee kind of sensed the sort of hopeless, dead feeling in me and came over and stood beside me for a while. He didn't say a word, but he looked over at the chaps who were yelling at me . . . and just stared. He was standing by me, I can tell you that."

Reese's gesture was not merely public grandstanding. It was an example of a deeper respect for Robinson as a person. Paul Wedley of *Independent* quoted Reese as saying, "He could have done anything he set out to do. It didn't have to be baseball. He was articulate and sharp and when he started to speak out, easy to dislike. But he taught me a lot more than I ever taught him." They were friends off the field as well, and often played bridge together.

The year 1947 was also significant for Reese for other reasons. He appeared in his second All-Star game, and would appear in it every year through 1954. Reese led the National League in walks with 104, and the Dodgers won the National League pennant.

Reese was such a good shortstop that when the Dodgers acquired another talented shortstop, Billy Cox, in 1948, they made him a third baseman. In 1949, Reese had the best season of his career. Appearing in 155 games, he had a batting average of .279 and scoring 132 runs (leading National League). The Dodgers again won the National League pennant.

Reese's leadership off the field was confirmed when he was named captain of the Dodgers in 1951. As the team continued to win the National League Pennant, in both 1952 and 1953, Reese was offered a bigger role in the team as player-manager. Reese turned the promotion down, in part because he felt he had been friends with his teammates for too many years.

In 1955, the Dodgers showed how much they appreciated Reese's importance to the team in a unique grand gesture. On the night before his birthday, the team declared the game "Pee Wee Reese Night" at Ebbets Field. During the fifth inning, the lights were turned out and 35,000 fans sang "Happy Birthday" to him.

Though Reese also received $20,000 worth of presents that night, he got a bigger gift later in the season. The Dodgers finally won the World Series. This was the only World Series victory for Reese in the seven times the team went to the championship while he was a player.

Before the Dodgers moved from Brooklyn to Los Angeles, California, after the 1957 season, Reese led the Dodgers in a number of offensive categories. He had the most stolen bases (231) and most runs scored (1,317). Reese was second in number of games played (2,107), hits (2,137), doubles (3,232), singles (1,612), and at bats (7,911). Reese's final season with the Dodgers was 1958. He appeared in only 59 games, primarily at third base.

When Reese retired after the 1958 season, he had appeared in 2,166 games, with a .269 batting average, 126 home runs, and 885 runs batted in. His career fielding average was .962. His totals would have been even better had he not missed those three seasons during World War II, for he had been in his prime at the time. After retirement, Reese was again offered the position of team manager, but he chose to take a coaching position instead. Reese worked as a Dodgers coach for only the 1959 season.

After leaving baseball playing and coaching, Reese turned to the booth. He worked as a baseball broadcaster for CBS, NBC, and the Cincinnati Reds, doing some broadcasts with Dizzy Dean, another former ballplayer. Reese had business interests as well. He owned a bowling alley and storm window business in Louisville, and was a banker. At one point, he worked for Hillerich and Bradsby Company, which made the Louisville Slugger baseball bat, as an executive (director of college and professional baseball staff).

Reese was inducted into the Baseball Hall of Fame in 1984. The same year, he was selected as a charter member of the Brooklyn Dodgers Baseball Hall of Fame.

Reese died on August 14, 1999, at his home in Louisville, Kentucky. The cause was cancer. Upon his death, perennial Dodgers' announcer Vin Scully told Jon Thurber and Jason Reid of the *Los Angeles Times*, "He was the heart and soul of the 'Boys of Summer.' He was the rare man who had the voice of authority and who was still loved by his teammates. I don't know of a modern-day player who was loved by his teammates as much as Pee Wee was, in all honesty."

Sources

➤ Books

Golenbock, Peter, *Teammates*, Gulliver Books, 1990 (opening quote).
Kahn, Roger, *The Boys of Summer*, Harper & Row, 1971.
Light, Jonathan Fraser, *The Cultural Encyclopedia of Baseball*, McFarland & Company, Inc., 1997, p. 608.
Porter, David L., ed., *Biographical Dictionary of American Sports: Baseball*, Greenwood Press, 1987, pp. 466-67.
Shatzkin, Mike, ed., *The Ballplayers: Baseball's Ultimate Biographical Reference*, Arbor House, 1990, p. 898.

➤ Periodicals

Columbian, August 15, 1999.
Dallas Morning News, August 15, 1999, p. 7B.
Gannett News Service, August 16, 1999.
Independent, August 19, 1999, p. 6.
Los Angeles Times, August 15, 1999, p. D1.
Orange County Register, August 19, 1999, p. D1.
Sports Illustrated, August 23, 1999, p. 54.
Washington Post, August 15, 1999, p. C6.

Bill Richardson

"Whether it's releasing prisoners or trying to bring nations that have deep divisions closer together, or protecting sacred sites, I think that's how I wish to express my faith."*

Born November 15, 1947, in Pasadena, California, Bill Richardson is a former congressman and U.S. Ambassador to the United Nations. Head of the Department of Energy under President Bill Clinton, he has been mentioned as a possible candidate for higher office. Address: U.S. Department of Energy, 1000 Independence Avenue SW, Washington, D.C. 20585-0001.

One of the most prominent Hispanic politicians in the United States is Bill Richardson, a former multiple-term representative in Congress from the state of New Mexico and U.S. Ambassador to the United Nations. In 1998 he accepted a cabinet-level post in the administration of President Bill Clinton as Secretary of Energy. Richardson has also been active in Hispanic causes and is sometimes touted as a potential member of a future Democratic presidential ticket.

Born on November 15, 1947, in Pasadena, California, William Blaine Richardson is the son of William Richardson and Maria Luisa Zubiran Richardson. His father was an American citizen who held an executive position with Citibank. His mother was a Mexican citizen, and it was in Mexico City, Mexico, that Richardson and his sister, Vesta, grew up amid the comforts and privileges of high society.

As a teenager, Richardson returned to the United States to attend Middlesex, a prep school located just outside his father's hometown of Boston, Massachusetts. There he was a standout baseball pitcher who was drafted right out of high school by the Kansas City Athletics in 1967. But his father discouraged him from pursuing a professional baseball career and urged him to go to college. Richardson later regretted his decision not to give baseball a try, but within a year after he had graduated, his elbow went out and effectively ended his pitching days for good.

Instead, Richardson enrolled at Tufts University and majored in political science. After earning his B.A. in 1970, he entered graduate school at the Fletcher School of Law and Diplomacy at Tufts. Richardson completed his studies in 1971 and headed to Washington, D.C., to work in politics. First, he spent a year (1971-72) as a staff member for the U.S. House of Representatives. In 1973, on the heels of his 1972 marriage to Barbara Flavin, an antiques restorer, Richardson became a staff member at the State Department, a position he held for three years before joining the staff of the foreign relations subcommittee of the U.S. Senate under the direction of Senator Hubert Humphrey.

Richardson's life changed dramatically in 1978 when he left Washington and moved to New Mexico. There he entered the business world as a trade consultant. However, he remained active in politics, becoming a member of the Bernalillo County Democratic Commission and, at the governor's request, executive director of the New Mexico State Democratic Commission. He also worked with Big Brothers-Big Sisters of Santa Fe and was a member of the

Santa Fe Hispanic Chamber of Commerce and the Santa Fe Chamber of Commerce Council on Foreign Relations.

In 1980 Richardson launched his first political campaign when he ran for a seat in the U.S. House of Representatives as the candidate for the Third District in New Mexico. He even set a short-lived world's record for the most number of hands shaken in one day (8,871) while on the campaign trail. Despite his efforts, Richardson lost the election to a popular incumbent, though not by much. Some of his opponents had accused him of being a carpetbagger—that is, someone who had moved to New Mexico just to obtain an elective office.

Two years later, Richardson ran again for the same seat, only this time, he won. The Third District was quite diverse, with a population that was 20 percent Native American, 34 percent Hispanic, and 44 percent white. Within its boundaries were 28 sovereign Indian nations. Richardson did his best to balance the needs of all his constituents. He was re-elected numerous times, representing the Third District through 1996.

Richardson served on a number of important committees as a congressman. In 1985, for example, he joined the House Energy and Commerce Committee. Among the topics he dealt with were pipeline-related issues and natural gas legislation. Richardson also promoted the increased use of natural gas and vehicles powered by alternative energy supplies. In 1990, he was instrumental in helping strengthen the Clean Air Act.

In addition, Richardson served on the Resources Committee on National Parks, Forests and Lands, the Select Committee on Intelligence, and the Helsinki Commission. Especially important to him were issues involving Latin America. In 1985, for instance, he voted in favor of sending aid to the new Sandinista government in Nicaragua, which was then at war with guerrilla troops known as *contras*.

Almost every year he was in office, Richardson also introduced a bill asking the president to formulate a free-trade agreement with Mexico. His persistence paid off in the early 1990s, when the North American Free Trade Agreement (NAFTA) finally came up for debate. Richardson himself had helped hammer out the agreement by negotiating with Mexico's president, Carlos Salinas de Gortari. His efforts on NAFTA's behalf prompted the Mexican government to grant him the Aztec Eagle Award, the highest honor the country bestows upon a non-citizen.

By the early 1990s, Richardson was a highly respected congress-man with a liberal voting record on social issues as well as on the environment. He served as co-chair of the Democratic Platform Committee in 1988 and was its chair in 1992, when Democrat Bill Clinton was elected president. Clinton considered Richardson for the cabinet post of Secretary of the Interior, but environmentalists balked, and the job went to someone else.

Instead, Richardson was chosen to be the chief deputy majority whip, a position he held until he left Congress. In this role, it was his responsibility to secure the backing of his fellow Democrats when it was time to vote on a particular piece of legislation. Though Richardson was successful at his job, he also thought occasionally about returning to New Mexico and running for governor.

During the mid-1990s, Richardson developed a secondary career in Washington that was an outgrowth of his work on the House Intelligence Committee. He became an unofficial emissary of the United States who met with important foreign officials to handle unusual predicaments, such as helping free Americans imprisoned overseas and promoting American foreign policy interests in espe-cially delicate situations. Richardson's access to the president ap-pealed to the foreign officials he met and greatly contributed to his success. He soon became known as the "Clark Kent of Capitol Hill" for his exceptional talents in this area.

Richardson's first mission was to Burma in 1994, where he met imprisoned democratic crusader Aung San Suu Kyi. He was the first outsider allowed to see her since she had been placed under house arrest in 1989. The meeting eventually led to her release. Richard-son's negotiating skills were also put to the test in North Korea that same year when he went there to talk about a nuclear disarmament agreement. While he was in the country, a U.S. Army helicopter was shot down during a flight over North Korean territory. The pilot, Bobby Hall, was captured, and his crewman died. Richardson spent days trying to secure Hall's release and to arrange for the remains of the other man to be turned over to U.S. authorities. In 1994 Richard-son journeyed to Haiti to try to persuade its military dictator, Raoul Cedras, to relinquish his post and allow the democratically-elected president to assume office.

Richardson attributed his success as an emissary to setting small goals before each meeting, going in with clear objectives, and doing extensive research about the people with whom he would be talking. As he told Tim Weiner of the *New York Times,* "I listen a lot. I try not to impose my views. It's important to listen, but important to be forceful, too."

Such attitudes served Richardson well when he met with Iraqi leader Saddam Hussein and other Iraqi officials in July 1995 to discuss the fate of American engineers David Daliberti and Bill Barloon. Both men were employed by defense contractors and had been jailed after accidentally crossing into Iraq from Kuwait. Richardson successfully negotiated their release by establishing a connection with Hussein on a person-to-person level. He also gained freedom for American prisoners in North Korea and Sudan as well as a Nigerian political dissident named Moshood Abiola. In addition, Richardson held talks with Cuban dictator Fidel Castro and observed elections in Nicaragua and Guatemala. In 1995, he was nominated for a Nobel Peace Prize in recognition of his work.

In 1996, following Clinton's re-election, Richardson was again under consideration for a cabinet post, this time as Commerce Secretary, but once again he was not nominated. Instead, at the end of the year, he was named the U.S. Ambassador to the United Nations. (He replaced Madeline Albright, who had been named Secretary of State.) After receiving Senate confirmation in early 1997, Richardson worked to advance U.S. foreign policy interests, including peace, human rights, democracy, and open markets. But his impetuous style did not work quite as well in this forum. For example, he made some mistakes in negotiations with Congo that affected U.S. relations with South Africa, France, and Russia. Overall, however, Richardson managed to perform well in this post while continuing his unofficial role as a roving diplomat for the United States.

Richardson's tenure as the U.S. Ambassador to the United Nations was short-lived. In the spring of 1998, he was named to replace Federico Pena as Secretary of Energy, a cabinet-level position in the Clinton administration. Despite his background in oil and gas legislation, he met with opposition from some critics who were not sure whether his overall knowledge of the subject was sufficient. Nevertheless, Richardson was confirmed for the post and almost immediately began raising the profile of the Department of Energy. Yet he faced a number of serious challenges along the way, including charges of nuclear science espionage at the Los Alamos National Laboratory in New Mexico. Though the events in question had occurred well before Richardson took office, he had to deal with the consequences as best he could.

As Richardson prepared to leave office at the end of the Clinton presidency, he faced a future filled with many possibilities. Though there was speculation that he might return to New Mexico and run for senate or governor, there were also hints that he was under consideration as a running mate for Democratic presidential hopeful Al Gore. In fact, Washington attorney Robert C. McCandless predicted that kind of scenario for Richardson, telling Lisa Leiter of *Insight on the News*, "He's going to keep climbing the ladder of American politics and sometime he'll end up on the Democratic [presidential] ticket."

Sources

➤ **Periodicals**

American Journalism Review, November 1999, p. 10.
Economist, December 13, 1997, p. 28; October 2, 1999, p. 32.
Fortune, May 27, 1996, p. 173.
Hispanic, March 1997, p. 18.
Insight on the News, October 23, 1995, p. 15; June 7, 1999, p. 10.
Los Angeles Times, June 18, 1998, p. A18.
Migration World Magazine, March-April 1997, p. 38 (opening quote).
National Journal, June 12, 1999, p. 1580; June 26, 1999, p. 1896.
National Review, August 30, 1999, p. 26.
New Republic, November 24, 1997, p. 22.
Newsweek, February 10, 1997, p. 29; June 29, 1998, p. 58.
New York Times, July 18, 1995, p. A3; December 14, 1996, section 1, p. 11; June 19, 1998, p. A26.
Oil & Gas Daily, June 29, 1998, p. 32.
Oil Daily, March 12, 1985, p. 1; June 12, 1985, p. 1; December 24, 1992, p. 1; December 10, 1997, p. 3; June 19, 1998; July 23, 1998; August 3, 1998; August 20, 1998; September 8, 1999; December 13, 1999; January 26, 2000.
People, August 7, 1995, p. 61.
Science, July 31, 1998, p. 623.
Time, December 23, 1996, p. 29.
U.S. News & World Report, December 9, 1996, p. 23; February 14, 2000.
Washington Post, December 13, 1996, p. C1; December 14, 1996, p. A10.
White House Weekly, June 7, 1999, p. 1.

Cal Ripkin, Jr.

"Sports for me has always been a combination of love and persistence. That's who I am, how I approach things. I was brought up a certain way. If I wanted to play, and I could play, then I would. With no questions asked."*

Born August 24, 1960, in Havre de Grace, Maryland, Cal Ripkin, Jr. is a professional baseball player who has spent his entire career with the Baltimore Orioles. He holds the record for most consecutive games played. Address: Baltimore Orioles, Camden Yards, Baltimore, MD 21218.

Known as a steady and reliable player, Cal Ripkin, Jr., played in 2,632 consecutive games, shattering the record previously held by New York Yankee Lou Gehrig. For many years, the record had been regarded as unbreakable. Ripkin became known as the "Iron Man" for his feat, one of the greatest players in professional baseball in the 1980s and 1990s.

Born on August 24, 1960, in Havre de Grace, Maryland, Calvin Edward Ripkin, Jr., was the son of Cal, Sr. and Viola Ripkin. His father was a minor league baseball player, a catcher, in the Baltimore Orioles' farm system. After an injury in 1961, Cal Ripkin, Sr., became a coach and manager in the same system, later managing the Orioles when his sons played. Ripkin had an elder sister, Ellen, and two younger brothers, Fred and Billy. Billy Ripkin also became a professional baseball player, who spent part of his career with the Orioles.

Ripkin always wanted to play baseball. By the time he was 12 years old, he knew he wanted to do it for a career. Because his father was often gone coaching and managing teams, Ripkin's mother encouraged her son's efforts, helping him with his swing. Ripkin grew up in Aberdeen, Maryland, but spent summers wherever his father was coaching or managing.

As a teenager, Ripkin often watched his father's minor league teams, observing the finer points of the game and asking questions of his father, and his father's staff and team. Ripkin told Ralph Wiley of *Sports Illustrated*, "I always had a hunger to learn the game. I had the hunger to play that all kids have, but it was more than that."

By the time Ripkin graduated from Aberdeen High School in 1978, he was a solid ballplayer. The previous year he had played in the Texas-based Mickey Mantle World Series. As a high school senior, Ripkin won his county's batting title with a .492 batting average, and his team won the state championship. Just after graduation, he was taken in the second round of the June amateur draft by the Baltimore Orioles.

Ripkin spent three seasons in the Orioles farm system, playing infield for four different teams. Though he began as a pitcher, Ripkin soon moved to shortstop. It took time to build his skills, and he struggled the first year, especially defensively. He did not hit a home run in his first minor league season. Ripkin hit his stride in 1980 with the AA team in Charlotte, North Carolina, but proved himself the next year in Rochester, New York, with the AAA Red

Wings. In his third season, he hit 23 home runs. Ripkin was called up by the Orioles in August of the 1981 season, playing third base.

In 1982, Ripkin played his first full rookie season with the Orioles. After a good opening day, Ripkin started out very slowly. At one point, his batting average was only .117. After getting advice from major league baseball star Reggie Jackson and Cal, Sr., Ripkin became a better hitter, learning how to anticipate pitchers during a game and becoming selective in what he would try to hit. He was named Rookie of the Year in the American League, leading rookies in numerous categories, including home runs (28), runs batted in (RBIs; 93), games, at bats, doubles, and runs.

While Ripkin began the season at third base, by mid-season he was back at shortstop, where he would spend the majority of his career. It was during Ripkin's rookie year that he began his consecutive game streak, on May 30, 1982. Ripkin also began another streak during the season. Beginning on June 5, 1982, Ripkin played every inning of every game through September 14, 1987, for a total of 8,243 consecutive innings, the longest in the history of major league baseball. Of his dedication, Ripkin told Steven V. Roberts of *U.S. News & World Report*, "My dad instilled in me very early that it's important in a team to go out there and be there for a team."

The following season, 1983, Ripkin continued to dominate. He was named the American League's Most Valuable Player and Major League Player of the Year. With 27 home runs and 102 RBIs, he had a .318 batting average. He led the American League in runs scored with 121, doubles with 42, and hits with 211. A team goal was also reached: the Orioles won the World Series, defeating the Philadelphia Phillies.

While Ripkin never matched his 1983 batting average and other offensive numbers, he did begin a rise in his defensive prowess. That year he led the league in defensive assists and double plays. While the Orioles struggled in 1984 (and 1985-88), Ripkin set an American League record when he had 583 assists out of 906 chances, best for a shortstop. His offensive output was still significant: a .304 batting average, with 27 home runs and 86 RBIs.

Ripkin's defense continued to improve in the mid-1980s. In 1985, he turned 32 double plays, tying the club record and leading the league. He also led the league in putouts and the voting for the All-Star game. In 1986 and 1987, he led the league in defensive assists. Ripkin's 1987 season in Baltimore was a family affair. His brother Billy played second base, making him Ripkin's double play partner, while their father managed the team. Ripkin was also married in 1987, to Kelly Greer. Eventually they had two children, Rachel and Ryan.

The family element in the Orioles was short-lived for Ripkin. The team played horribly, and Ripkin's father was fired after six games into the 1988 season. Ripkin continued to thrive, however, signing a four-year deal worth $8.4 million. By 1989, Ripkin was the team's leader, and the Orioles were in the race for the division title. That year he also broke the record held by Ernie Banks by having his eighth straight 20-homer season.

By June 12, 1990, Ripkin was second on the all-time consecutive games played list, having played in 1,308 straight games. He played in nearly every inning of these games as well. Some believed he would start to feel pressure as he came closer to Gehrig's record, but his father dispelled this notion. Cal Ripkin, Sr., told Ralph Wiley of *Sports Illustrated*, "There's no pressure on Cal. No pressure in it. You go to the ballpark and do the best job you possibly can that day. Cal always wanted to be as good a professional ballplayer as possible."

There were those who blamed "the streak" (as it became known) on Ripkin's offensive problems in 1990. His batting average was only .250. But Ripkin also set the major league records for fewest errors by a shortstop with three and most consecutive games without an error with 95.

During the 1991 season, Ripkin had his best season since 1983, and had the awards to prove it. He again won the American League Most Valuable Player Award and Major League Player of the Year, as well as Most Valuable Player of the All-Star Game. Ripkin had a .323 batting average, 210 hits, 34 home runs, and 114 RBIs. His field percentage of .986 earned Ripkin his first Golden Glove Award.

Though Ripkin continued to shine defensively in 1992, again winning the Golden Glove, he struggled offensively. He hit career lows with only 14 home runs and 72 RBIs. Still he signed a deal, after much tough negotiation, worth $30.5 million over five years. By this season, Ripkin was always asked about "the streak," and he continued to be criticized by some for keeping it going. He told Peter Schmuck of *Sport*, "It's been tough dealing with it, because it's not something that I set out to do. There aren't a whole lot of people I can talk to who have gone through the same things that I have, so I've had to deal with it on my own. I used to really disagree with the statements that I should take a day off, but now that I accept that it's someone's opinion and it's going to be there."

Ripkin's offensive output improved in 1993 and 1994, when he had batting averages of .300 and .315, respectively. He passed several milestones in 1994, appearing in his 2000th consecutive major league game on August 1. He also held the major league record for most career home runs by a shortstop.

On September 6, 1995, Ripkin became the consecutive games record holder, in a game against the California Angels. Despite his slumping batting average, he was named *Sports Illustrated*'s Sportsman of the Year. Ripkin was both annoyed and humbled by the attention "the streak" brought to him. He told *People Weekly*, "I cringe when someone calls me a hero. People make a big deal out of what I did. But I'm only a baseball player. I'm big on keeping things in absolute perspective."

In 1996, Ripkin was moved back to third base for a while. Yet he continued to set records, hitting more home runs than anyone in Orioles history with 334 on May 29, 1996. He also achieved the world record for consecutive games played (over a player in the Japanese league) on June 14, 1996.

At the beginning of 1997 season, there was pressure to end "the streak," in part because of his physical problems including back spasms and a herniated disk, but also because it became bigger than the team. Ripkin did not believe sitting out would help the club, despite the fact that he hit no home runs and his batting average was under .200. He also was moved to third base on a permanent basis.

"The streak" continued throughout much of 1998, as Ripkin's numbers improved. Through September, he had 12 home runs and 56 RBIs, and a batting average above .300. Ripkin was near 400 home runs and 3,000 hits. But in September 1998, Ripkin chose to voluntarily end "the streak" by sitting out a game. He remained, however, the heart of the Orioles.

As Tim Kurkjian wrote in *Sports Illustrated*, "Ripkin's life is about wanting to play, to win, to be the best. Some athletes share his simple philosophy, but no one in major league baseball lives it as vigorously or as passionately as Ripkin. That in part explains . . . why he's a future Hall of Famer. . . ."

Sources

➤ Books

Encyclopedia of World Biography: Supplement, volume 18, Gale Group, 1999, pp. 346-48.

Gareffa, Peter M., editor, *Contemporary Newsmakers: 1986 Cumulation,* Gale Research, 1987, pp. 326-28.

Porter, David L., editor, *Biographical Dictionary of American Sports: 1992-1995 Supplement for Baseball, Football, Basketball, and Other Sports,* Greenwood Press, 1995, pp. 984-85.

Shatzkin, Mike, editor, *The Ballplayers: Baseball's Ultimate Biographical Reference,* Arbor House, 1990, pp. 916-17.

➤ Periodicals

Esquire, April 1995, p. 48 (opening quote).

People Weekly, September 18, 1995, p. 68; December 25, 1995, p. 107.

Sport, May 1992, p. 22; March 1993, p. 16; June 1997, p. 68.

Sports Illustrated, June 18, 1990, p. 70; June 25, 1990, p. 13; June 10, 1991, p. 62; July 29, 1991, p. 24; June 28, 1993, p. 40; August 7, 1995, p. 22; September 11, 1995, p. 56; September 18, 1995, p. 98; December 18, 1995, p. 70; August 4, 1997, p. 83; September 7, 1998, p. 76; September 28, 1998, p. 10.

Tampa Tribune, September 3, 1999, p. 10.

Time, September 11, 1995, p. 68.

U.S. News & World Report, August 14, 1995, p. 6; December 26, 1994, p. 87; September 18, 1995, p. 16.

The Washington Times, April 1, 1999, p. B1.

Diego Rivera

"I stick to my idea of a clear, firm, simple and precise art that everyone can understand."

Born December 8, 1886, in Guanajuato, Mexico, Diego Rivera painted murals that celebrated the history of Mexico and its people, and also depicted contributions of working class Americans in murals in the United States. He died on November 25, 1957, in Mexico City, Mexico.

A dmired as an artist of the people, Mexican painter Diego Rivera is known for his murals that chronicle the rich history and culture of his native country and elevate the importance of the working class. Rich with allegory and politics, his works can be found throughout Mexico and the United States, and boast lush colors, expansive subject matter, and complicated yet masterful compositions. "He handled crowds and battle scenes with the flair of [legendary film director] D.W. Griffith, and pictured farmers and factory hands with so much natural rhythm that their work had the quality of a dance," commended a *Time* writer. "But all this skill was just the foundation for the best virtue of Diego's art: an atmosphere of joyful reverence for life, which onlookers could remember long after the details of the paintings had faded from their minds." Though he has been criticized for his Communist affiliation, his work is officially considered a national treasure of Mexico.

Diego Rivera was born Diego Maria de la Concepcion Juan Nepomuceno Estanislao de la Rivera y Barrientos Acosta y Rodriguez on December 8, 1886, in the mountain town of Guanajuato, Guanajuato State, Mexico, the son of Diego and Maria Barrientos Rivera. On his mother's side, he counted Indian, Spanish, and black heritage, and on his father's side, he counted Portuguese-Jewish and Spanish-Italian ancestry. Rivera's twin, Carlos, died when they were a year and a half old, causing his mother severe grief. She had already endured three other pregnancies that resulted in stillbirths.

To help her recover from her child's death, Rivera's mother studied obstetrics at the urging of her husband, who was then a city councilor and later became an inspector in the National Department of Public Health. She later had another child, Maria. By the time he was six, Rivera, a curious child who loved anything mechanical, longed to become an engineer. However, he had also been an avid artist since the time he could hold a pencil, drawing on doors, walls, and furniture. To prevent further destruction of the home, his father draped an entire room in black canvas, where Rivera recalled in his autobiography *My Art, My Life*, "I made my earliest 'murals.'"

Before he turned seven, Rivera and his family moved from Guanajuato to Mexico City, after his father raised the ire of other officials with his social activism, standing up for the underclass and editing a political journal called *The Democrat*. Rivera's mother enrolled him in a clerical school, then he transferred to another before trying out a military preparatory school at age ten, which he hated. At age 11, in addition to attending elementary school, he entered night classes at the San Carlos Academy of Fine Arts and began to win prizes for his drawings and paintings. When he was 13, on a scholarship, he began attending during the day, but at age 16 was kicked out for participating in a protest that turned into a riot.

Subsequently, Rivera traveled around Mexico painting natural landscapes. By age 20, he received a grant to study art in Europe, and arrived in Spain in January of 1907. Inspired by a wide range of European art, he journeyed around the continent and experimented with a range of styles, from the Spanish, Dutch, Flemish, and Italian classics to French impressionism. From 1913 to 1918, he produced mainly Cubist works, some of them with Mexican themes, like *Zapatista Landscape—The Guerilla,* 1915, depicting revolutionary leader Emiliano Zapata. This was an early indicator of Rivera's tendency to combine his art and activism.

In Europe, some of Rivera's pieces were displayed in galleries in Spain and Paris. His first one-person show was held in Paris at the Weill Gallery in 1914, but he was not finding fortune. After a brief return to Mexico in 1910-11, he went back to Paris and began living with a woman, Angelina Beloff, and in 1917 they had a son who died before he was two years old. In his autobiography, he also noted that he had an affair with a Russian female painter, Marievna Vorobiev, and she later gave birth to a daughter. In 1921, Rivera went to Italy, where he was inspired by the idea of painting murals for the masses. A *Time* obituary quoted him as saying, "I stick to my idea of a clear, firm, simple and precise art that everyone can understand."

Returning to his home country, Rivera's first commission was a mural for the National Preparatory School in 1921. While this showed the influence of the Italian mosaics and frescoes, it did not incorporate his own cultural heritage or the indigenous beauty of Mexico, which was perhaps the reason that it was not appreciated. He began to draw upon his native land in his 124 frescoes for the Ministry of Education in Mexico City from 1923 to 1926. These exhibited familiar scenes of peasants at work, local festivals, and class divisions. Though reaction was initially mixed, the works brought much attention to Rivera and established him as a storyteller through his pictures and thus a voice of the downtrodden and illiterate. Communist symbols began to appear in these works, giving blatant indication of his political sympathies. Though he belonged to the Communist party on and off, he was frequently absent at meetings and eventually asked to leave at least twice. However, this did not temper his enthusiasm for the doctrine.

Meanwhile, in 1922, Rivera had married Guadalupe ("Lupe") Marin, and they had two daughters, Guadalupe and Ruth. Rivera completed what many consider his masterpiece in 1927 in the Auditorium of the National School of Agriculture in Chapingo, about 25 miles northeast of Mexico City. Through these frescoes, Rivera delved into a more spiritual message. His basic theme concerns bringing order to the chaos of both the human realm and the natural world so that people can exist in harmony with both nature and each other. Up to this point, Rivera's work had featured nudes only on occasion, but they flourished in these murals and were modeled by his wife, who had appeared fully clothed in prior efforts. The complex spatial structure of this work, featuring baroque lines, lush scenes of the evolution of plants and agriculture, and the symbolic parallels in the development of society, presented extreme challenges. Rivera has been admired by other painters and critics for his expert handling of the various elements in this work.

Rivera and Marin divorced after five years, and he married artist Frida Kahlo in 1929. Also that year he took a position as director of his former art school, the San Carlos Academy of Fine Art, but left the next year. From the years 1930 to 1934, he painted six murals in the United States: in Detroit, New York, and San Francisco. These are among the best examples of his mature style, especially 1933's fresco at the Detroit Institute of Arts depicting industrial workers. Demonstrating Rivera's support for the working class, the work both celebrates technology and warns of it destructive effects. Afterward, business titan Nelson D. Rockefeller, Jr. hired the artist to complete a mural at Rockefeller Center, but when Rivera included a portrait of Soviet leader Vladimir Lenin, Rockefeller ordered him to remove it. The artist declined, but offered to add other figureheads as well, such as Abraham Lincoln. Rockefeller found the compromise unacceptable and had the work destroyed. As Rivera noted in his autobiography, "Thus was free expression honored in America." Another work in New York City, a series of movable panels representing American history for the Independent Labor Institute, survives.

In 1934, Rivera returned to Mexico City and executed the mural for the Palace of Fine Arts, replicating the one he began for Rockefeller Center, titled *Man, Controller of the Universe*. He then completed works on the grand staircase of the National Palace the following year. This effort chronicles the history of Mexico from the pre-Colombian era to contemporary times and includes scenes of the Golden Age of the Aztecs. The depiction of this great civilization, with its glorious pyramids, elaborate apparel, and native rituals, exposed a rich history to peasants who had never heard of the Aztecs, and pointed to Rivera's hope that someday Mexico would regain its former status as one of the world's great societies. He later continued frescoes in the corridors at the National Palace, but did not finish them.

In the 1940s, Rivera accepted a commission at a junior college in San Francisco for a mural which deals broadly with the future of culture and combines the artistic creativity of South America with the industrial accomplishments of North America. Two 1944 murals at the National Institute of Cardiology in Mexico City in 1944 concern the growth of the cardiology field and display portraits of pioneering physicians in that discipline. In 1947, Rivera completed *Sunday in the Alameda* for the Hotel del Prado in Mexico City, which caused controversy for its depiction of a figure holding an open book containing the words "God does not exist." In 1951, the Palace of Fine Arts held a retrospective of his career. His last works were mosaics for the National University stadium and Insurgents' Theater and a fresco in the Social Security Hospital No. 1.

Thanks to his many private commissions, Rivera became a wealthy man, and was able to purchase an estimated 57,000 pieces of pre-Colombian art, one of the biggest private collections known. He was also a celebrity, a rarity in the art world, and was popular with women. He and Kahlo, who was 20 years his junior, both had numerous affairs but remained devoted to each other. They divorced in 1939, but remarried in 1940. After her death in 1954, he married Emma Hurtado in 1955, but accounts claim that his heart remained with Kahlo, and her death led to his decline.

An imposing man at six feet tall and weighing 250 to 300 pounds, Rivera was intriguing enough of a figure simply for his artistic achievements and his volatile personal life, between his political leanings and succession of relationships. However, it was widely known that he had a tendency to spin fantastic tales about himself, which added to his reputation. In fact, one biographer, Bertram D. Wolfe, suggested that many items in Rivera's autobiography could not be taken as fact, since they were "calculated to offend and shock" his female coauthor. However, his active imagination and flamboyance were undoubtedly to thank for his vivid works of art, which made him one of the most revered painters of the twentieth century. After suffering in his later years from diabetes and cancer, he died at age 70 on November 25, 1957, at his home in suburban Mexico City.

Sources

➤ Books

Dictionary of Hispanic Biography, Gale Research, 1996.
Encyclopedia of World Biography, second edition, Gale Research, 1998.
International Dictionary of Art and Artists, St. James Press, 1990.
Rivera, Diego, with Gladys March, *My Art, My Life,* Citadel Press, 1960.
Wolfe, Bertram D., *The Fabulous Life of Diego Rivera,* Stein and
  Day, 1963.

➤ Periodicals

History Today, April 1996, p. 34.
Los Angeles Magazine, January 1997, p 60.
Newsweek, November 8, 1948, p. 76.
New York Times, November 25, 1957, p. 1; November 27, 1957, p. 31.
People, February 12, 1996, p. 83.
Time, April 4, 1949; December 9, 1957, p. 90 (opening quote);
  November 22, 1963, p. 100.

Mary Robinson

"There *must be accountability. Those who are responsible for human rights violations must bear responsibility."*

Born on May 21, 1944, in County Mayo, Ireland, Mary Robinson served as Ireland's first female president from 1990 to 1997. Address: Aras an Uachtarain, UN Palais des Nations, 1211, Geneva, 10, Switzerland.

As the first woman to be elected president of Ireland, Mary Robinson was ideally suited for the high-profile job. A constitutional lawyer and office-holder since the age of 26, Robinson had worked tirelessly to battle conservative, entrenched traditions in the largely Roman Catholic country over the past two decades. Inaugurated as president in 1990, she spent nearly seven years in the post, and has been recognized for helping usher Ireland into a newly liberal, prosperous, and peaceful era as a modern European nation.

Robinson was baptized Mary Theresa Winifred Bourke not long after her birth on May 21, 1944, in Ballina, County Mayo, Ireland. The third child of five and the only daughter of two physicians, Robinson grew up in an affluent, boisterous household full of boys, where she naturally developed a certain ruthlessness. The family was staunchly Roman Catholic, though there had been several notable Protestant marriages among ancestors. Sent to a private school in Ballina until the age of ten, she spent several years at a Dublin convent academy for young women.

Robinson's grandfather was a lawyer, and as a youth she made up her mind to follow in his footsteps. In her late teens, she was sent to a finishing school in Paris, and emerged with a solid fluency in the French language and an appreciation for intellectual freedoms, which she quickly put to use. Returning to Ireland, she planned to enroll at Trinity College in Dublin, a Protestant school founded by Elizabeth I, where her two older brothers were already studying. There was a semi-official injunction by the Church that banned Catholics from attending the famous college, and her parents were forced to drive to Dublin to speak with the Archbishop to secure permission for her.

Robinson entered Trinity College in 1963. There were many rules that restricted the comings and goings of women on its campus at the time, including a 7 p.m. curfew law, but her parents purchased a Regency home nearby—famously, one at which the poet Oscar Wilde had been born—and she and her brothers lived there under the supervision of their longtime nanny. She studied French language and literature and the law, and in the latter courses she sometimes encountered chauvinistic rebuffs from other students, since it was viewed as a traditional "male" field at the time. Nevertheless, Robinson persevered, and excelled in her classes. She was even elected to the Law Society as its auditor, and during her tenure made a provocative speech at a debate in which she urged reform of family laws regarding contraception and divorce.

While a student at Trinity, Robinson met her husband, Dublin native Nicholas Robinson, who hailed from a family that were barrel-makers to the Guinness brewery for generations. After earning her degree in 1967, however, Robinson departed immediately for the United States, where she began a one-year fellowship at the prestigious Harvard School of Law. She had been drawn to the United States in part because of its vigorous protest movements; civil-rights demonstrations, anti-war marches, and feminist calls to action seemed to predominate American news headlines, and much of the activity took place on college campuses. It was a permissive, extroverted, and completely different world for Robinson, and she later noted that her year at Harvard was the most influential event of her life. In Ireland, young people did not become involved in politics, partly because of the attitude that only with age came wisdom. In America, however, Robinson witnessed a young generation successfully working to eradicate unfair laws and implement liberal programs. "When I came home, I related all this to Ireland and have continued to do so," she told the *Sunday Independent.*

In Ireland, Robinson spent two years as junior counsel with the government judiciary, assigned to the remote rural counties of the western part of the island. Here, poverty and hardship were far more apparent than elsewhere, and sometimes even a woman arguing a case in court was a sheer novelty. In 1969, however, she applied for and received a plum assignment: Robinson was named Reid Professor of constitutional and criminal law at Trinity College. She was just 24, and became the youngest professor ever appointed at the university. She immediately caused a stir when she decided to run for political office: Trinity was allowed three seats in the Seanad, or Irish Senate. Though the Seanad is toothless—it can only introduce bills to the Daøl, the lower house of the Irish Parliament, and delay Daøl legislation by 90 days—it was nevertheless an honor bestowed almost exclusively on experienced older men. Robinson, however, thought that someone from the college's own age group should at least have one seat, and stood successfully for election on the national Labour Party ticket. She also became the first Catholic to represent Trinity in the Seanad.

In 1970, Robinson wed her husband, who was by then working as a newspaper cartoonist. Perhaps because of his profession, or the fact that he was Protestant, her family refused to condone the marriage, and did not attend the civil ceremony. The rift was quickly healed, however, after some diplomacy conducted by a great-aunt who was also a respected Catholic nun. Such attitudes were still prevalent in Ireland at the time, as were terrifically discriminatory customs and laws regarding women. Newly married women were expected to exit certain professions, such as banking, and a husband's signature was required to open a bank account. Impoverished families were given welfare assistance, but the checks were issued in the husband's name, and in some cases the funds were spent at the pub while the children literally starved.

Over the next two decades, Robinson worked ceaselessly to help change these laws, a battle for which she was sometimes vilified despite her professions of support for Church doctrine. Initially, she was not even allowed to introduce a bill to the Seanad in 1970 that would permit the limited sale of contraceptives; Robinson argued that to deny birth-control measures to Ireland's Protestant citizens was an impingement upon their civil rights. Thousands demonstrated in support of the reform measure, but she received hate mail and even used condoms through the post. It eventually passed after nine years of debate and contention.

As a senator, Robinson took on the even more controversial family-law matter, divorce, which was then prohibited by no less than Ireland's Constitution. She introduced a bill to legalize it in 1976, but ten years later, the question was rejected by voters in a referendum. Robinson also championed an equal-employment bill that vastly improved working conditions and pay for women, which brought Ireland into line with the more progressive policies of other European nations. Meanwhile, the dynamic politician also became part of an appointed legal team during the period that Ireland prepared to join the European Common Market (now the European Union).

When Irish politics geared up for the next election of a president in 1990, Robinson was nominated by the Labour Party, much to the surprise of many, since she had resigned from it a few years earlier over its support of a 1985 Anglo-Irish agreement that she construed as unfair to Protestants in Northern Ireland. The presidency was an apolitical but extraordinarily symbolic post, and usually went to a leader of the Fianna Fail (Republican) Party. Promising to work for reform on significant family-law issues, Robinson began campaigning vigorously, but bookmakers in Dublin gave her odds of 1,000 to 1. Scores of women voters, however, turned out at the polls and cast their ballots for her, and she was further blessed by a political scandal involving her main opponent that gave her, in the end, a majority of 39 percent.

After inauguration festivities at Dublin Castle, Robinson seized upon the opportunities her new job presented. She was legally enjoined from entering party politics or becoming involved in public policy issues under debate, but she used the platform to speak out on social matters and urge Irish citizens to become more involved. She crisscrossed the country tirelessly, making scores of public appearances, and even made an official visit to Buckingham Palace; in doing so she became the first Irish leader to meet with the British monarch in more than 70 years. At Arus an Uachtarain, her official residence in Dublin, she placed a lit candle in the window, the traditional Irish welcome sign at Christmastime. Hers, kept lit year-round, was designed to serve as a symbol of the Irish diaspora, and to remind her electorate that the Irish spirit had made a tremendous historical impact on the world.

Robinson became an outspoken advocate for human rights, and began traveling abroad, though technically she required the permission of the prime minister to do so. Once, she visited famine victims in Somalia, and went into war-torn Rwanda just months after its bloody civil war. She encouraged Ireland to commemorate the 150th anniversary of its Great Famine, and pointed out that in the modern era, the Irish are well-known for their contributions to a battery of international human-rights causes. "It is people who go through suffering that have an empathy for the suffering of others," Robinson told *Commonweal* interviewer Gary MacEoin. "Many people today in the developed countries are so far removed from poverty and suffering and starvation that they lack empathy for the sufferings of others."

During Robinson's tenure in office, Ireland changed dramatically. The economy rebounded and became one of the strongest in the European Union. A cultural revival was well underway, and a historic peace agreement with the IRA was imminent. She enjoyed tremendous popularity in the public-opinion polls. Robinson, asserted one leading newspaper, "has helped us to re-imagine Ireland," according to Lorna Siggins's biography, *Mary Robinson: The Woman Who Took Power in the Park*. In March of 1997, she announced she would not stand for re-election, and even left the post a few months earlier than scheduled when she was named the United Nations High Commissioner for Human Rights. She and her family, which includes three children with Nicholas—an attorney, professor and founder of the Irish Architectural Archives—then moved to Geneva, Switzerland.

In her new post, Robinson visits some of the most devastated sites on the globe, and works to address wartime violations of international law. She toured Serbia, attempted to meet with its president, and visited refugee camps across its borders for several weeks in the spring of 1999, just months after NATO planes began bombing the country. "There must be accountability," the *Irish Times* quoted Robinson as saying. "Those who are responsible for human rights violations must bear responsibility."

Sources

➤ Books

Siggins, Lorna, *Mary Robinson: The Woman Who Took Power in the Park*, Mainstream Publishing, 1997.

➤ Periodicals

Commonweal, March 14, 1997, pp. 8-11.
Europe, November 1997, pp. 42-43.
Irish Times, May 14, 1999 (opening quote).
National Review, November 24, 1997, pp. 46-47.
Sunday Independent, June 15, 1980.
Times (London), March 13, 1997.

Randall S. Robinson

"We should care about the black world be-cause it is the right thing to do. If we love ourselves, we love Africa and the Caribbean. We are indissolubly joined."

Born on July 6, 1941, in Richmond, Virginia, Randall S. Robin-son is the executive director of TransAfrica, an organization that promotes civil, social, and human rights for blacks in Africa. He is also interested in causes related to African Ameri-cans and other people of color. Address: TransAfrica, 1744 R Street NW, Washington, D.C. 20009.

As executive director of TransAfrica, Randall S. Robinson personally works to insure that the human, civil, and social rights of people of color are not overlooked in U.S. foreign policy decisions. His area of interest is not just Africa, however, but also the Caribbean and even the United States. Robinson has gone to extremes on several occasions to promote his agenda, including subjecting himself to a 27-day hunger strike to protest U.S. policy toward Haiti.

Born on July 6, 1941, in Richmond, Virginia, Robinson is the son of Maxie Cleveland Robinson, Sr., and Doris Alma Jones Robinson. Both of his parents were educators; his father taught history in an all-black high school and was an athletic coach, while his mother was employed at the elementary school level. Robinson and his siblings (including elder brother Max Robinson, Jr., who was the first African American television news anchor, and two sisters) attended segregated public schools in Richmond.

From an early age, Robinson loved to read. His parents instilled in him the values of pride, achievement, and having a social conscience. While attending Armstrong High School, Robinson was a standout basketball player. After graduating in 1959, he attended Norfolk State College (later known as Norfolk State University) on a basketball scholarship and began to become politically active.

During his junior year, Robinson dropped out of college and soon found himself drafted into the U.S. Army. During the 21 months he spent in the service, he managed to avoid being shipped out to fight in Vietnam. Instead, he remained stateside in Georgia. Upon his discharge, Robinson went back to school to finish his degree. Instead of returning to Norfolk, however, he entered Virginia Union University (an all-black institution) to study sociology and graduated in 1967.

Robinson decided that the best way to serve his burgeoning political interests was to become a lawyer. To that end, he entered Harvard University Law School. (It was the first time that he had ever attended school with white students.) He continued his political activities, including protesting South Africa's policy of apartheid, or strict separation of the races. Robinson received his J.D. in 1970.

Robinson then applied for and was granted a Ford fellowship and spent some time working in Tanzania. When he returned home in 1972, he settled in Roxbury, Massachusetts, where he spent the next three years working as a community development division director at the Roxbury Multi-Service Center. During this period, he married Brenda Randolph, a librarian. Together they had two children, daughter Anikie and son Jabari. In June 1987, Robinson married Hazel Ross, an advisor on foreign policy and head of the United Negro College Fund. They subsequently had a daughter, Khalea.

In 1975 Robinson left Massachusetts for a series of political positions in Washington, D.C. His first was as a staff assistant to Representative William L. Clay of Missouri, for whom he wrote policy statements. A year later, Robinson went to work as an administrative assistant to Representative Charles Diggs of Michigan. At the same time, he served as a staff attorney for the Law Compensatory Project on its Lawyer's Committee for Civil Rights.

Robinson made his first visit to South Africa as part of a congressional team while employed by Diggs. There he witnessed firsthand the dehumanizing effects of apartheid. The experience opened his eyes, especially when a white South African told him that he did not want blacks to vote because they were so childlike.

Robinson and other congressional employees involved in the Black Leadership Conference then decided to take action and work as advocates for Africans in international policy. South Africa was not their only area of concern, however. Though blacks constituted 98 percent of the population of Rhodesia (later known as Zimbabwe), they had no political power; the white minority ruled the country. Robinson and his colleagues were troubled by the fact that the United States not only tolerated this situation but also seemed to support it.

To combat such attitudes, they founded TransAfrica in 1977, and Robinson assumed the post of executive director. The agency lobbied on behalf of issues affecting blacks in Africa as well as those in the Caribbean. It was tough going at first; the staff consisted of just two people in a basement office, and funding from month to month was uncertain at best. Yet TransAfrica managed to survive and later added educational and research components to its agenda.

In 1981 the TransAfrica Forum was founded. It was a separate but related organization that collected information that was helpful to those formulating U.S. foreign policy in areas where people of color predominate. The Forum also held annual conferences and other programs and issued two quarterly publications, *TransAfrican Forum* and *Issue Belief.* Among its goals, the Forum wanted to show African Americans how such issues affected them.

While the work of Robinson and TransAfrica had attracted attention in Washington, it did not move into the national consciousness in a big way until the mid-1980s. From November 1984 to November 1985, TransAfrica staged a huge protest to highlight problems in South Africa. Called the Free South Africa Movement, it featured Robinson and others calling for the release of imprisoned activist Nelson Mandela and other political detainees as well as for the abolition of apartheid.

The protest was organized by Robinson and two other African American political activists, Walter Fauntroy, a former delegate to Congress from Washington, D.C., and Mary Frances Berry, a former member of the U.S. Commission on Civil Rights. The three met with the South African ambassador and then refused to leave the grounds of the embassy. Over the course of the yearlong sit-in, 5,000 people were arrested for protesting, including a number of prominent celebrities and politicians. The sit-in tactic eventually spread to 23 other cities across the United States.

Robinson's efforts earned him much praise. One of those arrested during the protests, U.S. Representative Don Edwards, told Barbara Gamarekian of the *New York Times,* "He's running the show and his leadership has been inspired. He goes to jail himself first. He doesn't sit in an office or hotel room. This is a movement that was lying there, almost dormant, that he almost alone picked up on. It's a movement that I am convinced will become a world event."

During and after the Free South Africa Movement, Robinson called for changes in U.S. policy toward South Africa. He wanted economic sanctions put in place, but President Ronald Reagan would not agree to do so. However, Robinson's work contributed to the passage in Congress of the Comprehensive Anti-Apartheid Act in 1986. It made provisions for economic and trade sanctions that would not affect South Africa's black population. Reagan vetoed the bill, but supporters drummed up enough votes to override his veto.

Robinson's efforts for South Africa continued even after Nelson Mandela was released in 1990. In 1992, Robinson and others went to South Africa at Mandela's invitation. Though apartheid had not yet been eliminated, the old system was slowly starting to crumble. Still, Robinson applied political pressure when American President George Bush wanted to ease sanctions. TransAfrica remained committed to continued U.S. involvement in South Africa even after the first free elections were held there in 1994 and Mandela became president.

As issues in South Africa appeared headed for resolution, Robinson and TransAfrica began focusing on the Caribbean and other African countries. For example, he lobbied for more American aid to countries like Somalia, which suffered from severe deprivation. He also pointed out that the United States gave more money to former Eastern Bloc countries (populated almost exclusively by whites) than it did to predominantly black countries that had also embraced democracy. In addition, Robinson asked Congress to decrease the amount of aid given to countries that did not have a strong human rights record. By 1992, TransAfrica had an $800,000 budget, and the following year its first headquarters was dedicated. Membership had grown by then to 15,000.

During the mid-1990s, Robinson and TransAfrica became increasingly concerned about events in Haiti. An embargo was put in place against the country's military rulers in 1993, but it had an adverse affect on the population at large, most of whom were black. Those who tried to escape to the United States via boat were denied entry and sent back to Haiti. At the same time, Cubans who fled their country for similar reasons were allowed to stay in the United States. Robinson denounced this as a racist policy because more often than not, the Haitian refugees were black.

In 1994, Robinson himself took a rather drastic step to highlight the struggles of the Haitian people. He went on a hunger strike, consuming just water and juice in an attempt to force a change in American policy. He said he was prepared to die for the cause. "I never doubted it was worth it," he told Karen De Witt of the *New York Times*. "No matter what the outcome, it's worth it always to try. It's better when you're successful, but it's always worth it to try."

After 27 days, Robinson claimed victory on May 8, 1994, when President Bill Clinton announced changes in U.S. policy on political asylum for Haitians and put in place more sanctions. Later that same year, the military leaders of Haiti were deposed, and Jean-Bertrand Aristide took office as the democratically-elected president of Haiti.

Toward the end of the twentieth century, Robinson continued to work on human rights issues in African countries such as Ethiopia, Kenya, Zaire, Liberia, and Malawi. In 1999, he met with Pope John Paul II to discuss relieving the debt of Third World countries. In 2000, he turned his attention to the United States and began a national dialogue on whether reparations should be paid to African Americans to compensate them for slavery, segregation, and other forms of discrimination in the past.

Over the years, Robinson has received numerous awards for his tireless efforts on behalf of those people who often have no one else to speak for them. As an *Economist* reporter once observed, "Say what you will about his tactics, Mr. Robinson is a man of deep convictions about foreign policy."

Sources

➤ Books

Bigelow, Barbara Carlisle, editor, *Contemporary Black Biography,* Volume 7, Gale, 1994.
Henderson, Ashyia N. and Shirelle Phelps, editors, *Who's Who Among African Americans,* Gale, 1999.
Robinson, Randall, *Defending the Spirit: A Black Life in America,* Dutton, 1998.
Smith, Jessie Carney, editor, *Notable Black American Men,* Gale, 1999.

➤ Periodicals

Black Enterprise, August 1992, p. 52 (opening quote); November 1994, p. 13.
Ebony, January 1992, p. 28.
Economist, May 7, 1994, p. A26.
Jet, December 28, 1992, p. 28; June 7, 1993, p. 34; May 2, 1994, p. 5; May 23, 1994, p. 4; June 13, 1994, p. 35; June 26, 1995, p. 12.
Los Angeles Times, June 10, 1984, p. E1.
National Catholic Reporter, May 20, 1994, p. 20; May 27, 1994, p. 10.
National Review, August 29, 1994, p. 22.
New Republic, January 7, 1985, p. 5; February 11, 1985, p. 11; July 9, 1990, p. 14.
New York Times, December 8, 1984, sec. 1, p. 9; August 22, 1991, p. C12; May 9, 1994, pp. A1, A7.
People, May 23, 1994, p. 85.
St. Louis Post-Dispatch, January 28, 2000, p. F3.
Time, November 25, 1985, p. 41.
Washington Post, June 23, 1994, p. C1.

Charles M. Schulz

"I *never realized how many Charlie Browns there were in the world. I thought I was the only one."*

Born November 26, 1922, in Minneapolis, Minnesota, Charles M. Schulz brought a wit and sensitivity to his *Peanuts* comic strip that has touched millions of readers for almost 50 years. He died February 12, 2000 in Santa Rosa, California.

Few creative artists have had the worldwide impact that Charles M. Schulz achieved with his comic strip *Peanuts*. From modest beginnings in 1950, it grew to reach millions of readers in 75 countries through syndication in 2,600 newspapers. Animated television specials, films, stage productions and numerous commercial licensing deals helped to make Schulz's work even more familiar to generations. Charlie Brown, Lucy, Linus, Snoopy and the rest of the *Peanuts* characters became enduring cultural icons thanks to the intelligence and subtlety that their creator brought to his cartoons. With understated, bittersweet humor, Schulz infused *Peanuts* with a compassionate, often spiritually-tinged message about human struggles and failings.

Schulz drew upon his own youthful disappointments in love, athletics and school for material in his strip. As much as anything, it was the poignancy contained in *Peanuts* that won him his massive audience. "Some of my best ideas have come from a mood of sadness, rather than a feeling of well-being," he wrote in his autobiography *Charlie Brown, Snoopy and Me*. "Strangely enough, pleasant things are not really funny. You can't create humor out of happiness. I'm astonished at the number of people who write to me saying, 'Why can't you create happy stories for us? Why does Charlie Brown always have to lose? Why can't you let him kick the football?' Well, there is nothing funny about the person who gets to kick the football."

The son of Carl Schulz, a barber, and Dena (Halverson) Schulz, Charles Monroe Schulz was born in Minneapolis, Minnesota on November 26, 1922. The family soon moved to nearby St. Paul, and by that time, he had received the nickname "Sparky" from an uncle, taken from a character in the comic strip *Barney Google*. By age four, he was sketching characters and winning praise for his talents. "I suppose I didn't realize that you could make a living drawing until I was in my early teens," he wrote in his autobiography. "Generally, comic strips were regarded as a very low form of art and something not worthy of a person's ambition."

Though his grades in elementary school were good, Schulz flunked classes in high school and even had his drawing rejected for the yearbook. As an athlete, he also had his frustrations; his team's losing streak in baseball was later immortalized in *Peanuts*. Painfully shy, he didn't have his first date until two years after high school. Despite all this, he continued to cultivate his gift. After a stint in the U.S. Army during World War II, he sought work as an artist, finally securing a teaching position at Art Instruction Inc. in Minneapolis.

Cartooning continued to be Schulz's first love, and he made his initial career breakthrough by drawing a weekly comic panel called *Li'l Folks* for the *St. Paul Pioneer Press*. In 1950, Schulz placed a strip derived from *Li'l Folks* with the United Features Syndicate, who renamed it *Peanuts* over his objections (he felt the title made it sound "too insignificant"). The strip began to gain popularity over the next several years, and in 1955 Schulz received a coveted Reuben Award from the National Cartoonists Society for being the outstanding cartoonist of the year.

The *Peanuts* cast of characters began to take shape during the strip's early years. The hapless but well-intentioned Charlie Brown emerged as its focal point. "I like to think of Charlie Brown as being a bit of Everyman," Schulz said in his autobiography. "Most people would admit to often feeling a bit like him. . . He tries to assume a perfect social image, but everything seems to go wrong. There is a lot of myself in his character, too." The irritable "fussbudget" Lucy and her philosophical, blanket-toting younger brother Linus appeared by the mid-1950s. Snoopy, the canine character based on Schulz's childhood dog Spike, gradually took on more human aspects as the strip progressed.

By the early 1960s, Schulz had published a series of *Peanuts* books and had earned a loyal cult following. Critics hailed the strip for its wistful, melancholy charm and insights into human character. "With the barely perceptible wriggle of a line, he can convey a pathos and tenderness beyond the reach of most of his colleagues," *Time* said of Schulz in April 1965. "The dots at either end of Charlie's mouth sum up six years of concentrated worry." Though Schulz avoided explicit political satire, *Peanuts* was viewed by many as a running commentary on the anxieties of the era. Italian author Umberto Eco, quoted in Schulz's obituary in *The New York Times*, described the strip's characters as "the monstrous infantile reductions of all the neuroses of a modern citizen of the industrial civilization."

Schulz acknowledged that he often dealt with spiritual issues in his strip. A member of the Church of God since high school, he was an active lay preacher who didn't smoke, drink or swear. On occasion, he would cite scripture and use his character Linus to make theological points. In 1964, seminary student Robert L. Short published *The Gospel According to Peanuts*, a best-selling analysis of the Biblical elements in Schulz's strip. Schulz wrote in the September 1963 issue of *Decision* that "all kinds of people in religious work have written to thank me for preaching in my own way through the strips. That is one of the things that keep me going."

The mid-1960s saw the *Peanuts* characters win new fans through a series of animated television specials. The first of these, *A Charlie Brown Christmas,* was first aired on CBS in 1965 and earned Emmy and Peabody Awards. More than 50 more animated specials followed, as well as a feature film, *A Boy Named Charlie Brown.* In 1967, the musical *You're a Good Man, Charlie Brown* enjoyed a successful off-Broadway run, and went on to win two Tony Awards after its revival in 1999. In addition, *Peanuts* greeting cards, stuffed toys, clothing and other licensed products earned Schulz millions each year. By 1999, some 20,000 *Peanuts*-related items had appeared on the market. *Peanuts* went on to inspire philanthropic as well as commercial endeavors, such as the Linus Project, which distributed blankets to children with serious illnesses to more than 300 cities in the United States, Canada, Australia and Japan.

Schulz's comic vision evolved with the times. In the late 1960s, he introduced the tomboyish Peppermint Patty and her bespectacled sidekick Marcie, as well as Woodstock, Snoopy's feathered friend. One character, a feline named Feron, was dropped because, as Schulz later told *Esquire,* "I learned that I couldn't draw a cat." Despite his enormous success, Schulz continued to maintain a diligent nine-to-four, five-days-a-week schedule until late in his life. He played golf and hockey as time permitted; his love for the latter sport led to his establishing the Empire Ice Skating Arena near his home in Santa Rosa, California in 1969.

Schulz's health began to decline in the 1990s. He continued to write and draw *Peanuts* on his own, despite the debilitating effects of Parkinson's Disease. When he was diagnosed with colon cancer in November 1999, he was forced to bring his strip to a close, and in a statement published on December 14, 1999, he announced his retirement. The announcement prompted a wave of fond farewells, including one from President Bill Clinton, who lauded, "Charles Schulz has shown us that a comic strip can transcend its small space on the page. It can uplift; it can challenge; it can educate its readers even as it entertains us." The last daily *Peanuts* appeared January 3, 2000, and the final original Sunday strip ran on February 13, 2000, carrying a signed farewell from Schulz: "Charlie Brown, Snoopy, Linus, Lucy. . . how can I ever forget them. . . "

On February 12, 2000, Charles M. Schulz died in his sleep, only a few hours before his last cartoon appeared in Sunday newspapers. Tributes to the cartoonist noted that he almost reached the half-century mark of publication, and *Peanuts* reruns continued to appear daily in thousands of newspapers after his passing. His achievements seemed secure and enduring. As James Poniewozik wrote in *Time*, "Sincere as a pumpkin patch, his lifework is a reminder that self-awareness and a refined sense of irony do not mean affectlessness, that being a loser does not mean being defeated."

Sources

➤ Books

Johnson, Rheta Grimsley, *Good Grief: The Story of Charles M. Schulz,* Pharos Books, 1989.
Schulz, Charles M., *Charlie Brown, Snoopy and Me: And All the Other Peanuts Characters,* Doubleday, 1980.
Short, Robert L., *The Gospel According to Peanuts,* John Knox Press, 1964.

➤ Periodicals

Christian Century, January 19, 2000, p. 53.
Christian Science Monitor, November 24, 1995, p. 10; December 16, 2000, p. 1.
Decision, September 1963, p. 9.
Editor & Publisher, May 28, 1994, p. 30; December 18, 1999, p. 5; January 3, 2000, p. 52.
Esquire, June 1996, p. 67.
New York Times, February 14, 2000, p. A1.
People, January 1, 2000, p. 130 (opening quote).
Time, April 9, 1965, p. 80; December 27, 1999, p. 95.
Weekly Compilation of Presidential Documents, December 20, 1999, p. 2623.

Margaret Chase Smith

"$\mathbf{S}$*ome of those who call us the weaker sex say that we possess such financial and economic control because we outlive the men and thus inherit the money. Did someone say something about 'survival of the fittest'?"*

Born December 14, 1897, in Skowhegan, Maine, Margaret Chase Smith was a prominent, outspoken Republican politician, the first woman elected to both houses of Congress. She died May 29, 1995, in Skowhegan, Maine.

Known as the "Lady from Maine," Margaret Chase Smith was one of the most influential female politicians in the United States during the 20th century. Smith accomplished many firsts in her more than three decades in politics, including being the first woman to serve in both houses of Congress and the first woman to seek the presidential nomination of a major political party. While serving in Congress, Smith introduced several key pieces of legislation, but was best remembered as being the first Republican to speak out against Senator Joseph McCarthy and his anti-Communist hearings.

Smith was born Margaret Madeline Chase on December 14, 1897, in Skowhegan, Maine. She was the eldest of six children of George Emery and Carrie Murray Chase. Smith's father worked as a barber, while her mother took part-time jobs, such as waitress, store clerk, and shoe factory worker, as needed to supplement the family's income.

While taking a commercial course at Skowhegan High School, Smith also worked on a part-time basis to help support her family. In addition to being a relief barber for her father, Smith was employed as a night telephone operator and dime store clerk. After graduating in 1916, Smith did not go to college because she could not afford it.

Instead Smith went to work full-time, beginning with a short stint as a teacher in a one-room schoolhouse, the Pitts School outside of Skowhegan. She went on to work her way through the ranks at the Maine Telephone Company, from clerk to operator, before taking managerial positions at other companies. She spent eight years working at the editorial, advertising and circulation sections at the local newspaper, *Independent Reporter*. She was also the manager at a woolen mill, the Daniel E. Cummings Company, and a local waste process company.

Smith was active in local women's organizations. In 1922, she established a chapter of the Business and Professional Women's Club in Skowhegan. Four years later, Smith was elected to a two-year term as president of the Maine Federation of Business and Professional Women's Clubs.

In May 1930, Smith married the co-owner and publisher of *Independent Reporter*, Clyde H. Smith. At 55 years of age, he was a wealthy businessman with interests other than the newspaper. He was the president of Bangor, Maine's Steward Goodwin Company as well as a local Republican politician who never lost in the 48 elections he entered.

After their marriage, Smith became active in Republican politics. She served on the Republican State Committee, representing her country through 1936. Smith also supported her husband's campaign for a House of Representatives seat in the 1936.

When Clyde H. Smith won the election as a liberal Republican, Smith served as her husband's secretary. Putting in 15-hour days, Smith did everything from filing and dealing with his mail to conducting research for his speeches and legislative proposals. In April 1940, Clyde Smith died suddenly of a heart attack, but before his death expressed his wish that his wife take over his seat.

Maine voters elected Smith into his seat in a June special election. Traditionally, most of the women who entered Congress were widows of men in who died while in office. Smith went beyond the norm, winning that fall's election as well. She spent the next 33 years in Congress as a Republican.

Smith served in the House of Representatives for eight years, but did not always vote along Republican party lines. Instead Smith voted with her beliefs and her conscience. With World War II on the horizon, she was one of the few Republicans to vote for the Selective Service Act (the draft) in 1940.

Smith also voted to arm the United States merchant marines, for the Lend-Lease Act (which gave armaments to European countries fighting against Germany and the Axis powers), and against the Republican-supported Smith-Connally Anti-Strike Act. Though she was denounced as a traitor for this negative vote, Smith believed her constituents in Maine, where many shipyards were located, did not support the act.

Smith was interested in military issues throughout her Congressional life. In 1943, she became a member of the Naval Affairs Committee, which was later renamed the Armed Services Committee. She made information-gathering trips to different countries and continents to view the state of American military forces first hand. She was the first non-military woman to sail on an American destroyer during a time of war.

During and after the war, Smith also did much to improve the status of women in the military. Smith proposed legislation that led to the creation of the Women Accepted for Voluntary Emergency Service (WAVES), which would send women overseas in noncombat roles so that more men would be freed for combat. Though some men did not believe women should be put in such difficult positions, Smith pointed out that female nurses were already there and the legislation was passed.

Smith also introduced the Army-Navy Permanent Nurses Corp Bill which gave women permanent status in the military. This became a law in 1947. The following year, Smith saw the passage through of the Women's Armed Services Integration Act of 1948. This was a very important law, giving female soldiers retirement benefits, equal pay, equal rank, and privileges. Much of Smith's work in this area changed how women in the military, and America at large, were viewed.

In 1948, Smith decided to run for one of Maine's Senate seats and won, becoming the first women who was elected on her own merits (not because she inherited or was appointed) and second woman elected overall. Smith was also the first Republican woman elected, though she had not been endorsed by her own party because they did not think she could win. Yet she won with 70 percent of the vote, the greatest majority win in the history of Maine.

Smith would go on win three additional terms in the Senate, always winning by large margins though she did not campaign much. She believed that doing her job in Washington was more important. Smith also kept the campaign promises she made.

Smith was a very active senator, securing memberships in key committees such as the Rules Committee, Appropriations Committee, and the Government Operations Committee. As she had in the House, Smith supported a strong military and taking a hard stance against the growing threat of communism. To that end, in 1949, she endorsed the formation of the North Atlantic Treaty Organization (NATO).

Though Smith was anti-Communist, she did not approve of the smear campaign and bullying of fellow Republican Senator Joseph McCarthy. In the late 1940s and early 1950s, McCarthy accused numerous government and public figures of being communists and subjected them to public "witch" trials. Many of Smith's colleagues feared McCarthy and his growing power.

In 1950, Smith made a courageous stand against him, the first elected official and Republican to do so. On June 1, she made a 15-minute long speech, entitled the "Declaration of Conscience" in which she denounced him, his tactics and his hearings. She accused him of abusing his seat in the Senate. Though McCarthy continued his campaign for several more years, until his 1954 censure, Smith eventually received the Chi Omega Award, also in 1954, for her stance.

Smith firmly believed that her fellow senators should be responsible. She favored legislation to promote voting among Senators that called for the expulsion of any senator who missed more than 60 percent of votes. Though this did not pass, Smith practiced what she preached. She did not miss a vote from June 1955 until August 1968, a record total of 2,941. Her streak only ended because she had to have hip surgery.

Smith's ambitions stretched beyond the Senate. In 1964, she ran for President, the first woman to run since Victoria Woodhull in 1872, and the first on a major party ticket. She received 27 votes at the convention, second to Barry Goldwater. Smith had previously been considered for the vice presidency in 1952 and 1956.

Some believed that Smith's presidential campaign failed in part because she had no real charisma and did not support anything specific. She was seen as responsible but dull. This issue resurfaced in her fifth Senatorial campaign.

By 1972, Smith was 74 years old and campaigning in essentially the same way as she had when she first ran for the Senate in 1948. Smith did not raise the same amount of funds as her opponents, nor did she propose specific solutions and programs to her voters. She only had a good voting record. Smith was upset by Democratic candidate William V. Hathaway.

When Smith left the Senate in 1973, she was the only woman to have won four terms. There were no other female Senators at the time. Smith remained active, however. With the sponsorship of the Woodrow Wilson National Fellowships Foundation, Smith spent three years going to colleges and universities and conducting seminars and discussion groups.

Smith's accomplishments were honored many times over her lifetime. Though she never attended college, she received between 85 and 95 honorary degrees. She was named Woman of the Year by the Associated Press in 1948, 1949, 1950 and 1957. When the National Women's Hall of Fame was founded in 1973, Smith was one of the original inductees. In 1989, she given the Presidential Medal of Freedom by President George Bush.

Even after Smith died on May 26, 1995 in Skowhegan, Maine, of complications from a stroke, her legacy remained relevant. In 1998, Smith was nominated by Maine Senator Olympia J. Snowe to appear on a new dollar coin to be issued in 2000. Ultimately, she was not used on the coin. But Snowe said of Smith, in a Capitol Hill Press Release, that "Margaret Chase Smith was a woman of countless firsts. Her importance to this nation was not a passing fad. Rather, her legacy extended across nearly a half-century as she blazed a trail for women in countless fields and professions while opening doors that had long been closed."

Sources

➤ Books

Adamson, Lynda G., *Notable Women in American History*, Greenwood Press, 1999, p. 344.

Cullen-DuPont, Kathryn, *The Encyclopedia of Women's History in America*, Facts on File, Inc., 1996, pp. 197-98.

Encyclopedia of World Biography, second edition, volume 14, Gale Group, 1998, pp. 299-300.

Garraty, John A. and Mark C. Carnes, eds., *American National Biography*, volume 20, Oxford University Press, 1999, pp. 253-54.

Graham, Frank, Jr., *Margaret Chase Smith: Woman of Courage*, The John Day Company, 1964.

Magill, Frank N., ed., *Great Lives from History: American Series*, volume 5, Salem Press, 1987, pp. 2106-11.

Magill, Frank N., ed., *Great Lives from History: American Women Series*, volume 5, Salem Press, 1995, pp. 1657-61.

Parry, Melanie, ed., *Larousse Dictionary of Women*, Larousse, 1996, p. 606.

Smith, Margaret Chase, *Declaration of Conscience*, Doubleday & Company, Inc., 1972 (opening quote).

Stineman, Esther, *American Political Women: Contemporary and Historical Profiles*, Libraries Unlimited, Inc., 1980, pp. 137-40.

Uglow, Jennifer, ed., *Dictionary of Women's Biography*, third edition, Macmillan, 1998, p. 501.

➤ Perodicals

Independent, October 27, 1999, p. 19.

Maine Sunday Telegram, July 4, 1999.

Minneapolis Star Tribune, May 30, 1995, p. 1A.

People, June 12, 1995, p. 67.

➤ Other

"Snow Advances Margaret Chase Smith Dollar Coin," Capitol Hill
  Press Releases, June 5, 1998.

Gene Stallings

"I hope people see that having a handicapped child is really not all that bad. It's what you make of it. Sure it's hard early on. You've got dreams. You want your son or daughter to do that. But they can't. Their accomplishments are little accomplishments, but they have great depth."

Born c. 1935 in Paris, Texas, Gene Stallings was a college and professional football coach from the late 1950s through the mid-1990s. He is active with numerous charities that benefit people with disabilities. Address: Hike-A-Way Ranch, Paris, Texas (some sources say Powderly, Texas).

Once described by Douglas S. Looney in *Sports Illustrated* as "one of the nicest men in college football," Gene Stallings accomplished much during his 40 years as a football coach at both the college and professional level. But he credits some of his success to the lessons he learned from his son, John Mark, who has Down Syndrome. On and off the field, John Mark—or Johnny, as he is more commonly known—has proven to be an inspiration, so much so that Stallings and his family devote a considerable amount of time working with charitable organizations that help people with disabilities and their families.

Born around 1935 in Paris, Texas, Eugene Clifton Stallings, Jr., is the son of Eugene Clifton Stallings, Sr., and his wife, Nell. The elder Stallings worked in a roofing business and as a storm adjuster for an insurance company, while Nell Stallings was employed by a title company. Gene and his older brother, Jimmy, grew up in Paris. He started playing football in fourth grade but was also interested in basketball and golf. Stallings continued to play football throughout high school, and in 1952 he became team captain.

In 1954 Stallings entered Texas A&M University, where he played football under legendary coach Paul "Bear" Bryant for four seasons and once again served as captain of the team. "I never thought of myself as a great player," he recalled in his book, *Another Season.* "I didn't think I was especially strong or fast, but I was sure passionate about the game and willing to give it everything I had." Stallings began playing during his sophomore year as a defensive end and at one point was named to an All-Conference team.

While Stallings did not intend to pursue a professional playing career, he was very interested in coaching. After graduation, Bryant hired him as an assistant for the 1957 season. The pair got along well. As Stallings told Geoffrey Norman of *Forbes,* "I learned a lot from Coach Bryant. Nobody could deal with people the way he did. He knew the right way to get to every one of them, and he knew that they all responded to something different. He was a genius, that way."

When Bryant was hired by the University of Alabama in 1958, he invited Stallings to go with him. Bryant remained at Alabama from 1958 until 1982, winning a total of 232 games (including six national championships), making him the winningest coach in college football history. In 1960 Stallings published a book on his mentor entitled *Bear Bryant on Winning Football.*

In 1962, however, his life was changed forever by the birth of his son, John Mark, on June 11. Stallings and his wife, Ruth Ann Jack, had been high school sweethearts who married during his senior year in college. They already had two daughters, Anna Lee and Laurie, and were delighted when their third child turned out to be a boy. But Johnny Stallings was born with Down Syndrome, a chromosomal abnormality that causes moderate to severe mental retardation and a number of physical problems, including heart ailments. Johnny fell into that category, too; he had a hole in his heart, a condition called Eisenmenger's Syndrome. Stallings passed out when he first heard the news. (He and Ruth Ann went on to have two more healthy daughters, Jacklyn and Martha Kate.)

At the time of Johnny's birth not much was known about Down Syndrome, and few people cared to discuss it. Doctors and others urged the couple to institutionalize their son, as was common in those days. Though they were warned he might not live past the age of four, the Stallings decided to keep their son at home and do the best they could for him. In return, the family received much more than they ever expected. "Johnny has given us love—total, unconditional love—and joy," Stallings told Susan Schindehette of *People*. "And what we thought was the worst thing that could ever happen to us turned out to be a true blessing for every single person in our family. He's been the cement that's made us so close."

Stallings believes that his son also helped him keep his life as a coach in perspective. "I developed a whole lot more tolerance for the less gifted," he explained to Schindehette. "If a kid wasn't big or strong enough, but gave his all, I let him be on the team to do what he could." Stallings began bringing his son to work occasionally when he became head coach at Texas A&M in 1964 after leaving his assistant position at Alabama. Though the team won the Southwest Conference title in 1967, then beat the University of Alabama (still coached by Bryant) by a score of 20-16 in the Cotton Bowl, Stallings was fired in 1971. His overall record was 27 wins, 45 losses, and one tie.

Stallings did not remain unemployed for long. In 1972 he moved into the ranks of professional football when the legendary Tom Landry hired him to be the defensive secondary coach of the Dallas Cowboys. Stallings regularly brought his son to work, and Johnny helped the trainer tape the players' ankles and do other small tasks. Though Stallings was initially uncertain about how the men would react to his son, he was pleased to see that Johnny soon became a part of the team and served as an inspiration to many players.

While Stallings was with the Cowboys, the team won two Superbowls. Though he was enjoying his tenure with Dallas, it was during this period that Bear Bryant retired from coaching at Alabama. University officials wanted to talk to Stallings about taking over the football program, but he could not because the professional season was still in progress. Another coach was hired before Stallings became available.

Stallings left Dallas in 1985 when he was hired as head coach of another professional team, the St. Louis Cardinals. (In 1988 the team moved to Phoenix and became known as the Arizona Cardinals.) At the time, the Cardinals were the worst team in the league, and nothing Stallings tried improved the situation. He was fired early in the 1989-90 season after posting a record of 23 wins, 34 losses, and one tie. One bright moment during his tenure with the Cardinals was a public service announcement for United Way that Stallings filmed with his son in 1987 that turned out to be extremely popular.

The firing proved to be a blessing in disguise, because it gave Stallings the opportunity to be considered for the head coaching position at the University of Alabama. The previous coach, Bill Curry, had had three successful seasons but chose to leave his post because he felt he did not quite fit in at the university. Though some were not sure if Stallings was good enough for the job (after all, he had a losing record as a head coach), and others thought that, at 55, he might be too old, many more were impressed by the fact that he had worked with the late Bear Bryant. It also helped that he looked and talked like the beloved coach. Stallings himself initially hesitated because the university wanted him to sign a long-term deal. Ultimately, he decided to accept the job. As sports journalist Paul Finebaum of Birmingham, Alabama, told *Forbes* writer Geoffrey Norman, "I think he knew that this was the last best chance he'd ever have to prove that he was a good coach. And Stallings has a lot of pride. . . . He believes he is a good coach. But when he got the job at Alabama, he might have been the only one in the state who did."

Stallings immediately came under fire at the start of the 1990 football season when his team lost their first three games, falling to Southern Mississippi, the University of Florida, and the University of Georgia. In retrospect, he believed that he could have won all of those games, but Alabama fans still fumed. The team eventually ended the season with seven wins and five losses. Two of those wins were over Alabama's biggest rivals, Tennessee and Auburn.

Under Stallings, Alabama improved over the next two seasons. In 1991, the team finished with eleven wins and one loss. It was ranked fifth nationally and beat the University of Colorado to win the Blockbuster Bowl. By the middle of the 1992 season, Alabama and

Stallings were riding a 17-game winning streak. Stallings was beginning to be regarded as the savior of the program, which was looking more and more like the glory days of Bryant. Later that season, the team became national champions by posting 13 wins and no losses and upsetting the University of Miami Hurricanes in the Sugar Bowl by a score of 34-17. Miami had won 29 straight games and was the defending national champion.

The 1992 season proved to be the pinnacle of Stallings' career as head coach at Alabama. Though the team continued to do well over the next few seasons and even contended for the national championship, they had problems rounding up good quarterbacks.

Of greater concern to Stallings, however, was the health of his son. Johnny had a job as a tour guide and audio-visual technician at the Paul W. Bryant Museum. But by 1993 he was slowing down. (After the age of 30, many people with Down Syndrome begin to suffer from heart problems and various other illnesses.) There were concerns about how much longer he would live. Meanwhile, his father used his high-profile position to help change public opinion and increase awareness in Alabama about those with disabilities.

During his days with the Cowboys, Stallings had established a charitable organization called Disability Resources. Once he relocated to Alabama, he became involved with Rural Infant Stimulation Environment (RISE), a public program for the early education of children under the age of six with disabilities, including Down Syndrome and cerebral palsy. The program had been housed in an old building on Alabama's campus and had little money. Well aware that his son would have benefited from such a program had it existed when he was a child, Stallings did his best to help RISE. In addition to paying frequent visits, he worked to obtain more funding. He donated his speaking fees to underwrite part of the cost of a new building and encouraged others to become involved as well. In 1995, RISE opened its new home, which was named the Stallings Center in his honor. Stallings also held a golf tournament every spring that benefited the Alabama Association for Retarded Citizens (ARC), the group that helped Johnny Stallings find his museum job.

Stallings retired at the end of the 1996-97 season, after his team beat the University of Michigan in the Outback Bowl. The losses had become especially hard for his son to take, and he felt it was time to call it quits after coaching for 40 years. During his seven years at Alabama, Stallings had won 70 games, lost 16, and tied once. Alabama went to six bowl games and averaged nine wins per season.

Stallings and his family then moved to their ranch near Paris, Texas. In 1997, he published a book about Johnny entitled *Another Season: A Coach's Story of Raising an Exceptional Son,* written with Sally Cook. Though he had collaborated on it with Cook for four years, Stallings was not entirely comfortable with the project. As he explained to a reporter for the *Fort-Worth Star Telegram* in an article that was reprinted in the *Omaha World-Herald,* "I didn't want to do it at all because some of those things are private thoughts. But they convinced us that it would be helpful to other people and that was the bottom line. Hopefully [the book] will make somebody that does have a handicapped child see that there is light at the end of the tunnel, especially when the child has just been born."

Though Stallings considered returning to coaching several times between 1997 and 1999 at schools such as Texas Christian University and Baylor University, in the end he opted to stick with retirement. Besides remaining active on the boards of several charities, he works on his ranch and spends time with his son.

Sources

➤ Books

Forney, John and Steve Townsend, *Talk of the Tide: An Oral History of Alabama Football since 1920,* Crane Hill Publishers, 1993.
Stallings, Gene and Sally Cook, *Another Season: A Coach's Story of Raising an Exceptional Son,* Little, Brown, 1997.

➤ Periodicals

Arizona Republic, August 18, 1997, p. C1 (opening quote).
Dallas Morning News, November 10, 1996, p. 22B; November 24, 1996, p. 24B; August 17, 1997, p. 8J; December 11, 1998, p. 10B.
Denver Rocky Mountain News, January 1, 1997, p. 9C.
Forbes, September 27, 1993, p. S190.
Gannett News Service, November 24, 1996, p. S12.
Houston Chronicle, August 30, 1997, p. 5; November 6, 1997, p. 5.
Los Angeles Times, August 28, 1990, p. C1; December 5, 1992, p. C1.
Newsday, December 29, 1992, p. 89.
Omaha World-Herald, August 30, 1997, p. 41.
People, February 2, 1998, p. 40.
Publishers Weekly, July 21, 1997, p. 195.
Redbook, June 1, 1998, p. G4.

Seattle Times, October 12, 1997, p. C9.

Sport, January 1993, p. 40.

Sports Illustrated, January 22, 1990, p. 48; September 24, 1990, p. 58; November 18, 1991, p. 108; October 26, 1992, p. 54; November 25, 1996, p. 90.

St. Louis Post-Dispatch, September 17, 1997, p. E1.

University Wire, January 14, 1999.

USA Today, April 21, 1997, p. C1; October 2, 1997, p. 3C.

Clyde W. Tombaugh

*"*F*or three-quarters of an hour, I was the only person in the world who knew exactly where Pluto was."*

Born February 4, 1906, near Streator, Illinois, Clyde W. Tombaugh earned a place in history as the discoverer of Pluto, the ninth planet of the solar system. He died January 17, 1997, at his home in Las Cruces, New Mexico.

On March 12, 1930, astronomers at Arizona's Lowell Observatory announced the discovery of a ninth planet, a tiny speck of light in the solar system that came to be known as Pluto. Located some 3.6 billion miles from the sun and not much bigger in diameter than Earth's moon, the mysterious "Planet X" had eluded astronomers for decades as they scanned the heavens for proof of its existence. In the end, it was a 24-year-old amateur sky watcher named Clyde W. Tombaugh who confirmed there was indeed a Planet X. Despite the fact that he lacked a college degree and had no formal training in astronomy, he possessed the kind of perseverance and painstaking attention to detail it took to accomplish such a feat. Tombaugh thus became only the third person in history—and the only one in the twentieth century—to discover a new planet.

Clyde William Tombaugh was born on an Illinois farm not far from the small town of Streator in the north-central part of the state. It was in this rural setting that he grew up as a confirmed stargazer, a love he shared with his father, Muron, and especially his uncle Leon. In fact, Clyde's first look through a telescope was at the age of 12 when Leon set up a simple, three-inch-diameter model in the field behind the family home. The youngster was amazed at how much surface detail he could make out on the moon, including numerous craters and mountains. He also saw the rings of Saturn and some of the many moons that circle Jupiter. Soon he was spending as many clear nights as possible observing the sky through his uncle's telescope. By day, after his chores were done, he devoured every astronomy book he could find and quickly became adept at identifying the planets and constellations.

In 1922, the Tombaughs moved from Illinois to another farm near Burdett, Kansas. Clyde, who was then 16, hoped that after graduating from high school he would be able to attend college and study his favorite subject. But his parents could not afford to pay for his education, and they still needed his help on the farm. So Tombaugh remained at home and continued reading and learning about astronomy on his own, looking forward to the day when he would be able to fulfill his dream.

Eventually, Tombaugh also longed for a bigger and better telescope. Because he was too poor to buy one, however, he decided to build one himself. Inspired by an article in the magazine *Popular Astronomy*, he rounded up the necessary parts (among them a crankshaft from his father's 1910 Buick and the stand from an old cream separator) and set about making a nine-inch reflecting telescope. Over the course of several weeks he carefully ground and polished the glass for the mirror, striving to fashion the proper curve required for sharp, clear images. Tombaugh's results were less than spectacular on the first try, but a second telescope he built soon afterward turned out to be a remarkably fine instrument that made his study of the heavens even more enjoyable. Around this same time, he started to make detailed drawings of what he saw through his eyepiece, including the moon and the planets Mars, Jupiter, and Saturn.

Meanwhile, the Tombaugh family's financial situation slowly improved. Three years after graduating from high school, Clyde was finally able to make plans to head off to college. Then a devastating hailstorm destroyed the year's crops, and once again he was forced to set aside his dreams while his family struggled to make ends meet.

Realizing more than ever that he was not cut out to be a farmer, Tombaugh vowed that somehow he would pursue a career in science. In 1928 he sent a sample of his astronomical drawings to Lowell Observatory in Flagstaff, Arizona. The director was so impressed with the quality of Tombaugh's work that he offered the young man a job taking long-exposure photographs of the night sky with the observatory's new telescope. Despite the promise of long, tedious hours at low pay, Tombaugh was thrilled to be given such an opportunity. Thus, on January 14, 1929, he boarded a train for Arizona.

Tombaugh's duties at the Lowell Observatory were quite varied at first. He gave tours to visitors, for example, and was also responsible for keeping the dome free of snow and ice. But his most important assignment involved taking pictures of the night sky so that astronomers could review them as part of the search for "Planet X," the elusive ninth planet that some believed orbited the sun well beyond Neptune.

The observatory's founder and namesake, astronomer Percival Lowell, had speculated several decades earlier that such a planet existed because of inexplicable aberrations in the orbits of both Neptune and the seventh planet, Uranus. He even predicted where in the sky it would probably be found. Years of searching had turned up nothing, but Lowell's successors (he died in 1916) were convinced that their new equipment would help them prove there really was a Planet X. Besides the photographic telescope, they had a special viewer called a blink-comparator that enabled them to compare two pictures of an identical section of sky taken several days or weeks apart. Looking through an eyepiece, the astronomers switched rapidly from one image to the other and back again, a technique that made it easier to spot movement among the hundreds of thousands of white dots in a single image. Once they detected some movement, the scientists then had to determine whether it signaled a planet or, much more likely, an asteroid or a comet.

Tombaugh spent night after night in the unheated dome of the observatory taking photographs of the sky, turning the images over to astronomers to analyze for any signs of planet-like motion. As time went by without any significant discoveries, the scientists grew discouraged and shifted their attention to other matters. Meanwhile, Tombaugh kept taking photographs that quickly piled up around the observatory. When the busy astronomers asked him if he would like to try his hand at evaluating the images himself, he jumped at the chance.

Over the next eight months, Tombaugh continued to scour the night sky in a systematic sweep of possible Planet X locations. At daybreak, he began pouring over the pictures he had taken. He discovered many asteroids and a few comets, but Planet X remained as elusive as ever. "There are 15 million stars in the sky as bright as Pluto," Tombaugh later explained. "I had to pick one image out of the 15 million."

Finally, on February 18, 1930, while comparing two photographs that had been taken in late January about a week apart, he came across a tiny white dot that had moved ever-so-slightly—more than a star would have, but not quite as much as an asteroid or a comet. To make an additional comparison, Tombaugh pulled out a third image of the same section of sky that had been taken earlier in the month. The amount and direction of the movement he saw convinced him that he had at last discovered Planet X. Recalling that historic moment years later, Tombaugh said, "It electrified me. When I saw that, I knew instantly that was it."

Once Tombaugh shared his findings with the astronomers at the observatory, they spent several weeks checking his data and calculating the new planet's orbit. (In the meantime, he managed to keep the exciting news secret, even from his own parents.) Finally, on March 13, 1930, the astronomers announced Tombaugh's amazing discovery to the public. In keeping with the tradition of naming planets after various Roman gods and goddesses (and to honor Percival Lowell, whose initials were PL), the new planet was given the name Pluto.

Having secured his place in history, Tombaugh remained at the Lowell Observatory for several more years before enrolling at the University of Kansas to obtain his long-delayed college education. (The work he had done to discover Pluto earned him a full scholarship.) After graduating in 1936 with a degree in astronomy, he returned to Lowell and resumed his systematic search of the heavens while pursuing his master's degree, which he received from the University of Kansas in 1939.

According to the logbooks, Tombaugh examined about 70 percent of the sky visible from the Lowell Observatory and in the process discovered nearly 4,000 asteroids, 1 comet, more than 1,800 variable stars, and almost 30,000 galaxies before taking a war-related leave of absence in 1943 to teach celestial navigation for the U.S. Navy. A budget crunch in 1946 resulted in the elimination of his position at Lowell and an unexpected change of careers. After brief teaching stints at Arizona State College (now Northern Arizona University) and the University of California at Los Angeles, Tombaugh went to work at White Sands Missile Range in New Mexico developing special optical guidance systems for tracking rockets in flight. In 1958, he joined the faculty of New Mexico State University as founder of the astronomy research program and professor of astronomy, a position he held until his retirement in 1973.

Tombaugh's stature in the scientific community increased with the passage of time and the growing recognition among his colleagues that his was no ordinary accomplishment. He spent his final years traveling extensively and lecturing at various universities and conferences, often to raise funds for a special scholarship program established in his honor at New Mexico State University. He also gave generously of his time and expertise to amateur astronomers who approached him for advice or just to chat.

Tombaugh remained passionate about astronomy until the end of his life and always kept an assortment of telescopes set up in his backyard. Among them was the original nine-inch-diameter reflecting model he had built on his parents' farm so many years before. (He once declined a request from the Smithsonian to donate it to the museum, explaining that he wasn't through using it yet.) Greatly weakened by congestive heart failure and related breathing difficulties, the man who "loved the sky like no other" died at the age of 90 on January 17, 1997, at his home in Las Cruces, New Mexico.

Sources

➤ On-line

"The Clyde W. Tombaugh Page," *Pluto Express*, http://www.jpl.nasa.gov/pluto/clyde.htm (January 21, 1997).

"DPS Article: Clyde Tombaugh," *Clyde Tombaugh (1906-1997)*, http://www.klx.com/clyde/dps.html (December 10, 1999).

"New Mexico State University Press Release," *Clyde Tombaugh (1906-1997)*, http://www.klx.com/clyde/mmsu.html (December 10, 1999).

➤ Books

Levy, David, *Clyde Tombaugh: Discoverer of Planet Pluto*, University of Arizona Press, 1992.

Vogt, Gregory L., *Pluto*, Millbrook Press, 1994.

Wetterer, Margaret K., *Clyde Tombaugh and the Search for Planet X*, Carolrhoda Books, 1996.

➤ Periodicals

Astronomy, April 1997.

Grand Rapids Press, January 19, 1997, p. B7 (opening quote).

New York Times, January 20, 1997.

People, May 12, 1980.

Science Digest, March 1980.

Sky & Telescope, April 1997.

Smithsonian, May 1991, pp. 32-36.

Walter J. Turnbull

"**E**verything I am as a person, the values, the kinds of things I believe are important for success, particularly for young black men in this society, are wound up into what I teach the children."

Born July 19, 1944, in Greenville, Mississippi, Walter J. Turnbull is the founder and director of the Boys Choir of Harlem. Address: The Boys Choir of Harlem, 2005 Madison Ave., New York, NY 10035.

Walter J. Turnbull has dedicated his life to both music and children. As the founder and director of the Boys Choir of Harlem, he has given boys (and more recently, girls) an alternative to the harsh realities of inner-city life while showing them the importance of hard work and education. In the process, Turnbull and the Boys Choir have achieved international renown.

Turnbull was born on July 19, 1944, in Greenville, Mississippi, the son of Jake "Jasse" Turnbull, Jr., and his wife, Lena Green. His parents separated when he was just a child due to his father's alcoholism and his mother's conversion to the Seventh-Day Adventist faith. Lena Green raised Turnbull, his brothers, Sam and Horace, and his sister, Mary, on her own. A very religious woman, she worked mostly as a cook and housecleaner for wealthy white families to support herself and her children. Her dedication and determination greatly influenced Turnbull.

Turnbull liked music from an early age and began taking piano lessons as a youngster. A fan of religious and gospel music, he also sang in church and school choirs. One school choir director in particular, Miss Jones, was especially influential in Turnbull's life. She was tough on her students but led them to statewide acclaim though practice and fierce discipline. The lessons he learned from her and from participating in other choirs shaped the course of his own future.

After graduating from high school, Turnbull had many options for continuing his education. He had been offered a number of scholarships due to his work with choirs and eventually chose to attend Tougaloo College in his home state. From the beginning, Turnbull was an outstanding student who was featured as a soloist during his first year. By the time he was a junior, he had decided to become an opera singer. To that end, he often spent summers in Chautauqua, New York, working to improve his musical skills.

In 1966, Turnbull earned his B.A. (with honors) in music education. After graduation, he headed to New York City, where he entered the Manhattan School of Music to obtain his master's degree. To support himself, Turnbull worked as a janitor. But music remained his primary focus. While spending summers at Lake George, a resort town in upstate New York, Turnbull continued working in opera, performing in productions such as *Die Zauberflöte* and *La Traviata*. He also performed regularly in church choirs, including Connecticut's Trinity Episcopalian Church. It was there that he saw their boys choir and began thinking about creating a similar group of his own.

After receiving his master's degree in 1968, Turnbull founded what went on to become the Boys Choir of Harlem (it had no official name until 1975) and began his uninterrupted tenure as the group's executive director. He launched his ambitious project with 20 boys in the basement of his church, the Ephesus Seventh-Day Adventist Church in Harlem. The choir was soon performing in other nearby houses of worship and quickly developed a positive reputation.

From the beginning, the Boys Choir did not just focus on the choral music of classical composers such as Bach, Handel, and Mozart. Turnbull also incorporated hymns, gospel tunes, and original compositions into their repertoire. As a result, their sound was distinctly different from that of traditional boys choirs. "Some people have in their ear an English boy-choir sound and they want us to sound like St. Thomas's Episcopal Church choir," Turnbull told C. Gerald Fraser of the *New York Times.* "We're not going to sound like St. Thomas. We never will and never want to, because the Boys Choir of Harlem has a sound that is characteristic of the people we serve and that sound is very different."

Despite its artistic success, the choir always faced financial problems. Furthermore, while it had become the focus of Turnbull's life, it did not make enough money to support him. Thus, to earn a living he continued his own musical career on the side, appearing with the Philadelphia Orchestra and the New York Philharmonic, among others. He also worked as a New York City public school teacher and taxi driver sporadically throughout the 1970s and 1980s.

While working as a teacher, Turnbull saw how music could change the lives of children. He used it to reach his students and provide them with positive role models and solid values. He hated to turn away children, but he did experience problems with some of the boys from time to time. Many were poor and from single-parent homes. It was difficult for them to adjust to his demands and to the rigors of being a member of the choir, though Turnbull did everything he could to help. As he told Mary Jo Palumbo of the *Boston Herald,* "Without the Boys Choir of Harlem, many of these kids just wouldn't make it. I see children blossom when they feel good about themselves. Music requires discipline and goal-setting. It's an important part of their development."

In 1975, the choir was incorporated as a nonprofit group and officially named the Boys Choir of Harlem. The decision to go with this particular name was a bit controversial because some people thought it sounded too "inner city." Funding and space were still a problem, too. The choir had to move twice in 1975, first to the

Marcus Garvey Community Center and then to the Church of the Intercession. But Turnbull remained committed to making the Boys Choir a world-class institution. During the late 1970s and early 1980s, the group gained an international reputation after it toured Europe for the first time, making appearances in London, England; Haarlem, Holland; and Paris, France; among other cities. The choir first toured the United States in 1983.

While the choir took up most of his time, Turnbull continued his own education as well. In 1984, he earned his Doctor of Musical Arts degree from the Manhattan School of Music. He also did some graduate work at the Columbia University School of Business Institute for Non-Profit Management to pick up skills that would help him run the choir more efficiently.

That same year, Turnbull decided that students would benefit even more from their association with the choir if they had their own school to attend. The Choir Academy of Harlem opened with about 150 pupils (boys as well as girls) in the middle elementary grades. As the years went by, Turnbull added more grades. By 1996, the academy included grades four through twelve, and it graduated its first class. The curriculum stressed academic excellence (all students had to maintain a certain grade point average) and also provided instruction in social and life skills.

Turnbull's work with the choir began to attract media attention during the late 1980s. In 1987, for example, he and the choir were profiled on ABC-TV's "Nightline" program. While such publicity made more people aware of the choir's existence, it often left them with a mistaken impression about the group's financial situation. As Turnbull told James R. Oestreich of the *New York Times,* "Perhaps we just look too successful. We're on television too much. The boys look good, and all the publicity is great. But people don't know what goes on, the time and energy it takes to make that happen. We have a problem getting the kind of money we need."

At the time, it cost approximately $800,000 a year to keep the choir going. It was somewhat self-supporting as a result of its concert appearances (100 in 1987) and performances on movie soundtracks and other artists' albums. But Turnbull sometimes paid for minor expenses out of his own pocket, and he regularly provided food and clothing to his neediest students. Thus, in 1987 he founded and chaired the Harlem Youth Development Foundation to help underwrite the cost of such "extras."

Despite money problems, the Boys Choir continued to grow and thrive; by 1992 it had about 250 members. That same year, the choir sang at Carnegie Hall, and the next year, it appeared on Broadway in "The Boys Choir of Harlem and Friends, Live on Broadway" at the Richard Rodgers Theater. (In fact, 1993 marked the twenty-fifth anniversary of the choir's founding.) By 1995, 500 boys and 100 girls were affiliated with the academy and either the Boys Choir or the Girls Choir.

Turnbull had originally started the Girls Choir of Harlem as early as 1979, but it did not last long because of funding difficulties and his inability to find a good director. It was re-established in 1989, however, and in 1997 it achieved a much higher profile after securing corporate sponsorship from Revlon. The Girls Choir made its performance debut that year and also made plans for a tour in 1998.

Turnbull has had an undeniably positive impact on the children with whom he has come in contact through the Boys Choir. About 98 percent of its members have gone on to college, though most do not study music. A few have returned to teach at the Choir Academy. Meanwhile, Turnbull's work has not gone unnoticed. He has received many awards over the years, including a Volunteer Action Award from President Ronald Reagan in 1986, the National Medal of Arts, and numerous honorary degrees. In 1998 *Reader's Digest* named him an American Hero in Education.

Turnbull has never married because the choir has been his life. Yet it is not a choice that he regrets. As he told Margaret Carlin of the *Denver Rocky Mountain News*, "God wanted me to do this work—it's my calling."

Sources

➤ **Books**

Henderson, Ashyia N. and Shirelle Phelps, *Who's Who Among African Americans*, 12th edition, Gale, 1999.

Phelps, Shirelle, ed., *Contemporary Black Biography: Profiles from the International Black Community*, Gale, 1997.

Turnbull, Walter with Howard Manly, *Lift Every Voice: Expecting the Most and Getting the Best from All of God's Children*, Hyperion, 1995.

➤ **Periodicals**

Boston Herald, June 28, 1995, p. 41.

Daily News, April 26, 1998, p. 18.
Denver Rocky Mountain News, October 15, 1995, p. 58A; February 3, 1996, p. 6D.
Newsweek, November 24, 1997, p. 74.
New York Times, December 24, 1987, p. C9; December 13, 1992, sec. 2, p. 25 (opening quote); November 24, 1999, p. B7.
USA Weekend, November 19, 1995, p. 10.

Barbara Walters

"I was the kind nobody thought could make it. I had a funny Boston accent. I couldn't pronounce my R's. I wasn't a beauty."

Born September 25, 1931, in Boston, Massachusetts, Barbara Walters became the first ever female co-host on a TV network news show when she was promoted to co-host of the "Today" show in 1974. Walters has endured sexual discrimination and hostility, but has overcome it to become one of the most powerful and popular news journalists of her time. Address: American Broadcasting Co., 1330 Avenue of the Americas, New York, NY 10019.

One of the most influential women on television, Barbara Walters became the highest-paid television news anchor in history when she signed a $1 million annual contract in 1976 to co-host the "ABC Evening News" with Harry Reasoner. Before that accomplishment, she had established herself on the "Today" show as a competent all-around journalist, with a knack for lining up important guests. Around the same time that she started hosting the "ABC News," she began airing her own brand of personal interview program, "The Barbara Walters Specials," which have made her a household name. Her probing yet nonaggressive manner, insightful questions, and obvious delight with her guests made those shows some of the highest-rated on television and have featured some of the biggest names in the news. She arranged the first joint interview with Egyptian President Anwar Sadat and Israeli Prime Minister Menachem Begin in 1977, and since then has covered a catalog of leaders and celebrities, from the late Princess Diana (after her split from Prince Charles) to Colin Powell to Monica Lewinsky. After leaving "ABC News," Walters joined the staff at "20/20," a prime time news magazine program designed to compete with "60 Minutes." She became a co-anchor with Hugh Downs in 1984 and has remained there since. In 1997 she began appearing in a much earlier time slot on "The View," which she and producer Bill Geddie created for the daytime talk show market.

Although Walters is a respected television professional with numerous awards and honors, she has endured her share of bumps in the road. From her humble beginnings behind the scenes on the "Today" show, she was eventually offered a spot as a ""Today" girl" in the early 1960s, a job previously held by attractive females functioning mainly as scenery. Walters was the show's first shot at putting an intelligent woman in the position, and she became popular with audiences, while facing daily tension with host Frank McGee. When McGee died, she was given his job. After her pricey appointment at "ABC News," Reasoner bristled at having to share the camera and acted hostile toward her. Critics were dubious of her credentials: despite her "Today" background, many felt her celebrity connections tainted her reputation. And she was reportedly hurt by the ribbing she got for her imperfect speech patterns, as exemplified in a recurring "Saturday Night Live" skit featuring late comedian Gilda Radner as "Baba Wawa." Walters rose above the obstacles and criticism, becoming more and more successful as her career continued. A *Working Woman* article quoted television critic Tom Shales of the *Washington Post* summing up Walters's success: "She became very splashy about her career. And she overcame a lot of male chauvinism in television." He added, "She simply got more intimate than anyone else had before her. She pioneered the style of getting the guest to cry. And she's genuinely nosy, which is a good thing for a journalist to be."

Walters was born on September 25, 1931, in Boston, Massachusetts, to Louis Edward and Dena (Selett) Walters. The Walters also had a son, Burton, who died of pneumonia at only a year old, and a daughter, Jacqueline, who was developmentally disabled. "She was a great influence on my life," Walters recalled to Allison Adato in *Life*. "I think she made me more understanding and compassionate because people were not as tolerant as they maybe are today." Walters' father, Louis, was a busy and well-known theatrical producer who booked vaudeville acts. Though he became quite wealthy, he also spent a lot, and then lost everything during the Great Depression. In 1937, he opened the Latin Quarter nightclub in Boston, and later expanded to New York City and Miami. Walters' father bounced his family from city to city as his business grew; she went to Miami at age 11 and New York two years later, then returned to Miami at age 15 and New York at 16. Her father's fortunes reversed again, however, and he lost his Boston Latin Quarter club in a card game. Walters decided that she would always be self-supporting in order to avoid this type of predicament later in life.

Walters went to Sarah Lawrence College and received a bachelor of arts degree in English. With help from her father's entertainment-world connections, she began working as a writer and producer for WNBT-TV in New York. In 1955, she began booking guests for the "Morning Show" with Dick Van Dyke on CBS, and after the show was canceled in 1956, she continued on its replacement, "Good Morning with Will Rogers, Jr." It eventually went off the air, and Walters found work at the public relations firm Tex McCrary Inc. as a publicist, trying to book clients on television shows and generate positive press. In 1961, she started writing for the "Today" show.

After managing to get on camera a few times to appear in the stories she wrote, Walters was given the chance to report a full story. Previously, the "Today girl" was an attractive young woman relegated to reporting on lightweight topics geared for female audience members. Walters started to change that. She was sent to India to accompany First Lady Jacqueline Kennedy and was the only reporter there to be granted an interview, albeit short. She continued writing and reporting, and although she was passed up twice to be a "Today" girl, the producer eventually realized he needed a woman with credentials, and hired Walters on a trial basis in 1963.

Walters fine-tuned her talents, especially for interviewing, on "Today," and in 1974 took a position hosting a daytime talk show, "Not for Women Only" (Walters insisted on adding the "Not" to the show's proposed title). Around the same time, she was promoted to co-host of the "Today" show when Frank McGee died of bone cancer, making her the first ever female co-host on a TV network news or public affairs show. However, she would soon break another barrier. In 1976, she was the center of attention when ABC extended an offer to co-anchor the "ABC Evening News" and produce four specials—for a salary of $1 million. No newscaster had ever made that much; most were making less than half that. NBC told Walters they would match the salary, but wanted her to stay on "Today." Walters moved to ABC and began anchoring the news with Harry Reasoner.

Walters came under fire for the salary as well as for her style. She was known for being more entertainment-oriented, and many questioned her hard news credentials. However, she was extremely popular with audiences, which was how she justified demanding such a hefty amount. Reasoner was reportedly unreasonable about her appointment to his desk. Though Walters made attempts to calm the waters, the duo's dynamics clashed. They never got along, and eventually would not even speak to each other. In addition, Walters did not help boost the third-place ratings (before cable, when there were only three competing networks), and ABC eventually abolished the anchor positions. Walters remained a correspondent, and began devoting more time to her specials.

Since her first "Barbara Walters Special" on December 14, 1976, with President and First Lady Jimmy and Rosalyn Carter and entertainer Barbra Streisand, Walter's shows have been ratings successes. Throughout the years, her slant has changed to focus mainly on celebrities and less on politicians, but she has interviewed every American president since Richard Nixon, as well as other world leaders, including Cuban leader Fidel Castro (he even made her and the crew grilled cheese sandwiches after the shoot). She is known for her incisive and intimate interviews with a bevy of stars, from Jim Carrey to Bette Davis. Usually informal and often held in the person's home, the interviews encourage public figures to reveal sensitive details about their personal lives. Her interview with actor Christopher Reeve after he became paralyzed in a horse-riding accident was seen by 29 million viewers and received the George

Foster Peabody Award. Walters told Melina Gerosa in *Ladies' Home Journal,* "I think this interview had a greater effect than anything that I have done in all the years at ABC, because there are not that many times when you come across that extraordinary true, shining love that Chris [Reeve] and his wife have for each other." In 1999, Walters conducted the first interview with Monica Lewinsky, which became the highest-rated news program ever broadcast by a single network.

Around the late 1970s or early 1980s, Walters began contributing to the news magazine program "20/20." Though the anchor, Hugh Downs, had originally suggested Walters for the spot on the "Today" show in the early 1960s that got her career moving, he was reluctant to have her on board as a "20/20" co-host. She was given the position in 1984 and remains a major presence. Her specials continue to earn high ratings, and the Lifetime cable channel in 1994 announced they would recycle Walters's past interviews for a new hour long series, "Barbara Walters: Interviews of a Lifetime." Throughout the 1980s and 1990s, thanks in large part to Walters opening the door, more and more women entered television. However, Walters noted in a 1996 *TV Guide* article that there were no women on the nightly network news.

After spending her career since the 1970s in evening time slots, Walters returned to morning television in 1997 with the premiere of "The View," which she put together with her longtime producer, Bill Geddie. Jane Hall in the *Los Angeles Times* described the effort as "the ABC daytime talk show that aims to combine 'Live with Regis & Kathie Lee' with 'This Week with David Brinkley,'" and noted that critics have applauded it "for being a positive, smart alternative to some dysfunctional daytime talkers." The show's panel features five women co-hosts who represent different stages of a woman's life: Walters, in her 60s, who appears twice a week, alternating days with Joy Behar; Behar, a comedian and radio show host in her 50s who is seen three days a week; Meredith Vieira, the moderator, a former "60 Minutes" correspondent who is in her 40s; Star Jones, a former prosecutor in her 30s; and Lisa Ling, a former Channel One News (a teenage news show) team reporter in her 20s. "The View" was nominated for eight Emmy awards in spring of 1998 after its first season. Despite the below-average ratings, ABC executives renewed the show for the 1998 season because it performed better that the show it replaced ("Caryl & Marilyn") and it had increased 38 percent in popularity with the coveted market of 18- to 49-year-old women. By 1999, "The View" was the highest-rated show for ABC in its time period since the 1993-94 season. Walters is involved in all aspects of the production. "I love doing this show, and I'm committed to it," she told Hall in the *Los Angeles Times.*

Walters has received numerous awards for her work over the years. She has won several Emmy Awards for her work on the "Today" show (Best Host or Hostess of a Talk, Service, or Variety Series, 1975); "Nightline" (Best News Program Segment and Best News and Documentary Programs and Program Segments, 1980); and "20/20" (Best Interviewer, 1983, and Best Interview Segment, 1988). In 1990, she was inducted into the Academy of Television Arts and Sciences' Hall of Fame, and was honored with the Lowell Thomas Award for a career in journalism excellence by Marist College. She has also received Lifetime Achievement Awards from the International Women's Media Foundation (1991) and Women's Project and Productions (1993), was honored by the Museum of Television & Radio for her contributions to broadcast journalism in 1996, and was awarded the "Muse" Award from NY Women in Film and Television in 1997.

Although Walters no longer commands the highest salary in television, she does not do poorly, with estimates ranging from $5 to $10 million per year. And, as Mansfield noted in *Working Woman,* "She may be the best value," with her highly-rated specials and the ongoing popularity of "20/20." Colleagues praise her skills and motivation, and she is a role model for many. In an industry where other female newscasters have been fired due to their age, Walters keeps working harder. Katie Couric, anchor on the "Today" show, told Mansfield in *Working Woman,* "What a lot of women in the business admire is that she is still hungry and so competitive. She will never rest on her laurels. She's in her 60s and still on the air. It gives all women a real boost." Steve Wulf in *Time* quoted ABC News president Roone Arledge commenting on Walters: "She just keeps getting better and better. She has a way that has matured over the years of getting people to say things on the air that they never thought they were going to say."

Walters married and divorced three times. Her first husband, Robert Henry Katz, was a businessman; they divorced shortly before their three-year anniversary. Her second marriage, to theatrical producer Lee Guber, lasted from 1963 to 1976. They adopted a daughter, Jacqueline, in 1968 after Walters had a series of miscarriages. She married a third time, to Merv Adelson, chairman of Lorimar Production Company, but it ended in 1992. She told Melina Gerosa in *Ladies' Home Journal* that she does not think her career caused her marriages to break up. "Maybe they broke up because I wasn't really happy in them," Walters mused. "I could walk away knowing that I could earn enough money. I could go places alone." Walters has remained single since her divorce from Adelson and now lives with two other women who provide friendship and help her at home. Revealing some of her regrets to Gerosa, Walters said that she wishes she had more children, and would have liked to have been more patient with her sister, Jacqueline, who died in 1988. However, Walters remarked, no one can have everything in life. "Along with living, there are always some regrets," Walters observed. "At a certain point, you say, 'It may not be the best, but it's what I chose, and you know what? It's pretty darn good.'"

Sources

➤ On-line

"Barbara Walters biography," *Mr. Showbiz* website, http://mrshowbiz.go.com/people/barbarawalters/index.html (March 30, 2000; opening quote).
"Barbara Walters biography," *The View* website, http://www.abc.com/theview (May 13, 1998).

➤ Books

Baldwin, Louis, *Women of Strength: Biographies of 106 Who Have Excelled in Traditionally Male Fields, A.D. 61 to the Present*, McFarland & Co., 1996.
Contemporary Theatre, Film, and Television, Volume 13, Gale Research, 1995.
Encyclopedia of World Biography, second edition, Gale Research, 1997.
Signorielli, Nancy, editor, *Women in Communication: A Biographical Sourcebook*, Greenwood Press, 1996.

➤ Periodicals

Broadcasting & Cable, April 9, 1997, p. 11.
Cosmopolitan, May 1994, p. 208.
Entertainment Weekly, December 16, 1994, p. 88.
Ladies' Home Journal, April 1996, p. 128.
Life, November 1997, p. 36.
Los Angeles Times, April 27, 1998, p. F11.
Maclean's, May 26, 1997, p. 36.
Mediaweek, July 21, 1997, p. 8.

Time, November 6, 1995, p. 68.
TV Guide, April 27, 1996, p. 24.
Vanity Fair, August 1994, p. 88.
Variety, August 25, 1997, p. 33.
Working Woman, November/December 1996, pp. 79, 81.

Dan West

"I *cannot eat cake when others in the world do not have bread."*

Born December 31, 1893 in Preble County, Ohio, Dan West organized the Heifer Project to help disadvantaged people become self-sufficient, and worked to promote world peace and volunteerism. He died January 7, 1971 in Goshen, Indiana.

An idealist who strove to live out his beliefs, Dan West worked as a humanitarian and peace activist in the United States and abroad. Though his efforts were often on behalf of the Church of the Brethren, he preferred to serve as a lay leader rather than as a clergyman. Mistrustful of powerful institutions, he believed in local self-empowerment long before such a concept was fashionable. West is best remembered for launching the Heifer Project International, a program that has helped supply needy families with livestock for over 50 years.

West was both a typical member of nineteenth-century rural American culture and a foresighted figure who anticipated late-twentieth-century social and ecological activism. Dedicated to a simple lifestyle that emphasized personal responsibility, he sought to uphold his values at home as well as promote them in his humanitarian work. "His message was, 'What do you need?'," his daughter Janet West-Schrock said in an interview. "He thought that if you had more than three pairs of shoes, then somebody was going without. He refused increases in wages; he thought we had enough money. According to him, we needed very few things to make us feel content. That meant we would be available to other people. His favorite thing was seeing people getting happy about what they could do for everybody else."

Born in Preble County, Ohio, Dan West was the son of Landon West, an itinerant preacher and elder in the Church of the Brethren (known popularly as the Dunkers) who ministered to African Americans from the Civil War era into the early 1900s. Landon West and his wife Barbara raised Dan and his five siblings in an atmosphere of piety and service, rooted in the Church of the Brethren's emphasis on community responsibility and the sanctity of individual life. After high school, West continued his education at Bethany Bible School and Manchester College, both Brethren institutions. He went on to complete work on a master's degree at Cornell University. Rather than follow his father into the ministry, he embarked on a career as a high school teacher in Ohio.

West was drafted by the U.S. Army in 1917, but served as a conscientious objector rather than participating in World War I. After his discharge, he increasingly became active in the Church of the Brethren as a lay leader. He applied his teaching skills toward building leadership potential among young people in the church. He stressed independent decision-making rather than blind acceptance of dogma in his talks with Brethren youth at outdoor gatherings and retreats. "His insistent and probing questions forced them to face their own beliefs," wrote author Glee Yoder in the book *Passing on the Gift: The Story of Dan West*. "He was always sorting through assumptions and cliches in order to arrive at the truth." Similarly, West-Schrock said that her father "would bring out people's ideas, rather than foist his own on them. . . . He liked to get people to wrestle with ideas, and he would do it in a provocative way, so that people wouldn't know what he was thinking."

In 1930, West had become National Director of Young People's Work for the Church of the Brethren. In that capacity, he urged a great social consciousness and activism beyond the confines of the church. Promoting an end to warfare was a particular concern for him. "When I see so much that the war makers are doing and so little that the peacemakers are doing, I wonder why the difference," he wrote in an article for *The Gospel Messenger* in June, 1931. "Find me one hundred Dunkers between the ages of twenty-one and thirty who will give as much for peace as a soldier gives for war, and we will change the thinking of Congress in three years' time." West encouraged young people to volunteer both in the United States and abroad to resettle those displaced by warfare and economic hardship. In 1936, West began working with the American Friends Service Committee's Emergency Peace Campaign, touring college campuses and recruiting students to promote peace.

West acted on his beliefs by going to Spain in the midst of its bitter civil war between the Loyalists and the Nationalists in September, 1937. Threatened by both sides, he and his fellow relief workers brought food and clothing to suffering families without regard to their political leanings. It was in January of 1938 that West claimed to have had the revelation that ultimately launched the Heifer Project. After serving cups of milk to long lines of war victims, he rested under an almond tree and thought of the abundant farmlands of his native Midwest. Then it struck him that, instead of more donations, what poor people in Spain and elsewhere needed were cows to supply milk.

Returning to the United States, West began organizing what became the first "Heifers For Relief" committee. This group enlisted the aid of farmers, academics and the U.S. Department of Agriculture in working out the logistics of sending cows overseas. The Church of the Brethren approved the project in 1942, but by that time World War II had broken out, making it impossible to make shipments to Europe. Instead, the Heifer Project Committee worked with needy families in Puerto Rico, sending its first 18 cows to the island in July, 1944. As shipments continued, volunteers went along to assist with care for the cows and to set up health and agriculture programs when they arrived. The project was a success, and the newly-founded United Nations asked for its aid in helping refugees in Europe after the end of World War II in 1945. From the start, families receiving heifers were asked to pass on the animal's first-born offspring to another needy family.

West retained his reputation as a maverick even as his role as a humanitarian increased. He disliked institutions and bureaucracies and believed in questioning authority. He condemned competition and the consumption-driven habits of modern life. His idealism could make him an exacting co-worker and a demanding parent. "He was not a team man," wrote Yoder. "He wanted to call his own shots. . . Not only did Dan not cooperate well with the organization; he often bucked it. . . He grew restless with any kind of routine, disliked being told what he could do, and was irritated at having to 'go through channels.'"

Training young people to help the disadvantaged continued to be among West's chief goals. Towards that end, he was a guiding force behind the Brethren Volunteer Service after its inception in 1948. This organization continued wartime efforts to aid refugees and the poor in peace time. West was also active in efforts to resettle European war refugees in the United States, and to promote humanitarian alternatives to military service.

West retired from his full-time work with the Church of the Brethren in 1959. Following a year-long trip around the world with his wife Lucy, he became the first lay person to moderate an annual conference of the Church of the Brethren in 1966. However, declining health forced him to curtail his activities by the end of the decade. Diagnosed with Amyotrophic Lateral Sclerosis (Lou Gehrig's Disease), he was too ill to speak at a ceremony honoring him on the twenty-fifth anniversary of the Heifer Project's founding. He passed away on January 7, 1971 in a hospital in Goshen, Indiana.

In the nearly three decades since West's death, the Heifer Project International has continued to thrive and expand. Based out of a 1200-acre ranch near Perryville, Arkansas, the program has reached 118 countries and launched self-guided affiliates in China, Tanzania and other nations. Within the United States, it has worked in such rural areas as Appalachia and established urban agricultural projects in Chicago. Besides heifers, it has distributed camels, llamas, goats, water buffaloes and other animals around the world according to local need. In 1999, the Heifer Project raised over $20,000,000 in donations, a 50 percent increase over the previous year's budget.

Dan West's lifetime commitment to helping others help themselves has been continued on in the work of the Heifer Project. His sometimes lofty idealism was tempered by a sense of the practical and an ability to draw out the best in others. "People loved him because he empowered people to think," said West-Schrock. "He didn't want to be at the head of the parade; he wanted to inspire other people to become leaders. He was always helping people to understand what they're worth."

Sources

➤ Books

Yoder, Glee, *Passing on the Gift: The Story of Dan West,* Brethren Press, 1978 (opening quote).

➤ Periodicals

Americas, November/December 1998, p. 40.
Country Journal, September/October 1995, p.9.
Detroit News, November 23, 1996, p. C1.
E Magazine: The Environmental Magazine, May/June 1999, p. 19.
Gospel Messenger, June 1931.
San Diego Union, December 23, 1999, p. E-4.

➤ Other

Additional information for this profile was obtained from a telephone interview with Janet West-Schrock in February, 2000.

Walter F. White

*"*E*very lynching, every coldblooded shooting of a Negro soldier . . . , every refusal to abolish segregation . . . , every filibuster against an anti-poll tax or anti-lynching bill . . . builds up a debit balance of hatred against America. . . ."*

Born July 1, 1893, in Atlanta, Georgia, Walter F. White was one of the major figures in the African American civil rights movement from the late 1910s through the mid-1950s. He spent much of that time as head of the National Association for the Advancement of Colored People (NAACP). White died March 28, 1955.

During a lifetime spent in the fight for racial justice, Walter F. White never shrank from doing whatever he believed was necessary to eliminate the bigotry and hatred eating away at America's soul. He is perhaps best remembered for risking his life to expose and denounce the horrific practice of lynching, an act of mob violence that involves putting someone to death (usually by hanging). Throughout the more than 40 years he was associated with the National Association for the Advancement of Colored People (NAACP), he made the crusade against lynching a top priority. He also spearheaded the group's legal assault on segregation, discrimination, and inequality. Under White's skillful administration, the NAACP increased its membership, improved its finances, and emerged as the preeminent African American civil rights organization in the United States.

The second of seven children born to Madeline Harrison White and George White, Walter Francis White was a native of Atlanta, Georgia. His mother had worked as a schoolteacher before her marriage, and his father was a mail carrier who had been forced to drop out of college after his parents died. Both Madeline and George White placed a high value on education and religious piety and raised their two sons and five daughters accordingly.

Determined to see that all of their children attended college despite their modest circumstances, the elder Whites made their home a center for studying and learning. Walter read voraciously as a youngster. He also regularly accompanied his father on his mail route after school, and the discussions they had during that time sharpened the young man's mind and whetted his appetite for knowledge.

At the time White was growing up, the so-called "Jim Crow Laws" then prevalent across the South demanded strict separation of the races in virtually all areas of public life, including housing, transportation, and recreation. Because of his fair skin, blond hair, and blue eyes (which he shared with his mother and siblings), White was often mistaken for Caucasian by whites and blacks alike. Yet no one in the family ever tried to "pass" as white; they embraced their African American heritage with pride despite the curious stares and sometimes outright hostility they experienced from members of both races as they went about their daily lives.

White's racial identity was cemented in his own mind as the result of a bloody race riot that rocked Atlanta for two nights in September 1906. The disturbances left 10 blacks dead and scores of others injured. The atrocities 13-year-old White witnessed created an indelible impression and demonstrated to him as never before exactly what it meant to be a black person in America.

A good student throughout his school years, White enrolled at Atlanta University in 1912. There he was a star member of the debating team and the popular president of his class. The summer after his junior year, he went to work for the Standard Life Insurance Company selling policies in rural Georgia. Often mistaken for a white man as he trudged on foot from house to house along the hot, dusty roads in his territory, White exuded a natural charm and friendliness that helped him gain the confidence of his customers. He easily conversed with them about racial matters, gaining valuable insights into their prejudices and fears that served him well in the future.

White took a full-time job as a clerk with Standard Life following his graduation in 1916 and was soon promoted to cashier. He seemed headed for a successful career in insurance until fate intervened later that same year and thrust him into the center of a bitter school controversy in Atlanta. Only two years after voting to eliminate the eighth grade in the city's black schools, the local board had taken up a proposal to drop the seventh grade as well. (Caucasian students received a free public education through the twelfth grade.) White emerged as the leader of a group of young black professionals who vigorously opposed the move. Their protests eventually forced members of the school board to modify their stance and also led to the founding of the Atlanta chapter of the National Association for the Advancement of Colored People (NAACP), a fledgling civil rights organization dedicated to promoting racial equality, securing voting rights for blacks, and fostering black pride and achievement.

White was elected secretary of the NAACP's Atlanta chapter and immediately launched a high-profile campaign to defeat a bond proposal that would have left the city's black schools (which were already severely underfunded) essentially destitute. His efforts quickly brought him to the attention of national NAACP leaders, particularly James Weldon Johnson. Impressed by his passion and drive, they offered White the job of assistant secretary in late 1917. Although he had never really considered living and working outside Atlanta, he accepted the offer and arrived at NAACP headquarters in New York City in January 1918.

During his first decade or so with the NAACP, White specialized in investigating race riots and lynchings. Such mob violence was widespread in the years following World War I and was, in part, a

response to mounting calls by frustrated blacks (especially returning war veterans) for justice and equality. Most lynchings, however,
were triggered by reports (often false) that a white woman had been
raped by a black man. This scenario inflamed southern white men in
particular; they regarded such behavior as an assault on their honor
as "gentlemen" charged with protecting their wives and daughters.
Because this sentiment was so commonplace at the time, the authorities rarely investigated reports of lynchings or bothered to
arrest the perpetrators.

Sometimes posing as a reporter, White relied on his Caucasian
looks to gather valuable inside information from people he never
could have approached as a black man. In more than one instance,
his deception came very close to unraveling, which would have
surely resulted in his own death. White followed up these investigations with published accounts and speeches detailing the most
heinous lynchings and soon found himself the target of death
threats from the Ku Klux Klan. But his reports succeeded in focusing national attention on racial problems and garnered more financial and moral support for the NAACP.

White became acting secretary of the NAACP in 1929 when James
Weldon Johnson took a leave of absence. Within months, he was
leading the organization's crusade against the nomination of a racist
North Carolina judge named John J. Parker to the U.S. Supreme
Court. Poor health forced Johnson to give up his post for good in
1931, and the NAACP board immediately named White to succeed
him as secretary.

Throughout the remainder of the decade and well into the 1940s,
White spent increasing amounts of time in Washington, D.C., on a
mission to force members of Congress and the Senate to address
racial issues. He lobbied ceaselessly for a federal law against lynching; although several versions were introduced over the years, none
managed to make it past southern legislators. Eventually, White
grew discouraged and disgusted by the stonewalling tactics and
hostility he encountered, but he never gave up trying to win support
for an antilynching bill. By keeping a spotlight on the cruelty and
barbarity of the practice, he finally convinced Americans to abandon it. His work was acknowledged in 1937 when the NAACP
awarded him its highest honor, the Spingarn Medal.

Among the other issues that preoccupied White during this same
period were voting rights and unequal funding for schools and
other public facilities used by blacks as well as whites. He fought
against laws intended mainly to deny the vote to blacks through the

use of poll taxes, literacy tests, and the like, and he battled attempts to allocate tax dollars in such a way that white institutions and services were well funded and black ones were left impoverished.

As the nation geared up for war during the late 1930s, White joined forces with prominent black labor leader A. Philip Randolph to challenge discriminatory employment practices in the defense industry. Such practices denied well-paying factory jobs to African Americans strictly because of their race. White and Randolph were eventually able to convince President Franklin D. Roosevelt to issue an executive order in 1941 that prohibited racial discrimination in the hiring of defense industry workers. The order also established the Fair Employment Practices Committee to monitor any abuses.

White then tackled the issue of racial discrimination in the armed forces. Blacks were routinely allowed to serve in only the most menial of positions, namely as cooks, food servers, and freight handlers. They were not issued weapons or trained how to use them. On military bases in the United States and abroad, they were also subject to mistreatment (including lynchings) and often had to deal with hostile local residents as well. Thus, in early 1944 White traveled overseas to document exactly what was happening. He came back with reports of low morale among black servicemen and clear evidence of segregation and unequal living, eating, and recreational facilities. White pressed for changes but made little progress until later in the war, when the need for more combat troops overruled objections some had to the notion of training and outfitting African Americans as true soldiers. But it was not until 1948 that President Harry S. Truman finally issued an executive order officially banning segregation in the armed forces.

During the late 1940s and early 1950s, White suffered from increasingly poor health but ignored suggestions from his doctor and his family to slow down. In 1945, for example, he served as a consultant to the American delegation at the founding meeting of the United Nations. An increase in the number of lynchings in the postwar period also demanded his time and attention, as did the activities of the busy NAACP legal department. (It had been leading the fight for equality through the courts since its creation in the mid-1930s and was at that time embroiled in a series of public school desegregation cases that culminated in *Brown v. Board of Education* before the U.S. Supreme Court.) In addition, White had to contend with rumblings inside the NAACP that too much of the organization's power was concentrated in his position and in him personally. Nevertheless, he continued to run the group as he saw fit and also lectured extensively, organized and attended rallies and conferences across the country, and wrote magazine and newspaper articles as well as a memoir, published in 1948 as *A Man Called White.*

In 1947, White divorced his wife of more than 20 years, Leah Gladys Powell, the mother of his two children. Two years later, he married a white woman, a writer named Poppy Cannon who was of South African descent. Their union touched off even more conflict within the NAACP; some members went so far as to demand that White resign, which he refused to do. Instead, the organization ultimately voted to strip him of much of his power and divide it among four new executives.

White subsequently turned down job offers in the business world and also declined requests to serve in the U.S. government as an ambassador to Haiti or India. His remaining years were devoted in part to working on a book that assessed the nation's progress in granting civil rights to all its citizens. Entitled *How Far the Promised Land?,* it was published after his death from a heart attack on March 28, 1955.

Some 10,000 people from all walks of life attended the funeral services for White. From the humble to the great, they acknowledged the many contributions of a man whose tireless efforts in the struggle for social justice brought about fundamental and lasting changes in American society. Although he could have easily chosen a different path, Walter White decided early on to identify with his black heritage no matter what the risks. In so doing, noted a reporter for the *New York Times,* he "made a special mockery of race discrimination."

Sources

➤ Books

Aptheker, Herbert, editor, *A Documentary History of the Negro People in the United States, 1933-1945,* Citadel Press, 1974 (opening quote).
Boulware, Marcus H., *The Oratory of Negro Leaders: 1900-1968,* Negro Universities Press, 1969.
Fraser, Jane, *Walter White,* Chelsea House, 1991.
White, Walter, *How Far the Promised Land?,* Viking, 1955.
White, Walter, *A Man Called White: The Autobiography of Walter White,* Viking, 1948.
White, Walter, *A Rising Wind,* Doubleday, 1945.

Wilson, Sondra Kathryn, editor, *In Search of Democracy: The NAACP Writings of James Weldon Johnson, Walter White, and Roy Wilkins,* Oxford University Press, 1999.

➤ **Periodicals**

New York Times, March 29, 1955.

L. Douglas Wilder

"I *worked on making myself the best lawyer and politician possible on the theory that I could best serve not by being a demonstrator in handcuffs but by seeking to get the handcuffs off the demonstrator and the repressive laws changed."*

L. Douglas Wilder, born on January 17, 1931, in Richmond, Virginia, became the nation's highest-ranking black office holder in 1985 when he was elected lieutenant governor of Virginia. He followed this achievement with his election to the governor's office, becoming the first elected African American governor in the nation. Address: Virginia Commonwealth University, 821 W. Franklin St., Richmond, VA 23284.

In the 1860s, L. Douglas Wilder's grandparents were plantation slaves in the South, but in the 1960s, he was elected to the Virginia State Senate, the first black to sit in that assembly since the Reconstruction after the Civil War. Wilder, a former trial lawyer, became a vanguard in southern politics with this win, using his seat to further civil rights issues in a state not known for its progressivism. Though extremely popular in his own mostly-black district and widely respected among his colleagues, many were doubtful that he would be successful in his next move, running for lieutenant governor. However, in 1985 he won the vote, becoming the nation's highest-ranking elected black official at the time. Subsequently, in 1989, he became the country's first elected black governor. Wilder's efforts blazed the trail for blacks to campaign in the future.

The second-youngest of eight children, Lawrence Douglas Wilder was born on January 17, 1931, in Richmond, Virginia, the son of Robert and Beulah Wilder. They raised their family in the city's segregated Church Hill neighborhood, and were devout Baptists. His father held a job with a black-owned insurance firm, and his mother worked at an apartment-hotel complex on the cleaning staff and in the kitchen. His grandparents on his father's side were slaves freed by the Emancipation Proclamation in 1863.

As a teenager, Wilder began taking odd jobs in order to save money for college, delivering newspapers, shining shoes, and operating an elevator in an office building in the days when attendants were needed. An advanced student who acted in plays, he was a sergeant in the cadet corps, drew cartoons for the student paper and yearbook, and graduated early from the all-black Armstrong High School. Up until this time, Wilder was only vaguely aware of racism, because he was firmly segregated and had never been around white people that often. After high school, though, he was hit squarely with first-hand knowledge of it when he realized he was not allowed to attend any of the state's public colleges. In 1947, he entered the all-black Virginia Union University, a private school, at age 16.

To pay his tuition, Wilder waited tables at some of the area hotels and country clubs. Oftentimes, being that he was in the capital city, he would find himself serving politicians, and he made sure to stick around to listen to the speeches being given. He had long held an interest in oration from the days of telling tales at Billy's Barber Shop while growing up. However, Wilder was considering becoming a dental surgeon, not a politician, and graduated with a bachelor's degree in chemistry in 1951. Though he was not an outstanding student, he later credited his college years with helping to develop his self-confidence.

Subsequently, in 1952, Wilder was drafted into the U.S. Army and began serving in the Korean War. On the front lines at Pork Chop Hill in 1953, he earned a Bronze Star for heroism for helping to rescue wounded soldiers and for capturing 19 enemy prisoners. He honed his leadership qualities in other ways during his military years as well. Though the troops had recently been desegregated by Harry S. Truman's presidential order, Wilder found that many African American soldiers were being passed over for promotions, so he took his concerns to his battalion commander. Soon, more promotions were handed out, and Wilder eventually reached the rank of sergeant.

After his discharge in 1953, Wilder returned to his home in Richmond, where he eventually found work as a chemist-technician in the state medical examiner's office. However, he had yearned to attend law school, and when the U.S. Supreme Court's historic 1954 *Brown v. Board of Education* decision outlawed segregation of public schools, he became fired up to pursue law himself. Ironically, though, law schools in Virginia remained unaccommodating to African Americans, preferring to give scholarships to blacks to enroll out-of-state, so he attended Howard University in Washington, D.C.

While in law school, in October of 1958, Wilder married Eunice Montgomery, an economics student at Howard. They would have three children: Lynn Diana, born in 1959; Lawrence Douglas, Jr., born in 1962; and Loren Deane, born in 1963. Upon graduating in 1959, Wilder went to work for William A. Smith, a personal injury lawyer in Newport News, Virginia, and commuted back to Richmond on the weekends to see his wife, who was employed at a bank there. After passing the bar exam, he set up his own practice in Richmond in his old neighborhood. Other colleagues felt that the area's residents were too poor to allow him to grow a practice, but Wilder thrived.

Building his business, Wilder established a reputation as a competent trial lawyer. Specializing in personal injury cases, he became quite wealthy and displayed a taste for flashy cars and fashionable clothes. During this time, the prime era for civil rights, he was involved with some pro-integration groups, but concentrated on his practice, figuring that Martin Luther King, Jr. would not accomplish much with his policy of nonviolence. "I've never been identified as an activist," he remarked to Laurence I. Barrett and Don Winbush in

Time. However, he also noted to B. Drummond Ayres Jr. in the *New York Times Magazine,* "I worked on making myself the best lawyer and politician possible on the theory that I could best serve not by being a demonstrator in handcuffs but by seeking to get the handcuffs off the demonstrator and the repressive laws changed."

An ambitious Wilder did want to try his hand at politics, though, and ran in a special election in 1969 to fill a vacant Virginia State Senate seat. No African American had ever served in that body since Reconstruction, but as a Democrat, he won a three-way race against two white candidates. Though he attracted less than 50 percent of the vote, he held on to his position unopposed over the next 16 years, representing a mainly black constituency after a 1970 redistricting.

Immediately, Wilder was pegged as an obvious liberal among his highly conservative colleagues. In his first month on the job, he caused consternation by introducing a bill to repeal the state's official song, "Carry Me Back to Old Viginni," which he chided for its racist lyrics. Some criticized his move to take up such a charged issue so soon, but as he told Barrett and Winbush, it "got under my skin so bad that I just couldn't resist it." The song would not be retired for 27 more years, but it established Wilder as a spokesperson for black causes. Another of his early platforms was to get more blacks appointed to the court system. Later, he would fight long and hard to get the state to declare a holiday in honor of Martin Luther King, eventually agreeing to allow the recognition of Confederate leaders Robert E. Lee and Stonewall Jackson on that day as well.

Due to his stance on racial issues, Wilder early on was pegged as being confrontational, but he soon changed direction and became one of the senate's leading compromisers. Known for defusing racial tensions with his wit, he charmed voters and other legislators. Eventually he became chairman of the committee that oversees state appointments—a powerful position—and was known as one of the top five most influential lawmakers in his state. As the years progressed, he became tougher on crime and less involved with civil rights issues. Although Wilder and his wife divorced in 1975, his rise continued, and he refused to remarry for his political image.

Despite Wilder's political prominence, many were openly skeptical when he announced his intention to seek the lieutenant governor seat in the 1985 elections, declaring that his presence would ruin the chances of a winning Democratic ticket. However, he won the seat, 52 to 48 percent, becoming the first African American in Virginia to hold a statewide office. Part of his success was attributed to a back-road station wagon tour, which helped him win over many rural white voters. Wilder's acceptance speech for lieutenant governor took place at the John Marshall Hotel, the same venue in which he waited on politicians four decades prior.

After four years in office, Wilder was the logical successor to run for governor on the Democratic ticket. Facing conservative Republican J. Marshall Coleman, the main issues appeared to be race and abortion. Coleman was vehemently pro-life, whereas the liberal Wilder was pro-choice. In the end, Wilder squeaked by with a margin of just 6,741 votes. He was inaugurated on January 11, 1990, as the country's first elected African American governor.

In September of 1991 Wilder announced that he was seeking the nomination for the 1992 Democratic presidential nomination, but withdrew his name in January of 1992, stating that he needed to focus on state affairs. During his time in office, Wilder cut back spending, got rid of a $2.2 billion deficit, and kept his promise of not raising taxes. In addition, he ordered all state departments and universities to eliminate any investments with ties to South Africa, thus becoming the first southern state to make such a move in protest of that government's apartheid policies. However, this action was partly in response to critics who derided him for opposing the creation of a new congressional district that would have held a black majority.

Since Virginia does not allow governors to hold consecutive terms, Wilder stepped down in 1994. Subsequently, he began hosting a two-hour weekday morning radio show that was broadcast on eight Virginia stations as well as one in Baltimore, Maryland, and one in Washington, D.C. By September of 1995, though, a *Jet* article reported that he cancelled his show, claiming it put "excessive demands on his time." Afterward, he began teaching political science at Virginia Commonwealth University and also returned to practicing law. He later accepted an offer to become president of his alma mater, Virginia Union University, but changed his mind. A fit man of five feet, nine inches in height, Wilder enjoys golf, chess, and traveling.

Sources

> **Books**

Contemporary Black Biography, volume 3, Gale Research, 1992.

Encyclopedia of World Biography, second edition, Gale Research, 1998.
Notable Black American Men, Gale Research, 1998.

➤ **Periodicals**

Black Enterprise, January 1989, p. 36.
Ebony, April 1986, p. 67.
Jet, September 11, 1995, p. 33; August 17, 1998, p. 20.
New York Times Magazine, January 12, 1992, p. 30 (opening quote).
People, June 11, 1989, p. 54.
Time, April 17, 1989, p. 26; November 20, 1989, p. 54; November 11, 1991, p. 49.
U.S. News & World Report, November 20, 1989, p. 48; May 13, 1991, p. 32.
Washington Post, June 11, 1989, p. A1.

Steve Wozniak

"I think if kids are going to have a hero in the computer world, they might as well have a good one."

Born August 11, 1950, in San Jose, California, Steve Wozniak invented the Apple computer and was a co-founder of the Apple Computer Company. He left Apple in 1985 to start his own company, and now spends his time teaching children about computers. Address: Axlon Inc, 252 Humboldt Ct, Sunnyvale, CA 94089-1315.

S teve Wozniak invented the Apple computer and helped found the Apple Computer Company. One of the wealthiest and most famous inventors in the U.S., Wozniak left behind the world of business to spend his time teaching children about computers.

Stephen Gary Wozniak was born on August 11, 1950 in San Jose, California, to Margaret Wozniak, a homemaker, and Jerry Wozniak, an electrical engineer. When he was eight, the family, including two other children, Leslie and Mark, moved to nearby Sunnyvale to be closer to his father's job at Lockheed Missiles and Space Company. Wozniak became interested in mathematics when he was in the fourth grade. The recognition and encouragement of a teacher helped to improve his self esteem. Wozniak loved to read; his favorite books were about Tom Swift, Jr., a young engineer who worked with his father inventing airplanes and rocket ships. In the fifth grade, after reading a book about a ham radio operator, Wozniak built his own radio transmitter and receiver from a kit. At 11, he built a machine he called a "ticktacktoe" computer. He also played on an all-star Little League team and ran in races. In junior high, Wozniak received a letter for swimming.

At Cupertino Junior High School, Wozniak won a blue ribbon for the best electronics project at the Bay Area Science Fair. He designed a binary adding and subtracting computer. At Homestead High School, Wozniak was too advanced for the electronics and math courses. His electronics teacher sent him to Sylvania, a large electronics company, to program its computers. He won an award as the best math student at Homestead in 1966, attended seminars at the University of Santa Clara, and scored an 800 on his math Scholastic Aptitude Test.

Wozniak attended the University of Colorado his freshman year of college, where he preferred skiing to studying. Because his parents could not afford the high out-of-state tuition, Wozniak returned to California to attend DeAnza Community College. For his junior year, he went to the University of California, at Berkeley. There, with the help of a high school friend named Steve Jobs, who was later to be his business partner at Apple Computer, he designed a "little blue box," a device for making illegal free telephone calls. They sold them to fellow students for $150. Wozniak, who had a talent for mimicry, said he used the box to call the Vatican, where only a sharp-eared bishop prevented him from talking to the pope by stating, "You are not Henry Kissinger."

At the end of his junior year, and short on money, Wozniak got a job at Hewlett-Packard (HP), an electronics company in Palo Alto, California. Within several months, he was a full engineer. At the center of the computer revolution, HP suited Wozniak because of its advanced technology and its laid-back atmosphere. The company allowed employees to work on their own projects at night. Doing so, Wozniak created some of the first graphics for computers and computer games. Steve Jobs, who worked at Atari, invited him to help design a spin-off of Pong called "Breakout." In four days, the two had designed it and split the $750 bonus offered by Atari. Wozniak learned many years later that Jobs had received substantially more money than he had. This discovery factored into the breakup of their friendship.

Wozniak and Jobs attended meetings of the Homebrew Computer Club where the Silicon Valley engineers exchanged ideas and showed off their inventions. These meetings led Wozniak to design an inexpensive personal computer. He decided that it should be easy to program, affordable, and fun. Wozniak also started a Dial-a-Joke service, where people could call for a joke of the day. One day he talked with Alice Robertson, a woman whom he married in January 1976.

Working at night at HP, Wozniak completed his computer design. When Jobs saw it, he thought it could be a commercial success and wanted to market it. While Wozniak would not leave his day job, he agreed to form a computer company with Jobs. According to Wozniak, "We never expected to make any money, but it was a chance to have a business once in our lives." Jobs came up with the name "Apple," because he had once worked in an apple orchard when he had experimented with vegetarianism in India. The Apple Computer Company was officially started on April 1, 1976. Having sold personal possessions to raise money, they decided to work in Jobs family's garage. By luck and determination, one month later they received an order for 100 computers for a total of $50,000. When he showed the computer at work, HP management decided that his personal computer did not match its business focus. The partners eventually sold 175 Apple I computers.

While Wozniak was still working for HP, he spent his nights improving the Apple, while Jobs figured out how to market it. Through contacts, Jobs recruited Mike Markkula, a marketing genius who had retired at age 33, to help run the company. After a short time, Wozniak's night-time efforts paid off in a much improved Apple II that was aimed at the average person rather than the electronic expert. It had sound, computer animation, high resolution images, and expanded game playing ability. The experienced Markkula wrote a business plan in which he anticipated sales of $500 million within ten years, and invested $250,000 of his own money in the venture. Finally, in October of 1976, Wozniak resigned from HP.

In January of 1977, the trio incorporated Apple Computer. The company moved to larger quarters twice, recruited an ever-growing staff, and acquired an eye-catching logo, a rainbow-colored apple with a bite taken out of it. The launch of the Apple II was scheduled to coincide with the first West Coast Computer Faire. Priced at only $1,298, the computer was a great success. By the end of its first year, the company had made almost three quarters of a million dollars in sales with a profit of $42,000.

At the same time that his business was taking off, Wozniak's marriage was floundering. His lack of social skills and his obsession with computers made his wife Alice feel increasingly isolated. Although they tried counseling for a year, they divorced after four years of marriage. Alice got one-third of Wozniak's Apple stock in a divorce settlement which quickly grew into a fortune.

After the initial separation, Wozniak became a workaholic. During this time, he developed a way to connect the Apple computer to a printer, thereby making it more useful. He also developed the floppy disk, a removable plastic disk with information on it that can be put into the computer memory for storage or for accessing without being stored. These innovations greatly increased the ability of average people to use the Apple computer. By the end of 1978, Apple sales had increased ten times, making Apple one of the fastest growing companies in the United States. Apple computers were now stocked by more than 300 dealers. By 1979, Apple employed one thousand people.

At this point, both Wozniak and Jobs were being eased out of the power structure by business people such as Markkula. Because Wozniak was so well known, he was frequently asked to give lectures and interviews with the press and television. While the Apple II was now the world's best selling computer, the company decided to plan ahead by developing the Apple III, a small business computer comparable to the IBM personal computer. Although it was priced at just under $3,000, the computer did not sell well because it experienced hardware failures, leading to bad reviews. Not much software was developed for it.

Frustrated with Apple management, Wozniak took up flying,

and started courting Candi Clark, a former Olympic kayaker and accountant at Apple. In December 1980, Apple stock went public and was sold out in minutes. Within a month, Wozniak was worth about $50 million. In February 1981, while flying Clark and other companions to Los Angeles, Wozniak crashed his plane, nearly killing everyone on board. He married Clark four months later and decided to take a leave of absence from Apple in order to return to college. Frustrations with Apple management and nearly losing his life made him reconsider his priorities. "The company had become big business, and I missed tinkering. I just wanted to be an engineer," Wozniak told *People* magazine.

Wozniak returned to Berkeley in 1981 to earn a computer science degree under the pseudonym of "Rocky Clark," the first name from one of his dogs, and the last from his new wife. Several credits shy of graduation, he left Berkeley, but received equivalency credits for work done at Apple. Wozniak was officially awarded a degree several years later, in 1986.

In 1982 and 1983, Wozniak produced two music concerts, called the US Festival, which combined the best music groups with the best computer stuff, a "hot tunes and high tech" event. Although he lost a lot of money on the festivals, he felt they were a success because both he and the concert goers had fun.

In 1982, Wozniak returned to the Apple II section of Apple Computers. In-fighting at the company was becoming bitter. Wozniak started designing a new computer called the Lisa, a cheaper version of which was later called the Macintosh. It had a mouse, folders, and pull-down menus and displayed pictures. However, the company had lost the camaraderie Wozniak liked so much. The development of the Macintosh led to more friction between the department led by Jobs and the Apple II department. There were strained relations between Jobs and Wozniak, who was hurt that the Apple II had not received its due recognition as a computer that had a billion dollars in sales by 1982. Jobs felt that the Apple II was obsolete. In February 1985, Wozniak left Apple for good.

Wozniak helped start a new company, CL9, to develop an infrared remote control device that would control household appliances. He continued to feud with Jobs, who felt betrayed because Wozniak had left Apple. When Wozniak discovered that Jobs had not evenly split the money earned from the development of the Breakout game, their relationship was further strained.

In 1989, Wozniak sold the unsuccessful CL9. Since then, he has spent most of his time donating money to various charitable organizations in San Jose, including the Tech Museum of Innovation, the Children's Discovery Museum, and the San Jose-Cleveland Ballet.

Wozniak and Candi Clark had three children, Jesse, Sara, and Gary; they were divorced in 1987. In 1989, he met Suzanne Mulkern, a mother of three, who shared his shyness, love of children, and sense of humor. They married in 1990.

Wozniak now spends his time teaching children about the wonders of computers. In 1992, he started an ad-hoc class for his son and four of his fifth-grade classmates, teaching them to build and dismantle computers and plug into information networks. "It was an experiment to see if they were given a lot, how far would they go?" Wozniak told *People*. A few years later, he started another class of 20 hand-picked fifth-graders, where the students learned advanced tasks like designing spreadsheets. He also challenges his students to gain new perspectives—he has taken kids in helicopter rides over the Grand Canyon, taught them how to fill Oreos with toothpaste, and even allowed them to drink cola from beer cans. "I don't want them to become nerds, thinking that only computers are important," he explained to *People*. "But I support anyone who's called a nerd. They are some of the most trustworthy people."

Sources

➤ Books

Gold, Rebecca, *Steve Wozniak: A Wizard Called Woz*, Lerner, 1994.
Greenberg, Keith Elliot, *Steven Jobs and Stephen Wozniak: Creating the Apple Computer*, Blackbirch, 1994.
Kendall, Martha E., *Steve Wozniak: Inventor of the Apple Computer*, Walker, 1994.

➤ Periodicals

Business Journal, November 16, 1992.
Forbes, January 22, 1990.
Maclean's, May 11, 1992.
People, May 30, 1983; February 19, 1996 (opening quote).

Photo Credits

Photographs and illustrations appearing in *Contemporary Heroes and Heroines, Book IV* were received from the following sources:

Abbey, Edward, photograph by Jonathan Blair. Corbis. Reproduced by permission. Ali, Muhammad, photograph by John Duricka. AP/Wide World Photos. Reproduced by permission. Allende, Salvador, photograph. AP/Wide World Photos. Reproduced by permission. Amory, Cleveland, photograph. The Fund for Animals. Reproduced by permission. Armstrong, Lance, photograph. Reuters/Eric Gaillard/Archive Photos. Reproduced by permission. Ashrawi, Hanan, photograph. AP/Wide World Photos. Reproduced by permission. Asimov, Isaac, photograph. The Library of Congress. Baekeland, Leo Hendrik, photograph. Underwood & Underwood/Corbis-Bettmann. Reproduced by permission. Belo, Carlos Filipe Ximenes, photograph by Muchtar Zakaria. AP/Wide World Photos. Reproduced by permission. Berners-Lee, Tim, photograph by Stephan Savoia. AP/Wide World Photos. Reproduced by permission. Blackwell, Elizabeth, photograph. The Library of Congress. Bohr, Niels, photograph. The Library of Congress. Brico, Antonia, photograph. AP/Wide World Photos. Reproduced by permission. Browner, Carol M., photograph. AP/Wide World Photos. Reproduced by permission. Byrd, Richard Evelyn, photograph by Underwood and Underwood. The Library of Congress. Capek, Karel (with Jozef Capek), photograph. Corbis. Reproduced by permission. Cech, Thomas R., photograph by Steve Senne. AP/Wide World Photos. Reproduced by permission. Clark, Joe, photograph. AP/Wide World Photos. Reproduced by permission. Cleland, Max (with Wilbur Gamble and Billy Griggs), photograph by Joe Marquette. AP/Wide World Photos. Reproduced by permission. Coachman, Alice, photograph. AP/Wide World Photos. Reproduced by permission. Cochran, Jacqueline (with Chuck Yeager), photograph. Archive Photos. Reproduced by permission. Coffin, William Sloan, Jr., photograph. The Library of Congress. Cole, Nat King, photograph. AP/Wide World Photos. Reproduced by permission. DeBakey, Dr. Michael, photograph by Donna Carson. AP/Wide World Photos. Reproduced by permission. Dellinger, David, photograph. The Library of Congress. Dith Pran, photograph. Corbis-Bettmann. Reprinted by permission. Dodge, Henry Chee, photograph. AP/Wide World Photos. Reproduced by permission. Dole, Elizabeth Hanford, photograph, The Library of Congress. Doolittle, James H., photograph. The Library of Congress. Durant, Ariel (with husband Will Durant), photograph by Bob Thomas. AP/Wide World Photos. Reproduced by permission. **Eisenhower, Dwight D.**, photograph. The Library of Congress. **Fang Lizhi**, photograph by Stringer/Andre de Wet. Corbis-Bettmann. Reproduced by permission. **Farmer, James**, photograph. The Library of Congress. **Faulkner, William**, photograph by Carl Van Vechten. The Estate of Carl Van Vechten. Reproduced by permission. **Fiennes, Ranulph**, photograph by Tony Harris. AP/Wide World Photos. Reproduced by permission. **Fitzgerald, Ella**, photograph by Carl Van Vechten. The Estate of Carl Van Vechten. Reproduced by permission. **Fong, Hiram Leong**, photograph. Courtesy of Hiram Leong Fong. Reproduced by permission. **Fuller, Richard Buckminster**, photograph. Archive Photos. Reproduced by permission. **Gale, Robert Peter**, photograph by Dennis Cook. AP/Wide World Photos. Reproduced by permission. **Gates, Bill**, photograph. AP/Wide World Photos. Reproduced by permission. **Gilbreth, Lillian M.**, photograph. The Library of Congress. **Goddard, Robert H.**, photograph. The Library of Congress. **Gonzalez, Henry B.**, photograph. AP/Wide World Photos. Reproduced by permission. **Graham, Katherine Meyer**, photograph. The Library of Congress. **Green, Maggie** (with her husband **Reg Green**), photograph by Susan Ragan. AP/Wide World Photos. Reproduced by permission. **Hamm, Mia**, photograph. Reuters/Rick Wilking/Archive Photos. Reproduced by permission. **Harper, Frances E. W.**, photograph. **Harris, LaDonna**, photograph. UPI/Corbis-Bettmann. Reproduced by permission. **Hayes, Denis**, photograph. Corbis-Bettmann. Reproduced by permission. **Hesburgh, Theodore M.**, photograph. The Library of Congress. **Hubble, Edwin**, photograph. The Library of Congress. **Hume, John** (with **David Trimble**), photograph by Bjoern Sigurdson. AP/Wide World Photos. Reproduced by permission. **Hunter-Gault, Charlayne**, photograph. AP/Wide World Photos. Reproduced by permission. **Hurston, Zora Neale**, photograph. AP/Wide World Photos. Reproduced by permission. **Hussein, King**, photograph. The Library of Congress. **Jarvik, Dr. Robert**, photograph. AP/Wide World Photos. Reproduced by permission. **Kaye, Danny**, photograph. AP/Wide World Photos. Reproduced by permission. **Keynes, John Maynard** (and wife), photograph. Archive Photos/Popperfoto. Reproduced by permission. **Kolbe, Maximilian**, photograph. AP/Wide World Photos. Reproduced by permission. **Lange, Dorothea**, photograph. The Library of Congress. **Le Guin, Ursula K.**, photograph. UPI/Corbis-Bettmann. Reproduced by permission. **Lewis, Carl**, photograph. AP/Wide World Photos. Reproduced by permission. **Lobo, Rebecca** (with Robin Roberts and Joan Jett), photograph by Adam Nadel. AP/Wide World Photos. Reproduced by permission. **Low, Juliette Gordon**, 1948, photograph. AP/Wide World Photos. Reproduced by permission. **Mahmoody, Betty**, photograph. Reproduced by permission of Betty Mahmoody. **Manheim, Camryn**, photograph. AP/Wide World Photos. Reproduced by permission. **Martinez, Vilma S.**, photograph. AP/Wide World Photos. Reproduced by permission. **McCarthy, Carolyn**, photograph. AP/Wide World Photos. Reproduced by permission. **Mink, Patsy T.**, photograph. UPI/Corbis-Bettmann. Reproduced by permission. **Momsen, C.B.**, photograph. AP/Wide World Photos. Reproduced by permission. **Motley, Constance Baker**, photograph. AP/Wide World Photos. Reproduced by permission. **Moyers, Bill,** photograph. Archive Photos. Reproduced by permission. **Muñoz Marín, Luis,** photograph. The Library of Congress. **Neruda, Pablo,** photograph by Jerry Bauer. Reproduced by permission. **Nhat Hanh, Thich,** photograph. AP/Wide World Photos. Reproduced by permission.**Ochoa, Ellen,** photograph. U. S. National Aeronautics and Space Administration (NASA). **O'Donnell, Rosie,** photograph. Archive Photos. Reproduced by permission. **O'Grady, Scott,** photograph. AP/Wide World Photos. Reproduced by permission.**Pankhurst, Emmeline,** photograph. The Library of Congress. **Pele,** photograph. Archive Photos. Reproduced by permission. **Peltier, Leonard,** photograph. AP/Wide World Photos. Reproduced by permission. **Perlasca, Giorgio, photograph by Marcy Nighswander. AP/Wide World Photos. Reproduced by permission. Piccard, Bertrand and Brian Jones,** photograph by Donald Stampfli. AP/Wide World Photos. Reproduced by permission. **Ramos-Horta, Jose,** photograph by Rick Rycroft. AP/Wide World Photos. Reproduced by permission. **Reese, Harold "Pee Wee",** photograph. AP/Wide World Photos. Reproduced by permission. **Richardson, Bill,** photograph by Joe Marquette. AP/Wide World Photos. Reproduced by permission. **Ripken, Cal, Jr.,** photograph. Archive Photos. Reproduced by permission. **Rivera, Diego,** photograph by Carl Van Vechten. The Estate of Carl Van Vechten. Reproduced by permission. **Robinson, Mary,** photograph. AP/Wide World Photos. Reproduced by permission. **Robinson, Randall S.,** photograph. AP/Wide World Photos. Reproduced by permission. **Schulz, Charles M.,** photograph. AP/Wide World Photos. Reproduced by permission. **Smith, Margaret Chase,** photograph. AP/Wide World Photos. Reproduced by permission. **Stallings, Gene,** photograph by Caroline Baird. AP/Wide World Photos. Reproduced by permission. **Tombaugh, Clyde W.,** photograph by Will Yurman. AP/Wide World Photos. Reproduced by permission. **Turnbull, Walter J.,** photograph by Frankie Ziths. AP/Wide World Photos. Reproduced by permission. **Walters, Barbara,** photograph. AP/Wide World Photos. Reproduced by permission. **West, Dan,** photograph. The Heifer Project. Reproduced by permission. **White, Walter Francis,** photograph. The Library of Congress. **Wilder, L. Douglas,** photograph. AP/Wide World Photos. Reproduced by permission. **Wozniak, Steve,** photograph by Bill Beattie. AP/Wide World Photos. Reproduced by permission.

Index

Personal names, place names, events, institutions, awards, and other subject areas or key words contained in *Contemporary Heroes and Heroines, Book IV* entries are listed in this index with corresponding page numbers indicating text references. Inclusive page numbers are given in bold type for each of the volume's main entries. Also cited are the names of people with main entries in the original *Contemporary Heroes and Heroines* (indicated by the abbreviation "CHH" in bold type after a name), *Contemporary Heroes and Heroines, Book II* (indicated by the abbreviation "CHH-2" in bold type after a name), and *Contemporary Heroes and Heroines, Book III* (indicated by the abbreviation "CHH-3" in bold type after a name).